Bengali Culture
Over A Thousand Years

Ghulam Murshid

Translated from
the original Bengali
Hajaar Bochhorer Bangla Samskriti

Sarbari Sinha

NIYOGI
BOOKS

Published by
NIYOGI BOOKS
Block D, Building No. 77,
Okhla Industrial Area, Phase-I,
New Delhi-110 020, INDIA
Tel: 91-11-26816301, 26818960
Email: niyogibooks@gmail.com
Website: www.niyogibooksindia.com

Editor: Mohua Mitra
Design: Shraboni Roy

ISBN: 978-93-86906-12-0
Publication: 2018
Reprint: 2022

Printed at: Niyogi Offset Pvt. Ltd., New Delhi, India

Dedicated to

Purabi Basu
Shafi Ahmed
Swarochish Sarker
—the first three readers of this book

CONTENTS

TRANSLATOR'S NOTE

We live in troubled times. Almost everywhere in the world, the walls are growing taller and more rigid as people turn away from history and ignore narratives that speak of shared destinies. More than ever before, this is the time to tell and share stories on the basis of recorded history instead of hearsay and social myths. If histories do not come out of the confines of academia and become part of everyday conversations, myth-making and bigotries inevitably usurp the intellectual space that is left vacant. Ghulam Murshid's *Hajar Bochhorer Bangla Samskriti*, (Dhaka, 2006) is perhaps the first book that offers ordinary Bengalis not connected with the pursuit of research an overview of their geopolitical history. The book is written for intelligent non-academic readers who might wish to dig deeper into their own history than what is retained in popular memory and dished up in school textbooks. Such a book, I felt, should be available in an English version that would be accessible to the Bengali diaspora from both Bengals.

I have retained in most places the writer's use of the expression 'East Bengal', even when he is speaking of East Pakistan or Bangladesh. This may be confusing to young readers and people outside Bengal. The use springs from a cultural context and orientation rooted in the shared history of undivided Bengal.

I have tried to retain Dr Murshid's racy, conversational style. In order to be able to do this, I have sometimes strayed from literal translation while remaining faithful to the content. Now and then I felt constrained to add, with Dr Murshid's approval, a few sentences to make the context clear to a readership that may not be familiar with certain aspects of Bengali culture. On the other hand, I have sometimes omitted, again with Dr Murshid's approval, details that might not make sense in translation, especially in the sections on language and music. But I alone am responsible for any errors that might have crept into the translation. I am grateful to Dr Murshid for allowing me to translate this wonderful book. Translating it was a great learning experience.

Sarbari Sinha

THE BEGINNING

When the Greek king Menander met the Buddhist sage Nagasena, the latter asked him, 'Maharaj, you have come in a chariot. But what is a chariot?' In reply, the king explained that a chariot was a vehicle on wheels drawn by horses. The sage asked, 'Is the horse the same as the chariot, then?' 'No', said the king. Were the wheels the same as the chariot? No again, and so it went. If it is so tricky to come up with a definition of a chariot, it may seem virtually impossible to define a culture. Indeed, the various definitions of culture offered by sociologists are by no means either simple or straightforward. Nor very concise. Culture is not something you can define in clear-cut, unambiguous terms. It is not made up of one or two things, it is an infinitely complex concept.

The definition of culture formulated by Edward Taylor in the second half of the 19th century is generally accepted as the classic definition. According to that definition, a comprehensive pattern of beliefs, conduct, behaviour and knowledge may be called 'culture'. Language, literature, ideas, religion and beliefs; codes of behaviour, social values and rules; festivals and rituals; art; and the tools needed in everyday life—all this makes up a culture. The refinements, accomplishments and habits that one picks up as a social being are also part of culture. Like the horses and the wheels of the chariot, these individual components of culture are visible enough. It is not quite as easy to define a culture in its entirety, which develops gradually over centuries. It is like the air that we breathe in, which we can feel all the time but cannot see.

We are born as animals. It is culture that makes us human. It makes us social creatures. It is through culture that we come to possess values, thinking minds and attitudes, as well as concepts and ideas. It is culture that refines our minds and tastes. On the other hand, certain kinds of cultural environment can turn human beings into beasts. In a word, it is culture that makes us what

Boats anchored by a river in Bengal
Photo courtesy: Suriajay (commoms.wikimedia.org)

we are. It is difficult to give a clear definition of culture, and I will not try to do so. Instead, I will straight away embark on writing a history of culture. I assume that readers will figure out what I am talking about as they make their way through the book.

But even if we do not attempt a definition of Bengali culture, it is necessary to set out the defining limits of this culture if one must write a history of it, though of course, I must say again, it is not an easy thing to do. Not easy, because though the myriad components of a culture catch our eyes, whether they combine into a clear pattern, and from what point of time in history they do so, is not always so clear. The flowers with which Time has strung the garland of Bengali culture are prominent enough, but the thing of beauty created out of them in the form of the garland is not as clearly perceptible. That is why I will start my discussion with the horse and the wheel, rather than the chariot. We will try to see when this culture started acquiring a character of its own, what its components were, when they became integrated and how they have changed with time. I trust that a general idea of Bengali culture will emerge from these discussions.

It is of course important to point out right at the beginning that Bengali culture is not homogeneous or monolithic. Just as Bengali society is fragmented into many sections, Bengali culture is also tinged with many hues. Going by political boundaries, this society can now be divided into two almost equal parts. On religious lines, too, this society is divided—mainly between the Hindu and Muslim communities. Yet, those are not the only divisions. For, within the same religious community there are many walls of separation. The community of upper-caste Hindus, for instance, does not at all resemble that of lower-caste Hindus, though their gods and goddesses may bear the same names. Even small differences in religious belief may be enough to create unbridgeable distances between different sections, and between individuals. So much so that people divided by such beliefs may not be able to accept food from each other.

A famous Bengali poet had the surname 'Dutt' and was a 'Kayastha' by caste (jati). This poet strung a new chord in Bengali culture. Yet, the act of adopting a different religion cast him far out of the pale of his own community. The Bengali society of his time did not exactly embrace him with open arms, despite his gigantic contribution to Bengali literature. Rabindranath Tagore was responsible for putting Bengali in the global literary map. But it took a long time for the Bengali Muslim community to accept him as one of its own. Even a section of Bengali Hindus took a long time to accept him without reservation. The fog of religious belief was able to cloud up even the sun-like brilliance of his genius. Differences of religion and caste apart, there are barriers between rural and urban Bengali communities. The differences in dialect between the different regions in Bengal are also not negligible. In sum, Bengali society does not signify a uniform, undivided community.

That is why one must see Bengali culture as one that belongs to Hindus, Muslims, upper-caste Hindus, lower-caste Hindus, Vaishnavas, Shaktas, Bauls, Ashrafs (lower-class Muslims), Atrafs (elite Muslims), Buddhists and Christians. The city dweller and the villager, the rich and the poor, this culture belongs to them all. It is therefore not possible to draw the outlines of this culture in simple, straightforward strokes. The cooking of eastern Bengal is quite distinct from that of western Bengal, and Bengali Hindu cuisine differs from Bengali Muslim cuisine. The folk songs of eastern Bengal are different from the folk songs of central Bengal; the folk songs of northern Bengal differ from those of western Bengal. The Baul songs of Kushtia are significantly different from the Baul songs of Birbhum. The dance steps of Santhals of eastern Bengal differ from those of western Bengal. These differences are not always subtle. In many cases they are sharp and unmistakable. Indeed, sometimes the gulf is so deep that it is hard to identify the different parts as pieces of the same culture.

Apart from everything else, this culture does not have a fixed or unchanging identity. Nor does it stand still at any particular point. It has evolved with time. Nevertheless, the most important thing that must be considered is whether there is some common ground despite all the widely differing components and particularities of this culture. Important, because it is the shared characteristics that give Bengali culture its distinctiveness. In the opinion of scholars, there are unmistakable similarities that mark many aspects of Bengali culture despite the differences. For instance, there is noticeable unity in the literature, music, eating habits, dwelling layouts, clothes, and even the facial features of Bengalis. The thatched huts of

Bengal are the same everywhere, for Hindus and Muslims alike. Rice and fish continue to be the staple of all Bengalis. In the 21st century era of globalisation, Bengalis are eating hot-dogs, drinking Coke and tucking into Thai and Chinese food, but the fish-and-rice meal has not lost its pride of place.

In the words of Rabindranath Tagore

> *The history of Bengal is the history of fragmentation. Eastern and western Bengal, Rarh and Varendra, these are not simply geographical divisions; divisions of hearts and minds were meshed up with them, and social unity was also absent. Yet through it all there runs a strain of unity, and that is the unity of language. What defines us as being Bengali is that we happen to speak Bengali.*

In other words, the most important shared characteristic of Bengali culture is the language. Despite all the social differences, Bengali is the language of all Bengalis. And so the point of origin of the Bengali language is what marks the beginning of Bengali culture. Which is not to say that we refuse to recognise the cultural attributes of the people who inhabited the landmass that is now home to Bengalis long before the Bengali language was actually born. Indeed, it is on the foundation laid in the pre-Bengali age that Bengali culture has been truly built.

Language apart, there is another important dimension to this culture —its geographical identity. Bengali culture belongs to the land where people speak in the Bengali language. One must accept Bengali culture as beginning at that point in history when a language called Bengali came into being and a region came to be identified as 'Bengal'. But when was the Bengali language born? When did a region come to be known as Bengal? And when did the people of that region start being called Bengalis?

Moment of Birth

Writers inspired by nationalist ideals have in recent times claimed Bengali culture to be very old, even as old as 5,000 years. In our view, the culture is not so ancient at all. For, not even the parent language of Bengali was born that far back into the past, let alone what we know as Bengali. In truth, it is doubtful if the Bengali language is even a thousandyears old. Doubtful, because a language does not acquire its distinctive features in a day—not even in a century. If this is accepted as a given, then what Nihar Ranjan Roy has called *Bangalir Itihash (The History of the Bengalis)* cannot truly be described as the history of either Bengalis or Bengali culture. For, in the time span that he has written about, the language of this region had not really come into its own as one recognisable as the Bengali language. In ancient times, even the region as a whole had not come to be recognised as Bengal or 'Vangabhumi'. The area that we now know as home to the Bengali-speaking people was then still divided into smaller areas known as Gaur, Varendri, Rarh, Samatata, Sumha, Vanga and so on. These smaller areas did not become integrated into an undivided 'Vanga' during the time of the Palas, the Senas and the Varmans. Therefore, it is not really logical to speak of the people who lived in these areas in those times as Bengalis. Of course, there is no gainsaying the fact that the cultural and anthropological traditions of those ancient pre-Bengali people were not washed away to make way for a new culture. Rather, it was on the basis of that ancient culture that in later centuries was built the edifice of Bengali culture with varied and new ingredients.

Thus, the blood of the Adivasis who lived here in the distant past still flows in our veins. It was before the birth of Christ that the Aryans pitched their first settlements in this land, initially in Rarh and then in Varendri. Before their time, it was not just the Austric people who lived here. The land was home to Dravidians and to people of Chinese-Mongoloid origin. There was much mingling of bloodlines and of languages between the peoples of these various anthropological groups. The bloodlines of the Aryans and later those of Semitic groups and of Central Asian communities enriched this great commingling. And it is not as if there was no fusion with European bloodlines at all. Just as the genes of the modern Bengali carry the history of this intermingling of races, so the present-day Bengali carries ingredients from the languages spoken by these varied anthropological groups.

The Aryans were not the rulers of this land when they made their first permanent settlements here. Later, however, it was they who ruled for centuries on end. And it was the language they spoke that the people of this region gradually made their own. Yet some words and other features of the older language inevitably influenced the language brought in by the Aryans. The Bengali language is surmised to have emerged, through a process of evolution, some 1,500 years after the Aryans arrived in the region, though the hill people inhabiting the northern and eastern reaches had not yet accepted the language as their own. And in fact they still retain their distinctiveness in the matter of language. But the people of the plains have embraced Bengali as their language, showing in this act of acceptance their willingness to assimilate influences from other cultures. When Muslims arrived from Central and West Asia, they were once again considerably influenced by the languages of the newcomers.

The people of this region have not been able to discard many aspects of the culture that existed before the birth of the Bengali language. For instance, people of the 'pre-Bengali' era ate fish and rice, which, as we have already said, is a habit we have not grown out of. The Aryans introduced new methods of farming and previously unknown foods among the older inhabitants of the land. The Mughals, the Pathans, the Turks and the Arabs also brought new food habits. Even the Portuguese and the English brought new kinds of food with them. Yet Bengalis remain as loyal as ever to their fish and rice. The cuisine, too, maintains a continuity with ancient times. The food described in 12th century *Udbhat Sloka*s is not much different from the food that Bengalis eat today. The pattern of thatched homes in the countryside has survived for centuries. So we must accept that the culture of ancient times forms the basis for the Bengali culture that has taken shape in the past 1,000 years. The structure is young, but it stands on the foundation of the 'pre-Bengali' tradition.

Let us now turn our attention to the time of the birth of the Bengali language, which forms the basis of Bengali culture. Scholars are divided on whether the *Charyapada* poems, which provide the oldest extant examples of the language, are a thousand years old. Haraprasad Shastri retrieved the text of the *Charyapada* from the library of the royal court of Nepal at the beginning of the 20th century and claimed that the poems were samples of Bengali that was a thousand years old. However, linguists such as Suniti Kumar Chattopadhyay and Sukumar Sen have not been able to accept that the *Charyapada* poems are quite so old. Analysing the history of how the literary variations of Prakrit, known as the *apabhramsha*s (deviations), developed into regional languages, they place the *Charyapada* poems between the 10th and the 12th centuries. On the other hand, Muhammad Shahidullah has claimed that the *Charyapada* poems were written between the 7th and the 8th centuries, going by references to people or facts in the poems. His analysis does not pay too much attention to the chronology of the evolution of the new Indo-Aryan language in northern and eastern India.

Though Muhammad Shahidullah and Haraprasad Shastri have tried to push back the date of the composition of the *Charyapada*, they acknowledge that the language of these poems cannot really be described as Bengali. In later discussions we shall see that despite the appearance of some distinctive traits of the Bengali language, this language still had many features in common with the Oriya and the Assamese languages. This means that the Bengali language emerged after the *Charyapada* poems were written. If these poems are a thousand years old, then Bengali must be younger. Therefore, if the Bengali language is taken to be the greatest common factor in Bengali culture, it is reasonable to suppose that this culture is less than a thousand years old. Still, let us push aside these debates and assume, for the sake of a round figure, that this culture is about a thousand years old.

Name of the Land

From when did the land that is home to Bengali culture come to be known as 'Bengal'? The extensive area that is known as Bengal, or 'Vanga Desh', was, even 700 or 800 years ago divided into various regions bearing different names. In the second half of the 14th century, Sultan Shamsuddin Ilyas Shah brought these areas under a single administrative regime. Until then, these areas were not recognised as forming an undivided political territory. The land had been divided into several small, politically independent units, and even their names were not constant. A few standardised place names, however, kept coming back in history. These were Gaur, Rarh, Vanga, Sumha, Varendri, Pundra, Harikela, Samatata and so on. Of these, Gaur, Varendri and Vanga appear to be the oldest and most frequently used place names. But exactly how old were they?

Though the famous ancient Indian grammarian Panini's *Ashtadhyayi* mentions 'Gaur', it does not mention 'Vanga'. Panini's time was some

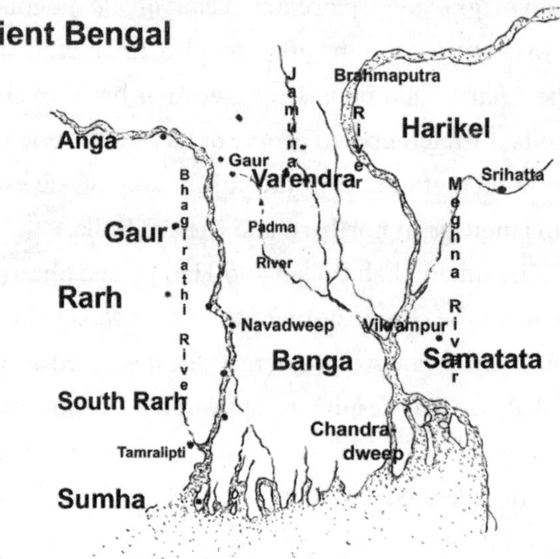

1.1 The kingdoms that together made up Bengal

five centuries before the birth of Christ. But when Patanjali wrote his annotations for *Ashtadhyayi*, 200 or 300 years later, he mentioned 'Vanga'. Not just 'Vanga', he also spoke of Anga, Sumha, Pundra, Magadha and Kalinga.

Aitareya Brahmana was also written before the birth of Christ. The text mentions Pundra, but not Vanga. Pundra was at that time taken to mark the eastern limits of Aryan settlements. Sukumar Sen has noted the use of the word 'Vanga' even in the Vedas. But his illustration involves a compound word of which 'Vanga' is a component, which leaves room for doubt about whether it is actually the same word. 'Gaur' and 'Vanga' occur even in the *Mahabharata*, which started being composed in the pre-Christian era. But the *Mahabharata* contains many interpolations and therefore cannot perhaps be completely relied on.

In the 4th century AD, – Samudragupta was the emperor of India. The eulogy of the king composed by the poet Harishen has a description of Bengal, but 'Gaur' and 'Vanga' are not mentioned; the word used is 'Samatata'. On the other hand, Kalidasa, writing just after the reign of Samudragupta, mentions Gaur, Vanga and Sumha while describing Rahgu's exploits in his *Raghuvamsa*.

But he does not mention Samatata. He describes Gaur as hugging the sea coast, which seems to imply that he saw Vanga as part of Gaur. Vatsayan, a near contemporary, praises soft-natured, romantic and lithe Bengali women in his well known work *Kamasutra*. But instead of Vanga, the word he uses is Gaur. Kautilya's *Arthashastra* also mentions Gaur.

The use of all these varied place names suggests that though there was an area called Vanga, the word 'Vanga', even if it was in use, was not very popular in areas outside the region known as Vanga in ancient times. It could also be that the part of Bengal that these writers were referring to was called Gaur and not Vanga, which was, in ancient times, clearly only southern Bengal. Several centuries later, even the Pala and the Sena kings were known not as rulers of Vanga but of Gaur. Whether eastern and southern Bengal were under their rule is also open to doubt.

At the end of the Sena dynasty's rule, when the Turks conquered Bengal at the dawn of the 13th century, the land was not yet known as Vanga. The region that the Turks conquered was called Gaur, not Vanga. Its capital, named after Lakshman (Lakkhon, as Bengalis would pronounce it) Sena, was Lakhnauti (Lakkhonabati). Bakhtiar Khilji had 'Gaur Vijay' inscribed in Sanskrit on the coin that he introduced after his conquest. The first Muslim historians did not also mention any area called 'Bangala'. But Vanga existed even then, and even the word 'Bangal' was in use. There are at least two pieces of evidence that prove this. Bhusukpada, one of the *Charyapada* poets writing around this time, mentioned a raga called 'Bangal' in one of his poems. There may be a difference of opinion over the time of Bhusukpada, but it is known for sure that Marco Polo visited India, if not Bengal, towards the end of the 13th century. He referred to 'Bangala' in his memoirs. He wrote that this land lay close to India (Bharatvarsha) and that its people worshipped idols and spoke a strange language. Some 60 to 70 years later, Shamsuddin Ilyas Shah for the first time brought Gaur, Varendri, Sumha, Samatata and Vanga under a single rule. He then declared himself 'Shahe Bangalian', meaning the 'Sultan of the Bengalis'. According to the 14th century historian Shams-i-Siraj Afif, he assumed this title after conquering Sonargaon. This conquest was made in 1352.

This, however, does not incontrovertibly support the conclusion that Shamsuddin Ilyas Shah became the sultan of the whole of Bengal or that he called his sultanate 'Bangala'. Rather, it could well be that he assumed the title to commemorate his conquest of 'Vanga' or eastern Bengal. Whatever that may be, it was after this event that that this extensive landmass was gradually brought under a single administration and started being known as 'Bangala'. But that did not happen in a day, or even in a century.

Alauddin Hossein Shah, Bengal's best-known sultan in the Middle Ages, ruled at the end of the 15th and the beginning of the 16th century. More than one Bengali poet have sung paeans in his praise. Vidyapati of Mithila also praised him in one of his poems. Remarkably, however, none of these poets called him the sultan of 'Vanga'. They described him as the king or sultan of Gaur. Vidyapati eulogised him as the ruler of 'Pancha-Gaur'. There is some debate on whether Vidyapati's couplet refers to Hossein Shah or his son Nasir Shah, but there is no room for doubt about what he means by 'Pancha-Gaur'. Though the expression does have another meaning, here the poet uses it to signify greater Bengal. It is noteworthy that he identifies greater Bengal not as 'Pancha-Vanga' but 'Pancha-Gaur'. This offers indirect proof of the greater importance and wider recognition of Gaur. After Vidyapati, Hossein Shah finds undisputed mention in the work of Jashoraj Khan or Maladhar Basu. He, too, spoke not of Vanga but of Pancha-Gaur as Hossein Shah's territory. Even when Mukundaram Chakraborty wrote his *Chandimangal* in the 16th century, he referred separately to Gaur, Vanga and Utkal while writing of Man Singh. From his description, it appears that Vanga in his time still generally meant southern Bengal. That means that 150 years after Ilyas Shah declared himself sultan of the Bengalis, Vanga still had not come to mean the whole of Bengal. Indeed, it was only in the Mughal period, in the late 16th century, that the entire region officially came to be known as Subah Bangalah. Contemporary European travellers also referred to it as Bengal.

But though the province was officially known as Subah Bangalah, it is only in the 18th century, and not before, that one notes the extensive use in written Bengali of 'Bangala' as meaning greater Bengal. It was probably the poet Bharatchandra who for the first time, and repeatedly, used the word 'Bangala' in this sense. Describing the raids of marauding Maratha gangs, called Borgis in Bengal, he wrote in *Annadamangal* (1752): 'Their plunders made paupers of the people of Bangala'. Describing Man Singh's meeting with Bhabananda Majumdar after the former's arrival in Bengal, he wrote: 'Man Singh ferreted out all information regarding Bangala by questioning him.' When seeking an account of Bengal from Man Singh, Jahangir says: 'Tell us Man Singh Ray, you travelled to Bangala—how did you find that land?'

So we see that Bharatchandra referred to the whole of Bengal as 'Bangala' in these lines. It is quite clear that he used the word Bangala, instead of Vanga, in imitation of the official Mughal name for the province, 'Subah Bangalah'. There is, however, no definite information about how Vanga became Bangala. According to some scholars, the word 'Bangal' was formed by the addition of the suffix 'al' to the proper noun 'Vanga'. According to Rakhaldas Bandyopadhyay and Sukumar Sen, the earliest use of the word Bangal can be found in an edict dating back to the 11th-12th centuries. But there may be some doubt about whether the word, occurring in a compound expression, was actually 'Bangal'. However, as we have already said, the first undisputed use of the word 'Bangal' can be found in a *Charyapada* poem by Bhusukpada, in which he referred to a raga as Bangal. In another couplet, he referred to himself as a 'Bangali': 'Today, Bhusuk, you are a Bangali/ A Chandal has made away with your wife' (adapted from a translation into modern Bengali by Sukumar Sen).

On a cursory reading, Bhusukpada appears to call himself a Bengali in these lines. In reality, however, the words 'Bang-a-li' or 'Banga-li' were not yet in use as meaning inhabitants of Vanga. Scholars surmise that Bhusukpada might have used the word here as meaning degraded, lowly, banished from the pale of caste. He says: 'A Chandal has taken your wife.' It appears, then, that he has become a 'Bangali' because he has lost his wife to a Chandal. In this interpretation, the word implies loss of caste, not his identity as a Bengali. The Sanskrit scriptures of the time also warned: Do not go to Vanga, for that is the land of the fallen. This, too, to an extent helps us to understand the meaning of Bhusukpada's use of the word 'Bangal'.

The first use of the word Bangal as meaning an inhabitant of Vanga can be seen during the 14th-15th centuries. It was not just Shamsuddin Ilyas Shah who was known as 'Shahe Bangalian'. A famous dervish called Nur Qutb-e-

Alam was also known as 'Alam Bangali'. He did not, however, live in southern Bengal. His grave was in Pandua. Why, in spite of this, he was called a Bengali is not known. But these were only a few exceptions, and the people of the region had not yet come to be called Bengalis. Mukundaram Chakraborty did use the word 'Bang-al' in his *Chandimangal* at the end of the 16th century. But he used it as referring to the people of southern or eastern Bengal, not the people of greater Bengal. He writes, for instance: '*Kandere Bangal bhai bafoi bafoi*' (The Bangal weeps loudly).

In the same century, 'Bangal' was also used in Brindabandas's *Chaitanyabhagavat* to refer to the inhabitants of eastern Bengal. Nearly two centuries later, it was Bharatchandra Ray who for the first time used 'Bangali' to refer to the people of the whole of Bengal: '*Bangalira kato bhalo pashchimar ghare*' (Bengalis are so much more sporting when they travel west, that is, the western provinces of India).

Elsewhere, he introduced Bhabananda Majumdar as a 'Bangali Baman' (Bengali Brahmin). According to the historian Tapan Raychaudhuri, the use of 'Bangali' as meaning the people of Bengal is not observed in written sources before Bharatchandra. However, Ahmed Sharif has claimed that the word was used in a work by Saiyid Sultan around 1584—'It is our misfortune to be born as Bengalis in Vanga. Bengalis use Arabic words without any clue to their meaning.'

Here, the word used for 'Bengali' is 'Bangali'. But Ahmed Sharif has not clarified whether the cited couplet was an interpolation, nor has he disclosed the date of the manuscript that he used. But the spelling and language do not suggest that the manuscript is quite so old.

Bengalis as Speakers of the Bengali Language

It will be easier to get a grasp of what we describe as Bengali culture if we know when it was that the language spoken in the land came to be known as 'Bangla' (Bengali), and the people who spoke it, as 'Bangalis' (Bengalis). We have said before that the language in which the *Charyapada* poems were written cannot really be called Bengali. It would be more correct to rather see it as a sort of proto-language that came just before Bengali. It was what the language of the Aryans had evolved into, after many changes, in the region.

The language spoken by the Aryans, according to philologists, was Prakrit. This spoken language took on a different name in each of the different regions of north India, defined by characteristics peculiar to that region. The Prakrit spoken in the east was known as Magadhi Prakrit. Muhammad Shahidullah described the branch of Prakrit prevelant in the Bengal region as 'Gauri Prakrit'. This Prakrit gradually evolved into *apabhramsa*, and then into *abahatta*, which is, more or less, the language of the *Charyapada*.

Just as some words and other characteristics of the Bengali language can be noticed in the language of the Charya poems, some words and other characteristics of the Assamese and Oriya languages are also evident in this language. We cannot, therefore, describe this language indisputably as Bengali. It was only in the 14th and 15th centuries that Bengali began to emerge as a distinct language. This is quite clear when one examines the language of Borhu Chandidas's *Srikrishnakeertan*. This means that roughly at the time when the regions of Gaur, Vanga, Varendri and so on became incorporated into greater Bengal (Bangalah), the language of the land became clearly recognisable as Bengali. It was not yet, however, known by any specific name. The Bengali alphabet also acquired its own peculiarities during roughly the same period. Some scholars, though, claim that the Bengali script is older. But that does not appear to be a very logical conclusion. Two things must be kept in mind in this context. One, the script of a language cannot evolve before that language acquires its characteristics. Second, the scripts of the north Indian languages evolved from the Brahmi script and, therefore, might well share similarities. If one or two characters in a manuscript here or a stone inscription there appear to resemble a character in the Bengali script, it does not conclusively follow that the script is Bengali or indeed that the writing was in the Bengali language.

Even if we accept the 15th century *Srikrishnakeertan* as an example of Bengali free from Assamese and Oriya influences, the language was not yet known as Bengali (or Bangla, as Bengalis would say). Just as we do not give specific names to the dialects spoken in the different districts of the Bengal region. Sanskrit scholars of those times described these different regional tongues simply as 'bhasha', meaning local languages. A Sanskrit sloka, for instance, proclaimed that anyone listening to the *Ramayana* or the eighteen

Puranas recited in bhasha – that is, in an unrefined local language – would be condemned to the 'Rourab Narak', the worst kind of hell.

Defying this scriptural injunction, many writers of the time translated the *Ramayana*, the *Mahabharata* and the other Puranas and produced works on religious themes, such as the Mangalkavya*s* in Bengali. Yet, remarkably, none of these writers referred to their bhasha or language as Bangla bhasha or Bengali language.

The Bengali poets of the time, in fact, described their language as just bhasha, *desi* bhasha (regional language), or '*loukik*' bhasha (spoken language). For instance, in the early 16th century, the *Mahabharata* translator Srikar Nandy called the language '*desi* bhasha'. What he wrote may be roughly translated as:

'Recite this tale in the regional tongue
And so spread word of my feat in the world'.

Kabishekhar, who came after Srikar Nandy, called it '*loukik*' bhasha instead of desi bhasha. He exhorted his audience/readers not to laugh at his use of '*loukik* bhasha'.

Even some 130-140 years after Kavishekhar, in the mid 17th century, 'Bangla' or Bengali had not gained currency as signifying the language of Bengal. Daulat Qazi referred to it as desi bhasha. Speak in the language of the land and in the rhythm of the panchalis, he said, so that everyone can easily understand. Abdul Hakim was a poet of the same century. Of all the medieval Bengali poets, it was probably he who took greatest pride in his Bengali identity and the Bengali language. But even he did not refer to it as 'Bangla'. He called it 'Bangabani' (language of Bengal), desi bhasha and 'Bangadeshi *bakya*' (language of the land of Bengal). For those Muslims who, even though born in the land, did not claim Bengali as their own and who bore ill will towards the language, his verdict was rather harsh. Not only did he cast aspersions on the legitimacy of birth of people who detested the local language (deshi bhasha) even after having lived in the land for generations, he also advised them to leave for other shores.

Though Abdul Hakim did not describe the language as 'Bangla' (Bengali), Ahmed Sharif has claimed that another poet of the same century, Muttalib, referred to the language as 'Bangala' in 1639.

In rendering Islamic themes in Bangala
I accrue many sins, I am sure
The only consolation in this clash is that
The faithful will bless me when the words make sense to them.

From the spellings and the words used in the passage, these lines may well be taken to be interpolations. In the previous discussion we noted that it was Bharatchandra Ray, the greatest poet of the 18th century, who for the first time, and repeatedly, described greater Bengal as 'Bangala', and, more importantly, called the inhabitants of this land 'Bangali'. Curiously, even he did not refer to the language of 'Bangala' as 'Bangla'. His definition of the Bengali identity was, therefore, based on the land and not on language. Bharatchandra finished working on *Annadamangal* in 1752. Even as late as that he did not call the language he was using 'Bangla' and referred to it as just 'bhasha'. Writing about his choice of Bengali rather than Hindustani or Farsi to report the conversation between Man Singh and Jahangir in *Annadamangal*, he wrote that those languages would be hard for his audience to understand, and so he would use 'bhasha' (in his case, Bengali) with a fair sprinkling of words from languages used by Muslims.

Even though Bharatchandra did not refer to the language of the Bengal region as Bengali, there is evidence in Portuguese and English works that it was more or less during his time that this language started becoming known as 'Bangla', or 'Bangala'. While the poet was still alive, Manuel de Assumpcao called the language 'Bengalla' in the Bengali grammar and dictionary that he wrote. This book was printed in 1743, in Lisbon. When Nathaniel Halhed published his Bengali grammar 17 or 18 years after Bharatchandra's death, he described the language as the 'Bengal language'. Six years after the publication of Halhed's grammar, when the East India Company's book of laws translated by Jonathan Duncan was published, 'Bangala' was still translated into English as 'Bengal language'.

Thereafter, the English titles in all the books of law that were published in Bengali translation until 1800 indicate that there was still some confusion among British officials on what the language of Bengal should be called in English. But there is no trace of uncertainty over the name of the language in the Bengali translations in these books of law. Jonathan Duncan's book of law published in 1784 uses 'Bangala' for Bengal and 'Bangla' for Bengali. Between 1787 and 1800, in the books of law translated by George Meyer, George Frederick Cherie, Neil Edmonstone and Henry Petes Forster, the Bengali language is sometimes called 'Bengal language' in English and sometimes 'Bengali'. But in Bengali texts, the language is always either 'Bangla' or 'Bangala'. In the 1790s, Henry Petes Forster consistently wrote 'Bangala' while referring to the province. He also used 'Bangladesh'. And in the title of his dictionary published in 1799-1801, he wrote 'Bongalee' to signify Bengali (a vocabulary, in two parts, English and Bongalee, and vice versâ).

Even outside the books of law around this time, the use of 'Bangala' and 'Bangali' can be noted. In Upson's *Engraji O Bangali Bocabulary* (English and Bengali Vocabulary) published in 1793, 'Bangali' is used to mean the Bengali language. But this seems to be rather an exception, since the use of 'Bangali' to mean the Bengali language cannot be seen in any other writer's work. Instead, some 4 years later, in John Miller's *Shikhyaguru* (The Educator), the word used for the Bengali language was 'Bangala'. The inhabitants of the land, the people who spoke the language, were called 'Bangali'. Introducing his book, John Miller wrote: 'Shikhyaguru is a new and suitable book in English (Engraji) and Bengali (Bangala) for Bengalis (Bangali) to learn English.'

From 1784 onwards, the words 'Bangala' and 'Bangla' started appearing even in the Bengali notices/advertisements that were published (I have discussed extensively the more than 2,000 advertisements that were published between 1784 and 1800 in my book *Kalantare Bangla Gadya*, or Bengali Prose at the Turn of the Century, 1993). Then, from 1801, when the authorities at Fort William started commissioning Bengali books, and the press run by Baptist missionaries at Serampore began printing books in the language, it was 'Bangala' that emerged as the standard word to signify the Bengali language.

As the above discussions make clear, Bengali as a language in its own right did not develop before the 13th-14th centuries. Nor had an undivided Bengal emerged before the 14th century. And the people of the province did not become known as Bengalis ('Bangali') before the 18th century. Hence, we may regard the culture that existed before the 13th-14th centuries as the bedrock of Bengali culture, but it was not yet truly Bengali in character. We have, therefore, focussed our attention on what came after that, the culture that is distinctly Bengali. But of course we must keep referring back to what came before, because we can only fathom the depths of this culture if we know about the culture that preceded it.

CULTURAL TRANSFORMATION IN THE INDO-MUSLIM ERA

Beginning from the early 13th century, Bengal was under Muslim rule for some 550 years. One must qualify 'Muslim rule' before attempting to give an account of it. The sultans of this period were immigrants from different areas of Central and West Asia and spoke different languages. They did not bring with them any single monolithic culture. What they all had in common was their religious identity. They had not, however, travelled to Bengal to preach Islam or to establish Islamic rule. Besides, the communication and administration systems of the times were not such as to make possible any direct exchanges between the highest ruling authorities and the people. Whether a sultan was a good ruler or not, his influence on the ordinary people of the land was scant. In reality, numerous small and medium kings, *dihidar*s, a service class of naibs and *qazi*s, and village elders held sway over the land and its people. The zamindari system had not been introduced yet, but the land was divided up into fiefdoms controlled by a landed gentry. These landlords/chieftains administered their own territories, and hence it was they who really ruled. It was not even as if a common law held good everywhere. The landlords made over revenues to the sultan and supplied troops at the time of war. There were also times when they joined battle with the sultan in order to defy his authority. When the Muslims first arrived in Bengal, they did not have any strength in numbers. So the land continued to be ruled directly by the old Hindu petty kings and chieftains even after the arrival of the Muslims.

The life of the most famous medieval Bengali poet, Mukundaram Chakraborty, provides a telling illustration. When state persecution forced him to leave his ancestral village, he blamed a Muslim *dihidar*, Mahmoud Sharip. Yet, a closer scrutiny will show that the man whom he named as Mahmoud's agent and held directly responsible for the harassment was not a Muslim but a 'Rayjada'. That is, the son of a certain Ray, literally meaning a king, but also used as a surname by Hindus.

The system of administration that evolved during this time can be described as being run by Hindus under the overall supervision of Muslim sultans and a handful of Muslim nobles, the amirs and omrahs. There were times, of course, when the sultan's wrath or his bounties touched lives in the countryside, but these were temporary and occasional events. It was really the old landowning families who ruled the land for generation after generation. It is thus more logical to see this age as one of Indo-Muslim rule rather than Muslim rule.

Indo-Muslim rule in Bengal started with Bakhtiar Khilji's conquest. He occupied the capital of Gaur in 1204. There is no authoritative account of his conquest. But some 40 years after the event, a Muslim historian, Minhaz us-Siraj, arrived in Lakhnauti. From the history that he wrote on the basis of anecdotal evidence, which he collected from the people living in the city, we learn that Bakhtiar attacked Gaur with a force of nearly 10,000 cavalrymen. The popular belief was that he led a front-line assault group of just 17 soldiers of this force, and with their help attacked the capital 'Nudia', encountering little or no resistance as he stormed into not just the capital but the king's palace itself. According to Richard Eaton, however, Khilji had with him not 17 but close to 200 soldiers. The old king, Lakshman Sena, fled through the back door as news reached him of the enemy soldiers trooping into the palace. This account may have some exaggeration, but there is no doubt that Bakhtiar Khilji defeated Lakshman Sena in a veritable blitzkrieg. The king subsequently moved to eastern Bengal with his close friends and followers.

This, then, was how the Muslim conquest of Bengal began. In the beginning, however, only a small part of what we now know as Bengal came under Muslim control. Much of eastern Bengal was then a swampy marshland and densely forested. Bakhtiar might have occupied Lakhnauti with remarkable ease, but he did not dare venture an assault on the forbidding forestland that lay to the east. Indeed, he was not alone in being thus thwarted. The sultans who came after him could not conquer eastern Bengal in the space of a century.

Was Lakhnauti Lakshman Sena's capital, or was it Nudia? It is not very clear. The exact location of Lakhnauti or Nudia is also not clearly known. Many scholars surmise Nudia to mean 'Nadia'. On the other hand, Lakhnauti has been identified as the contemporary name for Gaur. A site in the old city of Gaur has been identified as 'Ballal's palace' by historians (Ballal Sena was Lakshman Sena's father). The ruins found here are situated to the north of Gaur and south of Pandua. Gaur and Nadia are quite far apart from each other. The considerable distance between them has created some confusion on the question of where Lakshman Sena's capital really was. Dinesh Chandra Sen has even tried to prove that though Gaur was Lakshman Sena's capital, he had built a residence in Nadia, which was then an important hub of Brahmin scholars. This was where he was when Bakhtiar attacked, according to Sen, and that was why the conquest was made with such extraordinary ease. A more credible explanation has been offered by Abul Kalam Jakaria. He writes that 'Nudia' is actually 'Nauda' situated not far from Gaur, close to the modern-day Rohanpur railway station. Richard Eaton has also supported this inference.

Bakhtiar Khilji was a Turk. But not all the nobles (amirs and omrahs) and soldiers who came with him were Turks. Some of them had come from Arab lands, some from Turkistan, some from Uzbekistan, some from Iran and some from Afghanistan. In a word, they came from Central and West Asia. *Habshi*s from north and east Africa also arrived in Bengal in the 15th century. Those who had been driven from their homelands in Central Asia by the raids of Genzhis Khan and of the non-Muslim invaders after him initially established colonies in northern India. But many of them later moved to Bengal.

These immigrants from foreign lands were all adventurers and fortune-seekers. It was to turn around their own fortunes that they travelled to faraway Bengal. They did not come to preach their faith and thereby shore up their prospects in the next world. Almost all of them had left their families behind. It was not easy in those days to make the long journey across the difficult terrain from the Middle East to Bengal, and back again. Many died on the way. Still, there were probably many who managed to return to their homelands after making enough money. But the majority got married and settled down for good, in upper India or in Bengal. It goes without saying, of course, that most of those who stayed back married local women, using either brute force or the power of money. Consequently, they themselves partly turned into Bengalis within 40 to 50 years of their arrival in the land. Two or three generations later, there would be little, apart from their religion, to distinguish them from the local population. The elite among them, however, tried to retain their privileged social position by holding on to a linguistic difference.

We have said before that these conquerors from foreign lands had not brought with them any homogeneous, monolithic culture. And even though they were Muslims by faith, there is no reason to think that they shared similar Islamic values. For instance, after Islam spread to Iran, it assimilated many local religious rites and norms. We will discuss this in greater detail in the next chapter. It is enough to mention here that religion apart, these immigrants had significant cultural differences among themselves. Of the conquerors who came to Bengal, some spoke Arabic, some spoke Farsi, and some, Turkish. Their clothes, food and architecture were also not the same. In short, one might say that it was not just Islam that came to Bengal with its Muslim rulers, but the varied cultural and civilisational traits of a vast region of the globe.

Bakhtiar Khilji ruled Bengal for just two years. According to the historian Minhaz us-Siraj, within this short span of time he was able to run his writ over a large area through the might of the sword. In order to establish his own authority, he built mosques and madrasas (schools or colleges of Islamic education) for the ulema (Muslim scholars specially versed in Islamic law and theology) and *khanqah*s (retreats, or lodges) for the Sufis. He also arranged for the *khutba* (public prayers) to include his praises during the weekly namaz at the mosque. Besides, Bakhtiar Khilji reintroduced the use of coins in Bengal after a gap of several centuries when, according to Minhaz, there were no metal coins in Bengal before Bakhtiar Khilji's time. But it has been claimed that a coin of the time of King Sashanka has been found among the ruins of the Buddhist vihara at Mainamati. If this is true, then Khilji's coins were not the first in Bengal. But no coins belonging to the Pala and the Sena eras have been found. It may not, therefore, be unreasonable to surmise that for a few centuries before Khilji's arrival there were no metal coins in Bengal.

Khilji struck his gold coins not in his own name but in that of his overlord in Delhi, Sultan Muhammad Ghuri. Yet, he took care to maintain a certain difference from the Delhi coins. The message that he sent across through this was that these were coins of Gaur, and not of the sultan of Delhi. One side of his coins had inscriptions in Arabic. But the other side carried, along with Arabic inscriptions, the image of a soldier on horseback and two words in Sanskrit—'Gaur Vijay'. The sultans who came after him had their names, titles and dates inscribed on their coins in Arabic. It might appear on the face of it that Khilji chose to have 'Gaur Vijay' inscribed in Sanskrit because his were the first coins in Bengal after several centuries and the local population was not familiar with Arabic. His real intention, however, was to prove his own supremacy, both to the sultan in Delhi, and in Bengal.

In the seven years after Khilji, four rulers sat on the throne of Gaur. Even in this short span of time they all managed to introduce coins either in their own names or in that of the sultan of Delhi. Evidently, they were more interested in establishing their own supremacy than in restoring peace in the land. It also gives a hint of the kind of intense competition for power that was then under way within the ruling class. They had neither the time nor the opportunity to introduce reforms in the political establishment or the revenue system. However, Naseeruddin Mahmud was able to introduce a degree of stability after seizing the throne in 1213. He ruled for 14 years. No other sultan in 13th century Bengal was able to rule for that long. It can, perhaps, be assumed that it was he who, for the first time, tried to evolve a system of administration in close coordination with the local people. And he might even have been able to work out some kind of administrative structure. Moreover, though even in the 1st century of Muslim rule in Bengal the sultans tried every now and then to rule independently, they were all more or less under the sway of Delhi. They ruled in the name of the sultan of Delhi. Still, they seldom failed to seize upon moments of strife or weakness in Delhi to declare themselves as independent sultans.

Whether the sultans ruled independently, or with some degree of autonomy, the history of the 1st century of Muslim rule in Bengal is one of ruling with the sword. The sultans, their military officers and their nobles (the amirs and the omrahs) did not hesitate to shed blood or to desecrate places of worship in their efforts to subdue the local population. The most remarkable and iconic example of this tendency was Zafar Khan at the end of the century. He was said to be a pir (Sufi teacher and guide). Going by the size of his army of followers and soldiers, however, it would be more apt to describe him as a warrior pir. Besides, he helped the late 13th century ruler Ruknuddin Kaikaus to expand his sultanate. He might even have been a minor general under the sultan. He built a huge mosque at Tribeni. This mosque was a particularly noteworthy example of the use of the sword in the preaching of faith. Many of the stone slabs used in this mosque, built in 1298, have images of Hindu gods and goddesses carved on one side. In a stone inscription in the mosque, Zafar Khan boasts about how he destroyed kaffirs (infidels) with his sword. His mazar (mausoleum) was built close by, in 1313. This mazar was also constructed with stones that had been earlier used in temples of the kaffirs. Yet, the mosque and the mazar are not just symbols of the slaughter and subjugation of kaffirs. They are also beautiful examples of Indo-Turkish architecture. The minar (tower) that was built around the same time at the mosque in Choto Pandua in Hooghly district can also be recognised as Turkish architecture.

It is reasonable to ask in what ways the new rulers asserted their authority over the local population in the 1st century of Muslim rule. Is it possible to ceaselessly rule by the sword for years on end? Is it possible year after year to fill the treasury by plundering the wealth of petty kings and landlords? Perhaps not. It is more likely that the new rulers had to put in place some

Zafar Khan Gazhi's Mosque. *Photo courtesy: Biswarup Ganguly (commons.wikimedia.org)*

kind of an administrative system to govern and rule, and to do this they had to take the help of the local population. The new ruling elite did not know the local language. From the start, therefore, they were forced to depend on local collaborators to rule the land. It was the local kings and landlords who actually ruled in their name. In this way, before long there rose from among the local population an intermediate section of middlemen and brokers.

The exchanges that took place between the new rulers and this intermediate section, as well as the population at large, led, it seems within the first two or three centuries, to considerable co-mingling between the local language and culture and the language and culture brought by the Muslim immigrants. In particular, Arabic as the language of religious discourse, and initially Turkish and then Farsi as the language of administration slowly made their influence felt in the local language and literature. The English influence on Bengalis in the 18th and 19th centuries provides an inkling of the kind of impact that the newcomers must have made. If the 19th century produced an Anglicised Bengali society, then the 14th, 15th and 16th centuries produced a 'Turkish-Bengali' society. And just as the Anglicised Bengalis of the 19th century embraced foreign influences in their dress, language and in some food habits, it is reasonable to suppose that the Turkish-influenced Bengalis of earlier centuries had done the same. Many writers have left accounts of what the Anglicised Bengali society of the 19th century was like. Not much is known of the Turkish-Bengali society. But the descriptions that are available of Jagai and Madhai (two dissolute and meat-eating brothers redeemed by Chaitanyadev's disciples) of the early 16th century suggest that they belonged to this Turkish-Bengali section influenced by the Islamic world. The Jagais and the Madhais were of course different from the Anglicised Bengalis of the British colonial era, but the difference was quantitative rather than qualitative. Besides, the intermingling left its mark, more or less, on religion, architecture and various other aspects of life.

There is no specific information available about the section of people whose help Muslim rulers were constrained to seek in order to build up an administrative structure and a revenue system. It, is, however, possible to make inferences. Many of those who had been enthusiastic participants in the Brahmanic revival under the Sena rulers had followed Lakshman Sena into exile. Many of the king's warriors and aides would have also followed him. But there must have been a fair sprinkling of educated people among those who stayed back in and around the capital. Especially among the Brahmins and the Kayasthas, the two most dominant castes. They were the ones who presumably acted as the link between the rulers and the ruled in the initial years. It will not be illogical to assume that it was this section that was in the beginning most influenced by Muslim culture.

Almost all evidence of the kind of exchanges that took place between the cultures of the Middle East and Bengal in the first two centuries of Muslim rule, and of exactly when and how much the local culture was consequently influenced, is lost. But some pointers can be found in the architecture and the literature of the times. There are even indications of how the local culture influenced the rulers. Bricks, rather than stone, had to be used for the mosques, mazars and dargahs built by the rulers during this period. They had to come to terms with the fact that it was hard to come by stones in Bengal, even with the might of the sword to back them. Besides, they had themselves introduced the widespread use of lime and mortar to hold the bricks together. Many scholars say that the use of lime and mortar in construction was not known in Bengal before the time of the Muslim sultans. It is difficult to gauge how far this claim is justified. But even if the use of lime and mortar was not unprecedented, the style of domes, towers and arches introduced by the Muslim rulers was undoubtedly novel in Bengal. Their towers and domes were also quite distinct from those built in and around Delhi, partly because of differences in the ingredients used. Besides, though the Muslims gave their domes, towers and arches to Bengal, they in turn borrowed considerably from native architectural styles. The most remarkable of these was the use of terracotta. We will discuss this in the chapter 'Architecture, Art and Craft'.

The Era of Independent Sultans in Bengal

In the 14th century, the links between the local culture and the imported one grew relatively closer. One reason was that as the second half of this century began, the sultans of Bengal ceased to recognise the authority of their former overlords in Delhi and turned into independent rulers for good. After coming to power in 1342, Ilyas Shah gradually occupied, if not the entire swathe of land in eastern India between Assam and Bihar/Odisha, an extensive area in it. Some of these territories were part of the Tughlaq empire. It was easy for Ilyas Shah to establish his sway over them because they were situated far away from the imperial capital in Delhi. But these feats also bear testimony to his boldness, determination and ambition. Finally, in 1353, Sultan Firoze Shah Tughlaq of Delhi attacked Bengal with a huge force in an attempt to put a leash on Ilyas's increasing power. But Ilyas Shah was a shrewd military strategist. He did not put up any resistance at all and allowed Firoze Shah to advance deep into his territory. He himself retreated into the inaccessible Ekdala Fort away from the capital. Firoze sat on a prolonged siege outside the fort but could not occupy it. Eventually there was a pitched battle, but though Ilyas

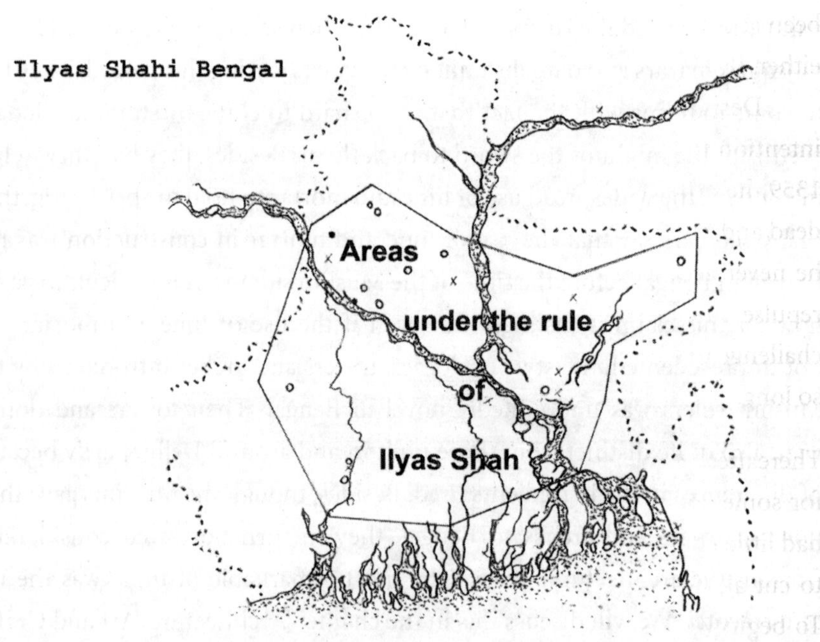

2.2 Areas that Ilyas Shah brought under his rule.

Shah suffered heavy losses, Firoze Shah was unable to win. Some historians claim that some two hundred thousand soldiers died in this battle. In the end, Firoze Shah decamped from Bengal in view of the impending monsoon. The two adversaries subsequently made truce, and Firoze Shah recognised Ilyas as an independent sultan. In his fight against the force from Delhi, Ilyas Shah was helped by local landlords and their private armies. These landlords were in those days known as 'Ray', meaning 'raja' or king. After repulsing the attack from Delhi, Ilyas Shah moved his capital from Lakhnauti to Pandua, some 20 miles to the north.

Partly because he had conquered eastern Bengal, and partly because he accepted Bengal as the land to which he belonged, Ilyas Shah proclaimed himself as 'Shah Bangalian', or the 'king of the Bengalis'. The limits of his kingdom, though, were not confined to Bengal. He had extended them to include stray fragments of Bihar and Assam. Among the Muslim-ruled territories in India thus far, his was the dominion with the most extensive borders. It does not look as if any Hindu or Buddhist ruler before him had been able to bring such a large stretch of land under a single administration either. Ilyas Shah was also able to establish peace and order in his territories.

Despite the truce of 1353, Firoze Shah Tughlaq never really gave up his intention to bring Bengal back under Delhi's domination. Six years later, in 1359, he attacked Bengal for the second time. By that time Ilyas Shah was dead and his son Sikander Shah was the sultan. Sikander was his father's son: he never accepted the domination of Delhi and, like his father, was able to repulse Tughlaq's army. After that, he ruled for 32 years, almost without any challenge to his authority. No other sultan in Bengal was able to rule for quite so long.

Thereafter, the period of independent rule by the sultans of Bengal continued for some 250 years. Having broken out of the control of Delhi, the sultans had little choice but to accept Bengal as their own land. For, they were forced to cut all ties with Delhi and to an extent with the rest of northern India. To begin with, Bengal lay at the margins of the subcontinent. Additionally, with the weakening of political ties with northern India, it was, not surprisingly, easy now for Bengal to develop a unique cultural identity. There emerged in this period opportunities for intimate connections to develop between the culture brought by the sultans from the west and the local one. Though the extent and nature of the consequent influence on the various aspects of culture is not very clear, the syncretic nature of the contact between the two cultures can be sufficiently gauged from the architecture of the times.

Between 1369 and 1375, Sikander built the great Adina Masjid in the capital Pandua. If his intention in building this mosque was to prove and flaunt his might to Delhi and Bengal, he did not fail in his objective. This mosque was not only bigger than Firoze Shah Tughlaq's Begumpur Masjid, it was the biggest mosque in India in the entire Muslim era. In the inscriptions on the walls of this mosque, Sikander proclaimed himself as the greatest ruler not only in Bengal or even in India, but as the greatest of all the sultans in the whole of the Arab world and Persia. More than its political symbolism, however, this mosque is important because of its significance in the cultural history of Bengal.

In the architecture of this mosque, Sikander Shah was able to bring about a remarkable synthesis of the traditions of the Middle East and Bengal. It bears testimony to the exchanges that were taking place between the culture of Bengal and the one that had arrived from distant shores. It also indicates the extent of the cultural synthesis that was accomplished by this time. Unlike Zafar Khan's mosque built 77 years earlier, this mosque did not replicate exactly the architectural styles of Delhi. Rather, its main structure, with some 370 domes and arches, brings to mind Persian architectural styles. Notwithstanding the imitation of Middle Eastern styles in the basic structure, however, the grooved shelves in the outer walls, the extensive use of terracotta ornamentation inside the mosque and the motifs used in them followed the local tradition. The ornamentation included suspended bells and chains and hanging lamps and lotuses, all considered symbols of the local culture. All in all, the mosque is an extraordinary example of contemporary Indian architecture. Whereas the sultans before him had blindly followed the architectural style of Delhi, Sikander brought about a synthesis of the architectural styles of West Asia's Al-Walid Mosque and Persia's Taq-i-Kisra with those of Bengal in the Pala and the Sena eras. This means that in a little over 200 years of Muslim rule, the two cultures had drawn close enough for the mutual borrowings to find unmistakable reflection in Sultan Sikander Shah's proud creation. No cause for surprise, then, if the exchanges went further and deeper in other areas of life.

Adina Mosque

Yet, it is also possible to see in the architecture of Adina Masjid signs of conflict between an alien power and the local culture. As in Zafar Khan's mosque, in this one, too, stones from older Hindu temples were used, though there was no exulting in the slaughter of infidels through stone inscriptions. This mosque also had a separate pathway to the sultan's private chambers and a raised platform for the king's throne. A higher seat for the king in a mosque is not endorsed in authentic Islamic tradition. It shows that Sikander considered himself superior not only to the local people but also to all other Muslims, including the elite Ashrafs.

Just as Sikander imported Persian styles of architecture in order to prove his own supremacy, that is, sought the seal of Middle Eastern endorsement on his own exploits, his son Giyasuddin Azam Shah established madrasas in Mecca and Medina as symbols meant to prove his primacy. He also tried to get the great Persian poet Hafiz to come to his court. In sum, the reign of the Ilyas Shahi sultans proved beyond dispute that they, and not the Sultanate in Delhi, held the reins in Bengal. Besides, the culture of Bengal quite noticeably influenced their activities. Nevertheless, all too often they turned to the Middle East for endorsement and legitimacy.

Meanwhile, Hindus had by this time started playing a more important role than ever before in administration. This was the route through which Ganesh, who came from an influential landowning family, acquired immense power and ultimately was recognised as the ruler and king. He did not seize power in a day and, most probably, never even sat on the throne at Pandua. Yet, towards the end of Giyasuddin's rule, he virtually arrogated to himself the highest administrative authority. After Giyasuddin's death in 1410, his son Saifuddin was nominally the sultan for a year. It was Ganesh who really held the reins. Around this time, a slave of Saifuddin rebelled and tried to seize power. But Raja Ganesh easily defeated him and started governing in the name of another of Giyasuddin's sons, Shihaduddin Bayjid.

At the height of his power, Raja Ganesh started directly opposing the Muslims in the land. He even took the symbolic step of razing a number of mosques at this stage. The assumption of power by a Hindu ruler and his symbolic opposition to Muslim authority through the destruction of mosques naturally had the Muslim nobility up in arms against him. Some of these amirs and omrahs even began to claim themselves as sultans. At this time some Muslim pirs invited the sultan of Bihar to occupy Bengal. In this situation Raja Ganesh realised that it would not be easy for a Hindu to rule the land in the face of direct opposition by the Muslim nobility. He therefore got his 12-year-old son, Jadu, to convert to Islam, installed him on the throne and thereafter ruled in his son's name. The boy henceforth became known as Sultan Jalal-ud-din Muhammad. Raja Ganesh was without doubt the most powerful man in Bengal at that time. Muslim opposition to him therefore dwindled immediately after his son's symbolic conversion. In fact, even a powerful pir such as Nur Qutb-e Alam now endorsed his authority. In this way the local zamindar class received institutional recognition as partners in power during the Muslim era itself. And this class, in turn, acknowledged that it was practically impossible to exercise authority without Muslim endorsement.

After his father's death, Jalaluddin did his best to establish his credentials as a religious Muslim. He rebuilt the mosques that his father had destroyed. That apart, he helped in the establishment of a madrasa in Mecca. In a stone inscription he proclaimed himself to be a *khalifa* of Allah. In order to receive endorsement from the Arab world, he even established contact with the ruler of Egypt. On the other hand, he also expressed his loyalty and attachment to the local culture. In keeping with an older tradition, he had the lion instead of the horse inscribed on his coins. This was probably an expression of his loyalty to Hindu traditions since the lion is the mount of the goddess Chandi.

Besides, it was not the architectural styles of Delhi, Persia or the Middle East but those peculiar to Bengal that were followed in many of the mosques and mausoleums built during his time or just after. A novel and fine example is Jalaluddin's mazar—the Eklakhi mazar in Pandua. It is built completely with bricks rather than stones, and instead of multiple domes it has only one large dome. Though notable, these traits are not all that novel. The quality that can be considered historic and innovative is that the mausoleum's structure imitates the quadrilateral sloped-roof cottages dotting the Bengal countryside. The curved cornice of the mausoleum imitates the sloping roofs of Bengal's thatched bamboo huts and henceforth it became so popular that it began to be widely copied—not only in mosques but also in temples and other constructions. This, indeed, became accepted as a standard architectural device in Bengal. Loyalty to native traditions can also be noted in the terracotta ornamentation and the square shape of the structure of the Eklakhi mausoleum.

The assimilation of Middle Eastern and native architectural traditions that took place in the Eklakhi mausoleum was further enhanced in the next 200 years. It was not just that native traditions influenced the constructions of the sultans. The architectural styles of the Bengal sultanate also influenced the styles followed hereafter in building temples. For instance, an architectural device such as the dome, which had been peculiar to mosques and mausoleums, now started being used in a modified form in temples and was known as *ratna*.

Dome modified as *ratna* in the Kantaji temple.
Photo courtesy: Shahnoor Habib Munmun (commons.wikimedia.org)

Jalaluddin did not patronise native traditions in architecture alone, he also actively encouraged scholarship in Sanskrit and Bengali. Richard Eaton has described this as the turning of an important corner by the Muslim nobility to embrace Bengali culture and discard the mindset that made them see themselves as outsiders in an alien land. In Jalaluddin's time, too, the local educated section, for the first time under Muslim rule, received positions of power and influence in the administration.

In 1433 CE, a year after Jalaluddin's death, the Ilyas Shahi dynasty's rule was established once again. Three sultans of the family – Nasiruddin Mahmud, Ruknuddin Barbak Shah and Shamsuddin Yousuf Shah – ruled for 48 years between them. But they were either unable to overturn the importance that native bureaucrats and local cultural traditions received under Raja Ganesh and Jalaluddin, or perhaps they did not try. Rather, they began extending their patronage to Bengali culture. This is evident in the way Barbak Shah patronised Bengali literature. It was during his rule that Maladhar Basu wrote his *Srikrishnavijay*. Based on the *Bhagavatpuran*, this was a work that played a particularly important role in the spread of the Vaishnava faith in Bengal. Some scholars say that Krittibas, too, wrote his version of the *Ramayana* during Barbak Shah's time, but there is no incontrovertible evidence supporting this.

Although they did look to the land of their origin in matters of culture, it was not from northern India or the Middle East that the Ilyas Shahi sultans recruited men to work for their armies. For this they cast their net even further away—they brought in *habshi*s from East Africa to fight in their armies, and in the process dug their own graves. These *habshi* slaves eventually got their masters out of the way and usurped the throne. Then followed a period of uncertainty and rapid changes of guard. Finally, in 1493, Alauddin Hossein Shah, a minister under the *habshi* rulers, seized power.

Hossein Shah was the most well known sultan in the entire history of medieval Bengal. Many historians have described his rule as the golden age in Bengal under the sultans. Bankimchandra is not known to have had much love lost for Muslims. Yet, he, too, claimed that a renaissance happened in Bengal under Hossein Shah. The sultan was not himself a Bengali.

Nevertheless, his extraordinary fame rests mainly on his patronage of Bengali culture, particularly of language and literature.

Just as he extended the limits of his kingdom, he also established law and order in the land to a remarkable extent. It was during his rule that the local educated community, that is, the Hindus, came to enjoy the maximum privilege and authority in the administration. His chief minister, chief security officer, chief secretary and even his chief medical officer were all Hindus. His trusted minister Sanatan (later famous as Sanatan Goswami) and his chief secretary Roop (later, Roop Goswami) were reputed scholar brothers. Roop composed a number of Sanskrit narrative poems under the Sultan's patronage. Hossein Shah was also the patron of Bidyabachaspati, the teacher and mentor of the scholar brothers. Other members of his court also composed poetic works in Sanskrit. Many poets ranging from Bidyapati and Maladhar Basu to Bipradas, Bijoy Gupta and even Mukundaram Chakraborty sang exuberant and fulsome praises of the Sultan. Even Kutban, the chief poet of Avadhi literature, praised Hossein Shah to the skies in his narrative poem *Mrigabati* (1503).

The patronage of language and literature that Hossein Shah started was not an isolated development. His son Nasiruddin Nusrat Shah also kept up the tradition. Two poems attributed to Bidyapati eulogised Hossein Shah's sons Naseeruddin Mahmud Shah and Giyasuddin Mahmud Shah. Their general and the governor of Chittagong, Paragal Khan, got the *Mahabharata* translated by Kabindra Parameswara. What is particularly noteworthy in these efforts is that unlike Dara Shikoh, that great admirer and enthusiast of Indian culture, they did not commission translations into Farsi but into the local language, Bengali. The reason for especially picking the example of Dara Shikoh in this context is that though Turkish was originally the language of the Mughal *badshahs*, living in India for several generations had slowly changed the language they used within the family. After an initial embrace of the Braj bhasha (a dialect of Hindustani then spoken in the western reaches of the Gangetic belt), they eventually adopted the *kharhi boli* (strong, masculine) Hindi spoken in and around Delhi. We learn from the letters of the hard-line Islamist *badshah* Aurangzeb that his eldest son called him 'Babaji' instead of 'Abba'. Shikoh himself surely spoke Hindi. Yet he translated the *Upanishad* in Farsi. He also commissioned other translations in Farsi. But sultans of the Hossein Shahi dynasty commissioned translations in Bengali. This suggests that not only were they familiar with Bengali, they must have been considerably attached to the language.

In an age in which reciting, or listening to, the *Ramayana, Mahabharata* and the 18 Puranas in local languages was considered blasphemous, it is doubtful if these poets would have dared to translate the sacred texts in Bengali without the backing of the sultans. It is at least beyond doubt that they received immense encouragement. Indeed, the sultans' cooperation helped to open up new horizons for Bengali literature. Foreign travellers have said that though Arabic and Farsi were the languages of administration, it was Bengali that was most volubly and widely heard everywhere during this period, beginning from the royal court.

Not only in language and literature, there is evidence of other kinds of exchange and assimilation between local and Muslim cultures during the Hossein Shahi regime. For instance, this cultural assimilation is evident in the surviving samples of contemporary architecture. The Chhoto Sona Masjid is one of the mosques that were built during Hossein Shah's time. An analysis of the mosque's architecture shows an extraordinary fusion between the two cultures. The mosque resembles the Eklakhi mausoleum in its curved cornice.

Chhoto Sona Masjid with its 15 domes; the three middle ones resemble *chauchala* huts. Its stone walls are decorated with native motifs.
Photo courtesy: Maun Sarwar (commons.wikimedia.org)

The ornamentations also bear sufficient testimony to cultural assimilation. Instead of the Islamic geometric patterns, floral and leaf patterns typical of Bengal appear on its walls. The Persian rose is inscribed at the main entrance of the mosque, and so is the lotus, symbolic of Indian tradition. The leaf of the lotus has 'Allah' inscribed on it in Arabic, showing the depth of the assimilation that had taken place. The syncretism is also clear in the domes of the mosque. There are 15 domes, arranged in five rows of three each, corresponding with the five entrances. The three domes in the middle row are shaped not like the semi-sphere that is typical of Middle Eastern tradition, but like the four-sided sloped-roof huts of Bengal's villages. Similar 'domes', obviously modified to suit local building traditions, are also there at the 60 Dome Mosque at Bagerhat. There can be few instances of cultural assimilation more conspicuous than this.

Meanwhile, an incident that took place some 2,000 miles away from Bengal during the time of Nusrat Shah before long shaped the course of politics there. In 1526 Babur came down from Central Asia to attack Delhi and sack its Afghan rulers. The defeated Afghans fled Delhi and made their way to the east. Nusrat Shah gave asylum to those who ended up in Bengal. Soon these Afghans began to play important roles in local politics. Nusrat Shah had in fact inadvertently darkened the future of his own descendants. In 1532, six years after his death, an Afghan installed himself on the throne of Bengal—he was Sher Shah. In this way, within the space of a single century, the throne and political power in Bengal passed from Turks to Bengalis, Bengalis to Turks, then again to Abyssinians, from them to Arabs and eventually to Afghans. Half a century after the Afghans seized power in Bengal, the Mughals came to hold the reins of authority there.

The dynasty founded by Sher Shah held the throne for 26 years, but power changed hands eight times during this period. These sultans were therefore busy consolidating their own power and had little time for cultivating links with the land or for any give-and-take with the local culture. The Karnani dynasty had an even shorter stint in power—the throne rotated between four sultans of the family in 11 years. They, too, were unable to make any contribution to the culture of Bengal.

End of Rule by Independent Sultans and Emergence of Colonial Rule

An immensely significant change was initiated in the politics of Bengal in 1575. That year the Emperor Akbar's army attacked Bengal for the first time. Meanwhile, during the weak rule of the Afghans, 12 powerful landlords, including Isa Khan, Pratapaditya Ray and Kedar Ray, had emerged as practically independent rulers in the territories under their control. They had become so influential that the real reins of political power in Bengal could be said to rest in their hands. They were also militarily so powerful that the Mughals were not able to secure an easy victory in Bengal. Though it was Akbar who began the Mughal military campaign in Bengal, it did not achieve success during his lifetime. The subjugation of Bengal took the Mughals more than 30 years. More precisely, it took a total of 12 governor-cum-generals in 33 years to complete this task. The man who eventually brought Bengal to its knees was Jahangir's childhood friend Islam Khan.

Once they had tightened their grip on Bengal, the Mughals introduced far-reaching and large-scale changes in the systems of administration and taxation. Ilyas Shah had shifted the capital of Bengal from Lakhnauti to Pandua. The capital was subsequently shifted again, almost 20 miles to the south—to Gaur. But Islam Khan moved the capital to Dhaka, probably to consolidate Mughal power in East Bengal. Yet the change of capital was in the main extraneous; the true transformation took place in the nature of the new ruling power. The sultans of the previous era were based in Bengal, and many of them had settled down permanently in the land along with their associates and followers. We do not know if the sultans themselves always married local women, but many of their aides took local women as wives over several generations. They had therefore become virtually localised. That apart, once they were independent of the authority of Delhi, the sultans and their aides became increasingly alienated from north India. They had no option but to identify themselves with Bengal. And in this way they became patrons of Bengal's culture.

On the other hand, the Mughals and the men in their employ who came with them from northern India could never make Bengal their own, nor did they ever become permanent residents of Bengal. Those who came did so on the understanding that it would be a temporary move. It was the power centre in Delhi that they were loyal to. The roots of their identity were in the soil of Delhi, or even perhaps in the Middle East. The Mughal officials serving in Bengal, along with their soldiers and other employees of humble rank, were not a happy lot and often complained about the climate, food and the people of the land. This mindset of alienation was quite distinct from the syncretism under the earlier sultans.

A pointer to how the Mughals felt about Bengal is available quite early on in Mughal rule – in 1579 – in a comment by Abul Fazl. He wrote that Bengal was a land of rebellion and strife. A pir called Shah Niamatullah Firozpuri arrived in Bengal during the time of Shah Jahan, ostensibly to acquire virtue through preaching religion. He founded a settlement in Malda. He, too, soon got fed up. There was no peace in Bengal, he wrote with poetic flourish, and one was food for either tigers or crocodiles. Quite a few of these pirs in fact proclaimed Bengal to be 'Dar-ul-Harb' or a land of strife not fit to be lived in. The mindset was not much different from the contempt in which the Aryans held Bengal many centuries earlier.

The Mughals never felt at home in Bengal. They regarded themselves as different and distinct from the people of the land in their language, clothes and food. They considered themselves to be superior to Bengalis, just as the British did in a later age. These roti-and-meat-eating outsiders of the Mughal age detested the fish and rice of Bengal. Even when the Mughal age was over and British colonial rule had been established, Mughal officials were not able to discard their old attitudes. There is unmistakable evidence of this in Ghulam Hossein Selim's comment in his 1786 book *Riyaz-us-Salatin.* He wrote:

> *The high and low of the land all love to eat fish, rice, mustard oil, curds, fruits and sweets. They like a lot of red chilli peppers and also salt in their food. They do not at all eat wheat and barley rotis. Goat meat and poultry cooked in ghee do not agree with them at all. The people of this land are inferior in their tastes, customs and clothes.*

Mughal officials looked down on Bengalis as lowly fisherfolk. They even described Isa Khan and his son Musa Khan as fishermen.

Indeed, the Mughal officials saw themselves as the rulers and Bengalis as the ruled. They regarded themselves as warriors from the Middle East or at least from upper India and Bengalis as the low-born inhabitants of a swampy lowland area. Islam Khan's naval chief was Ihtimam Khan, who was also the historian Mirza Nathan's father. He was born in northern India. Yet he saw himself as an outsider in an alien land and described Bengalis as 'natives'.

Some 20 years after Ihtimam Khan's time, a poet called Sadiq Isfahani came to work in Dhaka as an employee of the Mughal administration. He lived in Dhaka from 1629 to 1650. Isfahani kept a diary. We learn from his journal that the number of urban Ashraf, that is, elite Muslim, families grew in Bengal during the Mughal era. The ancestors of many of the elite families he encountered in Dhaka had come from Tehran, Shiraz, Isfahan, Mashhad, Tabriz and Bokhara. These people, living in Dhaka in Isfahani's time, had been born in northern India, and that was where they came from. Yet they still claimed to be Persians.

Many of these foreign-origin people were Shias. Shias grew further in number during Shah Jahan's time. This was because one of his sons, Shah Shuja, during his governorship of Bengal, brought with him 300 Shia families. There is anecdotal evidence suggesting that he, too, had become a Shia. As the numbers of city-dwelling Ashraf families swelled, their distance with native Muslims in the countryside also grew. The Portuguese monk Sebastiano Manrique travelled in Bengal in 1629. He was then not yet very familiar with the land and its ways. In his view, the land was inhabited by the Portuguese, Muslims and natives. Which is to say he was not able to identify native followers of Islam as Muslims. Or perhaps he did not regard them as true Muslims.

The Mughals and the Bengalis were not bound by any relationship other than that of the ruler and the ruled. The Mughal conquest of Bengal was entirely motivated by hopes of economic and military gain. Once Bengal was won, the Mughals for the first time had the province's total arable land measured. Todar Mal supervised this exercise. After the land was measured, Mughal officials worked out the taxes to be collected from the land. Not only that, they also worked out a system of land tenancy, that is, the 'zamindari' structure of landholding. This was the structure that, with some modifications, remained in place during British colonial rule. According to Abul Fazl, taxes on farmland were fixed at almost a third of the total produce. After the land measurement exercise, land revenue was fixed at 63,44,260 rupees in 1582. But land taxes were more than doubled in 1658 and fixed at 1,31,15,907 rupees. In Murshid Quli Khan's time the land revenue stood at rupees 1,42, 88,186. This earning from land went to the Mughal coffers in Delhi.

The men and women living in the countryside at that time did not have an exact estimate of the increase in land taxes. But the burden of the increase affected their lives. That the exercise of land measurement and the tax structure that followed were not quite just and pushed peasants into poverty is indicated in Mukundaram's *Chandimangal.* According to him

> *They measure the land diagonally to make a bigha with fifteen kathas (instead of twenty), paying no heed to the peasant's pleading. The king becomes the oppressor and his men mark/classify barren land as fertile. ...The piyadas (guards) keep an eye on everyone, lest people flee, and stand guard at their doors. Alarmed and upset, the peasants are selling off household stuff, they let go a rupee's worth for 10 annas.*

We learn from Abul Fazl's writing that tenants paid their taxes in cash. This, too, was perhaps one of the things that inconvenienced them. The zamindars were required to pay large sums of money as taxes, which they paid in gold and silver coins.

A more monetised economy, instead of the old barter system of exchange, came to prevail under the Mughals. Much buying and selling is seen to be going on in Mukundaram's imagined city of Gujarat. It is reasonable to suppose that all this buying and selling involved exchange of currency. In commenting on the taxes payable to Muslim merchants of faith, the poet mentions units of currency such as *siki, ganda, kurhi, burhi* and so on. Shells were widely used in small exchanges. The mention of the *siki* (a coin worth 4 annas, 16 annas being equivalent to one rupee or taka) suggests that the taka was also used. Agriculture, trade and industry improved in Bengal at this time. The Mughals played an active role in this growth story, and they did so to nurture their own economic interests. What they did can in fact be compared to the founding of a colony. Under their watch a huge amount of wealth was transferred every year to Delhi. After the end of the Mughal era, Bengal was turned into a full-fledged colony under British rule.

It was during Mughal rule, and not earlier, that the colonial character of the administration first manifested itself.

Mughal efforts brought about an immense improvement in the communication system. Northern India, in particular, became linked by better roads not only to Bengal but to other areas in the subcontinent. An indirect evidence of this is that Vaishnavas repeatedly travelled from Bengal to Vrindavan, and from Vrindavan Vaishnava religious ideals made their way to other parts of India. This improvement in communication facilitated progress in trade and business. In particular, Bengal's trade with western India and various other parts of the subcontinent as well as with the Arab coastal states grew by leaps and bounds. Trade links with South East Asia also grew. It was during Nusrat Shah's time that the Portuguese first came to Bengal to ascertain whether conditions suitable for trade existed here. Though trade with Portugal did not immediately take off very rapidly, it vastly increased under the Mughals. But a much greater volume of trade was established with the East India Company. Queen Elizabeth I sent Company envoys to Akbar with a letter requesting trade rights, and her successor, King James I, wrote to Jahangir. The Mughal state's volume of trade with the Dutch, Danish and French companies also grew. The growth in foreign trade spurred production, including textile output, and also pushed up the quality of the products. Just as industrial growth helps in the development of trade, growth in trade also helped in the development of industry.

Notwithstanding their policy of not patronising any particular faith, the Mughals exerted a significant influence on local culture. Two figures of this time show that though 73 mosques, with their dates of construction recorded, were built in the 16th century, the number of such new mosques dwindled in the 17th century. Only 24 new mosques were built in this century. Fewer, still, were built in the next half century—only eight new mosques. On the contrary, much enthusiasm can be noticed in the building of temples during the period under discussion. Whereas only seven new temples, with their dates of construction recorded, were built in the 16th century, 74 temples were built in the 17th century. Another 138 were built in the first six decades of the 18th century until the start of British colonial rule. As people became, with time, more and more familiar with Muslim rule, Hindus – in proportion – regained their influence and self-confidence. That apart, there is historical evidence to show that from the 15th century the sultans in some cases donated tax-free land for the upkeep of temples. The tide of enthusiasm that Chaitanyadev generated among Hindus might well have also contributed to the interest in building temples.

But what was the reason for the dwindling number of new mosques? State initiatives in building mosques, or even state help in building them, seems to have rapidly declined under the Mughals. On the other hand, though the Mughals may not have extended any direct cooperation to Hindus in building temples, they did not put up any opposition either. This was the reason why the number of temples went up. That the Mughals kept themselves dissociated from the local culture is evident in the way they refrained from patronising the local language and literature, unlike the earlier sultans. A far greater, and more visible, proof of their cultural detachment is that they did not accommodate local architectural influences in the mosques and mausoleums that they got built. The notable architectural edifices that were built in Dhaka under the Mughals, particularly the Seven Dome Masjid, Khan Mohammad's Masjid and the mosques in the Lalbag Fort, are not too different from the mosques in Delhi. The mazar of Pari Bibi is also built in the architectural style associated with Delhi. On the contrary, the temples built during this period followed the architectural styles that had developed under the sultans.

There is actually evidence to show that the Mughals followed a fairly rigid policy of separating governance from religion. Islam Khan himself was an orthodox Muslim. Since maintaining female slaves is endorsed in Islam, he is said to have had some 1,500 women in his harem. Yet he did not allow his ministers and bureaucrats to drink, not even on special occasions. For, Islam does not allow drinking. So whenever he was expected to attend a function, his amirs and omrahs finished their drinks before he arrived and concealed all traces of their forbidden pleasure by sprinkling attar. But even a hard-line Islamist like Islam Khan severely reprimanded and transferred an employee when he got to know how the latter had got a Hindu zamindar's son to convert to Islam after trouncing his father.

The sultans were generous with gifts of land to the Sufi pirs who came to Bengal to preach, even if they did not directly cooperate with them, especially in the first 200 years of Muslim rule. But the tradition of donating land to pirs almost came to an end under the Mughals. The ideal of rewarding efforts to preach Islam was in fact quite absent in this new dispensation. On the contrary, the practice, supported by law, was rather to not differentiate between Hindus and Muslims in the eyes of the administration.

When the shipwrecked Portuguese monk Sebastiano Manrique was travelling through western Bengal in 1640, disguised as a Muslim merchant, one of his Muslim employees secretly slaughtered a peacock one night, and then cooked and ate its flesh. Eating a peacock is not forbidden for Muslims. But the Hindus of the area were aggrieved. When they sought justice, the local Muslim administrator ordered the offender to be whipped and his arm to be amputated. Manrique, however, managed to save the poor man's arm through various clever ploys and costly gifts to the administrator's wife. The offender got away with just the whiplashes. In sum, far from meddling in the religious life of the local population, the Mughals seem to have been rather intolerant of even acts that might hurt their religious sentiments. They were aware that such acts did not help the cause of efficient administration.

This policy of non-interference stumbled for the first time during Aurangzeb's time. He imposed the *jiziya* tax on non-Muslims. This cannot, of course, be said to amount to meddling in religion. The Mughal reasoning was this: a Muslim administration was taking care of subjects belonging to other faiths, and non-Muslims were required to pay a price for the service through this tax. Non-Muslims, however, were unable to see this tax as anything but unjust, for the administration of any state was expected to take care of all its subjects. What this tax did, in fact, was to turn non-Muslims into aliens in their own land. The Mughals tried to enforce this tax with a firm hand. Not only Hindus, they tried to extract this tax even from the Portuguese.

The sultans of Bengal and their ministers had, in the 15th and 16th centuries, patronised the Bengali language and literature. This patronage of language and literature was stopped in the Mughal dispensation. No

Mughal subedar (governor) is known to have encouraged the pursuit of Bengali language or literature. It was rather the petty kings and landlords of outlying states such as Tripura, Cooch Behar, Bishnupur, Krishnanagore and Arakan who at this time started providing encouragement to Bengali literary activities. It was the patronage of the Arakan royals that made possible the extraordinary romances written by Daulat Qazi and Alaol. The influence of Islam is rather scant in the works of these poets because Arakan was situated at the frontier of Muslim governance, in fact, almost outside its pale.

Mughal rule had an impact on the Bengali language. The earlier sultans extended special patronage to Arabic, but Farsi came to be widely used under the Mughals. The stone inscriptions and writings on mosques in the Mughal age were in Farsi instead of Arabic. Farsi began to be so widely used in administration and tax collection at this time that Farsi words, and also Arabic ones through Farsi, found their way into Bengali in large numbers. These words gradually began to influence Bengali literature, too. A counterexample may serve to show the impact of the times on literature. The Bengali literary texts produced in the Arakan royal court, outside the Mughal sphere of influence, were written in a language dominated by *tatsama* words, or words of Sanskrit origin that had been retained largely in their old form. In Mughal-ruled Bengal, however, Ramprasad Sen used plenty of Arabic and Farsi words in the Hindu religious songs that he composed. There is relatively greater use of Arabic and Farsi words in some of Alaol's works, necessitated by the requirements of his themes. In comparison with the mainstream Muslim poets, however, he, too, used very few Arabic and Farsi words.

On the contrary, an analysis of the language in which Bharatchandra Ray or Ramprasad Sen wrote towards the end of the Mughal period will show more frequent use of Arabic and Farsi words than in earlier poets. Bharatchandra's theme in *Annadamangal* was religious. And Ramprasad Sen wrote Shyamasangeet, songs dedicated to the dark goddess Kali. But even while singing praises of Hindu gods and goddesses, these poets could not avoid what Bharatchandra called *jaboni mishal*, a language profuse in its content of Arabic and Farsi words. For, this was the language on which they had been brought up in the Mughal age, and this was the language in which they had learnt to think. Bharatchandra, of course, was extremely careful in his choice of words and there were some contexts in which he completely avoided Arabic and Farsi words. Ramprasad Sen not only used Arabic and Farsi words in his religious songs, he also freely used words employed in matters relating to ownership of and litigation over land in the Mughal age.

To sum up, then, we may say that Muslim rule had an impact not only in administration and the organisation of the tax structure, but in all areas of life such as architecture, literature and language. Elsewhere we will note how Muslim rule also produced immense transformations in the clothes and food of Bengal.

SOCIETY AND RELIGION

There is no clear picture of the people who lived in Bengal before the Aryans came. But the commonly held belief is that they did not belong to a single anthropological group. Many scholars have said that most of them were of the Austric group of people. Indeed, modern-day Bengalis show a marked physical resemblance to the people of this group. Besides, there were Dravidians who came from the south of the subcontinent. And there were people of the Bhot-Chinese group who had come from South East Asia. There were people of other ethnic groups, too. The diverse tribal groups, or the Adivasis, who still live here perhaps carry a hint of the presence of many different ethnic groups in Bengal in prehistoric times. Just as the people of prehistoric Bengal did not talk in a common language, they did not also follow a common religion. Many people did not even practise an institutionalised faith. Their food habits, their styles of building homes and their clothes largely differed from those in northern and central India, and the reasons lay predominantly in geography. Not only were these inhabitants of prehistoric Bengal racially quite distinct from the Aryans; their languages, faiths, festivals, rituals and other distinctive cultural traits were also completely different.

Judging by its climate and geographical position, ancient Bengal was not a very attractive place. Yet, people from other regions kept arriving here, in successive waves. This shows that this was a land of plenty, rich in food and grains. From the Sanskrit scriptures and literary texts of the pre-Christian era, we know that Bengal was deemed the land of the impure and the outcastes. Outcastes, because the people living here followed their own set of rituals and beliefs, the local *vrata*s (ritual propitiation of folk deities, usually performed by women), and not the Vedic ones. The scholars who wrote and interpreted the scriptures, therefore, condemned it as out of bounds for the faithful. Yet, the Aryans started arriving in this frontier region of the subcontinent a good few centuries before the birth of Christ, and with them came the Aryan culture. Interactions with these newcomers gradually influenced the local systems of production, agriculture and, generally, the local culture.

Among the totally unfamiliar cultural ingredients that the Aryans brought with them, religion was extremely significant. It is reasonable to suppose that as interactions between the two peoples became intimate, the Vedic faith started making an indelible imprint on the pre-existing faiths of the local non-Aryans. How much of the Brahmanic faith was accepted by the non-Aryans in those initial years of intermingling is, however, not known with any certainty. On the other hand, from the way in which the Vedic faith evolved in Bengal, it is evident that within a few centuries the Brahmanic tradition assimilated the local belief systems. In this way, non-Aryan gods and goddesses made their way into Brahmanism. And with them, local rituals and religious traditions also found a place in the Brahmanic faith. In particular, there is no doubt that the Aryans adopted many of the *vrata*s of the local population. To sum up, the coming of the Aryans produced interactions between the local and the imported cultures, and in the process the religious practices of both Aryans and non-Aryans began to change.

Whenever the Aryans may have first arrived in Bengal, their way of life began to make a forceful impact in Bengal in the Mauryan era. One reason for this was that the capital of the Mauryan empire was just next door, in Magadha. During this period, beginning in the 3rd century before Christ, the close interaction between the two cultures grew quite spectacularly in agriculture and in the system of production. Besides, Buddhism, as the state religion, began to rapidly gain currency. Second century BC inscriptions on the Sanchi stupa claim Bengal as Buddhist territory. A 3rd century BC stone inscription in Andhra also proclaimed Bengal as Buddhist territory. In 405 a Chinese traveller noted 22 Buddhist sanghas (monastic orders) in the town of Tamralipti (Tamluk, in present-day Midnapore) alone. It is clear, then, that Buddhism in Bengal was established on strong foundations much before the Pala kings came along.

Under the Gupta rulers, however, Brahmanism received proactive state patronage. The copper-plate edicts of this period mention that Vedic rituals and ceremonies were observed in Bengal. They also mention that land was donated to Brahmins for religious purposes. But though Brahmanism had state patronage, there is no evidence to show that Buddhism was up against any active opposition under the Guptas. There is evidence, however, that Buddhism faced a severe onslaught in the early 7th century under the indomitable King Sasanka of Bengal. The destruction of Buddha images, the razing of Buddhist viharas, the expulsion of Buddhist *bhikshus* (mendicants) from Bihar, and the chopping off of the Bodhi tree at Bodh Gaya were some of the outrages mentioned by the Chinese traveller Hiuen Tsang. He visited Bengal at the time of Sashanka, so his account was contemporary, and it is reasonable to accept it as true, although some exaggeration cannot be ruled out. Among the Vedic systems of belief, it was Shaivism that got the best deal under Sashanka. For, the king himself subscribed to this faith. Thereafter, Shaivism became very popular in Bengal.

From the 4th or 5th century onwards, the Hindu faith seems to have thrived on royal patronage while Buddhism gradually began to lose ground. That, at least, is the impression one gets from the information left behind by Chinese travellers. The table below gives the numbers of Vedic and Buddhist temples mentioned by Chinese travellers.

Count of Buddhist and Vedic temples as given in accounts left by Chinese travellers

Place	Fa-Hien 5th Century		Hiuen Tsang 7th Century		Yijing late 7th Century	
	Buddhist	Vedic	Buddhist	Vedic	Buddhist	Vedic
Tamralipti	22		10	50	5/6	
Varendra			20	100		
Samatata			30	100		

Table 3.1

The fortunes of Buddhism revived again under the Pala kings. Different parts of Bengal were at times simultaneously ruled by patrons of Buddhism as well as by Hindu kings. Jainism was never a dominant religion in Bengal, but there is no doubt that it had a presence, and Jain temples and viharas got built at many places. Besides, many people must have held on still to the old beliefs that had been prevalent in Bengal before the Aryans arrived. Bengal, in short, was a land of multiple faiths. Depending on state patronage, however, sometimes Buddhism, sometimes Brahmanism and sometimes a particular sect of these two principal faiths, gained predominance. With a change of rulers there usually came a change in the fortunes of the cults they espoused.

King Gopala established the Pala dynasty in the middle of the 8th century. An enthusiastic supporter of Buddhism, he played quite a proactive role in the spread of Buddhism in Bengal. After him, Dharmapala, too, helped Buddhism to prosper. Before the Palas, and also during their rule, kings of the Khadug, Deb and the Chandra families patronised Buddhism. Indeed, it was not only the Buddhist faith but also Buddhist-influenced institutions of learning that became widespread under the Palas. Two huge Buddhist viharas were built with Dharmapala's help: at Vikramasila in the west, beyond the boundaries of Bengal and the Sompur or Sompuri Vihara at Paharpur in North Bengal.

Somapur Vihara, popularly known as Paharpur Vihara.
Photo courtesy: Maun Sarwar (commons.wikimedia.org)

Buddhist viharas are known to have been built even earlier in the Comilla region, located south-east in present-day Bangladesh. But it is not known when the Salban vihara of Mainamati in Comilla was built. It is not known, either, whether it was built under the patronage of the Palas or the Debs or any other ruling family. Apart from the Salban vihara, several other viharas, both big and small, were built in the Mainamati area. These viharas were important centres for the practice of the Buddhist faith and also of Buddhist education. They were built, one after another, between the 7th and the 12th centuries. The large number of viharas and other Buddhist centres of learning that came up during the reign of the Pala kings shows how popular the religion was in Bengal at this time. It can also be inferred, from imitations of Buddhist architecture, that the Buddhists of Bengal wielded considerable influence well beyond the limits of the land. Buddhist temples modelled on the Paharpur Vihara were built in far-off Indonesia and other places in South East Asia in ancient times.

A central scriptural text of the Mahayana Buddhists is called *Astasahasrika Pragnya Paromita.* One of the manuscripts of this book, written in the 11th century, tells us about the main centres of Buddhism in Bengal at that time. Places that receive particular mention in the book are Haldigram and Deddapur in Varendri; Kanyaram, Ramjat and Baitrabana in Rarh; Jagnyapindi in Dandabhukti; Jayatungo and Champitala in Samatata; Shila Loknath in Harikela; and Sribijaypur in Subarnapur. Buddhists, clearly, occupied an influential position in society.

Notwithstanding their patronage of Buddhism and the various institutions connected with the faith, the Pala kings never opposed Brahmanism. Indeed, the Brahmanic tradition actually grew in strength under their rule. Among the masses, especially, there is evidence to show that Hindu beliefs became quite popular. And in fact some of the later Pala kings are even said to not have been Buddhists at all.

State patronage of Brahmanism increased under the Burman kings, who came after the Palas. But it was under the Sena kings that this religion got maximum support and patronage. The Senas had come as mercenaries from southern India and settled down in Bengal under the Palas. Towards the end of the 11th century, they seized power. Once in power, they started backing Brahmanism, especially the Shaiva cult. Vaishnavism, too, became quite popular towards the end of their short rule. And hand in hand with the spread of Hindu beliefs came a renewed interest in the study of the Sanskrit language, literature and scriptures. There is no reason to suppose, however, that Brahmanism spread evenly or at the same pace everywhere in the land, or that Buddhism and the local folk rituals and religious practices were completely wiped out. It is more logical to assume that it was among the elite that the Brahmanic faith, as the rulers' religion, found its chief patrons. From a geographical perspective, it was in the Rarh region that Brahmanism first made a strong impact, especially along the banks of the Ganga. For, this was where the Aryans found it easiest to set up their first colonies as they came down from the north. In the next phase, many of them chose northern Bengal to make permanent settlements. Much of eastern and southern Bengal still remained inaccessible and unfit for habitation. The agricultural methods followed by the Aryans were not yet followed in these areas. Bengal may not have been anymore the land of the outcastes that the ancients had believed it to be, yet the Brahmins who had come from northern India still seemed to have been rather contemptuous of much of southern and eastern Bengal. Many of them, therefore, did not think of these areas as liveable for decent people.

The Evolution of the Vedic and Buddhist Faiths

As persuasions of the conquerors, the Vedic and the Buddhist faiths rapidly spread their influence on local belief systems over several centuries. As early as the 7th century, Hiuen Tsang noticed how Vedic ritualistic forms of worship had become fairly widespread. It does not look as if he had any intimate acquaintance with rural society. But he did spend time in quite a few cities. From his accounts, it appears that among the city dwellers it was the Vedic and Buddhist faiths that prevailed most widely. Many people also observed the Jain faith. Hiuen Tsang has left descriptions of many *bhikshu*s, priests and devotees who served the religions followed in the cities. He has not, however, mentioned to what extent people beyond the limits of the cities practised institutionalised faiths or what their forms of worship were. But it would not be unreasonable to assume that the masses subscribed to a varied range of beliefs and worshipped many gods and goddesses. They would have had their own rituals and *vrata*s. That this was so is evident from the way in which these old rituals eventually got assimilated in the Vedic and Buddhist forms of worship. Just as the advent of Islam in the medieval period produced a process of opposition and assimilation between the local and the imported religions, the Vedic and Buddhist faiths in an earlier time must have produced a similar process between the pre-existing and the newly arrived belief systems.

The toiling masses of Bengal do not seem to have taken to authentic forms of the Vedic or Buddhist faith in a long while. And even when they did accept them, they do not appear to have been very strict in the observance of rituals and ceremonies. The accounts left by Hiuen Tsang and other Chinese travellers show that the forms of Buddhist worship that they observed in Magadha were quite different from what was followed in Bengal. It is possible to infer, then, that local beliefs and rituals had got assimilated in the Buddhism practised in Bengal. Bengal's geographical position as the frontier province must have played a role in this process.

This process of assimilation was not limited to the local belief systems but was at work even between the Vedic and Buddhist faiths. Some historians say that the Tantric mode of worship, in particular, made an impact on Buddhism in Bengal. Indeed, the spread of Tantric forms of worship does not seem to have been unlikely in a social life that was dominated by farming activities and the worship of mother goddesses. Roughly around the 8th century, under the influence of Tantric beliefs, first the Mantrayana tradition, and then the Bajrayana tradition that evolved out of it, developed in Mahayana Buddhism. Later, from the Bajrayana tradition was born a branch of the Buddhist-Tantric sect called Kalchakrayana. But it was the Sahajayana branch of Buddhism that became popular towards the end of the Pala regime and later during the rule of the Sena kings.

Buddhism in its initial days did not even have room for the concept of a Creator, let alone gods and goddesses. However, in a society where other religions sported innumerable gods and goddesses, Buddhists could not help but acquire some of their own along the way. Indeed, the Buddha himself came to be imagined as God. He even came to be represented in various forms, and each of these forms was given a name—such as, Amitabha, Bodhisatva, Manjusri, Abalokiteswar and Bajrapani. The Buddha was also imagined as Bajrabhairava with nine heads and 34 arms. What is more, the Tibetan deity Hebajra was converted into a god for the Mahayana Buddhists. There were goddesses, too, imagined as consorts for the Buddha or as creative energy. The goddess Tara was imagined in 13 forms in Tibet, such as Sittara, Shyamtara, Ugratara, Ekjata, Kurukulla, Bhrukuti, and so on. Tara was also imagined as a goddess ruling over snakes, much like Manasa, and in this form she was called Janguli.

It was the Sahajayana branch of Buddhism with which Hinduism engaged with particular intensity, especially its Shakta and Tantric branches. Whether the Buddhists actually worshipped any of the Vedic deities is not known. But from the terracotta motifs in the Paharpur Vihara and the images sculpted on the walls of the temple there, it can be inferred that they were respectful towards Hindu deities. Most of the 63 figures sculpted on the temple walls are those of Hindu gods and goddesses, with Krishna predominating. This might suggest that Vaishnavism had an impact on Buddhists, but historical evidence does not support this inference. These sculptures are a few centuries older than the temple. It is not impossible that they were brought in from some other temple and mounted on these walls. Or, it could even be that the vihara itself came up on the site of an older temple.

Krishna and Radha, Hindu deities on terracotta slabs. The Paharpur Vihara

The terracotta slabs on the temple walls offer a glimpse into the minds of the people of those times and also perhaps of the craftsmen who made them. On many of these terracotta slabs are images of Hindu gods and goddesses, for instance the different forms of Shiva and also Brahma, Vishnu, Surya, Ganesh, Krishna and Radha. Hindu deities on terracotta slabs also adorn the Mainamati Vihara. All this indicates a process of assimilation between the two faiths. But many researchers believe that Buddhism was influenced most by Tantric modes of worship.

For the followers of the Sahajayana tradition, the guru, or spiritual mentor, is deserving of the highest worship. In a way this was like a simpler form of the Bajrayana tradition, without the stress on ceremonies, in which the transformation of the heart was more important than rituals. But the practices and beliefs that crept into this sect in the name of spiritual seeking cannot be said to have been consistent with the highest ideals of Buddhism. The Acharyas, or teachers, of this sect were called Siddhacharyas. The *Charyapada* poems, the earliest samples of Bengali literature, were the work of these Siddhacharyas. Gradually, the Shakta, Tantric and Sahajayana traditions merged to give rise to the Sahajiya sect. Over a few centuries, this sect spawned several branches such as the Nathpanthis, the Abadhutas and the Bauls.

Hinduism in Bengal, just like Buddhism, assimilated many of the pre-existing local deities, rituals and other religious practices. It thus developed in a way that was quite distinct from Hinduism as it evolved in the rest of India. Not only did it make space for local folk gods and goddesses and deities worshipped in the Mahayana tradition, it also assimilated Buddhist and other local rituals. In some cases, the ancient gods and goddesses came to be equated with new deities, while some came to be imagined in various forms in keeping with local beliefs. Chandi, for instance, was imagined in different forms, each form representing one quality attributed to her. The images of gods and goddesses made in Bengal also unmistakably show the local influence.

In this context it may be mentioned that gods, rather than goddesses, predominated in the Vedic tradition. Though Shiva was a non-Aryan deity to begin with, he got incorporated into the Aryan pantheon quite early on. He was seen as the divinity in control of the endless cycle of creation, existence and destruction. He represented the highest ideal of manhood and pure consciousness. His was the seat deserving of the highest worship. In the non-Aryan tradition, on the other hand, mother goddesses predominated as embodiments of the primeval energy driving the world. Both gods and goddesses seem to have been worshipped in pre-Islamic Bengal. Not only did they live side by side in popular consciousness, they also formed family ties between themselves. As wives, daughters and daughters-in-law of Shiva, the non-Aryan goddesses became accepted as deities in the Hindu tradition.

For instance, the story of Manasa and the *vrata*s associated with it had been in circulation long before the Aryans came, especially among women in the Rarh region. She was not, however, a very popular goddess, nor did she receive worship from higher-caste Hindus. Eventually, however, as Shiva's daughter she gained more acceptability as a deity to be worshipped. Yet, the status of Shiva's daughter gave her only limited respectability. The goddesses who were recognised as wives of Shiva enjoyed a higher status—Chandi,

Durga and Kali. Each of these three goddesses was, again, imagined as having multiple forms, thus allowing many non-Aryan goddesses to be assimilated into the Hindu tradition.

The process was under way during the Pala and the Sena regimes and continued well into the Muslim age. Sukumar Sen, on the basis of linguistic analysis, has pointed to a difference between Vedic and folk deities. According to him, the Vedic deities and the Puranic characters continued to be known by their Sanskrit names in fairly unchanged form (*tatsama*) during the Middle Ages: Shiva, Vishnu, Ram, Lakshman, Yudhishthir, Arjun, Dasharath and so on. Whereas the folk deities and local mythological characters came to be known by *tatbhava* names, with Sanskrit root but modified to suit the phonology of the regional language: Kanai, Kanu, Rai, Aayan, Behula, Phullora, etc.

The Buddhist and the Vedic traditions can be said to have one thing in common: they both originated outside Bengal. The Vedic faith travelled several hundred miles before it arrived in Bengal from northern India. The Buddhist faith also came from territory well outside Bengal. Both traditions lost much of their pristine forms in this remote frontier region with tenuous geographical links with the lands of their origin. Local influences brought about changes in both, making for new characteristics that marked them out. The Islam that was preached in Bengal in later years also acquired a distinct local form.

The point in history that we have identified as marking the beginning of a distinctive Bengali culture was the time when the Pala regime was making way for the Sena dynasty. As we have said before, though the Palas were Buddhist kings, some of the later monarchs were more inclined towards the worship of Shiva. The Sena kings were Shaivas, but the last of them, Lakshman Sena, was a Vaishnava. Indeed, notwithstanding the personal loyalties of the Sena rulers to either Shaivism or Vaishnavism, no branch of the Hindu faith was neglected or mistreated under them. Even the worship of Shakti (the mother goddess as the source of creative energy) was quite widespread. Many scholars believe that the process of assimilation that had started a few centuries earlier between the Shakta (involving the worship mother goddesses) and the Tantric traditions reached a point of culmination at this time.

Though the Pala kings did not all share the same religious loyalties, they all patronised the Brahmanic faith and the Sanskrit language. On the other hand, the *Charyapada* poems that the Buddhist Siddhacharyas composed during the Sena regime and earlier were written in the local language. The Sena kings, however, ignored this local tradition and were more enthusiastic in their appreciation and patronage of the Sanskrit language and encouraged the writing of literature in it. Ballal Sena and Lakshman Sena themselves wrote quite a few books in Sanskrit. Halayudh and Sarvananda were the most well known scholars and experts in the scriptures of the time. Dhoyi, Sharan, Umapati and Govardhan were poets. But it was Jaidev who attained real literary fame. Though he was a Bengali, he did not write his *Gita Govinda* in Bangla. The other poets of his time also wrote in Sanskrit.

In spite of enough literary activity during the Sena regime, it was the study of the scriptures rather than the pursuit of literature that received more encouragement. There was particular interest in Smriti, Nava Nyaya and such subjects. It was also at this time that caste differentiation became quite entrenched. The southern part of India, where the Sena kings had come from, had a rigidly caste-differentiated society. This could be why these kings set such great store by a social order founded on caste hierarchies. They did not have much feeling, either, for the language in which the local population spoke. Partly because of this, and partly because it was the language of the scriptures, it was Sanskrit to which they were partial.

There is no concrete evidence to indicate how Buddhism, which received state patronage and gained widespread popularity under the Pala regime, fared under the Sena kings. There is no dependable evidence, either, to show what happened to the Buddhists, who formed a large section, under the new dispensation. There is no explanation on why the number of Buddhists reduced so drastically in just two centuries. Many scholars believe that the Buddhists became incorporated in the lowest rungs of caste-divided Hindu society. The more influential among the Buddhists began to move out to the frontier areas of Bengal at this time, especially towards the south-east and also northwards to Nepal. That Buddhist viharas stopped being built in the north after a certain point and were built only in south-eastern Bengal also suggests that Buddhists were gradually retreating in the face of the Brahmanic faith's march to power. There was another reason, too, for the way in which the Buddhists slowly lost their distinctiveness. Long before the rule of the Sena kings, Hiuen Tsang had written that Buddhism in Bengal had moved away from the original faith. It is not unreasonable to suppose that after another 500 years, the aberrations in Buddhism were more glaring than ever before. We have already noted how the Sahajia cult grew out of a process of assimilation between Buddhist, Brahmanic and Tantric beliefs. In sum, Buddhism in Bengal, after assimilating components from the Vedic and local systems of beliefs, had changed to an extent that paved the way for its predominant sect losing its distinctiveness during the Sena regime and in the years following immediately after it.

Advent of Islam

The ease with which Bakhtiar Khilji conquered the capital of Gaur, Lakshmanavati, in 1204 points to enemies within. It is not inconceivable that a section of the population might have sided with the Muslim conquerors against the ruling elite, thus teaming up, so to speak, with the enemy of the enemy just as, in the 18th century, there were those who collaborated with the British. The Turkish sultans may not have come to this land to shore up their share of virtues by preaching Islam, but there is no doubt that with them came a particular religion. And as the religion of the rulers, it did also find it relatively easy to gain acceptance among the people, just as had happened with other faiths under the Pala and Sena kings. Of course, it was not exactly as if Islam first arrived in Bengal with the Turks. Arab traders had started setting up colonies in the Chittagong area from as early as the 9th century. They, too, had not come to preach their faith. Like Bakhtiar Khilji, their objectives were entirely worldly.

Apart from the merchants and the mercenaries, there had also of course come the preachers. They came neither to trade nor to rule, but to earn virtue through conversions. According to Muhammad Enamul Haque, one such preacher, Baba Adam, came in the early 12th century. He is said to have died fighting against Ballal Sena in 1119. After him, Shah Muhammad Sultan Rumi travelled to Maimansingh (Br. Mymensingh) to preach. There is no evidence to support these claims, nor to indicate exactly when these pirs came. However, the claim that the famous Sufi Syed Jalal Uddin Tabrizi arrived in Bengal well before the start of Muslim rule seems to have some substance. But in the absence of state patronage, these early preachers are not known to have met with much success in their missionary efforts. But once the Turkish regime was in place, it must have helped in expanding the faith's reach and spread.

Preaching may not have been the objective of the sultans, but they were not impartial in respect of the religions of the land. Indeed, they had no compunctions about using religion and its symbols to reinforce their own positions and tighten their grip on power. Besides, as we have noted earlier, in the 1st century of their rule, the Muslim rulers liberally used the sword to establish their sway. It was also an accepted custom for sultans to build mosques and have the *khutba* read in their name. Though the numbers of Muslims in those initial years may not have been very high, the sultans of the 1st century of Muslim rule built, or helped in the building, of many mosques. At least six of these mosques survived for a long time. Indeed, the mosque became a symbol of the new regime.

No detailed or dependable account of the activities of the first sultans are available. Among the little that is known about them are stories of the destruction of Buddhist viharas. It is not known why they did this. They may have got wind of the treasures stored in the viharas. Or they might have faced some opposition to their authority from Buddhists. We have it from the contemporary historian Minhaz us-Siraj that Bakhtiar Khilji attacked the capital of Gobindapal Odontopuri (Adandapuri) and won it after a stiff fight. Bakhtiar and his soldiers were at once suspicious and tempted at the sight of the Buddhist viharas surrounded by moats and populated by the shaven-headed *bhikshus*. According to some historians, they were not satisfied by plundering the wealth of the vihara in the capital city but went on to finish off all the *bhikshus* there. Some historians even say that the massacre was so complete that no one was left alive to make sense of the manuscripts in the vihara libraries. As in an earlier time they had fled to escape persecution under the Sena kings, many Buddhists now again fled to the south-east and also beyond Bengal, especially to Nepal, to escape the terror unleashed by the new rulers.

Bakhtiar and the Sultans who came after him also destroyed many Hindu temples, again because of the wealth hoarded there. Another objective was to furnish ultimate proof of their authority by destroying holy sites and breaking the idols worshipped in the temples. And in this they would have found ideological support in their religion's opposition to idol worship. Some of these temples were like mini forts, ringed by ditches. There are detailed accounts of how much later – in the second half of the 16th century – Muslim troops led by Kalapahar plundered and razed the Jajpur temple. This gives an idea, if not actual proof, of the onslaught on Hindu temples in the two centuries preceding the incident. Historians like Asim Roy and Richard Eaton believe that stories of the destruction of temples are backed more by hearsay than by actual evidence. Also, that it is not at least true that Muslims destroyed every temple they came across.

One of the things that seem to back the claim that Muslims destroyed countless temples is that some mosques were built at the site of old temples. More importantly, stone slabs from old temples were used in the building of mosques. The mosques built in the first three centuries of Muslim rule, with stone slabs often carrying images of gods and goddesses, seem to bear out the theory. Such stone slabs with Hindu deities carved into them have been found at Bengal's oldest surviving mosque, that of Zafar Khan in Tribeni; and also at Adina Masjid. Stone slabs from Hindu temples were even found at the mausoleum called Eklakhi that the converted Bengali Sultan Jalal-Uddin Muhammad got built for himself. The mihrabs (ornamental arch-shaped niches carved out of mosque walls to indicate the direction of the Kaaba) from the Mahisantosh, and other mosques from an even later period, which have been preserved at the Varendra Research Museum also bear images of Hindu deities.

The explanation that historians like Asim Roy offer for the use of stones from Hindu temples to build mosques is that stones were always scarce in Bengal. Just as, in an earlier time, the use of ingredients taken from crumbling Buddhist temples in building Hindu temples was not unusual, it was nothing extraordinary that material from dilapidated Hindu temples should be used to build mosques. Nonetheless, it must be admitted that there is no reason to suppose that stone slabs from Hindu temples were used in mosques only because stones were not easily available. There were many who considered it virtuous to destroy temples and build mosques there and to get mihrabs made from stones that had Hindu gods and goddesses carved into them. Zafar Khan, for instance, quite proudly took credit for the slaughter of kaffirs. There were also those who considered such actions as the ultimate symbol of their assertion of power and authority.

Whatever might have been the extent of the destruction of Buddhist viharas and Hindu temples in the early years of the Muslim sultans' rule, it was this that created the impression that force was used to spread Islam. With time, however, the later sultans realised that this impression would not help them to rule. For, they were dependent on their Hindu employees for much of the administrative work. Countless small 'kings' and landholders, or zamindars, dotted the land, and they, too, were Hindus. Taxes collected from them filled up the Sultan's treasury. This is why the later sultans, with one or two exceptions, do not seem to have either taken any part in preaching their faith or to have actively backed any proselytising drives. Rather, there is evidence that the later sultans started donating tax-free land for the upkeep of temples.

Yet, there was nothing comparable in the preceding 1,000 years to the tsunami that broke upon the religious life of the people of Bengal with the advent of Muslim rule. The Muslims did not arrive gradually and quietly as the Aryans had done. Their arrival cannot even be compared to that of the Sena kings. Moreover, the fundamental difference between the religion that the Muslim sultans brought with them and the faiths practised by the local population was so obvious that there was no way it could escape the notice of even the least observant of witnesses. The new faith preached worship of a formless Creator rather than of idols, and it was flexible about rules and rituals. Indeed, the new beliefs and ideals from Arabia and Iran seem to have shaken up the very foundations of Bengali society and significantly influenced its people. Still, there is nothing substantial by way of evidence to explain why it was not before the establishment of Turkish rule, but after, that the numbers of converted Muslims began to rapidly grow in Bengal. There is disagreement between scholars on when Ramai Pandit's *Shunya Puran* was written and how much of it comprises interpolations. In the section called 'Niranjaner Rushma' (Niranjan's Anger) in this poem, the spread of Islam is described thus:

All the gods, in concert, happily donned izars
Brahma turned Mohammad, Vishnu turned Paigambar, Adam turned Shulpani
Ganesha became Gazi, Kartik became Qazi, all the munis became fakirs
Renouncing his own attire, Narad turned Sheikh, Purandar became Maulana.

Chandika Debi herself became Hawa Bibi, Padmabati became Bibi Noor
All the gods, in unison, entered Jajpur
They smashed the temple, grabbed things to eat, 'snatch it' 'snatch it' went the refrain.

The destruction of idols at Jajpur temple (in Odisha) described here refers to the vandalising of the temple by Suleiman Karnani's general Kalapahar. This happened in 1568. So the poem must have been written after Kalapahar had passed into legend, possibly sometime in the 17th century. As a result, there is a fair amount of exaggeration in this account. Islam did spread far and wide in Bengal, but it would not be right to assume that all the Hindu deities together decided overnight to switch to *izar*s (Arabic word for garment worn waist downwards, usually trousers with drawstrings, that is, salwars) and became Muslims. It is more reasonable to assume that the spread of Islam in the eastern and other parts of Bengal was slow and gradual. It did not take place at the speed of lightning.

Reason Behind the Spread of Islam in Bengal

Four theories are usually cited to explain why Islam made such spectacular headway in Bengal. The assumption that it was spread at sword's point is the one that is most popular among nationalist, non-Muslim historians. These historians believe that Muslims used state power to forcibly convert the local population. However, historians like Richard Eaton and Asim Roy refuse to accept this explanation. They point out that it is in east Bengal that Muslims form the majority, although this part of Bengal did not come under Muslim rule until much later, and even then the Muslim rulers had only a feeble administrative presence here for a long time. Had force been used to spread Islam, it would be more logical for Muslims to outnumber Hindus in the

Gaur-Pandua region. These historians remind us that it was in and around Delhi that Muslim rule was first established, yet the numbers of Muslims in Bengal far outstrip those around Delhi.

Citing letters written by contemporary pirs, these historians have tried to prove that the sultans in the 1st, 2nd or 3rd centuries of Muslim rule did not help in the preaching of their faith. This is inferred from the fact that the pirs and the dervishes were generally unhappy with the sultans. For instance, in 1397, Muzaffar Shams Balkhi, one of the foremost pirs, complained in a letter to Sultan Giyas Uddin Azam Shah that not much help was forthcoming from the sultan in the spread of Islam. Also that, on the contrary, Hindus were being installed in high posts. At the beginning of the 15th century, another leading pir, Nur Qutb-e Alam, urged the Sultan of Bihar, Ibrahim Sharki, in a letter to invade Bengal in order to cut the Hindus down to size and especially subdue Raja Ganesh.

Though there may be some debate about how actively the sultans promoted Islam, they were without doubt not indifferent to their own faith. Indeed, their enthusiasm about their religion is more or less clear from the way in which they had mosques, *khanqahs* and dargahs built some distance away from the capital. That apart, they dealt firmly with whoever came in the way of their conquests and the spread of their reach. And to that end, as historical records show, they sometimes forced vanquished petty kings and zamindars to convert. They also sometimes punished the defeated adversary by destroying and desecrating temples. Besides, there is no definite proof of any temple being built within the territory controlled by the Turkish rulers in the first two and a half centuries of their rule, though local kings are known to have built temples. It is not impossible to infer that the sultans opposed the building of temples because they were against idol worship. But nothing can be asserted with any certainty because there is no definite evidence to back such claims. However, though the sultans were enthusiastic about their own faith, there is nothing to show that they tried to preach on a regular basis. Whether it is possible to convert people on a mass scale through the use of force is also debatable.

The geographical position of the mosques built in the first few centuries of Muslim rule also point to limited state patronage for Islam. If preaching and acquiring virtue by doing so were the aim, the sultans might have built mosques all over the land. But that is not what actually happened. Until about 1500, mosques were built either in the capital or close by. The mosques built by Khan Jahan Ali in the Jessore-Khulna-Bagerhat area were notable exceptions. This was because Khan Jahan Ali was not just a ruler but also a pir. He can probably be compared to Zafar Khan and thus is not a reliable example of how the sultans behaved in general. What can be broadly said about the role of the sultans and their bureaucrats is that though they were interested in Islam and though their enthusiasm or wrath may have produced a few stray incidents of forced apostasies, this did not result in mass conversions all over the land and nor was this the chief factor in the spread of Islam.

Some historians, especially Muslim historians, attribute the wide reach of the new faith to Islam's promise of social equality. They contend that lower-caste Hindus in droves sought refuge from inhuman caste persecution in Islam, which does not subscribe to caste divisions. But Richard Eaton and Asim Roy do not agree. They say that the proportion of people of the lower castes in Bengal was not as high as in northern and southern India. Caste hierarchies in Bengal, they also point out, are historically not as repressive or rigid in Bengal as they are elsewhere. This argument makes a lot of sense when one compares the situation in present-day Bihar with that in Bengal. Caste divisions continue to be quite rigid in Bihar despite modern education and other forms of social development. It is in Bihar, then, that caste divisions should have produced mass conversions. Yet Muslims form a lower percentage of the population in Bihar than in Bengal.

Some historians have also raised questions about how equal the Muslim society was, pointing out that this, too, was a fairly divided society. The gulf was wide between the Ashrafs (the elite) and the Atrafs (the lower rungs). The Atrafs themselves were divided into four sections depending on their social status. There could not even be any shared meals between the Ashrafs and the Atrafs, let alone marriage. Then again, Muslims of foreign origin looked down upon converted Muslims. Highborn Muslims would rather forge marriage alliances with elite Hindus but never with lowborn Muslims. And so, these historians say, the argument that large numbers of people in Bengal embraced Islam to escape caste divisions does not quite bear scrutiny.

Others contend that there were anyway few Hindus belonging to the lower castes at the beginning of Muslim rule. The people at the bottom were mostly Buddhists, which takes the substance out of the theory of caste hierarchies leading to conversions. These historians believe that most of the conversions took place among Buddhists rather than low-caste Hindus. An indirect proof of this is that the Buddhists formed a large chunk of the population before the Muslims came. Within a couple of centuries, however, there seemed to be no trace of this huge section with the exception of a few shaven-headed men and women. Buddhists were now seen only in Bengal's south-eastern corner, in the hills and plains of Chittagong. This seems to suggest that most of the Buddhists converted to become Muslims. But then, as we noted before, the numbers of Buddhists started rapidly diminishing from the Sena era itself. There are no historical records to establish the proportion of Buddhists in society when the Muslims arrived or to determine whether most of them embraced the new faith. Thus the theory of mass conversions to escape social inequities does not really stand up to historical analysis.

The census of 1872 first brought to notice that the number of Muslims almost equalled that of the Hindus. Two decades later, the census of 1891 showed the number of Muslims to have outstripped the Hindus. Muslim historians started trying to rationalise the phenomenon soon after the 1872 census. Apart from citing the social justice inherent in Islam, they tried to explain the large number of Muslims with the contention that most of them had migrated from the Middle East and from northern India to settle down in Bengal. Most historians are unable to accept this explanation. In their perception, Muslims of foreign origin form only an insignificant part of the population. Even if the children of those who had married local women and stayed back permanently are taken to be of foreign origin, they would not account for more than 5 per cent of the Muslim population. From the census figures of 1872, Rafiuddin Ahmed has shown that Muslims claiming to be of foreign origin formed only 1.52 per cent of the population in the three divisions of Bengal.

Historians also point out that Muslims from foreign lands often did not find Bengal's food, climate and geographical position favourable enough to stay back permanently. Many of them, as we have noted, described the land as Dar-ul-Harb, or the land of strife. Though forced to come here in the course of seeking their fortunes, many went back to northern India to settle down.

There are also historians who underline the role of pirs and dervishes in inducing people to convert. According to them, many Sufi pirs, Jalal-ud-din Tabrizi (died 1244/45) for instance, started arriving in Bengal from the Middle East even before the start of Turkish rule. Tabrizi is said to have come at the time of Lakshman Sena, though it is not known how far this story is true. Lakshman Sena is supposed to have welcomed him in friendship and with high regard. Thereafter, the numbers of pirs and dervishes progressively swelled under Turkish rule. Sheikh Farid-ud-din Shakerganj and Abdullah Kirmani are known to have started preaching in Bengal in the 13th century. More such Sufi pirs came in the following century. Muhammad Enamul Haque mentions the names of Mir Syed Jalal-Uddin and Sheikh Alauddin Alaol Haque. However, the most notable preacher of the 14th century was Shah Jalal (died 1346). There are historical records to show that the sultans, even if they did not directly promote Islam, donated land to these pirs and helped them to settle down and establish colonies with their followers. This kind of help from the sultans may have encouraged the pirs to come in and settle down.

But it was not royal assistance alone that drew the pirs who came to earn virtue by preaching Islam. Many of them had been forced to migrate from Central Asia. In the 13th and 14th centuries, invasions by some non-Muslim Mongol monarchs including Jenghis Khan devastated the Muslim states of Central Asia. As a result, many Alims and Sufis moved, or were forced to move, to India along with other fortune-seeking Muslims. Many of these pirs made their way to Bengal through northern India. The fame and influence of the pirs and dervishes who had come before them may have attracted the ones who came later.

The pirs and dervishes who came at the time of the sultans did not settle down with their followers in or around the capital. In fact, they gave a wide berth to the towns and spread out in the countryside. Some of the earliest pirs about whom some historical information is available preached in the western part of Bengal. For instance, Abdullah Kirmani settled down in Birbhum, Makhdum Shah Mahmud Gaznabi in Burdwan (Bardhaman), Shah Shafiuddin in Pandua and Syed Abbas Ali Makki in 24 Paraganas. Many of the later pirs moved to North Bengal and the densely forested east. Badruddin preached Islam in Dinajpur, Makhdum Shah Daula in Pabna, Syed Ali Tabaraki and Shah Ali Baghdadi in Dhaka, Fariduddin in Faridpur, Ahmed Noori in Noakhali and Badar Shah in Chittagong. Later still, the numbers of proselytising Sufi pirs and dervishes grew rapidly.

The Sufi pirs and dervishes who made Bengal their home were of different sects. The Sufis of the Chishtia, Kalandaria, Madaria, Kaderia, Sohrawardi, Ahmadia and Nakshabandia sects became particularly popular in Bengal. It was the Chishtia sect, however, that received special favours from the sultans and also the nawabs who came after them. There is a hint of the Kalandari sect's popularity among the masses in western Bengal in Mukundaram's *Chandimangal* written in the 16th century. Mukundaram wrote: '*Kalandar haiya keho phire dibarati*' (And some turn Kalandar in right earnest). *Jog Kalandar*, a Bengali manuscript written in Arabic script that has been found in Chittagong, also furnishes indirect evidence that Sufis of the Kalandari sect were popular there. Alongside the Sufis, the Hanafis were the most popular among the Sunni sects. Though the Sufis and the Hanafis differ quite a bit in their religious beliefs, there are many among the converted who claim to subscribe to the belief systems of both.

These pirs and dervishes were not warriors. Besides, they knew that the sword was not the best instrument to spread Islam among the masses. They earned their popularity through their generosity and their leadership qualities. How popular they were can be gauged from the many dargahs scattered all over Bengal and the high regard these enjoy among the local people, including non-Muslims. There are innumerable stories and legends of pirs who dedicated their lives in the service of ordinary people. It can be seen in historical records that pirs who received gifts of land from the sultans used them to help the poor by setting up community kitchens and shelter homes. It is logical to suppose that many conversions took place among people emotionally overwhelmed by the generosity of the pirs.

From around the 14th-15th centuries, some religious leaders received from the sultans land in eastern Bengal with the brief to clear out forests and free up the land for farming. Khan Jahan Ali may have been an example. With the help of their followers, these men of religion cleared out marshy forests and initiated cultivation in previously inaccessible areas, earning in the process social influence and becoming revered as pirs. They also drew many to the fold of Islam by parcelling out the newly cultivable land among the poor. According to Asim Roy, the word of Islam spread in village after village and in Bengal's delta area through these cultivator pirs, and this despite limited state support from the rulers.

The texts of the time contain many a story of the spread of Islam through supernatural intervention. For instance, maybe a Brahmin and a pir have come together for a contest to determine which of them is superior. If the Brahmin is able to jump up high, the pir manages an even higher jump, and that induces the onlookers to embrace Islam. The 'jump', of course, is entirely symbolic. But what such exaggerated stories tell us is that the pirs converted many people to their faith through their own social influence and forceful personalities. There may be doubts about the veracity of the events described in Ramai Pandit's *Shunya Puran*, but there is no doubt that the so-called 'supernatural' influence of pirs and dervishes got many people to convert.

Besides, some of the Hindus who found employment with the new rulers are known to have converted in the hope of winning favours or high posts. Duarte Barbosa came to Bengal in the course of his travels in 1518. He has written that the vast majority of the population were Hindus. Every day, however, many of the Hindus were converting to curry favour with the sultan or his representatives. There is also historical evidence to show that vanquished rajas (petty kings/ zamindars) sometimes agreed to convert in order to save their lives or their 'kingdoms', that is, their landholdings or 'zamindaris'. That conversions generally pleased the sultans seems to be beyond doubt. In the Mughal regime the policy was by and large to separate administration from religion. Yet even then, as Eaton mentions, such conversions took place.

The most notable example of conversion for power is that of Raja Jadu, also known as Sultan Jalal ud-din Mohammed. As we have said before, when his father, Raja Ganesh, found it almost impossible to hold on to power in the face of opposition from pirs and dervishes, he got his son converted and continued to rule in his name. We also know of certain zealous pirs who were not just preachers. They occupied large swathes of land and reinvented themselves as feudal lords or even as politically influential personalities. The influence they wielded was both religious and sociopolitical, and they commanded a large number of followers. Whatever may have been the policy of the sultans, the pirs and dervishes preached their faith with zeal and seem to have used force at times to secure conversions.

Many people became Muslims through marriage. The Muslims who in those days arrived in Bengal from Central or West Asia or even from Delhi did not bring their wives with them and often married local women. A good example would be Shah Jalal Muzarad. He had come from Turkistan with a few hundred followers to the land of strife, Dar-ul-Harb, with the intention of doing good by converting infidels to Islam. It is claimed that he had 313 followers with him even when he reached as far east as Sylhet. All of them were single, and so was he. He defeated the local rulers, parcelled out the territory among his men and instructed them to marry and raise families. They all married local women, and it is not as if they found their wives in families that had converted to Islam. The call of Islam would not have reached the remote areas of Sylhet so early. It is possible to infer, then, that they got poor families to give them their daughters in marriage with the promise of material advancement or used force to get well-to-do Hindu or Buddhist parents to part with their daughters. And so it was that at least 313 families found themselves in a situation of losing their caste or ritual purity, assuming that each of Shah Jalal's followers took just one wife; it's probable that many of them took more.

The rape of women of a defeated people is widespread even today. This was much more rampant then. As mentioned before, Islam Khan was the Subahdar of Bengal and the historian Mirza Nathan was one of his generals. Nathan has recorded in his memoirs *Baharistan Gayebi* the imprisonment and rape of a few thousand women after a Muslim military campaign. When the general came to know of this 'feat' of his soldiers, he ordered them to release the women. But many of them had no clothes to cover their bodies when they were sent home. It is not hard to guess that many of these women would have no way of going back to their families. And the families themselves may have been unable to salvage their honour except through conversion.

Conversions necessitated by marriage could happen even among the elite. Aristocratic Muslims did not intermarry with lowborn Muslims. Rather, they often married their daughters into Brahmin or landowning families and also took their wives from such families. Kalapahar alias Raju was an example of such an alliance. He was a Barendra Brahmin and served as Suleiman and Daud Karnani's general. His marriage into an aristocratic Muslim family caused his own family to lose caste. Once condemned as an outcaste, he took up arms against Hindus and did his best to bring them to as much harm as he could. He destroyed many temples and broke idols. As we have said before, in 1568 he attacked Puri and partly damaged the Jagannath temple there. He is said to have picked up the Jagannath idol and thrown it into the sea. His soldiers broke some 700 images of gods and goddesses. After this, he became known as 'Kalapahar' in Hindu society, a name that might roughly translate as 'the black sheep' but literally means 'black hill', symbolising destruction. The name stuck, and his actual name is now long forgotten. But Kalapahar was not the only example of this kind of behaviour. Khilji's converted general Malik Kafur also went for the Hindus with great zeal. Isa Khan's father had converted to Islam after marrying a Muslim woman.

Many people lost their caste purity merely by coming into contact with Muslims. Peer Ali alias Mahmud Tahir was a Muslim administrator in Jessore. A handful of Brahmins lost caste through their interactions with him, and some of them later became Muslims. The others were known as *potit* (fallen) Brahmins and were called the Peerali Brahmins. Rabindranath Tagore happened to be the thirteenth generation descendant of one such Peerali Brahmin. The story runs thus: These Brahmins ate a meal in Peer Ali's presence during the month of Ramzan or Ramadan and claimed that his fast was broken because half of eating consists in sniffing the flavours of food. A few days later, Peer Ali once again invited them for a meal. This time he sat down to eat with them and ate beef. Now it was his turn to claim that his Brahmin guests had partaken of beef simply by inhaling its smell and had thus lost their ritual purity. It cannot be said with certainty whether the story has any historical truth. Yet it contains a greater social truth: many people found themselves losing caste for trivial and sometimes completely illogical reasons and were forced to convert.

The Sherkhanis, like the Peeralis, carried the stigma of impure contact, but they were able to hold on to their Hindu identity with support from local society. Debibar Ghatak, a *kulacharya*, that is, custodian/writer of the genealogical chronicles (*kulajis*) of caste Hindus, even issued an injunction to the effect that Brahmins would be able to retain their caste despite impure contact. Such prescriptions notwithstanding, hostile social elders often forced people into losing caste. In sum, a large section of the people of Bengal converted to Islam for varied reasons.

Muslims Swell in Numbers

There was no census in those days. So it cannot be said with any certainty how many converted to Islam and when. But the number of mosques and their locations furnish an indirect proof of when Islam began to spread substantially. There are only six surviving mosques that carry 13th-century dates. The proportional number of mosques did not go up at all in the following century: there were only seven. But the number of mosques rose rapidly in the 15th century. Sixty-six mosques were built in this century with dates carved on their walls, and 75 in the 16th century. The number of mosques in Dhaka, Mymensingh, Faridpur, Noakhali, Comilla and so on rose quite rapidly in the 17th century, though the Mughals are known to have followed a policy of no-intervention in the religious life of the people. Indeed, Mughal administrators did not play much of a role in building mosques outside the capital city of Dhaka. This seems to indicate that it was the preaching of pirs and dervishes that had by this time expanded the reach of Islam. The converts and their pirs and dervishes must have been the chief agents in the building of these mosques.

Graph 3.2 given on the next page gives an idea of when Islam became widespread in Bengal. It is apparent from the graph that there were only a handful of Muslims before 1500. Their numbers started rising rapidly from 1600.

Foreign travellers who came visiting in the 14th and 15th centuries wrote that they saw many Muslims in the cities. It is also quite clear that the

Population of Hindus and Muslims 1204-1901

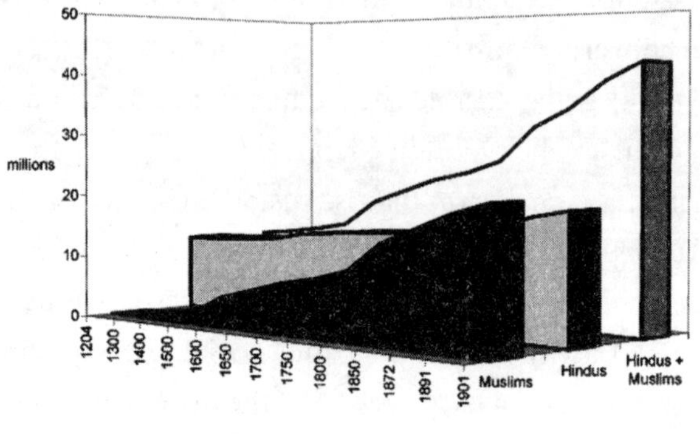

3.2 *Graph by Panini Murshid, based on population increase data found in Ulrich Cromer's research (1993). According to this data, the total population of Bengal in 1204 was 12.58 million (86 million in the whole of India). In 1872, this figure was 36.7 million (255 million in the whole of India)*

Muslims whom Ralph Fitch described at the end of the 16th century were all either Arabs or Persians. Fitch described them as being fair in complexion and having beautiful features. But foreign travellers do not mention the villages because, among other things, they may not have ventured out into the countryside at all. Also, it is reasonable to suppose that Islam did not make its way into the remote villages in the relatively early years of Muslim rule in Bengal.

From around the 15th century, however, the number of Muslims started swelling in the villages. That Muslims were by then a notable section of society in western Bengal is evident from Mukundaram's *Chandimangal* written in the 16th century and Brindavandas's *Chaitanyabhagavat.* In the seventh decade of the 16th century, Jayanandadas laments in his *Chaitanyamangal* that the numbers of Muslims were increasing. He fears that Brahmins would henceforth start growing beards and recite the Masnavi in Farsi:

The Brahman will sport a beard and read Farsi
Feet in socks, drawstring in hand, will mount the cannon
The twice-born will recite the Masnavi

There has been some research in recent times on patterns of population expansion in the past. Ulrich Cromer has an insightful study (1993) on how populations expanded in India and the rest of the world. From what we know of the time when Bengal came under Muslim rule, references to numbers of Muslims found in literature and other medieval sources, data on the rate of expansion of the Muslim population under colonial rule and on its eventual outstripping of the population of Bengali Hindus and from the graph 3.2 by Panini Murshid, it appears that Muslims started rapidly increasing in numbers roughly around the end of the 15th and the start of the 16th century.

Islam in Bengal

It would not be illogical to assume that as the numbers of Muslims increased, Islam in Bengal started changing in character. Here, too, one notices the role played by cultural life in a frontier province. In the past Buddhism and the Vedic tradition underwent changes after arriving in Bengal to acquire quite distinct forms. Islam in Bengal also went through a process of evolution to acquire a special character. But how did this process work?

In the initial years, foreign pirs preached Islam among the educated elite in the capital and in other cities. But as Islam gradually made its way through the villages and spread its word among the illiterate masses, it was no longer possible for it to retain its original character. Besides, Islam in Bengal was preached by Sufi pirs who came mainly from Persia and Central Asia. An indirect proof of this is that Allah is Khuda in Bengal, salat is namaz, Ramadan is *roza, zannat* is *beheseth* and *jahannum* is *dozokh.* So it was not through Arabic but Farsi that Islam came to Bengal. The Islam that these preachers brought was not quite the same as the Sunni faith of Arabia, especially that of the Hanafi sect.

Islam in Central Asia was a syncretic faith, having assimilated local religious customs and beliefs. In Persia, too, Islam could not remain unchanged even though its people embraced the faith. The Shias and the Sufis carried the day in Persia, and the faith they preached carried the imprint of varied influences. The exchanges between India and Persia meant that they were not free of Indian influences, either. It is said that the Sufis borrowed the idea of Anal Haq (I am He) from Indian philosophy. At any rate, the Sufi Islam of Iran with its devotional inclinations and its mysticism was quite different from the Islam of Arabia. And so it continues to be in the present day. Islam in its original form is dualistic. Allah is the lord and man his *banda* or slave. The Creator and the created are bound in a relationship of master and servant. But the Sufis believe in non-dualism. The created being is one with the Creator and has the potential to completely lose itself in the Creator. The Creator and his creation are bound in a relationship of love in the Sufi faith, not of master and servant.

There is another major difference between Sufism and the more conservative faith. Islam has no use for any medium between the Creator and the created. Pirs and murshids are, therefore, not required. There is scant room also for philosophy and mysticism. The main stress is on work. The Sufis, on the other hand, hope to draw close to the Creator through their pirs and murshids. Their religious philosophy follows the shadowy paths of mysticism.

It is this second stream of Islam that the Sufi pirs preached in Bengal. Moreover, Islam also acquired a new form through exchanges with local faiths, much like Brahmanism and Buddism in an earlier time. It does seem as if the Sufi philosophy of the created being merging into the Creator through the complete denial of self, or *fana*, is a product of Indian influence. Some scholars have noted resemblances between *fana* and the nirvana of Buddhism. It is easy to see similarities between the Sufi *latifa* and the Indian *kundalini*. Some scholars also claim that the Sufi *zikr* (the practice of chanting the names of God) underwent changes under Indian influence. Even the *muraqaba* or meditation in the Sufi tradition was influenced by the Indian method of meditation. And that is why the later Sufi tradition shows such close connections with the practice of *yoga* and *asanas*. But the most important influence was in the concept of *rabita*, the way in which the devotee can become one with the Creator through the medium of a 'guru'. The similarity with the guru cults of Bengal is unmistakable.

Faith in Bengal has always been devotional and inclined towards gurus or spiritual mentors and teachers. Not surprisingly, therefore, it was the non-dualistic, devotional and guru-dependent Islam that flourished in Bengal. More than the invisible and formless Creator, it was the accessible pir who drew reverence from the people. Countless mazars commemorating the mortal remains of pirs cropped up across the Bengal countryside, a testimony to the affection and awe they inspired. This devotional faith induced, through the centuries, the worship of pirs at the mazars.

Language was a major obstacle in the preaching of Islam in Bengal. The pirs who came from Central Asia or even from northern India did not know the local language. Even if they managed, men of letters as they were, to learn the language and start preaching in it in a few years, it was next to impossible for illiterate villagers to pick up enough Arabic, Farsi or even Hindi to learn about Islam in its authentic form from the pirs. The religious training that the pirs contrived to give them was at best Islamic in name. Let alone the philosophy of Islam, it was more or less beyond the unlettered villager to even memorise all the *surah*s that one would need to perform namaz five times a day, as required of a good Muslim. The pirs, however, kept up their efforts to teach the basics of performing namaz and *ozu*, as can be inferred from contemporary Bengali literature. Bipradas's *Manasabijoy* (1495-96) gives a picture of such attempts to teach the word of God (through the *kalma*/*ketab*) and train people to offer namaz and perform *ozu*. That the Syeds and the Mullahs were trying to convert Hindus is also mentioned. On the whole, however, regardless of the reasons for which a bulk of the illiterate rural population embraced Islam, whether to escape caste or other forms of persecution or to win favours, the act of conversion remained largely symbolic. In reality, life went on pretty much through the cycle of old beliefs and customs. Over time, Islamic tenets may have made a gradual and partial penetration through the filter of these beliefs.

Mukundaram at the end of the 16th century mentions Muslims in his *Chandimangal* while describing an imagined Gujarat city. Muslims, clearly, are of two classes in his description. There is one class of Muslims (obviously of foreign origin) who are very religious – they spread out their red mats to perform namaz five times a day, use Sulemani prayer beads, pay obeisance to the pir and *paigambar*, light lamps at the pir's mazar and sit in groups of ten or twenty to endlessly discuss the Quran and other religious books. These Muslims are sincere in their faith, do not prevaricate, and they never give up their *roza* fast even if it almost kills them. They do not converse with people who leave their heads bare and thrash them up with fuel wood. They wear white clothes. They don't grow their hair, but their flowing beards cover their chests. They never deviate from their own paths and always have their caps and *izar*s firmly in place.

The use of the word *beradar* in describing the meetings to discuss holy books is noteworthy. It gives some idea of the kind of language spoken by such Muslims. There is at least no doubt that they were descendants of foreigners and were fairly highborn. The expression 'make offers at the pir's mazar' (*pirer mokame sanj*) is also to be noted. This is obviously not the Sunni Islam originating in Arabia. Mukundaram also says—'There are those who roam around as *kalandars*' ('*Nana sthane bule keho Kalandar haiya*'). Here, too, is an indication of the predominance of Sufi pirs in the Muslim community. Mukundaram follows up his account of the highborn Muslims with a description of ordinary working-class Muslims. These Muslims 'don't care for *roza* or namaz . . . they lie all the time and do not grow beards' ('*roza namaz na koria keho hailo gola . . . nirontor mithya kahe nahi rakhe darhii*').

Bijoygupta's *Manasamangal* is said to have been written even before Mukundaram's poem. No definite conclusion can be drawn, however, and Sukumar Sen has raised pertinent questions regarding when the poem was written and on the language and dependability of the extant manuscript. But whatever may be the time of writing of Bijoygupta's poem, his description of rural Muslims gives an idea of the community's social life:

The Mullah called Takai has a good knowledge of books
He is the first to be called to the feasts the Qazi cooks.
He eases his dhoti as to pray he settles down . . .
And when done with prayers he slaughters a cock soon!
There is one Khalas; the Qazi's special man
This one is well-versed in the books and the Quran.

†

The Qazi now has faith in the Mullah's words
And all others come to take home his amulets, in hoards.

The Takai, or Taki Mullah we meet here does not appear non-native. He is dressed not in long flowing robes but in a dhoti—the tight folds tucked in firm at the waist, which he partly pulls out for greater ease when he sits down to perform his priestly rituals. What's more, he even believes in amulets and distributes these among the people. He commands greater social prestige than ordinary Muslims because of his familiarity with books. This seems to indicate that the others are not very familiar with books, or at best have a tenuous familiarity with them. The Qazi's associate, Khalas, on the other hand, has a good knowledge of the *Quran* and other books. He might well be a foreigner.

Both these trends persisted among Muslims in Bengal until the 19th century. It was under the influence of popular Sufi Islam with its pirs and dervishes that the mazars and dargahs were built. The influence of this devotional faith was not just limited to the countryside. Its impact was as strong in the higher rungs of society. For instance, in 1503 Alauddin Hosein Shah built the Qadam Rasul monument in the capital Gaur. A black stone with Prophet Muhammad's footprint on it was preserved there. This monument turned into a veritable pilgrimage site. There were even claims

Qadam Rasul

that the capital grew in prestige because of it. Hosein Shah himself not only visited Qadam Rasul, he also made an annual pilgrimage to Noor Qutb-e-Alam's dargah every year. Qutb-e-Alam had died in Pandua in 1459. A hundred years after Hosein Shah's time, Mirza Nathan also used to make pilgrimages to both the Qadam Rasul and Qutb-e-Alam's dargah from the capital Dhaka. Explaining the glory of the Qadam Rasul, Mirza Nathan wrote that the stone preserved there had been brought from Arabia so that the people of faraway Bengal could kiss the footprint of the Prophet and obtain his blessings. It is quite probable that this concept of worshipping a footprint carried the influence of the local practice of worshipping Vishnu's footprint. Similar expressions of devotion and the custom of pir worship were very much in currency in the mazars of famous pirs.

The tradition of seeking refuge with pirs rather than with one's Creator in moments of crisis, and of importuning with the divine at mazars with promises of obeisance, grew in strength through the centuries. Mirza Nathan pledged a three-day pilgrimage to Qutb-e-Alam's dargah if his father recovered from an illness. After his own wedding he paid his respects at the Qadam Rasul and at Sheikh Alaul Haque's dargah. Following the spectacular success of the Qadam Rasul at Gaur, another such monument was erected at Narayangunj. In Chittagong was built a mosque in which, it is claimed, a stone with the Prophet's footprint is preserved in a room. Hazrat Muhammad is not just the Messenger of God to Muslims, he is thought to be a friend of the Creator. Expressions of reverence for him, therefore, are quite in order. However, worshipping a stone that is said to be carrying his footprint is not really consistent with the Islamic ideal. Yet, such were the customs that came to be observed in Bengal. Many historians have seen this as indicating a limited and incomplete initiation into Islam.

It is clear, then, that Islam in Bengal was deeply impacted through its exchanges with local beliefs, customs and rituals. The changes these brought about in the Islam that was practised in Bengal were quite remarkable. Nor were Hindu beliefs immune to the new faith. Contemporary writing, especially Bengali literary writing, furnishes many proofs of Hindu assimilation of Muslim articles of faith. We will discuss this elsewhere. But it can be mentioned here that the give and take between Islam and local traditions turned pirs into gods and gods into pirs—Satya Pir, for instance. Though he was Satya Pir for Muslims, Hindus called him Satyanarayana. The worship of this pir/god was conducted more or less in the same way in the two communities. Gorachand was also a pir who belonged as much to Hindus as to Muslims. Panchpir was held in particular esteem by Muslim masses in the villages. As late as the 20th century, Muhammad Enamul Haque saw both Hindus and Muslims worshipping Panchpir in West Bengal. In East Bengal, too, he saw extraordinary devotion for Panchpir. According to Haque, the worship of pirs is an inseparable component of the cultural life of Bengal Muslims.

The Sundarbans of the Middle Ages were far more extensive than what they are now. The tigers of the forest were fearsome beasts. So were the crocodiles. To keep up their spirits in the face of this fear, if not to totally conquer it, the Hindus imagined Dakshin Ray as the king of the tigers. Among Muslims, however, he was known as Barha Khan Gazi, which was the name of a pir we have mentioned before. The god of crocodiles was Kalu Ray, while the pir was Kalu Shah. In a land criss-crossed by rivers, Badar Pir also occupied a special position. Nor could folk Islam keep Shiva at bay. Shiva, who from ancient times held pride of place in the religious life of Bengalis, appears in popular Islam in the guise of Manik Pir. Matsyendranath became Pir Machhlandi. Devi Mangalchandi became Bon Bibi.

Satyanarayana and Satya Pir, Dakshin Ray and Barha Khan Gazi, Sitala and Ola Bibi at least managed to retain separate names if not completely distinct identities. But there are instances elsewhere of even more intimate assimilation. Sixteenth century poet Saiyid Sultan in his *Nabi-Bamsa* imagined Vishnu, Brahma, Shiva and Hari as *nabi*s or prophets. Some Hindu poets, on the other hand, imagined Muhammad as an incarnation of Vishnu. In 1686, Krishnaram Das wrote his *Raymangal Kavya*, in which Dakshin Ray appears in conflict with Barha Khan Gazi. But the fight does not end in the victory of one over the other. God himself descends from the heavens to play mediator between them and save the world from destruction. He comes down to the earth as half Krishna and half Muhammad:

Half his head had flowing black tresses, a crown at a tilt on the other,
A garland of wildflowers adorns his chest and down further;
Suleimani prayer beads along with that, worn by Muslim fakirs.
Half his body the skin glows fair, the other half dimmed in clouds of darkness
He carries in his hands; both the Quran and the Puranas.

Saiyid Sultan calls Allah 'Prabhu' (lord) and 'Niranjan' (the flawless one). Haji Mohammad's word for him is 'gonsai'. Syed Murtaza has called Fatima 'Jagat Janani' or mother of the world. Thus the people of Bengal made Islam their own and brought it close to the toiling sons of the soil, making it look as Bengali or as Indian as was possible.

Even in their songs of praise introducing their works, medieval Bengali poets drew from both Hindu and Muslim traditions. Asim Roy claims that it was only through such Indianisation that Islam became accessible to the local population. The trend continued through the Middle Ages into the 19th century. Even fundamentalist movements such as the Faraizi and Tarikaye Muhammadia could not erase this syncretic tradition. Scathing criticism of Hindu practices in Muslim society appeared in magazines and journals produced by Muslims at the start of the 20th century. This shows how deep-rooted and strong the old tradition still was among Muslims, even after the spread of education.

Reforms in Local Religion

Just as Islam was assimilating local traditions and making them its own during the Middle Ages, Hinduism, too, was going through varied reforms. Starting from the Sena era, scriptural scholars (the writers of the Smriti texts and the *kulagranthas* or the genealogical chronicles of the patrilineal lineages, or *kulas*, of high-caste Hindus) recorded these reforms and gave them their seal of approval. These reforms were in large part a response to the challenge of Islam. In the face of this challenge, the guardians of the scriptures on the one hand pronounced against the loss of caste brought about by impure contact, and on the other tried to reinforce, with rigid fortifications, the ritual purity of Hinduism. It was at this time that the Brahmin clergy started laying down a stern set of rules governing the customs and rituals of Hindu religious life and insisted that these should be followed. The Smriti scholars exhorted Hindus to act like turtles in a world dominated by *mlecchas* (a derogatory term signifying people of an alien culture, deemed to be unclean and even barbaric). Hindus should, they were saying, retreat into their shells like turtles do when they see a threat. Raghunandan, one such Smriti scholar, tried to tie up the Hindu religious practice in a varied assortment of regulations in the 16th century. On the other hand, Debibar Ghatak prescribed that ritual purity be measured on a scale of diminishing transgressions instead of ritual status (*kaulinyo*) being granted to clans or *kulas* on the basis of exemplary religious conduct. He introduced the custom of *melbandhan* to prevent Brahmins from losing caste because of trivial reasons. This was a scheme that allowed 'tainted' or 'polluted' Rarhi Brahmin families to contract marriage alliances among themselves (many of the taints deriving from contact with Yavanas, or Muslims) and thus preserved the community from threats of extinction or expulsion from the Brahmanical social order. But these were feeble attempts at self-preservation. And in any case they were limited to the social groups at the top, among the higher castes. They were of no use whatsoever in resisting conversions and other kinds of transformation in society at large.

The attempt to keep the flock together among the lower castes and the lower classes, the social majority who had no right to read the Sanskrit scriptures, was being carried out through a different process. It was at this time that initiatives were taken to bring the lower orders within the pale of the Hindu caste structure, and this was done by forging ties between Aryan and non-Aryan deities. These initiatives were largely successful. We have narrated before how a local goddess such as Manasa found recognition as Shiva's daughter at the hands of the scriptural scholars and thus earned endorsement from the Brahmanic faith. Thus local and folk deities were subjected to a process of Sanskritisation and hauled up the ladder of ritual prestige. Manasa, though, did not straight away become a first-rung goddess, despite the scriptural endorsement. She was worshipped not at the puja mandap, which was the sacred space marked out for the worship of gods in people's homes, but in thatched huts outside the main dwelling and under the supervision of non-Brahmin priests. But in a land all but creeping with snakes, few could afford to ignore the goddess of reptiles. Manasa, therefore, slowly made her way into the worship of Hindus of the higher castes. In the 16th century, Brindavandas mentioned in his *Chaitanyabhagavat* that Manasa, along with Chandi and Basuli, was quite a popular goddess:

> *Dambha kori bishohari puje kon jane*
> *Puttoli koro-e keho diya bohu dhane*
>
> (Some people proudly worship the venom-remover/And some get her image made at great cost)

It was not, however, through Sanskrit scriptures or literary texts that non-Aryan gods and goddesses became popular in Bengal, but through the Mangalkavyas and the Panchalis. Bipradas Piplai wrote *Manasabijoy* at the end of the 15th century (1495-96), during the Hosein Shah regime. This was also roughly the time when Bijoygupta wrote *Manasamangal*, though there is room for debate over this. This was also more or less the time when Vidyapati wrote about Manasa. Manasa, therefore, appears to have turned into a popular deity in the 15th century.

Mangalchandi, like Manasa, was also initially a goddess worshipped only by Hindus of the lower castes. Indeed, she started out as not even a Hindu deity but a tribal one, worshipped in some parts of western Bengal. Within a few hundred years, however, she turned, as a Shiva consort, into a goddess worshipped by the higher castes and became quite popular in the 16th century. One of the factors that fuelled her rise was Mukundaram Chakraborty's *Chandimangal.* Sukumar Sen, though, has claimed that people in Bengal were fairly familiar with the story of Mangalchandi even before Mukundaram wrote his poem. Once Mukundaram's *Chandimangal* captured the popular imagination, other poets, too, came forward to write poems describing the goddess' glory.

The Hindu Puranas also mention a goddess called Chandi. But the Puranic Chandi is not quite the same as the Chandi that Mukundaram imagines. Mukundaram's Abhoyachandi was in large measure a folk deity. A few centuries earlier, Durga and also Kali had received scriptural endorsement as Shiva's wife. What is more, the worship of Durga started growing in popularity within a couple of hundred years of Muslim rule. By the 15th century, it is claimed in *Chaitanyabhagavat,* she was being worshipped in every home. Mukundaram in his *Chandimangal* has also described the worship of Durga as being quite popular. The surprising thing is that Durga worship is not prevalent in any other province of India, at least not in the form in which the goddess is worshipped in Bengal, as both the slayer of fearsome forces of evil and as a married daughter visiting her paternal home with her children. The latter myth, especially, marks her out as a goddess rooted in the local culture. The worship of Kali, too, is quite specific to Bengal. Kali, however, had to wait another few hundred years to get her dues. It does not look like the worship of Kali in its present form had started before 18th century, though she had been recognised as a goddess much earlier. Indeed, the Shakta community grew significantly under Muslim rule. Tantra beliefs, too, merged into the cult of the dark goddess. Kali, in a word, came to be seen as the predominant symbol of Adya Shakti, the Divine Mother, perceived as the primordial force that moves the world.

Even if Chandi and Kali had some Puranic antecedent, Dharma Thakur could claim no such heritage. He was truly a folk and local deity, worshipped only in the Rarh region, which was also where *Dharmamangal*, a narrative poem on the god, was written. The extraordinary thing about this folk god is that he was a product of the imagination of both Hindus and Buddhists. He is, therefore, an outstanding example of a culture of religious syncretism and assimilation. The local belief was that Dharma Thakur was able to grant male offspring and cure leprosy.

Like other folk gods and goddesses, Sitala and Shasthi were also sought to be included in the mainstream Hindu pantheon. Sitala was accepted as Shiva's wife and Shasthi as his daughter-in-law.

Attempts were being made at this time to extend scriptural approval to the folk god Dakshin Ray, the god of tigers, and co-opt him as a son of Shiva. Dakshin Ray, as a result, started receiving annual worship, though quite often with non-Brahmin priests officiating, as in the case of Manasa. Indeed, once semi-Puranic deities such as Manasa and Chandi had their places assured, it became easier for an ever growing brood of local and folk deities such as Dakshin Ray or Dharma Thakur to make their way into the cycle of worship. This was the route through which deities believed to be watching over crocodiles, tigers, rivers, and also the dreaded poxes, emerged.

As we have said before, it was not through Sanskrit literature or the scriptures that these local deities became popular, but through the Mangalkavyas and the Panchalis. It was partly the perceived glories of the goddesses and partly the narrative content and the literary quality of the poems that secured an audience for the Mangalkavyas that Bipradas wrote about Manasa and Munkundaram wrote about Chandi. After the success of these poets, others went on to write poems about other goddesses, both the famous and the lesser-known ones. Mangalkavyas such as *Kalikamangal*, *Annadamangal*, *Sitalamangal*, *Shasthimangal*, *Saradamangal*, *Raimangal*, *Surjyomangal*, *Gangamangal*, *Lokkhimangal*, *Panchananmangal*, *Subachanimangal* and so on are all paeans to the glories of these newly evolved local and down-to-earth folk deities. Even mainstream deities such as Shiva and Krishna became subjects of such poetry. Indeed, so popular did the Mangalkavyas become that some poets did not restrict themselves to writing just one. Besides, just as an initiative was under way to endorse and thereby co-opt Buddhist and other local belief systems, an effort to bring popular Muslim beliefs within the pale of Hinduism was also going on. This was how Satya Pir, as mentioned before, turned into Satyanarayana. It is not known whether Satya Pir was a historical character, but some popular pirs did turn into gods in the Hindu imagination and were worshipped as such. In this way, Hinduism managed to survive the onslaught of Islam, evolving and transforming itself in the process. But to survive is not the same thing as to get a fresh lease of life.

The Revival of Hinduism: The Arrival of Chaitanyadev

Chaitanyadev gave that fresh lease of life to Hinduism. He brought both strength and direction to Hindu society with his revolutionary message. The Vaishnava faith was not entirely new to Bengal. Even before the start of Muslim rule, Jaydev had written his *Gita Govinda* under Lakshman Sena's patronage. The appeal of *Gita Govinda* was not entirely because of its literary merit but also because of the popularity of Vaishnava beliefs. But it was Chaitanyadev who made Vaishnava beliefs truly acceptable to large sections of the population. It was not, however, through his rationalisation of the faith that he achieved this, though he did bring to it a new theory. Unlike the Smriti scholars, he did not try his hand at penning scriptural prescriptions. But he moved mountains with his powerful attack on lifeless religious regulations, bringing new life not just to Vaishnavism but to Hindu religious practice in general.

Chaitanyadev

Fortunately for him, the times were favourable. He was a contemporary of the liberal Sultan Alauddin Hosein Shah. He did not, therefore, have to preach in the face of administrative hostility. On the contrary, the sultans of Gaur had started patronising Vaishnava religion and literature. In the last chapter we took note of how, even before Chaitanyadev was born, Maladhar Basu wrote *Srikrishnavijay* under Sultan Ruknuddin Barbak Shah's patronage.

Borhu Chandidas's *Srikrishnakeertan* was also written before Chaitanyadev's time. Hosein Shah himself patronised Vaishnavas. His prime minister and his personal secretary – *dabeer-i-khas* – were two brothers who later became famous as Vaishnava gosains, Sanatan and Roop.

Chaitanyadev stormed the centuries old bastion of caste stratification with his message of love and equality on the one hand. On the other, he rescued faith from the mumbo jumbo of the scriptures and carried it away in a flood of deeply emotional devotion. There was no need for any mantras for the kind of faith that he preached. In his happily unceremonious cult, the only ceremony was the singing of the Lord's name. His other message was love for one's fellow creatures. The influence that this extraordinarily charismatic leader had on his followers was almost boundless. There is a story about how he once made them drink water that had been used to rinse the feet of a cobbler or a Muslim. If this is true, then one must say that he did at least temporarily bring down the insurmountable walls separating castes and communities. His teaching found its greatest acceptance among the lowest of the social classes. That even the infidel Haridas could be superior to a Brahmin through the sheer strength of his devotion was not an easy message to preach at that time. To actually translate such notions into appropriate action was even more difficult.

The conservative Brahmin community, of course, opposed his revolutionary teaching with all its might. Yet he managed to stir up the caste-divided society of his day by striking at the very root of its conservatism. In this way he succeeded in large measure in warding off the challenge posed by Islam's message of social equality. The flood of religious emotion that he released united the Hindus in a fervour of devotion. There may be debate about whether he borrowed this emotional content of faith from the Sufis, but that it completely overwhelmed the Hindus is beyond a shadow of doubt.

Language was a powerful tool. Instead of shutting up faith in the prison of the popularly inaccessible Sanskrit, Chaitanyadev freed it up for the masses by preaching it in their language, Bengali. The scriptural injunction of his time was that either reciting or listening to the *Astadash Purana* and/or the story of Ram in the regional language would ensure a place in hell (Rourab Narak). So afraid were the socially submissive poets of the time of falling foul of this warning that whoever wrote a Mangalkavya in Bengali always began the poem with an explanation of what made him write it. The usual excuse was that the goddess herself had appeared to the poet in a dream to command, and therefore compelled him to write it.

Even Muslim poets such as Saiyid Sultan started with an apology when they wrote Islamic poetry in Bengali. Chaitanyadev's use of language can perhaps be compared to the role that Martin Luther played in Europe to free the Bible from the chains of classical language. Chaitanyadev did not feel any need to couch his message in Sanskrit to make it glamorous and acceptable to Brahmins. On the contrary, by preaching in Bengali he succeeded in taking his message even to the completely down and out.

Unfortunately, Chaitanyadev died young. According to some accounts, he was murdered. Within 50 years of his death, his *goswamis* (disciples) left Bengal and settled down in Vrindavan, where they reversed all his reforms. Instead of Bengali, they now chose to codify their faith in Sanskrit. Chaitanyadev had freed up faith from the prison of books. Not only did his *goswamis* have their faith shut up inside books again, they also made those books inaccessible to ordinary readers through the wall of an unfamiliar language like Sanskrit. Chaitanyadev had rescued religion from the grip of caste divisions. His *goswamis* put the divisive caste structures back in place. In sum, they rejected Chaitanyadev's teachings about the efficacy of singing praises of the lord, love for fellow creatures and the spirit of loving devotion. Thereafter Vaishnavism earned endorsement from Brahmins through its adoption of sacred texts and a conservative world view. It now had more social prestige, but the flood of devotion and love that had swept away Bengali Hindus was dammed.

The efforts of a handful of committed preachers led to some social acceptance, though limited, for Vaishnavism as an organised religion, but the breath of life had gone out of it. Srinivas Acharya preached the faith in the Bishnupur area, Narottam Thakur in North Bengal, Nityananda's wife in Kharhdaha and his son in eastern Bengal. But though it did find some followers, its own internal contradictions prevented a wider reach. What's more, caste differences succeeded in dividing the Vaishnavas themselves. So there were the higher-caste Vaishnavas who abided by caste hierarchies and there were the lower-caste Vaishnavas who rejected them. Yet, despite these contradictions and regressions, Vaishnavism made a considerable space for itself in the lower rungs of society. There is indirect evidence of this in the temples built in the 17th and 18th centuries. From the account of the temples of this time given by David McCutchion, it can be seen that 110 Vaishnava temples were built between 1600 and 1760. During the same period, only 74 Shiva temples were built and other deities between them had 28 new temples.

Despite this relative edge in popularity that the faith enjoyed, lower-caste Vaishnavas, finding themselves adrift and leaderless, strayed quite far from mainstream Vaishnavism. Over time, some drifted so far away from the faith preached by Chaitanyadev that they identified themselves with other communities and eventually saw themselves as belonging to them.

Assimilation, and the Rise of the Sahajiyas

The indirect influence of Chaitanyadev's ideals of social equality and worship based on loving devotion continued to create ripples in society, even if mainstream Vaishnavism moved away from them. In post-Chaitanyadev Bengal, therefore, a tradition of unceremonious and syncretic faith started taking root. This tradition assimilated the Buddhist Sahajayana ideals, the Sufi world view in Islam and the stress on love in Vaishnavism, and it even drew on Tantric beliefs. A faith based on love triumphed over institutionalised religion. The tradition found its greatest expression in the Bauls.

The word 'Baul' was used in *Srikrishnavijay*, that is, as early as the 15th century. *Chaitanyabhagavat* and *Chaitanyacharitamrita* also mention the sect. The Bauls have close links with the Sahajiya community that existed even before the start of Sena rule. Like the Sahajiyas, the Bauls, too, seek that which is beyond the body within the temple of the body itself. Their search is for the formless, but they seek to experience it through the physical human form. They don't care for any codified chants or mantras. Refusing to recognise any religious regulations or sacred text, the Baul delves within through songs in search of the prince of his heart or *moner manush*. This *moner manush*, which roughly translates as 'the dearest one', is no god and has no name. In short, the Bauls seek a truth that is beyond all scriptures and reach out to an ideal of perfect manhood. Institutionalised religion is to them an obstacle in the way of attaining this ideal. It is this down-to-earth tradition of simple love which, much later, inspired a poet of the masses like Madan Baul to sing

Tomar path dhaikyachhe mondire masjide
Tomar dak shuni sain cholte na pai
Rukhe danrae gurute murshide

(The temples and mosques hide the road to You
I hear your call, Friend, but I cannot make my way through
The gurus and murshids block my path.)

The Kartabhaja and Sahebdhani sects were also influenced by the ideal of religious syncretism. The reverence for gurus always dominated the religious life of Bengal. Far from rejecting this guru culture, the Islam preached by the Sufi pirs reinforced this tendency, though after introducing some reforms. There is, indeed, little to distinguish between guru, murshid and 'karta', the object of search for the Kartabhaja sect, the word literally meaning 'lord'. The Kartabhaja community believes that Chaitanyadev was reborn as Aulchand sometime between 1694 and 1695. He was a foundling and, therefore, had no caste. As an infant he had been discovered in a stack of betel leaves. The adult Aulchand lived in various places in 24 Paraganas and the Sundarbans and attracted mainly casteless Vaishnavas with his preaching. But he also had some followers from other communities, including Muslims. The sect has many similarities with Bauls. Like the Bauls, the Kartabhajas worship no gods or goddesses. The 'karta' they worship is much like the *moner manush* of Bauls, and like the Bauls they seek him through songs. Apart from the Kartabhaja sect, some other smallish Sahajiya sects were Sakhibhabok, Kishoribhajoni, Ramballabhi, Sahebdhani, Pagolnathi, Matua, all of which practised a faith shorn of ceremoniousness.

To sum up, various kinds of changes and evolutions were quite evident in the religious life of Bengalis after the start of Muslim rule. On the one hand the advent of Islam and a Muslim ruling class initiated a momentous change in religious thought. On the other, a revolution seemed to be in the making in caste-divided Bengali society, though the values of that short-lived revolution did not reach all sections and were not equally forceful among all.

A fresh attack started in the 16th century as a new religion appeared on the horizon. This time, it was the Portuguese missionaries, who came with the message of Christ. By that time the era of independent sultans was over, but the Mughals had not yet consolidated their grip. Bengal was then under the sway of the 'Baro Bhuiyan', a group of petty chieftains and landlords who reigned supreme in the territories they controlled. Some of them may have welcomed in Portuguese missionaries in the hope that Portuguese help would be useful in their fight against Mughal domination. Among them were Isa Khan of Sonargaon, Ramchandra Ray of Bakla and Pratapaditya of Jessore. Pratapaditya did not stop at inviting the missionaries; he permitted Christians to build a church in his territory. He even made over some land surrounding the church to help with its expenses. On the first day of the year 1600, he visited this church with his son. But the most important thing that he did was to declare that whoever wanted to convert to Christianity could go ahead and do so.

Christian missionaries, like Muslim preachers, found most of their followers among the lower rungs of society. The numbers of people converting to this new faith soon started to swell. Francois Bernier visited Bengal in 1665. He has mentioned that at that time there were some 8,000 to 10,000 Christians living in Hooghly alone. According to him, the number of Christians in the rest of Bengal was by then around 25,000. These conversions were going on quietly, without anybody noticing. However, when the English missionaries started preaching, with a great deal of enthusiasm, in the beginning of the 19th century, there was much criticism of their activities, just as there had been of Muslim proselytising in an earlier time. One reason for this could have been the suspicion that Muslim rulers helped in the preaching of Islam, a common enough complaint. In the same way, in the days of British rule it was assumed that state power was in league with the proselytising efforts of the missionaries.

***

BENGALI CULTURE UNDER WESTERN IMPACT

The tired, sick and despairing sailors must have rejoiced when the coast of Calicut came into view on May 20, 1498, after 23 days of sailing a turbulent sea. Their leader was Vasco da Gama. He took more than 10 months to reach India from faraway Lisbon, losing many of his men on the way. But what made him embark on such a perilous journey? Was it only a craving for the kind of discovery that a few years earlier had made Christopher Columbus famous after he stumbled on to the Americas? Not really.

The First Contact

The silks and spices of India were then much in demand in Europe. Right rare and expensive those commodities were, too. But Europe was constrained to carry out this profitable trade with India through Arab merchants. A direct contact with India bypassing these middlemen would surely make it more lucrative. This was the thought that in 1492 led the King and Queen of Spain to give Columbus three ships, along with money and sailors, and send him on his way to find an easy route to India. Columbus knew that the earth was spherical. He believed, therefore, that he would sooner or later reach India even if he sailed west instead of east. He had not bargained for the fact that the earth was larger than he thought it to be or that some other landmass might block his way before he reached his destination. After weathering three weeks of growing despair, sickness and consequently mutinies by his sailors, he thought he was in India when on October 12 he touched land. It was, however, only an island in the Bahamas, and soon enough Columbus himself came to realise that. So it was that the land he discovered became known as the West Indies. He had found a whole new continent, but India dodged his quest. That is why five years after the discovery of the Americas, the King of Portugal ordered Vasco da Gama to find an easily navigable route to India.

Vasco started his journey from Lisbon on July 8, 1497, with four ships and three interpreters. It was already half a century since Portuguese and Spanish sailors discovered a southward route along the west coast of Africa, but they had been unable to get past the Cape of Good Hope. It was their old map, however, that Vasco relied on as he sailed along the west coast of Africa, past the Cape of Good Hope, travelling down a long route past Mozambique and Kenya, and finally found himself in the Indian Ocean. In Kenya he picked up a few Arab traders to show him the way to India. Twenty-three days after he set sail from there, he reached the west coast of India.

The contact that was thus established with Europe changed the course of history not just for Bengal but the whole of India. The Sakas, Huns, Mughals and Pathans who came before may have founded empires, but they had not been able to introduce modern ways of thinking, though it must also be admitted that Islam and the culture of Central Asia did significantly influence India over a few centuries. But the trail blazed by Vasco da Gama brought, for the next four and a half centuries, post-Renaissance modern European thought and myriad ingredients of a modern way of life. It so happened, for instance, that Vasco da Gama brought with him a printing press, one of the most important tools of modernism. In later years, the English merchants of the East India Company also came seeking their fortunes, in the hope of becoming 'nawabs' overnight through trade with the East. But with the commodities they brought also came, almost like a by-product, European learning and ways of thought.

The Portuguese secured a *sanad* (permit) to trade in Bengal in the time of Sultan Giyas-ud-din Mahmud Shah in the 16th century. Subsequently, Dutch, English and Danish traders also secured such *sanad*s, one after another. So did the French. The trading by these merchants opened up new markets for the commodities that Bengal had to offer. Exports to European markets increased manifold. As long as these European traders competed among themselves for monopoly over the trading, Bengal continued to benefit. But once the British established their monopoly over the trade and the competition was over, Bengal lost its edge. The time was ripe for colonial exploitation.

Muslin and other commodities from Bengal were then highly valued in the markets of Europe. European traders, however, did not just take back goods from India to Europe, they also brought European commodities to sell in India, especially woollen fabrics. The most important thing that they brought was, of course, knowledge in the current developments of science and technology. The Portuguese also brought with them many fruits, flowers and crops from distant lands. These they sourced mainly from Central and South America. Their most important imports, however, were tobacco and chillies. The chilli peppers brought by them quickly became widely available all over India. It seems almost incredible today, but peppercorns and ginger were the only source of heat in Indian food before the Portuguese introduced chillies. Tobacco, too, quickly became popular. Introduced by the Portuguese in the 16th century, it was in circulation as a commodity in trade in various parts of India by the first half of the 17th century. Emperor Akbar himself became quite fond of tobacco, though his son Jahangir, who was addicted to opium and wine, banned tobacco in his court. Indeed, so fast did tobacco earn its place as a luxury good that poems were written describing its virtues in 18th century Bengal. Round potatoes, also brought by the Portuguese, became quite popular as a cash crop.

The Portuguese did not stop at just trading. Many of them settled down in Bengal permanently. Some of them traded in slaves. Then again, there were many who served as mercenaries in forces maintained by local landlords (zamindars) or the sultan. A few became zamindars themselves. Some of them gave up trading and, in their eagerness to turn rich overnight, took to piracy. These men sailed the rivers of the land and the Bay of Bengal with their fleets to plunder and kill. A fleet of boats or ships is called 'armada' in Portuguese. This was the word that led to Portuguese pirates being called '*harmad*' in Bengali. Traders from Bengal in those days sailed to Sri Lanka, Burma, Indo-China and even as far as Indonesia. Most of the ships they used were made in the area around Dhaka. Ibn Batuta travelled on one such ship with Bengali sailors in the 14th century, from Sonargaon to Sumatra in 40 days. In the 17th and 18th centuries, however, the terror of *harmad*s all but put an end to domestic and foreign trade by Bengali merchants.

Notwithstanding this kind of notoriety, the Portuguese are still remembered in Bengal, partly because of the fruits and crops that came with them and partly because of their contribution to the Bengali language.

A kind of broken Portuguese was at that time spoken in India's coastal areas by traders who used it to do business with Portuguese traders. Bengali still carries the imprint of that makeshift language. Portuguese-origin words in Bengali may not number in thousands, as do Arabic, Farsi or even English words, but over a hundred Portuguese words for which there are no alternatives continue to be used all the time. There are words for many objects which are indispensable in modern lifestyles that we now borrow from English, but these were initially known by their Portuguese names. For instance, chair was once *kedara* and table was *mez. Baranda* (verandah), *janala* (window), *kamra* (room), *gudam* (godown or warehouse), *garad* (grill), *barga, ispat* (steel), *chabi* (key), *almari* (almirah), *perek* (nail), *alpin* (common pin), *balti* (bucket), *gamla* (tub), *pipa* (barrel), *pirich* (saucer), *boyam* (large china or glass container), *botol* (bottle), *canestara* (can), *saban* (soap), *towale* (towel), *kameez* (loose, long shirt), *saya* (in-skirt), *phita* (ribbon), *botam* (button), *istiri* (iron), ayah and many other words of everyday use have come in from Portuguese.

The words for a wide variety of foods and fruits are of Portuguese origin. For instance, the root of *anara*s (pineapple) is the Portuguese *ananas.* The fruit's wealth of juice or *ras* has tweaked the second syllable of *ananas* into *ras.* Other fruit and food names of similar origin are *aata* (custard apple), *peyara* (guava), *nona* (salty), *penpe* (papaya), *kaju* (cashew), *kopi* (cabbage), *ruti* (bread), *biskut* (biscuit), achar (pickle), *sagu* (sago), coffee, salsa (a kind of liquid medicine, much used by traditional healers), etc. *Kirich* (a kind of curved knife), *bombete* (ruffian), *mastul* (mast), *marka* (mark) and *kapten* (captain) are also words originating in Portuguese. It is amazing to think that even Lalon Fakir used the word *bombete* in his soul-stirring songs. It is a measure of how widely Portuguese words were used in those days. The Portuguese brought pistols and bombs, but with them also came the violin (*behala*). *Nilam* (auction) was another much-used word. The Bengali words for three European races, *ingrez* (the English), *farasi* (the French) and *olondaz* (the Dutch), are also borrowed from Portuguese.

It is said that Portuguese pirates abducted a Bengali prince and sold him to a missionary. It was this kidnapped prince who later became known as Dom Antonio and wrote a book in Bengali to preach Christianity. Titled *Brahman-*

Roman Catholic Sambad, the book was written in the form of questions and answers. It was never printed. The first book that was printed in the Bengali language was called *Kripar Shastrer Artha Bhedh* (Understanding the Scripture of Mercy). Published in Lisbon in 1743, the book was written by a Portuguese missionary called Manoel da Assumpçao. He seems to have dictated the book, which is about Christianity, to someone else who wrote it down. For, the book contains many things that do not quite go with Christianity. It was written sometime at the end of the 17th century or around the beginning of the 18th. There were no Bengali typefaces yet, so the book was printed in Roman letters. This was indeed an epoch-making event: a printed book of Bengali prose, and that, too, published in faraway Europe.

Just as the natives of the land picked up a broken Portuguese to converse with Portuguese merchants, so did Portuguese missionaries and traders learn Bengali to be able to communicate with the local people. They taught themselves Bengali grammar, in the belief that this would help them to master the language, and also put together a Bengali dictionary. In this, too, Manoel da Assumpçao played a special role. He started working on an encyclopaedia of Bengali words, which however he could not finish. He also tried to write a Bengali grammar in Portuguese. This was a truly pioneering work, because no other work of Bengali grammar is known to have been written before his. The attempt to analyse a language structure to discover its inherent rules could not have been easy for a foreigner.

The Portuguese were not just the first to come out with a printed book in the Bengali language or to write a Bengali grammar and an encyclopaedia of words, they were also the first to preach Christianity in Bengal. That Portuguese connection is evident in the way the Christian house of worship is *girja* in Bengali, Christ is '*Jishu*', Christian is *Christan*, the priest is *padre*, and the cross is *croosh*, all words borrowed from Portuguese.

The Portuguese were the first Europeans in India. They were also the first to secure a *sanad* to trade in Bengal. But they did not survive the competition with other European traders. Danish, Dutch and French traders, all of whom started trading with India before the English did, also could not hold their ground in the competition. India was a jewel that destiny had reserved for the British. And their first foothold in the empire they built in India was Bengal.

The Arrival of the English

At a time when Muslim rule was firmly consolidated in Bengal after five centuries and a half of uninterrupted domination, Nawab Siraj-ud-Daulah, quite unexpectedly, was defeated at the hands of English traders in 1757. Compared with the vast forces that he commanded, the East India Company fought with only a handful of soldiers. A number of factors brought about his defeat. As Alivardi Khan's favourite and pampered grandson, he had gone astray while still only a boy. Even the historian Ghulam Hussain Salim, who was sympathetic to Siraj, and the prince's loyal friend Jean Law, the chief of the French factory at Cossimbazar, have written about his debauchery and cruelty. He murdered his paternal uncle Hossein Kuli Khan in public view and had quite a few other close relatives killed. He also insulted Jagat Sheth and other influential members of his court. Jagat Sheth was India's most dependable banker of the time. One by one, Siraj turned his friends into enemies. His bonding with the people he ruled over was none too close, either. Most importantly, he had little administrative experience. Neither his ministers nor his employees had any heartfelt loyalty for him. The betrayal by his general, Mir Jafar, was what ultimately brought about his downfall. So treacherous was this betrayal that it was quite apparent to all. Even now, the expression *mirjafari* in Bengali signifies breach of trust.

Despite the heavy odds, the Nawab's forces under Mohanlal's leadership almost snatched victory on the first day of fighting against the Company's forces. But Mir Jafar's malicious advice got him to remove his forces from the battlefield. The following day his troops were defeated. The vanquished Nawab was caught as he tried to make his escape and he died at the hands of Mir Jafar's son Miran. On Mir Jafar's orders, a spectacle was made of his corpse as it was taken around the streets. Though the East India Company was the real winner, the rule of the nawabs lasted another 10 years, though much of it was in name only. The Company used these years to slowly tighten its grip on power and consolidate its position. The Brits started ruling directly from the time of Warren Hastings.

The East India Company obtained from the Nawab the *dewani* of Bengal, Bihar and Odisha, that is, the right to collect taxes in these provinces, in 1765. For the next few years, there was in place a kind of dual rule by the Nawab and the Company. The demand for revenue consequently soared overnight. Whereas in 1764-65 the total land revenue amounted to 81 lakh rupees, the very next year it increased to 1 crore and 48 lakhs. Seven years later, in 1773, the land revenue was fixed at 3 crores. This demand for revenue devastated Bengal's countryside and the agricultural system. A terrible famine ensued, and it is still remembered as the 'famine of the year '76' (*Chhiattorer Monnontyor*). This was in the year 1176 of the Bengali calendar, roughly corresponding to the first half of 1770. Many historians say that this famine wiped off one half of the farming community. One third of the entire population died. Many peasants fled, unable to bear the persecution unleashed by landlords out to extract the increased taxes that they were required to pay. A parliamentary report of 1781 said that in Rangpur alone, 30,000 families left behind fertile land to move to Coochbehar. Much of the land was left fallow as the tillers either fled or died. In the circumstances, the Company was forced to bring in reforms in the land revenue system.

Governor General Warren Hastings

The reform entailed an auction in 1772, through which landholdings were leased out for five years. Those who paid large sums of money to buy these leases often could not make the land yield the kind of revenue that they had expected. All the torture inflicted on peasants could not always ensure that collections came in on time for the zamindar to pay his dues to the Company. So this five-year settlement soon failed. After various experiments, Lord Cornwallis worked out a 10-year settlement with the zamindars in 1789-90. This settlement was more successful, and in 1793 it was made permanent. The Permanent Settlement recognised the zamindars and *talukdar*s as permanently owning the land. This meant that they would now be able to gift, sell, or pawn the land without requiring the government's permission. They would even be able to divide up landholdings among their heirs. Cornwallis correctly predicted, in one of his letters to the Company directors, that a permanent ownership would make rich traders invest their excess incomes in land because few other avenues were open to them. Yet, many zamindars were still unable to pay their taxes in time and thus lost their landholdings, which were bought, through auctions, by others who could afford them.

Many of the old land-owning class, people who had lived off the land for generations, lost their landholdings in this way. The trend continued after 1793. For instance, in 1796-97, the zamindars whose landholdings went under the hammer had together accounted for one-fifth of the total land revenue. A third of the zamindars lost their landholdings within 20 years of the Permanent Settlement of 1793 because they failed to pay their taxes. These properties were bought up by the nouveau riche of Calcutta, a new class of bankers (banias), brokers (*mutsuddis*) and traders. Thus, within 17 to 18 years of the Permanent Settlement, the number of landholdings substantially increased. The large landholdings got fragmented into many smaller ones.

In social prestige, however, the zamindars were far ahead of the men who made their fortunes through trade. It was also less risky to put one's money in land. Traders and businessmen, therefore, often aimed at buying up land and becoming zamindars. Even the exceptional Bengali merchant Dwarkanath Tagore, forever full of new initiatives and undaunted by the prospect of new risks, could not duck the trend. Though he engaged in trading and industry, he also invested his profits in land and became a '*zamidar babu*'. Prasanna Kumar Tagore was a professional, a well known lawyer. But he, too, became a landlord. In those days most of the people who made an impact in Calcutta bought landholdings in the countryside, large or small.

Yet, since most of these new merchant-landlords had business interests to look after in Calcutta, they hired others to run their landed properties. Thus was created a class of absentee landlords. There were yet others who, instead of supervising the running of the entire landholding, divided it up and leased out the fragments. These leaseholders leased out yet smaller fragments of land. In this way a large class of middlemen was created. Historians say that in some landholdings as many as fifty levels of middlemen were in place, an endless chain of zamindars, *pattanidars*, *ganthidars*, *talukdars*, *jotdars*, and so on. Within a hundred years, the number of such landlords, large and small, went up about a thousandfold. Whereas in 1772, at the start of Warren Hastings's time, the zamindars numbered only a few hundred, in 1872-73 there were 1,54,200 of them. Of these, 1,37,000 landlords had holdings that measured less than 500 acres. The pressure on peasants had mounted because so many levels of middlemen meant more taxes that would have to finally come from their produce. Whereas in 1772 the total land revenue amounted to 3 crore rupees, around 1872, the zamindars and their middlemen collected some 17 to 18 crore rupees between them. The peasants also had to cough up a fair bit of money whenever the landlord's family celebrated a marriage or held a funeral.

The Permanent Settlement thus produced, from around the beginning of the 19th century, a parasitic class of people dependent on returns from land. These people also started exerting quite an extraordinary influence in society. As we will later see, they became known as 'babus'. In the first three or four decades of this century, the zamindars and the big businessmen of Calcutta played quite a noteworthy social role. They spent lakhs on marriages and funerals and in religious festivals. In order to attract popular attention, they also spent quite lavishly on religious causes such as building temples and making donations to Brahmins. They also started making donations to various institutions, both to please their white colonial masters and to show off their own wealth. One of the major donors was Dwarkanath Tagore. When contributions were announced at any meeting or conference, his was usually the largest among those made by natives. There were others who may have given more money for religious causes, but no one made bigger contributions for charitable works than he did. He gave one lakh rupees to the District Charitable Society. He also donated a part of the money for his father's funeral on works for the public good. Rich people in those days often made donations in order to quickly climb up the ladder of social prestige. As we will see later, however, the contribution that this section made to Bengal's cultural life was extremely significant and far exceeded in scope and consequence the donations and gifts made by some of them. There was also another section that made an important contribution: the people who hauled themselves up into the new middle class through their knowledge of English.

The Muslims had lost out in the competition for social rank through the purchase of landholdings. Hindu zamindars in any case far outnumbered Muslim landlords even before the British seized power. If there were few Muslim zamindars, there were even fewer Muslim *baniya*s, *mutsuddi*s (brokers) and traders. The biggest banker and moneylender at the time of Alivardi Khan and Siraj-ud-Daulah was Jagat Sheth, not any Muslim. Indeed, the major part of the trading in those days was controlled by Hindus. As a result, few Muslims had any opportunity to become zamindars after the Permanent Settlement. They could not, therefore, play any very remarkable role in the culture of Bengal. The one exception was probably Haji Muhammad Muhasin, who donated one and a half lakh rupees for the education of Muslims.

Most of the Bengali-speaking Muslims in the countryside were dependent on agriculture. Or they were weavers (*jola*), tailors (*darji*), home-builders (*gharami*) and so on. As we will see in the next section, there were very few Muslims among those who came forward to receive an English education in the 19th century. Money, landholding, trade, education—none of these avenues for acquiring class or social prestige was open to Muslims, which also made them unable to contribute significantly to the culture of 19th century Bengal.

The Rise of the 'Babu' or 'Bhadralok' Class

Mukundaram Chakraborty mentioned Calcutta in his *Chandimangal* in the 16th century itself. At that time it was just a village. The city of Calcutta was founded by the English another 100 years later, at the end of the 17th century. Even then, however, Calcutta was only an import-export centre for the East India Company. It had no political significance as yet. But with the establishment of British rule some 60 to 70 years later, almost overnight Calcutta far outstripped Murshidabad in importance. It became the capital of India and the biggest centre of foreign trade. In modern education through the medium of English, too, Calcutta left the rest of the country behind. At the start of British colonial rule, there appeared in Calcutta a new class of English-knowing clerks and copyists. These people could not become 'zamindar babus' because they did not have the money to do so. But they, too, were known as 'babu'—they were the middle class babus.

It is not known exactly how old the word 'babu' is. The word is given different etymological histories in different dictionaries. Whatever be the etymology, the word 'babu' was first used in English in 1782 in a special sense. It meant an English-knowing Bengali clerk. It may seem incredible now, but many of those who made copies of English documents and official records at that time had no knowledge of the language. They had simply mastered the art of copying what they saw on paper. Such people were called munshis. Those who had even a smattering of English were known as 'babus' to their English masters. In the second half of the 19th century, however, the meaning of the word 'babu' changed once again for the English. It now signified a Bengali clerk who wrote incorrect English though he might use difficult and little-known words culled from dictionaries.

The British may have used the word 'babu' in jest and held in contempt the people they so described, but the babus who found employment with the colonial masters managed to turn around their own fortunes. Several members of the Tagore family became pretty rich working for the British. Ram Mohan Roy himself was for a while a clerk under an English master. So was Rajnarayan Basu's father. Those who did not find employment directly under English masters but still got clerical jobs in the new city of Calcutta also did quite well in life. The minimum wage for munshis working for the Company was then 25 rupees a month. Babus who knew English got much more. In those days it was not too hard to get rich with this kind of money.

There was quite a scramble to acquire an English education in Calcutta once it became evident that this would open the way to a respectable income. In this context, it should be borne in mind that high-caste Hindus of Calcutta founded the Hindu College with their own money and on their own initiative. In 1850, when Calcutta had forty schools and colleges that offered an English education, Madras had just one such institution. This, too, gives an idea of how advanced Calcutta was.

Though the English latched on to a special meaning for 'babu', Bengalis used the word in a quite different sense. The most widely used sense in which the word was understood was 'master' or 'employer'. But it had other meanings. Such as the one that is seen, for instance, in Bhabanicharan Bandyopadhyay's story *Naba-babu-bilas* (Affectations of the New Babu) in the 1820s. 'Babu' is the title that he gives young men with new money. The equivalent word that he used for women was 'Bibi'. About such women he wrote another story, *Naba-bibi-bilas* (Affectations of the New Bibi). At the start of the 19th century, those who had turned into the nouveau riche of Calcutta after buying up landholdings were respectfully called 'babus', a word that reflected their position in society. But the section of people who were described as babus in the newspapers in the 1830s were not just zamindars and traders. Idle young men of rich families were also counted among 'babus'. Besides, it was roughly at this time that the custom of suffixing proper nouns with 'babu' started, and the idea was to address people with respect. In the 1850s, it was general practice to refer to educated young men as babus. An indication of just how widespread the use of 'babu' had become is available in Michael Madhusudan Dutt's sarcastic skit *Ekei ki Bole Sabhyata?* (1860; Is This Called Civilisation?). The boss in office was also referred to as 'babu', and there were, for instance, '*barha* babu' (the big boss), '*chhoto* babu' (of lower rank than the *barha* babu) and so on. Over time, clerks also became babus. The eldest son of a family was referred to as 'Barha Babu', while the youngest was 'Chhoto Babu'. And because the zamindars, the traders and the educated, salaried people were all Hindus, the word 'babu' also acquired a communal dimension. The Muslim babus were 'sahibs'. The English were also respectfully addressed as 'Saheb'. The babus, too, were sometimes called 'babu saheb'.

The picture of the babu that Bankimchandra Chattopadhyay drew at the end of the century may be exaggerated, but it was not much off the mark. This babu is not a zamindar or trader; he is an English-educated babu—bespectacled, liberal-minded and a polyglot. According to Bankimchandra, these people hated their own language but were experts in an alien tongue. In their mother tongue they could not converse. They saved without any objective, earned money to save, pursued an education to earn, and stole question papers to pass examinations. Their hands were weak, but they were good at talking and even better at saving their backs, and they were never to be seen where they might be of some use. As children and adolescents they used their energies to study, in their youth to drink and in their old age to take refuge with their wives. The English were their gods, Brahmo preachers were their gurus, the newspapers were their Vedas, and the National Theatre was their site of pilgrimage. They were chameleons—to the missionaries they were Christians, to Keshab Sen they were Brahmos, to their fathers they were Hindus, and to Brahmins they were atheists. They drank water at home, alcohol at the homes of friends, and while they put up with being called names at prostitute quarters, they got far worse at the hands of their white masters. They despised using oils while bathing, fingers while eating and their mother tongue while speaking. And they sought to rescue their motherland from distress through their pan-chewing, tobacco-smoking habits and bilingual posturing.

There are similarities between this piece by Bankimchandra and the picture of the babu that appeared in *Somprakash Patrika* near about the same time. That article, too, pokes fun at the babu as wordy and fond of talking. 'The education that they receive makes them build ever more castles in the air, blow the bubbles of their talkativeness, and fan their easy excitability, much like the cotton blossoms that burst and scatter at the slightest breeze [a rough translation].' Notwithstanding such jibes at the babu from Bankimchandra and the editor of *Somprakash Patrika*, the babus left a huge contribution in the culture that took shape in 19th-century Bengal.

At the fag end of the century, and in the new century that followed it, the (pseudo) patriotic babus described by Bankimchandra started being referred to by another word. This word was 'bhadralok'. The class of bhadraloks is closely associated with modern Bengali culture, particularly the culture of the social elite. The bhadralok, however, is not necessarily '*bhadra*', that is, the word does not signify his possessing amiable manners or a good character. The word is used in a special sense and refers to the educated Hindu middle class that came into its own in the 19th century. At the end of that century, when the definition of babu covered a wide range of meanings and was used to refer to all kinds of people, from the domestic handyman who did the grocery shopping to the boss at one's workplace, the word bhadralok probably gained currency as describing a particular class of people. This changing sense of the word is somewhat apparent in the way in which it has been used in *Hutom Pyanchar Naksha* and in *Somprakash Patrika*. The word does not occur in its combined form in the 1862 edition of *Hutom Pyanchar Naksha*. That gives it the meaning of a 'man with good manners and of good character' (bhadralok). In a piece published in 1872 in *Somprakash Patrika*, the word again seems linked to human character: 'Here's a man who does not feed his family, does not go home, eats and sleeps wherever he can. Can such a man be truly a bhadralok?' William Hunter mentioned the word in 1872 in his *A Statistical Account of Bengal*, and he said that '*bhadra*' denoted aged elders in villages but that it had no connection with money or wealth. According to him, the equivalent word among Muslims would be '*matbar*'. This shows that the word still retained some association with good character.

But in two pieces carried in *Somprakash Patrika* in 1881 and 1883, bhadralok has been used in a way that clearly signifies a particular social class. This is what one of them says: 'Farming is not work that is fit for a bhadralok, it would make people call him a peasant. ... Even farmers are now trying to be *bhadra* by relinquishing their family occupation and securing jobs.' The other says: 'There are many sons of *bhadra* families who have no occupation, no education, and who cannot even do manual labour because of pride in their caste.' The same social class seems to be suggested in another piece published in 1885—'Those children of *bhadra* families who hanker after jobs on the basis of a limited knowledge of English...'

Indeed, the epithet bhadralok would not apply to an uneducated zamindar or a rich businessman. It is also hard to tell whether its meaning would extend to those of the lower middle class among clerks working in offices. The word was probably created to mean educated, middle-class people belonging to the higher castes. The word, of course, is easily recognised as a translation of the English 'gentleman'. But a gentleman in England was a wealthy and landed member of the aristocracy, the kind who did not need to work for a living. It is doubtful whether the word bhadralok in Bengali, even if it did carry some sense of the social elite, signified in any way the possession of either land or money. Rather, education was the crucial thing that was needed for inclusion in the bhadralok category.

Bhadralok takes on a particular meaning quite noticeably from the beginning of the 20th century. It now began to denote, specifically, people of the educated middle class. And this middle class was limited to the Hindus. There was a time when 'Bengali' meant 'Hindu'; in the same way, bhadralok meant educated, middle-class Hindu. Part of the reason for this was that there was no middle class yet among Bengali-speaking Muslims. Though a Muslim-run newspaper in 1903 referred to the 'Muslim bhadralok, the word had not yet gained currency as referring to Muslims. Indeed, the Muslim middle class started emerging only in the 1930s and came into its own in the East Pakistan era, towards the end of the 1950s.

From the definition of bhadralok that Meredith Borthwick has given in her book on the changing role of Bengali women, it would appear that this class started developing at the beginning of the 19th century. But Borthwick was probably unable to spot the difference that there was between 'babu' and bhadralok. David Kopf, on the other hand, has given a largely correct definition of bhadralok in his history of the Brahmo Samaj. But it might appear that his bhadralok is in some way linked with the Brahmos. The most comprehensive and accurate definition of bhadralok has been given by John Broomfield. Writing in the context of the first partition of Bengal, Sumit Sarkar, while he did not give a clear definition, gave quite a long explanation of what the expression means. It was the educated, Hindu, middle class that he referred to in his discussion, but he also included educated zamindars in the meaning of the word. And he took the 19th century as the time frame for the rise of the bhadralok. According to Broomfield, in 1901 the bhadraloks accounted for about 2.5 or 3 per cent of the population. In other words, among the 40 million people in Bengal at that time, a million and a half were bhadraloks.

One of the ironies of Bengal's cultural history is that most members of the educated community of the 19th century came from the new parasitic babu class, the zamindars, *pattanidars*, *talukdars*, *jotdars*, *nayebs* (managers who ran the zamindars' estates) and *gomostas* (petty officials involved in the running of these estates), who made their fortunes by exploiting the labour of the masses. Towards the end of the century, a new section joined hands with this class which lived off the labour of others. And this new section became known as bhadralok. In education, language, literature and music – in a word, in Bengali culture – the contribution of the babu and the bhadralok was colossal. These were two social classes that together produced, in the second half of the century, what historians call the Bengal Renaissance. Muslims, on the other hand, could not leave any significant contribution in the Bengal Renaissance, whether through inclusion in the landed gentry or through education.

India in a New Light

The establishment of Indo-Muslim rule, as we have already noted, made a far-reaching impact on Bengal's society and culture in the centuries following it. As a consequence there appeared remarkable changes in Bengal's religious life, administrative system, language and literature, music, architecture, food and clothes. In education and culture, however, Indo-Muslim rule had little to give beyond what was accomplished in the first four centuries. This was because in the pursuit of knowledge and science Muslim civilisation did not progress beyond its medieval milestones. The contact that was established between Europe and Bengal and also the rest of India, on the other hand, though colonial in character, brought about fast-paced changes. The ways of thought that the colonial forces introduced were not medieval. It was already a few centuries since the Renaissance brought about an epochal change in Europe's world of thought. Europe was then the most advanced in the world in knowledge and science, and in technology. So it is only a half-truth to say that the East India Company came with commodities to sell. More valuable than the merchandise they carried was the message of modernism they brought, along with the vehicle in which to approach it—comprising knowledge, science and technology. The changes introduced by the European colonialists were, then, steps towards the modern age and away from the Middle Ages.

We have already seen how Bengal first came in contact with Europe through Portuguese traders. But that was mainly a trade link. Historians do not talk of any influence in ways of thought. The nature of the contact that was established with the Portuguese seems to have been quite different from the one that was later established with the English. The impact was also different. The volume of foreign trade increased because of the Portuguese. There came in new fruits, new foods, new flowers and new kinds of clothes. Bengal got acquainted with Christianity through the Portuguese. Some Portuguese words, too, found their way into Bengali. But the Portuguese did not bring the light of modernism in the world of thoughts and ideas.

British rule, on the other hand, had Bengal's wealth siphoned off out of the country, but it also initiated a new age of knowledge and science. In the words of Tagore, it was an epochal change. It goes without saying, of course, that the East India Company did not establish its rule to take Bengal forward in the pursuit of knowledge, science and technology. Yet, a consequence of their rule was to take Bengal in a direction that its Muslim rulers or its Portuguese connection had been unable to illumine. This was the route in which Bengal travelled to have its education system completely transformed in the 19th century. There was an extraordinary development in Bengali culture, in language, literature and music, and the centre of this new flowering was Calcutta.

According to David Kopf, who has two extremely valuable books on the Bengal Renaissance and the Brahmo movement, the reawakening that happened in Bengal in the 19th century was an indirect consequence of the East India Company's initiatives to consolidate its rule. Warren Hastings himself had learnt several Indian languages and tried to study the local culture. He tried to grow many rare species of Indian fruits and flowers in his garden and even carried some of them back home to England. He realised that to spread British authority in India and establish it on a firm foundation, the men who ran the administration must acquire knowledge of the languages, customs and religions of the land and that they would also have to 'Indianise' themselves. This would help them to better understand the people they were ruling over and thus to rule more effectively. It would also make them more acceptable to the native population. David Kopf has described this policy of ruling on the basis of a close acquaintance with local culture as 'acculturation'.

Acquiring an intimate knowledge of the local language and culture was of course not quite as easy as defeating the Nawab in a staged battle. A major impediment was the Indian people's oblivion to their own history, language, literature and culture. The Bengalis had no real history-writing tradition to speak of. Though some kings did get their own histories written down, these were essentially made-to-order tributes to their personal achievements. It was in this intellectual climate of historical oblivion that Asoka, the greatest emperor of ancient India, had been pushed out of the memory of the people. Whatever little written history that Bengal had was limited to the accounts left by Muslim historians and travellers who had come from China and Europe. And most of these writings had not yet been translated into English.

The native language and literature were not any easier to learn. The languages spoken in different parts of the country were not the same, and most of them had, to a lesser or greater extent, literatures written in them. Yet, none of these languages apart from Sanskrit had any books of alphabet recognition or any kind of books to help learning. Nor did they have any written grammar or dictionaries. So the English administrators did not have access to any books while learning about the language and history of the Indian people. They had to write their own books as they mastered the local languages. And they had to depend on their own research to learn about India's history, culture, the nature of its people, its laws and its geology.

Warren Hastings encouraged Company officials to study the languages, culture and history of the land. Those who tried to learn native languages received regular monthly stipends to pay their munshis in each language. Rewards were offered for skills acquired in Indian languages. Henry Pitts Forster had mastered Bengali, Farsi, Oriya and Sanskrit. Every month he got 25 rupees for each of his munshis, or language teachers. A knowledge of the native languages also opened up promotions and other incentives. There were rewards for those who wrote books on Indian languages, religions, law, or history. Moreover, the government bought up most of the copies of such books. Fortunately, Warren Hastings had help in his project from quite a few scholarly officials who had an innate knack for research. The most famous of them was the Orientalist Sir William Jones. He was a judge in the Supreme Court in Calcutta. He was deeply interested in linguistics and literature, interests that he had picked up while at Oxford. He had published books in Farsi and Arabic even before he arrived in India and was already recognised as a scholar. Nathaniel Halhed, Charles Wilkins, Henry Thomas Colebrooke, John Borthwick Gilchrist, and Francis Gladwin are among the other names that may be cited in this connection.

Sir William Jones

In order to rule, it was important to master, before everything else, both Hindu and Muslim law. As soon as the Supreme Court was established in Calcutta, therefore, Hastings got Halhed to write a book called *Gentu Codes* (1776) on Hindu law. Ten Hindu scholars (pandits) were commissioned to prepare a gist of Hindu laws in Sanskrit, which was then translated into Farsi. Halhed had learnt Farsi and Bengali after he arrived in Calcutta in 1772. He now used his Farsi to translate the Farsi translation into English. This was how Hindu laws became available in English translation. Halhed also started work on a book on Muslim law. But a knowledge of law is not enough for effective administration, it is also necessary to know well the language spoken by the local population. It was this that Hastings had in mind when he requested Halhed to write a Bengali grammar. The grammar was written, but it was found that the Bengali typefaces required to print the book did not even exist, let alone a press where it could be printed. Hastings, whose own enthusiasm in the matter was

Nathaniel Brassey Halhed, who wrote the first Bengali grammar in 1778

considerable and heartfelt, got Bengali typefaces made by another Company employee, Charles Wilkins. And the first real Bengali grammar was printed, in 1778, in a small press in Hooghly with the typefaces that he created.

Sir Charles Wilkins, who first made Bengali types and printed Halhed's grammar

Wilkins had no previous experience of making typefaces or with printing. His maternal grandfather was, however, famous in England for his typefaces. During his visits to his grandfather, Wilkins had noted the process of making them. He had in fact managed to commit the process to memory even though he would not have watched it very closely. It was this memory that he used to create the first Bengali typefaces. Wilkins had also, besides, learnt Farsi, Sanskrit and Bengali. To create the typefaces, he found an extraordinary assistant in Panchanon Karmakar. Panchanon, after having learnt the skill of making typefaces from Wilkins, played a leading role in the making of typefaces in Bengal for the next 50 years, along with his son and grandson.

Though Portuguese missionaries had, a few decades before Halhed, taken the first initiatives to produce a Bengali grammar and dictionary, Halhed is not known to have seen their work. He was a linguist himself, which was why it was possible for him to learn Bengali and analyse the language to discover its inherent rules and discipline. His was a far more comprehensive grammar than the fragmentary one produced by the Portuguese. So reliable was it as a book of grammar that William Carey used it as a model to write his more complete Bengali grammar in 1801. Even Ram Mohan Roy was influenced by the structure and planning of this grammar.

Apart from Bengali, some scholars, encouraged by Hastings, started working with other Indian languages. Gilchrist wrote a Hindustani grammar. Colebrooke wrote a Sanskrit grammar. Mathew Lumsden wrote a grammar of the Farsi language. All these linguists, however, received direction and help from William Jones. Jones himself was at this time researching languages. His contribution in translating Kalidasa and in the study of Sanskrit and Farsi is, without doubt, remarkable. His greatest contribution, however, is the discovery of the unity between the Indo-European languages. He noticed that many words in the classical European languages such as Latin and Greek as well as many of Europe's modern languages had astonishing resemblances with words in the various languages used in Iran and in northern India, particularly Sanskrit. He and some of his colleagues including Halhed noted that there were unmistakable similarities between *saptam* (meaning seventh) and Septem (September) and seven; *astam* (eighth) and October and eight; *nabam* (ninth) and November and nine; *dasham* (tenth) and December and decimal; *mata* and mother; *akkhi* and eye; *bhru* and brow; *nasa* and nose... This constituted the beginning of comparative linguistics. Company officials such as Nathaniel Halhed, Colebrooke, Gladwin, Gilchrist, Jonathan Duncan, Neil Edmonstone and Henry Pitts Forster came forward to take up the study of Indian languages. To help other Company employees to learn native languages, these scholars wrote books in various north and south Indian languages, including Bengali, Hindustani and Urdu. They even wrote grammars in Sanskrit, Arabic and Farsi.

A decision taken by the Company a few years after the Supreme Court was established in Calcutta in 1773, further encouraged the study of the Bengali language. All government laws were ordered to be translated into Farsi and Bengali. Farsi was of course the official language at that time, so there was no option but to translate the laws into Farsi. But the Company had no special love for a language that was closely associated with the previous Muslim rulers. Nor for Muslims in general. Their distrust of and hostility towards Muslims was not in fact something that the English acquired after arriving in India. Animosities towards Muslims were nothing new in Europe. Over many centuries, Muslims and Christians had been caught up in numerous conflicts, including of course the Crusades. Muslims had conquered parts of south-west and eastern Europe. In this context, it would not be improbable for the British to see Muslims as enemies in Bengal after having usurped their seat of power. This may well have been what made them think of having Farsi replaced by some other local language and of using that language to the extent possible. Since the East India Company was headquartered in Calcutta, it was Bengali, which, as the local language, received their patronage.

It was not however easy to patronise Bengali, so weak was Bengali prose at that time and so stark the absence of books on the language. The number of Company employees who had picked up the language was also really quite small. Halhed, who had written a Bengali grammar, had gone home on leave at that time. The man whom the Company appointed for the translation was Jonathan Duncan. He arrived in Bengal in 1772. Halhed had come in the same year. Halhed mastered the language extremely well, and the legend is that people could not make out that he was not a Bengali when he dressed in local clothes and conversed with the natives in Bengali. The story is surely exaggerated. But Duncan never had any such legend circulated about him. It may be inferred that he gained middling proficiency in the language and got his munshis to translate the book of law. In 1784, the first book of law in Bengali, translated by him, was printed and published by the Company's press in Calcutta. This was the first printed book that was written completely in Bengali. The following year saw the publication of another Bengali book of law that was also translated by Duncan, that is, translated by his munshis and endorsed by him.

Thereafter, books of law began to be published in Bengali fairly regularly. Particularly since 1791, law books in Bengali were published every year. By that time, however, the task of translation had, in turns, devolved on George Meyer, Frederick Cherry, John Chauve, Neil Edmonstone and Henry Pitts Forster among others. Jonathan Duncan had by that time received charge of Varanasi and left Bengal.

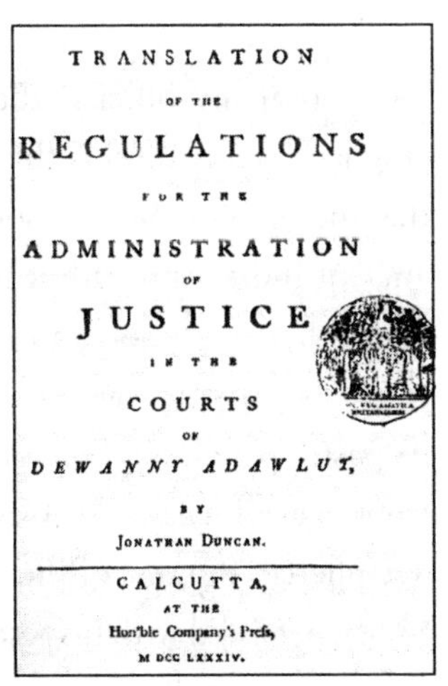
TRANSLATION
OF THE
REGULATIONS
FOR THE
ADMINISTRATION
OF
JUSTICE
IN THE
COURTS
OF
DEWANNY ADAWLUT,
BY
JONATHAN DUNCAN.

CALCUTTA,
AT THE
Hon'ble Company's Press,
M DCC LXXXIV.

The title page of the first ever printed Bengali book of law (1784)

Apart from legal translations, there were government notices and advertisements, which began to be translated into Bengali and printed from 1784 onwards. In most cases, a Farsi version was published along with the Bengali advertisement. These appeared in a weekly English magazine called *Calcutta Gazette.* Nearly 2,000 such notices and advertisements were printed until 1800. Some of these were very long, almost like small booklets. Bengali prose had acquired, through the translation of books of law, a certain power of expression and proficiency as a written language. These notices/ advertisements played a similar role in the development of the language. The quality of the printing of Bengali typefaces also improved at this time. (There is an extended discussion on the law books and the notices/advertisements in my 1993 book *Kalantare Bangla Godyo.*)

In the initial years, most of the books published by Company officials were, apart from the books of law, on the various Indian languages. Not limiting themselves to language, within a short while these scholar officials started researching India's history, geography, religions, and the lifestyles of its people. They published the results of their researches as essays and books. On January 15, 1784, the famous Asiatic Society was established in Calcutta, on the orders of Warren Hastings, in order to provide institutional help to these research initiatives. But though Hastings helped in its founding, it was Sir William Jones who breathed life into it. It was here that he started giving, from its very first day, his famous lectures on Oriental Studies. The journal brought out by the Society published the results of the researches by its members.

Company officials did not just acquaint themselves with the Indian languages and cultures through the Asiatic Society. Through the researches that they carried out in association with the Society, they were able to discover ancient India. And with it they also discovered India's geography, its geology and hitherto unknown information about its natural resources. It was these researches that revealed how wealthy a country India was and how glorious its past. Countless stupas and stone inscriptions were at this time discovered from the Himalayas to Ceylon. At first the writing on these could not be deciphered. But one of the members of Asiatic Society, James Princep (1799-1840), persisted with his researches into these until, in 1834, he deciphered the script. As a result, the mystery of the forgotten emperor Asoka was revealed, almost overnight. The countless stupas and stone inscriptions across the huge landmass of India were, it was learnt, built by a single emperor and bore testimony to his greatness. A huge chapter in India's forgotten history was now unearthed.

The Indian people's knowledge of their own history was extremely limited. Yet, the researches pursued by members of the Asiatic Society created in Indian minds, within 60 to 70 years of the start of colonial rule, an extraordinary awareness of their history, culture and heritage. This new consciousness produced a certain sense of nationhood. There was another way in which Asiatic Society researches stoked this sense of nationhood: the Company's researcher-officials did not stop at outlining India's glorious ancient past; they also marked out the Muslim era as an age of darkness. On the basis of this information and analysis, newly educated Indians began to derive a kind of comfort in blaming the Muslim age for the destruction of India's glorious past.

Admittedly, it was not out of any love for Indians or motives of doing good that the Asiatic Society was set up. It was set up to institutionalise research efforts on India, and the objective was to further the political interests of the colonial rulers. Until about the middle of the 19th century, the Asiatic Society was entirely a British organisation. Though the researches were on India, there was no collaboration with Indians. No Indian found a place at the Society's meetings. Even Ishwarchandra Vidyasagar was denied entry. But the researchers regarded Indian culture with respect and admiration. Many of them continued with their researches long after they had gone back home. Charles Wilkins, for instance, returned to London in 1786 but spent the rest of his life researching India. He also put together a collection of books at the India Office library. Those who loved the fruits and flowers of India, from William Roxburgh to Robert Kyd, took home saplings when they returned to Europe.

The Start of Print Culture

The advent of the printing press was one of the greatest contributions of British rule. We mentioned before that the Portuguese were the first to bring a printing press to the country, but that happened by chance. Vasco da Gama carried the printing press in the ship in which he sailed to India, and the plan was to drop it off in Ethiopia. Since he did not eventually stop at Ethiopia, the press made its way to Goa, and there it remained unused for a long time. The British, on the other hand, introduced the printing press because they had an interest in doing so. Within 15 years of the start of Company rule, a Company official called William Bolts tried to bring out a magazine in Calcutta. He even initiated efforts to have Bengali typefaces made in London. He was not, however, on good terms with the Company, which therefore regarded his efforts with suspicion. In the end, Bolts was not able to have his printing press.

Thus, even at the start of Warren Hastings's reign, the Company had doubts about having a printing press set up. The first printing press in Calcutta was established on private initiative, before there could be an official press. This momentous task was accomplished in 1777 by a fortune seeker called James Augustus Hicky. He invested his meagre resources in a box of typefaces and got a wooden printing press made. There being no other printing press in Calcutta at the time, he started to run a monopoly business with his press. All kinds of material were printed at this press on behalf of the East India Company and the armed forces that it maintained. Hicky also published what he called a 'calendar' at the start of 1778. Halhed's book was published in the second half of that year. From that perspective, Hicky's was the credit for printing a book for the first time in Bengal. In the following year he came out with another 'calendar'.

The Company started thinking of setting up a press only when Halhed's grammar required one. After it was published, the Company made plans of setting up a proper printing press under Wilkins's leadership. But this does not seem to have materialised very soon. From 1784, however, books began to be published and printed by what was called the Company Press. Besides, from 1780 onwards, printing presses were set up on private initiative. Once Hicky had shown the way, there came up at least a dozen printing presses in Calcutta before 1800. (There is an extensive discussion on these first printing presses and the printing assignments they took on in my 1986 book *Bangla Mudron O Prokashanar Adi Parbo*, Bengali Printing and Publishing in its First Phase.)

In the initial years, the printing press had nothing to do with the Bengali language and literature. Nor with Bengali society. Within a few decades, however, the printing press determined the direction of Bengali prose. That apart, Bengali culture, including religious practices, and other aspects of social life began to be influenced by the printing press. Halhed is said to have visited Nabadwip to collect samples of Bengali literature. Nabadwip was then one of the chief centres of education. Halhed, apparently, did not come across a single shelf of books there, which would not be unusual in an age when books were copied by hand. On the other hand, within a few decades of the advent of the printing press, there developed a tradition of Bengali printing which changed forever the look of Bengali language and literature.

A Bengali advertisement published in *Calcutta Gazette* in March 1784

Apart from the East India Company's books of grammar and law, the first Bengali book went to press in 1800. It was a religious text, a translation of the Gospels by John Thomas and Ramram Basu, a Bengali. This book of 125 pages was printed at a press at Serampore near Calcutta, then newly set up by Baptist missionaries. With this book the press started out on its long and memorable journey at the beginning of 1800. Over the next three decades, it played an unparalleled role in building up a tradition of printing in Bengal. In the second half of the 19th century, it went on to be recognised as the biggest press in the whole of Asia. By that time it had printed books in at least 34 languages, 30 of which did not earlier have any printed books. The typefaces for such languages were also made at the press, an extraordinary feat which was accomplished by Panchanon Karmakar, his son-in-law Manohar and Manohar's son Krishna Mistri.

Not just Christian texts, the *Ramayana* and the *Mahabharata* were also printed here within the first three years of the 19th century. Some textbooks used by the Fort William College were printed, too. These were books of history, legend, model letters and of spoken language such as could be used to communicate with different sections of the people. The curious thing was that the Serampore press was established in the teeth of fierce opposition from the Company. Once the missionaries started preaching, the Company felt, its chief objectives of trade and expansion of sway would be compromised. The locals might resent the spread of Christianity and revolts might surface. The Company, therefore, did not allow missionaries into the country for a long time, though it brought in chaplains to conduct religious ceremonies for its officials. These chaplains performed the religious rites for Company officials at births, deaths and marriages, but they did not preach. The missionaries, on the other hand, came to preach among the people and save their souls from the eternal fires of hell. Among the missionaries who came despite opposition from the Company was William Carey. He arrived in Calcutta in 1793. Carey put up with boundless hardships in order to carry out his preaching. The miseries that he was forced to undergo along with his family after arriving in Bengal would be too trying for anyone without his religious ardour. He did not, however, declare why he was coming to India and thus did not come with the Company's permission to preach. John Thomas, who had come before him with the intention of preaching, had also not declared his real objective.

After a period of hardship, William Carey found a job at an indigo factory in Malda. There he translated the Bible into Bengali and hoped to get it printed with the help of a wooden press that a friend had gifted him. But when he started looking around for Bengali typefaces, typeface-makers in London told him that it would take a few thousand pounds to get them made there. Carey now appealed to the English Baptist Missionary Society in London to send out to him people who had some knowledge of printing. Accordingly, William Ward and Joshua Marshman arrived in Calcutta at the end of 1799. But they took a detour, travelling first to America, so as not to arouse the suspicions of the East India Company. They then sailed to India in an American ship. They had, however, rather naively confided their missionary objectives to some fellow travellers, and their secret was eventually out. As soon as the ship anchored at the Calcutta port, therefore, they found themselves facing arrest. But the god-fearing captain of the ship refused to give them up to the police. A compromise was worked out, and Ward and Marshman sought refuge with their families at the Danish colony of Serampore. A few days after reaching Serampore, Ward went up to Malda to fetch Carey. In January 1800, these

Baptist missionaries set up the Serampore press, where Panchanon Karmakar and his son-in-law were engaged to prepare the typefaces. Carey and his friends avoided going to Calcutta because they feared arrest.

Hastings went home in 1785, but the policy of nurturing a close familiarity with the native culture that he initiated continued to be followed. Setting up the Asiatic Society and establishing a printing press were not quite enough. Keeping this in mind, Governor General Marquess Wellesley took a huge step in 1800. The 16 and 17-year-old boys who came out to India in those days to work as clerks for the company hardly knew anything about the country, and least of all, the language. The Governor General started the Fort William College in Calcutta to train them in the ways of the country they had come to work in, on the lines of Haileybury College in England.

The curriculum included, apart from Arabic and Farsi, different Indian languages, literatures, geography, history and Hindu and Muslim law. In sum, an education in the country's culture was offered, with the help of the scholar-officials associated with Asiatic Society. No one was, however, available to run the proposed Bengali department of the college. In 1801, the authorities got in touch with Carey through Claudius Buchanan. The understanding that was worked out was that in return for Carey's working for the college, his Baptist missionary friends would not be arrested if they visited Calcutta. Relations between Carey and the Company eventually improved so much that most of the textbooks of Fort William College were, in the initial years, printed at the Serampore press.

The credit of setting up and running the first printing presses in Bengal must of course go to the British, but the Bengalis themselves made no mean contribution to the process. True, it was Wilkins who taught Panchanon Karmakar how to make Bengali typefaces, but it was Panchanon who thereafter did the hands-on job. A 1790 statistic shows that only one of the presses then operating in Calcutta was run fully by English employees. In the rest, natives worked under a foreign master, and these were people who did not know English. Just as the munshis of those days copied English documents without knowing the language, these press employees composed English typescripts and printed them without any knowledge of the language. Since they did not know English, there were many errors, and proofs were not properly read.

William Jones was among those who criticised the quality of printing at these presses.

Among Indians, the first to be influenced by the possibilities that opened up with the introduction of printing in Bengal was of course Ram Mohan Roy, the man who played a pioneering role in so many areas of contemporary life. At the very outset of the 19th century, just when Baptist missionaries published a Bengali translation of the Bible, Roy turned to the printing press to express his views on religion. For the faithful he wrote *Tuhfat-ul-Muwahidin.* It was written in Farsi, with an introduction in Arabic. Roy had an extraordinary command over five languages, Arabic, Farsi, Sanskrit, English and Bengali. He had also learnt Hebrew. *Tuhfat* was an exposition of his monotheistic faith. In it, he even questioned whether Muslims, despite their profession of a monotheistic religion, actually did believe in a strictly monotheistic world order. Fifteen years later came his attack on Hinduism. Nor did he spare Christianity. But he used Bengali, not Arabic or Farsi, for his discussions on and criticism of Hindu beliefs. The language he used for his debates with missionaries on Christianity was of course English. Roy, indeed, was present with the shining sword of his faith wherever he spotted deviations from monotheism. Not that he did not make compromises in the real world, especially when faced with opposition from the Hindu society to which he himself belonged. But it is clear from the example he set that the will to express one's independent views and the effort to disseminate them among a wide community of readers started right at the beginning of the 19th century. And this was made possible by the printing press. Indeed, the changes that had started taking place in Calcutta's newly urbanised life made the printing press and the use of Bengali prose indispensable.

Another historic event occurred in January 1780, about one and a half years after the publication of Halhed's grammar. James Hicky, enthused by the success of his printing press, started publishing a weekly magazine called *Bengal Gazette.* As the owner of the only magazine in Calcutta, Hicky hoped, on the one hand, to make a lot of money through advertisements. He expected also to gain influence over Company officials and the Govenor General himself by criticising in his magazine the Company's practices and discussing the corruption rampant among its officials. Neither of these two expectations was fulfilled. He earned little through advertisements, for there was no tradition of advertisements yet. So not only did he not make much profit, he actually got into trouble by criticising Company officials. There might not have been much amiss if he limited himself to attacks on junior officials. But he spared no one, from Governor General Hastings to Chief Justice Sir Elijah Impey, publishing just, as well as not so just, criticisms of all. In consequence, he faced court-imposed fines for libel. Unable to pay them, he was forced to accept a jail term in 1782. When he continued to run his publication while still in prison, a furious East India Company confiscated his typefaces and thus silenced his magazine.

Though the *Bengal Gazette* failed, Hicky had shown what a powerful tool a magazine could be. Inspired by his example, two other Englishmen in Calcutta published another magazine in November 1780, probably with the Company's indirect help. A magazine published by Bengalis would take another 40 years to come, but the Europeans had shown them what a magazine could do. They saw that a newspaper/magazine was an extremely effective medium to establish contact with the rest of society. They noted, too, that a newspaper did not just present news but also carried editorial observations and opinions of its readers. That such a thing was possible had not been known to Bengalis before the British came.

The conflict between the government and the editor of the first magazine of Bengal, indeed, of India, tied up the history of India's print media with the question of that media's independence. The truth is that a tradition of complete independence of newspapers never really developed in Bengal. The colonial environment did not provide a favourable climate for it, either.

Development of the Bengali Language

As we said before, Governor General Wellesley established Fort William College in 1800. Like Asiatic Society and the print media, the college left a huge contribution in the cultural history of Bengalis. The aim of the college was to provide the Company's young employees a comprehensive idea of India and its people through lessons in the native languages, literatures, history and culture. Whatever might have been the real objective, the indirect benefits of the college were considerable. One of these was the varied textbooks on different subjects, such as the Indian languages, literatures and history, which were published by the college for its students. Among them were textbooks in Bengali.

These Bengali books were written under Carey's supervision. He had some knowledge of the language, though actually how much is open to debate. What he had in abundant measure was enthusiasm and diligence. He was especially interested in philology, and later acquired some mastery in the subject. His appointment as the head of the college's Bengali department turned out to be good for the Bengali language, and indeed, also for other Indian languages.

For some time after the college was started, the Governor General was unable to find a suitable person to be entrusted with the responsibility of the Bengali department. By that time, some seven to eight law books translated by Henry Pitts Forster had been published. An even more important publication was the first volume of his scholarly Bengali-to-English dictionary, the first of its kind. Yet, the Governor General refrained from appointing him as the college's Professor of Bengali. The reason was that Forster was identified with a section led by George Graham, president of the Revenue Board. This section did not get along with the Governor General. And so it came about that it was Carey, who had at that time published nothing in Bengali save a weak and short translation of the Gospels, who got the job. The appointment of Carey, rather than Forster, might have been discriminatory, yet it proved beneficial for Bengali and other native languages. Forster did not have Carey's boundless enthusiasm, willingness to overlook his own self-interest and organisational abilities.

Carey's role in the development of Bengali prose deserves particular mention because of his organisational abilities. His leadership in the writing of textbooks in Bengali was more important than what he himself actually wrote. As in the other language departments, quite a few munshis were appointed under him. The most well known among them were Ramram Basu and Mrityunjoy Bidyalankar. These munshis between them wrote books of sample letters, history and stories to train young Company employees in the Bengali language. Carey himself put together a collection of samples of spoken Bengali that could be used to communicate with different sections of people. With Mrityunjoy Bidyalankar's help he also wrote a Bengali grammar modelled on Halhed's work. These books were printed only in a few hundreds. And only the English officials read them. Yet, these were the books through which these men pointed to the direction that Bengali prose would take in the future.

The Bengali prose that was used until the end of the 18th century was dominated by Arabic and Farsi words. The sentences were short and simple. In the last decade of this century, however, Forster, while getting the law books translated, instructed his munshis to follow a style that would be closer to Sanskrit. As a result, even a much-used word like 'zamindar' became *bhumyadhikari.* Under Carey's leadership, the Fort William College munshis, particularly Mrityunjoy Bidyalankar, consolidated the trend. Carey himself became influenced by Mrityunjoy Bidyalankar's style, though in the initial years the Farsi-knowing Ramram Basu had had a greater influence on him. It was Ramram Basu whom he had appointed as his munshi after first arriving in Calcutta. Before that, Ramram had been John Thomas's munshi, too. The strong advocacy of a Sanskrit-dominated, stylised language that marked Carey's later years is not quite so evident in the Bengali grammar that he came out with soon after joining Fort William College to help his students learn the language. Nor did he have any axe to grind against Arabic and Farsi words in those early days. In the second edition of his grammar in 1805, however, the Sanskritised style was fully established. In this edition he described the style dominated by Arabic and Farsi words as an aberration of the pure and beautiful original style of the Bengali language. Carey not just determined the direction that the Bengali language would take, he also, as we have already noted, played a leading role in Bengali printing. The result was not just a speeding up of the

William Carey and Ramram Basu

development of Bengali prose, but also greater efficiency in Bengali printing. The textbooks that were prepared at Fort William College also in fact helped in the development of literatures in other Indian languages.

The new tradition of printing that took shape at this time also contributed a great deal in the development of Bengali and other Indian languages. No book was ever easily available before the tradition of printing was established because there could not be too many copies of books that were written and copied by hand. For ordinary people, such books were not easy to either come by or read. But once the printing presses started operating, books began to be printed by the thousands. It was now eminently easier for people to acquire an education and also for writers to have their say. It was thanks to the printing press that ordinary people now had access to samples of what a written language should ideally be like. The way they showed was soon followed by Ram Mohan Roy, Bhabanicharan Bandyopadhyay and other writers to come out with publications other than textbooks.

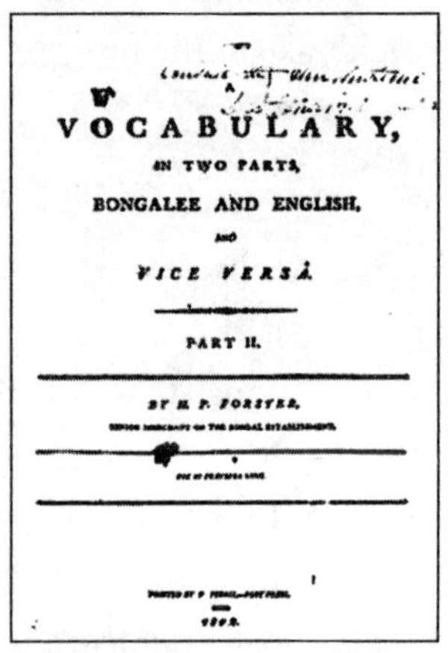
VOCABULARY,
IN TWO PARTS,
BONGALEE AND ENGLISH,
AND
VICE VERSÂ.
PART II.
BY H. P. FORSTER,

Title page of Forster's Bengali-English Dictionary, 1802. The first part – English-Bengali – was published in 1799

It may be mentioned in this context that because the publishing of textbooks was then considered a lucrative occupation, some of the professors at Fort William College started their own printing presses in the first five years of the 19th century. Gilchrist, for instance, opened a Hindustani printing press; Lamsden a Farsi one and Colebrooke a Sanskrit one. One Laluprasad, who was also associated with Fort William College, was the first Indian to start a printing press, in 1807. In this way, at the outset of the 19th century, Calcutta became the largest centre of printing in Asia.

Once English magazines had seen the light of day, thanks to the printing press, the publication of Bengali magazines became inevitable. The only question was when. The first Bengali magazine was eventually published 38 years after Hicky's *Bengal Gazette* came out. For this, too, the credit belongs to the British. This historic responsibility was fulfilled by the Serampore missionaries when in April 1818 they started publishing a monthly scientific magazine called *Digdarshan* (Determining the Direction). The following month they came out with a weekly newspaper, *Samachar Darpan* (News Mirror). This paper had a long life. Apart from reporting news, the Serampore missionaries' objective in publishing newspapers was to criticise Hindu beliefs and to prove how superior Christianity was in comparison with Hinduism and Islam.

Indians, not surprisingly, did not take kindly to the missionary attack on their religious beliefs. They were quick to follow the missionaries' example and come out with their own magazines. Ram Mohan Roy was among those who came forward to counter the missionary onslaught, and he published quite a few magazines. He believed in both liberal values and monotheism, so he criticised the conservative Hindus as well as the Christians. He did not hesitate to take on the Muslims, either. Conservative Hindu magazines such as *Samacharchandrika*, on the other hand, criticised both the Christians and Ram Mohan Roy. In this triangular contest, Bengali prose won hands down. The stiff Bengali of the textbooks now acquired an easy expressiveness that it did not earlier have.

Spread of Education

Researches to unearth the country's past had started through the Asiatic Society, and countless books and newspapers/magazines were published as the tradition of printing grew and strengthened. This was momentous, indeed, in the history of Bengal. What was even more important, however, was the influence of the West on Bengali minds and thinking. This influence came chiefly through the English language and literature. Bengalis had first started learning the language to trade with English merchants, and then to work for them. In the initial years after the arrival of the British in India, they were badly in need of English-knowing Bengalis. Those who could become interpreters found a way of making easy money. There is a story of how the captain of a ship that had anchored in the Hooghly asked the local people if there were any interpreters around. The locals, confused by his heavily accented speech, got hold of a washerman and took him to the sahib. The washerman is said to have quickly turned around his own fortunes by working as a middleman for the sahib. This may be an exaggerated story, but the truth that it points to is that with just a bare smattering of English, and sometimes even without it, contact with the English could turn around local fortunes.

A forefather of Rabindranath Tagore – Panchanon Kushari – had made his way to Calcutta from Khulna in search of his fortune. He came in the very first years of the city, soon after Job Charnock founded Calcutta, probably around the start of the 18th century. The fishermen of the area in which he made a home needed a priest to officiate in their religious rites. Panchanon was a Brahmin of flawed ritual purity, carrying the contamination of impure contact; he was a *pirali* (see previous chapter). The fishermen, however, were pleased to have a Brahmin in their midst and made him their priest or 'thakur'. So it was that Panchanon Kushari became Panchanon Thakur. This intelligent and enterprising priest, however, was not satisfied with just officiating at the fishing community's life-cycle rites. Looking to make some extra money, he went up to the banks of the Ganga and got in touch with the English merchants. He must have been a very handsome man, going by the looks of later generations in his family, and would have stood out among the crowd that usually gathered at the riverbank. The English traders took quite a fancy to him and called him 'Takur'.

Dwarkanath Tagore, the first modern Bengali entrepreneur

Panchanon had two sons, Jayaram and Sanatan. These two brothers developed even more intimate connections with the British. They picked up enough English to carry out their worldly affairs. Jayaram even learned some French. Both brothers found jobs with the English, and Jayaram also acted as a broker for French traders. In this way the two of them struck it quite rich. Their descendant Dwarkanath was not just wealthy but also earned the title of 'Prince'. So in less than a hundred years, the Kusharis graduated from the fairly lowly occupation of performing priestly duties for the fishing community to become one of the foremost families of the Calcutta elite.

Ram Mohan Roy's grandfather and great grandfather had gained money and influence in the employment of Bengal's Muslim rulers. His father, too, started out as a wealthy man. While Ram Mohan was quite young, however, his father's luck seemed to run out. Not only was he himself jailed for failing to clear his dues, so was his eldest son. Ram Mohan, on the other hand, was at this time taking his destiny in his own hands and building up a fortune. He had spent his childhood and boyhood carefully mastering Sanskrit, the language of religion, and Farsi, a language that was lucrative to know at that time. He also, with his father's encouragement, learned Arabic. Sanskrit and Arabic served him well in his studies of philosophy and religion, while his Farsi helped him a little to earn money. More importantly, it was his Farsi that brought him in close contact with the English. And once he came in contact with them he also picked up excellent English. It was this knowledge of English that brought him both worldly and intellectual success.

It is quite obvious, then, that knowledge of English was the chief tool to turn around fortunes. Munshis in the last two decades of the 18th century turned theirs around even without knowing the language, just by learning to copy documents written in English. We mentioned before how many people composed English typescripts without knowing the language. It was indeed enough to just somehow land up in Calcutta for one's situation to improve, even if fortunes were not always made. The title of Bhabanicharan Bandyopadhyay's 1823 book *Kolikata Kamalalaya* (Calcutta, the House of Lakshmi) was satirical, but it was not lacking in truth. Calcutta was actually seen by many people of the time as the abode of the goddess of wealth. In his book Bhabanicharan extensively described how to travel to Calcutta and, once there, how to seek out one's fortune in its lanes and bylanes. As for how many readers used his description as a modern guide book or how many actually felt impelled by the book to visit the city, that is of course a matter for conjecture. But there is no doubt that by that time many people had started arriving in Calcutta in search of a better life. One such person was Ishwarchandra Vidyasagar's father, Thakurdas Bandyopadhyay.

Thakurdas's family home was not exactly within walking distance of Calcutta. So he took a while to join the feast of opportunities that he knew, from hearsay, had begun there; he arrived in the city in the second decade of the 19th century. By birth he was a *kulin* Brahmin, that is, a Brahmin of high social status and ritual purity. But whatever be the ritual status of his lineage, his finances were in a mess. So he, too, came to the city to see what he could do with his luck. He came without any capital, because though he was conversant with the Hindu ritual chants (mantras), he had no inkling of the kind of knowledge that might bring success in Calcutta. Let alone having any knowledge of English, he had little or no education. So, whatever he might have heard of Calcutta as the city of opportunities, it did not in reality appear a very easy place to a man newly arrived from his village home. Indeed, he had to put up with many hardships and knock on many doors just to arrange for two square meals a day and a roof over his head. He was forced to fall back on charity to just survive in the big city. When he finally, after repeated attempts, secured a job with a monthly salary of Rs 2, his family was overjoyed. When his salary jumped to Rs 8 after a while, his family celebrated with a feast. Thakurdas would not have managed to find a job with even Rs 2 as the monthly salary had he not come to Calcutta. As a Brahmin, he would at best eke out a survival dependent on the kindness of wealthy householders.

Would his son Ishwarchandra do as well as he did were he not in Calcutta, notwithstanding his undeniable genius? Indeed, it was because he got a chance to study at Calcutta's Sanskrit College that his reputation spread so wide. One other thing should be kept in mind: this successful student of Sanskrit College took the trouble to acquire a good command over English even after receiving the title 'Vidyasagar' (Ocean of Knowledge). He had realised that the way to success would not be smooth without a knowledge of English, even if one were an ocean of knowledge. It is no use denying that he would never have made the kind of impact that he did had he been just a Sanskrit pandit. There were many others who were conferred the title 'Vidyasagar' by Sanskrit College, but none of them could come close to Ishwarchandra Vidyasagar in impact and influence.

In 1830, two years after Ishwarchandra came to Calcutta as a child of eight, someone from Jessore with a good grasp of Farsi came to the city to make a living in the business of law. He was Michael Madhusudan Dutt's father, Rajnarayan. The language of the courts was still Farsi, so Rajnarayan's was an almost overnight success. Yet, he never really reached the heights of Prasanna Kumar Tagore or Ramaprasad Roy because he did not know English.

Lalbehari Dey belonged to an orthodox Vaishnava family. The family lived at a fair distance from Calcutta. But his father had got wind of the key to success in the new age. In 1833, therefore, he brought his nine-year-old son to Calcutta in order to give him an English education. Lalbehari was among those who in those days really mastered the language well. In fact, so overwhelmed was he by his exposure, through English, to Western civilisation and religious ideals that in 1843 he got himself baptised by Alexander Duff. This was also the year when Madhusudan Dutt became Michael Madhusudan.

Ramkamal Sen (1783-1844) was born in Hooghly, near Calcutta. His father knew Farsi well and worked as a *serestadar* (court assistant). He knew how useful language was in practical life and had hence encouraged his son to learn English while he was still living in their country home. Fortunately, Ramkamal was able to get English lessons from a missionary in the village. This knowledge of English was what his father depended on when he brought his son to Calcutta. The following year, he started working in the city as a compositor in a printing press. He eventually learnt the language so well that he became the first among Bengalis to write an English-Bengali dictionary (1834). He was also the first Indian secretary of Asiatic Society. His knowledge of English was the tool he used to haul his family out of abysmal poverty and into a life of exceptional wealth. He left behind at least seven to eight lakh rupees when he died.

Men like Kashi Prasad Ghosh, Ramgopal Ghosh, Krishnamohan Bandyopadhyay, Dakshinaranjan Mukhopadhyay, Pyarichand Mitra, Kishorichand Mitra, Digambar Mitra, Radhanath Sikdar and Rajendralal Mitra all earned money and fame using their knowledge of English. A section of the mainly Hindu educated middle class that developed in the

19th century was produced by the Permanent Settlement; but a much larger section was produced by English education.

The people who at that time acquired an English education did so keeping in mind the money that it could bring. But there were also exceptions. There were people who were able to use English to navigate the world of thoughts and ideas. People like Ram Mohan Roy, Dwarkanath Tagore, Rasomoy Datta, Prasanna Kumar Tagore, Ramkamal Sen. Dwarkanath had enough English to carry out his business enterprises and to socialise. He also appointed an English teacher from whom he took piano lessons. Prasanna Kumar Tagore became the best known lawyer in the first half of the 19th century. The property he left behind was worth lakhs of rupees. Rasomoy Datta became a judge in the Small Causes Court. He realised how important English had become and played a significant role in the spread of English education. But Ram Mohan left all others behind to acquire such excellent English that he was able to use it not to trade but to gain a foothold in philosophy and other areas of higher learning. The standard of the English that he wrote was also quite high.

Indeed, the scramble to learn English started as early as the end of the 18th century. The first efforts were initiated outside the boundaries of schools or colleges. In those first years of contact with the Company, Bengalis usually tried to pick up their English by memorising word books, books of words. Some paid Anglo-Indians or even Englishmen for private lessons but they were very few in number. Many a foreigner inserted advertisements in newspapers seeking to teach English. I have seen such advertisements in the pages of *Calcutta Gazette*. Even the handful of Bengalis who had picked up the language started giving lessons in English. Ramkamal Sen mentions several such English-knowing persons in the introduction to his dictionary. He says, too, that English lessons given by

THE

TUTOR,

OR A

New English & Bengalee Work,

WELL ADAPTED TO TEACH

THE NATIVES ENGLISH.

IN THREE PARTS

সিক্ষ্যা গুরু

কিম্বা এক নেতন ইংরাজি আর বাঙ্গালা বহি

ভালোওপযুক্ত আছে বাঙ্গালি দিগেরকে ইংরাজি

সিক্ষাকরাইতে তিনখণ্ডে

COMPILED, TRANSLATED, AND PRINTED,

By JOHN MILLER.

1797.

John Miller's book, called *Shikshaguru*, a Bengali reader for the English private tutors cost between four to eight rupees a month at the beginning of the 19th century. This was not easily affordable in an age when people rejoiced over a job fetching Rs 2 a month.

So an English education was lucrative, but it was not easy to acquire. This was what led, on April 23, 1789, a group of men in Calcutta to place an appeal through the *Calcutta Gazette* magazine. The appeal was for someone to write an English grammar and dictionary that would contain English translations of much-used Bengali words. The very next week, a certain Stuart made it known in the *Calcutta Chronicle* magazine that he was almost through with his work on a Bengali-English dictionary. This dictionary was eventually published in 1793 as *Ingraji O Bangali Bokebilari* (An Extensive Vocabulary, Bengalese and English) from Aaron Upjohn's Chronicle press. In 1797 was published John Miller's *Shikhyaguru.* He had written this book to educate the natives, and he made his objective clear in the title and subtitle of his book—'Sikkhaguru or a new English and Bengali book that is good and suitable to teach English to the Bengalis in three volumes.' After this came Henry Pitts Forster's Bengali-English-Bengali dictionary in two volumes, in 1799 and 1801. Forster, however, had written his dictionary not for the benefit of Bengalis but to help Englishmen learn Bengali.

It was not possible for large numbers of people to learn English by taking lessons in private or reading books without an institutionalised system of education. Yet, though the East India Company needed English-knowing natives to work as clerks, it took no initiative to arrange for an education in English. Rather, in the interest of a more efficient administration the Company established the Kolkata Madrasa in 1781 and Sanskrit College in 1791. The initiative for an English education came from private enterprise. Within a couple of years of the start of the 19th century, two men started a school to teach English. One of them was a Scotsman, David Drummond. The other, surprisingly enough, was a Bengali. Besides, English missionaries started schools where English was taught, perhaps with the objective of eradicating superstitions and thus save the souls of heathens from eternal damnation in Hell. Among these missionaries, Robert May alone could claim

Hindu College in the 1830s

credit for founding 36 schools. Many other missionaries also opened schools. A military officer started a school in Burdwan on his own initiative.

The biggest role in introducing English education in Bengal was played by the first college founded by the natives—Hindu College. Notwithstanding the leadership provided by Chief Justice Hyde East in the project, funds for the college were pooled by Calcutta's rich, high-caste Hindus. These wealthy Hindu men were able to fathom that their sons needed a good grasp of English in order to fully avail themselves of the opportunities with which the new age had arrived at their doorstep. The conservatives among the Hindus as well as the progressives came together to establish the college. Work on the college started in January 1817.

Despite his sincere interest in the enterprise, Ram Mohan stayed away from it lest the involvement of an individual as controversial as he thwart the move in any way. Besides, he could not bring himself to totally support the idea of starting a wholly secular school. A few years later, therefore, he established a school on his own.

In the beginning the administration did not spend any money on Hindu College. The rich Hindus of the higher castes who had founded the college, on the other hand, assumed that the rest of society, that is, the lower castes and the Muslims, would never come forward to seek education. And even if they did it would not be proper for these disparate social groups, in view of the imperative of caste purity, to sit down to study together in the same room. From the beginning, therefore, right of entry at Hindu College was reserved only for high-caste Hindus. It was only much later that the Company administration started funding the college, and once that happened, an 1854 government order opened the doors of the college to all. Hindu College became Presidency College.

The founders of Hindu College knew that a college alone was not enough for the business of learning. They, therefore, also arranged for textbooks to be written and published at the same time. Calcutta Textbook Society was established right after the establishment of Hindu College, in 1817-18.

A large number of textbooks on various subjects were published on behalf of this organisation. The books that sold most were the English language books, which shows how conscious the people of Calcutta had become of the practical advantages of acquiring a modern education. It was this awareness that made even a conservative leader like Radhakanta Deb think of women's education in those early days of colonial rule, though orthodox sections of society fiercely opposed women's education. It was at Radhakanta Deb's request that Gourmohan Bidyalankar, a teacher belonging to the School Society, wrote the first book on women's education, *Stree Shiksha Bidhayak*. It was published in 1821.

It is clear, then, that the education effort that began with the Hindu College at its centre was limited to Calcutta and its immediate surroundings. In terms of caste and faith, it was confined to high-caste Hindus, especially those who were present in Calcutta and were wealthy enough to take part in this drive. The first to pass through the high gates of English education that now opened up and onwards along the road to a modern age were those who lived in Calcutta. Then came those who lived within walking distance of the city. An 1846 government report on education shows that there was then just one student from East Bengal at Hindu College, a boy from Jessore. It was only considerably later that students from further away travelled to Calcutta to join Hindu College and benefited from the education they received there. In the whole of Bengal, Hindus of the three dominant castes, the Brahmins, Kayasthas and Baidyas, constituted only 10 per cent of the total Hindu population. A minuscule proportion of this tiny group was able to use the opportunity for an English education at Hindu College. The large majority constituted by Muslims and low-caste Hindus were unable to make use of this, or any other, opportunity. Those who lived at some distance from Calcutta, particularly Muslims and Hindus of the lower castes, could not even take advantage of the other arrangements that were by now in place there for acquiring a knowledge of English.

Notwithstanding this limitation, the several thousand students who passed out of the college in its first three decades with a good knowledge of English became the most well known names in 19th century Bengali society. These men came to possess both learning and wealth. We will see in the next section how they became the new elite in the new age on the strength of their newfound social status. But whoever might have been the first beneficiaries of the new system, within a few decades even those who lived far from Calcutta, Muslims included, got to hear about the glories of English education as the key to success. And once they got wind of it, they did not hesitate to learn English if there was any opportunity to do so. In this way, though they were a bit late, even those Hindus and Muslims who lived far from Calcutta did in the end turn up at the capital city's feast of opportunities.

In 1821, Hindus in Calcutta numbered 1,18, 203. The city also had a sizeable population of Muslims, numbering 48,162. Most of the latter group were Hindustani-speaking. The educated among them used their knowledge of Farsi to make a living and support their families. This section made no move to acquire an English education. The consequence was that Muslims had no place among the educated 'bhadralok' section that developed at a later phase, the section that made the Bengal Renaissance possible. Though it is not as if there were no exceptions.

Speaking of the exceptions, the first name that comes to mind is that of Abdul Latif (1828-93), a Bengali-speaking Muslim from Faridpur. As we have already noted, very few people from faraway East Bengal in those days made it to Calcutta for the sake of an education. Latif, too, did not really travel to Calcutta for an education. Fortunately for him, his father, Kazi Fakr Muhammad, worked for the government in Calcutta, and that is why he found himself there as a boy, growing up with his father. His father must have realised how important it was to learn English. He got his son enrolled at Calcutta Madrasa, for, as we said before, none but high-caste Hindus were able to get admission in Hindu College. Latif acquired a good grasp of Arabic, Farsi and Hindustani at Calcutta Madrasa, and with it all he also learnt English. He even attracted Michael Madhusudan Dutt's attention as an English-knowing student. Thus armed with a knowledge of English, he started his working life as a teacher and then joined the civil service. At the time of his retirement in 1883, his were the highest rank and salary among Indian civil servants. The education he received possibly made him the best-known Muslim in the 19th century.

Another Muslim who like Nawab Abdul Latif made a name for himself was Syed Amir Ali (1849-1928). He, too, built on the capital of his knowledge of English. He got a chance to learn English because his family lived in Hooghly, right next to the first home of English education, Calcutta. In 1867 he passed out of Calcutta University with a postgraduate degree and then acquired an LLB degree. After practising as a lawyer for a while, he went off to England, where he was called to the Bar, and in 1873 he came back to Calcutta. Thereafter, he worked as a lawyer in Calcutta High Court and at one stage taught at Hooghly College and in Calcutta University. In the end, he served as a judge in Calcutta High Court for nearly 15 years. He also earned a reputation as a historian.

Delwar Hossein Ahmed (1840-1913) also got a chance to acquire an English education because his father was in Calcutta. And he made good use of that opportunity. When he passed out of Calcutta University with a B.A. degree in 1861, he was the first Muslim to have become a graduate. He started his working life as a Deputy Magistrate and went on to become the Inspector General of Registration. He was also recognised as a writer. He made sincere efforts to give a push to education among Bengali Muslims. More importantly, he displayed a progressive and liberal bent of mind, which was unusual among Muslims in those days.

Ubaid Ullah (1834-86) of Dhaka became Professor of Anglo-Arabic in Hooghly College. He wrote a number of books in English, Arabic and Farsi. Nawab Abdul Jabbar (1837-1918) became the Principal Sadar Amin. Abul Hossein (1862-?) of Hooghly studied in England and in the USA and attained the highest degree in medicine. Sir Abdur Rahim (1867-1952) of Midnapore topped the M.A. English examination of Calcutta University. He became the Chief Justice of the Calcutta High Court. Noakhali's Abdul Aziz (1867-1926) rose to the highest post in the Education Department.

Abdullah al-Mamun Sohrawardi (1870-1935) was probably the first among Muslims to secure a PhD degree in Calcutta in 1908. Comilla's Abdul Rasul (1872-1917) secured B.A. and M.A. degrees from Oxford and was called to the Bar. Burdwan's Abul Qasem followed the example of his uncle Abdul Jabbar when he acquired an English education. He served as the editor of several magazines including *The Musalman.*

In conclusion, Muslims also eventually came forward to acquire higher education, even if they were a bit late, once they witnessed the benefits of an English education. Abdul Khayer, Abdul Khalek, Abdul Bari, Izad Baksh, Taslim-ud-din Ahmed, Takrim-ud-din, Fazlul Qadir, Fazlul Karim, Fayez-ud-din Hossein, Farid-ud-din Ahmed, Mazharul Anwar, Mohammad Yusuf, Mohammad Ismail, Mohammad Wajed, Mohammad Dayem, Sirajul Islam, Syed Ali, Syed Hossein, Syed Khayrat Hossein, Syed Sakhawat Hossein, Hamid-ud-din Ahmed—they all passed out of Calcutta University between 1858 and 1881 with B.A. or M.A. degrees. Indeed, once they had tasted the fruits of English education, Muslims with a tradition of learning in their families and the means to pursue an education did not lag behind Hindus. There were also those who travelled to England to learn English, for instance Abdul Karim Gaznabi (1872-1939), his brother Abdul Halim Gaznabi (1879-1956) and Abdul Rasul. Gaznafar Ali Khan (1872-1959) travelled to England to write the civil services examination and became the first Muslim ICS officer. It was, however, only in the second half of the 19th century that Muslims started making such efforts. However, Hindus and Muslims at the lower end of the caste structure, especially those who lived in villages, did not get any opportunity to acquire a modern education. They are therefore absent from the canvas of the Bengal Renaissance.

Impact of Western Education on Minds and Thinking

The initiative to teach English in various schools set up in Calcutta, including Hindu College, soon began to produce quite remarkable consequences. A comment in *Samacharchandrika* in 1828 said that at least a thousand youngsters were at that time studying English in the city's schools. Some of them acquired quite a good command of the language. An indirect evidence is furnished by the fact that Kashi Prasad Ghosh published a book of English verses in 1830. We also know from comments published in *Samacharchandrika* that educated young men of those days wrote to other educated Bengalis in English. That this was so is also evident from the letters written by Michael Madhusudan Dutt, some years after the *Samacharchandrika* comments. All the letters that he wrote to his friend Gourdas Basak from 1841 onwards were in English. Gourdas, too, replied in English, though his grasp of the language in that phase was weak. The *Samacharchandrika* comments also inform us that young men even conversed with each other in English.

This preference for English continued in the latter half of the century. Bankimchandra Chattopadhyay, like Madhusudan before, started his writing career by writing in English. His first novel was written in English. He, however, wrote sarcastically about the trend of embracing everything Western and mentioned how English-educated people often spoke to each other in English. Even when the medium of conversation was Bengali, it was littered with many English words. Besides, the English-educated often did not know Bengali very well. The following dialogue, despite the element of exaggeration, reflects the attitude of the contemporary English-educated towards Bengali.

Husband: *Why do you read all that rubbish? Better not to read at all.*
Wife: *Why?*
Husband: *Those are all* ***immoral, obscene, filthy.***
Wife: *What do those words mean?*
Husband: ***Immoral****, do you know what that is? It's ...you know...meaning, whatever is against* ***morality****...*
Wife: *Is it a four-legged amimal?*
Husband: *No, no, ... you know... how do I get hold of a Bengali word for it? Whatever is not* ***moral****, that's all...*
Wife: *What is 'moral'? A swan? [A pun on the formal Bengali word for swan, which has a sound close to the English word 'moral']*
Husband: *Shame! Shame!* ***O woman! Thy name is stupidity.***
Wife: *What is it then?*
Husband: *Well, it is not possible to explain all that in Bengali. The long and short of it is that it is not good to read Bengali books.*

(The words in bold print appear in English in the original.)

According to Bankimchandra, the language of letters written by English-educated people was, without exception, English. He wrote that he was not aware of a single instance of English-educated people writing to each other in Bengali.

Debendranath Tagore, inspired as he was by a sense of nationhood, was an exception. He was particularly opposed to writing letters in English and is even said to have returned a letter addressed to him that was written in English. This exception, however, only points to what was the general rule.

An education in English bred a kind of contempt for Bengali among these young people. Early in the 1840s, Ramkamal Sen noticed, as external examiner at Presidency College, that the students there had picked up English quite well. He sadly noted, too, that no matter how well they knew their English, they were weak in Bengali. They were even actually contemptuous of the idea of learning Bengali and reading in the language. In the context of this report by Ramkamal Sen, Prasanna Kumar Tagore placed a proposal saying that students of Hindu College should be given rigorous lessons in Bengali: 'We trust that such a step would constitute a beginning for an excellent education in Bengali at Hindu College, and that the professors of the college will pay particular attention to the matter.' Former students of Hindu College ran a magazine called *Bengal Spectator*. They, too, complained, around the same time, that the teachers in the senior section of the college did not pay much attention to the teaching of Bengali. Even some Englishmen noticed an unwillingness to learn Bengali among young people. An English official called Hodgson published a booklet in 1847 in which he proposed that Bengalis should be educated through the medium of Bengali. The president of the Education Council, John Drinkwater Bethune, took the initiative in 1850 for Bengali to be taught at Hindu College. Accordingly, a professor of Bengali was appointed at the college three years later.

We also get to know of young people's indifference to Bengali from a letter written to Rajnarayan Basu in the 1860s by the greatest ever votary of Anglicisation, Michael Madhusudan Dutt. From 1832 onwards, Derozio's followers published several magazines called *Athenium, Parthenon, Enquirer* and *Gyananweshan* (Search for Knowledge). Most of the write-ups published in these magazines were in English. These people also spoke at meetings and conferences in English. (How embarrassed Madhusudan, the most famous Bengali poet of the day, was when he was asked to give a lecture in Bengali can be seen from one of his letters).

The long and short of it is that a large number of people seized, within two or three decades, the opportunities that an English education brought in tow. There is no reason to suppose, however, that the Anglicising tendency of those days was motivated solely by the lure of those opportunities. It was increasingly becoming fashionable to use English, as much as possible, in every sphere of life. Drinking, eating forbidden foods at hotels, adopting European clothes and imitating European lifestyles were all part of this new craze. As we shall see in the following section, this trend had its own limitations.

It cannot be said that the fruits of the development of Western education in Calcutta's social life brought about only lifestyle changes. Rather, varied changes were taking place, from the beginning of the 19th century, in the ways in which people thought and felt through their exposure to urbanisation, English education, contact with the British people, and Western thoughts and ideas. It was probably Ram Mohan Roy in whom before all else these changes were noticeable. He had first noticed in Islam the ideal of monotheism in which he came to repose his faith. But he had imbibed his thoughts and ideas in a large measure from European ways of thinking. He may not have studied English in school, but he had mastered the language very well through his contact with the Englishmen whom he came across in Faridpur, Jessore, Rangpur, Bhagalpur and Calcutta, benefiting particularly from his interactions with John Digby. Indeed, it was not just the language that he picked up. Through it he got himself acquainted with the rationalism, liberalism and thoughts on the freedom of the individual that crystallised in Europe in the 17th and 18th centuries. Not only did he acquaint himself with these thoughts, he practically made them his own. He learnt to look at the world and at life in an original way. So, though he was inspired by the monotheism of Islam, he could also detect flaws in the Islamic version of monotheism. And though he was influenced by European thinking, he was able to criticise the contradictions that he saw in Christianity and in the English character.

Ram Mohan Roy, the first moderniser

Ram Mohan set yet another example in the way he broke with the tradition of parochialism. No new ideas in philosophy and science had made their way into India from the Islamic civilisation in the last couple of centuries of Muslim rule. Even if they did, they made no noticeable impact in Bengal. The English, on the other hand, brought with them new knowledge from Europe and the harvest of the Renaissance in the world of thought, and Ram Mohan welcomed these new arrivals with open arms. Not only did he look beyond Bengal, he established contact, through letters, with the thinkers of Europe and America.

He was the first among Bengalis to embark on a global exchange of thoughts. He identified himself with progressive movements wherever he saw them. One event shows clearly how intimate his dialogue was with foreign thinkers and how highly he was thought of by the people with whom he had been able to establish communication. As early as in 1812, when he had not yet started living permanently in Calcutta, the progressives in Spain dedicated their alternative Constitution to a little-known man across the oceans, Ram Mohan Roy. Clearly, then, Ram Mohan was a familiar name to the liberal scholars of Europe even before 1812. Not just in Europe, thinkers in America were also acquainted with Ram Mohan's views. Especially the Unitarian theorists. Indeed, parochialism was what took the biggest blow from this establishment of contact with Europe through the medium of English.

A genius like Ram Mohan Roy is however rare in any society, and in Bengali society he was quite unparalleled. Ordinary people needed institutionalised education, and that was provided by Hindu College. When they sent their sons to study at Hindu College, wealthy Hindus of the higher castes hoped they would land good jobs at the new offices run by the English after they passed out, and might even, in time, become munsefs, deputy collectors or deputy magistrates. What they did not probably anticipate was that an English education would change the ways in which these young people thought and felt and even transform their ethical persuasions. But that is what happened. Hundreds of students passing out of this college may have secured jobs and earned good money, but there were many others who earned notoriety as they got carried away by Western lifestyles. Many of the newly educated generation were more influenced by the cosmetic side of Western civilisation and culture than by the values that these were built on. But some students of Hindu College, though these were few in number, were deeply influenced by Western values, especially some of the students of the famous teacher Henry Vivian Louis Derozio.

Henry Derozio, the influential young teacher of Hindu College whose students came to be known as Young Bengal

Derozio started teaching at the college at just 17. There were at that time many students who were actually older than he was. Yet he wielded an influence on his students that no other teacher in the 19th or 20th century could match in depth or permanence. He belonged to a family of Portuguese settlers and was born in Calcutta in 1808. His schooling, whatever it was, was entirely in Calcutta. His thinking, however, was European, no matter that he lived his life 6,000 miles away from Europe. He was especially inspired by the French Revolution, and probably by the American Revolution as well. Ideas of rationalism, freedom of the individual and cynicism also moved Derozio. He was particularly interested in philosophy and English literature and produced a remarkably mature essay on philosophy while still only 16. Apart from being a good literary critic, he also wrote poems of a fairly high standard. He was the first non-Indian to have identified himself with the country and, moved by the beauty of the land, wrote poems in its praise. One can only wonder how and where he imbibed this extraordinary value system. Even more amazing was his almost magical ability to attract the admiration and loyalty of his students.

Students were drawn to Derozio like iron to a piece of magnet. The education that he imparted, therefore, was not confined to the reading of books but became a part of the lives of his students. They reposed their faith in the Western rationalism and liberal thought that he taught them. It is known that they read, on his recommendation, Thomas Paine's *Age of Reason* (1794-96). Paine, who was involved in the American War of Independence and the French Revolution, analysed religion in this book. Though he had faith in religion, his analysis and evaluation of institutionalised religion was devastating. The book taught Derozio's students to look at religion in the light of reason. Derozio's students, indeed, adopted the ideal that he set before them: that of accepting nothing as a given truth but to question and analyse everything before arriving at a conclusion. He was also able to successfully sow the seed of liberal thought in their minds. Religious leaders are sometimes able to similarly establish a complete sway over the hearts and minds of their followers, working as they do with invisible forces of fear and temptation. The amazing thing about Derozio's far-reaching hold over his followers is that he achieved it through his advocacy of a secular world view. Many of the leaders of the 19th century Bengal Renaissance were his students. This alone shows how comprehensive and extraordinary was his role as an educationist. It is almost incredible that any single teacher should leave such a huge contribution in the building up of collective thought and emotion.

The thoughts and ideas with which he inspired his students did not remain confined to their discussions on the books on their curriculum. They sought to follow those ideas in their lives. Their endless discussions could not be exhausted within the boundaries of the college, so in 1828 they started a discussion forum called Academic Association. A few years later, as we have noted earlier, they came out with several magazines to criticise social norms and discuss their own beliefs. In 1838 was established the Sadharon Gyanoparjika Sabha (General Forum for the Acquisition of Knowledge). Derozio's lessons had cut right through the pages of textbooks and made their way into the hearts of his students, which was what made the education he imparted so self-fulfilling. His students had enrolled at the college with the objective of securing jobs as clerks for English masters. As it happened, however, though they did use their education to get jobs, they also moved far away from traditional society. Within 15 years of the establishment of Hindu College, these students mounted a powerful attack on social orthodoxies through their clothes, food habits, views and lifestyles.

The *Enquirer*, one of the magazines run by these young men, said in September 1831 that the spirit of liberalism had spread far and wide. It expressed the hope that education at Hindu College would remove the fog of ignorance and superstitions from the minds of youngsters. According to the writer of the piece, the 2,000 students who were at that time receiving an English education there were going through a comprehensive transformation after having freed themselves from the chains of custom. The superstitions that had for so long trapped them in the darkness of moral degradation were, so this magazine felt, now being erased quickly. This blanket claim could not have been true for everyone. There is however no doubt that many students of Hindu College, inspired by the ideals of rationalism and liberalism, had started to question everything—rules and ethics, customs and conduct, religion and values.

That attitudes to these things were changing was commented upon in *Samacharchandrika* magazine in 1829, that is, within 12 years of the founding of Hindu College. The young men concerned admitted as much in the *Enquirer* in September 1831. This transformation deeply shook traditional society. This was to some extent evident from a letter published in 1830 in *Samacharchandrika* magazine. The conservatives regarded the conduct of the young men as defiant and blasphemous. The letter in question said that the young people dismissed everything as 'nonsense', attended lectures and studied science.

The effort to impart an education in English was also under way at other institutions apart from Hindu College. Some of these schools were established by foreigners and were run like business ventures, with the sole motive of profit. These institutions provided courses in other European languages besides English. Michael Madhusudan Dutt studied in one such school for a few years before joining Hindu College. Some schools were established by natives, again with the objective of monetary gain. The well known missionary Alexander Duff opened a school where English was taught; so did Robert May, even before Duff established his school. People who passed out of these schools with a working knowledge of English must have secured jobs at government offices or merchant establishments run by Englishmen. But most of those who, inspired by Western example, brought about a revolution in the areas of thought and consciousness were students of Hindu College.

Outside this circle, too, there were a handful of individuals, such as Ishwarchandra Vidyasagar, who were not students of Hindu College but who played an extraordinary role in the history of Bengal. On a cursory assessment, the Sanskrit-educated Vidyasagar does appear like an exception. Yet, an analysis of his thinking, writing and actions reveals him to be a modern thinker, not an atavistic pandit. Indeed, he should be placed in the same bracket as the unparalleled Ram Mohan Roy.

The Birth of New Values

Making a show of respect towards elders and accepting their views without protest was not only customary in Bengali society but was something that was strictly followed. Even elderly people whom one did not know and was not related to were considered deserving of respect. There was, however, a noticeable drop in this unquestioning respect among the students of Hindu College. In a note to *Samacharchandrika* published on May 14, 1831, a letter writer wrote that educated youngsters called Brahmins names such as 'thief', 'robber' and 'cow' and abused their own fathers and uncles as fools. These youngsters were also, he said, stubborn and intolerant. These claims were most probably exaggerated. Despite the exaggeration, however, it is clear that noticeable changes were at that time creeping into the conduct of young people towards their elders. In another letter to the magazine that year, the parent of a Hindu College student claimed that his son had greeted the mother goddess with 'Good morning, Madam' instead of paying the customary obeisance to the deity. In all ages, the conduct of youngsters appears more or less boorish in the eyes of their elders. From the third decade of the 19th century, however, under the impact of the new English education and changed lifestyles, the disparities between the old and the young in Calcutta were a bit too obvious to escape notice. The trend continued throughout the 19th century. A write-up in *Prabhakar* in 1878 made the sweeping claim that youngsters defied their elders, kicked their own religion and what they shaped up as could not be described as Hindu, Muslim or Christian.

The loss of unquestioning respect for elders was directly linked to thoughts on the freedom of the individual. Contemporary Bengali society was extremely clannish. Individual lives were regulated by agencies such as the family, relatives, neighbours, village elders, priests, maulvis, in a word, by the entire society. Even in as personal a matter such as marriage, the decision of others rather than one's own was considered more important. Individual freedom was virtually non-existent. One of the main changes produced by Western education, however, was in the area of individual freedom. For the first time among young men, the freedom to think, worship and act according to one's conscience began to make itself felt. The *Enquirer* said in 1831 that the young men were striving to assert their own right to independent thinking and protect the right of conscience of others. We have already noted the way in which they had started displaying independent thought in matters of ethics and faith. This spirit of independence increasingly spilled over into other areas of life. The impact was felt first on the family and then on society.

An outstanding example was that of the father of zamindar Jayakrishna Mukhopadhyay of Uttarpara. He got a government job at Meerut at the start of the 19th century. It was not the done thing in those days to take one's wife and children along to one's workplace and away from the joint family. But he broke with that custom. In the same way, in 1830, Rajnarayan Dutt cut the chains of the joint family and moved to Calcutta from Jessore with his wife and son. But his son, Michael Madhusudan Dutt, far outstripped him in boldness of spirit. Not only did he not submit to the marriage that his parents fixed for him, he embraced Christianity to escape that alliance. Michael took this extraordinary step in 1843. Such a thing would have been unimaginable in the preceding centuries. Planning to move to England in order to become a poet, moving to Madras in search of his destiny, marrying a white woman there, travelling to England with the intention of studying to be a barrister—all this he did because he wanted to do it, without any thought for what others might have wanted for him. This expression of individual freedom in his character had taken shape under the influence of an English education and European ways of thought.

Ishwarchandra Vidysagar did not pursue an English education, but he too was influenced by the European ideal of individual freedom. That is why, though he disowned his son and denied him any share in his property, he did not disown either his daughter-in-law or any other relative connected to him through his son, and nor did he deprive them of their share in his property. This shows that he believed in relationships connecting one individual to another, not in clannish ties.

Though Debendranath Tagore was a conservative, the expression of individual freedom is also noticeable in his character. After his father's death in 1846, he decided not to observe the funeral rites despite opposition from his family and friends. He did this because he could not quite reconcile the prevalent Hindu funeral rites with his own beliefs. In 1851, Madhusudan's classmate Gyanendramohan Tagore ignored his family's diktat to convert to Christianity. He then married Krishnamohan Banerjee's (a prominent Christian convert) daughter. As a result, he did not inherit anything of his father Prasanna Kumar Tagore's vast wealth. Derozio was removed from his teaching position at Hindu College because he inculcated in his students this fearsome trait, individual agency. Rasamoy Datta, as we noted before, played a crucial role in his removal. But his son Gobindo Datta later became a Christian.

Yet another instance showing the surfacing of individual freedom can be given from a piece published in *Tatwabodhini Patrika.* Though conservative in character, this article published in 1875 describes the 'selfless protection of interdependent relations' among Bengalis as 'humanity' (*monushatwo*) but also admits that the protection of individual freedom by the English reflects the same quality. *Tatwabodhini Patrika,* therefore, was by that time unable to reject the value of individual freedom. Rather, this magazine accepted that while making personal sacrifices in the interest of others was the ideal of Bengali society, that of English society was the nurturing of one's own independence and freedom. Both these ideals, it said, 'bore testimony to humanity, and so neither could be rejected outright' (a rough translation).

As time passed, individual freedom progressively received greater social acceptance. Satyendranath Tagore married a girl chosen by his family. When he was old enough to understand how important the question of individual choice was in marriage, he wrote to his father from England in 1863 that he would accept his wife as a partner only if she accepted him of her own free will once she was an adult and had acquired an education. Three decades later he did not try to intervene in the marriage of his daughter, Indira Devi and acknowledged her independence. Marriages in the Tagore family were usually arranged by elders.

As long as Debendranath was alive, his wishes were usually binding. But with the idea of individual freedom slowly taking root, Indira Devi was able to choose her own partner. At the end of the 19th century, then, the concept of individual freedom was accepted in a section of society, even if its reach was not quite universal.

Individual freedom is linked with self-centredness and even selfishness. With the development of individual freedom, symptoms of both these qualities began to be quite forcefully manifest in Bengali society, at least in comparison with earlier times. This new trend was mentioned, and quite justly too, in *Tatwabodhini Patrika* in 1890. Those who travelled to England for an education in those days were considered selfish by their families and by society. There were many, however, who tolerated being thus maligned and went abroad to build up a life for themselves in the face of opposition from their families. Among those who crossed the 'black waters' (*kalapani*) to go to England were Surja Goodiv Chakraborty, Satyendranath Tagore, Manmohan Ghosh, Umeshchandra Banerjee and Taraknath Palit. Trying to follow the dreams of his heart ('*sadhite moner sadh*'), Michael Madhusudan Dutt in effect devastated his family life by moving to England.

Michael Madhusudan Dutt, the rebel poet and playwright who was the first moderniser of Bengali literature

This was also the time when ideas of personal friendship were taking shape. Intimacies in an earlier time were formed only with one's family and relatives; that it was possible to share joys and sorrows with anyone beyond the family circle was an unheard of idea. There was no concept of relationships based only on friendship. For, friendship does not grow without the development of individual freedom. When Kartikeyachandra Ray wrote his memoirs at the end of the century, he noted with wonder the development of this new relationship.

A probe into the history of friendships in the 19th century will show that Hindu College, which first witnessed the development of individual freedom, was also where the first friendships were formed. Derozio's students are the first to attract attention. Fast friendships grew between these young men. They were able to talk of their hopes and aspirations and exchange joys and sorrows not with relatives but among friends. Krishnamohan Banerjee, Madhav Chandra Ghosh, Rasik Krishna Mallick, Dakshinaranjan Mukhopadhyay and Mahesh Chandra Ghosh were close friends. But more intimate friendships can be noticed in the 1840s, when deep bonding developed between Madhusudan Dutt and men like Gourdas Basak, Bhudeb Mukhopadhyay, Banku Behari Datta, Shyamacharan Laha, Bholanath Chanda, Rajendralal Mitra. These men formed an intimate circle of friends. Instead of relatives, they spent their time with friends, meeting every day at Mechanic Institute. It appears from Madhusudan's letters that they felt restless if they were not able to go there. Rajnarayan Basu and Gobindo Datta were at this time very close. In the following two decades, Rajnarayan Basu formed firm friendships with men like Debendranath Tagore and Michael Madhusudan. In the 1860s, Keshab Chandra Sen broke with his relatives and built up close ties of friendship with Debendranath Tagore. Satyendranath Tagore and Manmohan Ghosh also became close friends. In this way, the circles of friendship became ever wider. Schools, colleges, workplaces and homes were the spaces around which they were built. People were no longer spending their entire lives with their families and relatives in one village. For education and for work, they were moving out to wider circles. And there they were forming, with people unrelated by family or blood, a new kind of bonding that was almost as close as familial ties.

Western Impact on Religious Thought and Customs

If we look at how religious beliefs fared at the beginning of the 19th century, we will see that in both the Hindu and Muslim communities, people blindly followed their religion and religious customs and rituals. A section of the Hindus did not even question inhuman practices such as suttee, (sati or burning of young widows at the funeral pyres of their husband) or the sacrifice of infants at Gangasagar. Ordinary Muslims followed religious customs, but that marked the limit of their religious consciousness. As we noted earlier, in village after village in Bengal, the Muslim masses were in reality only partially acquainted with Islamic ideals because of the incompleteness of the religious message that reached them. Though they did follow some Islamic rituals, they also in large part clung to their old beliefs and continued to be loyal to the old customs and rituals. In this situation had stepped in the new rulers, belonging to a different religion and an unfamiliar culture.

At first, both the Hindu and Muslim masses regarded them, that is, the English, with suspicion. But there was a significant difference between the Hindus and the Muslims. In the case of the Hindus, the previous rulers had also belonged to a different religion. So their position did not greatly change with the arrival of Christian rulers. Some of them even welcomed the enemies of the enemy. For the Muslims, on the other hand, the change was quite drastic. Islam had thus far received state patronage, to a greater or lesser extent. That state support vanished with the coming of the English. Many Muslims now feared that the new rulers would attack their religion. Because of these complexities, Hindus and Muslims came up with quite different responses in the area of religion from the start of the 19th century. Let us first look at the reaction of the Hindus.

British rule had a huge influence on religious thinking and social customs and ceremonies. Under this impact, Ram Mohan Roy began thinking about religion at the beginning of the 19th century. English-educated young men started thinking about it from the third decade of the century. This was not, however, initiated by the direct impact of Christianity. We do not know if Ram Mohan Roy read English literature. But he had got himself acquainted with European civilisation and philosophy through English. The students of Hindu College became familiar with European civilisation and thinking chiefly through English literature. Even conservative people noticed Western influences in their own society. As a result, Hindus, especially those based in Calcutta, started questioning their own religion and the customs and rituals associated with it. Was all that was being observed in the name of religion really sanctioned by the scriptures? Even if it were, was it human and logical? And was it relevant for present-day society? In the context of these questions, Ram Mohan and other forward-thinking men, to a greater or lesser extent, reformed their own religion. The other section rejected modernism outright and sought to establish the old customs on an even stronger foundation of scriptural approval. This reaction was not quite novel. A section of Hindu society had similarly retreated into a shell following the Turkish conquest.

Ram Mohan Roy raised questions on whether the practice of worshipping multiple gods prevalent in Hindu society was rational, even without going into the question of idol worship. He did not just question, he started a debate on it through his first book *Tuwafat-ul-Muwahidin* (1803-04). Such a thing would be unimaginable in an earlier age. Even in earlier times, many people would have found themselves questioning, under the impact of Islamic monotheism, the beliefs of Hinduism. No one however tried to express their views by writing a book. Bipin Chandra Pal has written in his autobiography that many of his forefathers had learnt Farsi and that they could only start their Farsi lessons with the maulvi after they had first recited the Kalema, that is, the verses containing fundamental articles of faith in Islam. Their teachers would explain the verses to them. The main message of the Kalema is: God is one and Muhammad is His messenger. Even if they failed to repose their faith in Muhammad, they were aware of the Islamic view on monotheism and may well have exercised their minds about whether this was logical. According to Bipin Pal, many of those who studied Farsi found cracks creeping into their faith in multiple gods. Even if faith in multiple gods was shaken, however, it was not as if all of these people wanted to embark on a war with their community. They had no compunctions about making compromises with society. If all it took to ensure that people did not try to scuttle one's daughter's wedding was making flower offerings to the gods, then, well, one might as well make them—so went the rationalising of religious loyalties. Otherwise, it was not as if belief in multiple gods was always unshakeable.

It took a stubborn and upright man like Ram Mohan to go against society to publicise his beliefs. This kind of rational thinking came from exposure to Western education. And it led him to question not just Hindu or Muslim beliefs, but also Christianity. If the truth of religion is questioned with rational thinking, no religion can be considered rational. Islam may have initially influenced Ram Mohan's thinking, but he could not continue to repose faith in it once he analysed it in the light of the rationalist thinking of the Mutazilah school of theology. Eventually he moved away from Islam. Indeed, his search for a religion based on reason and rational thought was tireless, but its object always eluded him. What he found, instead, was faith in monotheism. That is why he did not, or could not, found a new religion. Rather, he started a forum where people with faith in monotheism could meet and pray. The chief component of worship at this forum was reading from the Vedas. Ram Mohan used two central beliefs as the foundation of his religious thinking: the indivisibility of God, and dismissal of idol worship. He identified himself with the Unitarian Christians of England and America and established contact with them. He even started a Unitarian Society in Calcutta.

The most remarkable aspect of Ram Mohan's religious beliefs is that though he may have culled some of his thoughts from Islam, Christianity and Judaism, in the end he unfailingly sought endorsement for them in the Vedas and Vedanta. That is why he translated the Vedas anew and wrote his own commentary on them. But a return to ancient India was not his aim. Rather, his objective was to use the scared texts to reform the present. This, naturally, recalls parallels with the humanist scholars of the European Renaissance. Debendranath Tagore, too, used a modified form of the Vedas and the *Upanishad*, and with a new explanation. Later, Ishwarchandra Vidyasagar also used the ancient scriptures and literature in his reform drive for contemporary society.

After Ram Mohan, revolutionary changes in the world of thought in Bengal came chiefly through the students of Hindu College. These students did not confine their reading to English grammar and literature. They also kept themselves abreast of rationalist and liberal philosophies. The most important role in this was played by Derozio. He not only got his students acquainted with the writings of philosophers, he also taught them to analyse what they read. That many of his students had read David Hume, Thomas Reid and Dugald Stuart and were also familiar with Tom Paine's *Age of Reason* is clear from the evidence strewn in the magazines of the time. They were also familiar with the works of living philosophers such as James Stuart Mill and Jeremy Bentham. As a result, rational and liberal ideas started dominating the thoughts of the Hindu College students from the beginning of the 1830s. The effects were evident in the lives of these young men and also in wider educated circles.

Inspired by the ideals of rationalism and liberalism, these young men started questioning the customs, rituals, ways of conduct and values that they had inherited. That their attitude to these was changing was commented upon in *Samacharchandrika* within 12 years of the establishment of Hindu College, in 1829. The young men concerned admitted as much in the *Enquirer* 0in September 1831. They claimed that Ram Mohan's efforts and the education imparted at Hindu College had together dealt a severe blow to the tradition of idol worship. Many young men started questioning even religious values and analysed faith in the light of reason. Their gaze was gradually shifting away from thoughts of divinity to the living world of human beings. They now sought to adapt religion to the here and the now. In other words, they challenged in religion anything that they felt went against the fundamental rights of men and women. In this way, some of them had cracks creeping into their faith.

Some tried to come to terms with their loss of confidence in their own faith by seeking in other religions the values they cherished. In 1832, for instance, Krishnamohan Bandyopadhyay, Rasik Krishna Mallick, Mahesh Chandra Ghosh, Madhav Chandra Ghosh and others of Hindu College mounted a fierce attack on Hinduism. Madhav Chandra Ghosh wrote in the most widely circulated English daily in those days, *Bengal Hurkara,* that if there was anything that he and his friends hated from the bottom of their hearts, it was the Hindu faith. And that was not where they drew the line. That same year, Mahesh Chandra Ghosh and Krishnamohan Bandyopadhyay embraced Christianity. Some years later, in the 1840s, Rajnarayan Basu showed an interest in Islam, Bhudeb Mukhopadhyay expressed curiosity about Christianity, and Madhusudan Dutt, of course, converted to Christianity.

Ram Mohan's monotheism found its most ardent admirer in Debendranath Tagore. Ram Mohan in fact had an early influence on Debendranath while the latter was still a boy. He affectionately called him '*beradar*' and took him out for carriage rides. But whereas Ram Mohan believed in internationalism, Debendranath was to a large extent nationalist in his thinking. His greatest difference with Ram Mohan is that on a cursory assessment he appears anti-West. He did at any rate reject the glitter of Western lifestyles. Though Ram Mohan saw many good things in Christianity, Debendranath rejected it, at least outwardly. He reformed religion chiefly in the light of the Vedas and the Upanishads. For the Brahmo faith that he propagated, he chose from these sacred texts verses which had given him solace and which he found acceptable. Yet he was not able to accept the Vedas as revealed truth. Nor even the Upanishads. A close look shows that he based his religious reform on rational and modern thinking. These were ideas that he derived from his exposure to Western education and thinking. His thoughts on religion were independent, but the inspiration for independent thinking and the world view that made it possible grew out of interactions with the West. But once his thoughts had taken shape, he, like Ram Mohan, sought endorsement for them in the Vedas and the Upanishads. He did not even hesitate to sometimes refer to the 14th century Persian poet Hafez in attempting to explain his thoughts. Another major difference between Ram Mohan and Debendranath is that the former treated religion as a theory. He did not try to propagate his faith. Debendranath, on the other hand, sought to give an institutional shape to religion and convert it into an article of faith and emotion. Ram Mohan's Brahmo Samaj died with him, but Debendranath used the Brahmo ideal to propagate a new faith. He compiled a new sacred text for the new faith and gave it a shape that would make it possible for ordinary believers to practise it. Instead of just rational thinking, he brought emotion to his religious thinking. This was why the Brahmo community grew so quickly. Without the direct confrontation that eventually took place between him and Keshab Chandra Sen, the Brahmo Samaj might have developed into a major religious movement, apart from the social movement that it was.

Curiously enough, though Debendranath drew the fundamental tenet of the Brahmo faith from the Upanishads, he modified many of the verses (slokas) that he borrowed from the ancient texts. He rejected anything that did not agree with his devotional dualism, no matter what the source. He took only what he wanted and did not hesitate to chuck whatever he found unacceptable. The idea of symbolic worship, for instance. His views on religious life were drawn from his own felt experience. Thus, he used the ancient scriptures, but with a new interpretation and his own modifications.

Debendranath's religious consciousness was enmeshed with a certain cultural pride. This was where he differed greatly from Michael Madhusudan. He was not at all exercised about what the West approved of and what it didn't. On the contrary, he always attached greatest value to his own thoughts on religious customs and conduct. There were, therefore, not a few self-contradictions in what he did. He did not, for instance, forsake his caste identity. Nor did he reject the sacred thread, which it is the prerogative of Brahmins to wear. Yet he did away with all sorts of ceremonies. In an age when the nouveau riche fell over each other to acquire social prestige through lavish and elaborate pujas and funeral rites, he chose not to hold a funeral when his father died, though he knew that this would put off relatives. Debendranath was not afraid of direct confrontations with society.

Debendranath Tagore, who led the movement for the modernisation of Hinduism in Bengal

However weak its effect on Debendranath, Christianity in those days had its greatest impact on the Brahmos. On the young Brahmos this impact gathered momentum from the 1850s. These young men did not totally forsake their inherited faith to become Christians, unlike Krishnamohan Bandyopadhyay, Madhusudan Dutt, Lalbehari Dey, Gyanendramohan Tagore, or Gobindo Datta. Instead, they embraced the Brahmo faith. For, in their eyes the Brahmo beliefs, influenced as these were by Western values, particularly rationalism and liberalism, appeared far superior to Hinduism. Besides, it was easier to become a Brahmo than a Christian. Conversion to Christianity was regarded as an irredeemable moral fall, sinful in the extreme. Adopting the Brahmo faith was not considered quite as detestable. Many people regarded it as a modified form of Hinduism. Men like Rajnarayan Basu, Keshab Chandra Sen and Shibnath Shastri belonged to this category. It was such young Brahmos who were Bankimchandra's target when he said that they were known to their friends as Brahmos but were seen as Hindus by their parents.

There was a noticeably exaggerated consciousness of sin among many Brahmos. This was a mental habit they borrowed from Christians. The collective prayer meetings that they introduced also unmistakably reflected the influence of Christian congregations. This influence of collective worship in churches was felt even in the more conservative sect of the Brahmos led by Debendranath. They, too, were quite unshakeable in their custom of conducting their congregations with the singing of Brahmasangeet (songs in praise of the Brahma) to the accompaniment of organ music, much like hymns sung in churches; religious lectures by the Acharya on the lines of sermons by Christian priests; and collective prayers. This custom of collective prayers did not come from the Muslims. Bengali Hindus in the past 700 years, with the exception of Vaishnavas and Bauls to a limited extent, had remained largely unmoved by Muslim modes of worship. The ways in which the Brahmos, especially those of the Sadharon Brahmo Samaj, reformed the old religion were more noticeably influenced by Christian thinking and European civilisation.

Responses to religion in those days of social change and newly introduced modern education were quite interestingly varied. Two other names cannot but be mentioned in this context—Ishwarchandra Vidyasagar and Akshay Kumar Datta. Vidyasagar was born into an orthodox Brahmin family. Debendranath studied a secular curriculum at Hindu College, but Vidyasagar was educated at the conservative and religious educational institution of Sanskrit College. Yet, his first public exposure was through a write-up in favour of the remarriage of Hindu widows, published in 1842 under a pseudonym. In this article, and in countless articles afterwards, he repeatedly recalled the scriptures and came up with new interpretations to push through reforms in Hindu society. The strange thing is that he never openly professed his own religious convictions. He was probably an agnostic. As he grew older, his doubts grew, too.

Akshay Kumar Datta, on the other hand, rose above agnosticism and all but espoused atheism. He tried to show through a mathematical equation that prayers had no point. The equation was as follows:

Hard work = *Fruits of labour*
Again,
Hard work + prayers = *Fruits of labour*
Therefore,
Prayers = *0*

Some of his rational thinking comes across in this equation. This rationalist trend did not really become very strong in the 19th century. Yet we cannot ignore the handful of exceptional thinkers such as Akshay Datta while trying to understand how Bengali society reacted to the comprehensive and all-embracing impact of the West.

Among the educated Hindus, there were many who did not actually become Brahmos but were influenced by what they saw as the progressive, that is, Western, ideals followed by Brahmos. This section more or less saw Western civilisation as being synonymous with Christian values. The highly educated Durgacharan Dasgupta had a printing press. He wrote a number of books, which he got printed at his own press. He was not a Brahmo, but he was influenced by some of the ideals of Brahmoism. Those ideals, however, were social rather than religious. For instance, he believed in women's education and started coaching his child wife in secret. This child bride, Kailasbasini, eventually published a few books of her own in the 1860s.

There was another section to which belonged educated people like Bhudeb Mukhopadhyay, Dakshinaranjan Mukhopadhyay, Ramgopal Ghosh, Peary Chand Mitra, Kishorichand Mitra, Gourdas Basak, Pyaricharan Sarkar, Harchandra Ghosh, Rajendralal Mitra, Bankimchandra Chattopadhyay — all of these men had acquired an excellent modern education in English. They also came in close contact with the English. Yet they reserved a place of honour for the faith of their forefathers in their lives. But of course they, too, were forced to somewhat modify their religion in the light of reason, making it more liberal and rational.

The vast majority considered it sinful to even think of their faith in new ways, let alone reinterpreting it. They had no part in any revolution in religious thinking. Yet the winds of change did not leave them untouched. The lifestyle changes brought about by Western impact could not but leave an effect on their lives. This influence was social rather than religious. And hence they did not hesitate to make compromises with their religious beliefs in order to make their way in the world. They were happy to work in the offices of their colonial masters, and for many of them a dip in the Ganga in the evening served to wash off the sins thus accumulated. Many ate forbidden foods with the sahibs and made up for it by observing some expiatory rituals as part of their daily worship. In much the same spirit, many people tried to erase their sins, again through rituals of atonement, only on a much larger scale, after returning from educational pursuits in England that would help in the business of earning money. What shook the conservatives, even more than any challenge to faith, was the pooh-poohing of the caste system by the Western-educated section, especially the breaking of taboos to sit down and share meals with those outside the pale of caste and the eating of forbidden foods. The trend started as early as in the 1830s. In 1831, Krishnamohan Bandyopadhyay not only ate beef with his friends, he also flung the bones into his neighbour's yard. The incident raised much hue and cry. In the next decade, quite a few young people including Rajnarayan Basu and Michael Madhusudan Dutt started eating beef. Rajnarayan Basu has left quite a humorous account of this in his autobiography. Gourdas Basak was a Vaishnava and therefore not supposed to eat meat at all. Not able to escape the importunities of his friend Madhusudan, however, he became quite a seasoned meat-eater. Biscuits, too, were held in suspicion by Bengali Hindu society because Muslim workers made them. Besides, they were thought to contain ingredients that might compromise ritual caste purity. When Rajnarayan Basu became a Brahmo in the 1840s, his baptism in the new faith was accompanied by drinking alcohol and eating biscuits. It was a symbolic act, signifying the snapping of the chains of superstition. Bread was also forbidden. Apart from the eating of forbidden foods, drinking by educated people was frowned upon by the conservatives. Some of the conservatives, however, had begun to take to alcohol and meat-eating.

Even at the end of the century, the conservatives were not comfortable with the breaking of food taboos and the sharing of meals between castes, as, for instance, The *Somprakash Patrika* bears testimony. A write-up in the magazine in 1882 claimed that those Bengalis who had moved away from their own society did not hesitate to accept water from a Muslim or to eat biscuits and that they were no longer wary of social disapproval. Such people also apparently sat down to eat with others without any thought to caste rules, made a show of progressiveness, and grew beards. Yet they also joined their hands in prayer when they came back home and faced their household gods. That caste taboos on commensality actually continued beyond the 19th century and well into the 20th century is evident from the writings of many people including Rabindranath Tagore.

In the second half of the 19th century, once the initial impact of the West had dissipated, expressions of contempt for religion lost much of their earlier harshness among the Western-educated, no matter what the beliefs they may have privately held. Some, like Rajnarayan Basu, went back to the old religion. The newly aroused feelings of nationalism played a direct role in this. This tendency was further strengthened by the Hindu revivalist movements of the 1880s. Yet, a general lack of interest in, and also disparagement of, religion continued to prevail among Western-educated youngsters. So, also, their indifference to caste hierarchies. As late as 1870, a write-up in *Tatwabodhini Patrika* expresses regret about a general disdain for religion. In sum, then, with the spread of Western education in the 19th century, the section exposed to such education became quite secular in its world view. There was also a greater and more interested involvement with worldliness, the here and the now.

Social Reform

If the English-educated section turned its attention to religious reform under the influence of rational and liberal ways of thought, it also turned its gaze on social reform, particularly the various social rules, customs and rituals associated with religious beliefs. Ram Mohan started paying attention to this kind of work from the second decade of the 19th century. He took to writing books to raise awareness about the inhumanity of the custom of suttee (sati). In book after book, he tried to impress on his readers that suttee (sati) was a cruel practice and also held up scriptural evidence against it. He did not just stop at seeking out scriptural injunctions to bolster his position, he also came up with new interpretations for them. He appealed to the Company's government to prohibit suttee. The practice was eventually prohibited by law in December 1829.

The road map of social reform introduced by Ram Mohan continued right up to the 1870s. The new generation of English-educated people did not remain satisfied with saving young widows from the flames. In time they turned their attention to the way Hindu widows were compelled to remain celibate and to the forced austerity in their diet and lifestyles. Derozio's students first started raising awareness about this at the start of the 1830s through the pages of magazines such as *Gyananweshan* and *Enquirer.* The *Bengal Spectator* magazine joined the movement in the 1840s. Though this magazine belonged to the Young Bengal group, it was, curiously enough, Ishwarchandra Vidyasagar of Sanskrit College who wrote in it in favour of the remarriage of Hindu widows. Like Ram Mohan, he culled out old scriptural sayings to establish the reasonableness of widow remarriage and offered new interpretations of the ancient slokas.

Ishwarchandra Vidyasagar, first moderniser of Bengali prose and a leading rationalist

A strong public sentiment in favour of widow remarriage could not be built up in the 1840s. That had to wait for another decade. In the 1850s, Vidyasagar wrote a book advocating widow remarriage. He translated ancient sacred texts and reinterpreted them in his attempt to show that the remarriage of widows had scriptural endorsement. Like Ram Mohan, again, he appealed to the Company's government to make widow remarriage legal. He made this appeal through a petition, which he got others to sign. Thereafter, appeals to the government by progressive people from various corners of the country supporting his movement started pouring in. The Hindu Widows Remarriage Act was finally passed in July 1856.

The Act was passed, but it was not as if Hindu widows came forward on their own to remarry. Indeed, few men were actually bold enough to agree to such marriages. Six months after the Act was passed, Vidyasagar and his friends were able, with all their diligent efforts, to get one widow married.

The groom was a colleague of Vidyasagar—Srishachandra Vidyaratna, a professor of Sanskrit College. According to the grapevine, he agreed to the marriage in the hope of getting money and also the post of deputy collector. In the next half century, there were hundred-odd such marriages, chiefly among the Brahmos. It emerges, then, that very few Hindu widows could actually remarry, despite the new law. Yet, the law constituted an important symbolic victory against social conservatism. It also served to raise social awareness of the plight of Hindu widows.

To Vidyasagar and his friends, the passing of the Act was particularly encouraging. They now embarked on a movement to put a stop to polygamy among *kulin* Brahmins, that is, Brahmins recognised as being of exceptional ritual purity. But the Sepoy Mutiny of 1857 led the colonial administration to decide against intervening in native religious practices and social customs. Hence, no law against polygamy was passed. But the movement against the polygamy of *kulin* clans continued into the 1870s. Eventually, a *kulin* Brahmin from Dhaka, Rashbehari Mukhopadhyay, came forward to help in this mission. Though he himself had married multiple times, he was influenced by the reform movement and contributed a great deal to it.

Child marriage was at that time an almost universally accepted custom. We will discuss this extensively in the chapter 'Love, Marriage and Family'. Suffice it here to say that social awareness about it grew with the spread of education.

In the 1830s, drinking had become fashionable among young people. Many famous men of Bengal died early in the second half of the century as a result of excessive drinking. The social reformers saw drinking as a challenge to the stability that marked the middle classes of the time. That is why they also built up a movement against drinking.

But the movement that continued through the entire century was the movement to improve women's lives. It started with Ram Mohan's movement against suttee. After that, the fight was kept up and one after another came the movements against the forced celibacy of widows, polygamy, child marriage and dowry. All of them were movements to lighten the burden of women. But the movements associated with religion lost steam from the 1870s. A close analysis will show that a new awareness, a sense of nationhood, was then crystallising in society. (I have discussed this extensively in my book *Samaj Samskar O Bangla Natok*, or Social Reform and Bengali Drama.) On the other hand, social reformers, in their attempt to improve the situation of women, started movements to educate them and release them from the confinement of domestic spaces. The English-educated young men realised that men could not fully enjoy their own lives unless women could be educated and allowed outside restricted domestic spaces. And they were not far wrong. Indeed, it was partly in their own interest that the social reformers started their movement for women's education and against purdah (the custom of keeping women confined in homes). The fight for women's liberation spanned the entire 19th century and it has not reached its end even now, in the 21st century (For detailed information see my book *Sankochero Bihbholata: Adhunikotar Obhighate Bangaramanir Protikriya*, or The Bengali Woman's Response to Modernism).

Islam

In comparison with Hinduism or Buddhism, Islam is a young religion. From the very beginning, the rules and regulations of this religion were written down. In other words, there was little scope for aberrations in the scriptural sources of this religion. In spite of this, however, within two or three centuries of the propagation of Islam, at least four sects emerged in the main Sunni tradition, based on the teachings of four religious leaders. The Shia sect also emerged soon after the propagation of Islam. Besides, as we noted in the chapter 'Society and Religion' , when this religion spread in lands beyond the boundaries of Arabia, the influence of local beliefs and cultures on it produced a new religious philosophy. Still, it must be said that the followers of Islam reserved scant welcome for reform. Traditional Muslims had cruelly punished the Mutazilah sect for its dissenting views and its analysing of faith in the light of reason. Nor were they kindly disposed towards the Sufis. And if truth be told, they did not much care for debate on religion.

We have already noted that the Islam that was propagated in medieval Bengal was vastly different from Islam in the Arab world. Those who took to Islam in Bengal did not totally forsake their earlier beliefs and cultural values. It was not also easy for them to get acquainted with a sacred text written in an alien language and memorise verses from it in order to observe religious rituals. As a result of this compromise with local customs and rituals, there were many practices among Muslims in Bengal that had no real connection with Islam. The soil of India had an extraordinary syncretic ability to absorb the waves of humanity who arrived here, the Shakas, Huns, Pathans and Mughals. In the frontier province of Bengal, the Vedic, Buddhist and Muslim religions all moved away from their original forms. What emerged in Bengal was a syncretic Islam. The *khanqah*s (Sufi lodges, sort of monastic complexes) mazars (mausoleums) and dargahs (tombs serving as shrines) that cropped up in Bengal around its pirs and dervishes, within some 500 years of the propagation of Islam in the land, were not very Islamic in character. It was this aberrant Islam that reached the masses in village after village. But the new education that was being imparted under the colonial administration and the impact of Western civilisation could not but leave some imprint on Muslim society. In response, a section of the Muslims were forced to regroup and organise themselves.

Faced with the impact of the West elite Muslims had two options. They could either accept the new influence, or they could ward it off by strengthening the walls of Islam around them. They regarded the English, a foreign people of an alien faith, with suspicion. Very few Muslims in the first half of the 19th century were drawn to a Western education. Nor were they in a condition that was conducive to a Western education. Therefore, just as many Hindus in the 13th, 14th and 15th centuries had retreated into a shell, many Muslims in the 19th century reinforced the rules and regulations of their religion and clung to its customs and observances. A movement to return to the original form – a fundamentalist movement – now started in their midst, not in Bengal but in northern India. To be more exact, it actually started in the Arab world itself.

Titu Mir (1782-1831) started an Islamic reform movement in and around Barasat after his return from Arabia, where he had been inspired by Syed Ahmed to cleanse the faith of unIslamic components. He met with some success in 24 Parganas, Nadia, Jessore and Faridpur. Titu Mir linked economic issues to the religious movement. As a result, many poor Muslim peasants in these areas accepted his leadership in the fight against Hindu zamindars. He was eventually defeated and killed when his movement started to oppose the colonial rulers. With his death, the Wahabi movement was also halted for a while.

The jehad that was started by Shah Syed Ahmed (1783-1831) in northern India was brought to Bengal chiefly by two men, Enayet Ali (1794-1858) and Keramat Ali (1800-74), who expanded this movement through religious preaching. They unleashed a wave of preaching in the name of the Tariqa-e-Mohammadia, Enayet Ali in 24 Parganas, Jessore, Faridpur, Rajshahi, Malda, Pabna, and Keramat Ali in eastern Bengal, chiefly in Noakhali, Dhaka, Mymensingh, Faridpur and Barisal. The expression Tariqa-e-Mohammadia literally means the 'way of Mohammad'. These leaders tried to determine the way of Mohammad on the basis of the Quran and the Hadiths. This movement acquired many active supporters. More importantly, people in the countryside became familiar with the sacred texts and started observing Islamic regulations and rituals.

The Tariqa-e-Mohammadia movement had no objective other than an enthusiastic interest in preaching religion. There was, however, another arm of the fundamentalist movement that formed links with politics and economics. This was the Faraizi movement. Faridpur's Shariat Ullah (1781-1840) had become acquainted with the fundamentalist Wahabi movement when he went on a Haj pilgrimage to Mecca. He brought the movement to Bengal, where it was called the Faraizi movement. The Faraizi movement differed from the Tariqa-e-Mohammadia in its ideological content in that it laid greater stress on the teachings of the Quran, or *farz*, rather than on the sayings of Mohammad, that is, the Hadith.

After the arrival of the Muslims in Bengal in the 13th century, the Hindu *Smriti* scholars had retreated into a shell and laid down strict religious regulations for their flock. The two threads of the Islamic fundamentalist movement discussed above seem in some ways to be a throwback to what the *Smriti* scholars tried to do. The Hindu scriptural authorities tried to protect their faith by reinforcing old customs and rituals, introducing new forms of worship and ceremonies and even by creating new caste hierarchies (the system of marking out *kulin*s) to reward ritual purity. The Islamic fundamentalists saw British colonial rule and Christianity as constituting a grave assault and declared India to be Dar-ul-Harb, or land of strife. They issued fatwas saying that it was not possible to peacefully observe religious customs and rituals in this country. In effect, they, too, were asking the faithful to retreat into shells. In this way they tried to keep their distance from Western ways of thinking.

A purification drive was carried out among Muslims in Bengal through the Tariqa-e-Mohammadia and the Faraizi movements. These movements tried to ensure that ordinary Muslims conducted their religious lives in a strictly Islamic way. But unlike Enayet Ali and Keramat Ali, leaders of the Tariqa-e-Mohammadia movement, Shariat Ullah was not just a religious leader. He got himself involved in economic and political conflicts, in many ways like Titu Mir did. On Shariat Ullah's call, peasants, and particularly Muslim peasants, organised themselves against the colonial rulers and Hindu landlords. His son Dudu Mian led the movement after his death. The movement gained immense popularity in Faridpur, Barisal, Pabna, Jessore, Dhaka and Mymensingh around the middle of the 19th century. The peasants and sharecroppers who joined the movement hoped to be rewarded in their afterlives and also dreamed of liberation from the oppression of landlords. This dual aspiration for worldly and other-worldly gain was what made this movement so popular. But the movement lost its appeal and much of its steam after Dudu Mia's death in 1861.

Although the Faraizi movement petered out, individual and collective attempts to educate ordinary, illiterate Muslims in the ways of Islam and turn them into enthusiastic defenders of the faith continued, though these were not organised in the way a political movement is. This, however, provided the environment in which, at the turn of the century, Muslim writers such as Riazuddin Ahmed Mashhadi called on the faithful to practise Islam in accordance with the prescriptions in sacred texts. It appears from their writing that even at that time most Muslims were not able to offer namaz in the correct way or observe the Roja (Ramzan) fast. The sound of the azan, the Muslim call to prayer, was rarely heard in the countryside. Comments on the subject in *Rawshan Hedayet* magazine in 1926 give an idea of the Hindu customs and rituals that still prevailed among the Muslim masses:

> Many naïve Muslims join in the worship of Kali, Durga, Lokkhi, Saraswati, Bastu, Charak, chariot, stones, dargah, graves, Manik Pir, swamp bamboo, and so on.... They use ... mantras, and swear by the names of Kali, Durga, Kamguru, Kamakshya, etc. And through such sinful acts that go against the Shariat, they lose their priceless *iman* [faith] and turn into kaffirs [infidels] and so clear the way to *jahannam* [hell]...

In the way they conducted their lives and the clothes they wore, there was little to distinguish between the Muslim masses and low-caste Hindus. Rafiuddin Ahmed has shown in his book that many Muslims could not be identified as such from their names. Here is a handful of such names: Madan Sheikh, Nepal Gazi, Godhan Karigar, Gokul Mollah, Haru Biswas, Narayan Tarafdar, Pratap Shikdar, Rakhal Sheikh and Mandar Sarkar. And they, in fact, harboured no rigidity in their minds regarding their religious identity. But conservative Muslim writers at the start of the 20th century made a powerful call for awareness on such matters. These writers also played the role of social reformers. The religion of love that was preached by the medieval Sufi pirs continued to considerably influence rural society at the end of the 19th century and the beginning of the 20th. But social reformers like Mashhadi started a campaign urging people to embrace Sunni Islam and the teachings of the hard-line Hanafi sect in place of the lenient, devotional faith of the Sufis.

On the other hand, in the context of the changed political landscape, the unity that had slowly built up over centuries between syncretic Muslims and Hindus started to weaken around the same time. At the end of the 19th century, roughly from the 1880s, the revivalist and nationalist movements among the Hindus also helped to reinforce the conflicting identities of Hindus and Muslims. As we will see in the following discussion, it was the movement against the partition of Bengal that played the most important role in this respect.

Sense of Nationhood and Political Awareness

Western education had brought about remarkable changes among the young people in Calcutta from the 1830s, as we have already discussed. This left its imprint on religious rules and practices, social customs and behaviour, the hopes and aspirations of people and also their identities. The young men of the new age, however, did not just move away from traditional society. They also started looking at their country and their society in a new light. Western education had in fact helped a sense of nationhood to grow in their minds. The Asiatic Society researches, apart from the education provided at schools and colleges, played a huge role in this development. It was through these researches that the idea of a glorious Indian civilisation took shape. Colonial exploitation and the racism of the rulers also helped in the birth of this sense of nationhood. Beginning from the time of the Sena rulers, Bengalis had been ruled by outsiders for nearly a thousand years. The Sultanate era, though, is sometimes claimed to be one of Bengali rule. Still, Bengalis undeniably had accepted foreign rule over a prolonged period. In the 19th century, patriotic feelings and a sense of nationhood surfaced among them for the first time, under the influence of new ideas in a new age.

Shortly afterwards, in 1851, was formed the British Indian Association, India's first semi-political organisation. Its president was Radhakanta Deb, and its secretary was Debendranath Tagore. Thus, in the name of protecting financial interests and of nationhood, there began a collaboration between the conservative and progressive sections of society. The educated middle class in the 1860s was inspired by this sense of nationhood. They did not exactly carry out a political movement, but they started displaying pride in the glories of ancient India. And along with it, there also appeared anti-British, and even more powerfully, anti-Muslim sentiments. In this ideological environment, the Jatiyo Gaurabh Sampadani Sabha (Forum for the Attaining of National Pride) and the Hindu Mela were set up in the 1860s on the initiative of Rajnarayan Basu, Debendranath Tagore, Nabagopal Mitra and others. In the following decade came the Sanjeevani Sabha (Rejuvenation Forum). These organisations were largely communal in character. Even at that time, 'jati' or nation meant not much more than being Hindu. In spite of these limitations, however, these organisations certainly reflected a sort of nationalism and love of the motherland. Feelings of nationalism and patriotism came through quite unmistakably in the patriotic songs written at this time by Jyotirindranath Tagore and Satyendranath Tagore, two of Rabindranath Tagore's elder brothers.

Education had not yet taken off among Muslims. Still, they could not but organise themselves once they noted this communal sense of nationhood among the Hindu bhadralok section. Nawab Abdul Laitf established the Mohammedan Literary Society in 1863. Notwithstanding the 'literary' in its name, this Society was in reality only an attempt to organise Muslims. Syed Amir Ali's Central Mohammedan Association also reflected a similar attempt.

The movement for social reform in Hindu society was thwarted by the growing feelings of nationhood. For, Hindus inspired by a sense of nationhood naturally did not find it desirable that any outside force should intervene in their religious customs and practices. Instead of reforming their social customs and norms, they now started expressing pride in them. For instance, when the movement for widow remarriage was going on in the 1850s, most educated people considered it progressive to join it. Yet, in the 1880s, writers such as Akshay Sarkar rejected widow remarriage and praised the austerity practised by Hindu widows as something to be proud of. Thus, the tradition of social reform died out. An analysis of Bengali plays shows that many plays were written in the 1850s and 1860s in favour of social reform. Playwrights like Ramnarayan Tarkaratna, Michael Madhusudan Dutt and Dinabandhu Mitra contributed to this kind of literary tradition. In the 1870s, however, many a playwright wrote sarcastically about social reform. Even Jyotirindranath Tagore belonged to this group. A large number of sarcastic skits on women's education and women's liberation were published at this time.

Instead of focussing on the flaws in contemporary social life and calling for reform, playwrights writing from the 1870s onwards chose Puranic or patriotic themes. The English do make a fleeting appearance in some of these patriotic plays, but most of the criticism is reserved for the Muslim rulers of an earlier dispensation. In this context may be mentioned Haralal Ray's *Hemlata* and *Banger Sukhabosan*, Kunjabihari Basu's *Bharat Odhin*, Upendranath Das's *Sarat-Sarojini* and *Upendra-Binodini*, Jyotirindranath Tagore's *Purobikram* and *Sarojini*, Umeshchandra Gupta's *Maharashtra Kalanko*, Amritalal Basu's *Heerakchurna*, Harimohan Bhattacharjee's *Samare Kamini*, Mahendralal Basu's *Chitor-Rajsati Padmini*, Nabinchandra Vidyaratna's *Bharater Sukhosashi Jabanakabole* and Manoranjan Guha's

Bharat Bandini. Some of these plays were staged in the 1870s. So powerful was the sense of nationhood that came through in these plays that in 1876 the government felt compelled to pass the Dramatic Performances Act.

It was also in this decade that the once beef-eating Brahmo leader Rajnarayan Basu gave a lecture on the superiority of the Hindu religion. Debendranath Tagore, who by then did not usually attend such events, presided at the meeting in which this lecture, called 'Hindu Dharmer Shresthatwa' (The Superiority of the Hindu Faith) was delivered in 1873. In trying to prove that Hinduism was the best, Rajnayaran Basu ended up defending customs and practices that he himself had opposed some two to three decades earlier. His conservatism also came across quite unmistakably in his lectures on Bengali literature in this decade. Even Bankimchandra Chattopadhyay did not exactly display any very kind feelings towards Muslims in his novels in this and the following decade. All this reflects the increasingly nationalist sentiments of society.

India's first political organisation, the India Association, was set up in 1876 by Surendranath Banerjea. Two years earlier he had been dismissed from the Indian Civil Services amid a controversy and opposition from his British bosses. He might not, perhaps, have founded this organisation were he not thus forced to lose his job. Yet, in an environment of political awareness that had grown steadily in the years after the Sepoy Mutiny, someone or the other was sure to have started such an organisation within the next two years at the very least. In 1885 was formed the Indian National Congress, and Bengalis played a significant role in its establishment.

The Hindu revivalist movement was intimately linked with the development of a sense of nation. The progressive attitudes that could be seen in Bengal from the 1830s as a consequence of Western education and reformist zeal were quickly reversed as Hindu revivalist sentiments grew in strength. Indeed, this was the mindset that produced a powerful impulse to impose glory on everything about India's past. The tendency to describe Muslims as *jaban* started as early as the 1830s. From moderate Hindus like Ishwar Gupta to atheists like Akshay Datta, almost everyone at that time used *jaban* for

Muslims, to a greater or lesser extent. Without going into the question of how reasonable it was to describe as *jaban* or 'foreigner' people who were born in Bengal and whose language had been Bengali for generations, the tendency to bad-mouth the rulers of the previous era as *jaban*s is to an extent understandable. It is more difficult to understand, on a cursory assessment, the enthusiastic expressions of anti-*jaban* sentiments produced by the Hindu revivalist movements in the 1880s. There seems to have been generated at this time a general sentiment against all 'outsiders' by the newly developing sense of nation and by the growing political movement. Let alone Islam, Christianity, too, was not spared by the revivalists. Campaigners out to prove that Hinduism was the best could sometimes come up with such puerile claims as the one that said that the 'reverse' of G-O-D was D-O-G but that Nandan-Nandan remained Nandan-Nandan even if reversed. The regressive thinking that saw the Vedas as the repositories of all knowledge ('Everything is there in the Vedas') became popular at this time. Thus, a tidal wave of religious revivalism occupied the space earlier held by progressiveness and the renaissance.

Social Mobility

Social status depended upon one's familial status, not just in Bengal but in the whole of India. The accident of birth, thus, could determine one's place in society. In the structure of social hierarchies, the Sudras were on the lowest rung while the Brahmins were on the highest. People who managed to acquire wealth also earned some extra prestige in society. That did not, however, make any difference to one's inherited social status. The status of the ruling classes, and also in fact of the wealthy, was measured by a different yardstick. Muslims, too, had found a space for themselves in the caste-divided social arrangement of Bengali society. But if a Muslim was, for instance, a landlord, then a different yardstick was used to determine his status.

Social status was closely linked with hereditary family occupation. For generations, people in traditional society depended on their family trades to make a living. Over centuries, the fisherman's (*jele*) son became a fisherman; the tiller's (*chashi*) son, a tiller; the barber's (*napit*) son, a barber; the thatcher's (*gharami*) son, a thatcher. Such people picked up the skills of their trade from their fathers and grandfathers, generation after generation. In this way a priest's (*purut*, or *purohit*) son became a priest, a Baidya's (traditional healer) son became a Baidya and a potter's (*kamar*) son became a potter. It is not known if a mullah's son became a mullah in the Middle Ages, but a *jola*'s (*jola* was the Muslim weaving caste) son did become a jola and a butcher's (*kasai*) son became a butcher. So, then, Muslims too had hereditary family occupations. There were some family trades, however, where the supply of possible practitioners exceeded the demand for them. In such cases, people had to find alternative occupations. Not all Brahmins, for instance, became priests, and nor were so many priests required in society. Many Brahmins therefore found employment with zamindars, the amirs and omrahs and the sultans. The Kayasthas had even fewer options. They could not become priests. So they had to acquire an education and find jobs. In the Muslim age they learnt Farsi to work under Muslim masters. And they were no less enthusiastic about picking up English during British colonial rule.

This tradition of following one's family trade was very much in place until the first decades of the 19th century. But a certain social mobility began to manifest itself within 50 to 60 years of British rule, especially in and around Calcutta, with the result that many people began to forsake their family occupations and found other things to do. Brahmins, for instance, had no compunctions about adopting Vaishya (business class) occupations. Kayasthas started making their way into jobs traditionally held by Brahmins. And because social status was closely linked to family trades, this new social mobility had an impact on people's social status. *Hutom Pyanchar Naksha* has a sarcastic take on this social change: 'On witnessing the Bamuns [Brahmins] and Kayets [Kayasthas] becoming increasingly genteel, the cobblers and other lowly fellows in the city started crawling, too…in time, second Ram Mohan Roys, Debendranath Tagores and Keshab Sens started being born among the lower castes.' Then again, 'Whole dynasties began growing on fragile twigs. Nabo Munshi, Chhire Bene and Punte Teli turned kings.' (The surnames, signifying both caste and traditional family occupations, point to the incongruity between these people's traditional place in society and their newfound social prestige.) As a result of this social mobility, 'Money rose far above good birth. Rama Muddopharas and Kasta Bagdi, Pencho

Mullick and Chhuncho Sheel, started bossing over Calcutta's Kayets and Bamuns and became the most important people in the city.' The names mentioned with biting sarcasm in these passages are not all innocuous. Nabo Munshi was actually Nabakrishna Deb; Pencho Mullick was most probably Rajendralal Mullick and Chhuncho Sheel most likely was Motilal Sheel. All of them had risen from conditions of poverty to be counted among the super rich of Calcutta. As a result of this kind of social mobility, the steps of the old ladder of social stratification became rather unsteady, even if they did not quite break down.

There is an excellent account in *Hutom Pyanchar Naksha* of the way people from the lowest rungs of society slowly moved up in life. A 'babu' called Padmalochan Datta has no education but manages to make a lot of money and thus turns into a 'babu'. Born in an extremely poor family, he makes it to Calcutta from his village home and starts working for a family. The nature of his work is that of a domestic servant. Yet, he becomes one of the 'big people' of Calcutta by earning considerable wealth. He also acquires social status:

> In time, Padmalochan started making a fast buck through all sorts of tricks and trades, bought a new house to suit his current status, and his folks and mosahebs [hangers-on] soon filled up the house and their own tummies with all the good things that the big people of the city must have, while the Babu chose a whore for himself.

This is not just the stuff of made-up tales. Indeed, if we look at the social life of Calcutta in the first 60 to 70 years of the 19th century, we find that the non-Brahmins had outstripped the Brahmins in both wealth and learning. These were the *kulin*s of the new age, the people marked out for special social status. Let us try to understand the nature of this social transformation through some early examples.

As we said earlier, Rabindranath Tagore's ancestors arrived in Calcutta at the start of the 18th century to officiate as priests for the fishing community. But they gave up priesthood once they learnt Farsi and English and could use this knowledge to become rich. Though they were Brahmins, they now started pursuing business interests, traditionally the preserve of Vaishyas. This was the kind of change that was taking place across society. The 1901 Census shows that of the 44,000 working Brahmins then living in Calcutta, only 10,700 followed the family occupation of priesthood. The rest were all otherwise engaged.

Radhakanta Deb was not only a non-Brahmin, he was not even a high-ranking Kayastha. But he and his father, Nabakrishna Deb, acquired immense wealth and as a result his social prestige rose sharply. He also earned the distinction of Sanskrit scholarship, which too had once been the preserve of Brahmins. Consequently, he became the uncrowned king of conservative Hindus in Calcutta in the 1820s. Even Brahmin scholars accepted his leadership in all social matters. He acquired this social position through two things—first, his status as an extremely rich zamindar, and second, his formidable education.

Ramdulal Dey was very poor and started his life as a junior employee of a rich man. Yet, he later became one of the pillars of society on the strength of the money that he made. Measured by the yardstick of caste, Motilal Sheel was a lower-rung Sudra. He came to be considered one of the richest men of Calcutta after having turned around his fortunes through trade and brokerage. His social status, accordingly, changed. Whatever his caste identity might have been, he now turned into a respectable man.

Apart from wealth, the other route to social prestige in the new age was education. That so many non-Brahmins, ranging from Ramkamal Sen and Ramgopal Ghosh to Digambar Mitra and Rajendralal Mitra, came to be regarded as respected members of society was because of their learning and their wealth. Ishwarchandra Vidyasagar, who had been born into an extremely poor family, was one of the most famous personalities of the 19th century. His Brahmin birth had not earned him this stature. He earned it through his learning and his wealth. There were at that time hundreds of thousands Brahmins in Bengali society who somehow eked out a living as priests and lived almost like beggars. Sudras who followed hereditary occupations could acquire neither education nor wealth, and they thus remained forever below the Brahmins, Baidyas and Kayasthas. But not at the very bottom of the heap. That was where the untouchables were.

One might have expected Muslims, on account of their professing an alien faith, to remain outside this hierarchical caste-divided society. Curiously, however, they also had a place assigned to them in this ladder-like social structure. From the Middle Ages until late into the 19th century, Muslims shared social space with low-caste Hindus, below the Brahmins, Baidyas and Kayasthas, just above the lowest rung. However, Muslims who were amirs/omrahs, zamindars and those who were wealthy enjoyed the same social status as the high-caste Hindus of the upper classes. There was of course no question of commensality between even these Muslims and Hindus.

There is evidence of some social mobility at this time among Muslims, too. Muslims who did not have the advantage of good birth also acquired social prestige through education and wealth in the new age. Nawab Abdul Latif of Faridpur and Sirajul Islam of Chittagong naturally come to mind. The Muslims whom I mentioned earlier as having graduated from Calcutta University all secured good jobs. And they, too, came by some social prestige through the money they earned.

Bengali Language, Literature and Music

Apart from the commodities and the European ways of thinking that the British brought with them, the other most remarkable imports that came with them were English language and literature. At a cursory glance, this had nothing to do with Bengali language and literature. Amazingly, however, this had its greatest impact on Bengali language and literature. In the 19th century, Bengali language, particularly Bengali prose, and Bengali literature went through a phase of unprecedented flowering. What historians call the Bengal Renaissance has very little resemblance with the Italian Renaissance. Yet, the explosion of creativity that we see taking place in language, literature and music in the period under discussion does recall the European Renaissance. The way in which the literature at this time moved away from gods/goddesses and pirs/dervishes to focus on the human situation also seems to be, quite emphatically, a Renaissance trait. We will discuss the unprecedented development of language and literature in a later chapter dealing with the subject, and music in a separate chapter.

***

BENGALI CULTURE IN THE TWENTIETH CENTURY

Bengali society was, until the 20th century, fundamentally rural, and lifestyles in villages were simple and basic. Changes in this settled way of life had crept up very slowly over the centuries, almost like imperceptible changes in nature itself, without anyone taking much notice. But change picked up pace, and quickly, in the 20th century. There were a number of factors that brought this about—population increase, reorganisation of the family, social mobility, the development of education and communication, and epoch-making political developments including the Partition of India. We will briefly pause to look at these factors.

Until the 19th century, epidemics such as cholera and pox outbreaks and a high rate of child mortality saw to it that the population in Bengal did not significantly increase. We know from the magazines published in the 1820s and the 1830s that cholera and pox wreaked havoc in those years and thousands died of these diseases. Malaria wiped out entire villages. The situation changed quite radically in the 20th century with the discovery of life-saving medicines. The use of quinine shot up in Bengal after Ronald Ross, working in Calcutta, discovered the cause of malaria in 1898. Tuberculosis lost its sting after penicillin was introduced in 1944. Antibiotics of the sulfa group, or sulfa drugs, were already in the market by then. In sum, the discovery of vaccines and life-saving medicines significantly pushed down the rate of mortality, especially child mortality. So the total population rose in the 20th century, and so did average life expectancy. Whereas in 1901 the population of Bengal was 42.10 million (4 crore and 21 lakh), the combined population of the two Bengals in 2001 was over 210 million (21 crore). The average life expectancy in 1901 was 35 years, whereas in 2001 it was over 60.

At the start of the 21st century, West Bengal and Bangladesh form the most densely populated area in the world. The population count per square mile was 2,341 in West Bengal and 2,480 in Bangladesh according to the 2001 Census in India and Bangladesh, respectively. This means that the land available for every person is just one-fourth of an acre. Life in Bengal had always been predominantly rural, rooted in the land and dependent on agriculture. But when the explosion in population started exerting an unprecedented pressure on the land, the very nature of the culture it supported started to change. People started leaving the countryside for the cities in large numbers, looking for alternative livelihoods. Thus the big cities became ever bigger, and the small towns and market centres grew into cities. The population increase also swelled the numbers of landless peasants and unskilled labourers. The impact largely shattered the cultural environment that educated and well-to-do householders had once created in the villages. Not only did large numbers of people stream out to the cities, they kept coming back to their families in their village homes, importing urban ingredients in clothes, festivals and lifestyles and thus imposing a made-up, imitative quality on rural culture. Those 'shaded abodes of peace, the tiny hamlets' ('*Chhaya shunibir shantir neerh chhoto chhoto gramguli*') of Tagore's *Dui Bigha Jomi* were in reality mostly gone.

Family structures also changed in the 20th century. As the Hindu middle classes grew in the first half of the century, the joint family establishment flourished. The example made the joint family somewhat popular among educated Muslims, too. So family sizes grew in the first half of the 20th century as a result of population increase and so did the tendency of families to stick together, with brothers and their children sharing the same roof. But the families steadily dwindled in size as the century rolled on. The joint families started breaking up as members left to pursue varied livelihoods, and gradually families became nuclear or spread out in extended set-ups. Birth control through contraception also gained fairly wide currency among educated urban families in the second half of the century. This, too, brought down family sizes. The breaking up of joint families and the migration of people from villages to cities to set up nuclear households weakened the old ties of kinship considerably. Many family values including those relating to child rearing began to change in the nuclear and extended families, which gradually replaced the old joint family system.

The role of the family in the cultural life of a society or nation cannot be stressed enough. It is through the family that some values and expectations are handed down from one generation to the next. In areas left untouched by school education, family and friends fill the gap. How to behave with one's elders, the position of women and men in society, the distribution of housework, the role of husbands and wives in making family decisions—in a word, patriarchal values and the differing social images of men and women belong to the realm of the educative role played by families. The position and status of women in society have vastly improved in comparison with the past. Yet, Bengali society and culture remain largely patriarchal. The greater Bengali society still expects women to stay in and raise children, cook meals and take care of the house. Women who lead traditional lives are regarded with admiration and approval.

As we have seen in the Chapter 'Bengali Culture under Western Impact', social status and position in the 19th century was largely dependent on birth. This changed quite drastically in the 20th century. At the end of the 20th century, wealth and education were enough to propel people to the top. On the other hand, high birth was not of much help in acquiring social prestige. Yet, in the matter of having an edge in competition, success in life still remains pretty much linked to the accident of birth. The ease with which the children of educated middle-class people can compete in the race for education and wealth is not available to the poor. The poor, indeed, often give up the fight thinking their destinies will not change. The changes in the yardsticks used to select brides/grooms reflect the extent to which familial status has lost importance. Whereas familial status was once the most crucial factor in these decisions, now the most important things to look at in the prospective groom are education and income. And though familial status still counts in the selection of brides, education and good looks are considered more valuable.

Though education in the 19th century was centred, spatially, in and around Calcutta and flourished mainly among high-caste Hindu males, in the 20th century it no longer remained confined to the big cities and among high-caste Hindus. It now spread among people of other castes and other religious persuasions. Even women's education flourished at this time. The 1901 Census shows that the percentage of the educated among the Baidyas was then 53. Among Hindus in general, on the other hand, the percentage was just 11. It was much lower, however, among Muslims and low-caste Hindus. As the century progressed, more and more schools were set up in the villages and towns, and colleges in the district headquarters. Consequently, well-to-do Muslims and low-caste Hindus had better access to education.

Along with education, communication showed extraordinary development. In keeping with the growing number of books and magazines in this century, the number of readers grew, too. Radio transmissions began from the third decade of the century. And cinema started its journey around the same time. The gramophone had appeared at the turn of the century. The television arrived in the 1960s. Roads and transport also improved significantly. The pace of urbanisation increased almost tenfold. Whereas in 1901 the number of city dwellers constituted 2.7 per cent of the total population of East Bengal, in 2000 the corresponding figure in Bangladesh was 27 per cent. In West Bengal, city dwellers make up 30 per cent of the population. Though Bangladesh and West Bengal are still fundamentally rural societies with economies based on agriculture, industrialisation has remarkably improved. Trade has improved as a result of urbanisation and industrialisation. The collective impact of these changes has produced far-reaching changes in the economy.

A more important change in Bengali society of the 20th century came through politics. The impact of politics was noticeable in every aspect of social life in this period—in everyday life, the family, marriage, interactions with women and with others in society. Social rules and customs, values, patriotism, religious conduct and practices, architecture, entertainment—politics spared nothing. In a word, the fast-paced change in Bengali society and culture can be reasonably described as a smallish revolution. The concept of what constitutes 'Bengaliness' also changed as a result of these profound and widespread changes.

The undivided Bengal that had taken shape gradually over five and a half centuries was at first temporarily and then permanently partitioned as a result of political influence. Bengali society had in any case been divided along the lines of religious identity. Politics reinforced that division and made it stronger.

With religious identity was now joined a spatial and regional dimension. The Bengali domination in pan-Indian politics and culture that had developed in the 19th century slowly weakened in the 20th century. A Bengal dominated by high-caste Hindus was once well known outside Bengal, but that social group rapidly lost its influence. Though there was no significant change among low-caste Hindus, Muslim society now shot ahead with the speed of a meteor.

Muslim Awakening and Separatism

We have noted before how Hindu awareness of the land and nation in the second half of the 19th century on the one hand channelised itself through the pan-Indian institution of the Indian National Congress, and on the other expressed itself through Hindu revivalism. Among Muslims, however, there was at that time no organised sense of nationhood because of the limited spread of education in the community. But around 1900, a minuscule section of the community began to display awareness of a distinct identity. Their minds were now exercised over identity-related questions such as whether they belonged to Bengal and whether Bengali was their mother tongue.

The colonial government, which was keen not to see a repeat of the 1857 uprising, had adopted the policy of 'divide and rule'. Hindus and Muslims, it was decided, should be played off against each other. So some extra opportunities and favours were reserved for Muslims in education and employment.

In that early phase, however, it was religious movements such as the Faraizi agitations and the Tariqa-e-Mohammadia that played the biggest role in developing Muslim awareness of a separate existence and identity. The limited development of education in the community in the last three decades of the 19th century also helped. The community also responded to the Hindu sense of nationhood and the revivalist movement. For instance, Muslims were not exactly pleased with the intense loathing for *jabans* evident in books and magazines from the third decade of the 19th century. The Muslim-bashing in Bankimchandra Chattopadhyay's novels in the second half of the century hurt the pride of Muslims and helped to stoke thoughts of separatism. This new awareness of difference led a section of Muslims to claim that they were a separate community.

There were also economic factors at work. Though Hindus and Muslims lived side by side, the Hindus, as landlords, moneylenders, traders and government employees, were the dominant section. Muslims had previously accepted this without demur. But feelings of mutual abhorrence began to crystallise between the two communities once Muslims started becoming aware of their own identity. One of the main reasons for the popularity of the Faraizi movement in East Bengal was the lowly position of Muslims in society and the exploitation of Muslim peasants by Hindu zamindars and mahajans (moneylenders). It was this economic disparity and exploitation that the Faraizis used to successfully unify Muslims in the countryside. That they also organised Muslim Identity on religious lines posed a challenge to communal harmony and goodwill.

These feelings of loathing and distrust between Hindus and Muslims found expression in many ways. For instance, Hindus have always celebrated festivals and religious events with singing and music. Muslims have been eating beef for ages, whether as sacrificial (*qurbani*) meat or otherwise. But riots did not always take place over the singing and music of Hindus or the beef-eating of Muslims. From the start of the twentieth century, however, both communities appeared to be in a sweat to assert their rights. Many Hindus started, quite unnecessarily, singing and playing musical instruments in the vicinity of mosques. And many Muslims began to flaunt their sacred duty to slaughter cows in public at the time of *qurbani*. It is hard to say whether the British rulers provided any active incitement to this sort of thing from a distance. But at least in the early phase they made no attempt to prevent communal riots.

In the context of the increasing communal bitterness, the most remarkable application of the colonial government's policy of dividing the two communities in order to rule with greater ease came at the beginning of the 20th century. On the pretext of introducing a more effective administration, the government at the start of 1904 announced the official decision to divide greater Bengal into separate provinces. The 15 Muslim-majority districts of East Bengal were to be added to Assam to form a new province. It was to be called East Bengal and Assam and its capital would be Dhaka. Hindu-majority western Bengal would remain linked with Bihar and Odisha.

Whatever might have been the apparent objective of the proposed division, its real aim was to thwart the influence of the Hindu bhadralok class. A nationalist leadership had begun to emerge in this section and it nurtured dreams of greater participation in governance. The government was keen to check its dominance in national politics. Chief Secretary to the Government of India Herbert Hope Risley in a secret memo explained the real objective of the division of Bengal: 'Bengal united is a power, Bengal divided will pull in several different ways... One of our main objects is to split up and thereby weaken a solid body of opponents to our rule.'

Many of the Hindus who occupied positions of political leadership were zamindars, big and small. And most of their ancestral homes and landed property were in East Bengal. It was also the main hinterland for businesses and industries based in Calcutta. Besides, most of the clients of the lawyer-politicians were from East Bengal. All these people feared a challenge to their own interests in the event of East Bengal becoming a separate province. Above all, the politicians anticipated the loss of their power and influence in a Muslim-majority province. They would be defeated by the Muslims in the Legislative Council of East Bengal and lose political clout in West Bengal to the Biharis and the Oriyas. This was the common apprehension that united liberal leaders like Surendranath Banerjea and extremist politicians like Bipin Chandra Pal.

Surendranath Banerjea

On the other side of the divide, many among the educated Muslims of East Bengal hoped to gain both politically and economically in the event of a new province being formed. Muslims would constitute 58 per cent of the population of the new province and would thus lead the Legislative Assembly on the basis of numerical majority. On the contrary, they would constitute 32 per cent of the population in undivided Bengal. They also expected, not unreasonably, to gain from the new economic opportunities that would be available in the new province.

People like Rabindranath Tagore, who chiefly served the arts, were not any less shaken by the partition proposal. They realised that despite the differences, Bengalis of the two communities had lived in close proximity for centuries and were, more or less, partners in a common cultural inheritance. But now the colonial government's partition proposal was about to carve up undivided Bengal. They apprehended that in the two Bengals divided on religious lines with Hindu and Muslim majorities, Bengali language and literature would also eventually evolve into two distinct entities—one with Hindu and the other with Muslim characteristics.

Soon after talk of the partition plan first started in 1903, discussions to prevent it got under way. In their efforts to organise agitations on the issue, Hindu politicians realised for the first time that they needed the cooperation of Muslims to succeed. But there had not developed any sort of dialogue or communication between the bhadralok class on the one hand and Muslims and low-caste Hindus on the other. It was not easy for them, therefore, to adopt a joint plan of action on the basis of discussions with Muslim leaders. There weren't too many Bengali-speaking Muslims in positions of leadership, either. In any case these leaders were not really close to the Muslim masses in the villages. Still, a number of meetings were held in 1904 with leaders like Abdul Rasul, Shamsul Huda and Serajul Islam.

Apart from the political initiative against the partition plan, there were cultural events such as the one in which Tagore tied rakhis on the hands of Muslim labourers and coolies on the streets. He even composed and sang, in the name of the motherland, songs calling for the unity of Hindus and Muslims. But the people whose hands the bhadraloks sought to tie rakhis on because of political expediency, or the people whom they sought to organise in order to carry out a political movement, could not fathom what was going on. It left them bemused and wondering. A Bengal divided or undivided—it made little difference to them. On the other hand, the bhadraloks who now on their own initiative extended a hand of friendship could not really welcome Muslims into their fold with any heartfelt sincerity. It did not take a poet like Tagore long to detect this poverty of honest feeling.

In order to pressure the colonial administration into dropping the partition plan, educated Hindus started the Swadeshi agitation, which was chiefly a movement to reject British commodities. Many symbolic actions, such as not buying British goods and even setting fire to them, were undertaken at this time. But such efforts saw only a limited success. For, the movement resulted in some commodities becoming costlier or rarely available. Most Muslims opposed it, and many Hindus found it hard to bear with the inconvenience. Consequently, the conflict between Hindus and Muslims bared its teeth as soon as the partition of Bengal came into effect in October 1905. The political conflict that commenced at this time was, indeed, quite without precedent.

That Muslims form a significant community in Bengal and that they are distinct from the Hindus is of course a very old truth. Yet, it was the partition of Bengal that first made this undeniably obvious. That their support, or lack of it, was a significant factor was for the first time appreciated by educated and Hindus in leadership positions. The surrealism in the situation is captured in an essay by Tagore where he describes a meeting. Hindu and Muslim leaders at the meeting were discussing ways to prevent the proposed partition when one of the Hindu leaders felt thirsty. His religious proscriptions, however, ruled out drinking water in the presence of Muslims in the room. The courteous thing to do would be for him to leave the room to quench his thirst, but he, instead, asked the Muslims in the room to leave. Tagore found this incident extremely distasteful. He also realised that if this was the way Hindus felt about Muslims, then the claims of brotherhood and common cause were meaningless and ridiculous. Thus, the differences between Hindus and Muslims became quite obvious. Moreover, for the first time, in 1906, political causes triggered a riot between Hindus and Muslims. These riots and extremist political programmes were so unsavoury that before long even the liberal Hindu politicians grew disenchanted with them. Surendranath Banerjea, therefore, met Lord Carmichael, along with Muslim leaders to discuss the situation. A disillusioned Tagore also retreated far from the world of politics.

Muslims and low-caste Hindus largely did not support the movement to prevent the partition of Bengal. Nawab Salimullah of Dhaka actually came out in support of the Governor of East Bengal Bamfield Fuller. He made serious efforts to reinforce the belief that partition would benefit Muslims. Some said he had been bribed by the colonial government. Whatever his motivation might have been, on the day that the partition of Bengal came into force, the Provincial Muslim Union was set up in Dhaka under his leadership. Its aim was to unify the Muslims of East Bengal and Assam and represent them in politics. This was the first political outfit of Bengal's Muslims. Salimullah did not stop at this. In December the following year, he called a conference in Dhaka of notable Muslim leaders from across India. The Muslim League was established at this conference. It can be said that it was the Muslim League's leadership that first lent an institutionalised character to Muslim separatism. In an irony of fate, a Hindu Sabha was set up in the same year in Lahore. This was the first of a series of Hindu Sabhas in north India dedicated to the social and material uplift of Hindus, which eventually led to the formation of the all-India Hindu Mahasabha in the early 1920s. This organisation, informed by an ideology of communal politics and Hindu nationalism, was a hard-line advocate of the partition of the country on communal lines.

Nawab Salimullah

The hope expressed by Nawab Salimullah, that Muslims would gain from partition might have been politically motivated, but it was not a misplaced one. Many government institutions centred in the new capital of Dhaka were set up. The city's population improved remarkably in the years following the partition. As shown by the statistics given below, the number of educated Muslims in Dhaka also grew.

Proportion of Educated Muslims in Dhaka

Year	Percentage of Muslims in population	Percentage of educated Muslims	D
1901	45.50	9	1.1
1911	43.50	13	4

Table 5.1 *Source - Census of India, 1901, Vol VIA, Pt. II & Census of India, 1911, Vol. 1, Pt. 1*

The number of students in the schools and colleges of Dhaka increased between 1901 and 1911. In sum, a section of Muslims started taking advantage of the opportunities available in the new capital and expected more in the future. Hence the educated Muslims of East Bengal saw the anti-partition movement of the bhadralok Hindus as being against their interests. In spite of Muslim support for partition, however, the colonial government in December 1911 announced its reversal in the face of the forceful opposition and displeasure of Hindu politicians. The following year the two Bengals were reunited. But the cracks that had opened up between the two communities over the partition do not seem to have closed.

Terrorist Movement for Freedom

There was another movement that crystallised during the anti-partition agitations—the terrorist movement for freedom. Many young men of the time felt that the Congress movement through constitutional means would not bring freedom to the country, or at least not any time in the near future. These youngsters set up an organisation called Anusheelan Samiti in 1905 under the leadership of Barindra Kumar Ghosh. The aim of this group was to free India from colonial rule through a terrorist movement. Barindra Kumar's plan was to carry out a terror campaign with arms imported with the help of the French based in Chandernagore (Chandannagar) and with bombs that the group hoped to make, and in this way to get the British out of the country. Neither he nor his followers at that time appreciated how unreal and impractical the plan was of a handful of activists throwing out the Brits! Nor did the people in general. But no matter how removed it was from reality, the movement filled educated Hindus with hope and enthusiasm. Admittedly, the movement had a powerfully communal character. Muslims

Left: Khudiram Bose; Right: Jatindranath Mukhopadhyay, popularly known as Bagha Jatin (i.e. Tiger Jatin)

never joined the movement or even lent it their support. Indeed, they could not even tolerate the '*Vande Mataram*' song. The terrorist youngsters, on the other hand, could not accept the Congress decision to sing only the first two lines of the song in deference to forceful objections raised by Muslims.

In 1908 Khudiram Basu and Prafulla Chaki were arrested while trying to make a terror strike on behalf of the Anusheelan group. A few years later, Bagha Jatin (Jatindranath Mukhopadhyay) became famous for his participation in the terror movement for freedom. On September 9, 1915, he and four of his fellow activists faced a police contingent in an encounter; the following day, he died in hospital. His courage and valour became the stuff of legend. Nine years later, Gopinath Saha tried to assassinate the Police Commissioner of Calcutta, Charles Tegart, but ended up killing, unwittingly, a white civilian.

The terrorist movement started by Barindra Kumar petered out within a few years. Notwithstanding the movement's failure, however, it served to encourage violent, extremist and to some extent communal politics, along with the interest and enthusiasm that it awakened in people's minds. The tendency persisted, side by side with constitutional politics, right up to the 1947 Partition. Even a national hero like Subhas Chandra Bose chose this path after having failed to make his way in politics through constitutional means. The underground communist movement that started in the 1920s was also terrorist in character.

Constitutional Politics

Greater participation in governance, and not freedom, was the aim of the Congress movement in the first two decades of the 20th century under the leadership of liberals like Surendranath Banerjea. They tried to achieve this objective by obtaining more seats in the Legislative Council and having the Council's powers increased. The colonial rulers did not cooperate. Rather, as the statistics given in the table below show, the constitutional reforms of 1909, 1919 and 1935 in a planned way condemned the bhadralok politicians into being a minority for ever.

Distribution of Seats in the Bengal Legislative Council

Year	Total Number of seats	Reserved for Muslims	Reserved for Non-Muslims	European Members	Total Number of Voters
1909	54	5	0	18	9,289
1919	119	39	46	22	10,21,418
1935	250	117	78	33	66,95,483

Table 5.2

There are more seats for the majority community in a democratic system, but there are no provisions for reserved seats or separate electorates. Yet, these were the steps that the government took for the majority Muslim community through the Morley Minto Reforms of 1909 to ensure that caste Hindus lost their grip on power. In a move to further clip the wings of the Hindu bhadralok, the Government of India Act of 1919 had provisions for reserving seats for the Namahsudras, or Dalits.

The government also cut into the influence of the bhadralok class by increasing the size of the electorate. As long as the electorate was small and the voters were mainly educated and urban, it was easy for bhadralok politicians to assert their authority and make their influence felt. But the electorate increased 110-fold in size after the 1919 constitutional reforms, and people of the lower castes and classes in the villages also had the franchise. A large section of this expanded electorate comprised Muslims and lower-caste Hindus. The 1935 reforms further increased the electorate six times. The bhadraloks had no real working relationship with this huge body of voters. They had no way open to them to extend their sway over this newly enfranchised population.

Another cause for disenchantment with constitutional politics was the limited powers of the Legislative Council. There were, it is true, political debates in the House, but the Council had no real authority. In response to widespread demands from the natives, the 1919 reforms gave some powers of governance to Indians through the method of diarchy or dual governance in the provinces. In this diarchal system, the most important functions including home and revenue remained directly under the British colonial masters. Education and some other functions were placed in partial control of the Legislative Council. Yet, Indians were in reality unable to use even these very limited powers that were given to them. The failure to actively participate in governance bred disillusion and despair in both the liberals and the nationalists. The liberals, in particular, lost credibility. In their place, nationalists like Bipin Chandra Pal, Byomkesh Chakraborty and Chittaranjan Das now gained popularity.

The influence that Bengalis once enjoyed in national politics started to gradually ebb away after the first partition of Bengal. From the second decade of the 20th century, non-Bengalis such as Mohandas Gandhi and Mohammad Ali Jinnah seized the reins of politics in the country. In the 1920s and 1930s, first Chittaranjan Das and then Subhas Chandra Bose momentarily shot into the firmament of national politics like comets and dazzled all eyes with their brilliance, only to disappear overnight, for ever. Besides, political methods popular in Bengal were not in sync with pan-Indian politics.

At the start of the 1920s, Gandhi also realised that nothing much could be achieved by way of greater participation in governance through agitations following constitutional means. He, therefore, chose the strategy of non-cooperation with the colonial administration in governance, in economic activities and even in institutions like schools and colleges. He called for the establishment of indigenous institutions and an alternative economy. But the nationalists of Bengal were not prepared to close the door of collaboration with the West or to desert schools and colleges to take exclusively to the spinning wheel. For, it was through such collaboration and these institutions that they had built up a well-endowed community and society. It was not easy for them to willingly retreat from that position of advantage. Tagore opposed Gandhi's programme of total non-cooperation. So did liberals like Surendranath Banerjea. Even Bengali nationalists including Chittaranjan Das initially ignored the call for non-cooperation.

Gandhi tried to reinforce the ties between Hindus and Muslims in order to strengthen the movement. In order to attract Muslims to his cause, he extended limited support to the regressive movement to retain the institution of Khilafat or Caliphate in faraway Turkey. He also demanded the inclusion of untouchables in the Hindu fold in order to secure their support. By thus linking faith with politics, he temporarily brought spirit and enthusiasm to politics. But though this produced instant gains, there was no long-term benefit. The consequence, instead, was a significant increase in communal tension and bickering. More importantly, communal politics eventually pushed the country towards partition.

The cooperation of Muslim leaders and liberals like Surendranath Banerjea, while the non-cooperation movement was under way, somewhat eased the pressure on the Bengal government. In this environment Chittaranjan Das realised that Swaraj would not be achieved through non-cooperation. He got together with a few national-level leaders of the Congress to set up the Swaraj Party as a sub-group within the Congress. This party won most of the Hindu seats in the election to the Legislative Council of Bengal in November 1923. Indeed, Chittaranjan even managed to secure the support of most of the Muslim members of the Council. A young Subhas Chandra Bose, brilliant and indomitable, was at his side at this time. Subhas had secured the fourth place in the Indian Civil Services examination but had forsaken government service to join politics.

Chittaranjan Das

Chittaranjan understood that after the Montagu-Chelmsford Reforms of 1919, it was no longer possible for any group to win power without the cooperation of Muslims. That is why, in December 1923, the month following the elections, he arrived at the 'Hindu-Muslim Pact' with Muslim leaders. This agreement provided for major concessions to Muslims, including 55 per cent reservation in jobs. Other sensitive matters, such as the promise to not oppose the sacrifice of cows during *qurbani* and to ensure that there was no provocative singing or music near mosques, were also included. But the pact never came into force as Chittaranjan did not get a chance to assume power.

Apart from the support of most of the Muslim members elected to the new Council in the 1923 elections, Chittaranjan also secured the support of 19 extremist Hindu members. He thus had the confidence of 65 members in a House of 139. As the leader of the largest group, he was invited by Governor Lytton in January 1924 to form the Ministry. But his chief demand was the introduction of self-governance to replace the system of diarchy, for, diarchy was in fact a perpetuation of British rule. Lytton was unable to accept this demand for a change in the method of governance because the Montagu-Chelmsford Reforms did not provide for self-governance. The Swaraj Party's opposition all but rendered diarchy dysfunctional, but it was unable to push through any reforms in the system.

All that the Swaraj Party was actually able to achieve was centred around the Calcutta Corporation. As its first elected Mayor, Chittaranjan in 1924 took some bold steps. He appointed Subhas Bose as his Chief Executive Officer. He appointed five other leaders from the group supporting him as aldermen and adopted khadi (hand-spun cloth) as the official wear of the Corporation's officers. He also renamed the streets of Calcutta after well known Indians. But the most important thing that he did was to appoint Muslims in a number of important posts. He appointed Hussain Shaheed Suhrawardy as Deputy Mayor, thus providing the basis for his later rise. Chittaranjan appointed another Muslim as the Joint Executive Officer, while Maulana Akram Khan was made an alderman. In this way Chittaranjan halted for a while the constantly growing trend of Hindu-Muslim animosities. But

Subhas Chandra Bose, who later took to armed struggle and formed the Azad Hind Fauz

before he could play any greater role in Bengal's politics, he died suddenly in June 1925 when he was only 55. Prospects of Hindu-Muslim unity were virtually wiped out as a consequence of this untimely death. Surendranath Banerjea's death shortly before had also considerably weakened the liberals.

The death of these two leading lights produced a crisis of leadership in Bengal. Subhas Bose was in jail at that time. In this environment, the politics of extremism, terror and communalism gained in strength. On one side of the divide, the Arya Samaj and the Hindu Mahasabha reared their heads. On the other side, Muslim nationalists backed by the colonial rulers started asserting their rights under the leadership of Sir Abdur Rahim. The colonial government instructed officials in the districts to indirectly help in the constitution of Muslim organisations and associations. A policy of reserving jobs for Muslims in proportion to their share in the population was also announced. Abdur Rahim benefited considerably from the support he got from the government. Besides, young Muslim leaders like his son-in-law Huseyn Shaheed Suhrawardy also clustered around him.

Rahim's push for job reservation for Muslims and the colonial government's decision to concede the demand changed the nature of Bengal's politics for ever. Muslim communal politics marked the beginning of the end for the social and political advantage that the Hindu bhadralok class had for so long enjoyed on the strength of wealth and higher education. Besides, the number of voters at the lower social levels had increased manifold with the constitution of the new Legislative Council. Political power, as a result, slipped out of the grip of a handful of people in the upper levels of society and started moving down to the greater masses. This was an extremely significant milestone in the politics of Bengal. Thereafter, Hindu and Muslim communal politics progressively gained in strength. Curiously, in the late 1920s and also in the 1930s, the Namahsudras (Dalits, later called the Scheduled Castes) joined hands with the Muslims. As a class they identified themselves more with Muslim peasants and labourers than with caste Hindus.

What Abdur Rahim and his followers attempted by way of a specific political programme, consisted in nurturing the interests of Muslims and cutting into the political and social clout of the Hindu bhadralok class. He sought to achieve this objective by mobilising ordinary rural Muslims and by securing the support of Hindus of the lower castes. The Hindu-Muslim riots of April, May and August in 1926 helped his efforts by uniting the Muslims. The allegations that Suhrawardy mobilised Muslims for these riots were not backed by any clear evidence. Over a hundred people were killed and over a thousand were injured. The apparent cause for these riots was the playing of music in a political procession by Hindus while walking past a mosque. Whatever might have been the direct trigger, it goes without saying that communally motivated leaders, both Hindus and Muslims, had stoked the feelings of anger that led to the violence. The rejection of the Hindu-Muslim Pact at the 1926 Krishnanagore session of the Bengal Congress should be noted as marking a significant change in political thinking. Though this symbolic pact had never even come into force, its abrogation showed that Congress leaders were no longer able to tolerate even the idea of Hindu-Muslim unity.

In the elections held at the end of 1926, candidates of Abdur Rahim's party (Bengal Muslim Party) won 38 of the 39 Muslim seats. Kazi Nazrul Islam was then a very popular poet, and his was a loud and clear message of revolution for peasants and workers. Yet he failed to win in the election, which he had contested from Muslim-majority Faridpur. The reason was that he could not follow the communal agenda of Abdur Rahim. Meanwhile, government-nominated and private English members assured Rahim of full support in the Legislative Council. In this way, Muslim domination was on the rise, not just in the Legislative Council but in the Calcutta Corporation, the district boards and the local councils. The history of Bengal politics in the next 20 years is the history of extremism and communalism. Power moved out of the hands of the Hindus at this time into those of Muslims. And the Hindus did not get it back until the 1947 Partition. Their despair at this loss of power grew to an extent that instead of opposing the division of the country they actually welcomed it.

In order to reinforce the domination of Muslims and low-caste Hindus in politics, the government granted them a number of well-planned-out concessions. The Muslim and low-caste Hindu members of the Legislative Council themselves passed a number of laws designed to appeal to voters. Among these were laws to protect the interests of sharecroppers, bring down the steep rates of interest charged by moneylenders, and control microfinance in the countryside. A committee was formed in the Legislative Council to devise ways to abolish the Permanent Settlement and thus do away with the zamindari system, which had been the base for the rise of the Hindu bhadralok class. These new laws and moves went directly against the interests of Hindu zamindars and mahajans (moneylenders). They benefited Muslim and low-caste Hindu peasants and workers in some measure. Hindu members of the Council, therefore, expressed forceful opposition to these legislative moves. The proposal for job reservation for Muslims on the basis of population share that was placed in the Legislative Council was totally unacceptable to educated Hindus.

Thus, it became almost impossible for caste Hindus to play any meaningful role in the Muslim-dominated Legislative Council. Terrorist politics reared its head again in Bengal at this time. This violent stream of politics achieved its most spectacular success in the armed raid on the Chittagong armoury and the assassination of three district magistrates, one after the other, in Midnapore. Though the bhadralok class supported the civil disobedience movement led by Gandhi in 1930, it did not accept the ideal of non-violence and instead made emotional investments in the politics of violence. So inspired was this section, in fact, by violent political methods that when in 1932 Gandhi rejected the call for violent non-cooperation, Subhas Bose responded with sharp and strong criticism.

Meanwhile, civil disobedience and violent strikes were increasingly making effective administration difficult. The government responded on the one hand by incarcerating 10,000 Hindu youngsters and, on the other, by granting more concessions to Muslims, low-caste Hindus and European members of the legislative councils through the Communal Award of 1932. It was decided that in the Legislative Council of Bengal, 48.4 per cent of the seats would be reserved for Muslims, 39.2 per cent for Hindus and 10 per cent for Europeans. Ten of the Hindu seats were reserved for the lower castes. The caste Hindus, consequently, anticipated disaster. Gandhi started a fast-unto-death in protest against the move to constitutionally separate caste Hindus from the lower castes. Finally, under the Poona Pact, low-caste Hindus, described as the 'Depressed Classes' in the agreement, gave up the demand for separate electorates and seats were reserved for them within the Hindu quota.

Towards Partition

In the context of the Communal Award and the Poona Pact, the government introduced constitutional reforms for the third time through the Government of India Act, 1935. These reforms reserved 119 of the 250 seats in the Legislative Council for Muslims; 30 for low-caste Hindus; and 25 for Europeans. Only 58 seats were reserved for caste Hindus. The number of voters was increased, and it was now six times that in 1919. Among the newly enfranchised, too, there were more Muslims than Hindus. Low-caste Hindus also emerged as a political force at this time. In consequence, gradually but surely, the domination of the Hindu bhadralok in Bengal politics was destroyed forever. A significant example of this diminishing prowess was provided by the Calcutta Corporation elections in 1935. For the first time a Muslim was elected the Mayor of Calcutta—Fazlul Huq.

The communal movement that Abdur Rahim had started some years earlier received institutional recognition through the reforms of 1935. Still, even with separate electorates, a purely communal agenda was not enough for winning the election. In the elections that were held in January 1937, therefore, all parties tried to secure the support of the lower classes. Fazlul Huq turned out to be the most successful in this endeavour. He was Bengali-speaking and came from a rural background, whereas most of the other Muslim leaders were Urdu-speaking and city dwellers. They were also, besides, all zamindars, big or small. Fazlul Huq, therefore, had a special appeal for ordinary Muslims. It

A.K. Fazlul Huq, popularly known as Sher-e-Bangla

was this appeal that he capitalised on when he contested the elections in the name of the Krishak Praja Party. His party did not have an organisational structure across the province that could be compared to the Muslim League's. Yet it won in 34 seats. Even the former minister and Legislative Council member Khwaja Nazimuddin was defeated by him.

Fazlul Huq became the Prime Minister with the support of the Muslim League and the Namahsudras, the Europeans and some caste Hindus in the Council. But he was forced to compromise on quite a few things. Not pleased with this, the Krishak Praja Party members and the low-caste Hindus at once started putting pressure on him to pass laws favouring the lower classes. One by one, he tried to pass laws to reduce the burden of revenue and loans on peasants, initiate land reforms, bring in educational reforms in schools and universities and introduce municipal reforms in the Calcutta Corporation. But as the leader of varied interest groups, he tried to adopt a median position while introducing new legislation. Consequently, he could please no one, neither his own Krishak Praja Party nor the low-caste Hindus. Within a year, therefore, half of the Krishak Praja Party members and the low-caste Hindus withdrew their support. To hold on to power, he joined the Muslim League again at Muhammad Ali Jinnah's invitation. He also became a bit too dependent on the support of the European members.

All caste Hindus, and not just hard-line communal leaders like Syama Prasad Mookerjee, expressed apprehensions at the increasing clout of Muslims. In particular, there were some developments in the field of education which could not but aggrieve them. For instance, Calcutta University, which had always been controlled by Hindus, got Muslim vice-chancellors in 1930 and 1938. Even the university logo was changed because the old one carried Hindu associations. There were changes in the textbooks which Hindu leaders described as Islamic. Far more significant, however, was the recommendation to entrust the responsibility of conducting admission tests to an elected education board. Most of the members in the committee set up for this were Muslims and low-caste Hindus. It was not easy for caste Hindus to accept these changes. Even the patriotic scientist Prafulla Chandra Ray criticised the move in hard-hitting language. The protests notwithstanding, in August 1940, the Education Reform Bill proposing the above-mentioned changes was placed in the Legislative Council. It was also in that month that riots between Hindu and Muslim mobs started in Calcutta and went on for 10 months. The caste Hindus were also unable to accept the Bill on primary education brought by the Fazlul Huq government. They felt that making primary education compulsory would make the 'small people' too big for their boots and consequently diminish their own sphere of influence.

Muhammad Ali Jinnah got Fazlul Huq to propose the Pakistan Resolution at the Lahore session of the Muslim League in 1940. But Fazlul Huq, keen though he was to protect the interest of Muslims, did not particularly want to be seen as a communal leader. He also feared that low-caste and caste Hindu members might get together to remove him from power if he was perceived as protecting the interests of only the Muslims. He was, hence, obliged to make compromises all the time. Staying on in power was extremely important to him, and he thought nothing of repeatedly changing party loyalties to ensure that he did. He now left the Muslim League, complaining that Jinnah was meddling too much in provincial politics. Once again he formed a coalition with the Krishak Praja Party and a group representing the Topshili caste. Incredibly, he went to the extent of appointing Syama Prasad Mookerjee as his finance minister in December 1941. But Mookerjee left the coalition soon after, and once again Fazlul Huq found himself adrift in the powerful tide of Muslim nationalism under the League's leadership. Unable to resist that tide, Huq tried to return to the Muslim League and thus hang on to power. But the League did not welcome him back.

Nazimuddin of the Muslim League replaced Fazlul Huq as Prime Minister in 1943. Soon afterwards, Governor's Rule was declared in Bengal. After fresh elections were held in 1946, Huseyn Shaheed Suhrawardy was the new Prime Minister on behalf of the Muslim League. The two most remarkable things that happened under the watch of the Muslim League were, first, the famine of 1943, and second, riots on an unprecedented scale.

During the Second World War, the Japanese armed forces came knocking at India's doors in 1942-43 through Burma in the north-east. They were able to throw some bombs over even Calcutta. Subhas Bose's Azad Hind Fauj, too, advanced up to Manipur with help from Japan and Germany. Rice imports from Burma had to be stopped in this environment. In a move to prevent the Japanese army and the Azad Hind Fauj from taking advantage of the country's communication system and its food stocks even if they managed to enter Indian territory, the government had bought up huge amounts of rice and confiscated boats. The previous year Bengal had not had a good crop because of climatic conditions. More disastrously, despite the war effort the government had not kept any account of whether there was enough foodgrain in the province. As the supply of rice dwindled and prices shot up, traders started hoarding it. The rice stored in government granaries could not be distributed when it was most needed because there were not enough boats. In this way was caused a terrible man-made famine. One and a half million people died in it, according to official count. The unofficial count was three and a half million. There had not been a famine on this scale in 170 years.

The economic disparities between the rich and the poor and between the city-dwelling bhadralok and villagers became quite obvious during the famine. Thousands died on the streets of Calcutta while begging for rice starch. In this situation one section made quick profits and grew rich overnight.

With low-caste Hindus making common cause with Muslims, the Congress had in any case been made rather weak. Worse, it suffered from a crisis of leadership and internal bickering. Through the 1930s, the provincial Congress did not have any major leader to speak of. Subhas Bose was unable to play any very significant role in running the provincial Congress, partly because he was locked up in jail for much of the time and partly because of his conflict with Gandhi. Despite being twice elected as the national president of the Congress, opposition from Gandhi forced him to quit the party. In 1941 he started nurturing dreams of freeing India from her chains through violent means and by joining up with Japan and Nazi Germany.

Meanwhile, the Congress still had a strong appeal for the Hindu bhadralok, what though the party had no major leader in Bengal, and despite leaders from the province being unable to play a major role in the freedom movement. Congress politics, especially Gandhi's Quit India Movement of 1942, was still very popular. The movement also put the colonial government, caught up as it was in the war effort, in a spot. Consequently, at the end of

1942 Sir Stafford Cripps led a mission to India to work out a formula for the freedom question. But the talks did not yield a solution. The Cabinet Mission came in May 1946. The British government did not want a division of the country. But in order to grant Muslims greater political power, the Cabinet Mission proposed dividing the provinces into three groups in a united dominion, with the right to secede. The Muslim majority provinces to the east and the west would be bunched into two separate groups, while the Hindu-majority provinces would form another group. Apart from defence, foreign affairs and communications, which would be under the Union, the groups would manage all their own affairs. The Muslim League did not accept this, nor did Congress president Jawaharlal Nehru.

In its attempt to make partition inevitable, the Muslim League now called on Muslims to observe Direct Action Day on August 16 that year. The Prime Minister of Bengal, Huseyn Shaheed Suhrawardy, declared a government holiday on that day, so that the ordinary people could take part in this programme. There have been allegations that he organised Muslims to participate in riots. As the Home Minister, he was present that day at the police headquarters at Lalbazar in Calcutta. But it is not clear how hard he tried to stop the riots. If he did try, it must be said that he was not up to the job. Over four days following August 16, between 5,000 and 10,000 people, Hindus and Muslims, died in rioting in Calcutta. The violence also spread to other parts of the province, including Noakhali. Apart from the loss of lives in these riots, thousands of people were injured, women were raped and homes were plundered and burnt. The violence made it clear that Hindus and Muslims were no longer able to live side by side.

Hucoyn Shahood Suhrawardy

When the grant of Independence became inevitable after Clement Atlee became the Prime Minister of Britain in 1946, Jawaharlal Nehru and the Congress leaders of Bengal supported the idea of partitioning Bengal.

Even Gandhi, under the circumstances, accepted the proposal. The Hindu Mahasabha had already, a few years earlier, made a forceful demand for carving up Bengal. Only a handful of Hindu leaders such as Sarat Bose and Kironshankar Ray were in favour of undivided Bengal.

In an irony of history, Muslim leaders at this time demanded an undivided Bengal. In 1905, they had, as a weak group, supported partition. They were then far behind Hindus in both education and wealth. In the next 40 years, they took advantage of the colonial government's constitutional reforms motivated by the policy of 'divide and rule' to emerge as the majority presence in the province's politics. It would not be far wrong to say that the British led them by the hand to their newfound clout and political power. And it so boosted their confidence that they now demanded an undivided Bengal rather than a partitioned one. For, even in an undivided Bengal, in a democratic set-up they would, as the majority community, dominate the Hindus. Even Suhrawardy, who had sought to prove that it was impossible for Hindus and Muslims to live together, now expressed his support for undivided Bengal.

True, on the eve of Partition it was their own interests as a community that the Hindu leaders thought of more than anything else. But their contribution in the struggle for freedom had been invaluable. In a way it was the pressure of their movements for Swaraj and freedom that made the British government eventually accept the demand for independence. The Muslim League's politics did not traverse this path. The Muslim leaders were not quite as active and vocal about securing independence or Swaraj for the country as they were about seizing their share of power from the Hindus. And they had no compunctions about cosying up to the colonial rulers in order to get what they wanted. In other words, freedom arrived as a result of the movement carried out by the Congress; the Muslim League's contribution to it was extremely limited. What the Muslim League did was to wage a struggle for an independent homeland for Muslims in free India, that is, a struggle to secure the Muslim share of power.

Muslim Awakening

Despite burgeoning Muslim awareness about education and employment in the 1890s, curiously enough, educated Muslims occupying leadership positions in society still demanded a *maktab*-madrasa system of instruction for their children, rather than a general one. That is, they were asking for an Islamic education. The standard of education at *maktab*s (primary-level schools) and madrasas (secondary and higher-level schools) at that time was extremely poor. A contemporary report on education tells us that primary school students of the time could write letters and do basic sums. Students of *maktab*s, however, did not quite learn enough to write a letter or to do sums. Notwithstanding some awareness, therefore, Muslims were not yet trying to move towards a modern world view by following a mainstream education.

In the first two or three decades of the 20th century, however, the government took a few small steps to push Muslim society towards progressiveness. For instance, the number of Muslim appointments in the education department went up a little at this time. Some extra funds were also allocated for the *maktab*s and madrasas. In the 1920s, Muslims were made education ministers so that they would take a personal interest and initiative in the development of education among Muslims. Yet, there was no remarkable improvement in the condition of Muslims in the first part of the 20th century. The reason was that there was as yet no awareness about the situation among the huge population of Muslims in the villages. Even if any of them did acquire some awareness, they could not afford to educate their children in city schools that offered an English education. Moreover, many among them had chosen a suicidal regressiveness. For instance, they did not gladly accept Bengali as their mother tongue and were not even keen to study Bengali. Muslims, in fact, opposed Calcutta University's decision in 1922 to make Bengali the medium of instruction. This would still be understandable if only the non-Bengali city-dwelling Muslims had opposed the move. Surprisingly, however, even Bengali-speaking Muslim leaders were not in favour of Bengali as the medium of education. Instead, we see Fazlul Huq, at the Legislative Council in 1922, strongly opposing the move to make Bengali the medium of education. It was at his behest that a few months later a resolution was passed, at a students' meeting at Calcutta's Muslim Institute, against the move.

Fazlul Huq was not an educationist. His position, however unwarranted, is therefore understandable. But the educationist Sir Abdur Rahim also supported this position. He asserted at the Legislative Council in 1926 that making Bengali the medium of instruction would be catastrophic for Muslims. Not only the Muslim members of the Legislative Council, even many among the general educated Muslims at that time felt that Bengali was not quite as much a Muslim language as it was a Hindu one. So Muslims, they believed, would not benefit as much as Hindus would if Bengali was made the medium of instruction.

That Muslims lagged behind in the pursuit of Bengali might also have generated a sort of inferiority complex in them. They probably feared that they would not be able to compete with Hindus if Bengali was the medium of learning. This may have led them to believe that they would be better positioned to protect their interests if they could establish themselves as a community that spoke a different language. The table below makes it clear just how far behind Hindus the Muslims were in education, owing to the absence of a tradition of schooling, lack of awareness, poverty, and also their geographical distance from the capital.

A comparative count of the percentages of educated Hindus and Muslims, 1901

Districts	Hindu				Muslim			
	Educated		English Educated		Educated		English Educated	
	Male	Female	Male	Female	Male	Female	Male	Female
Calcutta, Howrah, Hooghly, 24 Paraganas, Midnapore, Burdwan, Murshidabad, Nadia	21.8	1.4	3.3	0.5	9.7	0.4	0.85	0.01
Dinajpur, Rangpur, Bogra, Rajshahi, Pabna, Mymensingh, Dhaka, Faridpur, Barishal, Comilla, Noakhali, Khulna, Jessore	18.4	1.2	1.09	0.02	6.1	0.15	0.16	0.001

Table 5.3 *Source: Report on the Census of India,1901, Vol VIA, Pt.II (Calcutta: Bengal Secreteriat Press, 1903), pp. 54-76*

The statistics show that western Bengal retained its edge on account of better physical access to Calcutta, where education started developing from the beginning of the 19th century, right up to the end of that century. This applied to Hindus, too. So it is not hard to imagine how handicapped Muslims would have found themselves, especially in the matter of higher education. The Calcutta University statistics given in the table below also clearly shows this.

Hindus and Muslims in higher education: number of graduates in Calcutta University, 1857-1901

Religion/Caste	% of Total Population	B.A. Number/%	M.A. Number/%	B.L. Number/%	M.B. Number/%	B.E. Number/%
Muslims	52	338 (4.50%)	45 (2.80%)	116 (3.10%)	2 (1.10%)	0 (0%)
Hindu	Two Selected Surnames					
Bandyopadhyay	< 1%	422 (5.70%)	104 (6.60%)	231 (6.60%)	9 (4.40%)	3 (5.80%)
Mukhopadhyay	< 1%	518 (7%)	125 (8%)	283 (7.60%)	11 (6%)	6 (10.70%)

Table 5.4 *Source: Calcutta University Calendar, 1901*

While analysing these statistics, it should be borne in mind that a majority of the Muslim graduates were not Bengali-speaking and did not even live in Bengal. This was because the geographical limits of Calcutta University then extended as far as the Punjab. On the other side, caste Hindus accounted for just 5 per cent of the population of Bengal. And the Bandyopadhyays and Mukhopadhyays among them numbered less than 1 per cent. Yet the Bandyopadhyays and Mukhopadhyays among the graduates made up 13 per cent of the successful candidates. This scale of disparity applied not just to the evaluation for the Bachelor of Arts degree but to all examinations.

Though the number of Muslim students in Calcutta University started rising a little in the last decade of the 19th century, Muslims fared comparatively better in education in Dhaka. Muslim leaders had been aggrieved at the 1911 declaration of reversal of the partition of Bengal. Their confidence in the colonial government was also considerably shaken. In order to mollify these indignant Muslims, the government announced in 1912 that a university would be established in Dhaka. It took another nine years for the university to be established. Once it was established, however, it was easier for well-to-do Muslims in East Bengal to acquire an education in Dhaka, which was nearer home, rather than in far-off Calcutta. This had quite a dramatic impact on lower middle class Muslims dependent on land. Some people also say that the increased demand for jute after the First World War also helped Muslim agriculturalists, who now came into a lot of ready cash.

The number of educated Bengali-speaking Muslims now grew. In the realm of thoughts, too, a remarkable progress was noticeable for the first time. Just as in the third and fourth decades of the 19th century, the young men of Calcutta displayed a tendency to brush aside conservatism and move ahead, the same trend was now visible, almost a century later, among Muslim youngsters centred in Dhaka. The 'Buddhir Mukti Andolan', or the movement to free up the intellect, was started at the initiative of Dhaka University students in 1926. Qazi Abdul Odud, Abul Hossein, Qazi Motahar Hossein, Abul Fazl and Motahar Hossein Chaudhury participated in the movement.

Just as the Young Bengal group tried to influence society by expressing their thoughts in magazines and journals in the 1830s, members of the Buddhir Mukti Andolan came out with the magazine *Shikha* (Flame) in Dhaka in 1926. Many of the Muslim writers, professors and intellectuals who earned a name for themselves in the next two decades had either actively participated in this movement or had been influenced by it. An important way in which these young men differed from the Young Bengal group was that the Western influence in the lifestyles of the latter had been quite excessive. Members of the Young Bengal group imitated the British in their clothes, language, conduct and even in their eating and drinking habits. But the Buddhir Mukti Andolan members were not much into imitating the West. One reason could be that by this time, an anti-British and anti-West mentality had taken root under the impact of the freedom movement, and a sense of nationhood had grown. So while these young people grew out of orthodox ways of thinking, they did not become Westernised.

Another important way in which the Young Bengal was different from the members of the *Shikha* group was that the former had declared a veritable jihad against their inherited religion. Some of them became Christians and they publicly opposed religious rules and regulations. But the *Shikha* group youngsters did not do that. Muslim society might have lacked the cultural environment that would make this possible, or perhaps they did not have the courage to do it. Besides, though they were influenced by rational thought, they did not have any doubt about their own religious identity. They seem to have nursed dreams of social reform while remaining very much a part of their own society. They, however, did not think it necessary to cling to values that they felt contradicted the exercise of free intellect. That is why they criticised any Islamic thinking that they found regressive. Qazi Abdul Odud, for instance, wrote that though the founder of Islam may have expressed extremely progressive thoughts 1,400 years ago, those thoughts may not fulfil the needs of people belonging to an age that was yet to arrive.

There was one remarkable way in which the Buddhir Mukti people differed from the generation immediately preceding them, and this was on the question of identity. The previous generation harboured doubts and contradictions on whether Bengali was the mother tongue of Bengali Muslims and whether they were Bengalis at all. Not so the young men of the *Shikha* group. They accepted Bengali as their language and Bengal, rather than Arabia or Iran, as their own land.

Another 15 to 20 years later, they welcomed the decision to partition Bengal on the basis of the two-nation theory. Indeed, there were few Bengali Muslims who did not welcome Pakistan or who did not move from Calcutta to East Bengal. The most well known among the few exceptions were Humayun Kabir and Qazi Abdul Odud. Kazi Nazrul Islam was healthy and writing until about a year after the Pakistan Resolution was accepted. In an editorial titled 'Pakistan, Na Fankistan' (Pakistan, or an illusion?) that he wrote during this phase, he opposed the prospect of another partition of Bengal that now loomed over the horizon. Abul Fazl, on the other hand, wrote a book praising the Quaid-e-Azam.

Those educated young Muslims who were not directly linked with the Buddhir Mukti Andolan but were rather known as nationalists did not just stop at demanding a separate homeland for Muslims. They also demanded that a different kind of Bengali should be developed for the Muslims of East Pakistan. Abdul Mansur Ahmed, Syed Sajjad Hussein and Syed Ali Ahsan were among those who belonged to this category.

Admittedly, it was not just through the route of education that separatism found a strong foothold among Muslims. The taste of political power was one of the chief causes of separatism. We have noted that from 1937, Fazlul Huq, Khwaja Nazimuddin and Huseyn Shaheed Suhrawardy became, one after the other, the Prime Minister of Bengal. This helped to boundlessly boost the self-confidence of Muslims. At the same time, it produced exasperation and disenchantment among Hindus. Until then, it was not numbers but merit that determined political dominance. From this time on, numbers replaced merit as the new yardstick. And the Hindus had no choice but to accept it.

Evolution of the Identity and Culture of Bengali Muslims

Only a minuscule proportion of Bengali Muslims, as we have noted before, were descendants of people who had come from foreign lands. Most of those who had arrived in Bengal in the Middle Ages and settled down permanently had married local women. Their offspring became Bengali within a few generations. There still remained, however, a tiny group among Muslims who could never accept Bengali as their own. Nor could they accept Bengal as the land to which they belonged. The percentage of such people became clear in the 1872 Census.

Statistics of Muslims claimed to have been abroad, 1872

Division	Muslim Population	Population of Muslims who have been abroad	Percentage
Burdwan	9,29,391	21,882	2.35
Presidency	31,57,026	80,828	2.56
Rajshahi	54,20,960	69,729	1.28
Dhaka	56,27,522	88,676	1.57
Chittagong	23,23,008	5,025	0.21
Bengal	1,74,57,907	2,66,136	1.52

Table 5.5 *Source: Rafiuddin Ahmed,* The Bengal Muslims 1871-1906: A Quest for Identity

These people lived in the city, talked in Urdu and claimed themselves to be *ashraf* or aristocratic. On the other hand, 98 per cent of Muslims lived in the villages, spoke Bengali and depended on the land for their livelihood. Many of them were also weavers (*jola*), tailors (*darji*), home-builders (*gharami*) and butchers (*kasai*). The *ashraf* regarded the rural Muslims as a blanket category of *atraf* or low-class Muslims and held them in contempt. These two distinct communities were also geographically separated. Most of the Urdu-speaking Muslims lived in western Bengal, while the Bengali-speaking ones lived in East Bengal. Non-Bengali Muslims also differed from the Bengali Muslims in matters of education and wealth. The former far outstripped the latter in both.

When Bengali-speaking Muslims came forward to acquire an education towards the end of the 19th century, their minds threw up many questions regarding their education and their identity. The ideal that they had before them was that of the educated Muslim elite who spoke Urdu. Even the Bengali-speaking Nawab Abdul Latif was constrained to disown Bengali and accept Urdu as his language in order to stake claim to an elite status.

As we noted before, Urdu, Farsi and Arabic had acquired such strong religious associations that even at the start of the 20th century educated Muslims did not consider a mainstream education to be relevant to their situation. Indeed, Bengali was not even taught as a subject in the *maktab*s and madrasas. The mullahs and the maulvis were the group most virulently opposed to Bengali. They had issued fatwas describing Bengali as 'Kufuri Jaban', or the language of kaffirs. Their opposition to Bengali was partly motivated by the intention of protecting their business interests and their social clout by using their knowledge of Arabic, Farsi and Urdu. The books written in Bengali that were available then and used as textbooks in schools and colleges were also partly responsible for the way they felt about the language. These books sported an excessive use of Puranic stories and Sanskrit words. The communal animosity that the Hindu writers of those days displayed towards Muslims made the ordinary, educated members of the community resentful of Bengali language and literature.

Grierson has remarked in his scholarly discussion on philology that the language of rural Hindus and Muslims of the lower classes might show some regional variations in dialect but was basically the same, apart from the use of some religious words. Differences, however, were quite noticeable in the language used by educated people. This had two broad categories—the Bengali of pandits and Muslim Bengali. According to Grierson, the Bengali of pandits abounds in the use of Sanskrit words, whereas Muslim manuscripts are liberally strewn with Arabic, Farsi and Urdu words. The colonial government tried to use this difference to reinforce its 'divide and rule' policy. At the start of the 20th century, therefore, the Bengal government recommended the teaching of 'Muslim Bangla' at *maktab*s and madrasas instead of the language in general use.

Despite this hostility to Bengali, many educated Muslims at the beginning of the 20th century appreciated the need to learn the language. They realized that without Bengali as the medium of instruction, the spread of education on a mass scale would not happen among Muslims. Out of this awareness grew a debate on whether Bengali was the mother tongue of Muslims, right at the start of the century. One of the earliest known instances is an essay titled 'Controversy' (*Bibad*) published in *Pracharak* magazine in 1900:

> It is inconceivable to think that the land in which we have lived for a thousand years through its winters, summers, its good times, bad times and famines, and whose wealth, joys and sorrows we have experienced in equal measure, is not our own and that we have a homeland somewhere beyond this one.

Three years later, *Noor-al-Iman* and *Nabanur* magazines published strongly worded remarks in favour of Bengali. *Nabanur* said: What but Bengali can the language of Bengali Muslims be? Those who seek to impose Urdu as the mother tongue of Bengali Muslims and thus obtain a single mother language for Muslims across India are only straining after the unattainable.

Noor-al-Iman appealed to Muslims to give up this wild goose chase and take more realistic measures: 'Instead of detesting Bengali as the language of Hindus, adapt it according to your situation and the times.' Around the same time, *Islam Pracharak* magazine played advocate for Bengali in even more hard-hitting language, though there are enough indications that even at this time there was fierce opposition to Bengali from several quarters. What Hamed Ali wrote in *Basana* magazine in 1909 deserves mention in this context:

> Wherever our forefathers may have come from, whether Arabia, Persia, Afghanistan or Tartar land, or even if they were indigenous Hindus, we are now Bengalis—and Bengali is our mother tongue.... What is stranger and more lamentable if we cannot accept as our own the land where we have been living for seven hundred years? ... The delusion persists for many of us. They might go to sleep in twig huts in the midst of Bengal's bamboo groves and mango orchards, yet it is Baghdad, Bokhara, Kabul and Kandahar that they dream of. And then there are those who are lost in the illusion of Urdu replacing Bengali as the mother tongue.

Syed Emdad Ali was one of the chief Muslim writers of the time. His point of view was also progressive. He, too, wrote of this same delusion in 1918: 'There should be no two opinions about the fact that Bengali is the mother tongue of Bengali Muslims.' Maulana Akram Khan also played a significant role in this debate. The language of his presidential address at the Bengal Muslim Literary Meeting (Bongiyo Musalman Sahitya Sammilan) in 1918 was forthright and hard-hitting: 'There are so many strange questions that are asked in the world. None more outlandish than this one: What is the mother tongue of Bengali Muslims? Urdu or Bengali?' Sheikh Abdul Gafur Jalali and Muhammad Shahidullah also spoke up in favour of Bengali around the same time. Such writings suggest a gradually growing popular opinion within Muslim society in favour of Bengali. But, as we have already noted, the opposition to Bengali at this time was also quite clear in the way a Bengali-speaking politician like Fazlul Huq played an active role in favour of Urdu being taught and against making Bengali the medium of instruction. But it was Bengali that finally carried the day in the debate concerning the Bengali language in Muslim society.

At the end of it all, Bengali Muslims not only accepted Bengali as their mother tongue, they also seemed to love and cherish it more than ever before. A piece by Mohammad Lutfur Rahman shows the nature and depth of this attachment: I might be reduced to begging on the streets, I do not even mind being shattered by the weight of sorrows and tears. I may be an orphaned, motherless boy, but I cannot forsake my ultimate possession, my language. Do not rob me of my all by stealing my language from me.

A deep and unequivocal love for the language is also evident in a piece by Nurunnessa Bidyabinod:

> We must always bear this in our minds that we have a greater claim on the word 'Bengali' than our Hindu neighbours. Which is to say that as we are a couple of steps ahead of the Hindus in our Bengali identity. ...If after having lived for ages within the boundaries of Bengal and having expressed our thoughts and feelings all the time in the Bengali language, we still cling to our pretensions of being an alien nation, then there is no hope of a better future for us but only the inevitability of a fall into a deep dark abyss.

Though the doubts and contradictions within Muslim society concerning the Bengali language were more or less resolved in the 1930s, these came back in a different form during the nationalist movement for Pakistan in the 1940s. Remarkably, however, the debate on whether or not Bengali was the mother tongue of Muslims was not revived again. The new debate was about how Islamic the language should become. It was a debate informed by a nationalist consciousness and political separatism.

Pakistan, constituted on the basis of the two-nation theory, was not formed at the start of the 1940s. Indeed, it was not yet very certain that it ever would be formed. Yet, some young Muslim writers at this time demanded that the Bengali in their independent state of Pakistan should be shorn of all 'Hindu' qualities, that is, it should be different from the standardised language. Writers such as Abul Mansur Ahmed, Syed Ali Ahsan and Syed Sajjad Hussein advocated this kind of Islamic Bengali. In their thinking, just as the literature of Ireland is distinct from the mainstream English literature, the language and literature of East Bengal should also be clearly distinguishable and different. These nationalist young men set up the East Pakistan Renaissance Society and Purba Pakistan Sahitya Samsad (East Pakistan Literature Council) even before the country was partitioned. They sought to lend a separatist character to the language by importing innumerable Arabic and Farsi words into it. Some of them went to the extent of proposing that Bengali should be written in the Arabic script. The inclination towards an Islamic Bengali was at this time unmistakably evident in the writings of people like Ghulam Mostafa, Farrukh Ahmed, Rawshan Yazdani, Talim Hossein, Mofakhkharul Islam, Mizanur Rahman and Shahed Ali.

Language Movement

Soon after the declaration, in June 1947, that Bengal would be divided as part of the Partition exercise, some young and older writers raised the question of what would be the state language of Pakistan. Among them, those who deserve special mention were Abdul Mansur Ahmed, Qazi Motahar Hossein, Muhammad Shahidullah, Adbul Huq, Mahmudur Rahman Zahedi and Farrukh Ahmed. The debate gathered steam almost as soon as Pakistan was formed after the Partition in August. In September, for instance, some students and teachers of Dhaka University set up Tamuddin Majlish, a cultural organisation, under Abul Kashem's leadership and published a booklet demanding that Bengali be made the state language of Pakistan. Soon afterwards, Syed Mujtaba Ali said in a written speech in Sylhet that there might well be more than one language in a state and that imposing Urdu on East Pakistan might one day result in Pakistan losing its indivisibility. This was, in a sense, the first stirrings of the language movement.

Indeed, though almost all Bengali Muslims had welcomed the formation of Pakistan, disenchantment soon set in because of a number of reasons. They could see neglect of Bengali and patronage for Urdu in government affairs. On money order forms, postal stamps, coins, in a word in all government transactions, Urdu was being used along with English, not Bengali. They also found themselves unable to put up with the proposal of using Arabic script for Bengali and the import of unknown and unfamiliar Arabic and Farsi words in the language. Nor did they receive just treatment from the Centre in economic matters. And they did not have any say in the administration of Pakistan. All this, together, made them resentful.

But it was the question of language, rather than economic unfairness, that first stoked resentment among Bengali-speaking Muslims. Political conflict on the language issue started at the beginning of 1948. In February that year, Dhirendranath Datta proposed in the Constituent Assembly of

Pakistan that Bengali be made one of the official languages of Pakistan. The proposal was scuttled because of opposition from the founder of Pakistan, Muhammad Ali Jinnah, and Prime Minister Liaquat Ali Khan. Once the information became public through the media, however, a controversy could not be averted. Even a nationalist newspaper like *Azad* published a number of arguments in favour of Dhirendranath Datta's proposal. An editorial was published criticising Liaquat Ali Khan.

More than the media, it was the students of Dhaka University who were extremely aggrieved by the government's anti-Bengali mentality. These students started a veritable movement in support of Bengali. In order to carry out this movement they got all the student associations to come together and form the Rashtra Bhasha Sangram Parishad (Association for the Struggle for State Language). On March 11, 1948, the Parishad observed State Language Day as part of this movement. That day, in an attempt to squash the movement, the government ordered police action on agitating students. The government was keen to put an end to the movement as soon as possible because Governor General Muhammad Ali Jinnah was scheduled to visit Dhaka in a few days. But the attempt to stamp out the agitation through repressive measures did not succeed.

Days after the March 11 incident, Jinnah brushed aside the demand for Bengali as an official language during his visit and told a huge public meeting in Dhaka that Urdu would be the only official language of Pakistan. Soon afterwards, in another meeting of students and teachers at Dhaka University's Curzon Hall, he made the same declaration. In both meetings, there were quite a few voices of protest, even if these were feeble. A delegation of students met him with a memorandum and he had an argument with them. This was how a political movement began around the question of language. In its initial days it was a weak movement. Besides, it was centred around the city of Dhaka, particularly the University of Dhaka. Only a handful of teachers provided encouragement for it and it was mainly the students who took part in it. Within a few years, however, awareness of the need for Bengali as an official language did not remain confined to educational institutions and spread all over the province.

In one phase of the movement, in 1948, the Chief Minister of East Pakistan Khwaja Nazimuddin worked out a compromise with the agitating students. He assured them that Bengali would be used as an official language in East Pakistan and that it would also be the medium of education. As for what would be the state language of Pakistan, that would be decided at the Constituent Assembly. Nazimuddin even hinted that he would put forth the claims of Bengali in that Assembly. However, this scion of an Urdu-speaking aristocratic family had little love for Bengali. He and his government, therefore, didn't do much to make good any of these promises. On the contrary, on a visit to Dhaka in January 1952 as the Prime Minister of Pakistan, he said at a public meeting that the people of the province would get to decide on the provincial language but that the official language of the state would be Urdu. Immediately afterwards, a strike was observed in protest on January 30 at the initiative of the students of Dhaka University. An all-party student committee decided that a general strike would be observed and agitations held on February 21.

In order to ensure that the proposed programme could not be held, on February 20 the government imposed Section 144 prohibiting meetings and processions. But the students were not disheartened. At 11 a.m. on February 21, they met in front of Kala Bhavan in Dhaka University in a huge meeting under Gaziul Haque's leadership. The participants were not just students of the university. Students of various schools and colleges also joined the meeting. The students decided that they would take out a procession towards the East Pakistan Legislative Assembly, which was in session at the auditorium of what is now Jagannath Hall. They came out in small groups of four through the gates of Kala Bhavan so as not to violate Section 144.

Police tried to stop the students once the procession reached the gates of the Medical College, and a clash ensued between the police and the students. Around three in the afternoon, when it became difficult to control the students, the security forces started firing. Quite a few students and some other civilians died as a result, though it could not be ascertained exactly how many. However, at least 10 of the dead could be identified. One of the students who died, Rafiq Uddin Ahmed, had his brains blown off in the firing. Abdul Jabbar and Abul Barkat died of their injuries later. Abdus Salam was one of the civilians who died in the firing. A nine-year-old boy called Ahiullah was killed. There were allegations that the police disposed of some corpses on the sly. This was the assumption that formed the basis of the play *Kabar* (Grave) that Munir Chowdhury wrote while in jail. The police and security forces also fired at the protest rally that was taken out the following day, on February 22. Shafiur Rahman and some others were killed in that incident.

The February 21 incident had a huge and extensive impact. As word spread of the police firing and the bloodshed, the employees of the Dhaka radio centre came out on the streets. Trains stopped running and shopkeepers downed shutters. The February 21 rally was of students, but the procession that was taken out the next day had people spontaneously joining it in large numbers. More importantly, emotional protests broke out in different parts of the province as the news spread. It was not just the towns and cities that thus responded. The ripples flowing out of the episode touched many villages, too. Never before had students and civilians given up their lives for language. This generated strong emotions around the movement.

Its impact was such that it deeply affected the politics of later years. In the 1954 provincial elections, for instance, the Muslim League was defeated miserably. They could win only nine seats in a House of over 300. Such a complete overturning of fortunes for a party that had brought Pakistan into being just seven years earlier was quite unimaginable.

Second, the Shahid Minar built at the site of the police firing on February 21 turned into a pilgrimage spot for Bengalis. It became a symbol for all struggle. This is where even now many a movement is started and pledges are made. Indeed, the biggest secular festival of Bengalis is Shaheed Dibas, Martyrs' Day, when homage is paid to the February 21 matyrs.

Third, the movement produced an awareness about language in the minds of ordinary people, and also a deep love for it. Writers started making extremely strong statements in favour of Bengali. People now upheld with pride their linguistic heritage which went deep into the past and the contribution of Muslims in Bengali literature. Suddenly there was a tidal wave of 'Bengaliness'. The birth anniversaries of Rabindranath Tagore and

Kazi Nazrul Islam and the Bengali New Year were now observed with greater fervour than ever before. Many people at this time chose Bengali names for their children and had house and shop signs written in Bengali, and even number plates for cars. People started signing official and also court papers in Bengali. Using Bengali in speech and even clothes turned into a fashion that people scrambled to imitate.

Shahid Minar, which has become the symbol of struggle for a good cause.
Photo courtesy: Roehl (commons.wikimedia.org)

Tagore, whom Muslims had never before really accepted as one of their own or as speaking for them, was in this changed environment loved and accepted by the Muslims of East Bengal. He was in fact now considered as an icon of East Bengal's language-based nationalist movement. The government, on the other hand, singled out the poet as an enemy of national integration. So in 1961 it tried to block his birth centenary celebrations. Yet many people in the province enthusiastically celebrated the anniversary. During the India-Pakistan war of 1965 the government prohibited Tagore songs on radio and television. But the pressure of popular opinion forced it to lift the ban just before Tagore's birth anniversary. Tagore songs were banned on radio and television once again in 1967. Through such prohibitions, the Pakistan government was trying to halt the tide of 'Bengaliness', or the assertion of a Bengali cultural identity. In reality, it managed to achieve just the opposite. The people of East Bengal laid claim to Tagore's legacy with ever greater enthusiasm. (I have discussed this extensively in my book *Rabindravishwe Purbabanga: Purbabange Rabindranath*, East Bengal in Tagore's World and Tagore in East Bengal'). That Tagore's *Amar sonar Bangla* was eventually chosen as the national anthem of Bangladesh also shows the strength and depth of the attachment that Bengalis at that time felt for him and for a secular Bengali culture.

Indeed, the harder the government tried to drive Bengali language and culture along a path of its own choosing, the greater the certainty with which it failed in the face of a strong resurgence of an assertive Bengali cultural identity, at the levels of state and culture and in social matters. In sum, the Muslims of East Pakistan had arrived at a confident realisation that they were first and foremost Bengalis. And that though they had joined up with West Pakistan to form a state on the basis of religion, in reality they had little in common with the country's western wing.

Awareness of this separatist nationalism was sharpened by some political developments. One of these was the dismissal of the United Front government within a few weeks of its being elected to power. This government had assumed power in 1954 after winning a huge majority in the election. The imposition of military rule in 1958 also throttled the democratic movement in East Pakistan. In the 1960s, the popular leaders of East Pakistan were repeatedly put in jail in an attempt to repress this movement. This, too, turned popular sentiment against West Pakistan. Eventually in 1966, Sheikh Mujibur Rahman gave up the vision of an indivisible Pakistan to start a movement seeking self-governance and autonomy for East Pakistan. The government of West Pakistan put it down with a firm hand, but the worst excesses came in 1971. That year, Sheikh Mujibur Rahman was prevented by West Pakistan leaders from forming the federal government despite his winning a clear majority in parliament. East Pakistan's battle for liberation was a direct fallout of this decision.

The language movement and the emergence of Bangladesh as a sovereign state are both extremely significant in the history of Bengali culture. The positive consequence is the way language is loved and cherished in East Bengal. The Bengali cultural identity has also been reinforced as a result of these developments. The future of the Bengali language and culture is hence more protected. But there is a negative side to it as well. The import of Islamic and East Bengal ingredients in the formal Bengali used in Bangladesh may lead the two Bengals to develop two distinct forms of the language, each with its own special characteristics. Besides, Bangladesh and West Bengal are bound to develop political and other identity-related differences. As a consequence, anything like a common Bengali culture is unlikely to exist. Indeed, the resurgence of love of language among Bengali Muslims may have built up a climax of 'Bengaliness', but it has also laid the ground for further fragmentation of Bengali culture.

Sheikh Mujibur Rahman, the founding father of Bangladesh

The Meaning of the word 'Bengali' after Partition

After Partition, the people of West Bengal acquired an all but monopoly ownership of the word 'Bengali'. One reason, of course, was that from the 19th century itself, Hindu Bengalis in the cities of western Bengal identified themselves as Bengalis. They did not regard Bengali-speaking Muslims as Bengalis at all. On the other side, the Muslims themselves did not claim to be Bengalis. This was the attitude that continued to prevail in West Bengal after 1947. That is to say, the people of West Bengal did not quite acknowledge all Bengali-speaking people to be Bengalis. And they themselves, though Bengali was their mother tongue, slowly moved away a little from their own 'Bengaliness' and became, to a greater or lesser extent, more Indian than Bengali. A couple of examples should make clear who in their eyes were Bengalis. Take, for instance, Suniti Kumar Chattopadhyay. Not only was he the finest ever Bengali linguist, he was also extremely culture-conscious. But from what he wrote in an essay titled *Jati, Samskriti O Sahitya* ('Nation, Culture and Literature'), his definition of 'Bengali' appears fragmented:

> The Bengali in his present-day culture is probably four parts European out of sixteen – his social and economic situation determines how European he is – and eight parts Indian; in the remaining four parts he is Bengali, and much of this is again just a Bengali aberration of Indianness—only the remaining portion is truly Bengali, that is, the rural Bengali.

Reading until here, it is not yet clear where Muslims stand in this definition. Soon after, however, he makes separate mention of Bengali Muslims. 'A section of the ethnic group called Bengali is influenced by Islam—it is up to Bengali Muslim historians to determine the extent of that influence; but it is not very extensive...'

More than one half of all Bengalis are Muslim. We noted in the previous discussion the depth of the influence that Islamic civilisation had on the religious thinking and overall culture of Bengalis. But according to Suniti Kumar Chattopadhyay, the Muslim influence on Bengalis is not very remarkable. He does not even find their contribution to Bengali culture important enough to merit mention. He has mentioned over a hundred names in this essay of people who made special contribution to Bengali literature, music, culture and to the arts and sciences. There is not a single Muslim name on the list. Which seems to suggest that by 'Bengali' he meant only the Bengali Hindu. Sukumar Sen's writings give the same impression.

The same mentality comes across in Jogesh Chandra Bidyanidhi's essay on the innumerable rituals and festivals of Bengalis. He has not mentioned in it a single Muslim festival. Panchkori Bandyopadhyay did not so much as use the word 'Muslim' while writing on Bengali culture. These men, of course, belonged to the first half of the 20th century. But contemporary writers show a similar thinking. Bhabotosh Datta, for instance. That he takes 'Bengali' to mean only the people of West Bengal and Hindus is unmistakably clear in his book *The Religion of Humanity of Bengalis* (1999). In this book he does not mention the direct or even the indirect influence of Islam in his discussion on Ram Mohan's religious thinking, nor in his discussion of the later Brahmo faith.

Similarly, Atul Sur in his book *Bangalir Bibaha* ('Bengali Marriages') has discussed only Hindu marriages. In the essay titled *Bangalir Nritatwik Parichay* ('The anthropological profile of Bengalis') there is not even a hint of the mixing of Middle Eastern blood in the Bengali gene pool. Ramakanta Chakraborty has written a book called *The Religion, Society and Culture of Bengalis*, which runs into 390 pages. It contains just 18 Muslim names, a number that includes Bengalis and non-Bengalis, well known and not-so-well known, of the past as well as the present, mentioned 24 times (according to the index). It must be acknowledged, of course, that there have also been thinkers like Annadashankar Ray, Shibnarayan Ray and Amlan Datta, novelists such as Sunil Gangopadhyay and Shyamal Gangopadhyay and unusual writers like Pabitra Sarkar who are aware of the larger definition of 'Bengali'. In general, however, religious and regional associations in the use of the word 'Bengali' have been reinforced following Partition.

On the other hand, though the Muslims of East Bengal did not earlier identify themselves as Bengalis, within a few years of Partition there was a dramatic reversal of their position because of political reasons, particularly in association with the language movement. Later, in the 1960s, it was their Bengali identity that came to the fore and became dominant. Indeed, their attitude seemed to even assert that they were more Bengali than the Bengalis of West Bengal. It was in this tidal wave of Bengali cultural assertion that religious identities lost significance and a new, language-based and nationalist Bangladesh could emerge. Seen from that angle, this particular time in the 20th century may be considered as marking the climax of 'Bengaliness' (*bangaliana*).

At the same time, however, there were a few individuals like Abul Mansur Ahmed or Syed Ali Ahsan who considered regional and religious identities to be more important than language. In their definition, the scope of the word 'Bengali' shrank instead of being expanded, as it had done in West Bengal. Syed Ali Ahsan's beautiful poem *Amar Purba Bangla* ('My East Bengal') provides an excellent example. The poem, written before the liberation of Bangladesh, reflects deep love for the land, particularly its natural beauty. Instead of looking at Arabia or Iran, in this poem he has turned his gaze at East Bengal, the land of his birth. Yet, it is clear from the title of the poem that he identifies himself not by language but by region. That means that though he has written his poem about nature in Bengal, he has not been able to see himself as belonging to all Bengali-speaking people or to the entire region that is the home of Bengali-speaking people.

In a slightly different form, this kind of limited identity is also evident in the work of writers like Abul Mansur Ahmed. By 'Bengali' such writers have meant the inhabitants of Bangladesh in a localised sense, not all Bengali-speaking people. Indeed, it is not even clear from their writing whether they include the non-Muslims of Bangladesh among Bengalis. Let us look at an example. Abdul Mansur Ahmed wrote after the liberation of Bangladesh: 'We, the Bengalis, have established an independent, sovereign Bengali state and a Bengali nation that is uniform in language and culture. Consequently, Bengali nationalism is contained within the boundaries of the Bengali state. The Bengalis of West Bengal, despite being Bengali in race, language and culture, are Indians.'

That the 'Bengali' he describes is exclusively Muslim is not yet clear. Further into the book (*Sher-e-Bangla Hoite Bangabondhu*), however, he unequivocally explains his definition of Bengaliness and makes it clear that Bangladesh is not a secular state but that it has in reality been established on the basis of the two-nation theory as a homeland for Muslims. Indian leaders had, in his opinion, kindly condescended to correct the wrong that Pakistani leaders had committed at the time of implementing the Lahore Resolution by rejecting the demand for more than one state for Muslims, and had gifted an independent and sovereign state to Bengali Muslims. In another book he has called Bangladesh 'Pak Bangla'. The word 'Pak' here is not meant to signify 'sacred' but a part of Pakistan.

Some writers of Bangladesh have used the word 'Bengali' to mean the Bengalis of Bangladesh, including Hindus, that is, the Bengalis occupying a certain geographical region. Examples can be given from two completely secular writers. Ahmed Sharif in his essay *Banglar Samskriti Prosonge* ('About Bengali Culture') analyses the crisis of identity in Bengali Muslims and chides those who hesitate to call themselves Bengalis. But when towards the end of the essay he says, 'If we can accept that we are 70 per cent Austric, 25 per cent Mongoloid, and the remaining 5 per cent Habshi, Turkish,

Mughal, Afghan, Iranian and so on of mixed blood....' it is hard to say whether he has included Hindus in his description because the list excludes Aryans and Dravidians. When at the very end of the essay he writes, 'Our gaze still wanders over the deserts of Arabia, Iran and Iraq, we still seek our heritage in the Sahara of our fellow believers and in the Gobi desert' it is clear that though he uses the word 'Bengali' it is the Muslims of Bangladesh who are the target of his attack. Abul Momen starts his book *Bangali Samskritir Itihas* (1992; 'The History of Bengali Culture') with the pre-history of the landmass of Bengal. Yet he does not include West Bengal in his discussions of the period after 1947. Here, too, it is a fragmented definition of Bengali culture or Bengaliness.

The definition of the word 'Bengali' changed once more after the Constitution of independent Bangladesh came into force in 1972. This Constitution termed the citizens of Bangladesh as 'Bengali'. So, the word then came to refer to inhabitants of Bangladesh. Hypothetically, those inhabitants of Bangladesh who are not Bengali are also Bengali by this definition, while the people of West Bengal are not Bengalis even if they speak in Bengali.

Politically, this new signification of 'Bengali' did not survive very long. Within a few years, the military ruler Zia-ur-Rahman did away with 'Bengali' in the Constitution and introduced a new word—Bangladeshi. In the Independence Day issue of the weekly magazine *Bichitra* in 1972, he wrote that Bangladesh was born as a consequence of the Bengali nationalist movement. But when he assumed power after the assassination of Mujibur Rahman, he played advocate for 'Bangladeshi' nationalism. Using the word 'Bengali' might appear inclusive of the people of West Bengal, so he dropped 'Bengali' to shut them out from the definition, though he did not hypothetically exclude the Hindus of Bangladesh. In truth, the 'Bengali' of Abul Mansur Ahmed and 'Bangladeshi' of Zia-ur-Rahman are the same. What is particularly remarkable here is that Zia-ur-Rahman's concept of 'Bangladeshi' does not draw upon linguistic associations. It is linked to geographical space. Those who speak Bengali or live in Bengal are Bengalis. But the adjective 'Bangladeshi' need not necessarily refer to people; it may well describe an animal or even an inanimate object.

In sum, then, the definition of 'Bengali' has repeatedly changed because of political and cultural reasons. And it may change again in the future. As the official language of the independent state of Bangladesh, Bengali receives a conducive atmosphere to develop there and consequently is likely to display some East Bengal characteristics and some Islamic influence. The rate at which the non-Muslim population is dwindling in Bangladesh may also reinforce the Islamic influence. The people of West Bengal, on the other hand, seem likely to become more and more 'Indian' with time. For the time being however, the word 'Bengali' is still very much in use, and it does not only mean Bengali-speaking. It signifies the inheritors of a composite culture irrespective of race, religion and state.

Partition and the Refugee Problem

The people of Bengal and Punjab were the most affected by the 1947 Partition. In both these provinces, the population was almost equally divided between Muslims and non-Muslims, even though they spoke the same language. It is hard to say how strong the idea of 'Punjabiness' was, but a concept of what constituted Bengaliness, that is, a Bengali cultural identity, had developed over the past several centuries. A glimpse of it can be detected even in Mukundaram Chakraborty's writing in the 16th century. A Bengali consciousness is quite clear in the writings of Bharatchandra Ray and Abdul Hakim in the 18th century. In the 19th and the 20th centuries, the consciousness of a distinct culture developed into a certain pride in that culture. Partition divided Bengalis and weakened them from inside, and sharp political differences emerged between them. Since Pakistan was founded on the basis of religion, no matter what the Constitution said, West Bengal was 'Hindustan' to East Pakistanis, while for the people of West Bengal, East Pakistan became synonymous with 'Muslim'. Thus, in a very short time the religious divide between the two Bengals became wide and clear. What the British had failed to do at the beginning of the century was now made a reality by India and Pakistan within a couple of years.

Immediately after Partition, educated Hindus from East Pakistan migrated in large numbers to West Bengal. Those who hesitated to leave made up their minds after the riots of 1950. Most of these people were Hindus of the higher castes and belonged to the middle class. Those who already had family in Calcutta or elsewhere in West Bengal could start their new lives with a roof over their heads. But those who had no one to seek refuge with in West Bengal, and no jobs to support themselves, now started a long, arduous struggle to rebuild their lives from scratch. An idea of the difficulties they faced is available in the films of Ritwik Ghatak and in novels such as Sunil Gangopadhyay's *Arjun* or Atin Bandyopadhyay's *Neelkantha Pakhir Khonje* (In Search of the Blue-Throated Bird). Though comparatively fewer in number, many Muslims from West Bengal were forced to migrate to East Pakistan. Muslims who worked in Calcutta also left for East Bengal, where many of them had families and family homes.

The state government of West Bengal tried to draw up plans for rehabilitating the uprooted families from East Bengal. Colonies of refugees sprang up on the outskirts of Calcutta, especially on the southern edges of the city, filling up large open spaces. There was in fact a scramble to occupy and claim tiny bits of land in these colonies. Once a family squatted on a piece on land, they helped relatives and even other refugees from their district back in East Bengal to claim and occupy neighbouring plots. For many long years, dialects from the different regions of East Bengal were spoken in different areas of these colonies. As a consequence, the language of general circulation in West Bengal slowly lost many of its own defining characteristics and absorbed innumerable East Bengal words, ways of speech and even pronunciations. In the initial years, these refugees did not find employment in keeping with their educational qualifications. The hundreds of thousands of refugees exerted an unimaginable strain on the economy and social order of West Bengal. It took West Bengal years to get over the impact of that pressure. Indeed, some 10 to 15 years passed before the people who poured into West Bengal were able to turn themselves into valuable human resources.

Political parties came forward to use these refugees to further their own political ends. Before Partition, leftists did not have any organised political outfit save the Communist Party of India, and it had only a limited popular support. But now, as resentment against the Congress government in power grew among the refugees, the leftist parties reaped the benefits and expanded their popular base. Even the number of parties on the left went up. The rise of the leftist parties in the last five decades of the century immensely affected the society and economy of West Bengal. On the one hand, leftist rule produced some marginal improvement in the situation of people in the villages, and the rural masses also got a taste of political power. On the other hand, the industrial climate in the state clouded over with leftist workers' unions gaining in strength. There was a flight of capital in the 1970s when many industries migrated to other states in the country. Many old values also broke down under the influence of leftist ideology, disregard for work and employer being the chief among them.

The Growth of the Muslim Middle Classes

As we noted before, the spread of education among Muslims started at very slow pace towards the end of the 19th century. Far greater educational opportunities were available to well-to-do Muslims in the 20th century, especially after the First World War. Muslims who acquired a higher education could, in the initial years at least, land government jobs with greater ease than Hindus because of the government's policy of appeasement. Yet, since there were not many educated Muslims around, an educated middle class did not develop among Muslims in the way it had among Hindus. There were very few Muslims in professions such as medicine and law. Bengali Muslims did not even do too well in trade. But Partition overnight opened up an extraordinary range of opportunities for Muslims.

As educated Hindus, uncertain of their future, migrated to West Bengal on a mass scale from an environment of insecurity in East Bengal, the sudden flight of competition created unprecedented job opportunities for Muslims there. From office clerks to senior managers and directors, countless positions lay vacant. At the same time, the creation of the new province of East Pakistan and its capital created many new positions that required people to fill them. Apart from the government offices, thousands of positions were vacant in schools, colleges and in the education department. Doctors, engineers, lawyers and skilled workers were all scarce. The people who came forward to fill these vacancies were comparatively less educated and less qualified Muslims. It was a simple game of demand and supply. The number of educated Muslims fell far short of the demand for educated people. So the clerks of Calcutta overnight became officers in Dhaka. Within a few years, local Muslims also benefited from the situation. The boundless demand in the job market encouraged Muslims to acquire educational qualifications.

Just how fast education spread at this time among Muslims of East Bengal is evident from statistics. Shortly before Partition, in the five years between 1940 and 1944, an average of 7,592 Muslim girls and boys from the whole of East Bengal and Assam appeared for the matriculation examination of Calcutta University every year. The ratio with non-Muslims was 3:14. This ratio was even poorer in the I.A., B.A. and B.Sc examinations. But the number and proportion of Muslim students went up significantly after Partition. In 1960-61, 54,667 students wrote the matriculation examination in East Bengal alone. If 75 per cent of this number were Muslims, then they numbered 41,000. After the liberation of Bangladesh, the number of students writing the entrance examination in 1974 was almost 3,75,000. If 75 per cent of these students were Muslims, some 2,81,000 Muslim boys and girls wrote the examination that year.

Muslims also took comparable strides in higher education. Hundreds of young men and women obtained university degrees, not just in B.A. and M.A. courses but also in medicine and engineering. Until the time of Partition, the number of Muslims with PhDs could be hand-counted. Within three decades after Partition, hundreds of Muslims in the same society secured doctoral degrees. This was made possible by the division of the country and the consequent flight of Hindus, which generated extra opportunities. The educational advances that high-caste Hindus had already made, on the other hand, continued to hold in both Bengals after Partition. The statistics given in the table below will show the unequal progress of education in Hindu-majority West Bengal and Muslim-majority East Bengal over the entire 20th century.

Educated population percentage (%)

Year 1901	Among Hindus	11
Year 1901	Among Muslims	4
Year 2001	In West Bengal	69
2001	In Bangladesh	45

Table 5.6

It was with the help of the progressively expanding reach of education that the number of people belonging to the lower middle classes swelled in both

Bengals. In particular, the lion's share of the lower middle class that developed among Muslims in East Bengal is made up of educated people.

Statistics also give an indication of a rising number of salaried people among Muslims. Of the 181 officials in the 1942 Bengal Gradation List, only 22 were Muslims. Only two of the 22 Muslim officials were Calcutta University graduates. The rest had passed out of Punjab, Delhi and Aligarh universities. Most of those 22 officials, then, were non-Bengali Muslims. On the other hand, 53 of the 181 officials were Bengali Hindus. Of the 37 officials in the Bengal Civil Service, 29 were Bengali Hindus, while the other eight were Muslims, both Bengali and non-Bengali. Within 15 years of Partition, in 1962, there were 714 Bengali Muslims in the East Pakistan Civil Service; 203 in judicial service and 844 in education service. This was how the numbers of salaried, middle-class people grew among Bengali Muslims in East Pakistan.

The process is also evident in trade. Bengali Muslims were traditionally excluded from trade and business. A Bengali saying carries a hint of this: A Sheikh selling oil is an example of a person attempting what is not his forte. Yet businesses, too, needed people to run them after Hindus left in large numbers. And once again unskilled Muslims with small means came forward to fill the gap. With employment and business opportunities opening up in this way, a Muslim middle class developed within 15 to 20 years. A social transformation of this scale does not usually happen in such short time. But a truly extraordinary situation made this possible.

In sum, if there was any one section that profited from Partition, it was the Bengali Muslims. High-caste Hindus found themselves disadvantaged, in particular the educated and high-caste Hindus of East Bengal. Muslims on the other hand were politically advantaged in the new situation and able to avail themselves of new opportunities. True, they now faced competition from non-Bengali Muslims; also true that they did not land the best jobs or become very wealthy and only moved up into the lower middle class. Compared with the situation in the previous century, however, this was not only progress but a meteoric rise.

Religion and Communalism

We have seen how religious reform occupied pride of place in Bengali society through the entire 19th century. People were trying to hold up their inherited faith and test it against the light of humanism, liberalism and rationalism. It began with Ram Mohan Roy. After him, Debendranath Tagore, Keshab Sen and even Ramkrishna contributed to this tradition. Among Muslims, too, reformist movements such as Faraizi and the Tariqa-e-Mohammadia gained immense popularity, though these were fundamentalist movements attempting a return to the original faith. But 20th century society, especially Hindu society, was not conducive to religious reform. On the one hand, nationalism encouraged an atavistic world view, encouraging people to look backward into the nation's past. On the other hand, new age education and lifestyles made people move away from questions of religion and spiritualism to engage with more worldly concerns. Indeed, it was now the politicians who showed a keen interest in using religion for their own ends. This new trend was reflected in the establishment of quite a few political organisations. The Muslim League and the Hindu Mahasabha, for instance. In the 1920s, the Arya Samaj, the Congress under Gandhi's leadership and the Muslim League under Abdur Rahim's leadership introduced religion into politics. Eventually Bengal was divided again on the basis of this kind of religious nationalism.

It is evident from Muslim-run newspapers and magazines that even at the dawn of the 20th century institutionalised faith in this society did not have very strong foundations. For, institutionalised faith presupposes a certain level of education. But as education started to spread among Muslims and as they became conscious of their own identity, the influence of institutionalised faith began to rise in Muslim society. The fundamentalists, especially, started movements to rectify what they saw as aberrations in the faith and revert it back to its original form. This movement was carried out in different parts of Bengal under different names. Its main aim was to reform rites and rituals associated with religion. Its leaders did not just stress the observance of *roja*, namaz, haj and zakat (alms-giving), they also insisted on Islamic dress codes, growing beards, circumcision and Muslim names. In short, they reinforced a distinct cultural identity for Muslims. This religious movement continued in East Bengal even after Partition. After the emergence of independent Bangladesh, proselytising organisations were also set up with foreign funding. Among Bengali Hindus, on the other hand, fundamentalist movements did not quite take shape, though sentiments of religious nationalism were strong among them. Instead, the impact of nationalism eroded some of the rigidity around rules of commensality and the practice of untouchability.

If religious politics gains in strength, communalism cannot but follow. The history of the 20th century is for this reason partly a history of communalism. We have noted already how strong were Hindu and Muslim communalism and religious injunctions regarding ritual purity and commensality at the dawn of the century. But the situation started changing quite dramatically in both Bengals after Partition. Many of the Muslims of East Bengal seized the increased opportunities on offer and caught up with their Hindu neighbours. With practically no competition from the Hindus and no displays of contempt, the old animosities and edginess about contamination through contact eased considerably. Though, of course, some Muslims began to bully and intimidate their Hindu neighbours and tried to frighten them into leaving their homes. In sum, communal feelings rose among Muslims and Hindus, but in other ways society became less polarised. The conflict that had arisen between the two communities over reservation for Muslims in jobs and in the Legislative Council under colonial rule was scaled down overnight. Pretty much as brothers tend to think more kindly of each other once they stop living under the same roof.

This changed mindset was reflected in many ways. For instance, during the riots of 1950, Altaf Mian gave up his life trying to save Hindus from rioting mobs at Agarpur village in Barisal district. This of course may well be more of an exception than a typical example of altered attitudes. It does not seem reasonable to suppose that all communal hostilities vanished with Partition and were replaced by communal harmony and goodwill. But the huge anti-riot peace procession in Dhaka in 1964 and the incident of Amir Hossein Chaudhury sacrificing his life did indeed reflect a change in thinking.

This new thinking manifested itself in the cultural world of East Bengal. Muslims began to express pride in their Bengali identity. In particular, Bengali language, literature and music were considered the chief ingredients in this proud assertion of identity. In this context, not only Tagore but also Bankimchandra, Vidyasagar, Michael Madhusudan Dutt, Atulprasad Sen,

Dwijendralal Ray and Saratchandra Chattopadhyay became cherished names. In the 1950s there had been an attempt to dress up the kaffir Nazrul to make him acceptable. But now his kaffir credentials became unimportant. Instead, his non-communal world view began to be praised and admired. To conclude, though East Pakistan was formed on the basis of religion, a non-communal way of looking at language, literature and music developed there. Admittedly, it was the exploitative rule imposed by West Pakistan and the language movement that made it possible for a secular and proudly 'Bengali' cultural environment to take shape.

The 1965 war between India and Pakistan also seems to have played a role. After the war, the Pakistan government locked and bolted all the doors and windows between the East and West Bengals. Not just the movement of people, all exchanges were sternly discouraged. The result was a surge in feelings of attachment between the two Bengals. I have seen a professor of Rajshahi University gaze with longing at the thin green line beyond the Padma, that is, at India, in 1968. This mindset was produced by the political and cultural atmosphere of the time. It was not as if the Muslims of East Bengal would be willing to give up the wealth of opportunities that Partition had brought them for the sake of a united Bengal. Nor would the Hindus of West Bengal be particularly keen on merging their identities with those of the Muslims of East Bengal.

In West Bengal, as in East Bengal, there were communal riots after Partition. Still, the communal mindset weakened among educated people. For, there were not enough educated Bengali Muslims there with whom Hindus might find themselves in a conflict of interests in everyday exchanges, or whom they might see as a threat in employment and education. This was the background in which progressive individuals like Maitreyi Devi and Gouri Aiyub set up anti-riot organisations. They also started two magazines, *Nabajatok* and *Brother's Face*, in order to foster feelings of communal goodwill and amity. In a novel by Asim Roy published in the 1960s, the protagonist was born in a village in East Bengal. Overwhelmed by nostalgia for his village, he makes his way to the border for a glimpse of East Bengal. As far as I remember, he was not able to set foot on the cherished land of his birth and instead was shot dead by border security forces. Around the same time (in the 1960s), I remember reading in 'Sunanda's Journal' published in *Desh* magazine about how the Bangals (people of East Bengal origin) of Calcutta yearned for the Padma *ilish* (Hilsa). The Padma *ilish* was not just a fish; it was a symbol of the motherland that was left behind.

This mutual attachment grew stronger at the time of Bangladesh's liberation war in 1971. The heartfelt sympathy in West Bengal for the East Bengal refugees, even for Muslim refugees, was quite unparalleled. In Calcutta, where I fled in 1971, I saw the Bangladesh flag displayed at the *Anandabazar* news editor Amitabha Chowdhury's home. He had been born in Sylhet. But it was not in the hope of one day returning there that he supported the Bangladesh movement. He supported it out of the wholehearted affection that he felt for Bangladesh. The same can be said of Shyamal Gangopadhyay, Sunil Gangopadhyay, Santosh Ghosh, Shankho Ghosh. Maitreyi Devi's father, the well known philosopher Surendranath Dasgupta's birthplace was Gaila in Barishal. But I doubt that Maitreyi Devi ever went to East Bengal. Gouri Aiyub's father was also a reputed philosopher. He had been born in Mymensingh. But Gouri Aiyub, too, never lived in East Bengal. Nor she did have any plans of returning there. Both of them suffered from fairly bad health at that time. But that did not stop them from coming out in support of the Bangladesh movement and extending valuable help to refugees.

A measure of how much the Hindu-Muslim relationship changed over the first seven decades of the 20th century is provided by an act of great symbolic value: Sheikh Mujibur Rahman's picture was hung at the community Durga Puja marquees (mandaps) of 1971, along with pictures of Hindu deities. I can cite from my own experience an example of the friendly relations that developed at the time between refugees and the residents of Calcutta. Amitabha Chowdhury's wife, Sunanda Chowdhury, welcomed me as a brother along with her own through the ritual of Bhai Phonta, the Bengali Hindu 'brother's day'. This was an unmistakable pointer to the heightened social exchanges between Hindus and Muslims in the 20th century. This increased exchange also made other differences insignificant—such as the differences between Bangals (people of East Bengal origin) and Ghotis (people of West Bengal origin), and differences of region, caste and dialect. The improved systems of communication also aided this social transformation, but education and a changed political context played a much greater role.

The same can be said of the examples set by various institutions. Take, for instance, the *Anandabazar* group of newspapers. This newspaper never seemed to have much love lost for Muslims. Indeed, before Partition its attitude towards Muslims was extremely communal, and it continued to be so even after Partition. Instead of dispassionately presenting news, the kind of reporting it published during the 1964 Hindu-Muslim riots can only be described as yellow journalism. Yet in 1971 it played a completely different role. Not only in building up popular opinion, this newspaper helped the Bangladesh movement in many other ways. Jadavpur University offered jobs to many teachers among the refugees. In order to ensure humanitarian help for intellectuals, several institutions including Calcutta University provided valuable help.

Ironically, though Bengal was partitioned on the basis of religion, religious loyalties among educated people in both Bengals were eroded after Partition under the impact of the spread of education, industrialisation and urbanisation. Besides, a secular nationalist movement crystallised around the language movement in East Bengal. That, too, helped in turning people's loyalties away from communal politics.

The Rise of Neo-communalism

The domination of petroleum wealth in international politics, the start of the Palestinians' struggle for liberation and its dependence on terror tactics and the spread of Islamic fundamentalism—all this generated a renewed interest in religion from the 1970s onwards. In particular, there is a new enthusiasm about observing religious rituals and customs and in pushing women back into purdah. The transnational Islamic terror network has also reinforced the religious identity of ordinary Muslims and strengthened pan-Islamic nationalism. This nationalist consciousness has, in turn, informed politics in the subcontinent. Besides, after the war of liberation, the anti-India sentiments that grew in Bangladesh because of political and economic reasons also strengthened anti-Hindu and anti-India nationalist feelings among Bengali Muslims.

The old Bengali tradition of religious tolerance and syncretism started changing at this time. Now, for instance, there is no longer any hope of the spread of the Baul movement. Nor can there be another movement like the Brahmo one. Indeed, the repeated use of religion for nationalist and political projects seems to have muddied the spiritual and humanitarian content of religion. Islamic fundamentalism in various forms and under various names is now extending its reach. Though Bangladesh was formed as a secular state, secularism in the country has progressively declined. Two military rulers have even seen to it that the very word 'secular' is dropped from the Constitution. Personal ambitions for power were only part of the motivating factor; the international resurgence of Islam and hard-line nationalist sentiments also played their part.

With the increased interest in religious rites and customs in recent times, amity and goodwill between communities have dwindled. Conflicts have surfaced again, and even riots. The rich are more eager than ever before to display their wealth through elaborate and extravagant observance of rituals and festivals. This tendency, so conspicuous among Calcutta-centred Hindus in the first half of the 19th century, now manifests itself among the nouveau riche of Bangladesh.

Going by the Constitution of India, West Bengal is secular. Secularism thrived in the state in the Left-documented environment. With the right-wing Bharatiya Janata Party seizing power at the Centre in the 1990s and consciously patronising a hard-line right-wing religious nationalism, the saffron flag slowly started being unfurled in West Bengal, too. Many people there are now once again adopting communal attitudes.

Internationalism and Leftist Politics

What is now meant by globalisation has close links to economics. In this sense, the impact of globalisation on Bengalis is not very great. But their connections with the wider world are now much expanded. The world views, values and lifestyles of Bengalis are no longer bounded by the limits of their homeland. International influences are now evident in many areas of their lives—in clothes, food, education, in bearing and in ways of using language, and also in music, cinema and theatre. Wealthy Bengalis now frequently travel abroad, use foreign commodities and decorate their homes with foreign goods. Hundreds of thousands of Bengalis now go abroad in search of jobs. To achieve this end, they are prepared to travel both the straight road and the not so straight one, too. Notwithstanding this close connection with the larger world, however, internationalism has left its mark largely on the external aspects of their lives.

International political developments left their impact on Bengalis from the beginning of the last century. The Bolshevik Revolution must be mentioned before all else. This revolution found followers among Bengalis almost as soon as it happened. Some people noted similarities with the terrorist movement in Bengal. Even a poet like Nazrul Islam became inspired by the communist ideal immediately after the revolution. I mention him first because he was a rather unlikely votary of the Russian revolution. He had little formal education. Moreover, he belonged to an orthodox Muslim family. More importantly, he was with the armed forces when the revolution happened. But that did not stop the young poet from being influenced by the ideology of the Red Army. Though he did not end up as a communist, he was enthused and influenced by the egalitarian ideal. Another glittering example is that of Muzaffar Ahmed. His family background, too, was not conducive to producing a revolutionary. However, not only was he inspired by the revolutionary ideal, he was one of the few activists who founded the Communist Party of India.

The Communist Party of India was formed in 1925 with the inspiration and assistance provided by communists living abroad, such as M.N. Roy, Abani Mukhopadhyay and Nalini Gupta. Three years before the party was founded, communist activists, having attracted the government's wrath, began to be put in prison. Leaders like Muzaffar Ahmed had realised from the beginning that it would be not easy to find workers or a large support base for a communist party. In the 1920s, therefore, they tried to work from within the Congress and influence it with their ideal.

Right from the start of the 1920s, the communist ideal began to exert a powerful influence on young people. Many young men influenced by it, started expressing sympathy for ordinary people, acquired an anti-government stance and rose above communalism. Soumendranath Tagore had been born into an aristocratic zamindar family. Bhupendranath Datta was also a member of the upper classes. But these men were influenced by communism. Those who did not actually read up Karl Marx or 'convert' to communism also showed awareness of workers' rights and sympathy for the poor. Many of the youngsters who had joined the terrorist movement displayed an inclination towards communism. Poets and writers were not outside this new sphere of influence. We have already mentioned Nazrul Islam. He brought coolies, labourers and peasants within the ambit of literature. Sailajananda wrote about coal mine workers. Poets like Subhas Mukhopadhyay and Sukanta Bhattacharya expressed heartfelt empathy for working class people. In the 1940s, the IPTA (Indian People's Theatre Association) gave expression to this empathy in theatre and songs about the working people's situation.

The Communist Party gained some organisational strength in 1935, though it was another few years before the government lifted its ban on the party—in 1942. Partly because of the government ban on it, the party did not manage to take deep root in Bengal before Independence. Nor did the situation significantly change in the first few years after Partition. In East Bengal, the party was completely illegal. That the communist ideology negated the idea of a Creator was also one reason why few youths from the more orthodox Muslim society were drawn to it. But the Communist Party was able to make a powerful impression on the refugees from East Bengal who tried to build a new life in West Bengal, as we mentioned before. Most of the workers of the Communist Party were idealistic and self-sacrificing. Individuals influenced by the communist ideal helped to thwart communalism in both Bengals.

In 1964, the Communist Party split, with one faction loyal to the Soviet Union and the other loyal to China. The Soviet followers were interested in politics through constitutional means, including the contesting of elections. The China-loyalists were hardliners and ready to take up arms and violent means if the need was felt. The Naxalite agitation at the end of the decade was also a violent movement. But none of the activists of the movement were peasants or dependent on land. They were all educated and middle-class people, and most were brilliant university students. They were all inspired by the revolutionary and egalitarian ideal. In the last chapter of this book, we will see that it has been a long tradition among educated Bengalis to express sympathy for the poor and to strike egalitarian postures. Still, the self-sacrifice and disinterested dedication among the sincere communist activists was, in a word, extraordinary. But just as the leftist movement generated awareness among ordinary people, especially ordinary wage-earners, of their rights, it also inspired many to choose the path of violence.

The most important political development in Bengal after Partition was the fall of the Congress and the rise of the communist parties, in particular the Marxist groups. Eventually it was under the leadership of the Communist Party of India (Marxist) that the longest surviving government in West Bengal was set up. The local governments were strengthened during this regime and ordinary people in the villages got some taste of political power. More importantly, ordinary people also saw a remarkable improvement in their financial condition. Non-communal sentiments also grew among them to an extent.

The communist movement never quite took off in Bangladesh. But radical extremist leftist movements have surfaced there, especially after Independence. More than one underground communist group, somewhat like the Naxalites, became active, but they left little mark in society or in politics. Indeed, their contact with ground realities was limited.

A negative aspect of the communist movement in Bengal is that though communism is atheistic, Bengali communists have practised both communism and religion. In order to secure votes, they have paid obeisance at the Kalighat temple in Calcutta as well as at the Baitul Mukarram mosque in Dhaka. There are also many for whom the ideal of equality did not quite work out in their personal lives though communism served as a way of securing political power. Idealistic and educated members of the middle class have been generally influenced by the egalitarian, if not communist, ideal, particularly in their youth.

Democracy

More than the communist ideology, the Western influence that had a longer history of contact with Bengalis was the democratic ideal. Ironically, this ideal produced a culture of liberalism and tolerance in Bengali society in the colonial era, in the 19th and early 20th centuries. But in the 20th century, despite the phased expansion of the electorate and the strengthening of the electoral system, it is doubtful whether democratic values have been able to exert much influence on society. Instead of democracy, it is intolerance and extremism that seem to progressively extend their reach in society. The development of politics and democracy in the two Bengals has also been unequal.

A close look will reveal that though political agitations started right at the beginning of the 20th century, true democracy was not initiated so early. This was partly because the land was under foreign rule. But, as we have already noted, the colonial rulers themselves were forced to slowly introduce some democratic processes. Widespread voting rights did not come before 1935. It was not as if democracy was established through enfranchisement, either. Neither colonial rule nor the violent agitations conducted against it in fact helped to nurture democratic ideals. Moreover, in East Bengal, a colonial regime was in place for another quarter century after Partition. This regime was not only colonial but also autocratic. The popular movement that developed against it was also not entirely democratic. Democracy in East Bengal, therefore, did not yet have an opportunity of growing out of its childhood. People enthusiastically participated in the 1954 elections, but that did not usher in democracy. Nor did democracy arrive through the 1964 elections. Though people spontaneously voted in large numbers in the 1970 elections, they were not able to establish democracy through the process.

In West Bengal, on the other hand, some sort of democratic ideal was established in 1947 itself. Right from the beginning, there was something called an 'opposition' in Indian democracy which played its role in the system. When the Congress weakened in West Bengal, however, it tried to somehow cling on to power, whether by might or by subterfuge, and in the process there surfaced all kinds of undemocratic activities. The movement by the leftists to oust the Congress was also in many ways undemocratic. The Naxalite movement, too, dealt a blow to democracy. The attempt to get political demands met through violent means and by taking the law into one's hands largely shattered the liberal and tolerant atmosphere. A degree of stability returned after the Left Front came to power and democratic values were also somewhat strengthened. For, during this regime a democratic system was established that reached right down to the village level. But in this case the party came in the way of a full and comprehensive development of democracy.

Indeed, true democratic values have never rested on strong foundations at any level of Bengali society, from the top to the bottom. Democratic values do not exist at the level of the family and institutions, not even at the level of the state, notwithstanding the extension of universal voting rights. The democratic process is hardly implemented in the way the political parties run themselves. Even the language used by political parties is in many cases undemocratic. Typical examples would be expressions such as 'We will dig the grave of that party' or 'We will skin that person alive'. The opposition parties, instead of engaging in constructive criticism of the government through a specific programme of action, tend to adopt violent means. None of the values associated with true democracy – the ability to accept the opponent's point of view, tolerance, liberalism, cooperation with others – is considered to be characteristic of Bengali society, though of course these values can be observed in individuals. As a result of the limited development of democracy, the atmosphere in both Bengals is not quite peaceful. A culture of bullying and intimidation clearly seems to prevail. Politics, of course, plays a role in this, but the absence of democratic values in society and in families is no less responsible for the growth of this culture. The flaw runs deep.

There was, especially in Bangladesh, a grave deterioration in law and order and in the judicial system towards the end of the 20th century. Not only were there more crimes than ever before, there was also scant respect for law and order. Heightened unemployment, economic want and the desperation for better living standards, often in competition with one's neighbours, have also combined to help create this situation. Children of educated and wealthy urban families seem to be going astray and falling prey to substance addiction. Along with this has emerged the criminal inclination to supply drugs. These tendencies have taken the shape of veritable subcultures in some groups. The absence of mechanisms of family control also seems to be greatly responsible for the spurt in crime. The values of courtesy, politeness and deference to rules that were traditionally passed down by families are now quite blatantly neglected and observed more in the breach. The limited independence of the news media and the vested interests of media houses have also seen to it that newspapers are not able to play the role that they might have.

Rise of Woman Power

Apart from the awakening of Muslims, the most fascinating thing about Bengali society in the 20th century is the history of the awakening of its women. The kind of women that one now sees in society and in families would have been unimaginable even 50 years ago. This change is nothing short of revolutionary. A number of factors have made this possible. The chief reason for the improved situation of women of course is the expansion of education. The statistics quoted below give an indication of the rate of expansion of education among women in the past century.

Year	Percentage of educated Hindu women	Percentage of educated Muslim women
1901	1.4	0.01
2001	62.22	44 (approx)

Table 5.7

The number of working women has also spectacularly increased. In the family and in society, women now play far more significant roles than they ever did before. Bengali society continues to be patriarchal, but its basis is weakening. We will extensively discuss the position of Bengali women in society in the chapter 'Bengali Women and their Culture'.

Conclusion

One side of the history of Bengalis in the 20th century is marked by the expansion of communal politics, famines, partition, riots and the problem of homeless people. None of this can be seen as positive in any way. The liberalism that thrived in the 19th century was also much reduced in this century. But the other side of this history is marked by two extremely positive developments—the awakening of women and of Muslims. High-caste Hindus, whose situation started improving in the 19th century, continued to do well in the 20th century. The advances they had already made in the previous century significantly quickened the pace at which they moved ahead, though they did lose political power in undivided Bengal in the early part of the century. What was completely new was the expansion of education among rural Muslims and the rise of a Muslim middle class. Muslims were at the heart of the first and temporary division of Bengal and also the second and permanent one. Eventually these were the people who brought into being independent Bangladesh. The expansion of education among Muslims and the rise of a Muslim middle class led to a comprehensive development of Bengali culture. Yet, Partition and the emergence of independent Bangladesh have also laid the basis for a division of Bengali culture into two distinct strands.

As a community, low-caste Hindus have seen an extremely limited improvement in their situation. They have not been recognised as a political power either in West Bengal or in Bangladesh. Nor did they get any extra opportunities in education or in livelihood. Moving ahead in life, therefore, has not been easy for them.

Urbanisation and industrialisation are extremely significant developments of the 20th century. Almost 30 per cent of the population in Bangladesh and in West Bengal now live in cities. That is to say, the percentage of city dwellers has gone up tenfold in a hundred years. Heavy and light industries in cities have seen huge expansion. In particular, Bangladesh as an independent state had no option but to industrialise. It was in fact relatively easy to bring about industrialisation there because of the availability of cheap labour. As a consequence of urbanisation and industrialisation, however, the culture that was once dependent on agriculture and rural cottage industries has undergone, and is still undergoing, large-scale changes.

The development of literature and music initiated in the 19th century not only continued apace in the 20th century but crossed ever more remarkable milestones. In the first half of the century, Bengali songs attained extremely high standards. What brought this about was the presence of geniuses like Rabindranath, Dwijendralal, Atulprasad and Nazrul Islam on the one hand, and technological strides and an increase in demand on the other. We will discuss this extensively in the chapters on literature and music.

***

LOVE, MARRIAGE AND FAMILY

There is no written history of romantic love in the thousand years of Bengali society. But in a society where one half defines marriage as an institution where a wife is taken for the sake of a male heir, the foundation of romantic love cannot be presumed to have been very strong. As for the other half, where there are provisions for a man to get himself four wives, it does not look as if there was a tradition of anything beyond physical love. Indeed, Bengali society was not very conducive for romantic love. It was not just mindsets or values that were responsible for this. There were other factors at play, such as the age of marriage, education, customs surrounding marriage, the unequal social status of men and women, clannishness, economic conditions, and so on.

Apart from a few exceptional cases, marriages took place very early in life in Bengali society until the 20th century, much before any feelings of romantic love got a chance to grow. Girls got married at eight or 10, and even many boys. The *kulin* girls were the only exceptions; some of them got married at a more mature age. But such marriages were relatively so few that they cannot be taken into account while commenting on marriages among Bengalis. With the age of marriage being so low, there was no scope for any pre-marital romantic involvement. Nor did people get to choose their marriage partners. Ballal Sena married the daughter of a Dom, one of the lower castes of Bengal, overwhelmed by her beauty. Chaitanyadev, too, married Lokkhipriya (Lakshmipriya) for love. Indeed, his stubborn persistence forced his mother to agree to the marriage. The poet Kanka in the 17th century fell in love with his guru's daughter. But these were exceptions, not the general rule.

Watching one's child wife grow into a woman or one's teenaged husband grow into manhood may of course generate some kind of emotional attachment, but that cannot be described as romantic love. Besides, the customs of the time required couples not to meet during the day once the wife reached a sexually active age. There is written evidence to show that this custom prevailed even in the second half of the 19th century. We know from Rasasundari Devi's autobiography how she only ever met her husband at night. From Debendranath Tagore to his youngest son, Rabindranath, this rule applied to everyone. In Dinabandhu Mitra's *Jamai Barik*, the sons-in-law were called inside to the women's quarters only at night, not at any other time. Couples met in darkened bedrooms and had sex, and hence also regularly produced babies. But this environment, needless to say, is not quite ideal for love. In Bengali society, therefore, husbands did not ponder over whether they had their wife's love. Wives, too, perhaps did not feel the need to ask whether their husbands loved them. In sum, there was no romantic love in Bengali society, and if at all it existed, it was rare.

Even in this environment, so completely hostile to romantic love, relationships did sometimes develop outside marriage. It was not unmarried young girls who got involved in such relationships, because they were not old enough to understand romantic love. It happened with married women or widows. This is why it can be said that whatever existed in this society by way of romantic love was in the form of illicit relationships. Medieval literature has many narratives of illicit love. A large part of such literature consists of the story of the love between Radha and Krishna. Besides, poets often told stories of their own relationships in the guise of writing about Radha and Krishna. This literature suggests that illegitimate relationships were not considered very unusual in Bengali society. But this love was not devoid of lust. On the contrary, sexuality seems to predominate in the depiction of such love in literature. The story of Vidya Sundar, as told by Ramprasad Sen and Bharatchandra Ray, is full of sexual titillation. It is reasonable perhaps to suppose from these narratives that however rare romantic love might have been, Bengalis were not averse to physical love.

There is also enough evidence of sexuality in real life, apart from literature. The nouveau riche of the 19th century did not hesitate to spend time or money on courtesans, whatever their relations might have been with their wives. According to a report in *Samachar Darpan*, a babu in the 1820s bought a courtesan called Niki for one lakh rupees. Shibnath Shastri wrote that babus boasted about gifting houses to their mistresses. Such women were not just sexual playthings. The men who 'bought' them also tried to get a taste of romantic love in such relationships. What was unattainable in marriage was thus sought after in illicit love and in relationships with courtesans.

It is said that the best-known social reformer of the time and the father of modern India, Ram Mohan Roy, also had a mistress. Dwarakanath Tagore was only in his thirties when he ceased to have sexual relations with his wife, who was extremely orthodox and finicky about rules of commensality. In the absence of a conjugal life with his wife, he formed intimacies with many women, some of them white. During his sojourn on the Thames on a boat, he lived with an Englishwoman. Indeed, maintaining a mistress was almost a socially accepted custom, and it persisted right up to the end of the 19th century. Dwarakanath's grandson Jyotirindranath is also said to have been involved in such a relationship. Binodini was the 19th century's best-known actress. But despite all her fame, she was also a 'kept' woman. She has left an account in her autobiography of how much she was loved by the zamindar who owned her before Gurmukh Roy bought her off. In sum, many men looked beyond marriage to quench their thirst for love. That many men went to their wives only with the sacred objective of producing children is known from both literary and real-life sources. The practice cannot be said to have totally ceased in the 20th century. As late as in the second quarter of the last century, I knew a well known judge who had a mistress, and this was not unknown to his family.

What is called romantic love was first initiated in Bengali society in the 19th century. It appeared in literature before it appeared in society. And what contributed most to bringing this about was Western education. From the 1830s, there was a steady trickle of young men passing out of Hindu College with an English education. In keeping with the social custom of the time, they had been forced to marry while they were only boys or in early manhood. Wedded to illiterate little slips of girls, they understood all too well that it was impossible to experience with their child wives the romantic love that they encountered in English literature in their college days. Indeed, English education may have fetched them financial success, but it also introduced the pain of unrealised longings in their private lives.

An indication of this is available in written sources belonging to the 1830s. A letter published in 1838 in *Samachar Darpan* said: 'The young men and little boys who are now engaged in learning will certainly secure good jobs when they grow up. ...Will the men so transformed be able to form ties of affection with their illiterate wives? After the day's mental and physical strain, will they get from those ignorant wives the succour and assistance that men need?' Only the wives' lack of education is mentioned here, but the age of marriage was also important. Even the way marriages were fixed was no less a problem.

A typically Bengali trait is to make a secret of love, though many other things may be publicly discussed. The habit persists to this day. Even when in love, couples do not easily come out with 'I love you'. Bengali men do not hold their wives' hands in public, let alone kissing, lest people talk—even today. It is therefore not easy to write a history of how romantic love slowly found acceptance in this society and expanded its reach. Yet, a hazy picture of the march of romantic love does emerge from some incidents and from literature.

Indirect evidence of romantic love is available in a couple of incidents that took place before Bengali novels, plays and autobiographies were published. The first example is that of Dakshinaranjan Mukhopadhyay. He was a student of Derozio. He participated in various progressive projects including social reform and women's education. He had realised from his reading of English literature that women were not an inferior species. The *Gyananweshan* magazine that he edited said in January 1833 that women and men were equal: 'There is no need to quote from the scriptures to try and improve the situation of women. Women must be seen as human beings and they are equal to men in every respect...'

Dakshinaranjan was also familiar with the ideal of romantic love in English literature. So influenced was he by this ideal that he could not be satisfied with the kind of arranged marriage that most men of those days had to accept. He married Basantakumari, the widowed wife of the Burdwan raja, for love. There was no provision yet for such a marriage within the frame of religious regulations. So he had to marry under the civil marriage law. He married in the teeth of overwhelming social opposition and was forced to leave Bengal.

The second example is of that colourful personality—Michael Madhusudan Dutt. Observing peculiarities in his son that set him apart from others of his age, Rajnarayan arranged to get him married. This was in November 1842. Madhu was then almost 18. A month earlier he had had a taste of calf love during a visit to Tamluk (in Midnapore district). But he was familiar with a far headier kind of love through his reading of English literature. He had observed a boundless outpouring of love, not only in the poetry of his hero George Byron, but in all his favourite Romantic poets. In Byron's personal life, too, he could see many instances of romantic love. He had therefore started writing poems about a blue-eyed beauty even before this episode. This, of course, was in the realm of imagination. But the marriage that was being arranged for him in real life got him truly alarmed. It was not possible for him to marry except for love. Yet, it was also impossible for a young man dependent on his parents to declare that he would not marry. To avert the marriage, therefore, he became a Christian. Though he did not yet love a woman, he was in love with love itself. This is the feeling that can be called romantic love. No expression of this kind of love is available before Madhusudan in Bengal's history or in literature. Madhusudan was eventually able to love a blue-eyed beauty, but that was another few years later. He married Rebecca for love. Within a few years he fell in love again, with Henrietta.

Madhusudan's classmate Gyanendramohan Tagore was not a poet. But he deeply loved English literature and was well versed in it. While still a boy, he had had to marry at his father's command. It goes without saying that he did not fall in love with his child wife, who died before attaining puberty. Gyanendramohan fell in love after that. It was not a very easy thing to do. For, where would he find a teenager or a young woman whom he could love? Luckily for him, however, he did find an unmarried teenager who had some conception of love. Her father, Krishnamohan Bandyopadhyay, was among the best known students of Derozio. Krishnamohan had converted to Christianity, and that was why his daughter was still single in early womanhood.

When Gyanendramohan married Kamalmoni on April 15, 1852, she was 15 years and two months old, and he was 26. Gyanendramohan did not write any autobiography. Nor did he ever write or talk about his love. But going by the age at which he married his second wife, he must have been, by then, consumed by the physical and emotional thirst for love. He had got Kamalmoni after weathering much hostility. Like Madhusudan, he had to convert to Christianity to get what he wanted. Presumably, he drank his fill of love.

The Hindu Widows Remarriage Act was passed in 1856. In the next few decades, with the help of Ishwarchandra Vidyasagar and some other distinguished social reformers, about a hundred-odd 'progressive' young men married young widows in the face of social opposition. Most of these widows got married to Brahmo men. Brahmo leaders such as Durgamohan Das encouraged such marriages. Reports of these marriages were published regularly in *Bamabodhini Patrika*. There are hints in these reports that it was not entirely the noble mission of social reform that motivated the grooms, but that some sort of pre-marital acquaintance (in other words, love) played a role.

Dwarakanath Ganguly was a progressive leader of the Brahmo Samaj. He was the first to publish, in 1869, a magazine, called *Abalabandhab*, aimed at the edification of women. After his first wife died, Dwarakanath married for love one of the first two Bengali women graduates. She was Kadambini Basu. As the surnames show, this was an inter-caste marriage. The Brahmos used to claim that they did not set any store by caste and that they believed in women's liberation and in independent choice in marriage. Yet when Dwarakanath married Kadambini, his friends were against it and did not even attend the wedding.

Krishnakumar Mitra married one of Rajnarayan Basu's daughters. He was a member of the Sadharon Brahmo Samaj and was keen to follow its marriage rites. Rajnarayan Basu, on the other hand, belonged to the Adi Brahmo Samaj and did not want the wedding to be conducted according to the Sadharon Brahmo Samaj rules. Yet he recognised his daughter's free will in the matter of her marriage. And since she loved Krishnakumar Mitra, he allowed the marriage to take place though he was not present at it.

Notwithstanding a few such examples, it must be admitted that there were not too many marriages that were made for love in those days. There is, however, indirect proof in the literature of the time that young men had gradually started to nurse hopes of marrying educated girls, and for love. Of the many plays of Shakespeare, the first to get its story retold in Bengali was *Romeo and Juliet* (1848). A translation of *Merchant of Venice* was also published at the start of the 1850s. In original Bengali plays, too, ideas of love and independent choice in marriage started appearing in the 1850s. The first such play was *Swapatni Natok* published in 1858. In Dinabandhu Mitra's play *Leelabati* written in the following decade, a picture of love and marriage is sketched through attractive plot and characterisation. Both the hero and the heroine, Lalit and Leelabati, are educated and they fall in love while they are still single. Contemporary readers particularly liked this play with a happy ending. The dramatisation of the play was also very popular.

Lakshminarayan Chakraborty's *Kulinkanya ba Kamalini* and Debendranath Bandyopadhyay's *Swarnalata* were written around the same time. Both these plays support the love between man and woman and the human right to freely choose a partner. Sarojini and Sukumari of Upendranath Das's *Sarat-Sarojini*, and Binodini and Birajmohini in his *Surendra-Binodini*, both plays written in the 1870s, wanted to marry men of their own choosing. At this time, Jyotirindranath Tagore was quite conservative. But the Oilobalas, Sarojinis and Hemanginis of his plays were also in favour of choosing their own partners in marriage.

It is clear from these plays that attitudes to love and marriage were changing among a section of educated people. When this change was taking place is also indicated by the dates of publishing of these plays and in some cases from the dates of dramatic performance. How effective these plays were in actually influencing society is, however, doubtful. On the other hand, many people read with deep interest the novels that Bankimchandra Chattopadhyay wrote. Even the little-educated women of the time read them. Readers, both men and women, waited eagerly for the next issue of *Bangadarshan* to find out what happened to the hero and the heroine. Bankimchandra depicted both married love and love outside marriage. Indeed, no one before him had narrated stories of romantic love in Bengali literature quite in the way that he did. And there were few to match him even later. Many people say that it was he who transformed Bengali thinking about love. There is no dearth of truth in the observation. But of course this was not an easy task. Little slips of girls conducting romantic relationships would be ridiculous and strain credibility too far. Bankimchandra, then, was forced to imagine heroines who were young adults. He made this possible by putting his heroines in unusual situations. *Kapalkundala*, for instance, grew up far from traditional society in a secluded forest. She was raised by a *kapalik*, a sadhu in the tantric tradition. Kundan-nandini and Rohini in the novels *Bishbriksha* (Poison Tree) and *Krishnakanter Will* (Krishnakanta's Will) were widows. Rajani was blind, and this was why she did not get married at the usual age. Indira, though an adult, was a virgin because of the special circumstances of her life.

In the 10 years following the publication of his first novel in 1865, quite a few of his well known novels and novellas were published. Professors of literature and critics had not yet turned him into a saint. He himself had also not quite reinforced his Hindu nationalist image. At that time he was still popular only as a storyteller who told stories of romantic love. Very few Bengali women had any sort of education in those days. Still, they started reading Bankimchandra. This was the subject of much derision in contemporary plays and skits fired by reformist zeal. The derision apart, it is evident from these plays and skits that educated people were taking lessons in romantic love from Bankimchandra's books. The men encountered this kind of love in English literature too, but for Bengali women, the chief, indeed the only, source was Bankimchandra's writing. True, in two of his famous novels Bankimchandra punished two beautiful widows for falling in love. Yet those who read the novels loved these widows more than they did his morally perfect heroines. He kindled an interest in love among Bengalis.

A story by Prabhat Kumar Mukhopadhyay is set at the start of the 1870s. This was the time when the movement around the proposed Brahmo Marriage Act had just begun. This story gives an unmistakable indication of a changed thinking about wives among Brahmos. Its protagonist believes that in the absence of love, a wife should be like a sister to her husband and not a true marriage partner. In sum, the literature of the 19th century made it quite clear that social attitudes to marriage and love were changing.

Let us look at a couple of extraordinary instances from real life in the latter half of the 19th century. The poet Dwijendralal Ray's father, Dewan Kartikeyachandra Ray, admitted in his autobiography that he was loved by a prostitute, and that he regarded her love with sympathy and respect. He defended his stance by saying that a flower was not defiled by the filth in which it might grow. Girish Chandra Vidyaratna was a junior colleague of Vidyasagar at Sanskrit College. He wrote not about illicit love but about his deep love for his wife. He even hinted at the physicality of this love. He worked in Calcutta, while his wife lived in the family home in his hometown. He visited his family at weekends or at fortnightly intervals, driven by the pangs of emotional longing and physical separation. On one occasion he went home to find the house was under repair. He had to sleep with his newly married wife in a room where the floor was freshly caked with mud and was quite uneven. Yet, he wrote in his autobiography, the couple made love through the night.

Another remarkable instance of married love can be glimpsed in the letters of Satyendranath Tagore. He wrote to his child wife from London in 1863-64 that they had been married at an age when they were not old enough to give informed consent. Until Jnanadanandini Devi grew up and accepted him with love of her own free will, therefore, he did not wish to enter into a conjugal relationship with her. There is no gainsaying the fact that the way he wrote about kisses at the end of his letters was also quite uncharacteristic of Bengali husbands.

Rabindranath Tagore was 19 years younger than Satyendranath. But he far outstripped his elder brother in the matter of love. In the one year between the time he was 18 and 19, he fell in love with three young women, Anna Tarkhar and Lucy and Fanny Scott, in quick succession. He also loved his sister-in-law Kadambari Devi (I have extensively discussed the many loves of Tagore in an article published in *Desh*, November 21, 2002). His, however, was an entirely romantic love. He wove his dreams of love in the realm of the imagination, not in the down-to-earth world of everyday life. There was desire in his love, but not much room for lust. After those initial romantic encounters, the love that he wrote of in *Mayar Khela* at the beginning of the 1880s was almost suicidal, so absolute that the heart does not hesitate to put everything at stake; yet it was devoid of the body. This shows how Bengali society was waking up to a new kind of love.

Love outside the realm of marriage became far more common in the 20th century because of the spread of education and the raising of the age of marriage among other things. There is however no detailed information about this. In keeping with the Bengali tradition of secretiveness about love, writers have not written about their own relationships. Indeed, many of them have regarded romantic involvements as being shameful and scandalous. Even in 1910, Tagore wrote about social outrage in connection with love. The imagined subject of one of his songs pledges her love despite the scandal it will cause ('*Ami tomar preme hobo sabar kalonko bhagi*'). Love, for the poet, was not confined to the realm of imagined characters: he was attracted to a number of women in real life. One must remember, however, that it was only because he was so famous that his loves are known about. It is known that he loved Victoria Ocampo and Ranu Adhikari. It is also known that there were others who were attracted to him.

That he was famous was also why Nazrul Islam's relationships are known about. He himself did not write about them. He seems to have been in love with someone when he joined the army at 18. He carried with him a woman's hairclip when he joined his posting. Shortly after leaving the army, he fell in love with a girl in Comilla. In an impulsive decision, he married her, only to run away on his wedding night. He fell in love once again with the teenaged Ashalata, with whose family in Comilla city he took refuge after his flight from his first bride. She was pregnant when he married her in April 1924. He lost his heart several times afterwards, too. He became especially attached to the brilliant and beautiful Faziltunnesa, a student of Dhaka University. Qazi Motahar Hossein's account gives some idea of the depth of this attachment, and it seems unlikely that it was only a fleeting fancy. Some years later, Nazrul wanted to dedicate his collection of poems *Sanchita* to Faziltunnesa. When she objected, he dedicated it to the 'Poet of the World, Rabindranath Tagore'. Nazrul, according to some reports, also fell in love with Ranu Som in Dhaka. No other names are known in connection with him, but there are fairly clear indications that he experienced other romantic encounters.

Faziltunnesa withdrew midway from her involvement with Nazrul. Later, she fell in love with a Bengali student, Shamsuzzahar, while in Dhaka. She cut short her studies to come back to the country with this gentleman and married him. She was then nearly 30.

We know of Maitreyi Devi's love life from her own writing. She entered into a relationship with an overseas student of her father, a well known philosopher, sometime around 1930. The relationship does not appear to have been entirely platonic, going by what she wrote in her autobiographical novel *Na Honyote* (The Indestructible). That she could write about their stolen kisses in the novel is a testimony to her immense courage. The poet Amiya Chakraborty also formed a strong attachment. He was then a married man, but he left his family for a while to live with the lady, a foreigner, with whom he had fallen in love.

Jasim Uddin wrote about a platonic attachment in his memoirs. He loved a girl who was a distant cousin. She was extraordinarily beautiful. The weaver whom she was married to was lazy and, partly because of this, also very poor. He did not pay much attention to his beautiful wife, either. Jasim Uddin did not particularly notice this girl when she was younger. But on a trip to Faridpur while studying in Calcutta, he visited her family home, and there he fell in love with her extraordinary beauty. He found his thoughts always straying to this simple, unlettered girl. On one occasion Jasim Uddin lost control while visiting her when she was unwell. He told her that had he known that he would one day grow to love her so, he would never have let her become someone else's wife. But the girl was hurt and said such words were sinful. She also returned the little money that Jasim Uddin had given her to buy food and medicine. Jasim Uddin asked for forgiveness and left, but he never quite got over his love for her. The episode ended with the girl's untimely death. The great tenderness with which Jasim Uddin narrates it in his memoirs reflects the depth of his feelings. Abu Rushid in his autobiography wrote about his experience of love during his student days in Calcutta. He even mentions his visits to prostitutes.

Contemporary writers have written about how attitudes to love and marriage were changing with the transformation of social mores. They also criticised loveless marriages. An essay published in 1873 in *Bamabodhini Patrika*, for instance, said: 'Successful and educated young men are deeply unhappy in one respect. They do not get any succour from their wives, their family lives are painful and distressing.' A similar comment was made two years later in an essay titled 'Women's Education' in *Jnanankur* magazine. It was this feeling of dissatisfaction and incompleteness that spurred many young husbands of the time to try and educate their unlettered wives. The 13-year-old Kailasbasini Devi was married to Durgacharan Gupta in 1849. She was completely illiterate at that time. Durgacharan, on the other hand, was not only educated but the author of several books. He felt he would not be able to find happiness with a wife like this, so he set about educating her.

Satyendranath, Jyotirindranath and Rabindranath also married very young and uneducated girls. They, too, educated their wives and brought them up to quite a high level of reading and refinement, keen as they were to establish relationships of love with their wives.

Marriage

There is nothing to show that the institution of marriage in Bengal was significantly different from what it was in other parts of India. As a result of the arrival of the Vedic and Buddhist faiths, the varied marriage customs prevalent among the different groups of the original inhabitants of the land slowly evolved into a standardised and somewhat homogeneous form. Some local influences certainly persisted in marriage rites and ceremonies, like, for instance, the custom of smearing turmeric paste on the bride and the groom and the rituals surrounding it. After the advent of Muslim rule in Bengal, some Islamic customs were imported into the marriage rites of native Muslims. But that did not significantly transform the institution of marriage. There was no tradition of love or the exercise of free choice in the matter of marriage, whether among Hindus or Muslims. Even the age of marriage for girls was roughly the same in both communities. Since the Muslims of foreign origin were forced to marry local women, local customs and rites more or less persisted in their weddings, too.

Some information about marriages in ancient Bengal can be gleaned from the *Charyapada* poems. Both marriages within caste restraints and inter-caste ones are mentioned in these poems. Even sexual unions outside marriage are mentioned. In some circumstances, high-caste men married women of lower castes. As we mentioned earlier, Ballal Sena married the daughter of a Dom. After the arrival of Muslims in Bengal, marriages between Hindus and Muslims, especially between Hindu women with Muslim men, began to take place on a large scale. This was because the Muslims who came from distant lands did not bring their families along. Apart from real life, instances of marriages between Hindu women and Muslim men are found in medieval literature. We know from these sources that wealthy and influential Muslims used force to marry beautiful Hindu women. But again, in the court literature of Arakan, we find a Muslim 'king' or 'prince' marrying a Hindu princess at her wish. There is also evidence that aristocratic Muslims married their daughters into Hindu families rather than with Muslims of the lower classes. Suleiman and Daud Karnani's general Raju, also known as Kalapahar, had married a Muslim woman. Isa Khan's father was a Hindu. He, too, had taken a Muslim bride.

The custom of taking many wives may not have been widely prevalent in Bengali society, but more than one wife was fairly common, especially among the rich. One of the main characters in Mukundaram Chakraborty's *Chandimangal* is Dhanapati. He was rich and had two wives. The hero, Kalketu, on the other hand, was not rich. He had one wife. Mukundaram has written about Muslims taking many wives. In Bipradas's *Manasabijoy*, we hear of some hundred wives of Hassan, not just one or two. He also had female slaves. Daulat Qazi's hero 'Raja' Lor had two wives. Bharatchandra's hero Bhabananda Majumdar is rich, and he, too, has two wives. Besides, 'Suo Rani' and 'Duo Rani', two queens married to the same king, one pampered and the other neglected, are quite ubiquitous in Bengali folklore. Not just literature, real life also provided enough instances of the polygamous family.

The father of modernism in India, Ram Mohan Roy, himself married thrice, though he did so at his father's behest. Shibnath Shastri, one of the leaders of the Brahmo Samaj, was forced to make a second marriage and spent the rest of his life in severe repentance and anguish. Two wives were not, however, the norm in poor families.

The custom of taking multiple wives was fairly common among the *kulin* Brahmins and the *kulin* Kayasthas, the groups believed to possess exceptional ritual purity. But the practice does not appear to have gained popularity before the second half of the 18th century. The *kulin*s generally married for money. And they had enough opportunities to do so. For, Brahmins and Kayasthas of the lower orders tried to climb up the caste ladder by getting their daughters married into *kulin* families. There were *kulin*s who considered making money through marriage an excellent way of making some profits on zero capital. Popular custom, if not religious regulation, endorsed the practice. But getting hold of a *kulin* groom was not always so easy. When a groom was available from a family with which marital union was ritually sanctioned, he was sometimes found to be much younger than the bride. Yet the marriage would still take place. Sometimes, if something as rare as a *kulin* groom presented himself, the bride's family sought to get all their unmarried daughters married to him and thus free themselves of a grave responsibility. This practice of multiple marriages, though it reached a pinnacle in the 19th century, was fast abandoned in the 20th century. Some traces, however, might have lingered. The 1901 Census reported 108 marriages of a *kulin* man.

Muslims could not, under the religious regulations that bound them, marry 50 or 60 wives in the way that *kulin* Brahmins could. But taking four wives was quite common among well-to-do families. Besides, since sexual relations with slaves is endorsed in Islam, the practice of maintaining female slaves was widely prevalent among the rich in the Middle Ages. The Portuguese traveller Duarte Barbosa visited Bengal in the second decade of the 16th century. While describing urban, rich Muslims, he wrote that they all had three or four wives, and some of them even more. Twenty-five years before Barbosa arrived, multiple marriages of Muslim men were mentioned in poems by Bipradas Pillai, Mukundaram Chakraborty and Dwij Hariram. Indeed, many wealthy Muslims married, if not four wives, at least more than one. This was not rare even in the 20th century.

Though multiple marriages were a serious problem, an even bigger problem in the 19th century was child marriage. Girls were generally married before they were 10. It was also not entirely unusual for girls to be married off at three, four, or even when they were a few months old. Marrying off eight-year-old girls (*gouri daan*) is much praised in the Hindu scriptural text *Parasara Samhita. Manu Samhita* pronounces damnation in hell for parents who fail to marry off a daughter before she starts menstruating. Parents, therefore, were desperate to get their daughters married off before they turned 12, fearing the onset of puberty. Only the highest placed *kulin* Brahmins were exempted from this custom.

Since girls were married so young, the child wives were sometimes left with their parents for a while. The girl would be sent to her husband's family home after she menstruated for the first time. But most child wives grew up with their husbands' families. When such a child wife started menstruating, a 'remarriage' ceremony was held to celebrate the occasion. It was after this ceremony that she was required to share her husband's bed. Until then, the child wives slept with female relatives of the husband. Bankimchandra, Rabindranath, Prabhat Kumar Mukhopadhyay – the writers who wrote the first stories of romantic love – none of them was able to escape this custom.

Marriage at such a young age naturally led to myriad problems, particularly for girls. Sometime around 1820, Rasasundari was married at the age of 10. She has left a vivid account in her autobiography of how terrified she was, and how heartbroken, when she was sent off to her husband's home. Most families welcomed the child bride with a sort of animosity. She was a witch out to get their son. As young as eight or at the most ten, she was assigned household chores. Another negative consequence of child marriage was widowhood. Child mortality rates were then higher than they are now. Husbands like Bankimchandra Chattopadhyay whose wives died in girlhood were not inconvenienced in any way, for they soon remarried. But the child brides whose husbands died young were forced to remain unmarried all their lives. For the rest of their lives they had to carry the burden of widowhood, with all the regulations that made it a living hell. (I have discussed extensively the many marriage-related problems in my book *Samaj Samskar O Bangla Natok*, Social Reform and Bengali Theatre.)

How widespread was the custom of child marriage is evident from the lives of the famous men of the 19th century. Dwarakanath Tagore married at 15. Though he was extremely modern for his time in his thinking, he got his son Debendranath married at 17, and the bride was 11 years old. Ishwarchandra Vidyasagar, Rajnarayan Basu, Bankimchandra Chattopadhyay, Keshab Chandra Sen, Satyendranath Tagore, Kaliprasanna Sinha, Ramesh Chandra Datta—all these well known individuals of those days married before they turned 17. Their brides of course were even younger. The girl whom Bankimchandra married was only five years old. The wives of Debendranath and Bijoykrishna Goswami were six. Satyendranath Tagore's bride was seven years old, Vidyasagar's was eight, Keshab Sen's and Jyotirindranath's were nine, Shibnath Shastri's was 10, and Rajnarayan Basu's wife was 11 years old.

Social custom was a chief pressure factor in the matter of child marriage. For, marrying off a daughter at a slightly mature age led to social disgrace. The Tagore family at Calcutta's Jorasanko was one of the most educated and aristocratic families of Bengal at that time. Debendranath Tagore had carried out reforms in the marriage ceremony, ignoring the orthodoxies of Hindu society. But even he did not raise the age of marriage for the girls of his own family. Nor did he get his sons married to adult women. The only exceptions were two of his granddaughters, Indira Devi and Sarala Devi. Indira Devi had the support of her liberal father, Satyendranath. And Sarala Devi was a rebel herself. She did not pay attention to Debendranath's opinions.

The age of marriage for men, however, went up quite remarkably after the spread of Western education. For, by the time men completed their studies or passed out of the university (established in 1857), they were almost 25. It was not customary yet for women, on the other hand, to pursue higher education. So they continued to be married off very young. Even at the end of the 19th century, therefore, educated young men were forced to marry 10- or 11-year-old girls. Generally, it can be said that the age difference between men and their wives increased rather than decreased at the end of this century.

Romantic and smart, handsome and young, aristocratic and England-returned—Rabindranath was perfect in every way as a prospective groom. Even he, however, was forced to marry at the wish of his elders an illiterate, village girl who was just 11 years old. 'Forced to marry' may not perhaps be quite right. For, the invitation that he designed for his wedding and sent out to friends is testimony not just to his sense of humour and wit but also to his happy consent to the match. At the turn of the century, he married off two of his daughters very young, and it was not even as if they were unlettered girls like their mother had been at the time of her marriage. One of the girls was 13, while the other was even younger—six months past 10. Surely he would not have tried to ascertain what such little slips of girls felt about getting married.

But though Tagore compromised with social custom in his own life, there are indications in his writing of the transformation that was taking place in a section of society. None of the heroines we meet in his collection of short stories, *Galpoguchchho* ('Bunch of Stories'), from the last decade of the 19th century is exactly a small girl. He wrote the novel *Gora* a few years after marrying off his own daughters, in 1910. Even at that time, it was not possible for his educated heroine, Sucharita, who was also a member of the Brahmo Samaj, to be over 15. What should be noted here, however, is that Sucharita is remarkably mature in her personality. That Kalyani in his short story *Aparichita* ('The Unknown One') was 16 was considered scandalous by other characters in the story. But Kalyani herself refused to hide her own age. The heroine of the short story *Haimanti* was also 16 and her parents-in-law tried their best to keep it a secret, but not Haimanti herself. Both these stories were written in 1914. By that time, indeed, there was some awareness on such matters as a consequence of the movement against child marriage and the spread of education.

New attitudes also surfaced in his stories on the matter of the exercise of free will in marriage. The hero of his short story *Samapti* (1893; 'The End'), Apurba, ignored his mother's preference and brushed aside her pleadings to marry a young girl of his own choice. He did not, however, try to ascertain the girl's opinion. This is not just one isolated case of a fictional character. The opinions and preferences of men began to gain importance in educated society as the age of marriage went up for them, but not those of girls. Educated Hindu men in the new age sought to marry, if given a chance, girls who would be able to somewhat grasp the concept of love and so respond, to an extent, to the new kind of love offered by their husbands. But such girls were rare.

Though the age of marriage for girls was not substantially raised in society as a whole, it did go up a little among Brahmos, Hindus influenced by the Brahmos and Christians towards the end of the 19th century. This was particularly noticeable in the case of women who obtained a higher education. For instance, the first women to pass out of the university, such as Chandramukhi Basu, Kadambini Basu, Kamini Ray, Jamini Ray, Indira Devi and Sarala Devi, all married late. Some highly educated women did not get married at all. The table below demonstrates how higher education affected the age of marriage for women.

Name	Education	Profession	Age of Marriage
Kadambini Basu	B.A, Medicine, Edinburgh	Doctor	21/22
Kamini Sen	B.A.	Teacher	30
Virginia Mary Mitra	M.B	Doctor	39
Chandramukhi Basu	M.A	Teacher	41
Indira Devi	B.A		26
Sarala Devi	B.A	Teacher	33
Jamini Sen	L.M.S, F.R.C.S	Doctor	Unmarried
Hemaprabha Basu	M.A		Unmarried
Lajjabati Basu	B.A.	Teacher	Unmarried
Radharani Lahiri		Teacher	Unmarried
Surabala Ghosh	B.A.		Unmarried

Table 6.1

Muslims lagged far behind in education. In their society, therefore, the age of marriage was even lower. But since there was no Islamic injunction making it mandatory for girls to marry before attaining puberty, there was no social scandal if girls were married at a slightly older age. Rokeya was 16 when she was married to Sakhawat Hossein in 1896. It did not cause any scandal. Men and women in Muslim society, especially women, did not in fact have any scope to choose their marriage partners. It is unlikely that Rokeya's opinion was sought when she was married off to a widower more than twice her age and suffering from diabetes. None of her writings expresses either love or any enthusiasm about her husband. (I have discussed the question of whether

Rokeya was happy in her married life in my book *Rassundari Theke Rokeya: Nari Progotir Eksho Bachhor.*)

The taste and preference of men in choosing a bride began to be deemed important in Western-educated urban society from the start of the 20th century, but the preference of women in selecting husbands was not taken seriously for many more years. One reason for this was that it took longer for their age of marriage to go up. They had not yet made significant strides in education either. Consequently, their personalities did not develop sufficiently. They did not, at this stage, contribute to the family finances with their own earnings. Their opinions in the matter of marriage, therefore, were not considered important.

The practice of fixing matches on the basis of preferences expressed by the man and woman concerned might not have acquired popularity in ordinary Bengali families, yet romantic involvements maturing into marriage began to happen in ones and twos right from the start of the 20th century. We have already mentioned this before. It was not just Western education that made this possible; the enactment of the Civil Marriage Act in 1872 also helped. (The Brahmos were not too keen to identify themselves as Hindus, and so under Keshab Sen's leadership a petition was presented to the government seeking a separate marriage law for Brahmos. After much debate and discussion, the government passed, not a Brahmo Marriage Act, but the Civil Marriage Act. This law was known as the 'three laws' or *teen ain* of 1872.) A notable example of an early love match in Bengal was the marriage of the poet Atulprasad Sen. A barrister by profession, he must have seen in England marriages where the partners chose each other. In the Brahmo Samaj, too, this was an ideal that was slowly but surely taking root. After coming back to Bengal, he fell in love with a first cousin, Hemantakumari, who was his maternal uncle's daughter, and wanted to marry her. But even under the Civil Marriage Act there was no provision for marriage with a first cousin, and surely not under Hindu laws. He, therefore, travelled to England with Hemantakumari with the intention of marrying her there. Unfortunately, even under English laws he was unable to marry his first cousin. A crestfallen Atulprasad subsequently discovered that it would be possible to marry her in a Scottish village under the laws of that village. So that is what he did and was happy for the time being. The close blood ties between him and his wife made this union so difficult to achieve. Meanwhile, in the Brahmo Samaj, marriages were preceded by some sort of acquaintance between the prospective partners and mutual consent, if not exactly courtship. We have already mentioned Kadambini Basu and Rajnarayan Basu's daughter Kumudini.

Courtship followed by marriage was rare among Muslims in those days. Love did not have much of a chance in this society, mainly because of the general orthodoxy, the purdah system and lack of education among girls. We have, however, already mentioned the many relationships of Nazrul Islam. Indeed, he played quite a pioneering role in Muslim society in this respect and eminently made up for its absent tradition of love. We must also remember how Faziltunnesa married for love.

At the end of the 20th century, instances of university students, colleagues and in some cases neighbours marrying after a period of courtship were on the rise. Yet, conservative society still frowns on such unions. Muslims are perhaps more conservative than Hindus in this respect. The reason is that education among Muslims is still relatively narrower in reach than among Hindus. They have been late, too, in taking their first strides on the way to modernism. Religious conservatism is also more entrenched among them. Even now, the opinions of family elders matter most in marriages, though in educated families the groom is consulted when a bride is chosen for him. The bride's opinion is also sought by her family, thought it may not always be taken seriously.

The giving of dowry was for centuries accepted as a standard practice in Bengali marriages. It still is among sections of this society. In some small Hindu communities, the custom of giving dowry for a bride was prevalent in the 19th century. But this was an exception to the general practice. Whether among Hindus or Muslims, the prevailing custom is to give dowry for a groom. Until recently, parents considered it a misfortune if a daughter was born instead of a son. One reason for this was the system of dowry. A lot of money was required to get a daughter married to a suitable man. A 'suitable' groom would belong to an elite and educated family and hold university degrees. The amount of the dowry would depend on how many of these degrees the groom held—matriculation, intermediate, B.A. and M.A. The dowry was given in the form of jewellery, cash, and money to pay for the groom's education. The expenses were sometimes so high that the bride's parents found themselves burdened by debt. In a short story by Tagore, the bride's father planned to sell his home to pay her dowry. Tagore himself paid dowry to his sons-in-law. Apart from paying for their overseas education, he also had to pay them in cash. The poet's relations with one of them broke down because he was unable to meet his demands.

At the end of the 20th century, dowry began to consist almost entirely of gifts rather than cash, with jewellery predominating. In some cases, the weight of the jewellery to be given is fixed between the two families before the marriage takes place. Another modern fad is to gift furniture and domestic gadgets. Marriage gifts range from bicycles, radios and watches among the poor to television sets, refrigerators, sofas and so on among the rich. The super rich even gift houses and cars. In educated sections, however, the custom is on the decline. It is not just good taste that is bringing this about but the fact that women are educated and, increasingly, financially independent. In villages, though, the custom does not seem to be dying at all. On the contrary, very often there are reports of women in villages who face cruel torture at the hands of their husbands who are out to get more dowry. The short story *Nirupama* that Tagore wrote more than a hundred years ago is still enacted in many a Bengali home.

Bengali society is deeply fragmented along the lines of religion, caste and financial status. In a society of so many divisions, not too many marriages take place across the social barriers, between castes and communities or between the rich and the poor. In the golden age of the Brahmo faith in the second half of the 19th century, many people had been able to rise above caste divisions. A few of the Brahmos married outside their own caste. From the 1860s and right up to the 1890s, several such marriages were reported with much fanfare in *Bamabodhini Patrika*. Yet, society did not take to these marriages very kindly. Those who became Brahmos, therefore, and even those who converted Christianity, did not easily marry outside caste. The caste that the converted to had left behind in their past lives in their parent communities was kept in mind when marriage alliances were made. Krishnamohan Bandyopadhyay, therefore, married his daughters either to Englishmen or to Brahmins.

There was stiff resistance among Bengalis to marriage with people from other regions and other communities. In spite of this, in the 19th century such marriages began taking place once in a while. In 1848, Michael Madhusudan married an Anglo-Indian woman. Within a couple of years, Surja Goodiv Chakraborty married an Englishwoman. Khetramohan Datta also married an Englishwoman, in 1866. Rokeya Sakhawat Hossein's father married an Irish woman during the Sepoy Mutiny. But all these examples are of Bengali men. The first Bengali woman to marry a foreigner was probably Hariprabha Takeda. She fell in love with and married, in 1907, a Japanese employee of her father's soap factory—Uemon Takeda. Another unusual thing that Hariprabha did was to travel to Japan, where she spent a few months. After returning from there she wrote a book titled *Bangamohilar Japan Jatra* (A Bengali Woman's Japanese Sojourn). Jatindramohan Sengupta married Nelly Grey during his stay in England, in 1909.

Marriage between the two main communities, Hindus and Muslims, was very rare at that time. There is a list of the registered marriages since 1852 at the India Office Library. This includes a few marriages between Hindus and Muslims, but until the year 1869 all such marriages took place outside Bengal. I was not able to gather evidence of when the first such marriage in Bengal took place. But there are reports of such marriages from the 20th century. The first such union that was highly publicised was Nazrul Islam's marriage with Pramila, also known as Ashalata Sen. A few years later, Humayun Kabir married Shanti Das. In the first few marriages between Hindus and Muslims in those initial years, the men were all Muslim and their brides were Hindus. Even at the end of the 20th century, there were not too many marriages between Hindu men and Muslim women. Unions between Muslim men and Hindu women are, however, no longer very unusual.

There was a time when marriages between the Ashrafs and the Atrafs were inconceivable. Yet, there is no Islamic injunction that might come in the way of such marriages. Muslim-run newspapers and magazines at the start of the 20th century, therefore, criticised the custom. Marriages started taking place between elite Muslim families and the more ordinary ones only after Atraf Muslims started climbing up the social ladder through education. When this started happening, aristocratic and wealthy Muslims had their daughters married to educated young men and got them to move in with the bride's family.

This kind of pride in family status is now seen as hollow andmeaningless. What counts more than family status while choosing a groom is education, career, success and so on. In the selection of brides, too, family status is less important than the girl's looks, education and career. This is particularly the case among the middle class. The preferences of the bride and groom themselves are also taken quite seriously. Individual freedom and personal likes and dislikes, then, are slowly occupying the space once dominated by society and collectiveness.

Once individual freedom assumes the deciding role in marriage, the married couple's relationship, and generally the question of how successful the marriage turns out to be, become important. That is why, in the last half century, the number of divorces has been fast rising. There are no reliable statistics on this. But that the number is rising is not debated. Society still largely sees divorces as being scandalous. In most cases, the woman is blamed. It causes social embarrassment for her family and affects the marriage prospects of her younger sisters. Many women, therefore, try to keep their marriage going despite being tortured by their husbands in order to protect her own and her family's honour.

Divorces are still relatively fewer among Hindus. This is because in Hindu society, second marriages are unusual for women. Writer and editor Nirupama Devi (1895-1984) was probably the first Hindu woman who divorced her first husband and remarried. She had been married into the Coochbehar royal family. Later she married the political activist Sisir Kumar Sen. The story of the writer Jyotirmala Devi is similar. She went to England in 1924 and got married there. But this marriage did not last very long. Many years later she fell in love with and married Birendrakishore Roychoudhury. But this marriage did not get social recognition.

When a marriage fails, men find it fairly easy to move on and marry a virgin again. It is not quite so easy for women to remarry. For, double standards still apply to the sexuality of men and women. Even men who have had multiple sexual encounters want their lovers and wives to be virgins and chaste (*sati*). That is why divorced women seeking to remarry often end up with much older men or widowers. Or maybe even divorced men with children from the previous marriage. The situation of financially independent women or women who enjoy some sort of social recognition or fame is different. This is true of women in both Bangladesh and West Bengal.

In this context it must be mentioned that remarriage is also problematic for young widows. Hindu widows were prohibited from marrying again even in ancient times. The child wives who became widowed at three or four also had to remain celibate for the rest of their lives. Even now, remarriage for widows is not very common among Hindus. But Muslim widows could remarry even in the Middle Ages, and they can do so now, though it is not as if there aren't any exceptions. Two of my close relatives lost their husbands in the early 1930s; one of them was 16 or 17 and the other was 21. Though they both lived to a ripe old age, neither of them ever married again.

The marriages that were fixed by family elders were in many cases little more than a licence for the couple to produce children. The husband went out to earn money while the wife took care of the house. The situation is changing fast with the spread of education, stress on individual freedom and the economic independence of women. In many households now, the wives would not quietly put up with unacceptable behaviour from husbands and in-laws. Many men, on the other hand, cling to the old attitudes and values. In sum, what men and women expect from marriages often does not match what they actually get. There is, as a result, a lot of unhappiness. Earlier, marital quarrels remained private, but they now come out into the open. Men and their wives once shared a kind of master servant relationship. Although men still arrogate greater authority and have louder voices, their position is not unchallenged anymore. Marriages fall apart more often now, yet it must be acknowledged that there is generally more love and understanding in marriages now than there was earlier. It is hard now to find an educated husband who is satisfied with just sex with his wife and does not seek her love. Or one who has not repeatedly asked her if she loves him. Wives, too, are much more curious and conscious about their husbands' feelings for them. Courtship before marriage, and even pre-marital sex, are now far more common. Not all such relationships end in marriage, either. To conclude, in the last 150 years love in Bengali society has been established on solid foundations. The institution of marriage has also been vastly, if not fundamentally, transformed.

Family

There is no mention of even large families in medieval Bengali society, let alone joint families. Treatment of diseases was then quite primitive, and child mortality rates were very high. It was not easy, therefore, for families to grow in size. Cholera and pox epidemics were among the factors that caused sudden and untimely deaths. There was hardly any treatment for malaria and other kinds of fever. At the end of the 18th century, a number of senior English officers including William Jones died young in Calcutta, despite having access to the best medical treatment available then. In 1831 Derozio died of cholera when he was just 23. In 1842 David Hare also died of cholera. But the overall situation started somewhat changing around this time. Vaccines arrived in Bengal in the 19th century. Hospitals were established. Treatments for malaria were introduced. In short, there was a slight improvement in healthcare, especially in a big city like Calcutta. It could be because of this improved medical situation that a family as large as Debendranath Tagore's was possible in the 19th century.

One does not encounter in medieval literature the kind of joint families seen among wealthy and middle class Hindus in the 19th and 20th centuries. The only exception is the story of Chand Saudagar. In *Manasamangal*, his adult children live with him. In the 16th-17th centuries, the poets who, like Mukundaram Chakraborty, left some account of their lives in writing, or even the autobiographical literature left by the Vaishnavas, do not give any information of large or joint families. There is in fact no specific information of when exactly the joint family began to appear in Bengali society. But it does not look like it happened before the 18th century. The custom of sharing the family home with adult brothers may not have developed by then, but there are many mentions of people living with aged parents in extended family set-ups from around that time. From the early 19th century, the joint family started being recognised as the ideal family structure among well-to-do Hindus.

This ideal became so firmly entrenched among the bhadraloks that in an article published in *Somprakash* in 1885 the joint family was referred to as a timeless custom. The article also blames the joint family set-up as being a harmful aspect of Bengali society. The joint family seems to have evolved as an incidental outcome of the Permanent Settlement. Rather than allow an established zamindari to get fragmented, many landed families accepted the alternative of adult brothers living together as a single family. Presumably, this was how the institution of the joint family developed within a short time. Other wealthy and middle class families imitated the example of the zamindars and started living in joint families. The family of Madhusudan's father can be cited as an instance of how this process happened. Rajnarayan Dutt's father was quite poor. But once Rajnarayan's eldest brother, who was educated, secured a job in Jessore and saw better times, all the four brothers set up home together. In the late 19th century, the institution of the joint family became an ideal that Hindus of the lower middle classes also tried to follow. The custom was so widely prevalent even in the 20th century that those who transgressed it had their reputations tainted. The joint family system found acceptance among some Muslims who copied their Hindu neighbours' way of life. But this was more of an exception rather than a general rule. There were far fewer zamindars among Muslims than there were among Hindus. Their laws of inheritance were also very clear. So the joint family never got a chance to become a widely prevalent institution among them. The joint family never quite took off among the poor, whether Hindu or Muslim. The economic environment conducive to the growth of the joint family never existed among the poor. Nor was the need for such a family structure ever felt among them.

The novels of Saratchandra written in the first three decades of the 20th century furnish indirect proof of how widespread and popular the joint family had become. There were many positive things about such families. Their members often had extremely strong ties with each other. Children brought up in such families grew up with values of cooperation and sacrifice. Saratchandra depicted these good things about the joint family in his novels. This was one of the reasons for his popularity among the educated middle class. Despite this glorified image of the joint family, however, many people were made quite miserable within its confines. Families were sometimes devastated by the pulls and pressures of difficult relationships. This aspect, too, can be seen in Saratchandra's novels. Individual freedom, in particular, was seriously compromised in these families. A melancholic example would be Mrinal in Tagore's *Strir Patra* ('Wife's Letter'). Flattened under the wheels of the joint family system, she was forced to give up even her own personality. In stories such as *Haimanti*, too, Tagore drew subtlely outlined sketches of animosities within joint families. In families of insufficient means, fights could break out even over food. Jealousies, greed and sometimes the narrow-mindedness of some members of joint families generated strong resentments.

So rigid were the rules that held the joint family together that members who lived away for the sake of a job or some other economic activity sent home their earnings and could spend time with their wives and children only during visits to the family home on vacations. They were not permitted to take their wives and children to live with them where they worked. Ishwarchandra Vidyasagar's father followed this custom, and even Ishwarchandra adhered to it. Some men were able to visit their families so infrequently that they could not do without a 'kept' woman. Those who were not moneyed enough to do so fulfilled their physical needs by visiting prostitutes. Yet they did not break the joint family rules.

There were, however, some men even in the 19th century who set aside the shackles of the joint family to take their wives and children along to wherever they worked and set up nuclear families. In this context we have already mentioned Madhusudan Dutt's father Rajnarayan Dutt, the zamindar of Uttorpara Jayokrishno Mukhopadhyay and Satyendranath Tagore. Jyotirindranath Tagore also stayed apart from the joint family off and on.

Though the joint family has increasingly been breaking down, the concept of the extended family continues to be quite strong among the educated middle classes. Even at the end of the 20th century and the beginning of the 21st, the educated eldest son is expected to take up a job in the city, oversee the education of younger siblings and take care of ageing parents. People are generally expected to help out nephews and nieces, other distant relatives and even those related by marriage – such as one's wives younger siblings – sometimes by providing them a home where they can pursue their studies and build a life for themselves. That children continue to live with their parents at least until they get married is not only the norm, it is also what is expected of them. Those who move out to live on their own in rented accommodations are criticised by their families and relatives.

A different kind of extended family has now emerged, which in the language of sociology is called the neo-extended family. Members of a family living within manageable distances who visit each other frequently and stay in constant contact over the telephone make up these new extended families. Such families can be noticed particularly in the cities. These families enjoy the benefits of both nuclear set-ups and extended families. The modern trend, however, is inclined towards the nuclear family, where parents make a home with their children. This is now so normative that people hesitate to share domestic space with relatives and see it as an imposition when they are forced to do so. Many families seriously consider, when fixing a match for a daughter, whether a prospective son-in-law will set up home independently or whether he will continue to live with his parents and siblings after marriage.

Values regarding the family size are also fast changing in Bengali society. Until the early years of the 19th century, family sizes remained small because of the high rate of infant mortality. Information about families growing in size is available from the 19th century, though even then there were few families quite as large as Debendranath Tagore's. Family sizes grew significantly in the 20th century, a time of unprecedented population increase sustained by the arrival of vaccines and life-saving medicines including quinine. We have already noted this in the chapter 'Bengali Culture in the Twentieth Century'. In some Muslim families in Bangladesh in the mid 20th century there could be 10, 12 or even 14 siblings growing up together, even among the educated. But the trend showed a significant decline in the late 20th century. Around the time when Muslim families in East Bengal were growing in size, awareness about family planning started appearing in the Calcutta-based educated Hindu society. Consequently, families became smaller in size. From the 1960s, some families in Calcutta started opting not to have a second child if the first was a son.

In 1951, the population of East Bengal was slightly over 40 million (4 crores). Hindus formed 20 per cent of the population. Notwithstanding the large-scale migration of Hindus to West Bengal and other areas of India, the 1961 Census showed that the population was rising at an alarming rate. The government now started showing some awareness of the problems of a fast growing population. Family planning campaigns started being undertaken by the government in the 1960s. The pressure on the land was also increasing. The lower middle classes now found it difficult to raise and educate children. The large urban families had a new problem to cope with—the problem of housing.

As increasing numbers of women joined the workforce, from the 1950s in West Bengal and the 1970s in Bangladesh, having a large number of children was no longer considered feasible. It was also increasingly difficult to hire help for childcare and housework. Many people therefore became more or less aware of the need for family planning. The limited spread of education and religious orthodoxies prevented family planning ideas from taking root immediately. Still, the urban educated family started getting smaller in size in the 1970s. The effects of family planning were not yet noticeable in rural families.

Family planning has been extremely successful in West Bengal. The people of West Bengal had already experienced the problems of urbanisation. That apart, conservatism regarding family planning is relatively less pronounced in Hindu society. There are now one or two children in most families in the cities of West Bengal, though sometimes there are more if the older children are girls. Even in the villages of West Bengal family sizes are smaller than in Bangladesh. Among Bengali Muslims on the other hand, the birth rates were always high. Industrialisation was slower in East Bengal. Family planning programmes also started later there. So the average family size in Bangladesh is relatively larger. There are few instances in Bangladesh of families with a single child and that child a daughter. Many people would not be happy with an only son, either.

Indeed, in both Bengals sons are still valued more than daughters. A daughter leaves her parental family behind when she marries, but a son can stay on with the parents. Even if he does not, he can always help them out in need and look after them in their old age. This is the hope that perhaps leads parents to stake greater claim on the son's affections and duties. That the family lineage is carried forward through sons is also an article of faith for Bengalis. This is why most families in Bangladesh hope for not one but at least two sons. In a land where life is relatively uncertain, parents can't quite feel secure with just one son. Despite this preference for a son, however, attitudes to daughters have changed significantly. The birth of a daughter no longer displeases her parents and other relatives as much it once did. On the contrary, some families actually rejoice if a daughter is born after a son. Many families now bring up their daughters in the same way, or almost in the same way, as sons. Daughters are educated and their opinions are taken seriously when the time comes to choose a marriage partner for her. Many daughters, on the other hand, support their parents financially before they marry, and sometimes even after they are married. Though husbands and their relatives do not generally take kindly to married daughters helping out their parents with their expenses.

BENGALI WOMEN AND THEIR CULTURE

In the religious life of ancient Bengal, mother goddesses reigned supreme. It is not unreasonable to infer from this that women played a leading role in society and family. From the time when some historical proof is available, however, the indications suggest that women occupied a subordinate position in family and society. Indications, because though we know of kings, scholars and writers of religious texts from the evidences available in history, history does not tell much about famous women and their lives in ancient times. Nothing is known about how important a role women played in family and in society or what kind of contribution they made. Though women make up half of human society, they are missing from the pages of history. Missing, likewise, are society's lower orders. An attempt to look into how this came about will show that men have always dominated women with their superior physical strength and their appropriation of the forces of production. They have also sought to perpetuate the subordination of women through religious regulations.

The situation did not significantly change with the introduction of Indo-Muslim rule at the dawn of the 13th century. For, there was nothing in Islamic faith and culture to radically improve the condition of women. Whether in education, economic role or social status, Muslims were not able to contribute any new ideas or traditions in the lives of Bengali women. When compared with the changes that occurred several centuries later during the British colonial regime, it is easy to see how scant the effect of Indo-Muslim rule was in the lives of Bengali women. What we see during this era is a continuation of the old tradition. Moreover, most of the Muslim noblemen (the amirs and omrahs) and the Sufi preachers and pirs used force or bribes to take local women as wives or concubines. There is no written evidence to show that these women, who became converts to Islam, were able to occupy high positions in family and society. In sum, there were no opportunities in the male-dominated society of ancient and medieval Bengal for women to realise their promise and potential. Nor indeed can it be said that even in modern times women get the same opportunities as men to grow to their full potential. It is possible to guess the heights that women might well have climbed, if given a chance, from the advances that they have made in education in the modern age. They no longer trail behind men in education, not even a bit. Yet there was a time when it was believed that women had no intellect.

Despite the lower social status of women, the contribution of women in Bengali culture is not at all negligible. From behind the curtains they played a fairly equal role in building up family and society. Not only did they inspire and motivate the men, they also enriched certain branches of culture. In this chapter we will follow the gradual progress of women to their present situation and see how their contribution nurtured different aspects of Bengali culture. But as we have already observed, the main obstacle in this task is that though the histories of kings and emperors were more or less written down, there is hardly any written history of women, just as there is none of the lower orders.

Position of Women vis-à-vis Society and Family

Religious identities might not have made any difference to the position of women in Bengali society, but divisions of class did make a significant difference. For instance, women in the poorest families in villages were somewhat better positioned. These women helped their husbands in economic activities and so were not confined to the house. Indeed, they could not really afford to stay confined in domestic spaces. They had to work in the fields or take part in buying and selling in the marketplace. They were not in a position, then, to shut themselves up in their homes or to observe purdah. In wealthy families the situation was quite different. Women in these families were not required to participate in economic activities, and so their husbands guarded them like property and practically kept them imprisoned at home.

Women's standing in their marriages also varied according to class differences. It appears from Nihar Ranjan Ray's descriptions that even in ancient Bengal it was customary among the poor to take only one wife. But the rich indulged themselves with more than one wife. Nor were concubines unheard of. Marriages took place within caste boundaries, but the rich could marry outside their own caste if it so took their fancy. Austerities were prescribed for widows even in those early times. Indeed, austerities started being imposed on even Muslim widows in the Middle Ages. Writing about Hossein Shah's regime, Mamtazur Rahman Tarafdar mentions that Muslim widows, at least for a period following their bereavement, abstained from indulgences in food, dress, jewellery, and so on. From medieval literature and other historical evidence, marriage as an institution does not appear to have particularly changed; it remained much like what it was in ancient times. In marriages, too, women did not command much respect and their personal autonomy was not recognised. Men were the dominant and controlling partners.

Women in wealthy families did not have even the limited rights in decision-making that women in poor families did. The rich dressed up their women in expensive clothes and jewellery and provided them with all the comforts of life, but in exchange they expected servile obedience. These women were, in a word, glorified slaves. They had no right to come out of their marriages no matter how unbearable things might get. That apart, Hindus had no religious sanction for divorce. For men, however, the situation was different. They could exile forever a wife they did not like in her parental home, or they could reduce her to the position of a servant and take another wife. Poor women, on the contrary, helped out their men in economic activities and did not receive bribes of expensive clothes or jewellery, and hence they expressed their opinions and protests quite loudly. They could not match their men in physical strength but they made up for it with their high-decibel voices. The samples of women's conversations and quarrels that William Carey collected at the start of the 19th century indicate that they had decidedly sharp tongues. From the pictures of women drawn by poets ranging from Borhu Chandidas to Bharatchandra, women appear to have been lively and rather shrewish, notwithstanding their subordinate position in the family.

There were major differences between rich and poor women in the way they dressed. Poor women usually made do with a single piece of clothing. In the chapter on the sartorial aspect of culture, we will look at the kind of clothes that women wore and the changes that were introduced in ways of dressing in the 19th century. It will suffice here to say that the clothes that women wore might have covered their shame at home but were not suitable for venturing out of the house or in the presence of men. This scant clothing was in fact one of the chief reasons for observing purdah, the custom of keeping women in seclusion.

It cannot be said with any certainty exactly when purdah started being observed in Bengali society. But with the emergence of a sense of Hindu nationhood in the 19th century, there also appeared a tendency to blame an 'other' for everything that was flawed about the past. The Muslim rulers were blamed for purdah. No historical evidence has been found to support this attribution of responsibility. On the contrary, the information presented by Nihar Ranjan Ray seems to indicate that even in ancient times women of rich and aristocratic families did not venture out into the open and stayed indoors. On the other hand, as already mentioned, the lifestyles of poor women precluded the possibility of such seclusion. But there are also indications that the poor families which managed to turn around their fortunes resorted to purdah to protect the 'honour' of their women. In the second half of the 19th century, an English civilian called James Wise wrote in his memoirs that in the villages what people did as soon as they made a little money, particularly the Muslims, was to fence the portion of the house marked out for women and put in a pucca toilet.

No matter when it was first introduced, in the late 18th and early 19th century purdah was observed quite strictly in Bengali society, particularly in well-to-do, educated and genteel families. Rasasundari Devi was born in 1810 in a village in Pabna. She has not left any description of the kind of purdah that was observed in this village. Married into a family that owned a small zamindari (landholding) in Faridpur, she has described in detail the rules of privacy that were strictly followed in this family. As we discussed in the previous chapter, her husband could not meet her during the day, nor was she able to access spaces where he was present. Her husband did not even talk to her during the day. In those days men coming into the women's portion of the house had to first send in warning signals such as by clearing the throat or coughing, so that the women could remove themselves out of sight or rearrange their clothing and make themselves presentable. On one occasion Rasasundari fell ill and almost died. When word reached her husband, he came into the house accompanied by others of the family. He did not, however, try to feel her body temperature or make any attempt to find out how she was doing. Remaining at respectable distance from his wife, he expressed his anxiety by asking, 'Is she dead?'

Rasasundari Devi was 12 years old when she got married. Though so young, she wore a long veil in the presence of her mother-in-law and her two sisters-in-law in deference to the rules of purdah. As for her husband, she was all along terrified and extremely shy of him. So extreme, in fact, was this shyness that she was reluctant to even venture out before his horse. Once this horse was nibbling at the paddy left out to dry in the courtyard. Rasasundari wanted to drive it away. But she could not do so, despite being somewhat exercised over the paddy being eaten up, because she could not bring herself to go out before her husband's horse. Rasasundari was a rural woman. It might be supposed that seclusion rules for women were more rigid in rural society. This, however, is not true. The purdah was actually far more lax in the countryside. We know, on the other hand, how strictly purdah was observed in the most educated, cultured and elite family of Calcutta, the Tagores of Jorasanko, half a century later. When Tagore's mother wanted a bath in the Ganga, she was taken to the river in a closed palanquin. She never got out of it, though. The bearers carrying the palanquin dipped it into the river with the lady sitting inside.

Women had no permission to go out of the house in those days. Once in a while married women visited their parents. An example of how confined women were can be given from Keshab Sen's life. He was an extremely enthusiastic member of the Brahmo Samaj. Impressed by his zeal and his abilities, Debendranath Tagore made him the Acharya of Brahmo Samaj in the early 1860s. Keshab Sen wanted to take his wife along with him to the anointment ceremony at the Tagore family house. But his family could not accept the thought of his wife coming out of purdah to visit unrelated people, and they forbade him to take her out. When he tried to defy their diktat, they did not hesitate to get a watchman to try and stop him. Eventually, Keshab cut off his family and moved in with the Tagores along with his wife.

In Dinabandhu Mitra's play *Jamai Barik* written in the 1860s we see a household where the sons-in-law lived in separate quarters away from the women's portion. They did not meet their wives during the day. Sometimes at night they were called inside. In the Tagore family, too, the husbands went into the women's portion only at night. Both Tagore's sister Soudamini Devi and Satyendranath's wife Jnanadanandini Devi have mentioned this. Debendranath himself was not an exception to this rule. He went into the inner chambers of the house around 10 at night where his wife, Sarada Devi, waited for him, all decked-up and perfumed.

Satyendranath Tagore was as aware of women's rights as one could be in his time and sensitive about possible companionship in marital relationships. But even he could be with his 'Genu' only at night, not earlier in the day. Once he decided to introduce his close friend Manomohan Ghosh to Jnanada Devi. But it was not such an easy thing to do. The first obstacle was that the household rules would not allow Jnanadanandini Devi to leave the women's quarters or Manomohan to go in there. So one night Satyendranath put his arm around his friend's neck and marched in step with him to the women's portion, so that no one could make out, from the footsteps, that two men, and not one, were coming in. Once inside Jnanada's room, Satyendranath shoved his friend inside the mosquito net along with Jnanada. But in an age when there was no tradition of men and women mingling and talking freely, there was no conversation or even exchange of niceties between them. Stiff and faint with embarrassment, Jnanada could not utter a word. After a while, Satyendranath marched out with his friend. A few years later, in 1864, Jnanada went to Bombay with her husband. There, too, gawky and extremely shy, she behaved unnaturally on some occasions. By the time she was back in Calcutta in 1866, however, she had turned into a self-possessed and sophisticated woman who had completely left the purdah behind. In this phase she even attended a party at the Governor General's house without her husband.

Since women were not able to meet their husbands during the day, and since there wasn't much conversation between couples even at other times, normal marital relationships could not always develop. Nirad Chaudhuri has mentioned an almost incredible example of this kind of marriage. A mother of three apparently did not know what her husband looked like. So she did not recognise him when one day she saw him during the day. They had until then met only at night, and their only exchanges had taken place in bed. In Nirad Chaudhuri's opinion, in the sexual encounters that women had with their husbands in such circumstances, the two bodies made contact and achieved sensual gratification, but there was no pleasure of sight. For, neither could see the other in the darkness.

The example that Satyendranath set by bringing his wife out of domestic confinement enthused many young men of the time. For instance, two zamindar brothers from Barisal, Rakhalchandra and Biharilal Ray, brought their wives out of the purdah in the Barisal Brahmo Samaj. They even startled the people of Barisal out of their wits by riding with their wives in open horse-drawn carriages. Earlier, in 1866, Jnanadanandini Devi caused a social scandal when upon her return from Bombay she rode home in a car (phaeton) after her ship docked in Calcutta. Upset by such outrageous behaviour, Debendranath did not speak to his daughter-in-law for a long time. The Ray brothers did not stop at riding with their wives in open carriages. From reports in *Bamabodhini Patrika* we know that they invited local European officers for a meal at their house. The Ray wives joined their guests at the meal. A much impressed Cecil Beadon, then Lieutenant Governor of Bengal, wrote to the Barisal Collector praising the Ray brothers.

In Calcutta, too, the Brahmo Samaj set two historic examples in breaking the rules of purdah. The first was in November 1866 when young Brahmos held a reception for Mary Carpenter. The men and women who gathered on the occasion disregarded purdah to meet and hold discussions. Mary Carpenter in turn invited them to a function in December, and there, too, men and women met and talked. But the leader of these young Brahmos, Keshab Sen, did not approve. They, however, ignored his disapproval and carried on encouraging such acts of defying purdah. In the same year, two Bengali girls - the two daughters of Gobindachandra Datta, Toru and Aru Dutt – set sail for England to pursue higher studies. In another few years, the wives of Sashipada Bandyopadhyay, Satyendranath Tagore, Manomohan Ghosh and

Umeshchandra Bandyopadhyay travelled to England. Jnanadanandini went by herself, without her husband. Even without travelling to England, people like Durgamohan Das, the three sisters of Jagadish Chandra Bose, Rakhalchandra Ray's wife Kusumkumari, Rajkumari Bandyopadhyay and Radharani Lahiri set shining examples of rejecting purdah. *Bamabodhini Patrika* reported that a young woman turned up for Calcutta University's convocation ceremony in early 1871. The magazine, established though it was to improve the condition of women, was critical of this act. When, the following year, Ramtanu Lahiri attended a lecture by Keshab Sen with his daughter and nieces, even someone as concerned about women's situation as Peary Chand Mitra sharply criticised the action.

Eventually, it was over the breaking of purdah rules that the Brahmo Samaj split in 1872. Differences of opinion cropped up with Debendranath Tagore over whether women should join the men during prayer meetings without any curtain to separate the two sexes. Some people objected that the women sharing the same space during religious services might prove distracting for the men. Debendranath was in favour of women continuing to sit behind a curtain. But Keshab and his young followers were in favour of doing away with the curtain. In the end, this dispute split the Samaj. Debendranath and his followers remained in what was called the Adi (original) Brahmo Samaj; the sect formed by Keshab's supporters was called the Naba Bidhan (new dispensation) Samaj. The name that they were popularly known by was 'Unnoto Brahmo' (progressive Brahmo). But though the Adi Brahmo Samaj did not recognise women's right to pray without purdah, Debendranath's sons Satyendranath and Jyotirindranath did not show any regard for purdah. Jnanada Devi was not the only one to defy purdah by riding a phaeton and going to a party attended by men. Jyotirindranath went out horse-riding with his wife in the open fields surrounding Fort William (called Garher Math) in the 1870s, the two of them mounted on separate horses. In the 1880s, the Tagore women started taking part in the family's theatrical performances. Not with all the force of his formidable personality could Debendranath stop this tide of modernism.

The example of rejecting purdah set by the Brahmo Samaj was later followed not just by other Brahmos including those in the smaller towns. English-educated Hindus were also influenced by them. At the fag end of the 19th century, the rigidities of purdah slowly eased. The change became inevitable with the spread of women's education and with women starting to join the workforce in ones and twos. From the early 1880s women started seriously pursuing higher education and even taking up jobs after passing out with university degrees. They were in fact partly forced to ignore the tradition of purdah in order to acquire an education. Kadambini Devi had actually travelled to England to study medicine, and in 1889 she joined the Congress session as a delegate along with Swarnakumari Devi. Krishnabhabini Das was not a Brahmo. But she spent a few years in England with her husband Debendranath, and after returning to Bengal she organised several programmes for the liberation of women. She, too, did not observe purdah. Many English-educated young men at this time brought their wives out of purdah in order to seek greater fulfilment in their own lives. And so it came about that Hindu society shed the purdah in the early 20th century.

Purdah for Hindus was a civilisational thing. But for Muslims it was also linked to religion. That is why purdah rules were more rigid among educated and well-to-do Muslims than among Hindus. The 47 instances of purdah that Rokeya Sakhawat Hossein described in her *Abarodhbasini* (Life in Confinement) were, unless exaggerated, not just strict but quite heart-rending. At least in one instance it was life-destroying, for the woman concerned died in her effort to cling to purdah norms. Rokeya herself was rigidly bound by purdah as a child. She has described how she had to take refuge in the attic when women came visiting. So it was not only in the presence of men that she had to observe purdah but also unrelated women. As an adult Rokeya was able in some ways to wholeheartedly embrace modernism. Yet she never gave up the burkha and other rules of purdah. It must be mentioned in this context that the burkha was a necessary part of purdah for Muslims. Hindu women did not wear burkhas.

Partly because of religious reasons, and partly because of the delayed spread of education among women, Muslim society took a long time to discard purdah. From Rokeya's description of her school, it is clear that purdah was quite rigid among Muslims in the first two decades of the 20th century. There is no specific information about how exactly purdah eventually broke down among them. But one or two incidents do give us some idea. For instance, Kazi Nazrul Islam does not seem to have deferred to purdah rules when he met the well-read and beautiful Faziltunnesa in Dhaka after arriving there in 1927. But only a year earlier, when he was Habibullah Bahar's guest in Chittagong for a month, he probably did not even meet his host's sister, Shamsun Nahar, though she deeply admired the poet. Very slowly, the iron grip of purdah gave out as instances of people defying it began to come to the fore, even if they came in ones and twos. Eventually, educated Muslim women in the cities completely discarded purdah in the 1950s and 1960s. The process of acquiring an education weakened the purdah among both Hindu and Muslim women. Among the consequences of education was a further weakening of purdah.

Women's Education

Ancient and medieval Bengal had no tradition of educating women, whether rich or poor, though there were exceptions. For instance, an aged Buddhist nun of Gaur called Bilasbraja earned fame as an author of Buddhist scriptural texts during the reign of the Pala kings. We also hear of a 15th century poet called Indramukhi. In the 16th century, Advaitacharya's wife Sita Devi and Nityananda's wife Jahnavi Devi were scholars of Vaishnava scriptural literature. We know about a poet called Chandravati, roughly belonging to the same time, who composed narrative poems on the *Ramayana*, the goddess Manasa, and so on. Her father, Banshidas Bhattacharya, was a poet. It was his interest and encouragement that made Chandravati learn to read and write, and it was his example she followed when she started writing poems. We also know of a few other women poets. Early in the next century, for instance, Priyamvada Devi mastered literature and grammar. In the middle of the century, Vaijayanti Devi acquired scholarship in poetry, literature, philosophy and the scriptures. She helped her husband to write a work of poetry. Srinivas Acharya's wife Padmavati also acquired knowledge of the scriptures and music in the 17th century. In the 18th century, women poets Anandamoyi and Ganga wrote some songs. Apart from these women, there are some educated female fictional characters such as Vidya in medieval Bengali narrative poems. These examples, few and far between though they are, prove only too well that women had the intellect to acquire learning and to produce literature. It was the social arrangements of the times they lived in that prevented them from acquiring an education and hence from gaining the kind of position in society and history that men did.

Many women, however, were trained in music and dance even if they could not acquire an education. For, women trained in dance and music have always been in demand for the entertainment of kings and landlords. So a tradition of music and dance always existed among a certain section of women. Notwithstanding the joy that these professionals brought to men and the contribution they made to music and dance, they were not respectable in the eyes of society. We hear of amateur women artists, on the other hand, who earned fame with their skills in music and dance. One such woman was the poet Jayadev's wife, Padmavati. The names of other such women in the Middle Ages are not known, but sculpted figures of dancing women bear testimony that dance was popular in the upper stratum of society.

As for women's education, some changes began to appear right from the early years of British rule. Women started, in ones and twos, to come forward and acquire an education. Three women can be cited as examples. Rani Bhabani, Hoti Bidyalankar and Rupmanjari alias Hotu Bidyalankar. All three were educated. Hoti and Hotu Bidyalankar, in particular, were able to hold their own against the pandits of the day. Almost all of the handful of women who in those days managed to acquire an education were widows. Their aim was to either read religious texts or to look after landholdings. There were, of course, exceptions. Rupmanjari, for instance, was not a widow. Her father decided to educate her because he noticed that she was exceptionally intelligent.

The few exceptional women who learnt to read and write in those early years did so with the help of relatives or pandits. There were no institutional arrangements yet to educate girls. Most men actually doubted whether they even had the intellectual abilities to acquire an education. In 1819, Ram Mohan Roy challenged this male assumption in a book and asked whether men had ever put women to test in order to ascertain whether they had intellect. Rasasundari Devi would have been nine or 10 years old when he wrote this. Her uncle used to leave her for a while every day at the household pathshala (an informal school with a pandit teaching young boys) to protect her from bullying by other little girls. Boys were taught at the pathshala, but no one, not even the teacher, thought of teaching her. They did not even suspect that she had the ability to learn. Yet she silently grasped what she watched the boys learning. When, many years later, she learned to write, she became known as the first woman to write an autobiography in Bengali. In 1821, Gourmohan Bidyalankar wrote a book entitled *Stree Shiksha Bidhayak* (Arguments in Favour of Female Education) advocating women's education. He, too, tried to persuade men that women had the intellectual abilities to acquire an education and that they should be educated.

There is nothing to show that the books of Ram Mohan or Gourmohan inspired anyone right away to encourage efforts to educate girls. There is in fact nothing to show that these writers themselves made any arrangements to educate the women in their own families. We know from the newspapers and magazines published in the 1820s, however, that Christian missionaries tried to establish some schools for girls in and around Calcutta. But girls from decent families did not attend these schools. Rather, some educated and aristocratic families of Calcutta got Englishwomen to come home and educate their girls. Shibsundar Roy's daughter Harasundari was one of those women who were educated in this way. Prasanna Kumar Tagore arranged for the women in his household to be educated at home. Ishanchandra Mustafi also got his daughter Shibsundari Devi educated at home. Shibsundari later wrote a play entitled *Tarabati*. Chandicharan Tarkalankar educated his widowed daughter Drabamoyee. This private enterprise of educating women at home was in those days known as 'zenana shiksha' or zenana education. This was how the educationist Faizunnessa, growing up far away from Calcutta in a Muslim family in Comilla, learned Bengali and English, apart from Arabic and Farsi. This instance shows how far the ideal of privately educating women at home had quietly spread.

That women must be educated so that they may become suitable partners for men and properly raise children was an idea that took hold from the 1830s. As we noted in the previous chapter, the young men who were at that time receiving an English education in Hindu college perceived the difficulties of building meaningful lives with uneducated spouses. But none had the courage to openly educate girls. Women's education would result in girls being widowed, bring harm to the family, make women promiscuous and disobedient, turn them off housework—such and many more were the prejudices that circulated in those days. Nevertheless, members of the Young Bengal group and social reformers such as Akshay Kumar Datta and Gourishankar Bhattacharjya started writing in newspapers and magazines in favour of women's education from the start of the 1840s. What they wrote might have got a few individuals interested in women's education, but opposition from orthodox society did not ease. When Bethune School was established for girls of high-caste Hindu families, conservative sections virulently criticised and opposed the move. A few of the families who brushed aside these objections to send their girls to this school faced social ostracism. Nevertheless, at Vidyasagar's initiative in the 1850s more girls' schools were established in the districts.

That apart, around this time some English-educated young men, especially the Brahmos, started secretly educating their wives. This was how Kishorichand Mitra educated his wife Kailasbasini Devi. Many years later, Kailasbasini wrote an autobiography. Krishnamohan Bandyopadhyay was able to give an excellent education to his wife and daughters. Another shining example of this kind is that of Kailasbasini Devi (Gupta). We have noted earlier that when she got married to Durgacharan Gupta at the age of 12 (in 1849), she was not even familiar with the alphabet. Under the caring supervision of her husband, however, she acquired a good education within 10 years. In the 1860s she published three books, in both prose and verse. (I have extensively discussed this in my book *Rassundari Theke Rokeya: Nari Progotir Eksho Bachhor*, 'From Rassundari to Rokeya: Hundred Years of Women's Liberation'). Bamasundari, Brahmamoyee and Kumudini were some other learned women of the time. They, too, were educated at home, at the initiative of their families.

There was, to begin with, very little government enterprise about women's education, informal or institutional. English-educated young men and members of the Brahmo Samaj were in fact far more enthusiastic about this. Thanks to their efforts, the reach of women's education began to slowly expand, however low the standard. The government started a miserly patronage of female education in the late 1850s. How far-reaching this turned out to be can be inferred from the statistics in the table below.

Girls' Schools and Number of Female Students

Year	Number of Schools	Number of Students
1863	95	2,486
1871	344	6,717
1881	1,042	44,096
1890	2,238	78,865

Table 7.1 *Source: General Report on Public Instruction in Bengal for the years 1863-64, 1871-72 and 1890-91*

Though primary education for girls thrived at government and private initiative, there was at that time no system in place to impart higher education to women. Parents, too, were not really keen to look beyond primary education for daughters. Girls got married at 10 or 12 years of age, and with marriage ended their studies. Annette Akroyd initiated some efforts towards higher education for women in the 1870s, but these could not be sustained for too long. Later, institutional arrangements centred around Bethune School were made for imparting higher education to women. In 1878 Calcutta University recognised women's right to write examinations. In the initial years, however, no one but Brahmos and Christians availed themselves of this opportunity. Admission to Bethune School was also limited to high-caste Hindus and Christians; other communities, including Muslims, did not have entry. Once the doors of higher education were thrown open, within a few years – in 1883 – Chandramukhi Basu and Kadambini Basu passed out with B.A. degrees. Kamini Sen, Priyatama Datta, Kumudini Khastagir, Suprabha Gupta, Leela Sinha, Sarala Ghosal, Sarat Chakraborty, Jibonbala Datta, Indira Tagore and Priyambada Bagchi graduated in the next 10 years—a total of 12 women, counting the first two graduates. Chandramukhi Basu and Nirmalabala Shom also acquired M.A. degrees. Nirmala Shom obtained the degree in two subjects. Bidhumukhi Basu and Violet Mary Mitra got M.B. degrees. This was how women's education started and spread in Bengal. In the early 20th century Sarojini Naidu's younger sister Mrinalini Chattopadhyay graduated in the Philosophy tripos from Cambridge University. Surama Mitra was the first woman to secure a doctorate degree from Calcutta University, in 1941. In the late 19th century Nagendrabala Mustafi (1877-1906) managed to learn several languages on her own initiative. (I have extensively discussed this in my book *Reluctant Debutante: Response of Bengali Women towards Modernization*, 1983.)

Though the English-educated families of Calcutta started educating their women, it took much longer for women's education to spread outside the capital. Besides, even among high-caste Hindus, the spread and development of education was not even. The table below will show how unequal the expansion of women's education was among the different castes.

Percentage of Educated Women among High-caste Hindus

Caste	Education Percentage	English ediucation Percentage
Brahmin	5.6	0.1
Kayastha	8	0.4
Vaidya	25.9	0.8
Brahmo	55.6	30.9

Table 7.2 *Source: Census of India, 1901, Vol VIA, Pt II, pp 60-61;100-04,106-11*

(In connection with this data, it must be remembered that expansion of education was limited among Brahmins because they had a family occupation. Education expanded relatively much faster among the Kayasthas, Baidyas and Brahmos. As for the Brahmos, it should be kept in mind that in the census count of 1901 most of them identified themselves as Hindus. So the data on Brahmos in this census is not very reliable.)

Just as Muslims were some 50 to 60 years behind the Hindus in acquiring an English education, women's education among them was also delayed by some 50-60 years. The handful of Muslim women who were educated in the early years were exceptions. *Bamabodhini Patrika* started publishing in 1833. Writings by women, mostly immature, were regularly published in this magazine. Only one Muslim writer was published in the magazine's first 40 years, in 1865. She was Taherannessa. Faizunnessa was taught Arabic, Farsi, Bengali and Sanskrit by home tutors. She later published a book of poetry. Rokeya Sakhawat Hossein's elder sister, Karimunnessa, acquired some knowledge of Arabic and Farsi at home. But she started learning Bengali and English only in 1869, after her marriage, encouraged by her husband and helped by her in-laws. In the 1880s, Rokeya educated herself in complete secrecy, with help from Karimunnessa and her elder brother. She also picked up English quite well from her England-returned husband after her marriage in 1896. When after her husband's death she founded a girls' school to educate Muslim girls, she faced strong social opposition despite the strict purdah maintained in her school. (Interested readers can consult my aforementioned book *Rassundari Theke Rokeya: Nari Progotir Eksho Bachhor* for a detailed account.) Masuda Rahman, a writer deeply admired by Nazrul Islam, was also tutored at home.

How narrow the reach of women's education among Muslims was in comparison with that among Hindus is clear from the statistics given below. While looking at the data about Muslims, it is important to remember that Muslims who could read the Quran were also considered educated in those days. But even if they could read the Quran they did not always have any real knowledge of Arabic. Besides, they were not tutored in Bengali at all. Many of the Muslim women included in the data, therefore, did not have any proper education.

Percentage of Educated Hindu and Muslim Women, 1901

District	Hindu		Muslim	
	Educated	English educated	Educated	English educated
Calcutta, Howrah, Hooghly, 24 Paraganas, Midnapore, Burdwan, Murshidabad, Nadia	1.4	0.5	0.4	0.01
Dinajpur, Rangpur, Bogra, Rajshahi, Pabna, Mymensingh, Dhaka,Faridpur, Barisal,Comilla, Noakhali,Khulna, Jessore	1.2	0.02	0.15	0.001

Table 7.3 *Source: Report on the Census of India,1901, Vol VIA, Pt.II, pp. 54-76*

Just as institutional education had a delayed start among Muslim women in comparison with their Brahmo, Christian and high-caste Hindu sisters, the speed with which it spread was also very, very slow. There was no separate school for Muslim girls, and there were many schools where they had no right of entry as we have already noted. Nawab Faizunnessa was the first Muslim woman to open a primary school for girls in Comilla, in the second half of the 19th century. Long after her death, this institution became a high school. On the other hand, the school started by Rokeya Sakhawat Hossein in 1909 grew into a high school within a few years.

Rokeya Sakhawat Hossein

Even at the dawn of the 20th century, there were hardly any Muslim girls in high schools. From 1911, however, educational efforts among Muslim girls started gathering momentum, especially in Eden School in Dhaka. It was from this school that Faziltunnesa topped the school-leaving examination of 1921. In 1925 she graduated with distinction from Bethune College. Two years later, she secured a first class first in Mathematics from Dhaka University. The following year she went to England for further studies, though she left halfway to come back and marry. Notwithstanding the example set by this exceptional woman, however, Muslim girls did not generally show a great deal of interest in higher education. As late as 1937, of the nearly 1,100 women students in the colleges of Dhaka only 37 were Muslim. Educated Muslim women such as Malekunnessa, Sarah Taifur, Mamlukul Fatema, Nurunnessa Khatun, Zobeda Khatun, Shamsun Nahar Mahmud and Sufia Kamal had mostly acquired their education through home schooling and were taught by relatives. In the initial years many women even refused to take lessons from Hindu teachers.

Despite the late start of women's education, many of the women who received higher education came forward to teach. Once this happened, the process of women's education was relatively hastened. From this perspective, therefore, women made an extremely significant contribution in the spread of education. Among the women who played significant roles in the spread of education in the early years were Bamasundari, Durgamohan Das's wife Brahmamoyee Devi, Nistarini, Rajalakshmi Sen, Radharani Lahiri, Manorama Majumdar, Chandramukhi Basu, Kamini Ray, Jyotirmoyee Gangopadhyay, Tatini Das, Durgapuri Debi and Rokeya Sakhawat Hossein.

Jobs, Manly Jobs, Economic Roles

We have noted how in the initial years the objective of women's education was to produce ideal life partners for educated men and competent mothers. But once women received some education, what they would do at the end of their learning lives also emerged as a problem. Not all women were happy at the prospect of a lifetime of just housework, reading novels and knitting. There was also pressure from social reformers for women to play an active role in the spread of education. For, they felt that the appointment of women teachers in the place of men would get conservative families interested in female education. Social reformers repeatedly petitioned the government for a 'normal school' for women teachers, that is, a teachers' training school for women. Finally, in the late 1860s, the government decided to allot Rs.1,000 a month for such a school in Calcutta. Even before that a normal school for women was started in Dhaka in 1863. But this school did not run beyond a few years.

Though there was sufficient demand for women teachers, women of bhadralok families, wary of social disapproval, did not readily respond. That is why probably the first women to start working for pay did so in the smaller towns and belonged to the lower Hindu castes. We know from a report in *Bamabodhini Patrika* that a woman from Dhaka called Radhamoni Devi got a job with the Sherpur *Stree Shiksha* Bidhayini Sabha in 1866 at Rs.40 a month. She had been educated at the women's normal school in Dhaka, established three years earlier. Seventeen Hindu women, mostly from the lower castes, are known to have been educated at this school. Some years later, in the 1870s, Ramtanu Lahiri's niece Radharani Lahiri (her father was a Christian) made bold to start teaching at a school in Calcutta. She later became the principal of Bethune School. Manorama Majumdar of Barisal also started teaching in the early 1870s. But these early examples did not immediately influence others.

The first woman to secure a prestigious government job on the basis of her educational qualification was Krishnamohan Bandyopadhyay's daughter Manomohini Wheeler, in 1876. She, too, had not received any institutional education and had been educated at home by her father and sisters. After Calcutta University recognised the right of women to pursue higher studies, more opportunities for women to receive institutional education and secure jobs became available. The first woman to secure a job, in 1884, after passing out with a university degree was Chandramukhi Basu. After completing her master's, she started working in Bethune School as Assistant Superintendent. A few years later she became the principal of Bethune College. She did not much feel the pressure of orthodoxy from her own society because she was a Christian. But her educational qualification and her status as a working woman seems to have come in the way of her getting married at a suitable age. She married unusually late for her time, after she was 41.

Notwithstanding the effect of education and a paid job in Chandramukhi Basu's personal life, the example she set made it easier for others to accept paid jobs. For instance, when Kamini Sen graduated a few years after this, she considered taking up a job. Her father initially objected, but because hers was a Brahmo family she did not have to face much social opposition.

Some years later, Kumudini Khastagir, Hemaprabha Basu and Surabala Ghosh passed out of Bethune College and got jobs in the same college. Sarala Ghosal got a high-paying teaching job in Hyderabad. On the other hand, her cousin Indira Tagore also did her bachelor's from Bethune College, but she did not take up a job.

When the right to work became somewhat established for women of bhadralok families, teaching was still the only kind of work that they could do. Apart from teaching, the only other profession in which women were first seen to be making a living was acting. From 1873, several women including Binodini and Golapsundari were appointed to act in professional theatre. None of them, of course, had much education to speak of. I have discussed this extensively in the chapter on theatre and cinema.

The most respectable profession for women outside teaching was medicine. But though female doctors were much needed, society did not readily accept women as doctors. Kadambini Basu went to England for higher studies in medicine and started practising as a physician after she came back. But she was derided and slandered in the newspapers and magazines of the time, and a libel suit was fought in court. Like Kadambini, Kamini Sen's sister Jamini Sen also started practising medicine after acquiring university degrees first in the country and then in England. She, too, met with social disapproval. Also, she remained unmarried. As Christians, Chandramukhi Basu's sister Bidhumukhi Basu and Violet Marie Mitra were able to work as physicians with relative ease. In those early years, no women apart from Brahmos and Christians came forward to study to become doctors. But the example set by these early pioneers inspired and encouraged later generations of women.

According to the census data of 1901, more than 1,150 women were then engaged in teaching and the practice of medicine (Europeans probably made up the bulk of this number). There were over a thousand girls' schools at that time, but only six high schools. It is not known if the teachers at the smaller schools were paid. But the data suggest that they were not listed in the census as holding salaried jobs. Women's education in itself was the subject of much derision among Muslims, so it is not hard to imagine how much they would have detested the idea of working women. It is not known who the first Muslim woman was to work for pay. But I wouldn't be surprised if it were Faziltunnesa. She taught at a school for a short while before leaving for England in 1928. After her return she landed a prestigious job in the Education Department.

Thus, slowly, women started working. But social resistance to women working persisted for a long time. Even as great a writer as Bankimchandra Chattopadhyay could not imagine women working, let alone ordinary orthodox people. In the following discussion we will look at how contemporary dramatic literature poured ridicule and venom on women's education and possible participation in the workforce. The extent of the resistance offered by family and society can be inferred from examples drawn from the lives of some famous women. Chandramukhi Basu was the first and foremost highly educated woman of her time. Yet she could not carry on working after her marriage. Her younger sister Bidhumukhi Basu qualified as a doctor. But she did not treat anyone except her doctor husband's female patients. Jamini Sen was also a doctor. She never got married. Her elder sister, Kamini Sen, married late. She, too, did not continue working after her marriage. Kadambini Ganguly had studied medicine in England, but she faced bitter criticism and derision from Hindu society. Rokeya Sakhawat Hossein's was the strongest position, in her time, in favour of women joining the workforce. Yet, she was not able to work as long as her husband was alive. Even after his death she never held a salaried job.

With the spread of women's education, and especially higher education, the situation started changing fast in the middle of the 20th century. Political and social developments played a crucial role in bringing about this change. In West Bengal after Partition and in Bangladesh after it gained independence, an epochal transformation was initiated.

In the chapter 'Bengali Culture in the Twentieth Century' we discussed how caste Hindus were forced to migrate from East Bengal at the time of Partition and immediately after it. These Hindus waged a hard struggle to survive in West Bengal. This was when educated women in large numbers came forward to keep the boat afloat for their families. They seized whatever was available, no matter how low-paid the job. Then again in 1971, when after the liberation of Bangladesh the middle classes there were thrown into a sharp financial crisis, the women of Bangladesh did the same thing. The Mujib government's decision at that time to reserve 10 per cent of jobs for women also helped women to find work.

Once women came forward to work, it was not just the sheer numbers of working women that rose. Women in fact started working in more and more senior positions. They began to be seen as judges and lawyers in the courts, secretaries and deputy secretaries in the secretariats, pilots in aircraft, commissioners in the income-tax departments and chairpersons in local councils. Such examples, on the one hand, boosted women's confidence in themselves and raised their aspirations, and on the other they made women acceptable in these posts to men. Bengali women at the end of the 20th century no longer fit the image of Bengali womanhood that had prevailed at the dawn of the century. The kind of working and financially independent women one now meets all the time had never existed in Bengal before. Many of these women initially faced, in society and workplace, all kinds of ridicule, indecent jokes and even sexual harassment. Male-dominated society could not at first accept that women were capable of taking on responsible roles or that they deserved respect. But slowly male attitudes to women changed, and so did women's own self-perceptions. Now women have secured social acceptance as colleagues and members of the workforce. What is particularly remarkable is that it was not just educated women who came forward to work, hundreds of thousands of uneducated or little educated women also started working under the pressure of financial hardships. Women are now seen digging roads, crumbling bricks, sewing in textile-manufacturing units and generally doing all sorts of work that had never been associated with women. Women now play significant economic roles in society.

Women's Liberation

The concept of women's liberation started forming more or less around the same time when awareness about women's education emerged in Bengali society. But the Bengali language did not have words to express this idea. It was probably a woman who first used the adjectival form of *swadhinota*, meaning independence, in this connection, in 1842. In a letter written under a pseudonym to *Bidyadarshan* magazine edited by Akshay Kumar Dutta, she spoke of travelling to Calcutta with an 'independent mind' (*swadhin mone*). Akshay Datta was not able to support her idea of independence, but a hazy definition of independence does emerge from his own comment. He wrote: '... women will be independent like the men, that is to say, eat everywhere, visit all places, talk and converse with everyone....' He was not able to support independence for women because, in his opinion, women had not yet acquired the kind of education and other kinds of preparedness that were needed for independence. Another seven years later, in May 1849, the editor of *Sambad Bhaskar Patrika* wrote an essay on the occasion of the founding of Bethune School. It was titled *Hindu Strilokdiger Swadhinotar Shubhanushthan* ('Auspicious Ceremony for the Freedom of Hindu Women'). A somewhat more comprehensive view of women's independence and subordination can be seen in this essay. Still, the idea of women's liberation was not yet popular.

Nor was the expression '*stri-swadhinota*' (women's independence) coined. It is in the 1860s that we notice this compound noun being used.

Though the concept of liberation was beginning to take root, it was not yet very clear what men and women perceived as independence. It was in fact an idea that gradually evolved and changed, and its implementation in family and society happened in phases over time. In 1863, an enthusiastic young member of the Brahmo Samaj – Umesh Chandra Gupta – started publishing *Bamabodhini Patrika* for women. Educational pieces meant for the edification of women used to be published in this magazine. News of women and their activities was also published. More importantly, the magazine published poems, essays and letters written by women. Right from its inception, the expression *stri-swadhinota* was used in this magazine. Though the editor did not define the word, it is apparent from the essays published in the magazine that it meant the right of women to come out of seclusion and to meet and converse with men.

Whatever 'women's independence' might have stood for, the educated women of the Brahmo Samaj started playing a social role outside the confines of the family. In the mid 1860s, for instance, some 50 women participated in the annual Maghotsav festival held at Debendranath Tagore's family home (marking the anniversary of the founding of the Brahmo Samaj in January 1830). This would have been unthinkable earlier. We have already noted the fierce opposition that Keshab Sen had faced only a few years earlier when he tried to take his wife to visit the Tagores. Undoubtedly, then, the permission to take part in a religious function was a major event. Even after this, however, Debendranath did not recognise women's right to share the same space with men during Brahmo religious services. Notwithstanding Debendranath's objections, many others including Keshab Sen, Durgamohan Das, Dwarakanath Ganguly, and Annadacharan Khastagir strongly supported women's right to participate in prayer meetings. As we have already seen, the Brahmo Samaj split into two over this issue. Thereafter, women found a life beyond the home and the spaces marked out as feminine. They also started mingling much more with other women, if not yet so much with men.

We have mentioned an instance of men and women meeting socially and conversing with each other—at a reception held for Mary Carpenter in November 1886. Quite a few young Brahmo men and women met and spent some time together on the occasion. Unused as they were to conversing with men, however, many of the women were unable to utter a word. But the men were fulsome in their appreciation of what was happening. One of them delivered a longish speech aimed at the women:

> Sisters! If your husbands are apprehensive about opening the doors of well-being for you, take heart, march ahead, overcome their meanness of spirit, and once again wear around your necks the garland of freedom that is God's gift to you. … You are not inanimate objects, and nor are you beasts that you must do only what your husbands ask you to do. … You have as much freedom of thought and action as we do.

Keshab Sen was critical when he heard about this gathering. But he could not stem the tide. This same set of men and women got together again the following month when Mary Carpenter invited them back for another gathering. This was how women slowly moved out of the four walls of their homes. Within a few years even Keshab Sen accepted this 'freedom' of women. Not only that, he turned his back on the Adi Brahmo Samaj over women's right to participate in religious services without purdah and founded a new Samaj with his young followers.

These ideas began to spread beyond Calcutta among progressive men. This is evident in Kaliprasanna Ghosh's book *Narijati Bishayak Prastab* ('Proposal Regarding the Female of the Species') published from Dhaka in 1869. He wrote:

> Freedom is God's gift to all men and women and is their natural state. One human being cannot make a gift of freedom to another or take it away. … Freedom for women, it is apprehended, will result in evil consequences, and surely it is arrogant on our part to deprive women of their freedom on the basis of this imagined fear. … When God has granted freedom to men and women, no evil consequences will ever flow from freedom of women, not even if the world is shattered.

Although this sort of positive thinking about women's independence was initially limited to Brahmo men, it slowly started to receive endorsement from other English educated men and they began to set their wives free from the prison that domestic spaces once was for women.

Freedom for women did not initially mean much more than venturing out of the house and conversing with men. What women themselves thought about this was even more curious. What Kailasbasini Devi wrote in her book *Hindu Mohilar Heenabastha* ('The Degraded Condition of Hindu Women') in 1863 was probably the oldest definition of women's independence. She wrote that men and women had been created equal but that men had kept the women imprisoned. She added that men had kept women in a state of illiteracy in order to perpetuate their bondage. Within a few years, Sarada Devi wrote that men considered women to be a degraded species and kept them tightly shut at home. What a woman from Rajshahi wrote in an article in *Bamabodhini Patrika* in 1871 was much the same—that women were forced to remain confined at home and that they had no right to talk to men. Freedom had an even narrower definition in what Mayasundari of Calcutta wrote in 1875. 'Women have no permission to look at anything. They built a bridge over the Ganga in Calcutta, and the men praised it to the high heavens, but all we women could do was to hear about it, not for a single day could we see it with our own eyes.'

But though women had a narrow perspective of freedom in the beginning, the meaning of freedom did slowly change and expand. Apart from breaking with purdah, the other examples that were being set by the elite section of women, particularly the Brahmo women, also expanded the meaning of freedom. These included, for instance, the right to work for pay, an opinion in the choice of one's own marriage partner and a role in decision-making in the family.

Apart from the example she set by coming out of seclusion, Jnanadanandini Devi also devised decent clothes for women. Many women in the last two decades of the 19th century became 'modern' by following her example. She also expanded the meaning of women's independence by giving her daughter a higher education and by recognising her right to choose a husband. But in the 1880s it was Krishnabhabini Das who made the strongest demands about the equal rights of women and their right to play meaningful economic and social roles. Her sojourn in England with her husband, who was liberal in his world view, had helped to shape her comprehensive thinking about women's independence. She expressed her views in her 1885 book *Englande Banga Mohila* ('A Bengali Woman in England') and in several articles published in the *Bharati* magazine in the next few years. She also worked to expand the reach of education among women and initiated programmes to make women financially independent.

Rokeya Sakhawat Hossein educated herself within the constraints of rigidly observed purdah. Indeed, she observed the rules of purdah all her life and never stopped wearing a burkha. But in the books and the many essays that she started publishing from 1904 she expressed strong and extremely bold views on women's rights in family and society. Remarkably, she did not just speak of the 'acceptable' and the so-called 'decent' professions for women such as teaching and medicine. Women, she said, could also work the soil. She said that men kept women in bondage with their superior physical strength and money power and in the name of religion, and also that women were downtrodden—thus anticipating later feminist positions. She also took practical steps to expand women's education. She may not have talked of marriage or of women's sexual rights, but the strength of the views she expressed on other aspects of women's independence remains unmatched.

Changing Roles, Expectation and Reality

The image of women in family and society that had taken shape over centuries started crumbling in the late 19th century as a result of the spread of education, the discarding of purdah and the economic and social roles increasingly assumed by women. In 1849, the popular Bengali poet Ishwar Gupta heaped ridicule on girls in a poem written on the occasion of the founding of Bethune School. The social resistance to women's independence reflected in the poem has certainly eroded, but it is not completely gone even after 150 years. Ishwar Gupta wrote:

> *They were all good girls once, they kept the fasts and followed the rituals.*
> *Bethune has single-handedly dispatched them all, will they ever be the same again?*
> *Now that the lasses put on airs and flaunt their books,*
> *No doubt they will pick up their 'A's and 'B's, dress like* bibis, *and babble in English.*

Ishwar Gupta also feared that girls would start using forks and give up the traditional wooden seats used for eating meals and air themselves out with carriage rides in Calcutta's Garher Math (the fields surrounding Fort William). In another poem, he wrote:

All the good girls will now ride horses
Street smart they will be, a little civilised, too …
Shedding the purdah and the veil, they'll go partying
Down with Hinduism, they'll declare, and drink drops of brandy.

The example of ridiculing women's modernism that Ishwar Gupta set was followed in the last three decades of the 19th century by innumerable conservative writers in their essays, plays, poems and stories. The dramatic literature of the time deserves particular mention in this connection, for example, Manomohan Basu's *Nagasramer Abhinoy*, the anonymous *Meye Monster Meeting*, Biharilal Chattopadhyay's *Khandaproloy O Achabhuar Bombachak*, Rakhaldas Bhattacharya's *Swadhin Zenana O Rukminiranga*, Radhabinod Haldar's *Pass Kora Mag*, Siddheshwar Ray's *Boubabu*, Amritalal Basu's *Tajjob Byapar O Bouma* and Durgadas Dey's *Chhobi Ba Barhadiner Pancharanga* and *Miss Bino Bibi, B.A.* The most remarkable skit of this kind was Jyotirindranath Tagore's *Kinchit Jalojog* (1872). Remarkable, because he was a member of the Brahmo Samaj and his brother Satyendranath was an ardent advocate of women's liberation. That someone who later went out horse-riding with his wife could write such a play is also astonishing enough. It is evident from his example that society was fast changing despite the initial orthodoxies.

Women have not left too many written accounts of what they thought of their own roles in family and society. But a look at the admittedly small body of writing that they did leave shows how their roles kept changing. It can also be seen how their thinking and their self-perceptions changed. The wife and mother that one meets in Rasasundari Devi's autobiography probably corresponds to the traditional Bengali image of wife and mother. This image requires the ideal wife to keep herself immersed in housework from morning till night even if she has hired help, to uncomplainingly put up with hardships, to eat only after everybody else has eaten and to tolerate all impositions by her children, husband and his relatives with a smile on her face. Whether there is love in the marriage or not, this ideal wife is expected to look up to her husband like a god.

In later decades, the changing roles of women in family and society is evident in the writings of Kailasbasini Devi (1860s), Jnanadanandini Devi (1870s and later), Krishnabhabini Das (1880s and later), Rokeya Sakhawat Hossein (from 1904) and Maitreyi Devi (1930s and later). Changing, too, were women's expectations from their husbands and in-laws. Husbands and their families also probably slowly stopped expecting the older patterns of behaviour from women. The nature of housework, ways of relating to husbands and children, clothes, the way women treated relatives and even what they did with their time, were all changing. In a word, the lifestyles of women were transforming remarkably.

We discussed in the previous chapter how married couples in the 19th century frequently failed to develop close relationships. But with the spread of education in the late 19th century married couples started sharing greater closenessand the nature of relationships within marriages changed. A shining example would be that of Jnanadanandini Devi. She has written in her memoirs that her husband, Satyendranath, fell in love with her even before she turned 12. He did his best to educate her and inculcate in her a modern outlook and thus turn her into a suitable life partner for himself. This inevitably resulted in pulls and pressures within the joint family. It is not known how put off her mother-in-law, Sarada Devi, was by all this. But the father-in-law, Debendranath, stopped talking to her for a few years. Jyotirindranath's relationship with his wife, Kadambari, was not very old-fashioned, either. Debendranath Das had taken his wife Krishnabhabini to England with him against the wishes of his family. Their relationship also changed, transformed by both Krishnabhabini's acquiring an education and the examples of married relationships that they had before them in the West. Saratkumari Choudhurani grew up in the Punjab, and her relationship with Akshay Choudhury was modern. Earlier, husbands were 'gurus' and revered figures, but now they were slowly turning into lovers and friends. Examples of this happening increased in number with time. These women were able, with their husbands to support them, to break away from joint families and establish nuclear units.

Not everyone was so lucky. Many women were forced to go on living in joint families. This led to misunderstandings, and sometimes quarrels, with other members of the family. Conservative society blamed daughters-in-law, and not mothers-in-law or other relatives of the husbands, for family discord. An essay published in *Jnanangkur* magazine in 1873 provides a hint of how much conservative society opposed and detested 'modern women'. In this essay titled *Bidyabirombana* ('Farce of Education'), the writer, a Calcutta University graduate called Chandrasekhar Basu, wrote that even hell was preferable to living with educated women. Not just the men, many women were also quite vociferous in their criticism of modern young wives. This mindset of conservative women can be noted in many articles published in *Bamabodhini Patrika.* One of them wrote that young wives were losing respect for elders in the family and that their conduct was increasingly reducing mothers-in-law to tears.

A chief cause of conflict was over who was the mistress of the household, the mother-or the daughter-in-law. Another was the sharing of housework. No matter how tied up young wives were with the rearing of their children or looking after husbands, they were expected to bear the bulk of the burden of housework including cooking, even if they were indisposed. Even the very young wives, and also those who had no previous experience of housework, had to accept this responsibility. Wives actually fared worse than household servants. In some families, mothers-in-law expressly forbade employing help. A marriage ritual required the bridegroom to tell his mother, before he left home to marry, that he was going out to fetch a maidservant for her. That daughters-in-law no longer brought the old dedication to housework was a complaint that featured in many write-ups published in magazines and newspapers in the late 19th century. Mankumari Basu was a poet. She interpreted the neglect of housework by women as resulting from hedonism and selfishness. In her opinion, modern women were more taken up with dolling themselves up than with keeping house. That women were paying more attention to their clothes, wearing shoes, keeping themselves well-groomed and were more concerned with cleanliness also drew criticism. In a write-up by a conservative woman in *Bamabodhini Patrika* in 1901, it was claimed that a woman's duty and even her own good lay in silently tolerating rude or even heart-breaking behaviour from her husband. Most exemplary wives still believed that husbands were the ultimate guides and teachers (the '*param debata*' and '*guru*') and that disobeying a husband was sinful.

Many people disapproved of the way women now spent time reading novels and sewing, instead of gossiping and chatting. Conservative society also did not regard kindly women's new awareness, in the late 19th century, of the need for medical attention in illnesses, in contrast to the women of older generations who never thought of seeing a doctor in times of sickness. There are humorous yet pitiful scenes in some Tagore stories that depict this mindset. No one ever heard of calling in a doctor for a sick wife in past generations, says one of his characters and asks why, then, should a doctor be fetched for the daughter-in-law? Indeed, society spoke ill of highly educated women if they so much as spoke in English. On the contrary, it was commendable for English-educated men to speak in English or Bengali with many English words thrown in. As for sartorial choices, men were not criticised for wearing Western clothes, but it was blameworthy for women to even wear shoes, let alone Western clothes.

Educated women, of course, did not silently put up with the censure from conservative society. One of the foremost among the modern women was Saratkumari Choudhurani. She may have acquired her dissenting values from her upbringing outside Bengal. She wrote that mothers-in-law did not see their sons' wives as daughters but rather as opponents and with envy. Jnanada Devi, Swarnakumari Devi and Krishnabhabini Devi also supported the educated women. What they said was, in sum: keeping house may be the chief responsibility of women but by no means their only or most important task. Many women also appreciated the care that modern women took with their clothes. That they were now better groomed and had acquired good taste and decent manners was commended by educated women. Saratkumari Devi said in her criticism of male society that ways of life were bound to change for women if they changed for men.

The kind of 'new women' that we see at the end of the 19th century, especially in educated, urban families, as a result of education and other social transformations, were different from the women of earlier generations in their work roles, self-perceptions and in their attitudes to relatives. Though it was not as if misunderstandings or even violent fights did not earlier happen in families; relationships within them began to be significantly redefined in the new age. The women who once put up with wrongs without complaining now started protesting. We can point to Tagore's *Strir Patra* (1914; A Wife's Letter) in this context. The expression of personal autonomy that we see in the protagonist, Mrinal, would have been unimaginable even two decades earlier.

Many of the women in Tagore's 20th century stories, novels, plays and poems are rebels who reject prevalent values. That does not however mean that society now happily accepted the changing roles of women. On the contrary, an analysis will show that Tagore himself did not wholly accept it. Though in his creative writing he depicted women as rebellious, he continued to endorse the traditional role of women in his essays—ideal women would be long-suffering, self-sacrificing, caring, and faithful and devoted to their husbands. It is at once ironic and symbolic that the changing roles of women and the unchanging social attitudes to this transformation can both be noted in Tagore's writing.

Another self-contradiction in Bengali society is that its men have changed under the impact of contact with the West – in education, attitudes, clothes, food habits, tastes – but they continue to expect women to fit traditional roles. They have educated women in order to make their own lives more enjoyable, not in order to improve the lives of women. They have hesitated, too, to allow their women to take up jobs and establish contact with the greater world waiting outside the limits of home. The truth is that they have used one yardstick to evaluate themselves, and quite a different one to evaluate women. The most important application of this double standard happens in love and in the sexual lives of men and women. It does not matter if men are dishonest in love or if they have multiple sexual encounters; but nothing compensates a woman's infidelity.

Yet, there is no escaping the changes that have come about in women in the 20th century. The development of individuality in women, as a consequence of education, improved clothes, easing of seclusion rules, and also partly economic independence have vastly changed male perceptions of women and women's own self-perceptions. Even if women are not exactly liberated, they are surely independent in their thinking. The change first appeared in the educated women of Calcutta, but it gradually trickled out to the smaller towns and even villages. And in this way, the social values and customs formed over hundreds of years started to crumble. When compared with the women from a century earlier, the Bengali women at the early 21st century may well appear to have come from a different planet altogether.

Women now seek to take independent decisions and act independently in many areas of life. Inevitably, this leads to clashes with male-dominated families and society. Such clashes not only cause quarrels but sometimes also result in divorces. Divorces among Hindus, in particular, are extremely significant. For, there is no religious sanction for divorce among Hindus. A divorce in a Hindu family was earlier considered to be a scandal. But not only are there now more and more divorces, divorced women are marrying again. Earlier, only men could think of obtaining a divorce. Now women, too, initiate divorce proceedings in some circumstances. There was a time when women had no opinion about who they would marry. Now they do. And in some cases they choose their own partners.

In sum, the idea that women are no longer what they used to be has taken deep root in society. Apart from education and economic factors, the empowerment of women in politics has been instrumental in the transformation of women's image in society. At the start of the 20th century, women cooperated with men in political movements. But in the last three decades of the century, women in increasing numbers chose the path of active politics. The taste of political power they have got as members of local governments and local councils have made them ambitious. In Bangladesh, especially, the instance of two women, notwithstanding their political limitations, becoming prime minister one after another could not but bring about a major change in society's way of looking at women. Many women in West Bengal have become ministers and members of the Legislative Assembly. Men are now more willing to accept the authority of women and treat them with respect.

Bengali men have not changed quite as visibly as the women, who have been transformed by education, the breakdown of purdah, economic want and political developments. The extremely timid, shy, helpless and mute sari-clad figure that once formed the image of the Bengali woman no longer exists. The purdah-bound image of Bengali Muslim women is also in shreds, notwithstanding the partial comeback that the purdah has made on the back of Islamic revivalism. The self-confidence that women have now acquired was unimaginable earlier. The women that one now sees in offices and courts, in public transport, office canteens, shops, meetings and public platforms, in informal gatherings and in social functions did not exist even 50 years ago.

The position of women in educated families has changed in many ways. Parental neglect of girl children is now much reduced. Girls are raised and educated with the same care that is lavished on boys. The conduct of husbands with their wives, and that of their relatives, is also quite different from what it used to be. Wives are no longer expected to be unquestioningly submissive. Women themselves, though they still largely see themselves as subordinate to the men in their families, now expect much more from their husbands and in-laws than they once did. They also take active part in family decisions. In a word, the personalities and self-perceptions of women have undergone drastic change.

Contribution of Women in Bengali Culture

The contribution of women in Bengali culture, like that of society's lower orders, is not immediately evident. The main part of rural and land-based Bengali culture has been shaped by farmers, yet the names of the farmers whose contributions enriched and defined this culture is not known. Women, likewise, have built up this society and its culture alongside the men, but there aren't any names that can be cited to mark their contribution. Women have remained invisible in the processes of administration, production, distribution, education and other activities of male-dominated societies. The responsibility for this lies not with the women but with men. It was the men who deprived women of their right to education and kept them confined to domestic spaces, thus restraining them from realising their potentials and proving their capabilities. Women could not therefore play the roles they might have played if given a chance.

The exceptional women who could buck the trend only proved that women did not lack capabilities but a conducive environment to realise them. Take governance, for instance. Bhabashankari of the 16th century was an extraordinary woman. The raja of Bhurshut, impressed by her valour, married her. She took on the task of governance after his death and fended off an attack on her territory by the Pathan chieftain Osman Khan. The Mughal Emperor Akbar bestowed on her the title of Raibaghini when he heard of her prowess. In the 18th century, Debi Choudhurani joined the Sannyasi rebellion. Rani Shiromani owned a large zamindari. In the last couple of years of the 18th century she assisted the rebellion of the Chuar peasants and the Paiks. Rani Bhabani, also of the 18th century, owned a large zamindari, too. She was reputed for the efficiency with which she managed her landholding. Rani Rasmoni was a well known zamindar in the 19th century. So it was not as if women could not govern and rule. They had the same capabilities that the men did, but scant opportunities to use them.

Though the men drew a line around the work roles of women, their contribution in the Bengali culture based on agriculture and cottage industries was by no means inferior to that of men. Women of peasant families in the countryside have from time immemorial played a crucial role in producing crops. In paddy cultivation, for instance, they played equal, in some cases greater, roles in sowing, harvesting, bundling, threshing, boiling, drying and milling. Almost every household in rural Bengal grows vegetables and fruits in the backyard, and these, too, are tended by women. It is women, again, who rear livestock and poultry. Women's contribution in the economy may not be evident at a cursory glance, but in fact a closer analysis will reveal it to be no less than the men's. If the services that they render without pay, such as cooking and the raising of children, are taken into account, their contribution to the economy might well appear to be greater than that of men.

An analysis of different aspects of Bengali culture shows assimilations from and exchanges with other cultures in literature, music, painting, architecture, dramatic performances and clothes. External influences working on native traditions have in fact shaped a new culture. There are however some aspects of this culture that are peculiarly its own and belong exclusively to the region. These include Bengal's cottage enterprises. There has developed over centuries a rich tradition of making such handicrafts as the *sheetal pati* (a naturally cool, cane mat), the *nakshi kantha* (a quilt made with old saris and decorated with running stitches), *nakshi pakha* (embroidered hand fans made of cloth, cane, palm leaves), embroidered pillow covers, cane and bamboo artefacts, clay dolls, *pat*s (scroll paintings, and also painted clay disc; the subjects were mostly mythological, but the scroll paintings of the 19th century also drew upon contemporary themes) and painted mud pots. Many of these are made exclusively by women. Particularly, *nakshi kantha, nakshi pakha,* pillow covers and many different kinds of embroidered linen, *alpana* (floral patterns drawn on floors with a solution of rice powder), paintings or coal sketches on mud walls, *sheetal pati,* cane and bamboo artefacts, clay dolls, painted pots—these are all creations of women. In making terracotta artefacts and objects, scroll paintings and in weaving fishing nets, too, women have worked along with men.

Cooking forms one of the chief arts in Bengali culture. There are many different kinds of steamed and fried sweets, with or without coconut fillings, milk sweets, pickles, an assortment of vegetarian dishes, condiments like kasundi (the Bengali mustard sauce), sweets made of puffed rice, which are all peculiarly and exclusively Bengali, different from the foods of other regions in the subcontinent. And it is in the hands of women that these have evolved to their present forms. Women have perfected the art of making them through centuries of experimenting with food. Some areas of Bengal are distinguished for their cottons and silks. In textiles, too, women have worked alongside men. The famous Dhaka muslin was an intricately worked chikan, which was the handiwork of women. The contribution of women deserves mention at every stage of textile manufacturing, from spinning and dyeing of threads to weaving cloth.

It is difficult to gauge the contribution of women of past ages in the arts of painting and drawing. Though no names have come down to us, the artistry with which women execute *alpana*s and wall drawings, stitch and embroider, turn out *nakshi kanthas* and paint on pots and scrolls suggests that their contribution in this area of culture might have been formidable. We can also guess how skilled women might have been in drawing and painting from the achievements of Sunayani Devi in modern times.

What we do know, of course, is that women in recent times have played significant roles in literature, music, dance, dramatic performances and so on, and we know who they are. There are enough hints in history to suggest that there were such women in the Middle Ages, too. We have, for instance, already mentioned the poet Jayadev's wife, Padmavati. We know, too, of Hemalata Devi in the 17th century. She was famous for her renderings of kirtans, devotional singing accompanied by the telling of religious myths and legends, and in Bengal an important strand in the Vaishnava tradition. She joined the second Vaishnava religious congregation at Kheturi (in Rajshahi, North Bengal) as a delegate. She also had vast scholarship in the Vaishnava sacred texts and wrote a book called *Manabi Bilas.* Many Vaishnavas accepted her as their Acharya, in deference to her mastery over Vaishnava literature. In the 19th century, of course, many women acquired a fine artistry in dancing and singing.

The tradition of educating girls at home that started in the 1830s in highly educated families began to produce a direct and noticeable result in the 1850s. It was in this decade that Krishnakamini Dasi published a book of poems called *Chittobilasini* (1856). Thakurani Dasi wrote poems that were published in *Sambad Prabhakar.* Kailasbasini Devi published three books, in verse and prose, in 1863, 1865 and 1869. Rakhalmoni Gupta published a book of poems in 1865. Kaminisundari Devi and Shibsundari Devi published two plays, in 1866 and 1873, respectively. Rasasundari Devi, Nabinkali Devi, Faizunnessa Khatun, Birajmohini Dasi, Girindramohini Dasi and also Swarnakumari Devi published their first books in the 1860s and 1870s. It was around this time, too, that Kailasbasini Mitra wrote her autobiography. In the 1880s Krishnabhabini Das wrote a travelogue. These must be deemed as extraordinary achievements since none of these women had received any institutional education. They overcame the myriad obstacles of domesticity to attain the unattainable.

In the 20th century women have made their mark in the different genres of literature including poetry, novels and short stories. With the spread of education, women have not hesitated to pick up the pen. Notwithstanding the limitations imposed on them by society and environment, hundreds of women have written in newspapers and magazines and published books. Women such as Mankumari Basu, Kamini Ray and Kusumkumari Das became well known names because of their poems. Going by the number of books, Prabhavati Devi Saraswati surpassed even Tagore. Priyamvada Devi, Nirupama Devi, Pankajini Basu, Prafullamoyi Devi, Shailabala Ghoshjaya, Sarojini Naidu and many others deserve mention for their contribution to literature. Toru and Aru Dutt may not have written in Bengali, but they left testimony to their extraordinary genius. Toru Dutt was only 21 when she died, yet by that time she had published several English poems and a short novel in French. Her work earned praise from English and French critics of the time.

Apart from writing, women have played significant roles in running and editing magazines from the 19th century. When the first women-related magazines started coming out in the 1860s, many women used them to publish their writing for the first time. Within a few years, women had acquired enough confidence in themselves to come forward to edit magazines in the 1870s. It was in this decade that Mokshadayini Devi edited *Bangla Mohila* magazine. In 1875 Thakomani edited the *Anathini* magazine. In 1881 Kamini Sheel started editing *Khrishtio Mohila* magazine. Sometime later Mohini Sen edited *Paricharika* magazine. In the same decade Swarnakumari Devi took over the reins of the *Bharati* magazine and creditably edited the magazine for 10 years. Sarala Devi, too, had a stint at editing *Bharati*. Both *Bharati* and *Balak* were creations of the Tagore women.

As early as the 1830s, when institutional education for women was absent, a woman called Radhamoni acted as Vidya in a dramatic performance of *Vidyasundar*. She proved that women were capable of a high quality of acting. To be able to further prove their credentials in the field, however, women had to wait for another 40 years. In the 1870s, when the stage was finally open to women, quite a few women became famous for their performances. Among them were Golapsundari a.k.a. Sukumari Datta, Khetramoni, Jadumoni and Elokeshi. But the most well known of them all was Binodini. Among the women who appeared on the stage shortly after Binodini were Tarasundari, Tinkori, Gangamani, and Norisundari. There is an extensive discussion on them in the chapter titled 'Theatre and Cinema'. The women of the Jorasanko branch of the Tagore family were the most remarkable among those who participated in dramatic performances outside professional theatre. Among women of (bhadralok) families, Pratibha Choudhuri was both an accomplished actor and singer.

When we consider the extent of contemporary social opposition to women acting on stage, women appear to have been more gifted than the men. Actresses were regarded as prostitutes in those days. Educated women of decent families were not willing to risk earning this appellation by acting on the professional stage.

The number of actresses rose in the 20th century, and so did their standard of acting. Along with the theatre, they also began to appear on the silver screen. To women surely belongs half the credit for the heights that Bengali theatre and cinema have climbed in the last hundred years.

In music women have all along had a place beside the men. The so-called fallen women of the 19th century warmed the hearts of men, rather than women, with their gifted singing. When, at the turn of the century, it became socially acceptable for girls to take music lessons, sing in public and even to bring out their songs in records, the female singers soon surpassed the men in numbers, and sometimes in quality. Yet they often did not grow to their full potential. Marriage, child rearing and other demands of domesticity led many to give up singing or seriously cut into their time. Gaharjan, Binodini Dasi, Amala Das, Manadasundari Dasi, Neeharbala, Kamala Jhoria, Indubala, Angurbala, Uma Basu, Maloti Ghosal, Kanak Biswas, Sati Devi, Sahana Devi, Amiya Thakur, Premalata Devi and Deepali Nag were some of the women who enriched the tradition of Bengali music. Women have also proved their genius in classical music. I will further discuss the greatest women singers in the chapter titled 'Traditions of Music in Bengal'.

Dance is one of the most important forms of the performing arts. Even those who have scant respect for women admit that women show greater artistry than men in this form of art. This is not just because of the beauty of the feminine form. Women seem to have a natural affinity for dance. The women who in the 19th century earned notoriety as '*baiji*s' (courtesans) were all skilled practitioners of dance and music. So were the actresses. Kusumkumari, an accomplished singer and dancer, was one such actress and dance director. Uday Shankar is renowned for his extraordinary contribution in the history of dance in the 20th century. His wife, Amala Shankar, was not only his partner but also an able colleague. Sreemati Tagore also contributed a great deal to the Bengali tradition of dance. She invented new dance forms by assimilating Manipuri dance and the Gujarati garba.

Contribution in Religion and Philosophy

Though women of the upper and middle castes had no social visibility in the Middle Ages, they did not only encourage their men in religious observances but acted as true life partners in carrying out religious duties. In some cases, women even gave leadership in religion. We have mentioned before a Buddhist *bhikshuni* (nun), Bilasbajra of the Pala era, who was a scholar of scriptural literature. Another Buddhist nun in the 8th century, Leelabajra, translated religious texts into the Tibetan language. Around the same time Lakshinkara authored a few texts and introduced the Bajrayogini technique of worship.

With the start of the Brahmanical era shrank the rights of women in religious life. Hindu scriptural texts were studied extensively during the Sena era, but women are not known to have made any contribution to that tradition of scholarship. The situation changed after Vaishnavism started gaining strength in the Middle Ages. Probably because of the close links of Vaishnavism with Bengal's folk culture, women enjoyed considerable rights in this religious tradition. We know of Madhabi Dasi, a contemporary of Chaitanyadev, who was well-versed in the scriptures. After Chaitanyadev's death, there were women who took it upon themselves to preach the Vaishnava faith and contributed a great deal to its reach and spread. Advaitacharya's wife, Sita Devi, Nityananda's second wife, Jahnavi Devi and his daughter Ganga Devi deserve special mention in this context. Srinivas Acharya's wife Padmavati also acquired a good grasp of the Vaishnava sacred texts. It might be supposed that these women were exceptions and that women generally did not play any very significant role in the religious life of the Vaishnavas. But that would not be quite true. For, the participation of women in Vaishnava religious observances and in Vaishnava scholarship seems to have survived into the 18th and 19th centuries.

If women enjoyed considerable importance in the world of Vaishnava scriptural scholarship, their position was even more assured in the folk tradition of Vaishnavism, that is, among the Boshtams. Women played active roles in the religious life of this sect. In the Baul and other Sahajya cults, too, women emerged as equal partners of the men in religious observances and in the arduous seeking of the divine that marked these faiths. In the 18th century Sati Ma was revered as 'Guru Ma' in the Kartabhaja sect. Among the Shaktas, too, women had a special position, even apart from the cult of the Bhairavis. In the 19th century, women like Sarada Devi and Gouri Ma were deeply revered by fellow believers for their wisdom and devotion. Manorama Majumdar was a preacher among the first-generation Brahmos. But though Hindu women could leave some mark in religious life, no Bengali Muslim woman is known to have played a similar role.

Contribution of Women in Politics

Bengali women's contribution to the freedom movement was nothing short of extraordinary. Soon after the Indian National Congress was established in 1885, women started taking part in its activities. Women like Swarnakumari Devi and Kadambini Ganguly joined the first session of the Congress as delegates, and this despite the limited spread of women's education at that time. It would of course be an exaggeration to describe their participation as very active. But the example they set makes it evident that women were at this time acquiring a political consciousness. Swarnakumari Devi's daughter Sarala Devi was in fact far more politically aware than her mother was. She sought to shore up nationalist feelings among the youth by introducing festivals such as Pratapaditya Utsav and Beerastami Brata. She also tried to stoke popular interest in indigenous commodities and industries. But her activities also had their limitations. At a time when efforts were under way to promote peace between Hindus and Muslims, her progammes had a strong Hindu leaning. Even the man she married, around the time of the first partition of Bengal in 1905, was a leader of the Arya Samaj in the Punjab—Rambhaja Datta.

Women truly started playing an active role in politics for the first time during the swadeshi movement against the 1905 partition. Special mention must be made of names such as Kumudini Mitra, Hemangini Das and Sarala Devi's sister Hironmoyee Devi. The swadeshi movement was particularly strong in Barisal under Ashwini Kumar Datta's leadership, and many women joined it spontaneously. Their efforts were not limited to rejecting foreign commodities and campaigning for indigenous products. Women poets and writers at this time published works aimed at reinforcing nationalist feelings. Among them were Swarnakumari Devi, Krishnabhabini Das, Girindramohini Dasi, Kamini Ray, Mankumari Basu and Hironmoyee Devi.

The terrorist movement started around the time of the movement against the Bengal partition. Women did not just encourage and cheer the youthful terrorists, many women helped them by providing refuge. Such as, for instance, Dukhoribala of Birbhum. In 1916 she was jailed for three years after a pistol belonging to terrorists was found at her house. She was probably the first Bengali woman to be incarcerated for political reasons.

Sarojini Naidu played a crucial role in the constitutional politics of the second decade of the 20th century. She had a keen interest in English literature and was a talented poet. She joined the Congress formally in 1915. Unlike most women in politics at that time, her political participation was not limited to being a silent worker. Indeed, she repeatedly made strongly-worded and incisive addresses at Congress sessions. She visited the United States in 1927 in order to create awareness among Americans about the situation of Indians and their demands and aspirations. She also addressed a parliamentary committee on the rights of women. In the 1921 Congress session she read out Chittaranjan Das's presidential address. Shortly after, she presided over the Kanpur session. She was jailed for her participation in Gandhi's breaking of the salt laws. Sarojini's sister Mrinalini also participated in constitutional politics. Generally, however, women did not play a major role in constitutional politics in the first two decades of the 20th century. For, they did not have the right to vote. Rather, it was in the non-cooperation and satyagraha movements that they actively participated.

When Chittaranjan Das joined the non-cooperation movement of the 1920s, he received the support of not just men but also many women including his wife, Basanti Devi. She toured the districts campaigning for the movement, earned people's support for it and raised money. In this she was helped by her sister Urmila Devi and Hemaprabha Majumdar. They enthused people to adopt the charkha and sell hand-spun cloth (khaddar). When the chief leaders of the Bengal Congress including Chittaranjan were incarcerated, Basanti Devi took on the presidential responsibilities of the provincial Congress.

Jyotirmoyee Ganguly actively participated in politics in the 1920s and 1930s. After having taught at school and college levels for quite a few years, she formed the Congress's team of women volunteers. Urmila Devi and Jyotirmoyee were both jailed for six months. This was the first time that women accepted prison terms for their role in the non-violent movement. Jyotirmoyee was imprisoned for a second time in 1932. In an irony of fate, she died of her injuries after being hit by an army vehicle.

Jatindramohan Sengupta's wife, Nelly Sengupta, played a particularly active role in the non-cooperation movement in East Bengal. She also contributed a great deal to constitutional politics. She was twice arrested, in Delhi in 1930 and in Calcutta in 1933, for speaking in banned meetings. Even more remarkably, she assumed the presidency of the Congress after the organisation was declared illegal in 1933. In 1940 and 1946, she was elected member of the Bengal Legislative Council. In 1937, Hemaprabha Majumdar had been elected from Dhaka as the first woman legislator. Nelly Sengupta stayed back in East Pakistan after the Partition of 1947. In 1954 she was elected unopposed to parliament from Chittagong. An Irish lady may also be mentioned in this context—Sister Nivedita. Along with Vivekananda, she had inspired the young men of Bengal in the early 20th century.

Among the women who did not stop at helping terrorist politics but also actively participated in such politics, the most well known was Preetilata Waddedar. She became the principal of a school in Chittagong after graduating with brilliant results from Calcutta. In 1930 she teamed up with Surjya Sen and his revolutionary colleagues and joined the raid on the Chittagong armoury. She was able to escape, but Kalpana Dutta was arrested and sentenced for life. Two years later, Preetilata took part in an encounter with the army. That same year, she attacked an European club in Chittagong and killed herself, by consuming poison, before she could be arrested. In 1931, school students Shanti Ghosh and Suniti Choudhury of Comilla shot dead District Magistrate Stevens. They were tried and sentenced for life. Two months later, Beena Das shot at Governor Stanley Jackson at the convocation ceremony of Calcutta University. She missed her target but was still sentenced for life.

Preetilata Waddedar

Charushila Devi was initiated into politics by Khudiram Das. She was incarcerated several times in the 1930s. Nirmalnalini, the first woman to become a satyagrahi, was imprisoned for taking part in the Civil Disobedience movement of 1931. Parulbala Mukhopadhyay served time in jail in 1932. Pratibha Gangopadhyay was an active communist worker and in 1940 became a party member. She worked among peasants, especially women, in the districts of Howrah and 24 Parganas to create political awareness. In 1949, she objected to police torture while in jail and was shot dead, along with Latika Sen, Amiya Dutta and Gita Sarkar. Another woman connected with the communist movement must be remembered with respect—Ila Mitra. She, too, worked among peasants. Not only did she serve time, but was subjected to extreme torture and humiliation in jail.

Women did not just take part in constitutional and terrorist politics. Leela Nag in Dhaka took an extraordinary initiative to help women gain financial independence, through her organisation Deepali Sangha. Those who came in contact with her became politically aware, too. Leela Nag, however, did not believe in politics as much as she did in the awakening of selfhood.

Politics, education, production processes, the arts—participation in none of these was as easy for women as it was for men. Nevertheless, women's contribution to Bengali culture has been extraordinary. What Sarojini Naidu said in this connection may be quoted to give an idea of how valuable this contribution has been: 'In times of trial, Indian women have always been the refuge of men. When men are weary and confused, it is women who, torch in hand, will show them the way.' Women, truly, have inspired men in politics and in cultural activities, and have themselves enriched them. At the heart of the Taj Mahals built by men has always been a Mumtaz, though the Shah Jahans might have been at the forefront.

BENGALI LANGUAGE AND LITERATURE

A glance at Bengali culture shows up more diversity than unity. The greatest unifying factor is quite evidently the Bengali language. To get an idea of the emergence and evolution of this culture, therefore, it is essential to dig into the history of how the Bengali language was born and how it evolved to its present-day form.

Old Bengali Language

As we have noted before, the *Charyapada* poems are considered to be the oldest extant samples of the Bengali language. The full name of *Charyapada* is *Charjashcharjabinishchoy*. These were poems composed by the Buddhist Siddhacharyas. Every verse is accompanied by a mention of the melodic modes (raga, ragini) in which they were sung. A mention of the raga/ragini also accompanies some of the verses in the later Charya poems that Rahul Sankrityayan collected in Nepal. Shashi Bhushan Dasgupta heard slightly modified forms of some of these songs being sung by Buddhist *bhikshu*s in Nepal. He recorded those and some other songs. These verses are extremely valuable in the history of Bengali culture. They constitute samples of the oldest forms of the Bengali language and the language that immediately preceded it; they also furnish nuggets of information about the society that produced them.

The meaning of these songs is not always very clear. They often have a dual meaning, an apparent one and an inner one. Using the apparent meaning as an allegory, Buddhist Siddhacharyas tried to express the inner truth of their spiritual seeking. Scholars therefore have described this language as a kind of light-and-shadow or twilight language. Though a total of 56 Charya verses have been found, only 46 and a half have been deciphered. The curious thing is that Haraprasad Shastri retrieved these verses not from any place in Bengal but from the royal court of far-off Nepal. When he published these songs in a book, *Hazar Bachhorer Purano Bangla Gan O Bauddha Doha* (1909; 'Thousand-year-old Bengali Songs and Buddhist Couplets'), he provided meanings and interpretations on the basis of Tibetan annotations.

Scholars have come up with varied theories to explain why these early samples of Bengali were found in Nepal and not in Bengal. There is no debate over the inference that Buddhists carried the Charya poems with them when they fled to Nepal from Bengal. There is also not much dispute over the hypothesis that the Buddhists were forced to leave the land in adverse circumstances or in the face of persecution. It is not however certain exactly when they left. It does not seem unreasonable to infer that they fled after the rise of Brahmanism during the Sena era. In that case the blame falls on Hindu kings. On the other hand, if it is assumed that they migrated in the time of Indo-Muslim rule, then Muslim rulers become partners in the crime. There is historical evidence to show that these rulers destroyed Buddhist viharas and that countless Buddhists converted to Islam. It is perhaps logical, therefore, to conclude that the stream of Buddhist migrations continued into the Muslim era. But it is rational to suppose that the flight started during Sena reign, which was the age of Brahmanical revival and Buddhist decline.

In the first chapter we noted that though Haraprasad Shastri claimed that the Charya verses were a thousand years old, according to Suniti Kumar Chattopadhyay, these were composed between BCE 950 and BCE 1200. In Sukumar Sen's opinion, these verses might have been composed even later. He believed that Bhusukpada, one of the chief poets of the Charya verses, belonged to the late 13th century. Rakhaldas Bandyopadhyay felt that these poems were composed even later, around the 14th century. At the other extreme is Muhammad Shahidullah's view that the first Charya poems were composed during the 7th-8th centuries. In sum, going by what various scholars say, these poems belong between the 8th-9th centuries and the 12th-13th centuries.

In the age in which the Charya poems were composed, there was no language called Bengali yet. These poems are written in a sort of proto-language that eventually developed into Bengali, Assamese and Oriya. Oriya got detached from this language as it slowly developed distinct characteristics of its own. After that Bengali acquired its special characteristics and became known as a separate language. And finally, Assamese, too, separated from Bengali. Consequently, within a few centuries a single language in north-eastern India had bifurcated into three distinct languages. Which means that just as we notice in the *Charyapada* certain Bengali words and Bengali linguistic peculiarities, Assamese- and-Oriya-speaking people are also able to detect some words and other characteristics of their language. Just as Bengalis claim that *Charyapada* poems constitute the oldest extant samples of their language and literature, Assamese- and-Oriya-speaking people also make similar claims. But some scholars say that though the *Charyapada* does show some characteristics of Oriya and Assamese, it is more closely related to the later Bengali.

Indeed, the similarity with Bengali is not limited to some distinctly familiar words but also extends to certain linguistic characteristics. For instance, in the words *rundhela, bhoila, bhoili, bhoile, leli* in poems by Kanhapada and Bhusukpada, the past tense is indicated by the use of *-ila, -ili, -ile* added to the verbs. This is undoubtedly a characteristic of Bengali and not of Oriya or Assamese. Elsewhere, verb forms like *aila* (came), *gela* (went), *cholila* (got going), *chorhila* (climbed), *porhila* (fell) have been used, all indicating the past tense, and all still recognisably Bengali. The expression *chore nilo* (thief took [it]) in a poem by Kukkuripada is significant. Not only is the verb form *nilo* (took) distinctly Bengali, the –e suffixed to *chor* (thief) is peculiar to Bengali. Verb suffixes *–ibo* and *–ibe* have been sometimes used to indicate future tense, again as in Bengali. For instance, in words like *koribo, koribe, kahibo, hoibo*. The use of genitive suffixes such as *–era, -or, -ara* (*tokkhar, tohori*) and the locative –ta (*harhita, gharoto*) is also peculiarly Bengali.

Some words have come down to Bengali unchanged. Some examples are: *uthe, kopat, koribo, koribe, kaj, kee, khai, khade, khal, gabhi, ghorini, ghare, chorhile, chore, chharhi, jani, dal, tini, tula, dui, dharo, dhuni, nal, nahi, niti, nid, paran, pane (pani), boitha, balod, bohi, bibaho, bhat, majhe, michhe, mor, rajsap, rate, sakol, sahoje, sali (shali), heri.* Then there are words and compounds that are remarkably similar to ones now used in Bengali. The table below lists some examples.

In *Charyapada*	In present-day Bengali
aiso	*eso* (come)
ailo	*elo* (came)
sukhedukhe	*sukhedukkhe* (in joys and sorrows)
dhoke	*dhoka dei* (cheats)
taher	*tahar* (his/her)
chanda	*chand* (moon)
nanando	*nanad* (sister-in-law, husband's sister)
sahi	*soi* (friend, usually in friendship between women)
nahi	*nai* (absent; nor there)
bhoyo	*bhoy* (fear)
horinar khur	*horiner khur* (deer hooves)
omon dhan	*aman dhan* (lowland rice grown in the rainy season)
koriho	*koriyo* (do)
alo	*olo*
chorhi	*chorhia* (having climbed)
pasara	*pasra* (merchandise)
bhomora	*bhomra* (bee)
on upae	*onyo upae* (by other means)
choushothi	*chousatti* (sixty-four)
du-ar	*duar* (door)
kori	*koria* (having done [something])
ghin	*ghrina* (hatred)
opna	*apna* (on one's own)
niti	*nityo* (every day)

These words and parts of speech show that though the language of the Charya poems was not exactly Bengali, many characteristics that would later mark the Bengali language were already present in it. Apart from their extraordinary linguistic and etymological value as constituting the earliest extant samples of Bengali, the Charya poems are also valuable for the fragments of contemporary social life that they reveal and what they tell us about the ordinary people of those times. The ordinary men and women we meet in these poems fished, ferried boats, hunted birds and animals, separated cotton fibres from seeds, brewed alcohol, sold curds. The *Charyapada* poems have images of people crossing rivers, setting off on trading trips, attending weddings. They tell us how people built homes on mounds and lived in them. They tell us, too, of thieves, watchmen, robbers, and of waylaying of travellers by dacoits. There is mention of music and singing and of games of chess. And then there is that age-old lament: *Haarito bhaat nanhi niti abeshee* (there is no rice in the pot, but there are guests every day).

Of course, only a small number of Charya poems have been found. Besides, the Siddhacharyas did not write these poems to describe social life. Yet we get to know of musical instruments, dramatic performances, chess games, deer-hunting, objects of everyday use and human relationships from these songs. The poets have left hints of the regulations of commensality then prevailing and of fastidiousness about contamination of caste purity through touching. A Dom woman lives on the edges of town and her shaven-headed Brahmin admirer passes by touching only the thatch of her cottage. Such images provide a window into the social and cultural life of the time.

Bengal at the time of the *Charyapada* poems was not yet an urban civilisation and we are used to thinking of the lifestyles of those times as having been rural. Yet the Charya poems do not so much provide a peek into life in the countryside. Rather, they suggest a world of trade and business and an urban life in a very basic sense. This indicates that the poets who wrote these songs probably lived in ports and small market towns. It might also be inferred that village settlements had not yet colonised the whole of Bengal, especially East Bengal.

The Emergence of Authentic Bengali

No works of Bengali literature belonging to the two centuries following the last of the *Charyapada* poems have been found. This is why many scholars describe this period as the dark age of Bengali literature. Yet, the absence of extant literature does not mean that no literature was created in that period. Very little was actually written down, because the tradition of writing was not yet very strong. And whatever did get written down could not be preserved. Neither the kind of materials used for writing nor the climate of the land was conducive to the survival of the manuscripts. The *Charyapada* poems survived by chance. They might well have been lost if the Buddhists had not carried these, their religious songs, with them to Nepal. The links of Buddhists with Tibet might also have helped these to survive. The climate of Nepal, too, would have been friendlier to the manuscripts than that of Bengal.

Some historians of literature have tried to establish that no literature was produced in the first two centuries of Muslim rule because of the persecution unleashed by the new rulers and the lawlessness that prevailed. There is, however, reason to doubt this inference. Indo-Muslim rule may have started in the early 13th century, but its reach did not extend to the whole of Bengal in the first 150 years. Also, in view of the poor communication of those times, it must be assumed that the vast rural population that lived outside the city limits did not come into direct contact with the new and alien ruling elite. There is at least no reason to assume that the kind of police state that we are now familiar with could exist then. In this context we may cite the instance of an educated poet like Mukundaram Chakraborty. After another three centuries had passed and Mughal rule was firmly established and communications vastly improved, he believed Man Singh to be the monarch of the land rather than Akbar. This should give an indication of how negligible the impact of Indo-Muslim rule was in the lives of ordinary people. The inference that the establishment of this rule put an end to the production of literature for 200 years seems, therefore, to be erroneous. A more logical assumption would be that while a vast body of literary and scriptural texts in Sanskrit were produced under the patronage of the Sena rulers, in the first 200 years after the introduction of Muslim rule, Sanskrit literary and scriptural texts were not produced with court patronage. No Bengali texts, either.

The second most notable sample of old Bengali literature after *Charyapada* is Borhu Chandidas's *Srikrishnakeertan*. This text, too, was lost. It was discovered not very long ago, and quite by chance, in a village in Bankura in the barn of a descendant of Vaishnava goswami Srinivas Acharya. Basantaranjan Ray published the narrative poem on behalf of the Bangiya Sahitya Parishad in 1916. It is not known when it was written. It is not even very clear from the manuscript what its actual title was, because the

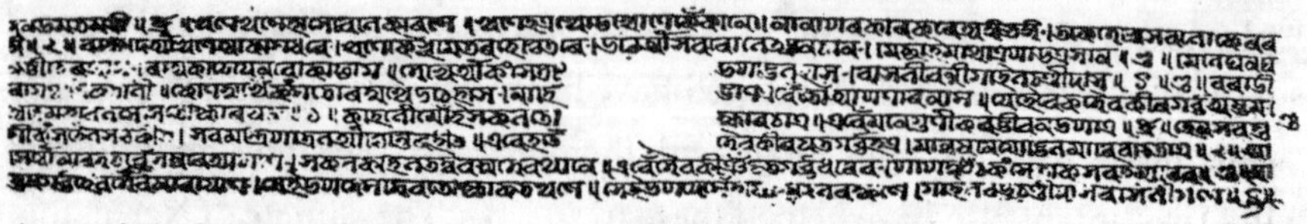

A page from *Srikrishnakeertan*, the earliest manuscript in Bengali

first and the last few pages are missing. Basantaranjan Ray found the name 'Srikrishnakeertan' (songs sung about Krishna) written on a small piece of paper tucked into the manuscript and decided to use it as the title.

When compared with the other Bengali manuscripts that have been found, the script of this one appears to be older in style. Most scholars have placed it in the 15th century, though Suniti Kumar Chattopadhyay, analysing its language, regarded it as belonging to the latter half of the 14th century. Scholars have generally acknowledged it to be the earliest extant example of a text written in a language that is close to Bengali as we know it. But Sukumar Sen has claimed it to be a much later composition on the basis of his examination of the paper and ink used in the manuscript and pointed out modifications of two or three Arabic and Farsi words in the poem. He has also hinted, without saying it in so many words, that the manuscript found might even be a copy made sometime in the 18th century. He doubted the authenticity of the manuscript and whether it was a single poet who wrote the poem.

The innumerable *Vaishnava Padavali* poems (collections of Vaishnava poems on the life of Krishna) composed in the Middle Ages survived mostly through an oral tradition of singing, though a few were also written down. The language of these poems, therefore, has evolved with time and become modern. An example of this transformation is seen in Dwija Chandidas's Padavali. His were possibly the most-loved among the *Vaishnava Padavali* poems. His *Padavali* therefore does not appear very dated at all and might even be taken to have been composed in, at the most, 18th century. *Srikrishnakeertan*, on the other hand, retains many characteristics of an older form of Bengali. This suggests that the poem possibly lost its popularity and ceased to be sung by people. The poem survived as a written text. Assuming that the text lost popularity, many scholars infer that Borhu Chadidas composed the poem before the time of Chaitanyadev. The story of *Srikrishnakeertan*, based on physical love, could not retain its popularity after Chaitanyadev came up with his novel interpretation of Vaishnava philosophy. This story thus was shut inside the pages of the manuscript and no changes could creep into the language of the written text. A comparison with the *Charyapada* poems shows the language of the poem as much more recognisably Bengali.

Not only is the *Charyapada* language difficult to understand because of the old and unfamiliar spellings used, but most words, barring a few stray ones, are so different from present-day Bengali that they are not immediately recognisable as Bengali at all. The language of *Srikrishnakeertan*, on the other hand, can be immediately recognised as Bengali. Only a few vowel sounds added to words, including verb suffixes, and some pronouns are different. For instance, *amhe* is used for *amra* (we). *Antore* is used for *ontore* (inside).

Some scholars claim that old Bengali has survived in another poem. It is called *Yusouf-Julekha* and was written by Shah Mohammad Sageer. Muhammad Enamul Haque has said that he worked for Giyasuddin Azam Shah (1389-1410). If this claim is true, then the poem *Yusouf-Julekha* might well be older than even *Srikrishnakeertan*. But the evidence on which Enamul Haque bases his claim is justifiably open to doubt. Sageer has written that the sultan called 'Gyech', that is, Giyas, for whom he worked, had defeated his father to become king. Now, Giyasuddin Azam Shah had defeated and killed his father Sikander Shah. So if Sageer was his employee then he must have been a late 14th century poet. On the other hand, Giyasuddin Mahmud Shah (1533-38) of the Hossein Shahi dynasty also rebelled against his father, Naseeruddin Nasrat Shah. Nasrat Shah was also killed, though whether at the hands of his son is not clear from historical evidence. But there is no doubt that a year after his father's death Giyasuddin Mahmud Shah killed his nephew and seized the throne. If Sageer was in the employ of this Giyasuddin, then he belonged to the first half of the 16th century. There is no categorical mention of the date of composition of the poem. Enamul Haque has not said anything about the authenticity of the manuscript on which he based his claim. However, there is some evidence of both antiquity and regionalism in the eulogy that he quotes to press his case. But the evidence of antiquity is not substantial. Apart from the words *karon, tinho, loilento, jenho* and *kahonto*, there is little other evidence to support the claim of antiquity. The use of the word *mui* and its unusual spelling probably point to regionalism rather than antiquity. Sageer belonged to the Chittagong region. The version of the poem retrieved by Enamul Haque, even if it is undistorted, cannot be accepted as being older than *Srikrishnakeertan.* Indeed, its language does not seem to belong to a period before the 17th century.

Another early text is Krittibas's *Ramayana.* The date of this poem is also not known. There is an opinion that it was written in the 15th century, during the reign of Raja Ganesh. Its language is not quite as archaic as that of *Srikrishnakeertan.* Moreover, thanks to a series of copyists, the spellings and grammar used in this text kept on significantly changing. Consequently, traces of the original language are scant in the edition published in the Serampore press in the early 19th century. This is more or less true of other works of the 15th and 16th centuries, such as *Manasabijoy, Chandimangal, Mahabharata.* To get an idea of what early Bengali was like, therefore, the most important source after the *Charyapada* is *Srikrishnakeertan.* It is also important to understand the changes that came into Bengali after the stage marked by the *Charyapada*; no other extant text records these changes. A comparison of the language of the Charya poems with that of *Srikrishnakeertan* shows how this language had by then branched off from the other East Indian languages.

Bengali literature flourished in the three centuries that followed, first during the reign of the sultans and then in the Mughal era in Bengal. A major factor that helped to bring this about was that the sultans started patronising the writing of Bengali literary texts. We have seen in the second chapter how and why state patronage produced a rich literary tradition. In the discussion below, we will see how the popularity of the Vaishnava faith produced thousands of Vaishnava poems during this time. The age also produced plenty of Mangalkavyas, biographical works and translations. The natural process of evolution in the language combined with the constant writing of literature to bring about significant linguistic changes in Bengali. It is not however possible to determine the exact stages through which the language changed and evolved. For, the literary texts that have come down to us did not remain undistorted but underwent repeated changes at the hands of copyists over several centuries. Still, among the linguistic transformations that can be detected are changes in pronunciations, spellings, pronouns and in vowel sounds added to verbs to signify tense.

The pronouns used in *Srikrishnakeertan* are archaic: *ahme, ahmar, mo, tomha, tomhe, tomhak*, etc. So are the verb suffixes: *ailanho, jaon, chorhilon, geli, korian*, etc. This kind of archaism is largely absent in works ranging from Bipradas Piplai to Mukundaram Chakraborty. The pronouns used in these works are not very different from the ones in use today: *ami* (I), *amar* (my), *tumi* (you), *tomar* (your, yours), *tomare* (to you), *toma, tok, tar* (his/her), *tare* (for him/her), *jahar* (whose), *se* (he/she), *ke* (who), *apni* (you, respectful), *apnar* (yours, respectful), etc. Verb forms in present-day Bengali have shed the old nasal sound: *korian, jaon, chonrhilo*, etc. have become *koria, jao, chorhilo*. The vowel sounds added to verbs to denote past, present and future tense are almost modern: such as *jai* (go, first person), *dekhi* (look, first person), *kohi* (say, first person), *kori* (do, first person), *kaho* (say, second person), *pao* (get, second person), *kahe* (say/says, third person), *kohiche* (is saying, third person), *jae* (go/goes, third person), *kare* (do/does, third person), *bole* (say/says, third person), *loy* (take/takes, third person), *dei* (give/gives, third person), *palae* (escape/escapes, third person), *kande* (cry/cries, third person), *bandhe* (tie/ties, third person), *chilo* (was/were, third person), *likhilo* (wrote, third person), *gelo* (went, third person), *ghuchilo* (ceased to exist), *anilo* (brought, third person), *koilo* (said, third person), *hoilo* (happened), *dile* (gave, second or third person), *koribo* (will do, first person), *katibo* (will cut, first person), *niba* (will take, second person), *loibe* (will take, second and third person), *haube* (will be), etc.

Apart from these linguistic changes, the language of the Middle Ages saw a major shift in vocabulary. The use of *tadbhava* words multiplied. Much increased, too, was the use of loan words from foreign languages. As we have already noted, Farsi was the official and court language in the Mughal era. A very large number of Arabic and Farsi words therefore found their way into Bengali. These words took on local styles of pronunciation and grammatical properties to become indispensable parts of Bengali. As a result, we find many Arabic and Farsi words that are used not just in official documents, deeds, and letters but also in literature and even in Hindu religious literature. Portuguese merchants came in to trade long before the Mughal era was over, and with them came words from their language. In the chapter 'Bengali Culture under Western Impact' I discussed how loan words from Portuguese blended into Bengali and are still very much in use.

Apart from changes in vocabulary and grammar, Bengali acquired greater expressiveness during this period and became simpler. The lucidity and easy gracefulness of the works of Krittibas, Mukundaram, Alaol, Kashiram Das and Bharatchandra Ray could not have been achieved with the language of *Srikrishnakeertan.* Looking away from these learned poets, the same can be said of the other writers of this period. Even village ballads such as *Purbabanga Geetika* and *Mymensingh Geetika* bear testimony to the richness that the language had acquired by this time.

Beginnings of Prose

Though we know from extant literature what the language of poetry was in the Middle Ages, we have no idea what the spoken language was like or the language that people used if they needed to write letters. The reason is twofold. One, literary texts were written in verse, never in prose. Two, though prose was used in letters, documents and deeds, these have not survived. The administration and the revenue department of the Mughals, however, were far more organised and institutionalised than they had been in earlier regimes. The use of written documents and deeds also correspondingly increased. All official writing was in Farsi, but many of the local people used Bengali in exchanges between themselves. For instance, the Raja of Coochbehar writing to an Assamese ruler used not Farsi but Bengali. The ruling family of Tripura used Bengali as their official language. They used Bengali prose in their official transactions. Bengali was also used in the court of Arakan in what is now Myanmar (Burma).

Vaishnavas initiated efforts to write books in Bengali prose as early as the 17th century. This early prose can be sampled in Roop Goswami's *Karika,* Chandidas's *Chaitanyaroop-prapti,* Narottom Das's *Dehakarhcha,* etc. An analysis of the language of *Karika* gives us an idea of this early prose. A random sampling will show the use of *tadbhava* words and short, simple sentences. The sentences are even shorter and simpler in *Chaitanyaroop-prapti,* and sometimes they have no verbs. Later Vaishnava literature followed this tradition, and sentences were sometimes written shorter still. Also, since the subject of this prose concerns Vaishnava religious beliefs, Arabic and Farsi words are absent. As we noted in the previous discussion, there were many Arabic and Farsi ingredients in the poetry that got written at the same time.

As in poetry, so in Bengali prose samples in the 18th century deeds, documents and letters, Arabic and Farsi words have been used liberally. The sentence structures are simple. There were Arabic and Farsi words in letters written by Brahmin pandits (such as *jabab* [*jawab*, or answer], *marfat* [through], *haqiqat* [current condition/reality]) but not in excessive measure. In the Bengali text of a letter quoted in Halhed's grammar, however, we can clearly see a strong Arabic-Farsi influence such as: *shelamat, zamindari, pargana, doriyashikeeshti, jabardasti, dakhol, sharbaraho, amin, chopdar, sharejomin, talab, hakdar, hak.* The letter in which these words are used does not contain any unfamiliar words, and the sentences are also short. Yet, one keeps stumbling while reading it, and its powers of expression are limited. Indeed, Bengali prose was not yet a mature medium capable of carrying ideas. Prose that can be considered literature had not yet developed. This situation changed with the start of British colonial rule.

Prose in Colonial Times

The import of Arabic and Farsi words during the time of the sultans and then the Mughals enriched Bengali vocabulary and also heightened the expressiveness of the language. Yet these words were not able to initiate any epochal change in the language. On the other hand, Bengali went through an epochal transformation during British colonial rule. The British did not enrich the language by producing written works in Bengali. But lifestyles and the use of technology changed so much during their rule that large-scale and revolutionary transformations in the language became inevitable. Administrative functions at this time brought the British rulers in close and intimate contact with Bengalis.

Although exchanges with the Muslim ruling elite had taken place over a prolonged period, the effect could not be very widespread or far-reaching because of the limited development of communications. The local population in the Muslim era would not have been able to establish the kind of large-scale and extensive contact with the rulers that they achieved during British colonial rule. The unprecedented development of the educational system under colonial rule also brought about drastic changes. The British did not extend the kind of state patronage to Bengali literature that the sultans had done. Yet English language and literature hastened the development of Bengali language and literature.

The British rulers retained Farsi as the court language to begin with. English was introduced as the official language after almost 80 years. This might lead us to believe that the British presence did not produce any significant impact on the Bengali language in the initial years of colonial rule. A closer examination, however, will show that an epochal transformation came about in the use of words and in sentence structures within 50 years of the establishment of British rule. An analysis of the Bengali deeds and documents going back to year 1770 that have been found at the India Office library in London shows that even in those early years of colonial rule English words had started getting incorporated in the language. Words such as company, *mestor* (mister), seal, *effon* (apron), *kang* (captain), *kes* (cash), *raspinjori* (respondentia bond), August, Sitamber, Dejamber, etc. Some English ideas also got translated into Bengali: *fiskora* from per cent, '*ratri aat/noy ghorhi*', meaning 8 or 9 o'clock at night. The biggest change, however, began to appear in the sentence structures. Bengali sentence structures in these deeds and documents closely followed and imitated English ways of constructing clauses. The sentences in these deeds also showed a tendency towards greater length.

The use of Bengali prose was not limited to deeds, documents and letters. With the establishment of British rule Bengali prose began to be used for legal and administrative purposes. The government decided to translate into Bengali, as well as Farsi, the laws that were promulgated after the foundation of the Supreme Court in Calcutta in 1773. The first such book of law in Bengali translation was published in 1784. Thereafter, such translations of law books, slim or voluminous, began to appear every year right up to the first few years of the 19th century. From 1784, arrangements were made to publish government notices and advertisements in Bengali newspapers along with English and Farsi versions. Consequently, the amount of Bengali prose that was written and published between 1784 and 1800 had no parallel or precedent in any of the preceding centuries. (I have discussed the law books and the Bengali advertisements of this period in my book *Kalantare Bangla Godyo,* 1993; 'Bengali Prose at a Turning Point'.)

The import of technology also made it easier for Bengali prose to gain wide currency. The first printing press in Bengal was established in the 1770s at the initiative of an Englishman called James Hicky. Subsequently, another printing press was established with the East India Company's help, and this was where Halhed's Bengali grammar was printed in 1778. Charles Wilkins devised Bengali typefaces for the Bengali examples that were used in the book. Once the Bengali printing infrastructure was in place, the development of Bengali prose was a natural and inevitable outcome. It must be borne in mind that verse may be created and enjoyed even without it being written down because verse can be committed to memory and can even be set to tune and sung. But prose is only possible if it can be written down. A printing press is a necessary precondition for the development of prose.

The exercise of translating books of law and notices/advertisements into Bengali brought about fundamental changes, in the few years between 1784 and the foundation of Fort William College, in the language and style of Bengali prose. In the extant samples of prose-writing up to this period, Arabic and Farsi words were liberally used. The sentences, too, were short. The translation of legal books produced two kinds of change. First, the proportion of Arabic and Farsi words was now much reduced. In their place we now notice more Sanskrit words. Among the company officials, Nathaniel Halhed and Henry Pitts Forster believed that Bengali had lost its purity because of the import of Arabic and Farsi words and that this lost purity could be retrieved and the language reformed through the use of Sanskrit words. Halhed presented his opinion in his introduction to his grammar. Forster actually applied this principle in the translations that he supervised. And thus started the Sanskritisation of Bengali at the end of the 18th century.

The Fort William College became the principal agent of this process of Sanskritisation after its establishment in 1800. Quite a few Bengali munshis were employed under William Carey's leadership in the Bengali department of the college. These men wrote books that were used to teach the students of the college. One of the munshis was Mrityunjay Tarkalankar, a Sanskrit pandit who was a hardline supporter of Sanskritisation. Another munshi, Ramram Basu, was in favour of an easier Bengali with its happy blend of Arabic and Farsi words. William Carey himself used to take Bengali lessons from him before the foundation of Fort William College. He, too, was a patron of the easier, Arabic-and Farsi-influenced Bengali to begin with. And for good reason. Carey learnt Bengali to preach Christianity among the native population. The belief that preaching in a laboured, Sanskritised language would not be effective made him advocate a language that was closer to the spoken language of the people. But the influence of Mrityunjay turned him into a supporter of Sanskritisation. The prose used in the textbooks written at the college under his leadership is generally far more Sanskrit-influenced than the earlier Bengali prose. Later writers including Ram Mohan Roy were not able to ignore the tradition of prose writing that was established in these textbooks.

The sudden flowering of Bengali prose came at a price. Not only were Arabic and Farsi words weeded out, as far as possible, in the tradition of written language that developed in the 19th century, the simple sentence structures also took on more complex forms. A comparison of the law books translated by Forster with personal letters that have survived from the years narrowly preceding them will show how the kind of Sanskritisation promoted by Forster made the language difficult and removed it from the tongue actually spoken by the people. Long, complex sentences with multiple clauses are used in Forster's translations. Juxtaposing the two writing styles, we can say that until the 18th century Bengali sentence structures were generally simple, and the style followed the spoken language. From the time of Jonathan Duncan and Henry Forster, however, sentences became long and compound, and the style bookish. Thus the written language branched off from the spoken language and became quite different. Admittedly, however, the language could not but change at this time in keeping with the changing realities and ideas that it was required to express.

The Language Thrives

Bengali prose came into its own in response to the demands of a new age and a new way of life. The British brought new thoughts, new ideas and new kinds of work to the land. The kind of language that was now in demand to deal with these new realities had not formerly existed. The conditions that would make this language a necessity did not exist in pre-colonial times and the contexts that made this language necessary had not existed in everyday lives. But when a heretofore unknown prose was called for in society, in government jobs, in educational efforts, in the new print media, and in the business of everyday life, a virtually new language had to be 'midwived'. Consequently, in the decades between the 1780s and the publication of the first modern Bengali novel (Bankimchandra's *Durgeshnandini*, also probably the first novel in any modern Indian language) in 1865, Bengali prose went through a veritable revolution. This long road from Jonanthan Duncan to Bankimchandra's arrival in Bengali literature might have measured only 80 years in the human calendar, but the two limits of this short period are separated by a light year if measured by the linguistic transformation that was achieved in it. The change happened in phases, a step at a time, and it did not take place at the hands of any single individual. It came about in part through the efforts of Forster and Carey, in part through the writings of Ram Mohan Roy and his contemporaries, a little again at the hands of the Derozians, and then through the writings of Ishwar Gupta, Vidyasagar, Akshay Datta, and then again in Peary Chand Mitra's *Alaler Gharer Dulal* ('The Spoilt Son'; published in 1858; claimed by some scholars to be the first Bengali novel, written in a language that was close to the spoken tongue), and in Kaliprasanna Sinha's *Hutom Pyanchar Naksha* ('Sketches of Hutom the Owl'). Each of them expressed some new idea or the other, and the work of each threw up new aspects of the evolving prose. And thus, through the collective efforts of all these writers developed a new prose style.

Discussions on textbooks, newspapers, religion, philosophy and other such matters started right at the start of the 19th century. These are subjects that, when written about, require words that are not used in everyday life. Complex ideas need suitable definitions to be properly expressed. In the process some differences are bound to develop between the language of talking and the language of writing. In the age of Fort William College, however, language moved from one pole to another. The munshis of the college did not knock at the doors of Sanskrit only to give words to new ideas. They also consciously tried to avoid Arabic and Farsi words by increasingly using Sanskrit words in their place. One of their objectives was to make sure, through the profuse use of Sanskrit, that Bengali was able to make the cut as a sophisticated language. The social scientist M.N. Srinivas has described this process as 'Sanskritisation'. A considerable amount of artificiality crept into the language as a result of this process. Mrityunjay was quite an artist in the use of language and was fairly skilful in writing. Many more *tatsama* words are used in his writing than is common in oral speech. Arabic and Farsi words are not used at all. More remarkably, the sentences are extremely long. Yet, his prose makes smooth reading and the judicious use of punctuation ensures that the reader does not have to stumble through it. But the language could also occasionally become much more complex and jarringly artificial at the hands of less accomplished writers.

Once the pandits of the Fort William College set the trend, even writers of the stature of Ram Mohan Roy followed it. The early newspaper editors, too, were forced to adopt this language though it was not really suitable for the medium. In the 1820s, however, Bengali prose acquired a degree of expressiveness through a debate on religion that was carried out in several newspapers. Even Ishwar Gupta made his first public appearance through the medium of the daily newspaper. The 1840s produced two prose writers of immense stature, Ishwarchandra Vidyasagar and Akshay Datta. They were not able to check the use of *tatsama* words. What they achieved was to make the language smooth-flowing. They were able to master the inner rhythm of prose and the natural punctuations that make it easy to understand, and these they put to excellent use. Their prose, consequently, acquired readability and lucidity. After some initial experimenting, Vidyasagar's language became that of a literary artist, particularly in *Betal Panchabingshati* (1847; a collection of 25 stories retold from a pool of folktales). Debendranath Tagore was not exactly a writer of great literary stature. Nor did he get much of a chance to influence readers through his writing. Yet he, too, wrote an easy-flowing prose.

The prose style dominated by *tatsama* words that these writers brought into vogue was not well suited for all kinds of subjects. There are many things connected with everyday life that cannot be expressed gracefully in this language. Peary Chand Mitra, a one-time student of Derozio, wanted to write a story about the problems of the time, and he had in mind a readership of little-educated women. He found that a language weighed down by *tatsama* words might fit the speech of educated gentlemen without straining credibility too much, but it would not at all do as the language of ordinary people and of women. Not even for describing the trivia of ordinary everyday lives. In parts of *Alaler Gharer Dulal* (1854-58), therefore, he used a language that was not too literary, nor exactly the language of everyday speech, but something in between and closer to spoken language. The vowel endings and the pronouns follow the more literary style. But the onomatopoeic expressions that he uses to create an atmosphere give the language a flavour of everyday speech. Besides, everyday speech is used for some dialogues, such as one between a barber and his wife, and in these the spoken forms of vowel endings and pronouns are used. The realistic language of the dialogues and the onomatopoeic words impart a racy liveliness to the text. Then again Arabic and Farsi words are used in the dialogue between the Muslim Thak Chacha and his wife, which enlivens their characterisation and makes them real. Ramnarayan Tarkaratna wrote the play *Kulinkulsarbaswa* in the same year that *Alaler Gharer Dulal* was published as a book, that is, in 1858. He, too, wrote his dialogues for commoners and women in spoken and regional dialects. But it cannot be said of him, as it can be for Peary Chand, that he played a shaping role in the creation of a new prose style.

The writer of *Hutom Pyanchar Naksha* (1862-64) surpassed Peary Chand's achievement. The subject of this book is such that it could be written only in spoken language. It could not have been written in bookish or written language, and even if it were it would not have any life in it. Nor would it survive a hundred years later. The extraordinary use of spoken speech brings to life scenes from contemporary city life: The church bell ringing at dawn, *tung, tang, tung, tang,* the babus returning home after a night of debauchery, Oriya Brahmin cooks kneading dough in sweet shops, the street lights losing their glare, cuckoos trilling from the verandahs of prostitutes' quarters, a city still quiet and slumbering except for a few stray dogs barking, a city coming to life slowly with stray bits of conversation floating out of the houses, women coming out for a dip in the river, butchers carrying loads of mutton chops, all the sergeants, patrol officers and constables, that is, all those who make a living out of terrorising the urban poor, reporting at the police station after night shift, their pockets bulging with small change, the night's haul of petty bribes. No other language but the one that was used would have worked for this description. Around the same time as Peary Chand and the author of *Hutom*, Michael Madhusudan Dutt and Dinabandhu Mitra established the potential of spoken speech through their satirical skits. Even an accomplished practitioner of Sanskritised prose like Vidyasagar recognised the promise of spoken language by weaving it into some of his anonymous satirical writing. Still, no writer of that period staked their entire reputation on spoken language by making it their only medium. Nor did they accept the premise that it could be used to create great literature.

Bankimchandra Chattopadhyay, mindful that language must match the subject and include ingredients from spoken speech wherever necessary, crafted a prose style of exceptional beauty, though he did not directly use spoken language. His language is sometimes solemn and sometimes simple and easy in the manner of spoken speech. Sometimes it shines bright with humour, and sometimes cuts with sharp, glittering satire. His language is not just a medium to express ideas, it is an art in itself. No one wrote more beautiful prose in the 19th century.

Rabindranath Tagore said of himself that he was above all a poet. It was with poetry that he began his long creative life. The oldest samples of his prose that we have were written in spoken language—*Europe Prabaseer Chithhi* (Letters from Europe). He was only 18 when he wrote these. And these were written as letters, that is, informally. When in the mid 1880s he started writing creatively in prose, it was the stylised, written language that he chose, though it soon began to appear artificial to him. He was not comfortable writing in this language. When in the early 1890s he wrote a series of letters to his niece Indira Devi describing his life in rural East Bengal, he used spoken language. The first stories of *Galpoguchho* ('Bunch of Stories'), the collection of Tagore's short stories, are from this period. In writing these stories he could not make up his mind about which style to follow. These therefore show a certain conflict between the two competing styles. The pronouns follow the spoken tongue: for instance, *tar* is used instead of the more formal *tahar*, both meaning his/her. But the vowel endings are used in their stylised forms instead of the informal ones, *jaitechhe* (is going) and *khaitechhe* (is eating), instead of *jachche* and *khachche* as people would say in spoken speech. In another few years he firmly embraced the spoken language as his chosen medium, though by that time he had also mastered the style followed by Bankim.

At the dawn of the 20th century Tagore had already established his position as a poet, author and music aficionado. Then in 1913 came the Nobel Prize, though *Gitanjali* was not his greatest work. Only one other writer in the entire British Empire had got the Nobel Prize for Literature before he did—and that was Rudyard Kipling. The prize, therefore, brought extraordinary prestige and honour for Tagore. Even those who disliked him with all their hearts were now forced to acknowledge his supremacy as a writer. In this atmosphere of adulation, Pramatha Choudhury, writer and also the husband of Tagore's niece Indira Debi, launched a monthly magazine called *Sabujpatra* ('Green Letter'). The name carried a hint of the changes that Choudhury was seeking to bring about in the feast of Bengali literature, signifying the claims of youth, and, therefore, innovation. He wanted to publish in his magazine writing that exclusively used the spoken language. He persuaded Tagore to also write in the spoken language. At that particular moment in history, Tagore dominated the Bengali literary firmament, standing tall over all others. Though *Sabujpatra* turned out to be an extremely short-lived venture, the prose style that Tagore introduced through this magazine was perpetuated as the standard and permanent medium of literature. It was a style that closely followed the spoken tongue.

In this way, the artificial stylisation that had crept into Bengali through the efforts of Duncan, Forster, Carey, Mrityunjay and the like slowly made way for a more natural, smooth-flowing style. But of course written language cannot ever be identical with spoken language. Bengali, therefore, started following the spoken tongue in its pronouns, verb endings and some vowel sounds, but without erasing the expressiveness that writers such as Ram Mohan Roy, Ishwarchandra Vidyasagar and Bankimchandra Chattopadhyay had endowed it with through sentence structures and definitions that allowed it to carry complex meanings. Nor would it be desirable to erase this rich legacy.

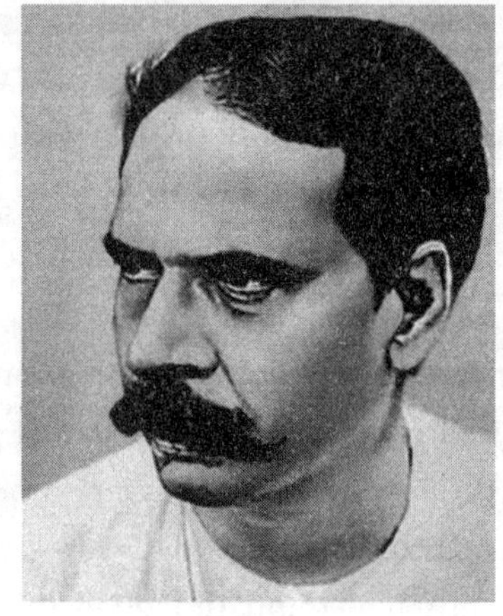
Pramatha Choudhury

Many writers after Tagore have tried to introduce individualised prose styles. Pramatha Choudhury, Rajshekhar Basu, Abanindranath Tagore, Bibhutibhushan Bandyopadhyay, Gopal Haldar, Syed Mujtaba Ali, Jasim Uddin—none of these writers followed any single style. Later still, a new kind of language took shape to meet the demands of science, technology and administration. Much variety was introduced in the use of words and the construction of sentences through the efforts of various writers. But the kind of novelty that was brought about in Bengali prose through the innovations of Forster, Carey, Mrityunjay, Vidyasagar, Tagore and Pramatha Choudhury has not been replicated in recent times. The combined efforts of Bengali writers made the language a suitable medium for subjects ranging from literature, philosophy and science to satire and comedy, and through language they created many an edifice of beauty. And so it was that an epochal change was brought about in the Bengali language, especially in Bengali prose, by a series of writers over a period of some 150 years beginning in the late 18th century.

Early Bengali Literature

Religion was from the beginning at the heart of Bengali literature. Buddhism was the predominant faith in the age when Bengali was only just emerging as a language, and so Buddhist spiritual seeking was the subject of the literature produced then—the *Charyapada* poems. During the Sena regime, however, Brahmanism replaced Buddhism as the state religion. Literary and scriptural writing in Sanskrit thrived under state patronage in the new regime. Even the Bengali poet Jaydev wrote his *Gita Govinda* in Sanskrit, not in the regional language. Indeed, the scriptural scholars decreed it blasphemous to even listen to the scriptures or the Puranas recited in the regional languages. Nothing comparable to the *Charyapada* was therefore written under the patronage of the Senas. In this context it must also be borne in mind that the Sena kings were not Bengalis. This could have been an important reason for the drying up of the tradition of early Bengali writing that had produced the *Charyapada* poems. There is at least no extant Bengali creative writing, which was produced under the Sena rulers' patronage.

In the period following the Sena regime, rigidities of Brahmanism eased on the one hand, and on the other, Muslim sultans started patronising the local language. In this changed atmosphere, literature was produced on various aspects of the Hindu belief system. *Srikrishnakeertan* belongs to this tradition, and its subject is the story of Radha and Krishna. Borhu Chandidas did not however make any pretence of the Radha-Krishna story being an allegory for the bond between the Creator and the created. Instead, he gave himself up to describing their love. In Vaishnava philosophy, Radha is symbolic of the spirit of the created being, and Krishna of the Creator. In this scheme of things, Radha does not seek union with Krishna to gratify her senses, she offers her whole being to be united with her Creator. This philosophy also talks of physical union, but this union is not for Krishna's sensual gratification or for the fulfilment of Radha's desire.

Srikrishnakeertan, on the other hand, is a simpler story of love and lust. The teenaged Radha we see at the beginning of the poem is not familiar with the import of love. Krishna reveals his godhood to her to get not her love but her body. The young Radha not surprisingly sees his overtures as an irritant and rejects them straightaway. The first few sections of the poem describe how Krishna, with the help of an old go-between called Barhayi and using a range of strategies such as subterfuges, tricks and even force, is finally able to seduce Radha. The last two sections show how Radha, her sexual instincts now aroused, repeatedly seeks intimacy with Krishna. It is not union with her Creator that she seeks, but physical union with her lover with its embraces and kisses. But a sexually gratified Krishna loses his attraction for her and departs on the pretext of work. The poem ends with Radha's heartbreak, and it is her grief that the poet depicts with the greatest empathy. Borhu Chandidas had composed *Srikrishnakeertan* as a ballad that could be sung, in the form of dialogues by Radha, Krishna and Barhayi. Each dialogue is preceded by a mention of the raga (melody) and the tala (rhythm) to which it should be sung.

Chaitanyadev started preaching the Vaishnava faith in the early 16th century. In the chapter 'Society and Religion' we noted how his faith of simple love and devotion, unencumbered by ritualism and regulations, overnight won the hearts and minds of the people. True, not all Hindus got themselves formally initiated into the ways of Vaishnavism, but Chaitanyadev triggered a flood of religious emotion that swept across the community. This torrent left its mark on Bengali literature. The political climate of the land was also conducive.

In the 16th and 17th centuries, Dwija Chandidas, Govindadas, Jnandas, Balaramdas, Vidyapati, Vrindabandas and hundreds of poets composed thousands of Vaishnava poems, known in Bengali as the *Vaishnava Padavali*. These poems are intensely emotional in nature. Also, they were not read as poems but sung as songs. The kirtans, or musical renderings of the Vaishnava poems, blended folk tunes with contemporary classical melodies to produce a novel style, and this became as popular as the Vaishnava faith itself. One of the things that drove so many poets to this genre was that it provided many of them an opportunity to use the Radha-Krishna story to tell their own love lives. The literary mores of the time did not permit the recounting of personal experience. Apart from the Padavalis, a vast body of Vaishnava literature surrounding the faith and also Chaitanyadev's life was produced at this time. The story of Radha and Krishna was of course universally known. So the poets were not able to add to it at will to create ever new narrative poems. What they did do, however, was offer many subtle interpretations of the narrative and depict, through the various Padavalis, the many shades, moods and forms of love. The Radha of these poets was very different from Borhu Chandidas's Radha. Krishna in *Srikrishnakeertan* used subterfuge to seduce Radha, with Barhayi's help. The Radha of the *Vaishnava Padavali* poets beginning with Dwija Chandidas was from the start madly in love with Krishna. Dwija Chandidas's Radha, for instance, felt a great rush of love for Krishna at the mere mention of his name, even before she saw him. Overwhelmed at her own reaction, she said: 'If I am so swept away by his name, what will his touch do to me!'

Through their fragmentary imaging of the first stirrings of love in Radha, and later the range and depth of her feelings, her love dates, her waiting, her unions with her lover, and then again her anguish at separation, the Padavali poets have explored the various stages of love and the emotions that accompany them. Just as Vatsayan has described every imaginable posture and process of coitus, the *Vaishnava Padavali* poets illumined all the varied emotions that form part of the experience of love. An old saying, '*Kanu charha geet nei*' (no song without Kanu, Kanu being an affectionate shorter form of Krishna), reflects the kind of all-encompassing influence that the Vaishnava Padavalis had on Bengali literature, in their subject, their range of feeling and their poetic merit. So great in fact was the popularity that the *Vaishnava Padavali* acquired that even poets who were not Vaishnavas wrote and sang these poems, including quite a few Muslim poets. The Padavalis are perhaps the greatest literary creations of the Middle Ages. Even the Shaktas, who were not only not Vaishnavas but actually opposed to them, followed the Padavali ideal to compose Shakta Padavalis.Around the same time and a little later, fringe communities such as the Bauls and the Sahajiyas also produced innumerable poems in the Padavali mould.

Apart from the Vaishnava Padavalis, Chaitanyadev's impact on the religious environment led to the writing of many books on the philosophy of Vaishnavism and on other aspects of religion. Some of these religious texts were written in Sanskrit. But an even more important tradition of writing was founded at this time, the tradition of biographical literature. Until the time of Chaitanyadev, poems were written about gods and goddesses or about imaginary characters. Now for the first time books were being written about a living or contemporary individual and society. This was how the tradition of writing history started in Bengali, though hagiographies written by devotees are not really objective or impartial as biographies ideally should be. Unrestrained imagination and the emotional excesses of hero worship often push facts out of view.

Songs, poems and dramatic literature on Chaitanyadev's life started being written during his lifetime, in both Bengali and Sanskrit. It was a tradition started by his disciple Advaita Acharya, and it continued to grow and thrive after Chaitanyadev's death. By that time, of course, he and even some of his disciples had turned into veritable gods in popular belief. Murari Gupta wrote the first book about Chaitanyadev's early life, in the form of a *karhcha* (a sort of catechism, in question-and-answer format). Chaitanyadev was still alive at the time. Though the work is full of devotional fervour, it is taken to be largely factually correct because the writer was familiar with his subject. But the printed edition called *Srikrishnacharit* that is now available is deemed to be heavily distorted by Sukumar Sen.

Vrindavandas, on the other hand, wrote his *Chaitanyabhagavat* mainly on the basis of facts collected from Nityanandadas. It cannot be ascertained how much of his account is exaggerated or anecdotal. The excess of devotional fervour in this long work running into some 25,000 lines often blurs the line between fact and fiction. Vrindavandas believed with all his heart that Chaitanyadev was an incarnation of Krishna. He believed, too, that his own guru, Nityananda, was an avatar of Balaram.

After Vrindavandas, Churhamonidas wrote the second biographical work on Chaitanyadev – *Gourangabijoy* (The Triumph of Gouranga) – between 1542 and 1550. This book is as full of emotional excess and exaggeration as *Chaitanyabhagavat*. Krishnadas Kaviraj's *Chaitanyacharitamrita* is relatively more factual. Sukumar Sen believed that as a young man Krishnadas Kaviraj had travelled with Chaitanyadev in the Deccan. This would have brought him into intimate contact with Chaitanyadev, and so his biography was based on personal observation. Some of Chaitanyadev's close associates such as Jeeb Goswami did not like his work. One reason for this could be the absence of devotional fervour about Chaitanyadev in the book. Whatever that may be, this is the book that is considered to be the most reliable biography of Chaitanyadev.

Lochondas and Naraharidas were not only Chaitanyadev's contemporaries, but they had also come in close contact with him. Both these men wrote biographical works on Chaitanyadev. Lochondas's *Chaitanyamangal* is one of the foremost biographies of Chaitanyadev. Jayanandadas's *Chaitanyamangal* is a significant text in this tradition. Many others in later years wrote books on Chaitanyadev's life and teaching. Some of these works are meant to be read, others to be sung as songs.

Mangalkavya

Towards the end of the 15th century, another tradition took root in Bengali literature—the tradition of the Mangalkavyas. Poems of this category are basically paeans to gods and goddesses through mythological stories. The first text in this tradition is *Manasamangal*, written by Bipradas Piplai in 1495-96. The merchant Chand's trading trip is used as a framework to describe the glories of the goddess Manasa. The story shows how Chand Saudagar is forced to worship Manasa despite being a believer in Shaivism, that is, a Shiva devotee. Bijoy Gupta also used this story for his *Manasamangal*. According to some scholars, his work preceded Bipradas's and was written in 1494 or 1484. But Sukumar Sen has raised doubts on whether Bijoy Gupta was quite such an early poet. Analysing evidence such as how the manuscript was found, when it was published, the language used in the text and other internal evidence, he has identified the poem as a much later work.

Just as the goddess Manasa received worship in a swampy, marshy Bengal infested with snakes, Mangalkavyas sung in her praise also easily earned popular interest. In the next 200 years, many poets including Narayan Deb, Ketakadas Khemananda, Bishnu Pal, Kalidas, Rasik Misra, Bangshibadan Chakraborty composed their own *Manasamangal*. Like the Vaishnava Padavalis, *Manasamangal*, too, was meant to be sung. Very often these songs would be sung through the night. That is why it acquired another name by which it was known, Rayani, from *rajani* meaning night.

Though *Manasamangal* was the first Mangalkavya, far surpassing it in popularity was Mukundaram Chakraborty's *Chandimangalkavya* written almost a century later. The reason was twofold. First, as Shiva's wife Chandi was considered far more important a deity than Manasa. Second, Mukundaram was a greater poet than the other Mangalkavya writers. As poetry, therefore, Mukundaram's *Chandimangal* (1589) became the most renowned of the works in this genre. Apart from being a competent poet, Mukundaram was also extraordinary in his social awareness and his gift of storytelling. Indeed, not only was his *Chandimangal* the best among the Mangalkavyas, it was also, in language, plot, descriptions, literary merit and social consciousness, one of the greatest literary creations of medieval Bengali literature. Mukundaram himself may be taken as the greatest poet of the 16th century. There were a few others who composed *Chandimangal* after him. Among them, Dwija Madhav, Dwija Hariram, Akinchan Misra deserve special mention. But other works in the genre pale by comparison with Mukundaram's work.

Once *Manasamangal* and *Chandimangal* became popular, poets started composing Mangalkavyas on other gods and goddesses. Goddesses like Kali, Annada, Sheetala, Lokkhi and Shasthi and gods such as Shiva and Krishna turned into subjects for Mangalkavyas. Even the tiger deity Dakshin Ray and the crocodile deity Kalu Ray were not left out of the tradition. But the strand of Mangalkavya that was the most popular after the *Manasamangal* and *Chandimangal* poems was that of *Dharmamangal*. Many writers including Khelaram, Srishyam Pandit, Roopram Chakraborty, Ramdas Adak, Seetaram Das, Ghanaram Chakraborty and Manikram Ganguly tried their hand at *Dharmamangal*. The most well known among them was Ghanaram Chakraborty. His *Dharmamangal* was written in 1711.

The Mangalkavyas about the various gods and goddesses became so popular in the 17th century that some poets wrote more than one. Krishnaram Das was the most notable among such poets. He was the author of five such works: *Kalikamangal* (1676), *Shashthimangal* (1679-81), *Raymangal* (1686-87), *Sheetalamangal* and *Lokkhimangal*. The Panchalis (verse narratives meant to be read aloud and usually accompanied by rituals of worship) about Satyapir or Satyanarayan, meant to bring out the glories of the pirs, also belong to this genre.

The tradition of the Mangalkavya lost its glory and slowly dried up in the 18th century. Yet it was in this century that Bharatchandra Ray wrote an extraordinary work in this tradition of narrative verse. Divided in three sections, the poem is called *Annadamangal* (1752). The work is not only the greatest of the 18th century Mangalkavyas, it commands a distinctive place in the entire history of Mangalkavyas. Bharatchandra wrote this narrative poem at the command of his patron, Krishnachandra Ray, an influential zamindar based in Krishnanagar, Nadia. Though the poem is in praise of the goddess Annada, its main objective was to present the glories of Krishnachandra Ray's ancestor Bhabananda Majumdar. This is done in the third part of the poem.Krishnachandra was so impressed with this work that he had it sung in his court. Also, it was after *Annadamangal* was written that he started a tradition of Kali worship that was close to the modern annual ritual of worship of the goddess.

The story of Vidya and Sundar is recounted in a section of *Annadamangal.* It was not as if Bharatchandra was the first to narrate this story. Yet, in language, rhythm, plotline and metaphors, his treatment clearly has a claim of superiority to all previous renderings of the story. The humour and sophistication of his style is absent in the other medieval Bengali poets. In the use of language, especially, he displayed extraordinary skill and artistry, employing with practised ease Bengali, Hindustani, Sanskrit and Farsi words in his work. Many scholars consider Bharatchandra to be the greatest pre-modern Bengali poet. He was well versed in both Sanskrit and Farsi. The influence of Sanskrit literature and figures of speech is clearly evident in his work. This is also what sometimes subjects his work to criticism. For instance, he is often accused of obscenity. His description of sexual union in the second section of *Annadamangal,* that is, in *Kalikamangal,* while telling the story of Vidya and Sundar, or of the feminine form in *Rasamanjari* may well expose him to the charge of obscenity. He also makes some crude jokes about women. Yet it cannot really be said with certainty how much of this was a result of the Sanskrit literary influence and how much a reflection of his own taste.

The first to tell the story of Vidya and Sundar in poetry was Sridhar, 200 years before the time of Bharatchandra – in the second half of the 16th century, during the regime of Hossein Shah's son Nusrat Shah – at the behest of Nusrat Shah's son Firoz Shah. There is little by way of eulogies to goddesses in this narrative, which is chiefly a love story. It is about the love and eventual union of a foreign student called Sundar with a Bengali girl called Vidya. This could be why a Muslim prince encouraged the writing of this story. It might also be why at least one Muslim poet wrote a narrative poem on the story. His name was Sabirid Khan. Enamul Haque has claimed that he belonged to a period earlier than the 16th century. But his language does not bear him out to have been quite so early a poet. The language of two of his four narrative poems is relatively modern, but it does not help in ascertaining his dates. It is clear that he had a good knowledge of local traditions and knew Sanskrit quite well. Another poet called Kabikanka is known to have told the Vidya-Sundar story in verse in the 16th century. Gobindadas and Balaram Chakraborty deserve special mention among those who told the story of Vidya and Sundar before Bharatchandra. Balaram belonged to the 17th century, but nothing is known about Gobindadas. According to Sukumar Sen, he might have been a 16th century poet. In Bharatchandra's own time, Ramprasad Sen also composed a version of the Vidya-Sundar story.

Translation Literature

Translations formed a significant tradition in medieval Bengali literature. Both Hindu and Muslim poets contributed to the translation literature of the time. Krittibas is held by some to have been the first to try his hand at translation. But exactly when he translated *Ramayana* is open to debate. In one opinion, he wrote his work during Raja Ganesh's reign, that is, at the start of the 15th century, and under his patronage. Not all historians have been able to accept this hypothesis. According to Haraprasad Shastri, Krittibas did not belong to a period earlier than the 17th century. Sukumar Sen in a long and well-argued discussion also identifies him as more or less belonging to this period. Going by the language of the version of the Krittibas *Ramayana* that is now available, it is in fact hard to think of him as pre-dating the 17th century. Indeed, it would not be unreasonable to place him in the 18th century. But of course it must be borne in mind that as a popular literary work it might well have undergone many changes at the hands of the copyists.

Krittibas did not make a literal translation of the *Ramayana*. His was a retelling of the *Ramayana* story on the basis of the original epic. In size, too, Krittibas's *Ramayana* is far shorter than Valmiki's work. More importantly, though Krittibas stuck to the basic storyline of Valmiki's version, he introduced many subtle changes in the characterisation of Ram, Lakshman, Sita and even the *rakshasas*. He in fact made these characters quite recognisably Bengali, and that is why Bengalis so deeply loved his work. This localisation is also evident in descriptions of nature, social rules and customs, festivals, food and clothes. No matter how much it differed from Valmiki's version, it was through Krittibas's work that Bengalis became familiar with the *Ramayana* story. And it was Krittibas's Ram, Lakshman and Sita who for several centuries dominated the Bengali imagination as characters to be revered and worshipped.

Many other poets apart from Krittibas retold the *Ramayana* story under many different names in the 16th and 17th centuries. Some chose to deal with only parts of the story. In sum, the *Ramayana* story acquired much popularity in medieval Bengal. Ramchandra is regarded as a god by Hindus, and the belief that reading the *Ramayana* would lead to the accumulation of virtue also added to the popularity of the text.

Though there may be doubts about whether Krittibas wrote his *Ramayana* in the 15th century, there is no room for doubt that the *Bhagavat Puran* was translated in this century. The translation, though, was not quite literal. Maladhar Basu based his *Srikrishnavijay* broadly on the *Bhagavat Puran.* His work also shows the influence of *Harivamsa.* Maladhar Basu wrote his book between 1473 and 1480 with the Sultan's patronage, and the Sultan, pleased with his translation, rewarded him with the title Gunraj Khan. Rukunuddin Barbak Shah was the Sultan of Bengal at this time. The Sultan of Gaur praised by Maladhar Basu, therefore, must have been Barbak Shah, although he is not named. A few decades later Chaitanyadev praised Maladhar Basu's work. After Maladhar Basu, Jashoraj Khan wrote *Krishnamangal* based on the same bank of stories. He, too, translated from Sanskrit with the ruling sultan's patronage. But neither his full name nor the exact date of composition of his book is known. But he must have written it during Hossein Shah's rule or just afterwards.

Jashoraj Khan also wrote a Padavali. The text of *Krishnamangal* is not extant, but a few stanzas of the work have been found. Dwija Madhav, one of the *Dharmamangal* poets, also wrote *Srikrishnamangal* on the basis of the *Bhagavat Puran.* Another poet, Krishnadas, had a version of *Srikrishnamangal.* In sum, once Maladhar Basu had shown the way and Chaitanyadev swept

Bengal with a tide of Krishna devotion, many different kinds of books on the Krishna story got written.

The story of the *Mahabharata* does not revolve round a god or a god-like figure in the way that the *Ramayana* does. This could be one of the reasons why the *Mahabharata* never found the kind of adulation that the *Ramayana* did in Bengal. Kabindra Parameswara seems to have done the first Bengali translation of the *Mahabharata*, at the command of Paragal Shah, an officer of Hossein Shah. Like the Bengali *Ramayana*s, this, too, was not really a translation but rather a retelling of a part of the *Mahabharata* story in Bengali. He called it *Pandavvijay*. This was followed by Srikar Nandy's translation of the Ashwamedha Parva of the *Mahabharata*, commissioned by Paragal Khan's son Chhuti Khan. A century later, Ramchandra Khan and Dwija Raghunath also translated the Ashwamedha section. Ramchandra Khan's title seems to suggest that he, like Parameswar and Srikar before him, was patronised by the Sultan or one of his officers. The poet whose *Mahabharata* found the greatest popular acceptance was Kashiram Das. He wrote his book before 1643, during the reign of Raja Damodar Singha of Bishnupur. Like others before him, he retold parts of the *Mahabharata* instead of labouring at a literal translation. The *Mahabharata* that was published from the Serampore press in his name is not wholly his. The language, too, cannot be accepted as belonging to the first part of the 17th century. This popular text was copied so many times that repeated changes by copyists have made the language relatively modern.

In the chapter 'Society and Religion', we noted how Islam in the 16th century gradually spread to interior and remote villages of Bengal. When this religion became assimilated into the lives and traditions of the Bengali-speaking people, Muslim poets started writing in Bengali. The earliest extant writings by them were influenced by Arabic and Farsi literary models. Muslims do not have collections of mythological stories like the Hindus have in their Puranas. The imagination has not much room to thrive and spread its wings in Islam. Muslim poets, therefore, have borrowed sparsely from Arabic literature and traditions, particularly the Quran. Even where they have borrowed from the Quran, they borrowed only the basic storyline and filled it out with their own imagination. They borrowed far more extensively from Persian mythology and literature. This was because Farsi had a rich literary tradition and a trove of mythological stories. Besides, it was not Arabic but Farsi that was the court language of the Muslim rulers, which could have been one of the reasons why the poets relied more on the Farsi literary heritage. The nature of the translations followed a pattern across the communities. Just as the Hindu poets retold the original stories instead of literally translating their Sanskrit sources, Muslim poets, too, took many liberties with the Farsi texts they translated.

The medieval literature that we have so far discussed, beginning with the *Charyapada* poems, had religious subjects. Even the Muslim sultans patronised this religious literature. Where they differed from the rulers in the Sena regime was that they encouraged the retelling of Hindu mythological stories in the local language, that is, Bengali, instead of Sanskrit. As I mentioned before, the scriptures forbade listening to Puranic tales in the regional languages. Encouraged by the sultans and their officers, however, poets ignored the prohibition and started writing in Bengali. Both the Bengali language and literature thrived as a result. But the religious content and nature of the literature did not change. The task of introducing novelty in the content fell on some Bengali Muslim poets. They could do this because of the absence of gods and goddesses in Islam and of any legends to speak of, and also because the texts they translated, whether Arabic and Farsi or Hindustani, did not have religious narratives. The earliest extant verse narrative written by a Muslim was *Yousuf-Julekha.* As we noted before, going by Enamul Haque's claim, Mohammad Sageer wrote this poem in the 15th century. A linguistic analysis, however, would place this as a much later work. The story of *Yousuf-Julekha* was not original, Sageer borrowed it from Farsi literature. He did not also attempt a literal translation and filled out the story with his own imagination, thus blending many local elements into the narrative. The most remarkable thing about this work is that Sageer wrote it as a story of human love, not as a religious tale. Thus Muslim poets in the Middle Ages introduced a new strand in contemporary literature.

In the 17th century, other Muslim poets carried forward the tradition of translation and verse romances. Syed Sultan and Alaol are particularly memorable names in the context of translations; Daulat Qazi and Alaol in that of verse romances. The works of poetry that they wrote, backed by the munificence of the royal court of Arakan, may be considered exceptional in the entire gamut of medieval Bengali literature. Somewhat surprisingly, these poets did not borrow stories from Arabic or Persian sources, they got their stories in the subcontinent itself. And what they took from the subcontinent were not stories of gods and goddesses but of men and women. Also, in an age when the use of Arabic and Farsi words was fast increasing in mainstream Bengali literature, even in texts with Hindu religious subjects, Syed Sultan, Daulat Qazi and Alaol wrote their verse narratives in a language dominated by *tatsama* words. Daulat Qazi and Alaol wrote their poems away from the mainland, which may have influenced their style. But Syed Sultan was very much in Bengal when he wrote his work in a language dominated by *tatsama* words. That Daulat Qazi and Alaol wrote their works away from the mainland, in the royal court of Arakan, may also have influenced their content.

Daulat Qazi wrote his narrative poem at the request of Ashraf Khan, the general of the king of Roshang, sometime before 1638. The source of his *Satimayna* ('The Faithful Mayna') was a story prevalent in Bhojpuri, but he is not known to have directly translated from any particular text. His hero is Lor, the king of Gohari. The poem describes the story of Lor's two loves and his marriage with two women. He first married a princess called Maynabati, and they were quite happy. But Lor hears of the extraordinarily beautiful princess Chandrani of Mohra and is attracted to her. He travels to Mohra and has a secret union with Chandrani. Later he kills Chandrani's husband in battle and marries her. He then occupies Mohra and stays back there with Chandrani. Years later, Maynabati sends him a message through a bird. Reminded of his past, Lor puts his son on the throne and comes back to Mayna, taking Chandrani with him. Daulat Qazi died before he could finish the poem. Alaol finished the incomplete work in 1659.

Alaol had landed up in Arakan as a slave, after he was kidnapped by Portuguese pirates. He knew several languages and was accomplished in the musical arts. These talents soon earned him the favours of many of the nobility in the Arakan royal court. First he was patronised by a minister of the king, Suleiman. Then one by one he was patronised by courtiers Magan

Thakur, Syed Mussa, and the king's *qazi*, Syed Masud. Alaol wrote quite a few books, but the most remarkable was *Padmavati.* He wrote it in 1659 at the behest of Quraishi Magan Thakur. It was also at his request that Alaol started writing *Saiful Muluk Badiuzzamal.*

Padmavati Panchali was not an original work. Alaol's poem was a retelling of the Ayodhya poet Malik Muhammad Jaisi's *Padmavati.* Jaisi wrote this poem some 125 years before Alaol, and the background of his story is set not in Bengal but in Chittor. The poem tells the story of the king of Chittor Ratnasen and one of his wives, Padmavati. Alaol introduced some changes in the storyline of his translation. He also made his characters quite recognisably Bengali. Alaol was undoubtedly a much greater poet than Jaisi, and his translation significantly improves the standard of the poem. It is possible to read a spiritual meaning into the poem, but that would be a somewhat laboured exercise. It is basically a love story that Alaol has told. The artistry of language, metaphors and plot construction that Alaol has shown in *Padmavati* has led some scholars to call him the greatest Bengali poet of the 17th century. He wrote of his own writing that his language sprinkled divine nectar on the lines of the poem and made them delicious, and he was not too far from fact. When it comes to narrative poems, it must be acknowledged that between Mukundaram and Bharatchandra, Alaol was the greatest poet.

Alaol's *Saiful Muluk Badiuzzamal* was also not an original work. The story is sourced from the *Arabian Nights.* But he took the story not from an Arabic text but, most probably, from a Persian one. Alaol wrote *Tohfa* in 1663-64, at Suleiman's request. This is not a romantic tale; it is a religious text that he translated from a Farsi original. *Haptapaykar* was also a translation, of a Farsi work of the poet Nizami. So was Alaol's last work, *Sekandarnama.* The subject of this work is Greek emperor Alexander's conquest of Persia. One of Alaol's patrons, Quraishi Magan Thakur, himself wrote at least one narrative poem, *Chandravati.* The hero is the prince of Bhadrabatinagar, Beerbhan, and the heroine is the Sinhala princess Chandravati. The poem narrates how the lovers overcome various obstacles to be finally united with each other.

Syed Sultan was a 16th-17th century poet. He was a mainland poet, and therefore he did not follow the example of the poets of the Arakan royal court. Intead of writing romances, he wrote several religious books. His most famous book was a collection of tales of *nabi*s, or prophets—*Nabivamsa.* The similarity of the title with the Sanskrit *Harivamsa* is not coincidental, and he did to some extent imitate this text. As we have already noted, he did not just write about the Islamic prophets in this book. He also included Brahma, Vishnu, Shiva and Hari in his pantheon of prophets. There is a debate about exactly when he wrote this narrative poem. In Sukumar Sen's opinion, he most probably wrote it in 1654-55. Enamul Haque, on the other hand, dates the work around 1585-86. Just as the narration of Puranic tales in local languages was forbidden by the guardians of the scriptures in the Middle Ages, Muslim religious leaders also forbade writing about religion in the local language. Syed Sultan defied this diktat to write his *Nabivamsa.* In the last section of *Nabivamsa* – 'Shab-e-Mairaj' – he wrote that native Muslims were unable to make any sense of religious texts written in Arabic and Farsi. Their knowledge of the faith was also extremely limited. He had therefore written this book in order to uphold for such people the main message of Islam. Apart from *Nabivamsa,* he also wrote a few other religious books, the most remarkable of these being *Rasulvijay.* Sabirid Khan before him had also written *Rasulvijay.* Another remarkable thing about Syed Sultan was that his language, like that of Daulat Qazi and Alaol, had few borrowings from Arabic and Farsi. In some passages he used a language dominated by *tatsama* words.

Syed Sultan was probably a Haji, that is, a Muslim who had undertaken the Haj pilgrimage to Mecca. Yet he was considerably influenced by Indian religious thinking. Not only did he include Brahma, Vishnu and Shiva among his *nabi*s, he also regarded the four Vedas as '*asmani ketab*' or heaven-sent scriptures. His *Jnanchoutisha,* written when he was young, and *Jnanpradeep,* a product of more mature years, show how influenced he was by the subcontinent's traditions of yoga and spiritual seeking. In these two works he effected an assimilation between Sufi teachings and the theories of yoga and spiritual seeking. His deep interest in and knowledge of the Hindu Puranas is quite evident in *Nabivamsa.* Notably, he depicted the Middle Eastern prophets much like Bengalis. Syed Sultan also wrote Vaishnava poems.

We have already mentioned the name of another 17th century poet, Abdul Hakim, in the context of Bengali as a language. His was the strongest voice in the medieval debate on whether Bengali was the language of Muslims. His contribution to literature was no less significant. He wrote quite a few long works in verse, including *Yousuf-Julekha, Leelabati-Saifulmuluk, Noornama* and *Shihabuddinnama.* The first two were romances. Among those who wrote romances outside the Arakan royal court, Abdul Hakim can claim particular mention for his *Yousuf-Julekha* and *Leelabati-Saifulmuluk.* The content of his other poems was religious. *Karbala Kahini* ('Story of Karbala') was one of the religious books he wrote.

We have mentioned before that Muslims did not have any stock of mythological stories. Nor did they have any gods and goddesses. But they did have a prophet who had founded the faith, and a lineage that he left through his daughter and her sons. The Muslim way of relating to these charaters is not much different from the Hindu way of relating to their gods and goddesses. Muslim poets therefore wrote many poems based on the lives of these people. In particular, the story of Hossein's piteous death moved quite a few Muslim poets to write narrative poems, the plotline filled out with their own imagination. That the number of Shias increased under the Mughals might well have had something to do with this. A closer look will show that the Muslim poets of the earlier centuries were not as attracted to this story as the later poets were. In the 17th and particularly the 18th century, quite a few Muslim poets wrote narrative poems based on the Muharram story. Among them, the names of Abdul Hakim, Muhammad Khan, Hayat Mahmud and Garibullah deserve special mention. *Jung Nama, Muktul Hossein, Karbala, Hanifar Larhai* (Battle of Hanifa)—such were the titles of these narrative poems. This literature was, in a word, known as Morsia.

Folk Literature

In the modern age we think of literature as written. But in the Middle Ages written literature did not have the reach and spread that oral or folk literature did. Yet its oral nature was what caused this second category of literature to get lost for ever. Some writers, though, did write works based on oral literature. A comparison of the two kinds of literature will show that oral literature did not have the refinement and the learning that went into written literature. One reason for this of course was that written literature was the work of educated writers. But oral literature was created extemporaneously with happy abandon by even unlettered villagers. This kind of literature was rich in a kind of simple beauty, and in human values. In written literature the subjects were predominantly religious, but it was human love that was most important in oral literature. Even when faith crept into it, it was the message of a humanitarian religion rather than any institutionalised belief system that found expression in this kind of literature.

For the little of Bengal's oral tradition of folk literature that has been preserved for posterity, the credit goes mainly to Dinesh Chandra Sen and Dakshinaranjan Mitra Majumdar. At the start of the 20th century, they themselves and with the help of assistant researchers, collected a wealth of samples of oral literature. Moved by the simple beauty of this literature, Tagore, too, wrote about folk literature and lauded the efforts to collect samples. It was he who for the first time collected samples of Lalan Fakir's songs and got them published in the *Prabasi* magazine. Afterwards, a number of scholars including Chandra Kumar Dey, Jasim Uddin, Mansur Uddin and Upendranath Bhattacharya collected and published samples of folk literature from different regions of Bengal. Some samples of this literature have been preserved in two collections, *Mymensingh Geetika* and *Purbabanga Geetika.* Dinesh Chandra Sen published these samples of folk literature in a book. But the originals got somewhat distorted in the process because of the partial editing of village dialects in the published version, and because of the intervention of the researchers who collected these samples.

In the chapter 'Society and Religion', we noted in the discussion on religion that a certain syncretism in medieval Bengal marked by the plurality of religions and communities led to the development of a faith based on simple devotion and love. This simple faith also more or less got identified with a number of fairly institutionalised cults and thus its followers got fragmented into sects that were known by different names. Baul, Kartabhaja, Nathjogi, and so on. The songs that the followers of these cults wrote may also be considered folk literature. More important than these songs are the lyrics and ballads on love themes composed by unlettered villagers, for religious and communal divides get blurred in these songs.

These poets did not build their work on Puranic tales or on themes drawn from institutionalised religion. They sang instead of the joys and sorrows of ordinary rustic people. Taking an instance from *Mymensingh Geetika*, we can say that Mohua, one of the protagonists in a verse narrative, is truly Bengali. Her Bengaliness comes across in her clothes and her behaviour, and this is where she is so different from the Puranic characters in medieval literature, though even they are also frequently 'Bengali-ised'. Mohua is above all a woman. She does have a religious identity, but that identity is not so much religious as it is a social one, signifying her status as belonging to a low caste. She belongs to a family of snake charmers, but she loves Naddar Thakur, who is not outside the caste pale as she is but a Brahmin. This caste identity is what comes in the way of their love. Naddar is willing to abandon his caste identity to get Mohua, but her snake charmer community is unable to accept him. This piteous story eventually ends with Mohua's suicide and the murder of Naddar Thakur. The love stories of Kajalrekha, Molua, Madina, Leela and Chandravati in *Mymensingh Geetika* and that of Bhelua in *Purbabanga Geetika* do not in any way pale beside the romances in written literature, and indeed, these simple tales of love and sacrifice are in a way more heart-warming. Folk literature is even more remarkable in its assimilative and syncretic tendencies, which makes such literature ignore the regulations of institutionalised religion to engage with the human situation. And this is the true historical inheritance of Bengalis.

Modern Bengali Literature

Just as a barren period followed the start of Indo-Muslim rule in Bengal, which some literary historians have described as a dark age, a barren period also seemed to follow the establishment of British colonial rule. Bharatchandra died five years before the start of British rule, in 1752. It was in the 1850s that Ishwar Gupta published his first book of poems. The only extant samples of Bengali literature of the period in between are the works of some Hindu *kabiyal*s (men with a gift for extempore versification who engaged in literary face-offs with rival poets) and multilingual manuscripts by Muslim writers who used a language littered with Arabic, Farsi and Hindi words. But a great deal of literary writing started being produced from the middle of the

19th century. This was literature of the new age, and not just in the calendar sense; it was truly modern in form and content. Before this, the long tradition of Bengali literature, from the oldest extant samples in the *Charyapada* poems to Bharatchandra Ray shortly before the start of British rule, was almost entirely based on religion. The subjects were gods and goddesses for Hindu writers, and *nabis*, *rasools* and pirs in the case of Muslims. The only exceptions were some narrative poems and translations by Muslim poets. In less than a hundred years of British rule, however, Bengali literature was transformed. In the place of gods and goddesses appeared, first, rajas and *badshahs*, and then ordinary flesh-and-blood men and women. Puranic tales were replaced by everyday events. Even when gods and goddesses do make an appearance they are humanised, as we see in the works of Michael Madhusudan.

The burst of creativity that we see in 19th century Bengali literature is astonishing in both intensity and range: it is like waking up at daybreak one day to find a huge open space suddenly filled with a burst of colours and covered with flowers. Historians of Bengal have often claimed that the land witnessed a Renaissance or rebirth in the 19th century. But then again many historians are unwilling to recognise the Bengal situation as a Renaissance since it did not very closely resemble the Italian Renaissance that ushered in modernism in Europe.

The Italian Renaissance found expression chiefly in architecture, painting and literature. In Bengal, on the other hand, there was no flowering of the visual arts in the 19th century. Indeed, Bengal did not come up with art of international standards in the next hundred years. Nor were there any outstanding developments in architecture. Bengal did not also experience the kind of worldly progress that the Renaissance brought about in Italy, in economy, science and technology on the one hand and in thoughts and ideas on the other. In a relative assessment, the extent to which individuality replaced collectivity in Europe had no parallel in Bengal. The expression of personal autonomy that we see in individuals such as Ram Mohan, Vidyasagar, Michael Madhusudan, Keshab Sen, Satyendranath Tagore, Shibnath Shastri, etc., was exceptional when seen in the broader perspective of contemporary society. In society at large, it was medieval collectivity that remained far more deeply rooted. Those who insist that there was no Renaissance in Bengal, therefore, cannot be totally dismissed.

But of course there is no denying that the revisiting and re-evaluation of ancient literature that happened early in the Italian Renaissance and the birth of a secular literary tradition had a parallel in Bengal. The emergence of humanism and individuality that we see in Ram Mohan, Vidyasagar and Michael are also Renaissance traits. These men, like the humanist scholars of Italy, reinterpreted ancient scriptures and literary texts to cull lessons in humanism for contemporary society. So did Bankimchandra. An even greater resemblance can be noticed in the extraordinary flowering of language and literature. Indeed, the explosion of creativity that we see in the development of the local language and in literature is certainly in sync with the Renaissance. We have already discussed the development of language under colonial rule. We will be able to appreciate the strength and nature of this creativity if we now look at some branches of literature. We will also see how English education and literature brought about this burst of creativity.

The new literary tradition of writing about present-day human beings rather than about deities or Puranic tales began at the start of the second half of the 19th century. But even before that, fragmentary images of contemporary life had appeared in the work of Ishwar Gupta. He was not able to totally forsake the old world view or the old subjects. We do notice imitations of the old style in his language, metaphors and other figures of speech, but everyday life started peeping through his writing. Instead of gods and goddesses, he wrote poems on the English New Year, pineapples, potatoes, sesame seeds, jaggery, thickened milk dessert, coconuts, fried sweets, the beauty of the seasons and other such subjects. Even mutton and fish have not escaped mention in his writing. On the other hand, he also described the persecution of small farmers by the indigo merchants and sufferings caused by famine. He expressed heartfelt tenderness for his mother tongue and for his country. Even women's education moved him to write poetry, though his orthodoxy provoked him into using ridicule and satire to say that women's education would destroy traditional social values.

Ishwar Gupta was in fact like a bridge between the old literature and that of the new age. On the one hand he could not wholly cut himself off from the old themes and rhetorical devices; on the other, he also introduced novelties in his subjects, style and use of words. This tendency of keeping his face turned both to the past and the future that we see in him has led to comparisons with the Roman god Janus, who has one face turned backwards and the other turned forward.

A number of extraordinary individuals arrived in the 19th century literary scene, informed as it was by the spirit of the new age. Not only did the new age favour them, they were in a sense products of the new age. Their own extraordinary genius in turn led them to shape the new age through literature. Their golden touch immensely enriched Bengali literature. Michael Madhusudan Dutt, Bankimchandra Chattopadhyay and Rabindranath Tagore at the end of the century were among these towering personalities. Vidyasagar, Peary Chand Mitra, Dinabandhu Mitra, Rangalal Bandyopadhyay, Nabinchandra Sen, Biharilal Chakraborty, Jyotirindranath Tagore and Girish Ghosh were also undoubtedly writers of considerable stature. On the strength of their collective contribution, Bengali literature outstripped in 50 years the progress that it had managed to make in the previous 500 years.

The first to usher in this revolutionary transformation was Michael Madhusudan Dutt. But this transformation was not the product of a single decade. In other words, the divide between Bharatchandra and Madhusudan was not bridged overnight, there were many stepping stones in between. The language of deeds and documents did not in a day turn into Bankimchandra's language. The same holds true for poetry. Hundred and eight years after the completion of *Annadamangal* in 1752, Madhusudan's *Tilottamasambhav Kavya* was published in 1860. The change was not wrought by any single individual's magic touch. A new way of thinking had struck root in the Hindu College premises, and its medium was the English language and literature. Derozio brought to his students a different way of looking at life. Kashi Prasad Ghosh brought a new insight in politics. The Young Bengal group had a novel message. Vidyasagar humanised the Puranic characters in his creative writing. Ishwar Gupta imported contemporary realities in literature. Rangalal laid the ground for modern verse narratives. Madhusudan arrived only then, after the soil had been thus cured and prepared by many. He might have chosen historical characters for his English works, but it was not of their past glories that he sang of but their human qualities. In sum, our language and literature were fundamentally transformed under the combined impact of the new kind of city that was Calcutta, the process of urbanisation that it involved, western education and literature and the contact and exchanges with Europe that were taking place.

The modernistic trend in Bengali poetry was exclusively the handiwork of former Hindu College students who were committed readers of English literature. Michael Madhusudan Dutt's may be the foremost name in the context of how Bengali writers delved in the stream of European thought and perception to create literature in their own tongue. Yet a long line of poets such as Rangalal Bandyopadhyay, Hemchandra Bandyopadhyay, Nabinchandra Sen, Biharilal Chakraborty, and Tagore in late 19th century, all wrote poetry modelled on the work of English poets. A certain literary tradition is clearly evident in their works. Then again in prose literature, English writers inspired and influenced Peary Chand Mitra, Bhudeb Mukhopadhyay, Bankimchandra Chattopadhyay and Rabindranath Tagore.

Rangalal published a new kind of verse narrative before Madhusudan did. But of course it was Madhusudan who single-handedly and in a very short time brought about an epochal change in the genre. He himself confessed that he did not know Bengali very well. The remark reflects a lack of self-confidence and also, rather uncharacteristically for Madhusudan, a certain humility. Yet it was not lacking in truth. Nor did he have any experience or practice of writing Bengali verse. How then did he almost overnight come up with *Tilottamasambhav Kavya*, then in quick succession *Meghnadbadh Kavya* (1861), *Veerangana* (1862) and *Brajangana* (1861)? It was his extraordinary genius that made this possible. Along with his own unusual powers, his capital was his grounding in English and European classical literature. There were two Italian poets whose work he especially loved—Dante and Petrarch, Renaissance poets both. Petrarch especially was one of pioneers of the Renaissance. Michael used Dante's style in his epic poem, while Petrarch inspired him to write sonnets. Above all what Michael had was original perception and values. So thoroughly had he internalised European classical literature that success came easily to him when he took up the challenge of writing in Bengali.

On the surface, Michael Madhusudan seems to be clinging to the old Bengali literary tradition of writing of gods and goddesses. Yet the most remarkable way in which he differed from the earlier poets was that not only did he serve up the old themes in new packaging, he also turned a religious narrative into a human one in the mould of the Renaissance humanist scholars. The names were old and familiar, so was the plot. Yet the well known story, the characters and the message were all recast in the light of the poet's subversive world view. This is true of all his four long narrative poems. In *Tilottamasambhav Kavya*, the two *asura* brothers, Sunda and Upasunda, attract his sympathy much more than the gods do. His point of view in *Meghnadbadh Kavya* is quite startling and subversive from a religious perspective. Not only does Ravana and not Ram, the god lovingly worshipped by all Hindus, have the poet's sympathy, he is depicted as a superior 'human being' in comparison with Ram. Madhusudan's Ravana is greater than Ram. The subject of *Brajangana* is, in the poet's own words, "Mrs Radha" and her heartbreak. His Radha is not the Hindu symbol of the *jeevatma* or the created soul. She symbolises wronged womanhood, a woman in love deserted by her lover. Thus Madhusudan reinterpreted old Puranic themes.

He did not however stop at reinterpretation. He created a language and poetic forms suited to his poetry. There are plenty of Sanskrit words in his writing, and he even occasionally uses unfamiliar words. Yet these words are twisted and reworked to yield new meanings and nuances. He also creates new words out of some of the root words. We see a similar process at work in the matter of meter. He could not be confined within the old *payar-tripadi* meter of medieval Bengali poetry, a rhymed meter with six or eight syllables to each line, but wrote in blank verse—a meter that broke out of the limitations of punctuation and ignored rhyming in line-endings. He did not use the blank verse in *Brajangana*, but here, too, he introduced novelties that would later, at the hands of Biharilal Chakraborty and Rabindranath turn into the refined cadence of lyrics. Not just meter and language, he also introduced poetic forms suited to the new era in literature. In epic, sonnet and epistolary poetry, he has left ample testimony to the Western influence that shaped his creativity.

Michael Madhusudan, in sum, was a true Renaissance poet. What he built on the old foundation was new not only in form but also in spirit.

Ram Mohan and Vidyasagar before him had of course reinterpreted ancient sacred texts and presented a modern message with old ingredients, and their medium was Bengali. But Michael was not influenced by them, and in fact he was not familiar with their writing. He was influenced by European civilisation and literature.

Though Bengalis had village ballads and also *jatra*, a kind of rustic theatre, there was nothing like plays or their dramatisation in Bengali. The students of Hindu College studied English drama, their syllabuses were structured to include the subject. We also know that they watched the dramatic performances of English plays. Yet Bengalis did not come forward in the 1830s and 1840s to write plays, notwithstanding the existence of English theatre. It is hard to say why. One major reason of course was that the reach of education was still quite limited. More importantly, the environment was not yet conducive to the dramatisation of Bengali plays. Besides, Bengali prose had not yet reached a stage at which plays could be written in it. So it was a little late – in the 1850s – that two men assumed pioneering roles in this respect: former Hindu College student Taracharan Shikdar and another gentleman whose identity is not known, possibly G.C. Gupta. In 1852 they published, respectively, *Bhadrarjun* and *Keertibilas*, five-act plays both. *Bhadrarjun* was somewhat traditional, but *Keertibilas* was quite modern in both form and content. The following year another former Hindu College student, Harachandra Ghosh, published a play. His play, *Bhanumati-Chittobilas*, was based on Shakespeare's *Merchant of Venice*. And thus began the journey of Bengali dramatic literature, though not yet of theatre.

Once the first plays were out in print, several plays were published within a few years. A new strand within this genre was introduced by Ramnarayan Tarkalankar. Using sharp ridicule and biting satire, he drew attention to the ill effects of multiple marriages common among *kulin* men. Notwithstanding the absence of dramatic tension in his play, it had plenty of humour. This was why his play *Kulinkulsarbaswa* (1854) became popular as a widely read text even before it was dramatised. This popularity led to its dramatisation in March 1857. This was the first stage performance of a Bengali play. After the success of Ramnarayan's play, Umesh Chandra Mitra wrote *Bidhababibaho* (1856), a play on the problems of Hindu child widows not being allowed to remarry. This play, too, was very popular in its time. Not only was there a second edition in 1857, the play was successfully staged in April and May of 1859.

The success of these two plays moved many other writers to produce dramatic literature on contemporary social problems. We describe such writing as 'dramatic literature' rather than plays because though these were written in the form of dialogues, in most cases they were not really successful as plays that could be performed. Some were so short that they could not even be considered as one-act plays. Though the plays of Ramnarayan Tarkalankar and Umesh Chandra Mitra were divided into acts and scenes, neither of them seems to have been overly familiar with English theatre.

It was Dinabandhu Mitra, a former Hindu College student and well-read in English literature, who first wrote a notable play on a contemporary theme that was recognisably modelled on the genre of English drama. Like Ramnarayan and Umesh Chandra, he culled his theme from contemporary society, but the problem he chose was a socio-economic one, rather than socio-religious. English indigo planters were at that time forcing peasants to grow the crop. *Hindu Patriot*, an English-language newspaper run by Bengalis, was publishing news of this unfair persecution, as well as editorials sharply criticising it. Even a religio-social magazine such as *Tattwabodhini Patrika* published criticisms of this persecution by indigo planters. Dinabandhu Mitra published his play *Neeldarpan* (1860) to draw people's attention to the nature of this persecution through a different medium. He would have marked the success and social usefulness of *Kulinkulsarbaswa* and *Bidhababibaho*.

It is difficult to say how popular this play would have been after publication if it was left to itself. But a magazine and the indigo planters moved a libel suit against Rev. James Long over the publication of an English translation of the play. James Long had published the translation. The play received so much publicity during the court case which followed that even after 150 years it remains known as a notable play in Bengali literary history despite its exaggerated histrionics.

Dinabandhu Mitra's play, modelled though it was on English theatrical examples, was not too successful as a work of art. The play that registered success even before *Neeldarpan*, and which is still considered the first play worth its name in Bengali literature, was Michael Madhusudan Dutt's *Sharmistha* (1858). The subject of this play was not drawn from contemporary society as *Neeldarpan*'s was. Michael took his theme from a Puranic tale. But he, too, presented a human story behind the façade of his mythical characters. He had no conscious aim of social reform. Nor was he protesting against any sort of persecution. His engagement was purely literary as he wrote *Sharmistha*, *Padmavati* (1860) and *Krishnakumari* (1861). These plays are still included among the best plays of Bengali literature.

Michael Madhusudan Dutt could not totally keep away from the tidal wave of enthusiasm for social reform through drama that arose in society at this time. In early 1860 he wrote two satirical skits called *Ekei ki Bole Sabhyata?* ('Is This Called Civilisation?') and *Burho Shaliker Gharhe Ron*. In *Ekei ki Bole Sabhyata?* he ridiculed the blind imitation of the West by English-educated young men. In *Burho Shaliker Gharhe Ron* the subject of his satire was the hypocrisies of conservative society. These two skits may still be considered the best in the history of Bengali dramatic literature. A few years after these two skits were written, Dinabandhu Mitra wrote *Sadhabar Ekadashi*, *Jamai Barik* and *Biye Pagla Burho*. These still live on in Bengali literature as memorable examples of reformist dramatic literature. *Sadhabar Ekadashi*, especially, can probably be considered the greatest Bengali skit ever written.

Dinabandhu Mitra died at just 43. By that time, however, he had written plays and skits which were considered eminently suitable for stage performance. Eventually, it was the theatrical production of one of his plays that gave Bengalis their first professional stage for dramatic performances. A number of plays were written in the 1870s in response to the requirements of professional theatre. Upendranath Das, Jyotirindranath Tagore, Manomohan Basu, Girish Chandra Ghosh, Amritalal Basu, Kshirodprasad Bidyabinod and other playwrights of varying abilities wrote a large number of plays in this period. Not that all of these passed the test of literary merit. But these were plays written for the professional stage, and consequently most had enough dramatic tension to make them suitable for dramatisation. Especially the plays of Girish Ghosh, Amritalal and Kshirodprasad, men who were directly linked to professional theatre, ran successfully on stage. We will discuss this in the chapter 'Theatre and Cinema'.

There was an inclination to write plays on Puranic, religious and historical themes when in the 1870s nationalist thinking started to harden and crystallise. In the patriotic plays of the time, however, it was the Muslims rather than the British who were identified as the 'other', the alien enemy. Someone had to be scolded as the 'outsider', and it was safer to scold Muslims than the British. The same tendency can be seen in the Bengali poetry of the time.

Two years after the first Bengali plays came out in print, what can be called the first Bengali novel started being serialised in 1854—Peary Chand Mitra's *Alaler Gharer Dulal* published under the pseudonym of Tekchand Thakur. But Tekchand Thakur did not suddenly arrive from nowhere, and nor could he have done so. One could hardly write a novel using the language of the Fort William munshis. It was not in a day that a language suitable for novel-writing came into being. In the 1820s, Bhabanicharan Bandyopadhyay laid the foundations for storytelling in Bengali prose, making in the process an important contribution in the development of the language needed for such writing, even though his 'Nabababu-Bilas' and 'Nababibi-Bilas' were not stories in the true sense. Ishwar Gupta in the 1830s and Akshay Datta in the 1840s and 1850s kept up the work of crafting a prose capable of expressing everyday realities. In his *Betalpanchabingshati* (1847), *Shakuntala* (1852) and *Sitar Banobas* (1854), Vidyasagar shaped up Bengali prose for storytelling. It was in this environment that Peary Chand Mitra, a fond reader of English literature, gave Bengali its first novel by writing *Alaler Gharer Dulal.* So novel indeed was this venture that he did not dare to publish it in his own name.

His novel had many limitations. The story is ordinary, and indeed the book is better described as a series of scenes than as a novel. The characters are typecast and not rounded enough to appear as flesh-and-blood human beings—the good guys are perfect, whereas the bad guys could not be worse. Still, the story of *Alaler Gharer Dulal* is based in contemporary society and reflects the everyday lives of many Calcutta families of those days. The problems of a nouveau riche family, the kind then sprouting in the city, form the subject of this novel. It reflects a certain reformist zeal of doing good but is not really able to express the conflicts between human desires and instincts on the one hand and conscience on the other. But Peary Chand Mitra had no doubt in his mind that the age of medieval fairy tales was over, and he resolved all doubts on this score through his prose style. Another former Hindu College student of his time, Bhudev Mukhopadhyay, also influenced by English literature, refined the language of story-telling in his *Anguri Binimoy* ('Exchange of Rings'). No one recognised *Anguri Binimoy* as a novel. Yet it is questionable whether Bankimchandra would be able to produce *Durgeshnandini* out of nothing had *Alaler Gharer Dulal* and *Anguri Binimoy* not come before it.

The Bengali novel, and indeed Bengali literature, became truly modern at the hands of Bankimchandra. His novels make great literature by any standard and indeed they bear no comparison to anything in contemporary Bengali literature. More than a hundred years after his death, many scholars still consider him to be the greatest Bengali novelist. Like Michael he too was a former student of Hindu College, intellectually and aesthetically nourished by English literature. He too made his literary debut by writing in English. He realised quickly enough that Bengali and not English was the medium through which he would be able to open his heart and display his artistry.

Bankimchandra did not write anything in Bengali that led up to his first novel *Durgeshnandini* in 1865. This very first novel from his pen brought about a veritable revolution. While writing *Krishnakumari*, Michael Madhusudan Dutt had explained to a well known actor of the time, Keshab Ganguly, why his hands were tied and why he was forced to draw his women characters within certain fixed parameters. Bankimchandra was also forced to operate within similar limitations while writing his novels. In outlining his female characters, especially, he had to voluntarily submit to many proscriptions. His heroines were either widows or compelled to remain celibate because of some unusual

Bankimchandra Chattopadhyay, one of the best novelists and prose writers of Bengal

circumstances in their lives. He could not write of romantic relationships preceding marriage, because no such thing existed in society. Had he allowed his women characters to get into such situations, society would reject them as unreal.

Bankimchandra borrowed from history for his first few novels, and he also wrote a few historical novels towards the end of his writing career. In between and in his later years he wrote about contemporary society in *Bishbriksha* ('Poison Tree'), *Krishnakanter Will* ('Krishnakanta's Will') and some short novellas. We encounter the good guys and bad guys in these books too, but these cannot be compared to Peary Chand's typecast characters. Even the character whom he punishes by getting her shot dead at the end of the novel is carefully and lovingly sketched, his artist's brush filling her out in many different shades. The ideal of social good that he believed in imposed some limitations on his imagination. His sense of nationhood and his distaste for Muslims also thwarted the spontaneous flow of his creativity. Notwithstanding all his limitations, however, Bankimchandra is the first and the greatest novelist of Bengali literature.

Sanjibchandra Chattopadhyay, Ramesh Chandra Datta, Lalbehari Dey, Swarnakumari Devi and other late 19th century writers produced some notable novels. Tagore, too, tried his hand at this genre. Yet none quite matched up to the standard set by Bankimchandra.

Like the novel, the Bengali short story also came in the wake of English literary influence. But the short story took somewhat longer to truly come into its own. If *Durgeshnandini* is taken to be the first true novel in Bengali, then the first real short stories arrived after another quarter century—the first stories of Tagore's *Galpoguchho*. Thousands upon thousands of short stories have since been written, and the Bengali short story has undoubtedly scaled great heights. Yet the *Galpoguchho* stories are still considered as the greatest Bengali short stories of all time.

Contribution of Muslim Writers

We have so far mentioned not a single Muslim name in the context of modern Bengali literature. For, Muslim writers did not arrive so early in the history of modern Bengali literature. In the chapters 'Bengali Culture under Western Impact' and 'Bengali Culture in the Twentieth Century' we discussed the social and political background of Muslims' regressiveness. Let us just recall here that the community remained educationally backward until the end of the 19th century. It was not as if they could have acquired an English education even if they wanted to or come forward to create a new kind of literature in the way their fellow Hindus did. They could not therefore make any contribution to the modern Bengali literature that got written in the British colonial era. They lagged behind the Hindus by at least 50 to 60 years.

Medieval Muslim poets had left significant contributions in verse narratives, translation literature, religious literature and so on. One reason for this was that many of them received the patronage of zamindars, amirs and omrahs, and even the sultans. Such patronage was no longer available in the colonial era. There then grew a lot of interest in a certain kind of manuscript described as 'bilingual' in literary history. Bilingual, because these were written in a language that blended Bengali and Urdu components. Because plenty of Arabic and Farsi ingredients also crept into this language through Urdu, many scholars describe these manuscripts as being of a mixed language. When at the beginning of the 19th century, Hindu writers under Western influence started experimenting with a new kind of literature, Muslim writers worked away at their bilingual manuscripts with medieval themes, but even that tradition slowly dried up.

Mir Mosharraf Hussein, the first Muslim prose writer

Mir Mosharraf Hussein (1847-1912) was the first Muslim to write within the mainstream of Bengali literature in a standardised language. His is the most notable name among the handful of Muslims of his time who left a contribution in Bengali literature. His first book, *Ratnabati*, was published in 1869. By that time all of Vidyasagar's books had been published, and even a couple of Bankimchandra's novels. That is to say, Bengali prose was by now a refined and powerful tool. All of Michael

Madhusudan Dutt's books were also out by then. Indeed, Bengali literature was now quite modern, thanks to the influence of English language and literature. A suitable language and prose style were also ready and waiting for the writing of literature. Yet, moderately educated Bengali Muslims were still busy writing their bilingual manuscripts in medieval-style rhymed meters. There were no evident efforts to write prose. The only example of prose writing by a Muslim writer before Mosharraf Hussein that I have seen is an essay by Taheran Nessa that was published in *Bamabodhini Patrika* in 1865.

Mir Mosharraf Hussein of course did not just write one essay like Taheran Nessa, he produced more than 25 books of drama, poetry and prose fiction. So refined was the prose of his *Ratnabati* that Bankimchandra while criticising the book made a comment that may now seem laughable. He wrote that Mosharraf Hussein's prose was like the prose written by Hindus. What he was trying to say was that it was not at all like the language of the bilingual manuscripts but was a standardised prose dominated by *tatsama* words.

The book in which Mosharraf Hussein still lives on is his *Bishaad Sindhu* (1885-91; 'Ocean of Melancholy') in three volumes. In it he tells the piteous story of Karbala. Many writers had told this story before he did, in many names, right from the Middle Ages. None of these previous works can bear comparison with Mosharraf Hussein's book. Though written in prose, many consider *Bishaad Sindhu* as poetry, so lyrical is the language. In the beauty of its narrative and language, the book can be considered a canonical text of Bengali literature. The prose style recalls Bankimchandra's in its predominance of *tatsama* words. The rhetorical devices also reflect a continuation of older styles, as in Ishwar Gupta's works. It is not just the words and the figures of speech that draw the reader, the rhythm and arrangement of punctuation are also among the attractions of Mosharraf Hussein's prose. His sentences, sometimes long-winding and sometimes brief, are beautiful. His prose is free-flowing and racy, thus marking him out as a mainstream writer in Bengali literature. He is remarkable also because he was the first Bengali Muslim to become aware of the true identity of Muslims. A close look will show that he was fully conscious of his identity as a Muslim, but his Bengali identity was also quite unmistakable. Another important aspect of his work is that he aspired for Hindu-Muslim unity and assimilation, though this quality is not carried over into his later work.

Once Mosharraf Hussein had shown the way, many other Muslim writers started writing both prose and verse. Among them were Kaykobad (1858-1952), Mozammal Haque (1860-1933), Nazibur Rahman (1878-1923), Syed Ismail Hossein Siraji (1880-1931), Sheikh Fazlul Karim (1882-1936), Qazi Imdadul Haque (1882-1926), S. Wajed Ali (1890-1951) and others. Mozammal Haque published a handsome number of books in both prose and verse. In particular, his narrative poem *Jatiyofoara Kabya* and *Lahri*, the journal of poetry edited by him, inspired and enthused Muslims. He also wrote novels. Kaykobad was the most notable among the Muslim poets of the time. His *Mahashamsan Kabya* published in 1904 was an important attempt in the genre of epic. It was based on the third battle of Panipat. He might have received a wider readership than he did, but for the fact that by that time the tradition of epic poetry had dried up in Bengali literature and made way for a flood of lyric poems.

After Mosharraf Hussein, the prose writer who in those days was most well-received by Muslim readers and most prolific was Ismail Hossein Siraji. He took up the pen largely in reaction to the Hindu revivalism of the late 19th century. In particular, Siraji responded vociferously to the disdain for Muslims that Bankimchandra's writing betrayed in some of its weak moments. This nationalist position was what made him so popular with Muslim readers. Like most other Muslim writers of the day, he did not write just for the sake of writing but out of concern for his community. The chief objective of contemporary Muslim writers was to hold up the past glories of Islam for their readers. Siraji was among those who did this competently and well.

It can be said of this first batch of modern Muslim writers that they had forever bid adieu to the bilingual manuscripts of the *jungnama* kind that were woven around battles fought by the Prophet and his relatives. The language in which they started writing was the standard language of literature of the time. Mozammal Haque, Sheikh Fazlul Karim, Ismail Hossein Siraji, S. Wajed Ali—this can be said of all of them. They did not presumably adopt this prose style solely in the hope of making a place for themselves in the mainstream of Bengali literature. What it shows, indeed, is their awareness of the new age. They were trying to set aside the pulls of the past to match their steps with the changing times and move ahead. Their religious identity, however, still formed the chief strand in their self-perception. They could not therefore completely grow out of the mental habit of looking backwards to the past. They could not also quite reject the Muslim habit of clinging to real and imagined Islamic glories of the past and of imagining Arab territories and Iran as Muslim homelands. This regressive mindset is evident in the way they debated, well into the 20th century, whether Bengali or Urdu was the mother tongue of Bengali Muslims. It also took them long to shed religious loyalties in choosing literary themes. It was Nazrul Islam who performed this impossible task. Once he surmounted this obstacle, others more or less followed suit. But Bengali literature would have to wait another quarter century for Nazrul Islam's arrival.

Twentieth Century Bengali Literature

As the 19th century drew to a close, the Renaissance that in a limited way had unfolded in its middle years grinded to a halt. Notwithstanding this untimely demise of the Renaissance, even before it could attain maturity, the stream that kept flowing with the same or rather renewed vigour was Bengali literature. In making this happen, the role of one man surpassed the efforts of all others. He was Rabindranath Tagore. His prolific output nourished all branches of literature, giving them perhaps an edge that they might otherwise have taken a century to acquire. He truly transformed the image of Bengali literature. He also immensely enriched the Bengali language. He made Bengali prose turn round an important corner and forever changed its course. He broke with the traditional bookish idiom and brought the language of literature closer to the spoken language, at the same endowing it with beauty and greater expressiveness. What is even more important is that many other writers came forward at this time to fill the literary basket with myriad hues.

Tagore himself has claimed that his truest identity is that he is a poet. It was for his book of poems, *Gitanjali*, that he received the Nobel Prize in Literature. *Gitanjali*, though, is not his best work. Bengalis today perhaps read little of his poetry beyond what is taught in textbooks, but his songs have become inseparable from Bengali lives. In their bereavements and sorrows,

Rabindranath Tagore, the poet, lyricist, composer, short-story writer, novelist, playwright and essayist

and in all festivals and ceremonies, Bengalis cannot do without his songs. In every situation and on all occasions, his songs inspire and soothe.

Half of Tagore's life was spent in the 19th century, and the other half in the 20th century. The greater part of his success, however, came to him in the 20th century. Particularly after he received the Nobel Prize, he turned into a sort of yardstick by which all others had to be measured. Others trying to establish themselves as writers saw in him an ideal of what literature should aspire to be. The 20th century did not of course produce a second Tagore. Collectively, however, innumerable poets and writers have together brought about such immense progress in 20th century Bengali literature that the work produced in all the previous centuries together cannot match up to it. The improvements in the printing press, the publication of countless magazines and journals and the spread of education have all combined to make this happen.

Tagore transformed prose fiction, the genre that ushered in modern Bengali literature, at the start of the 20th century through novels such as *Chhokher Bali* (1903). There may be doubts about whether Tagore's characterisation of human nature was more subtle than Bankimchandra's, but Tagore did not punish his widowed protagonist for falling in love in the way that Bankim did. In his social perceptions Tagore was without doubt more progressive than Bankimchandra, and his liberal outlook is reflected in his novels. He kept on at his experimenting with this form in a series of novels after *Chokher Bali—Gora, Ghare Baire, Chaturanga, Jogajog, Dui Bon, Char Adhyay,* etc. In placing the inner lives of his characters above complications of plot, Tagore imparted a flavour to his novels that is rare not only in the novels that came before his but even those that came after.

After Tagore, the novelists Saratchandra Chattopadhyay, Bibhuti-bhushan Bandyopadhyay, Tarashankar Bandyopadhyay and Manik Bandyopadhyay left extraordinary contributions in Bengali literature. These novelists brought in village lives and ordinary people in their novels. Sharat Chandra showed in his sketching of women characters a tenderness and sympathy not seen before in any writer. Not only sympathy, the wealth of experience he brought to his delineation of women characters is also astonishing. His other remarkable quality is his gift of storytelling, imparting to his books a fairytale-like attraction that induces a willing suspension of disbelief in the reader no matter how unreal the events described. His novels are too high on sentiment, but that quality is concordant with Bengali character. Besides, readers found in his books a world that they could recognise and identify with, something which they missed in Tagore's work. The world that he recreated was a dream world of life in joint families among educated middle-class and lower-middle-class people.

The village society that he drew in his novels had not been seen in the books of Bankimchandra or Tagore.

Writers who came after Bankimchandra, Tagore and Saratchandra were able to hold up in their novels aspects of life that their predecessors could not, including sexuality. Bibhutibhushan Bandyopadhyay turned a dreamy, loving gaze on the Bengal countryside and its simple people, filling with nostalgia city dwellers who had forever left the village behind. Naresh Chandra Sengupta, Premendra Mitra, Shailajananda Mukhopadhyay and Annadashankar Ray introduced more variety in theme and thoughts. Manik Bandyopadhyay was influenced by Marxist ideology. But when he brings rural working-class people into his novels, class conflict is eclipsed by the situations of human love and play of instincts in which he places his characters. A novel like *Padmanadir Majhi* can be considered great by any yardstick.

Although novelists of the calibre of the writers mentioned did not appear after Partition, a great many middle-order novelists compensated the loss. Many of them wrote new kinds of novels in which we find, for instance, the clash of the individual with society, the use of the stream-of-consciousness technique, and varied depictions of love and sexuality. In sum, the Bengali novel came of age in the first half of the 20th century. Compared with the number of novels written during this period, however, it is debatable whether quite as many successful short stories got written. Admittedly, though, the short story after Tagore was taken forward by writers such as Prabhat Kumar Mukhopadhyay, Rajshekhar Basu, Jagadish Gupta, Banaphul, Manik Bandyopadhyay and Narendra Nath Mitra.

Though Muslim writers did not initially try their hand at the short story, writers such as Nazibur Rahman came forward in the early 20th century to write novels. But the novels they produced did not particularly enrich Bengali literature. Just as Muslims trailed the Hindus by some 70 to 80 years in education, so also in literary creation they remained behind by half a century or perhaps more. Syed Waliullah was the first Muslim writer to write a first-rate novel like *Lal Shalu* (1948). Subsequently, too, he wrote a couple of notable novels. Syed Mujtaba Ali also became quite popular and earned recognition as a travel- and short-story writer.

Notwithstanding the significant development of the genre of prose fiction, the 20th century belonged even more to Bengali poetry. Perhaps this says something of the Bengali character. Tagore alone was equal to a whole army in the history of Bengali poetry, and he left behind some hundred thousand lines in verse. His greatness however lies not in the number of lines he wrote but the quality of his poetry. The heights that he scaled in his poetry were such that there were subsequently others who despite writing fairly good poems were pushed out of view by the dazzle of his brilliance. For 65 long years, between the ages of 15 and 80, he wrote poems, wide-ranging in their sheer variety. He experimented continuously with the language and meter of poetry. The poet also endlessly explored love, nature, and his relationship with his Creator in his poems. Subtle emotions, beauty and a belief in the greater good have repeatedly found reflection in his poems. Looking back at his life and his work at the end of his days, Tagore said that his life was a 'garland of many Rabindranaths'. Considering the immense variety of his work, the remark must be accepted as true.

Satyendranath Datta and many other poets following in Tagore's footsteps appeared on the literary scene after Tagore. These poets produced very many readable and enjoyable poems, but in the space of a hundred years have largely been consigned to oblivion. On the contrary, the poets who started writing in the 1920s tried to come up with something new instead of just imitating Tagore. Kazi Nazrul Islam, Premendra Mitra, Mohitlal Majumdar, Jeebanananda Das, Buddhadeb Basu, Bishnu Dey, Sudhindra Nath Datta and Amiya Chakraborty deserve particular mention in this context. Not only did they write a new kind of poetry in terms of style and theme, they introduced many novelties in the language, meter and rhetorical devices that they used. These young poets came into public view through magazines such as *Kallol, Kali O Kalam* and *Kabita.* Some of these poets decided to have nothing to do with the idealism and sense of greater good that we find in Tagore and chose instead to focus on the harsh realities and the dark sides of life. In particular, love, sexuality, poverty and life struggles are themes that have repeatedly appeared in their poems. Instead of following Tagore, these poets tried to build up a post-Tagore stream in Bengali poetry.

The poets of the 1930s experimented not only with subject and point of view, but also with the language of poetry. In place of the simple beauty of Tagore's language, they crafted a style that can be called the language of modern Bengali poetry. Most of these poets had been students of English literature. They were deeply influenced by their reading of English poetry as they worked at their language, metaphors and style. A certain level of education is a prerequisite for making sense of this language. Hence, the work of these poets created for a while a certain distance separating them from ordinary readers.

In the previous discussion we have noted how the subject of Bengali literature moved away from religion to the human situation and the individual. From the third decade of the 20th century, however, the nation, society and politics also turned into subjects to be explored in literature. Nazrul Islam played a significant role in this process. Before he came along, too, Bengali literature had a powerful voice of revolt in Michael Madhusudan Dutt. In terms of theme and form, he had broken down all the old and established rules. This is why there is no greater rebel in Bengali literature than he. Nazrul Islam, however, mounted a different kind of revolt. He called for an assault on religion, politics, government and society, everything that thwarted or undermined the individual's freedom as a human being. He asserted the rights of those at the lower orders of society who had so far been neglected and persecuted. No one else in Bengali literature had spoken of the supremacy of the human being in a louder voice. No one, too, had made a stronger demand for the country's freedom. This new message in his poems inspired many of the later poets. Just as among poets Nazrul was inspired by the egalitarian ideal, Premendra Mitra and Shailajananda Mukhopadhyay were among writers of prose fiction who were similarly enthused. These writers brought the lower classes into their stories and their novels.

Kazi Nazrul Islam, the rebel poet, lyricist and composer. He is the symbol of Bengali Muslim pride

Nazrul gave a push forward to the Muslim community, too. On the one hand he sang of the awakening of Muslims. On the other, he reminded

Muslims of their past glory and inspired them by using Islamic ingredients in the language and subject of his poetry. He also boosted the self-confidence of Muslim poets and writers through his own success. Indeed, once he had arrived on the literary scene, Muslim poets and writers no longer trailed behind or remained caught in complexes of inferiority. Quite a few Muslim poets now started writing eminently readable poems.

A few years after Nazrul's arrival, another Muslim poet overnight acquired success and fame in the mid 1920s: he was Jasim Uddin. He did not at all follow the way that Nazrul had shown. He did not write poems with urban themes or on poverty. It was rather the style of the medieval Mangalkavya and verse narratives that he followed to some extent. He brought the life and society of rural Bengal on the high table of literature. Using rural ingredients and the language spoken in villages, he created a completely different kind of poetry. His success was also a source of inspiration to Muslim poets. The Muslim poets who joined the literary feast in the 1930s and 1940s largely wrote poems either on nationalist themes as Nazrul had done or on the countryside that Jasim Uddin had brought into focus. Besides, as we have already noted, even before the formation of Pakistan, writers such as Syed Ali Ahsan, Abul Mansur Ahmed and Farrukh Ahmed called for the creation of a new kind of literature in a language dominated by Arabic and Farsi words and reflecting an Islamic tradition influenced by the old bilingual manuscripts.

We note a faster-paced development of poetry in the 1950s. More important than how mature this poetry was in terms of quality was the fact that innumerable books of poems and magazines were published. The Muslim poet who at this time appeared in East Bengal now for the first time started writing poems on secular themes. Of this bunch of poets, the names of Shamsur Rahman and Al Mahmud are the first to come to the mind. In West Bengal Shakti Chattopadhyay, Shankha Ghosh, Niren Chakraborty and Sunil Gangopadhyay were among those who earned maximum popularity. But none of them appears to have been able to establish a particular stream or movement in poetry.

Going by just numbers, poetry eclipsed the other branches of literature in the second half of the 20th century. Modernist poetry had once earned notoriety as being indecipherable, but by the end of the 20th century that impediment was removed and modern poetry has now reached a large readership outside the academia. Jibanananda Das may not have contributed to this development while he was alive, but he made a major contribution posthumously. The language of his poetry, simple on the surface, and the anthology *Rupasi Bangla* ('Beautiful Bengal') published after his death were responsible for this. Notwithstanding the deep emotion that he invested in the poems in this collection, the poet himself did not consider *Rupasi Bangla* worthy of publication. When it did finally come out in print some seven years after his death – in 1961 – it touched the hearts of readers. Even those who so far had not been able to make much sense of the language and style of modernist poetry could appreciate to an extent the flavour of these poems. Many successful and not-so-successful poets imitated his language and style. Indeed, no other poet apart from Tagore and Nazrul Islam had quite as many imitators.

Jibanananda Das, considered the greatest of the post-Tagore era poets

Other branches of literature could not keep pace with the immense strides taken by poetry and prose fiction in the 20th century. This is particularly true of drama. As in the 19th, it underwent only a limited development in the 20th century. Many critics have with enough reason blamed the absence of the professional stage for this. But there are others who say that the Bengali genius and mental traits are not of the kind that is best suited for the writing of drama. Notwithstanding this limitation, however, men like Tagore and Dwijendralal Ray wrote some notable plays early in the 20th century. Though Tagore wrote such remarkable plays as *Bisarjan* and *Raja o Rani* in the 19th century, it was in the 20th century that he wrote most of his plays. His was predominantly a poetic genius. His plays, too, are therefore imbued with a poetic quality. That is not at odds with the nature of drama, but his plays lack in hard realism and the control that comes from a fidelity to material truth. Yet the extraordinary genius that he possessed made his contribution to Bengali drama brilliant and significant. In particular, his allegorical plays such as *Raja, Raktakarabi* and *Muktadhara* are rich in their literary content, though some critics might perhaps contend that these are not as successful on stage as they are as dramatic literature, that is, they are better read than performed. The experimenting that he did with the dramatic form was in keeping with his genius.

Dwijendralal Ray, poet, playwright, lyricist and composer

Dwijendralal Ray started his writing life as a poet. In the chapter 'Traditions of Music in Bengal' we will see that he also left significant contributions as a lyricist and musician. He started writing plays from the beginning of the 20th century. The patriotism that emerged around the movement against the first partition of Bengal was the inspiration for his historical plays. Apart from *Shah Jahan*, however, it cannot be said that his plays were of a very high standard.

Dwijendralal's contemporary Kshirodprasad Bidyabinod wrote a number of plays. No other playwright of his time perhaps wrote as many plays as he did. The greatest quality of his plays is plot and dramatic tension, making them suitable for stage performance. He first earned popular attention with his musical play *Alibaba* (1897). He subsequently wrote a number of other plays based on stories from the Middle East. In 1918 he even wrote a play about Aurangzeb—*Alamgir*. The movement against the 1905 partition enthused him to write plays on events in Bengal's history. These plays included *Pratapaditya, Chandbibi, Palashir Prayshchitto, Bangalar Masnad* and so on. Under the influence of the anti-partition movement, Girish Ghosh wrote *Siraj-ud-Daulah* and *Mir Kasim* (1906). Apareshchandra Mukhopadhyay's *Karnarjun*, Baradaprasanna Dasgupta's *Misharkumari*, Jogesh Chandra Choudhury's *Sita*, Rabindranath Maitra's *Manmoyee Girls School* and Banaphul's *Srimadhusudan* were among notable plays in the first half of the 20th century. Starting in the 1940s, Tulsi Lahiri, Bijon Bhattacharjya and Utpal Dutta wrote a significant number of plays that made a mark. In the second half of the 20th century, innumerable plays were written to meet the requirements of the professional stage as well as of television. Many of these playwrights made use of their exposure to and experience of Western theatre. Syed Shamsul Haque and Badal Sarkar should be particularly mentioned in this connection.

It was not just that the different branches of Bengali literature thrived in this century, they also witnessed veritable revolutions. Through, for instance, transformations in theme and language. In attempting to bring ordinary people and the countryside into literature, writers imported many ingredients from regional dialects. A major development in this century was the arrival of Muslim writers and through them the introduction of East Bengal rural life and Muslim society as literary subjects, which brought along many components of regional dialects into literature. With the rapid expansion of education in the 20th century, Muslims started publishing many magazines and journals. Muslim writers now had to respond to the requirements of these magazines. In the beginning, though, their contribution in creative writing was negligible. Absence of confidence, and some initial fears, may perhaps have been responsible for this, at least in part. The subjects of Muslim writers who started writing at the dawn of the 20th century were drawn from the past. These writers were trying to stand upright and hold high their own heads by recalling the past glory of Muslims in various lands and at the same time wake up fellow Muslims from their slumber. This Muslim habit of looking to the past did not easily give way to modernist thinking. It was the members of the Shikha group in the 1920s who for the first time tried to relate to their lives and to the world in a truly modern way. We have discussed them in the chapter 'Society and Religion'.

***

TRADITIONS OF MUSIC IN BENGAL

More than 200 years ago, Gerasim Lebedoff, who wrote the first Bengali play, commented while writing about the Bengali character that Bengalis loved songs and clowning. Notwithstanding their love for singing, Bengalis have not recorded the history and evolution of songs in their culture. Not that such recorded history can be reasonably expected. Yet songs have always been in the air of Bengal. There are various ways in which human beings express emotions, and modulation of voice to reflect states of the mind is one of them. This is the soil from which songs spring, but it is only later that they become songs, having acquired a specific structure through rhythm and melody. This is how songs were born everywhere in the world. Just as speech arrived before written language and the rules of grammar, so also for songs. The tunes and melodies that had currency among ordinary people became, at the hands of musicians, refined into structured melodic patterns of classical music. It did not happen the other way round, that is, folk music did not evolve from classical music.

There is not enough evidence to determine how much of the tunes and rhythms of the songs sung by the earliest inhabitants of the land, and the musical instruments they used, survived into later ages. It cannot even be ascertained what kind of songs and instruments the first Aryan immigrants brought with them. It is however reasonable to suppose that just as the faith of the Aryans got assimilated into the local belief systems and customs and was thus transformed, their music is likely to have undergone a similar process. The music of the Aryans was assimilated and syncretised with that of the older inhabitants of the land. Though we do not know which melodic tunes were born out of this assimilative process, the names of melodies such as 'Bangal' and 'Bhatiali' provide hints of this syncretism and blending. Even now the names of many melodic tunes have 'Gaur' prefixed to them, such as Gaur Mallar, Gaur Sarang, etc. Such names suggest that these melodic tunes are local variations of the original tunes. Bengal is located on India's eastern fringes. The tunes of the Aryans were unable to retain their original forms in this frontier province and most probably had to submit to extensive assimilation with local tunes.

As in present-day Bengal, different kinds of folk music were prevalent in different parts of Bengal in ancient times. Some of the later folk songs may indeed have developed from much earlier versions. Though this cannot be vouched for, there is some evidence in the *Charyapada* that the music brought by the Aryans has to an extent survived through lineages of music gurus. Each Charya poem carries mention of the melodic tune to which it was sung, and there are 19 of them in all. If Gabrha and Gaurha, and Sheebari and Shabari are the same then there are 17 of them, and not 19. The most common melody, mentioned with the maximum number of poems, was Patamanjari. Among the other melodic tunes are Gaurha, Malasi, Mallari, Ramkiri, Kamod, Bararhi and Bangal. Some of these melodies are no longer used. They do not exist anymore in Indian classical music. These were perhaps formed through the blending of Aryan and local tunes.

Whatever that may be, just as the *Charyapada* poems are the earliest extant examples of the Bengali language, they are also the earliest extant examples of Bengali music. The Buddhist Siddhacharyas sang these poems to tune. The Siddhacharyas who composed these poems were perhaps proficient in classical music. It would not however be reasonable to suppose that all of their disciples were trained in classical music and were able to sing these songs. Most people must have chanted the poems to some basic tunes, just as people still recite or sing religious poems in a monotonously rising and falling inflection of the voice. Faith is associated with deep human emotions, which is why the custom of chanting religious poems is noticed in all religions, to a greater or lesser extent. Even in Islam, which is otherwise opposed to music. The relationship of music and emotional thinking is indeed extremely close. Bengali music is no exception to the pattern. That is why we will see that the history of Bengali music is inseparably linked to the history of the rise and fall of different religions in Bengal.

Apart from the *Charyapada*, many poets in ancient Bengal must have composed religious songs. In the court of the Sena kings, for instance, the greatest poet of the time, Jaydev, composed *Gita Govinda*. The name itself makes it clear that this work is not a verse narrative, it is a ballad that could be sung. The language of *Gita Govinda* is not Bengali but Sanskrit. But it was in Bengal that it was sung, that is, *Gita Govinda* belonged to Bengal. Compared with the *Charyapada*, *Gita Govinda* makes greater use of melodies common in the rest of India. Indeed, most of these melodies are still in use. *Gita Govinda* does not however use a great variety of melodies, the total of melodies used is only 12. Every poem also carries a mention of the rhythm and meter, though there are only five kinds of meter used—Ektala, Ashtatala, Yati, Rupak and Nihsaar. Four of the melodic tunes used in *Gita Govinda* show similarities with the ones used in the *Charyapada*—Gurjari (or Gunjari), Deshakh, Bararhi and Bhairavi. One of the melodies mentioned in *Gita Govinda* is Malavgaur. The name suggests that this was a local version of the Malav melodic tune of north India.

In the history of Bengali songs, the next important written source is Borhu Chandidas' *Srikrishnakeertan*, which was written some 250 to 300 years after *Gita Govinda*. This was what we would now call a musical, a play in verse set to tune. The dialogues of Radha, Krishna and the go-between Barhayi are written in the form of ballads. These, too, carry mention of the melodic tunes to which they should be sung, and in fact these show a clear continuation of the musical tradition to which the *Charyapada* poems and *Gita Govinda* also belong. Among the melodic tunes, for instance, Gurjari, Bararhi, Deshakh, Bhairavi, Patamanjari, Mallar, Bhatiali and Bangal, which are used in the *Charyapada*, are also used in *Srikrishnakeertan*. Some of these are also found in *Gita Govinda*. There are similarities with *Gita Govinda* in the use of Malav, Deshbararhi, Ramkiri, Basanta and Bibhas melodic tunes. Apart from these older ragas and raginis, *Srikrishnakeertan* uses some newer ones, such as Dhanushi, Aher, Lalit, Gouri, Sree, Paharhi and Belabali. Some new meters are also mentioned.

In sum, *Srikrishnakeertan* makes it clear that complex musical structures were firmly established in Bengal before the 15th century. What is not so clear is how far folk music had developed in Bengal alongside this kind of classical musical tradition. The Bhatiali ragini is mentioned in the *Charyapada*. This mention seems to suggest that a particular kind of folk music called Bhatiali was sung in southern Bengal from much earlier times. A thousand years on, Bhatiali is still a particular kind of folk music. Musicians turned the tunes used in these songs into a refined melodic structure and passed it on as the Bhatiali ragini. Even now this ragini is used in north Indian classical music, though it now has two forms. One is somewhat like Baul tunes. The other one, though it carries hints of folk tunes, bears no resemblance with the Bhatiali of Bengal. There is no information on what other forms of folk music were prevalent in other parts of Bengal in ancient times. But names of ragas such as Bangal and Gaur carry hints of local tunes. At the root of these two ragas perhaps lay two separate strands of Bengali folk music.

The existence of a certain kind of folk music native to western and middle Bengal can also be sensed in the kirtan songs. We have already mentioned that Chaitanyadev preached his faith in Bengali. There was indeed little stress on the scriptures in the religion that he preached. He stressed kindness to living beings and the merits of chanting. He encouraged and led *naamkirtan*s, the collective chanting of the names of Krishna, so that people could together engage in an emotional outpouring of devotion. No refined or complex tunes were used for such singing. It was, presumably, a sort of chanting of the names of Krishna in a steady and monotonous rising and falling rhythm, performed with deep devotion. But musically trained people soon found their way into these singing congregations of the Vaishnava faith, and they started using sophisticated ragas and raginis in what was once simple chanting. Somewhat in the way that Chaitanyadev's ideal of love and devotion evolved into a scriptural canon at the hands of his *goswami*s, or Vaishnava religious scholars and preachers. Kirtan thus took on the contours of a structured and refined musical tradition. This happened in the 16th century.

Particularly in the *padavali*-kirtans, the singing of Vaishnava verse renderings of the Radha-Krishna story, complex musical structures made a far deeper penetration. This kind of singing no longer remained a simple and direct medium for the laity to chant the names of Krishna. It became indeed a veritable school of music in its own standing. There is no reason to suppose that those who wrote the poems also set them to tune. Or indeed to assume that the tunes they chose necessarily stuck. Kirtan became recognised as a refined musical tradition. And this tradition was built on the melodic tunes, the ragas and raginis and the meters used in north Indian classical music. But Bengali folk music, particularly that of the Rarh region (western Bengal) and middle Bengal, also got assimilated into it. The distinctive style of kirtan is not of north Indian classical music, it belongs to Bengal. Narottom Thakur had played a crucial role in evolving a standardised form of this style. He himself had received training in classical music in north India. So, just as the six *goswami*s imparted a scriptural form to Chaitanyadev's message, Narottom Thakur established kirtan singing on a foundation of classical music. In order to do this, in 1585 he held a congregation of distinguished musicians from Bengal and beyond, at Kheturi in Rajshahi. Discussions were held at this conference on finalising a standard form of rendering kirtan.

Despite the discussions and general consensus, at least five different gharanas, that is, schools or methods of music, emerged within kirtan soon after the Kheturi conference. The style introduced by Narottom Thakur in the mould of classical music became known as the Garanhati gharana, Garanhati being a pargana, or a district subdivision, in the Kheturi region. The other popular gharanas were the Manoharshahi, Raneehati, Mandarni and Jharkhandi gharanas. After returning to his native Birbhum from the Kheturi conference, Jnandas Manohar reformed the kirtan style prevalent there, and the kirtan of this area later became known as the Manoharshahi gharana. Bipradas Ghosh started the Raneehati gharana in the Burdwan region. Sarkar Mandaran's gharana was called Mandarni. The distinctive singing style of Jharkhand gave rise to the Jharkhand gharana.

The names of these gharanas show that kirtan in those initial years was prevalent mainly in the Rarh region (in western Bengal) and northern Bengal. At least, no separate gharana emerged in East Bengal. But when in the 16th, 17th and 18th centuries Vaishnavism rapidly spread all over Bengal, these songs also found their way all over the province. Kirtan therefore can be said to be the first truly Bengali school of music. It was, however, owing to its very popularity that the basic classical form of kirtan, whatever it might have been in its original form, could not remain undistorted. Spreading extemporaneously from one person to another, a simplified form slowly gained currency. A tradition of such simplified kirtan developed in the 18th century, and it was called *dhap*-kirtan. It carried the influences of the medieval *Panchali* (verse narratives recited in monotonous rising and falling rhythm); *kathakata* (literally meaning narration, this consisted of the recital of mythological stories; it was at once a popular rural entertainment and a source of religious knowledge); and Baul music. As kirtan spread to the various regions of Bengal, the folk tunes and folk singing styles in each region blended into the kirtans sung there. Some composers and singers also influenced and changed the ways in which kirtan was sung. And in this way kirtan too acquired variety as it evolved.

Around the time when kirtan established itself as a popular musical tradition, another body of songs was sung in some parts of Bengal with a fair degree of regularity. These were the *Panchali* songs. If kirtan was refined music with its ragas and carefully structured meters, the *Panchali* song was folk music. Its words and tunes did not carry much sophistication. This form of folk music tried to entertain its simple audience by importing recitals and drama into the performance. The *Panchali* song did not have a specific subject and theme. It could be about the Radha-Krishna story, but it could also tell tales from the *Ramayana* and the *Mahabharata* and other Puranic stories. It was somewhat like a village ballad. The Mangalkavya songs were probably a part of this tradition of musical performance.

The popularity of the Vaishnava faith was driven by the impact of a single personality—Chaitanyadev. No such forceful or charismatic individual arrived to preach and expand the reach of the Shakta faith. Yet the Shakta belief system goes much further back into the past than the Gaur school of Vaishnavism does. This religious philosophy had grown out of the assimilation of the Buddhist, Vedic and local religious beliefs. The pre-Aryan society in Bengal was probably matriarchal. There is a hint that this might have been so in the predominance of the mother goddess in the religious life of Bengal. This tradition must have left its mark on society, and hence the evident attraction of the Shakta faith among the people of Bengal. In this context we can cite a very modern example. Tagore did not believe in idol worship and was in fact quite opposed to it. Yet he seems to have subconsciously imagined the motherland in the image of Kali in the song '*Aji Bangladesher hridoy hote kakhon apani; Tumi ei aparup roope bahir hole janani*'. The 'mother' is for Bengalis a fond and powerful idea, and this was what made the Shakta faith so popular. The way in which the idea of Shakti, a primordial force, got assimilated into other belief systems also bears testimony to its hold on people's hearts.

The Shaktas and Vaishnavas have a long history of mutual opposition. So when the Vaishnava faith and kirtan songs reached the remote nooks and crannies of Bengal, the Shaktas felt impelled to write their own padavalis. Besides, in the 18th century, Raja Krishnachandra Ray, a big landowner in Nadia, started an extravagant annual ritual of Kali worship. The combined effect of these two things produced at least two famous writers of Shyamasangeet, a body of songs devoted to the dusky mother goddess Kali. One of them was Ramprasad Sen, the other was Kamalakanta Chakraborty. A close look at the work of these two musicians shows that both of them were well trained in classical music. Most of their songs are composed on the basis of the ragas and raginis of north Indian music. But the songs attributed to Ramprasad clearly reflect a continuous tradition of folk music alongside the classical school. Folk tunes have made their way into many of these songs. Tunes used in Baul songs, for instance, and even simplified forms of kirtan styles. It was through these songs that Ramprasad made his place in the hearts of the people, much more than through his classically structured compositions.

Those who stopped short of becoming Shakta worshippers but reposed faith in tantra were divided into many sects. One of these was the community of the Bauls. Bauls believe that the human body symbolises the cosmos and it is in the body that the '*moner manush*', the perfect being sought by the human self, resides. The limitless, in their thinking, lives within the limited body, and for this reason they seek the '*moner manush*' through the body and through love. It is the echo of this philosophy that we find in Tagore when he says, *Roopsagare dub diyechhi aroopratan asha kori* ('I have plunged in the ocean of beauty in the hope of attaining that formless core of beauty'). The medium of the spiritual seeking of the Bauls is music, the Baul songs. In this sense there is a similarity between Chaitanyadev's stress on chanting and the Bauls' exploring of their spiritual ideal through their songs. Then again, though the Bauls believe in using their bodies in their quest for a greater truth, there are subtle differences between their thinking and that of yogis and tantriks.

The community of Bauls did not appear before the 17th century. It was in fact in the 18th century that Baul thinking acquired some hold on people's hearts, and its greatest flowering took place after the arrival of Lalon Fakir. But it was not as if a new singing style and tune suddenly appeared at this time out of nowhere. Rather, Baul melodies seem based on the Bhatiali. The melodic variation in the north Indian Bhatiali that I have already referred to as 'Baul tune' is the basis of Baul music of Bengal. But it also carries the influence of kirtan, especially in the Birbhum region. Thematic similarities also naturally lead to a certain resemblance between Baul songs and kirtan in Birbhum.

Bauls do not have any sacred text or scriptural literature. Nor do they have an institutionalised religion. But they believe in devotional worship and in the mediation of gurus. The Bauls apart, several such devotional and guru-centric sects emerged in the 17th and 18th centuries. It is possible that this was an indirect result of the devotional faith of Vaishnavism. Kartabhaja (literally, the word means devotee of the guru, or *karta*) was one such devotional sect that became prominent in the mid 18th century. Like the Bauls, Kartabhajas do not see themselves as either Hindus or Muslims. And they, too, understand religion as faith based on simple human devotion.The Kartabhajas have their own songs.

The similarities between the Kartabhajas and Sufi Muslims are quite obvious. The difference is that the *karta* of the Sufi Muslims is the pir, whom they call murshid, or guide. The songs dedicated to murshids are known as 'murshidi songs'. But murshidi songs are so called because of their subject, not because of any particular musical trait that binds them into a body of songs.

Not all songs associated with religious movements found their way uniformly into all parts of Bengal. For, all religions were not uniformly accepted everywhere in Bengal. When a particular sect or community remained geographically confined to a particular region, its songs also remained confined to that region. Baul songs, for instance. Baul music is seen as belonging to two regions of Bengal—Kushtia in central Bengal and Birbhum in the west. A certain type of songs in north Bengal are also known as Baul songs, but in mood and tune these do not show any close family resemblance to the Baul songs of Kushtia and Birbhum.

This is more or less true also of the various traditions of folk music in Bengal. These songs belong to specific parts of Bengal and are in that sense local, and not all-Bengal in character. Bhatiali songs, for instance, belong to the southern part of East Bengal. Bhaoayia, again, are a body of songs belonging to North Bengal, particularly Coochbehar. We have no information about how long it is in history that Bhatiali and Bhaoayia songs have been sung. A certain kind of songs used to be sung in the Mymensingh region, which are now known as *Mymensingh Geetika.* These songs were about human love. There is however no way of determining whether these songs were bound together by any common musical traits, in the way that Baul, Bhatiali and Bhaoayia songs are.

All the Bengali musical traditions we have looked at so far were closely linked to religious beliefs. These songs, indeed, were born out of religious movements. Only the folk songs such as those of the *Mymensingh Geetika* and the Bhatiali and Baul songs were exceptions, though religious thought does run through folk music like a secret stream. The first truly secular Bengali songs that we have are the songs of Nidhubabu, known as 'Nidhubabu's tappa'. In the late 18th century, Nidhubabu worked in Chhapra near Lucknow. There he trained in classical music under an ustad called Ghulam Nabi. But the musical tradition that drew him most was tappa. Tappa songs were based on a certain kind of Punjabi folk music. Some six years before the turn of the century, Nidhubabu a.k.a Ramnidhi Gupta came back to Calcutta and started singing his tappa songs.

Initially, he sang the songs he had heard in Lucknow. He turned the original Hindi songs into Bengali and sang them. Soon, however, he started writing his own songs in Bengali. And in these songs he showed his originality in two ways. He slowed down the rapid modulations of tune in the Punjabi tappa and thus made the form better suited to his Bengali songs. He also added a sort of dramatic expressiveness to his songs. The greater novelty that he introduced, however, was the fundamental transformation that he brought about in the subject of his songs. Ignoring the examples of all his predecessors in Bengali music, he wrote his songs about human beings rather than gods. Nidhubabu took this extraordinary step at a time when the Bengal Renaissance had not yet started its journey under Ram Mohan Roy's leadership. Literature was still under the complete sway of gods and goddesses. Some four decades later, mortals made their entry in literature through the agency of another Gupta, the poet Ishwar Gupta. In Ramnidhi Gupta's songs, however, human love found expression as early as the first decade of the nineteenth century. We might form an idea of his themes by quoting one of this songs:

We meet after many days
Separation had felt like poison, and fire
The heart knew no hope
But then the heart found its refuge in our union, it found you
Are there words to express this happiness?
The heart floats in a sea of happiness, the eyes are moist.

Nidhubabu incurred much criticism for bringing human love into his songs. Many people found his songs obscene, an idea that grew in strength especially after Brahmo squeamishness took hold in the second half of the 19th century. Apart from love, there were also the first faint hints of patriotism in the songs he wrote. In this context it is enough to refer to just one song—'*Nanan desher nanan bhasha bine swadeshi bhasha mite ki asha*'. (There are so many different languages in different lands, but is the heart warmed by any language other than one's own?)

Nidhubabu's contemporary Kalidas Chattopadhyay alias Kali Mirza also wrote tappa songs. He lived in his village home in his younger days, and that was where pursued his interest in music. He moved to Calcutta a few years after Nidhubabu did. His songs differed from Nidhubabu's in that he did not write songs on secular themes. He wrote and composed Shyamasangeet in the tappa form. His Shyamasangeet became so popular that very soon others started writing Shyamasangeet in the tappa style. Even kirtan started imitating the style to an extent. Once tappa became well-received, singers like Sridhar Kathak, Gopal Urhe, and many others helped make it popular.

We need to give some background information on the term tappa. Though Nidhubabu's songs became known as tappa, he himself had written that he had no intention of composing anything on the lines of the Hindustani khayal or tappa. Indeed, the songs that he started writing and setting to tune within a few years of coming to Calcutta were, in his own opinion, *akhrhai* songs. *Akhrhai* songs were based on classical music with its structured meters and melodic discipline. It does not however have the complex melodic structures of Hindustani khayal or the rapid modulations of tappa. In a word, it is much simpler and easier. Partly because of this simplicity, and partly because of their themes, Nidhubabu's songs became popular. But since he had first gained recognition for his renderings of tappa songs in Bengali translation, his later songs also came to be known as tappa. His tappa has, however, subtle differences from *akhrai* songs.

Nidhubabu wrote and sang his songs in Calcutta, that is, in the capital. His songs were able to find an audience and earn acclaim in the large population supported by the city. The song-writers of past ages, on the contrary, had not been based in any thickly populated centre. That their songs still earned popularity was because of their religious appeal. It was the followers of the various religious sects who passed on their songs from one region to another and from one generation to another. Nidhubabu's secular songs did not have this advantage. But the capital, Calcutta, made up for it. It was indeed with Calcutta at its centre that Bengali music began to thrive in the 19th century. Several socio-economic factors brought this about.

The Bengali language and literature had developed partly under the patronage of rajas, sultans and zamindars. Curiously enough, the same cannot be said about Bengali songs. Bengali songs thrived without royal patronage. Perhaps because songs were nurtured by faith and life, not by the hope of court favours. Besides, many of the Muslim sultans who ruled the land in the Middle Ages were opposed to music because of religious reasons. Even if some of them were fond of music, there is at least no evidence that any of them patronised the writing of songs. For this reason Bengali music developed away from the capital and other urban centres, in the countryside.

We notice a fundamental change in the situation, however, in the colonial era. Bengali music now drew nourishment in and around Calcutta and, in the beginning, under the patronage of the nouveau riche.

The population of Calcutta started rapidly increasingly once it became the capital of the British-ruled territories. Word spread from village to village that the city turned fortunes around. In the chapter 'Bengali Culture under Western Impact' we noted how people from various regions of Bengal started arriving in Calcutta in search of their fortunes. Trade with the English and other European merchants created overnight a nouveau riche section in Calcutta at this time. These newly rich people started observing pujas and other ceremonies with great pomp and extravagance in order to gain social recognition. In their pursuit of pleasures and amusements, these people who suddenly found themselves turned into 'babus' needed songs and music, too. They had courtesans (*baiji*s) performing for them, but that did not quite satisfy them. And not everyone had the musical training to be able to appreciate Hindustani classical music.

Various simplified forms of serious genres of music became popular at this time. Tappa was of course one of them, and so were *akhrai* and *half-akhrai* songs. Besides, many different kinds of village songs made their way to Calcutta from nearby areas. Such as *dhap*-kirtan, *Panchali* songs, *kheur*, *tarja* and so on. Despite some similarities, the songs of the *kabiyal*s (itinerant singers who engaged with rivals in extemporaneous singing matches) were superior in quality than *tarja* songs and also had a fair bit of variety. *Kabiyal* songs therefore became quite popular in Calcutta and also in rural areas. It was this popularity of *kabiyal* songs that turned Antony Firingi, or Antony Hensman, into a *kabiyal* though he was Italian-born. Like the *kabiyal* songs, another type of songs was very popular in Calcutta: these were the *jatra* songs. Now *jatra* has come to mean a sort of open-stage theatre. But in those days jatra was mostly about songs though it did have some prose dialogues. It is therefore more apt to describe these performances as '*jatra* song' rather than just '*jatra*'. The most popular of these *jatra* songs were the ones telling the Vidya-Sundar story. It is not hard to see why. The descriptions of physical love in the Vidya-Sundar narrative must have attracted audiences. *Jatra* songs, of course, cannot be placed in any specific musical genre, unlike tappa or *akhrai* songs. All kinds of songs were used in them. A type of songs called *pokkhidaler gaan* (songs of birds) acquired currency among the debauched and bibulous babus of Calcutta.

The songs that in those days made the rounds in Calcutta, such as *Panchali, kheur, tarja, kabiyal* songs, *half-akhrai, jatra,* and *pokkhidaler gaan,* were all more or less obscene in their subjects. Even Nidhubabu's songs were considered obscene by some, though he only spoke of human love. That his songs were nevertheless seen as obscene was because songs in the past had always been the medium of religious emotion. When songs suddenly turned into a medium for talking about human love, many were unwilling to accept them as being within the bounds of decency.

There was another way in which Calcutta stoked the culture of singing and songs. The huge population that gathered in the city then and for another 100 years after that brought with them many different kinds of singing from the different parts of Bengal. These songs, on the one hand, enhanced the wealth and variety of melodies used in Bengali music and brought to the fore many upcoming and talented singers. On the other, these rough songs acquired a degree of polish and refinement in order to meet the requirements of the Calcutta babus. And the songs thus refined in turn made their way back into the various regions where they had originated. Bengali music thus developed through a process of give-and-take.

Singers who came to the capital city of Calcutta did not just bring with them local songs from the regions of Bengal. Many ustads also brought with them Hindustani songs from other provinces. There were also many Bengali musicians like Kali Mirza and Nidhubabu who were trained in north Indian classical music. These non-Bengali and Bengali ustads together created an environment for classical music in Calcutta at the start of the 19th century. In particular, *dhrupad,* khayal and tappa songs were sung then. Thumri came later. The ustads from beyond Bengal also introduced instrumental music: sitar, *surbahar,* sarod, sarangi, and *shehnai,* among others. The singers who in those days became well known for their rendering of *akhrai, half-akhrai, dhap*-kirtan, *kabiyal* songs and so on were all more or less trained in classical music. Singers such as Dasharathi Ray, Sridhar Kathak, Gopal Urhe and Madhu Kanh – though none of them made their reputation by practising classical music – all had received a classical training. Indeed, the days of flaunting untutored skills were over. In this way Bengali music improved its standard through efforts centred in Calcutta.

It was not just the nouveau riche who lived in Calcutta at the dawn of the 19th century, many educated people and scholars also flocked to the city. Ram Mohan Roy, for instance. He arrived in the city right at the start of the century. A musical training was in those days considered to be a necessary part of education. How strong this notion was can be inferred from a comment of Tagore's. He wrote that anyone who was unable to nod his head at the right moments while listening to classical music was considered as worthless as an unlettered country bumpkin without an English education. It was this contemporary stress on a musical education that probably made Ram Mohan Roy and Dwarakanath Tagore take formal lessons in music.

Ram Mohan Roy trained under Kali Mirza. Besides, he also had an ustad called Rahim Khan staying at his house. One of the disciples of Rahim Khan was Bishnu Chakraborty, who later gave music lessons to Rabindranath. As we mentioned before, Kali Mirza was, like Nidhubabu, a virtuoso in tappa music. He had also trained in *dhrupad*. He himself in fact composed songs in the tappa and *dhrupad* styles. Rahim Khan was also a *dhrupad* master. Ram Mohan Roy found the *dhrupad* and not tappa better suited to his taste. One reason for this was that the more solemn *dhrupad* was considered more apt for use during prayer services. Having trained under two *dhrupad* masters, Ram Mohan in later life wrote songs in the *dhrupad* style. These songs were sung at the Brahmo Samaj that he founded. *Dhrupad* music thus became linked with the Brahmo faith, and this was a tradition that continued to be followed later in Debendranath Tagore's Adi Brahmo Samaj and Keshab Sen's Nababidhan Samaj.

Dwarakanath Tagore had also, like Ram Mohan, received a musical training. He learnt not only Indian but also Western music. He was taught to play the piano by English masters. Later we will see how playing the piano became a tradition in his family. Debendranath also received formal lessons in classical music. He arranged for all his sons starting from Dwijendranath to receive a musical education.

There were other things about 19th century Calcutta that encouraged music and a culture of singing. One of these was the European influence. It would not be right to say that the Bengali musical tradition was influenced by European singing styles and melodies. But the musical instruments that arrived from Europe certainly did influence our music. The first to arrive was what Bengalis call the *behala*, an instrument similar to the violin but larger. It came much before the British did, thanks to the Portuguese. This early arrival is also hinted at in its name. *Behala* originates not in violin but in viola. Terracotta temples built close to Calcutta in the 18th century have terracotta slabs carrying images of the *behala*. The bands that were formed during the colonial era also influenced Bengali musical sensibilities. Bengalis started forming their own bands and their members learnt to play European musical instruments. The English theatre and church music also more or lesss had an impact. The custom that grew at the Brahmo Samaj of singing hymns at religious services certainly recalls the hymns sung during church services. The tradition of piano and organ music accompanying the hymns at the Brahmo Samaj also stemmed from imitating church music. Indeed, Western melodies and styles can be detected in some of the Brahmo hymns that Jyotirindranath Tagore wrote.

The introduction of notations in music was another result of the European impact. India had never had before any custom of noting down in written symbols the melodic tunes used in songs. Songs were passed down through a chain of gurus and their disciples, from one generation to another. Changes and distortions therefore crept into the tunes. Training in vocal music depended completely on what was taught by music gurus. But with the English example of using written notations in music before them, Bengalis figured out a way of committing their own tunes in written symbols. The two Tagore households at Jorasanko and Pathuriaghata made significant contributions in this effort.

Sourindramohan Tagore (1840-1918) of the Pathuriaghata Tagores was trained in both Indian and Western music. Just as Ram Mohan played the role of a humanist scholar by retrieving ancient sacred texts, bringing them back into public discussions and reinterpreting them, half a century later, Sourindramohan Tagore played a similar role in music. Unprecedented arrangements were made at his family home for the pursuit of classical music. Ustads gathered there from far and wide, and this was the environment in which he received his musical education from childhood. He trained in both vocal and instrumental music. A German musician taught him to play the piano.

Sourindramohan retrieved ancient classical music and gave it fresh currency. He even retrieved old musical instruments that were all but lost and forgotten and preserved them. He also tried to uphold the wealth of Indian classical music to the West through the medium of the English language. He wrote a number of books in English on Indian music. It was through these books that the West got to know about Indian music for the first time. The United States and many European nations recognised his extraordinary knowledge of music with honorary titles. Several universities including Oxford conferred on him honorary degrees of Doctorate of Music.

In order to give new life to ancient classical music, Sourindramohan got one of the ustads who lived with the family, Kshetramohan Goswami, to prepare notations and made them available in the public domain. His *Sangeet-Sar* was published in 1869. This was the first time that Bengali notations got written. However, around the same time Dwijendranath Tagore also independently innovated a way of recording notations.

The style of notations that Jyotirindranath devised on the basis of Dwijendranath's is still considered the standard model for Bengali notations. Krishnadhan Bandyopadhyay (1846-1904) had also, like Sourindramohan Tagore, received a thorough education in Indian and Western music. On the one hand he leant to play the sitar and the piano, on the other he also learnt vocal music. He used his extraordinary knowledge in music to experiment andinnovate. Krishnadhan Bandyopadhyay made Indian music available in European notations, and he also used Western singing styles in Indian music.

Beginning from just before the foundation of their rule, the British in Calcutta established quite a few theatres. It would not be correct to say that these theatres influenced Bengali songs or dramatic literature. But when Bengalis started acting in dramatic performances in the 1850s, the example of the English theatre influenced Bengali music. The burgeoning Bengali theatre needed songs that were dramatic in quality and would go well with a particular situation and incident. Plays in those days contained a number of songs. These songs had to have variety, too. Songs in theatre must be counted among the performing arts. They are linked to particular dramatic situations in a way that sets them apart from songs in general.

In the chapter 'Bengali Culture under Western Impact' we noted how a sense of nationhood grew in and around Calcutta after the Sepoy Mutiny. It was this that was reflected in the activities of the Hindu Mela. Songs played a major role right from the start of the Mela in 1865. The older Tagore brothers, Dwijendranath, Satyendranath and Jyotirindranath, started writing patriotic songs at this time. Even the teenaged Tagore started contributing to this tradition within a few years. This was how patriotic Bengali songs were born. The phenomenon was not limited to songs. Poets such as Hemchandra Bandyopadhyay and Nabin Sen at this time wrote patriotic narrative poems. Many other writers including Jyotirindranath and Upendranath Das wrote patriotic plays, as we have already noted in the preceding chapter.

In sum, in the new age and new environment ushered in by the 19th century, Bengali music seemed all at once to emerge from its slumber. The creative outburst that we see in Bengali literature during the Bengal Renaissance had its parallel in Bengali music. The first expressions of this creative outpouring were centred in a few families and some individuals. The Tagore family branches of Jorasanko and Pathuriaghata, for instance, played an outstanding role.

Tagore was born in 1861. Within the next 10 years, Bengal saw the birth of a series of geniuses who changed forever the history of Bengali music. The birth of so many famous individuals within so short a time is no doubt extraordinary. Dwijendralal Ray was born two years after Tagore; Rajanikanta Sen after four years; and Atulprasad Sen after 10 years. These four men were all lyricists, composers and singers. They immensely enriched the Bengali musical tradition within a very short time. Playwright Girish Chandra Ghosh was born 17 years before Tagore. He was also a lyricist, composer and singer, and he, too, enriched Bengali music through his innovations.

Bengal has not had a second genius as great and as many-sided as Tagore. But Tagore did not scale the heights that he did by dint of his genius alone. The family and environment that he was born into stoked his genius and encouraged it to grow. This is true not just of his literary creativity, but also of all other aspects of his genius. We have seen before how Dwarakanath received an excellent education in instrumental and vocal music. So did Debendranath. He could sing, and he also wrote many songs and set them to tune. His sons Dwijendranath, Satyendranath and Jyotirindranath also received musical training. Among the brothers, Jyotirindranath was quite a virtuoso. This was the environment in which Tagore was born. It would indeed have been impossible for him not to acquire singing skills. Tagore did not show any interest in a formal academic education. Nor was he too enthusiastic about his music lessons. But the elders in his family left nothing to chance in their efforts to give him a musical education. The Tagore family was, during the poet's childhood, frequented by many musicians of the day. Famous ustads such as Jadu Bhatta, Bishnu Chakraborty, Radhikaprasad Goswami, Shyamsundar Mishra were the family's music tutors. Tagore, therefore, had no option but to learn to sing. He did not however go through a systematic method of learning music. He picked up many ragas and raginis by just listening. It was the greatness of his genius that made this possible.

The way in which Tagore received his musical education, and the people from whom he received it, gave a particular direction to his taste in music. This taste, and this education, both deeply influenced his creativity later in life. Most of the ustads under whom he trained sang *dhrupad* compositions. In the Brahmo Samaj, too, the hymns that were sung at prayer meetings were *dhrupad*-based. The songs that Tagore started writing while still a boy were hymns (Brahmasangeet) with the *dhrupad* structure.

Tagore followed the *dhrupad* structure. *Dhrupad* songs have four stanzas, called *tuk* in the language of music: *sthayi, antara, sanchari* and *abhog. Antara* and *abhog* generally share the same tune, which is why the *abhog* is often described as the second *antara*. This was the structure that Tagore replicated in his songs. Apart from a few exceptions, he retained it in all his songs. Indeed, this was the structure that he used even in songs based on folk tunes instead of classical melodies. This gave his songs an extraordinary distinctiveness. Just as sonnets with their octets and sestets have a definite structure that regulates their shifts in mood, Tagore songs likewise have their words and tunes bound within a particular structure that sets them apart and makes them stand out. He thus created a new form in the genre of Bengali poetry. We can provide an example to explain this observation.

Have you then brought home the wayfarer
My road dipped in the hues of mercy!
He is here, he is in my yard
His chariot is at my door.

Messages from across the seas/ Does he bear for my heart
On his eyelashes seem to sing the forests and the hills
The mind swings gently between joy and sorrow
The eyes fill with unexplained tears.

The cruel road, I know/Will again take away
Him who filled me up, he will pass like a dream.

Here, the *sthayi* exuberantly announces the arrival of the desired wayfarer. The *antara* says how he comes bearing messages from across the seas and how forests and hills sing in his eyes. The soft-tuned *sanchari* tells of the joy that the arrival has brought and also anticipates the bleakness that departure will cause. The departure takes on a definite finality in the *abhog*: the ruthless road will again take away the wayfarer on a journey into the unknown. The tonal modulations reflect the changes in mood and emotion. Poems often do not have any definite conclusion. At the end of this song however there is a certain ebbing of emotion, a finality of mood, a cathartic sense of resignation. With a few exceptions, almost all Tagore songs perhaps would be amenable to this way of reading them.

Dhrupad songs also have this quality that they are usually solemn and devotional. This is a quality that we generally see in Tagore songs. He also of course wrote many other kinds of songs, but a comparison of the mood of his poems and his songs will show that his poems do not always reflect the unshaken faith in divinity that his songs do. He touched on varied themes in his poetry, but in his songs he went back again and again to God. His sense of the divine is in fact also enmeshed in his songs on nature and love. The *dhrupad* influence on Tagore was so comprehensive that for years he did not take to khayals, and nor did he write many songs in the khayal mould. The thumri moved him even less, though he did write many tappas.

Dhrupad was not the only musical influence on Tagore. Jyotirindranath played the piano at home, and there is no reason to suppose that he played only Indian music; he was also interested in Western music. At 18, Tagore went to England to study, and there he was naturally exposed to Western music. Indeed, it is not enough to say that he became familiar with Western music. He had grown up in a musical environment and he loved music. He was also talented enough to pick up ragas and raginis just by listening to them. Tagore was thus able to soak himself in the wealth of the Western musical traditions that opened up for him during his time in England. As we said before, his musical education at home had consisted as much of just listening to music as it did of formal training. The towering genius that he was, his knowledge of Western music also mostly came from listening, much more than from formal lessons.

He got a chance to pursue his musical interest at the home of his host in London, John Scott. In the chapter 'Bengali Women and their Culture' we noted that the younger Scott daughter, Lucy, was in love with Tagore though she was eight years older than he was, and Tagore, too, seems to have been infatuated with her. They agreed that Tagore should give her lessons in Bengali while she would teach him Western music. So he learnt Irish and Scottish folk songs from Lucy, though these were not typically the kind of village songs that we understand as folk songs in Bengal. Tagore also deeply admired opera music. We can't tell how exposed he was to Western classical music. We will see how Western music soon wielded an immense influence on his creative genius.

Tagore did not stay in England for long. His family called him back, partly after reading the pieces that he wrote for the *Bharati* magazine on English society and its women, but also for other reasons. A few months after his return he wrote *Balmikipratibha* ('The Genius of Valmiki'). *Balmikipratibha* introduced virtually a new form in Bengali literature. No such work had ever existed in Bengali before. It was, quite clearly, written in imitation of the operas that he had watched in England. Tagore at that time called it '*sure natika*', meaning a play set to tune. Later such works came to be known as '*geetinatya*', or musical drama.

Balmikipratibha directly reflects the cultural influence of his overseas trip. It contains three songs set to Western tunes, but the indirect influence of Western music is even more comprehensive and significant. The dramatic tension that he introduced in the work came from his exposure to the Western opera. Besides, the folk songs that he heard and learnt in England were long-winded, voluble outpourings set to tune. Apart from kirtan and Baul songs, Bengali music did not have this kind of songs dominated by word. Melodies and tunes were more important than words in Bengali vocal music. This can be illustrated by comparisons with Nidhubabu's songs. Inspired by the Western ideal that he encountered in England, Tagore started writing songs in which words dominated the aesthetic experience. He could never quite walk away from this ideal, though he did also write a few songs memorable mainly for their melodies. That he was a poet might also have had something to do with this. Whatever that might be, words, and not just melodies, started playing a major role in his songs.

Some 10 years after coming back from England, Tagore started living more or less permanently in rural East Bengal. In Calcutta he moved in elite urban circles. But in Shilaidaha (in Kushtia, then undivided Nadia district), Sajadpur (in Pabna district) and Patisar (Rajshahi district) he became acquainted with a wider Bengali society. This vastly influenced his work, particularly his poems, short stories and songs. (I have extensively discussed this in my book *Rabindrabishwe Purbabanga: Purbabange Rabindranath.*) In particular he was fascinated by the Baul songs that he heard in Kushtia. The Bauls' simple faith in love and their seeking of the '*moner manush*' drew him as much as did the simple and emotional melodies in their singing. He did not of course start writing Baul songs as soon as he moved to Kushtia, but he did realise that simple tunes can also attract, far removed though they might be from the rigid structures of ragas and raginis. Baul melodies seemed to show him the way towards what he himself has described as the 'liberation' of music. He could feel that Baul tunes came right from the hearts of simple people unburdened by any knowledge of classical music. An indication of how deeply he was influenced by Baul songs was that he collected the songs of Lalon Fakir and published them in the magazine *Prabasi.* He also encouraged others to collect folksongs.

Tagore started using Baul tunes in his songs almost 15 years after he moved to Shilaidaha. Most of the patriotic songs that he wrote for the movement against the Bengal partition were based on Baul melodies. The patriotic songs that he had written before this phase followed the classical structure. There was in fact little to distinguish those songs from his hymns for the Brahmo Samaj. He had written, for instance, a song like '*Tomari tare Ma sonpinu e deho*' (a hymn to the motherland, in which the poet dedicates his body and being to the country evoked as a mother goddess), strictly classical in form and style, without sparing much thought on who and how many such songs could attract. But when he wrote his inspired songs on the partition of Bengal, driven by a need to reach out to a wide audience, he chose Baul tunes.

Later of course he used Baul tunes not just in patriotic songs but also extensively in his songs of love and devotion. More significantly, he blended in Baul tunes even when he was working with ragas and raginis, consciously or otherwise. Then again, he sometimes used the four-stanza pattern even when he wrote Baul songs. Many critics believe that even in his religious philosophy he was progressively influenced by the Baul ideal of simple love. Sashibhushan Dasgupta has for good reason called him the greatest Baul of Bengal. Apart from Baul melodies, he was not much influenced by other folksongs. Kirtan tunes of course had an extensive and deep impact on his songs, as much as Baul songs did. But not everyone may be willing to accept kirtan as folk music.

Tagore's greatest achievement is that he wrote songs that were truly Bengali, that is, he did not just render Hindustani music in the Bengali language. Just as kirtan and Baul belong truly to Bengal, he introduced a new tradition of music that was not just Bengali in its language but also recognisably Bengali in tune and style. Yet this was not an easy thing to do from the position that he started out with as a boy poet. That he had not actually submitted himself to the rigid discipline of a classical education in music perhaps turned out to be a blessing in disguise. His intimate exposure to Western music also helped. He drew even more deeply from Baul and kirtan songs. But his greatest inspiration came from within. Those who are touched by genius are drawn out and up to heights that ordinary mortals cannot even fathom. Tagore transformed Bengali music through what he called the liberation of music. The older he grew, the more his songs stood out in their brilliant distinctiveness, and with ever greater abandon he threw away the rigidities of classical structure. And so, even when he based his songs on classical melodies in these later phases, they bore his unmistakable imprint. He set his songs to tune in a way that liberated them from fixed classical patterns. Those who recorded the tunes in notations therefore added a note here and took away another there in order to keep intact the grammar of music.

Many critics claim that Tagore created an extraordinary combination of words and melodies in his songs, one in which neither the words nor the melodies are any less important than the other. On a closer look, however, this generalisation may not stand up to the songs of his last years. Notwithstanding a few exceptions, it is the words that seem to dominate his last songs, rather than the melodies. The words seem to form a recital, only they are set to tune. Tagore in fact transformed Bengali music with the new form of song-writing that he introduced. More than 135 years since the publication of his *Balmikipratibha*, even now many Bengali songs are divided into four stanzas and words dominate the aesthetic experience that they provide.

Tagore was not only the greatest Bengali poet, he was also the greatest Bengali lyricist. It is however my belief that several factors combined to make his songs as attractive as they are to educated middle-class Bengalis. The biggest reason of course is the poetic wealth of his songs. Bengalis hear echoes of their own hearts in Tagore's songs. In our laughter and in our tears, the words of his songs seem to play around in our conscious and our subconscious minds. The second reason is that he liberated music from the rigid classical structures based on ragas and raginis and made it accessible and comprehensible to those who have not had the benefit of a musical education. It is possible to sing his songs with a little effort, but not, say, the songs of Nazrul Islam. The latter require a rigorous classical training.

That Tagore was endowed with a beautiful voice and could present expert renderings of his own songs also initially facilitated their wide acceptance. If we look at the history of musical recordings, we will find that in the first years of the 20th century no one had more songs recorded in gramophone than he did. This was not just because he belonged to the influential Tagore family, but because there was magic in his voice. We are no longer able to enthusiastically praise his voice when we hear it, because the definition of what constitutes a melodic voice has changed. It is what is called a 'deep voice' in English that is now received well. In the time of Tagore, on the other hand, the 'tenor', or the high-pitched male singing voice, was considered ideal. There is another reason for his recorded voice losing appeal—the records that survive are all from a time when he was fairly advanced in years. He was then past 60. The technology used in the recordings was also not very advanced. Apart from the poet himself, the greatest other repository of his songs at that time, his grand nephew Dinendranath Tagore, also had a voice as high-pitched as his own. So was Shantideb Ghosh's voice. From what has survived of Bengali songs other than Rabindrasangeet that were recorded in those days, we can see that Dwijendralal Ray, K. Goswami and Radhikaprasad Goswami also did not possess deep voices. Even Nazrul Islam had a high pitched voice. This gives us an idea about what kind of singing voice was popular then. The first to use a baritone in Tagore songs, in the 1930s, was Pankaj Kumar Mullick. It was in fact Pankaj Mullick, and then Hemanta Mukhopadhyay and Debabrata Biswas, who made it fashionable to sing Tagore songs in a deep voice. Whatever that may be, in the history of Bengali music Tagore remains the greatest lyricist ever. And in view of the unprecedented combination of poetry and melody in his songs, also the greatest composer.

Dwijendralal Ray also left an extraordinary contribution in Bengali music. But he came from a background very different from Tagore's, and for that reason his songs are in many ways different from Tagore's in the aesthetic experience they provide, the cultural taste that they reflect, and also in form. Unlike Tagore, Dwijendralal was born, not in Calcutta, nor in a very elite or even a Brahmo family, but in a traditional Hindu household in Krishnanagar. His father, Kartikeyachandra Ray, was highly educated and scholarly. He worked as the dewan of the raja of Krishnanagar. He had trained not in *dhrupad* but in khayal. He is considered to have been one of the greatest early exponents of the khayal in Bengal. Dwijendralal did not have the kind of versatile and musically accomplished brothers that Tagore had, but both his two older brothers were writers, if not musicians.

Dwijendralal received his musical training from his father. His, in fact, was a far more formal and rigorous training than Tagore's. In the 1890s, when he worked away from Bengal, he received formal training in khayal and tappa from his friend and distinguished singer Surendranath Majumdar and other ustads. This formal training turned out to be both a strength and a weakness. Weakness, because he never could quite shake off the limitations imposed by classical music. Strength, because he wrote many beautiful songs within the bounds of the classical form. Dwijendralal was not influenced by the *dhrupad*. His songs therefore do not have the four-*tuk* structure that Tagore songs do. Though his songs are divided in many stanzas, the same tunes are repeated through all of them, again and again.

Dwinjendra Lal was also inclined to experimenting and innovating in music. As in the case of Tagore, he became alive to these possibilities when he went to England to study. As a music lover he could not help enjoying Western music. He, therefore, seriously pursued his musical interest during his years in the West and trained in Western music. He was also attracted to the theatre. How deeply Western music influenced him can be gauged from that extraordinary song, '*Dhana dhanyo pushpo bhara*' (This earth filled with the bounties of grain and flowers). The Western influence makes itself felt not only in the tune but also in the singing style. Under the impact of the West, Dwijendralal introduced the humorous song in Bengali music, an extraordinary innovation. Later, Tagore, Rajanikanta Sen and even Nazrul Islam wrote humorous songs. Some of Tagore's humorous songs make great music. Yet it is Dwijendralal Ray who remains at the top in the genre of the Bengali humorous song.

His years in England also left their mark in his plays and the songs he wrote for them. As the 20th century dawned, he wrote a number of social, historical and Puranic plays. These were very popular, too. Dwijendralal liberally used songs in these plays and was also able to make them fit harmoniously into the relevant dramatic situations. In my opinion, he outshone Tagore in this respect. Unlike Tagore, however, Dwijendralal was not able to inspire a committed circle of followers who imitated his style. The songs of Dwijendralal are exclusively his own: he has no followers, whether in tunes or in form. On the contrary, post-Tagore Bengali songs have followed Tagore in language and in structure. Even his melodies have left their mark in these songs.

The lyricist who nourished the Bengali musical tradition with musical trends borrowed from outside Bengal was Atulprasad Sen. He was not born into an aristocratic family in the way that Tagore or even Dwijendralal was. The extraordinary and rich musical environment that they benefited from in their own families was not part of Atulprasad's inheritance. Orphaned in childhood, however, he was brought up by his maternal grandfather and it was from him that Atulprasad received his musical training, though his grandfather was not any famous musician. Atulprasad went to England as a young man and came back after being called to the bar. There is something here that sets him apart from Tagore and Dwijendralal—unlike them, he was not influenced by Western music despite spending a few years in the West. His workplace was in Lucknow, and it was there that he received a proper musical education. The Hindustani musical tradition that most influenced him was that of the thumri. Most of his songs were modelled on the thumri, which had until then not found its way into Bengali songs. Ghazal styles can also be detected in Atulprasad's songs. A few of his songs also clearly show Tagore's influence. But this influence is limited to style and does not extend to structure. In structure, his method is largely similar to Dwijendralal's; the four-stanza song is not the ideal that he follows.

Atulprasad wrote some 200 songs in all. It is not as if his songs are particularly rich in their poetic merit. Though he married for love, he was virtually separated from his wife. He deeply loved his estranged wife, however, and his anguish over the split is repeatedly reflected in the pathos of his songs. In their ability to speak from the heart and in their appealing tunes, his songs are considered to form a distinct category in the mainstream of Bengali music. That his songs, written in the early 20th century, are still well received in Bengali society show how distinctive they are.

The songs of Rajanikanta Sen are also recognised as constituting a separate and distinctive strand in the tradition of Bengali music. He too did not leave behind a prolific output. His songs are not very remarkable in their form and other musical qualities. Yet they move the heart in their simplicity and devotional sweetness. Like the songs in Tagore's final years, he too did not attempt to create classical compositions though he generally based his songs on ragas and raginis. He wrote and composed what we would describe as ordinary Bengali songs, some of which were humorous and patriotic, like what Dwijendralal composed. Yet it was the devotional emotion that found strongest expression in his songs. As in the songs of Atulprasad, a certain melancholy pervades his songs.

Among those who wrote songs in the second half of the 19th century, Girish Chandra Ghosh was a distinguished lyricist and composer. He wrote 1,300 songs, that is, he wrote more songs than Dwijendralal, Atulprasad and Rajanikanta together produced between them. But he was not a poet of the stature of these men. The poetic quality of his songs was therefore not quite as high as that of these later song-writers. Nor was he as accomplished a musician as they were. But he wrote widely varied songs to meet the requirements of theatre. These included a good number of religious songs, too. Though a Vaishnava himself, the Shyamasangeet that he wrote reflected genuine feeling. The songs that he wrote with specific dramatic situations in mind also show a certain dramatic quality.

The five men discussed above were all lyricists, composers and singers. Though it was not as if they were all equally accomplished in all these capacities. It can be said of all of them that were products of the Bengal Renaissance. Their geniuses were nurtured in the very special musical atmosphere that developed in Calcutta in the second half of the 19th century as a consequence of the contact with the British. And they in turn enriched this world of music with their own insights and innovations. The situation changed drastically in the 20th century. In this century we encounter only one individual who wrote, composed and sang. He is Nazrul Islam.

Going by numbers, he was the greatest Bengali song-writer. It is often claimed that he wrote nearly 4,000 songs. But this claim cannot be verified with any degree of certainty. The songs that survive number less than 3,000. Though it is true that many of his songs got lost, it is not possible to guess the number of the lost songs. The legend of his having written 4,000 songs is perhaps not true.

There is a significant way in which Nazrul Islam differs from the five great song-writers we have discussed. Let alone Tagore, the other four were also born in educated and wealthy urban families, at least Dwijendralal and Atulprasad were. Rajanikanta was also born in an educated middle class family. But the family into which Nazrul was born was uneducated, rural and extremely poor. Apart from Rajanikanta, all the others had enough opportunities to acquire a musical education in childhood. Nazrul did not have such luck. The scraps of music that he picked up as a boy came from his association with a '*leto dal*' (see page 423). The most that this would have done for him was to give him a sense of rhythm and meter. How in spite of these limitations he became such a great lyricist and musician is a wonder. The only explanation is that he was an extraordinary genius, which made the conditions applicable to ordinary mortals irrelevant for him. This much at least we know beyond a doubt that just as he became a great poet without the benefit of a formal education, he also turned into a great musician without any formal musical education or training. Like Tagore, he, too, had learnt his music mostly by listening. In a way this helped to introduce a certain distinctiveness in his songs. He found and made his own way in music, instead of treading in the way that a musical education might have shown.

When he was 25 or 26, at a time when he was already well established as a poet, he trained in classical music for a while under an ustad called Zamir Uddin. This ustad specialised in thumri. But Nazrul wrote many different kinds of songs. The tunes to which he set his songs were based on a wide array of ragas and raginis. There is no clue as to where he might have picked up the familiarity with classical music that the songs reflect. Though he did learn to sing ghazals while in Karachi, it was not under any ustad that he did so. The other kind of songs that he is known to have sung at that phase was Rabindrasangeet. In this, too, he was not coached by a tutor. He learnt mostly by listening. We know that after moving to Calcutta he sang in the company of his friends, but no one has said that he took lessons in singing. Moreover, in the first few years of his literary career he neither wrote songs, nor composed. He wrote poems. And then all at once he became a musician overnight, because he needed money. This was an extraordinary episode in the history of Bengali music.

He was initially influenced a great deal by Tagore. That is perhaps why the aesthetic experience of many of his songs is dominated by words.

The initial songs even show the influence of Tagore's four-stanza structure. But once he became seriously drawn to classical music, he started writing many different kinds of songs. No longer did he confine himself to the four-stanza division. Besides, it was not *dhrupad* but khayal and thumri that had a particular influence on him. Even tappa did not influence him to any great extent. The more Tagore advanced in age, the more he shed the rigidities of classical music and created his own melodies. On the other hand, the more Nazrul's familiarity with classical music grew with the passing years, the more he embraced its bounds, a few exceptions apart.

He differed from Tagore in another important way. Tagore gave equal importance to words and tunes in his songs. Yet, if there was any one that he placed above the other, then it was surely words. Nazrul's stress, on the contrary, was clearly on the melodies rather than the words. And once he immersed himself in the world of music, he moved away from poetry, and he himself admitted as much. Indeed, he ceased to be a poet and turned into a musician, a lyricist and composer at the same time. Upon a close scrutiny, many of his songs give the impression that he wrote the words to give body to the tunes instead of creating the tunes to fit the words. The observation of course does not quite apply to the songs that he wrote on commercial demand after joining Gramophone Company. Most of such songs were nothing more than commercial productions, they did not turn out to be works of art in their combination of words and tunes. There were exceptions—heartfelt inspiration sometimes endowed his commercial songs with a different kind of beauty.

Carrying the comparison with Tagore further, we might also say that they were artists of very different tastes. Nazrul wrote few devotional songs apart from his formalised religious songs, and these were different from the songs that Tagore wrote exploring thoughts on divinity. Nazrul wrote songs on gods and goddesses, on Krishna, Kali and Mohammad. But he did not write songs expressing love for a formless divinity in the way that Tagore did. Yet his songs, too, whether Islamic, kirtan or Shyamasangeet, reflect a deep faith. It was this faith and a powerful religious emotion that brought him close to the hearts of the ordinary people of Bengal. This is particularly true of his Islamic songs. He made music acceptable to Muslim society with his Islamic songs. As for his Shyamasangeet, it can be said that though many others had written songs in this genre both before and after, Nazrul's songs are the greatest ever.

His love songs also clearly show how different he was from Tagore. In songs such as '*The black bee is here, open your petals o rose*' or '*Oarsman slowly row your boat*' love is superseded by lust. We may in this context look at the words in '*Oarsman slowly row your boat*':

Alas, you have sailed midstream on the plea of taking me to the bank
How do I resist the overflowing stream of my youthful desires?
The restless wind steals the covering of my shame
You seek to destroy me, you naughty one
I fall at your feet, my friend, I am another man's wife.
The river is rough, my body is rocked,
I am drunk in body and soul, my eyes are dreamy
The river is stormy, the winds rage, the boat rocks
How do I hush my heaving heart
Now water fills up the narrow vessel, and I a helpless girl!

A song like this, and the kind of taste that it reflects, could not have come from Tagore's pen, nor from Dwijendralal's. Even Atulprasad or Rajanikanta could not have written this song. No one writing before the 1920s could perhaps come up with a song like this. To use a counterexample, we might say that love is helplessly defeated by lust in this Nazrul song, whereas love is sublimated and goes beyond the body in Tagore's songs—even his embraces do not quite have a flesh-and-blood quality in them.

Three kinds of songs among the many different kinds that Nazrul wrote deserve particular mention—the *ragpradhan* songs, based on classical ragas, ghazals and *kavyageeti.* His *ragpradhans* are better described as songs in broken Hindustani rather than Bengali. In the 1930s these songs were made popular by singers such as Jnanendraprasad Goswami, Bhishmadev Chattopadhyay, Tarapada Chakraborty and even Sachin Dev Burman. A close look will show that though these songs beautifully bring out the ragas and raginis on which they are based, their words are not very compelling. It might even seem as if the writer's aim was to build an edifice of melodies on a foundation of commonplace words. Often, the singers who sang these songs also seemed to pay scant attention to their words. To use a counter example: Nazrul wrote the song '*Shunyo e buke pakhi mor aay phire aay*' from a depth of anguished feeling; the song sprang from personal experience; but the sharp pain of loss in its lines is hardly reflected in Jnanendraprasad Goswami's rendering of the song, it is rather the melody that stands out. Yet many years later when Ajoy Chakraborty sang the song, the words took on a different life and meaning.

Nazrul moved effortlessly across different branches of Hindustani music. Using his familiarity with Hindustani music, he created some extraordinary songs that have no parallel in Bengali music. A song like, say, '*Sakhi, bandhlo, bandhlo jhulania*', is not only one of a kind in Bengali music in tune and form, the way the words are used also set it apart as an unusual creation. The romantic atmosphere that Nazrul is able to create in this song through poetic devices such as the rhyming line-ends is the mark of a great artist. Admittedly, however, though Nazrul wrote a few thousand songs, there are not too many songs that match up to this standard. The words are weak in many of his songs and the rhythm even weaker.

Notwithstanding the novelty that he introduced though his *ragpradhan* songs, his greatest contribution to Bengali music consists of his ghazals. Ghazals are extremely popular in north India. Ghazals arrived in Calcutta in the 19th century along with the exiled Nawab of Oudh, Wajed Ali Shah. No one, however, attempted to adopt ghazals into the Bengali musical tradition in the way that Nidhubabu embraced tappa by giving it a Bengali contour. This was the task that Nazrul took up. He started singing ghazals in the company of friends after his return from his army posting. And then one day he ended up writing ghazals in Bengali. Not only was he a pioneer in showing the way for Bengali ghazals, he was the greatest writer of ghazals in the language. There was a time when his ghazals acquired an immense popularity. It is said that the reach of his ghazals spread beyond the city into the villages and small market towns of Bengal.

Some of the songs of the last phase of Nazrul's creative life must also get particular mention in the history of the evolution of Bengali music. These songs have become known as *kavyageeti* ('songs in verse'). Songs such as '*Tumi sundor tai cheye thaki priyo*' are important because they belong to a category that immediately precedes what we know as modern Bengali songs. These were the songs out of which 'modern' songs were born. The structure is not in fact very different from that of Tagore songs, in both tune and words. A major difference, however, was this: many of these songs were set to tune not by Nazrul himself but by his colleagues at Gramophone Company, such as, for instance, Kamal Dasgupta. This practice initiated a major shift in the history of Bengali music. The function of writing songs and that of composing music for them became separated. Nazrul subsequently composed music for many of his own songs, but it was with his songs that the new tradition was established. This turned out to be both good and bad for Bengali music.

Nazrul became famous for yet another kind of song—his inspirational and patriotic songs. He did not actually write too many of them. Yet songs like '*Kaaraar oi lauha kapaat*' are in a class by themselves in the history of Bengali music. Tagore had made the beauty of nature pre-eminent in his patriotic songs. Nazrul however has few patriotic songs of that type. He does not have too many nature songs, either. Notwithstanding their small number, however, his inspirational and patriotic songs acquired immense popularity. The need for such songs grew in proportion to the strength of the freedom movement in the 1930s and 1940s. In response to this demand, other song-writers of the 1940s also wrote patriotic songs.

Nazrul is the last notable milestone in the history of Bengali songs. The tradition of musicians who were at once lyricists and composers slowly dried up after Nazrul. Only a couple of names such as Salil Choudhury come to the mind, individuals who both wrote songs and composed music for them. But none of them introduced new streams of music in the way that Tagore, Dwijendralal, Atulprasad or Nazrul did. Nor did they write very many songs.

Songs became commercial commodities from the time of Nazrul. As we have already mentioned, he became a musician in pursuit of commercial success. It is doubtful whether he would otherwise forsake the world of poetry in order to become a full-time musician. Gramophone Company was established in Calcutta in 1901-02; songs started getting recorded on a commercial basis after another seven or eight years. In consequence, a demand arose for many different kinds of songs, including local and religious songs. And hence also the need to write songs to meet this demand. From this time, too, arose the need for bands of instrumentalists to turn songs into attractive commercial commodities. It would not be unreasonable to suppose that a market for music records did not spring up as soon as Gramophone Company was founded. It took nearly two decades for this market to develop.

Calcutta Radio was also established around this time—in 1928. The era of Bengali talkies started in 1931. These three media together produced a much increased demand for Bengali songs in the 1930s. Nazrul to an extent met this demand by writing a varied array of songs ranging from lusty working men's songs to religious compositions. To an extent, but not entirely. So in the 1930s many other lyricists, composers, trainers and associated professionals gravitated towards the gramophone and cinema. Then, all too suddenly, Nazrul's voice fell silent in 1942. Yet the demand was still there, and was if anything, progressively increasing. In this environment a number of mediocre lyricists and composers took on the task of filling the vacuum.

Among those who entered the musical scene in the 1940s were Shailen Ray, Ajoy Bhattacharya, Bani Kumar, Subodh Purakayastha, Anil Bhattacharya and Pranab Roy. Poet Premendra Mitra and the writer Sajanikanta Das also participated in the work of writing songs. These song-writers accepted Tagore's four-stanza structure. The words and themes they borrowed from Tagore and Nazrul. However they might have been as musicians, the task did not prove too difficult for them because they had no need to write the music for their songs. To fulfill this function came forward men like Dilipkumar Ray, Raichand Borhal, Krishna Chandra Dey, Sachin Dev Burman, Kamal Dasgupta, Sudhir Lal Chakraborty, Himangshu Datta, Anil Bagchi and Anupam Ghatak. These men also had an easier task than the earlier composers, for they did not have to write the songs. Most of them based their tunes on Tagore's four-stanza structure. They even followed Tagore's frequent habit of using softer tunes for the *sanchari.* Tagore's innovation of mixing up ragas and raginis also made their work easier.

A bunch of male and female singers came forward to sing the new Bengali songs that were produced during the 1930s and the early 1940s by the combined efforts of lyricists and composers, and some of them were also composers. Singers such as Sachin Dev Burman, Krishna Chandra Dey, Kamal Dasgupta, Pankaj Mullick and Santosh Sengupta belonged to this category. Most singers, however, were happy with just their singing roles. Kundanlal Saigal, Kanan Devi, Angurbala, Indubala, Kamala Jharia, Jaganmoy Mitra and Shaila Devi were chiefly singers. Just after this crop of singers arrived Hemanta Mukhopadhyay. He, too, was chiefly a singer, though he also composed music for many songs in the 1950s and 1960s.

Krishna Chandra Dey, Pankaj Kumar Mullick and Hemanta Mukhopadhyay were extremely popular singers in their time. In one very important way, they differed from their fellow singers—they possessed deep voices. Debabrata Biswas also found himself a place in this category, though he sang mainly Tagore songs. These great charioteers of Bengali music made the deep voice fashionable and normative. In fact they established it as the ideal of the male singing voice and thus transformed the definition of what constituted a good singing voice.

The 1940s were a decade of strong political movements. There was the Quit India movement against the colonial rulers on the one hand, and the communist movement on the other. A new tradition of writing *gana-sangeet*, or 'people's music', started under the impact of these two movements. The people's theatre movement was also a part of this tradition. Though known as people's theatre, the movement drew much of its life from its songs. A number of popular songs got written at this time which were about contemporary politics and life's harsh realities. In form and content, the songs of this new tradition were noticeably different from the tradition of romantic songs that Tagore had founded. In this environment, Jyotirindra Maitra, Salil Choudhury, Hemanga Biswas, Mohini Choudhury and other lyricists wrote very different kind of songs. These lyricists took forward Nazrul's tradition of songs of awakening. Some of these songs became very popular, indeed. Songs such as, for instance, '*Hein Samalo!*' It was Salil Choudhury who started a whole new tradition of songs in the late 1940s. A bunch of songs, including '*Ganyer bondhu*' and '*Runner*', sung by Hemanta Mukhopadhyay and set to tune by Salil Choudhury were considered as constituting an atypical tradition in the history of Bengali music.

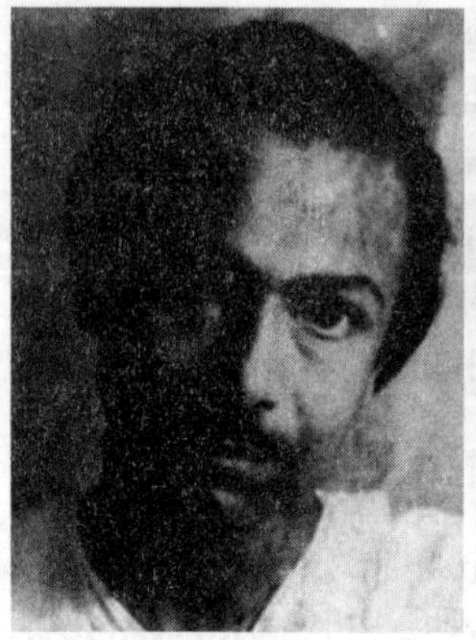
Salil Choudhury

Hemanta Mukhopadhyay

Sandhya Mukhopadhyay

Yet this tradition of 'people's music' did not turn out to be very long-lasting. A major reason for this was the departure of the British colonial rulers. Some songs consequently lost relevance and overnight lost their popular appeal. That apart, the greatest music writer of this tradition, Salil Choudhury, and its greatest singer, Hemanta Mukhopadhyay, left the world of Bengali music and took their talents to the Bombay film industry.

The 1950s brought new life to the world of cinema. It was love that dominated the new movies that got made in this phase. Many romantic songs were consequently written to meet the demand created by the film industry. Apart from the lyricists who had successfully produced songs for the 1940s, others such as Gouriprasanna Majumdar, Pulak Bandyopadhyay and Shyamal Gupta came forward to write songs in this phase. New composers arrived, too. Among them were Sudhin Dasgupta, Dilip Sarkar and Prabir Majumdar. The romantic cinema of the 1950s, in particular the films starring Uttam Kumar and Suchitra Sen, helped to make modern Bengali songs very popular indeed. Some extraordinary singers, apart from of course Hemanta Mukhopadhyay, also made their appearance at this time—Sandhya Mukhopadhyay, Satinath Mukhopadhyay, Manna Dey, Shyamal Mitra, Manabendra Mukhopadhyay, Dhananjay Bhattacharjee. This unprecedented success of Bengali music drew even an artist of Lata Mangeshkar's calibre to Bengal. Asha Bhonsle, Kishore Kumar, Talat Mahmud and even Mohammad Rafi, notwithstanding his extremely poor Bengali pronunciation, were drawn to the world of Bengali music. This was the time when the modern Bengali song found itself riding

Lata Mangeshkar

Sachin Dev Burman

Satyajit Ray

a rising wave of popularity, helped in part by innovative tunes, in part by racy lyrics, and also to an extent by movie plots and situations and the charismatic images of individual actors. Slowly, and without anyone noticing, the songs of Tagore and Nazrul were carried away in this flood, far from the hearts and minds of ordinary listeners.

There were at this time many experiments and innovations aimed at introducing variety and novelty in music. The Bombay influence was of course a powerful one, but folk and Western music also impacted the new developments. A certain kind of classical-influenced songs also acquired popularity. In this environment Satyajit Ray produced new kinds of songs. The influence of Tagore songs, folk music and the classical tradition is evident in the songs that he composed for his films. Yet the one aspect that remained unchanged in Bengali music was the predominance of words in Bengali songs. The tradition that Tagore, and to an extent Nazrul, had brought into being, of a musical experience dominated by words and their meaning, remained entrenched for decades.

The spread of education was speeded up after Partition. Radio, too, became far more popular than before and reached more people. New radio centres were set up to meet governance needs. New songs, in turn, had to be produced to meet the needs of radio. Music was not always very well received among the Muslims of East Bengal. Many of them in fact saw the act of listening to music as blasphemous or anti-religious. Now, however, music started gaining popularity even in East Bengal. It was chiefly Nazrul and

Abbas Uddin who made music popular among Muslims in the early 1930s. Before that, Kasem Mullick was constrained to sing as K. Mullick. Even in the 1940s Talat Mahmud recorded his songs as Tapan Kumar.

In sum, all kinds of songs gained greater reach after Partition. But it was local and folk music that particularly grew in popularity. Men like Abbas Uddin and Jasim Uddin contributed a great deal to this development. Abdul Alim also played a role in making the Bhatiali popular. Folk songs became popular in West Bengal too. Baul songs were in particular made popular by Purnadas Baul. Nirmalendu Choudhury made various folk traditions popular by blending modern styles with them.

The East Pakistan policy was to stoke communal polarisation and patronise Muslim culture. This led to administrative opposition to the broadcasting of Tagore songs on radio. Nevertheless, since few records were actually available in the 1950s, Tagore songs were played on radio in programmes of recorded music. In the 1960s, however, the government started actively opposing Tagore songs while at the same time promoting Nazrul songs. As we have already mentioned, the songs of both Tagore and Nazrul had somewhat lost their sheen in the 1950s in the face of the rising popularity of modern Bengali songs. Nazrul songs almost entirely lost currency in West Bengal. His name was generally left unmentioned when his Shyamasangeet and other devotional songs were played on Calcutta Radio. It is strange to think how within a decade the songs of Nazrul, which had dominated Bengali music, suddenly lost popularity.

In East Pakistan, on the other hand, Nazrul started receiving official patronage after some initial indifference. So though there were not too many artists who sang his songs, Dhaka Radio started broadcasting them in earnest. Calcutta Radio could not for long remain unresponsive to this flood of Nazrul songs being broadcast from Dhaka. Some Nazrul songs therefore began to be broadcast by Calcutta Radio as well. Firoza Begum helped this effort in the early 1960s. Then in 1964 HMV came up with a long-playing record of Nazrul songs at the initiative of Santosh Sengupta. It was a huge commercial success. After this Nazrul songs started regaining their popularity, a trend in which artists such as Manabendra Mukhopadhyay played a role. Despite his rich promise, Manabendra had not been able to survive the competition in the market for modern Bengali songs. He firmly embraced Nazrul songs, which thus staged a comeback from oblivion and near death.

Firoza Begum

Likewise, the acclaim and acceptability that Tagore songs have had in East Bengal also have a history. For a number of reasons Tagore songs did not always hold much appeal for the Muslim community in East Bengal. In any case Muslims considered it sinful to listen to and enjoy music. Besides, many of them had been unable to accept Tagore as one of their own. As we said in the chapter 'Bengali Culture in the Twentieth Century', even the Pakistani government took a position against the promotion of Tagore songs. But the situation started changing rapidly after the language movement of 1952 owing to political and cultural factors. When the Muslims of East Bengal put their linguistic identity above their religious one, the non-Muslim poets and writers of Bengali literature not only became acceptable to them but were also particularly cherished and held dear. Thus Tagore songs found a space for themselves in East Bengal and in the 1960s they became very popular indeed. (I have extensively discussed this in my *Rabindrabishwe Purbabanga: Purbabange Rabindranath*, 'East Bengal in Tagore's World: Tagore in East Bengal'.) It was in this cultural environment that the people of Bangladesh chose Tagore's '*Amar Sonar Bangla*' as the national anthem of their future state even before Bangladesh became independent.

Bengali music took a new turn once again in the 1970s. Technological progress was responsible for this. The cassette recorder was now in the market, pushing up the demand for music in practically every home. Innumerable singers, composers and lyricists came forward in an attempt to meet this demand. It is hard to say how much of their efforts were driven by inspiration.

And in fact they are better described as professional artists. Many of them chose music as a means of livelihood. That apart, none of them were artists of the stature of Tagore, Dwijendralal, Atulprasad, Rajanikanta or Nazrul Islam. Rather, they were all craftsmen of middling abilities.

We have so far roughly sketched the history of Bengali songs. Songs have been the most important aspect of music in Bengali cultural history. Needless to say, however, that the history of music in Bengal was not limited to Bengali songs. A tradition of classical music, both vocal and instrumental, also always existed alongside. But it is not possible to reconstruct that history anymore. We can only tell, from the evidence of medieval Bengali poetry and late medieval terracotta slabs, which musical instruments were used in Bengal. The string instruments that are known of are the veena, tanpura, sarangi, and, going by 18th century slabs, the *behala*, modified from the Portuguese viola. There are also images of an instrument with seven strings, but we do not know what it was called. Several leather-covered percussion instruments are known of. These are the *karha, nakarha, dhak,* dhol, *srikhol, mridanga, dugi-tabla, tasa, dompho, jagajhampa, khonjuri, domru,* etc. The bamboo lute or windpipe was always there in Bengal. Another musical instrument made of bamboo and belonging entirely to Bengal was the *ektara*, a single-stringed instrument. Singers play on just the one single string as they sing. Yet, when Bauls and *bairagi*s (Vaishnava ascetics) sing to the accompaniment of the *ektara*, they create an uplifting aesthetic experience of an extraordinary and simple beauty. The *dotara* (double-stringed instrument) also belongs to Bengal. The Bhatiali and Bhaoiya songs are unimaginable with the *dotara*. That is why Bhaoiya songs are often also called *dotara* songs. Another musical instrument typical of Bengal is the *sarinda*. Though bearing some similarities with the *sarangi*, the *sarinda* is built in the villages of Bengal with entirely indigenous and local material. It is played by village artists, too.

The only known history of the pursuit of classical music by Bengalis lies between the 19th and 20th centuries. We have noted that people from far and wide had converged in 19th century Calcutta in search of their fortunes. Non-Bengali musicians, both Hindus and Muslims, were also among these fortune-seekers. Some of them were vocalists, and some were instrumentalists. Right from the start of the 19th century, these artists were part of an attempt at nurturing classical music in Calcutta. We have already mentioned how this attempt gained momentum through the efforts of a handful of wealthy families.

Among the Bengali classical singers who became famous after Nidhubabu and Kali Mirza, the names of Vishnu Chakraborty and Kaliprasad Chakraborty may well be the first to pop up in one's mind. They were well known *dhrupad* artists. They had trained under Hosnu Khan, Delwar Khan and Miyan Meeran. Jadu Bhatta trained first under his father in Burdwan and later under Ganganarayan Chattopadhyay in Calcutta. But it was to north India that he went for further studies in music. He turned into an extraordinary *dhrupad* artist. He not only sang Hindi *dhrupad* songs but also Bengali *dhrupad* that he himself wrote. Both Bankimchandra Chattopadhyay and Rabindranath Tagore were tutored by him. Tagore wrote about Jadu Bhatta's Bengali *dhrupad* songs that these had certain distinctive qualities that were absent in Hindi *dhrupad* songs. Kshetramohan Bandyopadhyay learnt to play the veena from Lakshmiprasad Mishra of Benaras. Krishnadhan Bandyopadhyay learnt to play the sitar in Gwalior. Kartikeyachandra Ray was tutored in khayal by Hochchu Khan. Kaliprasanna Bandyopadhyay acquired remarkable skill in playing the sitar, *surbahar* and *nastaranga*. In sum, quite a few Bengali classical musicians made their appearance in the second half of the 19th century. That gives us some idea of the pursuit of vocal and instrumental music by Bengalis.

The territories of the Nawab of Oudh Wajed Ali Shah had been annexed by Lord Dalhousie, who exiled the deposed ruler to Calcutta. The Nawab himself was a musician. He could sing and play musical instruments, and he even danced well. The Nawab along with the musicians of his court had made the thumri popular. Yet, he made an even greater contribution to music by patronising musicians. There were some 200 salaried singers, instrumentalists and dancers in his Calcutta court. Among them were exponents of the *dhrupad*, khayal, thumri and tappa. And of course there were many instrumentalists. The coming together of so many classical musicians created an extraordinary cultural environment in Calcutta. Indeed, no other Indian city or royal court of the time had a comparable convergence of musicians. At a cursory assessment, it might seem as if these non-Bengali musicians had no contribution in Bengal's history of music. But that is not true. They might not have made a direct contribution. But it was they who trained the Bengali musicians who went on to create history in Bengali music. Even in the 20th century the famous Bengali classical musicians we hear of received their education under non-Bengali musicians. Indeed, the city of Calcutta drew famous classical musicians even in the 20th century. Many stayed back permanently in the city, and some even made their homes in mofussil towns. One such musician was the extraordinary sitarist Emdad Khan. He became music tutor at the home of the zamindar of Gouripur.

It must be admitted however that no classical vocalist of all-India fame emerged from among the Bengalis. Bengalis produced instrumentalists. And the musician who played the role of pioneer in this genre was Alauddin Khan. In a parallel trajectory with that of Nazrul, who became a great poet and musician by dint of sheer genius against heavy odds and despite being born in an extremely poor, rural family, Alauddin Khan was also born in a poor, uneducated, rural family and realised his potential in spite of many obstacles in his way. He must have also faced religious orthodoxy working against him. For, music is often said to be prohibited in Islam, particularly instrumental music. Yet it was instrumental music that he practised.

Modern India did not perhaps have a greater musician. Not only was he one of the greatest instrumentalists of the 20th century, his was a many-sided genius, which is another thing that sets him apart. Many artists had become famous through their skill in playing more than one instrument of the same kind, such as the sitar and the *surbahar*, but Alauddin Khan could play many different kinds of instruments. The two instruments that he played with particular dexterity were the sarod and the *behala*, two very different instruments with very different methods of playing them. But Alauddin Khan was not happy playing just these two instruments. He also played the veena, *surashringar*, the lute (*banshi*), *shehnai*, cornet, clarionet and many other instruments including even the tabla, *pakhwaj* and dhol. He was also a proficient singer. The rare genius that he was, he innovated quite a few ragas and raginis. He even invented some musical instruments on his own.

Alauddin Khan faced many hostilities when as a young man he was trying to learn music. Many ustads refused to accept him as a student. There were also some who imparted a general training but would not share the particularities that marked their gharana—a particular musical style practised by a particular clan. Even his greatest teacher, Wazir Khan, was initially unwilling to teach him the style of his gharana. But after his son died he decided to pass on his knowledge to Alauddin Khan. Alauddin Khan was pained by this miserliness on the part of musicians in sharing their knowledge. This was why he threw open the doors of musical education to all after joining the court of the princely state of Maihar, now in Madhya Pradesh. Especially for the poor, he arranged both musical training and food. It was with these artists from very ordinary families that he set up his Maihar Band. With his musical pedagogy so generously available, many future musicians were able to take advantage of it—Ravi Shankar, Timir Baran, Nikhil Bandyopadhyay, Pannalal Ghosh, Shyam Ganguly, Neeharbindu Choudhury, Indranil Bhattacharjee and many others. As for his own family, his younger brother Ayat Ali Khan, son Ali Akbar Khan, and grandsons Bahadur Hossein Khan and Ashish Khan were all his students.

A separate gharana centred in Gouripur also took shape under Emdad Khan's leadership. No outstanding instrumentalist really emerged from among the disciples of Emdad Khan himself or of his son Enayet Khan. But Emdad Khan, Enayet Khan and Vilayet Khan left a significant contribution in classical music.

Indian classical music has now spread far beyond Indian shores. A close look at the phenomenon shows that this has been made possible almost entirely through the efforts of Alauddin Khan's disciples. Vilayet Khan also played a role. We might say, therefore, that classical music played a crucial role in the cultural history of Bengalis and also that Bengalis have made an outstanding contribution in the nurturing and spread of Indian classical music.

Timir Baran deserves special mention because he played a pioneering role in making the orchestra popular. He trained under Alauddin Khan to play the sarod and then followed his ustad's example by setting up a band with others of his family, in Calcutta. Later he joined Uday Shankar's dance troupe. The orchestra music that he was exposed to during his visits to Europe inspired and influenced him. In 1934 he left Uday Shankar's troupe and started working with the theatrical company Calcutta Art Players. He composed a number of original pieces of music, such as his orchestra composition based on Tagore's *Kshudito Pashan* ('Hungry Stones'). Krishnadhan Bandyopadhyay, Kshetramohan Bandyopadhyay, Kaliprasanna Bandyopadhyay and others also experimented with orchestra music. But there was no one in Bengal who came anywhere close to the kind of work that Timir Baran did.

The definition of 'sangeet' includes dance along with vocal and instrumental music. The sculptures and terracotta slabs in temple walls indicate that dance was widely practised in Bengal. Yet Bengalis do not seem to have made a very remarkable contribution to dance, or at least there is nothing to show that they did until the 19th century. It is hard to tell why. It is known that women were required to observe purdah in the 18th and 19th centuries. It is however not known whether the practice existed in the Middle Ages or if it was as rigidly observed as in the later centuries. There were many women in the harems of the sultans, but history gives no information to indicate that women gave dance performances in the courts of the sultans. Indeed, dance did not find much currency among Bengalis even when music thrived so spectacularly in 19th century Calcutta. The hordes of *baiji*s or courtesans who thronged Calcutta in response to the newly created demands of urban life had all come from other provinces. In the second half of the century, though, Bengali actresses acquired some dance skills, thanks to the arrival of professional theatre. But apart from Kusumkumari and Sadhana Bose, no famous dancer emerged from among them. (I have discussed this in greater detail in the chapter 'Bengali Women and their Culture'.)

It is in the 20th century that we come across the initiative and contribution of two individuals in promoting dance—Tagore and Uday Shankar. It is my belief that both of them had found their inspiration in the West. Tagore made the Manipuri dance form popular and also developed a new dance style on the basis of kathak, though he himself did not dance. Uday Shankar, on the other hand, was a trained dancer and he introduced a new style of dancing by assimilating what he saw in the West with Indian dance traditions. What is now called choreography started in India with Uday Shankar. His disciples, too, kept up the tradition after him. Music had once been unacceptable to Muslims, and dance even more so. More, because dance is linked to expressions of feminine beauty. A few Muslim young men had however come forward to learn dance in the initial years. One of them was Bulbul Choudhury, another was Gauhar Jamil.

No dance gharanas developed in Bengal in the 19th century, notwithstanding the emergence of a few dancers. Nor did dance play any very significant role in Bengali culture. In the 20th century however, probably thanks to Tagore's efforts, dance became acceptable among educated and elite urban families. Though women do not usually dance after marriage, many young girls take dance lessons, just as they take music lessons. Besides, the needs of cinema and professional theatre have also made dance acceptable within an ever-widening circle.

THEATRE AND CINEMA

Excellence in drama did not happen in India very early, and certainly not in Bengal, unlike in Europe where drama flourished from ancient times. Kalidasa was the only brilliant exception in India. In discussing his and other ancient Indian plays, however, it must be kept in mind that these constituted dramatic literature rather than drama as it was understood in Europe, which could be enacted on stage. Nonetheless, we have to say that a dramatic tradition did take shape in ancient India, at a time when drama had not yet developed in Bengal. Nor was it possible for it to develop. For, the Bengali language had not yet emerged. Bengalis did not produce any well known dramatist even after the Bengali language acquired its own distinctiveness in the Middle Ages. We may say that there was no tradition of drama in the early Bengali language. Even when literary writing started being produced in Bengali, the sultans did not encourage the writing of drama. They were, for religious reasons, hostile to drama in the way that they were also opposed to music and art.

Following Jaydev's example, Borhu Chandidas wrote *Srikrishnakeertan* in the 14th-15th century, another 'musical', or *palagan*, as it was called—a series of songs assigned to characters in a narrative. The theme of *Gita Govinda* and *Srikrishnakeertan* is more or less the same, the love of Radha and Krishna. In the *palagan* form, each singer sang the songs assigned to a particular character, and the performance was held in a kind of open theatre. A stage was not required, and there were no dialogues. The device of distributing the songs among the performances lent a dramatic quality to the performance, and this also had a visible dimension. But this was still far from drama.

It was not as if Bengalis were not aware of the greater effectiveness of enacting something before an audience rather than just saying or reciting it. The inclination to act is also a natural human tendency. That is why Chaitanyadev in the early 16th century got the Radha-Krishna story enacted through songs. From *Chaitanyacharitamrita* we know that he himself took part in the acting, in the role of Rukmini. His *goswamis*, who witnessed his interest in drama, later wrote quite a few books in the dramatic form. Most of those books of course were written in Sanskrit. There were also Bengali books written in the catechism form, as questions and answers, called *karhcha.* But though constructed in the form of dialogues, these were not plays at all.

Bits of dialogue and acting added to the early *palagan* gave rise to the tradition of the *jatra* in medieval Bengal. But the *jatra* also mainly consisted of songs, which is why it was also called *jatragan, gan* being the Bengali word for song. This *jatragan* did not even have any resemblance with what we now know as *jatra* (rural theatre with loud histrionics), let alone having any similarities with drama. The modern *jatra* is largely a product of the influence of drama. The *jatra* has in turn influenced drama. Whatever that may be, until the 18th century *jatra* largely resembled the old *palagan.* The performance was interspersed with rhymes/poems, and also bits that were almost prose-like. There were more characters than the old *palagan* would have, and greater scope for acting. A narrator, called the *adhikari*, held together the plotline and filled the gaps. That apart, another kind of dramatics started during the 17th and 18th centuries, practised by what were known as *leto* or *neto* groups. The name is derived from *natuke*, the Bengali word for 'dramatic'.

The drama emerged during British rule and under the influence of English literature and English theatre. A few thousand Englishmen lived in Calcutta in the middle of the 18th century. In the provincial town that Calcutta then was, there were few avenues of entertainment for them. A theatre was built in the city to fulfil this need, even before the British defeated Siraj-ud-Daulah and seized power. This theatre later became known as Old Playhouse. Later, in 1775, the East India Company allowed a fairly well-equipped theatre to be built not very far from Writers Building. Though initially this theatre was in some financial distress, in the 1780s it started to run regularly and well under the management of Francis Rundell. The price of tickets was raised to range between one gold *mohar* and eight. Rundell got some actresses from London to join his theatre to make it more attractive. The theatre survived until 1808. From the advertisements published in Hicky's *Bengal Gazette*, the semi-government publication *Calcutta Gazette*, *Mirror* and other contemporary magazines, we find that most of the plays staged in this theatre, written by local 'playwrights', were pantomimes or humorous plays, though some plays by well known playwrights were also staged. A band of instrumentalists was also set up for this theatre.

An even better-equipped theatre called Chowringhee Theatre became popular with the English society of Calcutta in the early 19th century. This theatre ran from 1808 to 1839. Professional actresses acted in the female roles in this theatre, but most of the male roles were played by amateur actors. It was quite a big theatre for its time—it could seat nearly a thousand viewers. A dramatic performance was held every week.

Let alone writing plays, it is extremely doubtful if any of the native Bengalis even watched a play in the theatre of the English. We cannot also be sure whether they would be allowed to enter even if they wanted to watch. In this situation a Russian living in Calcutta – he was Gerasim Lebedoff – did something unbelievable. He had arrived in Calcutta in 1787. He found a good tutor in the city to teach him Bengali. He had learnt some other Indian languages, too, including Hindi. He even wrote a Bengali grammar, though it was not published. His Hindi grammar was however published. It is from the introduction to his Hindi grammar that we learn about his incredible feat. He wrote that he had written two Bengali plays based on English originals in 1795. One of these was *The Disguise* (written by Richard Paul Jodrell), *Kalponik Sangbadol* in the Bengali version; the other was *Love is the Best Doctor* (written by Moliere)—*Prem-i Shrestha Chikitsak* in the Bengali version.

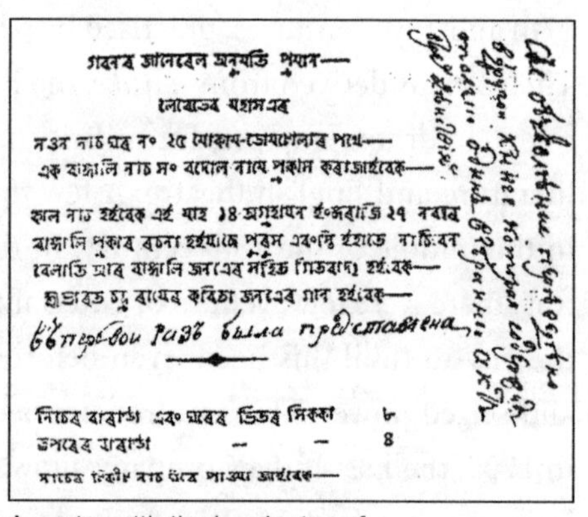

A poster with the handnotes of Gerasim Lebedoff

What was even more extraordinary and astounding than the fact that he wrote the plays in Bengali was that he managed to stage *Kalponik Sangbadol.*

His Bengali tutor, Goloknath Das, fetched native actors and actresses to act in his play. It was not however possible for Lebedoff to stage this play in the Englishmen's theatre. He therefore spent three months building a stage in the Radhabajar neighbourhood, where he lived. This theatre could seat some 200 people. He conducted rehearsals to get his actors and actresses ready for the performance. On November 27, 1795, the first Bengali play went on stage. It was staged once again on March 21 in the following year. On both occasions his theatre was packed, which shows that the performance was quite successful. Yet Lebedoff did not make any attempt to stage his second play. Nor did he try to write any other play in Bengali. In 1801 he left Calcutta.

For many years after Lebedoff's solitary effort, no one, native or European, took any initiative to stage plays in the Bengali language. Yet the English theatre and Lebedoff's enterprise were a bit like birdsong just before daybreak. Bengali society still took some time to stage its own plays, but it could not forever continue to slumber. The first time that Bengalis organised a dramatic performance was in 1831. Prasanna Kumar Tagore played a pioneering role in this. A number of factors made it possible for him to do so. For one, he had money to spend on the stage performance. For another, he had an English education and so was familiar with English drama. He was also young, about 29 years old at that time or maybe slightly older. He set up an organisation called the Hindu Theatre. From contemporary magazines and journals we learn that whole or parts of English plays were dramatised at the initiative of this organisation. But in December 1831 this theatre staged *Bikramurvashi* in Bengali. The last act of *Julius Caesar* was also staged alongside the performance. *Bikramurvashi* does not seem to have been a proper play, not at least what we understand to be a play. Sukumar Sen infers that it was more like the old *jatrapala*. The report in *Samachar Chandrika* seems to corroborate this assessment. Magazine reports tell us that the 'play' ran successfully and got its audience interested in dramatic form.

Apart from the efforts of the Hindu Theatre, there are reports of another notable dramatic performance around that time, in October 1835. The Vidya-Sundar story was staged at Shyambazar in Calcutta at the initiatve of Nabin Chandra Basu. This too was a *jatrapala*, rather than a play. From the scant information that survives, we learn that a stage was erected for the performance and women, and not men, acted in the female roles. Even the names of two of these actresses are known—Radhamoni and Jaydurga. Radhamoni played Vidya. A lakh was supposedly spent on the show. This interest in the enacting of the *jatrapala* later drew Bengalis to drama.

These bold attempts in the 1830s notwithstanding, dramatic performance in the Bengali language did not immediately strike root. One reason for this was surely that the staging of plays was an expensive affair. And among the wealthy there were not too many men such as Prasanna Kumar Tagore or Nabin Basu who were seriously interested in drama. Another important reason was that no original Bengali play had been written yet. But the Hindu College students were reading English plays, and they were required to do so by the syllabus that was followed. There are also reports that many well known individuals of the time, including Ramtanu Lahiri and Rajendralal Mitra, who, with the help of Hindu College and other institutions, acted in fragments of plays by Shakespeare. It is also known that in 1850 the students of a college in Calcutta now and then put up performances of English plays. All this shows that an interest in watching dramatic performances and in acting in them was slowly growing among Bengalis. But still no Bengali play was written before the 1850s.

We noted in the chapter 'Bengali Language and Literature' that the first Bengali play was published in 1852. Once this first play was published, a number of plays, both long and short, got written in the same decade. However limited these plays might have been in terms of their literary merit, they served to open the doors on dramatic performance. Some reformist plays in particular stoked strong interest in the form. The first proper stage performance of a Bengali play took place in January 1857. The initiative for this first dramatic performance was taken by a wealthy man—Ashutosh Deb. Nanda Kumar Ray's *Abhijnan Shakuntalam* was performed at his house on January 30. The second dramatic performance took place at the home of another rich man—Ramjay Basak. The play that was staged here was Ramnarayan Tarkaratna's *Kulinkulsarbaswa.* The staging of this play was far more significant, and attractive, in comparison with that of *Abhijnan Shakuntalam.* For, in this play the viewers saw a direct visual representation of their own times. The episode enthused many people to initiate efforts towards dramatic performances in Bengal.

The man who organised a dramatic performance after Ashutosh Deb and Ramjay Basak himself wrote the play. He was Kaliprasanna Sinha. In the same year, that is, in 1857 he put up his own play *Vikramurvashi* and Ramnarayan Tarkalankar's *Benisamhar* on the stage of the Bidyotsahini Sabha (Enthusiasts of Knowledge), a group of 'knowledge seekers' established by him. All at once, the staging of these four plays in 1857 seemed to breathe life into Bengali dramatics. Many people now came forward to take part in the efforts to stage plays. There were people available who were willing to help with funds as well as individuals who were able to act on stage. Even more significantly, organisers of dramatic performances now had access to plays that had reached a certain standard.

This extraordinary convergence of factors happened in 1858. Michael Madhusudan Dutt was then in Calcutta, making ends meet on the lean salary of a petty job. Two brothers of an influential family in Paikpara, Pratap Chandra and Ishwar Chandra, were out to make an impression on the sahibs by putting up a dramatic performance. They arranged for Ramnarayan Tarkaratna's play *Ratnabali* to be staged in Belgachhia Theatre established by them. In order to make sure that their English guests were able to follow the dialogues during the performance, they sought to get the play translated into English. The responsibility fell on Michael, who through this exercise became interested in writing plays in Bengali. He had noted that the educated drama enthusiasts of Calcutta were immersed in the entertainment offered by low quality plays. He, on the other hand, had a close familiarity with the best dramatic tradition of European, including English, theatre. During his years in Madras, he had in fact started work on a play of great literary merit. Though he quit writing the play midway owing to some particular circumstances, he had acquired some experience of writing a play. Making use of that experience and his extensive scholarship in European dramatic literature, he now turned his attention to writing a path-breaking Bengali play.

His first play was *Sharmistha* (1858). Before the publication of this book, Bengali did not have any play of comparable dramatic quality or stage-worthiness. Apart from *Kulinkulsarbaswa*, no other play even had such smart, racy dialogue, too. Fortunately, he got the Paikpara brothers' help to stage the play. Of the two brothers, Ishwar Chandra Sinha was himself interested in acting and drama. Jatindramohan Tagore, who was familiar with Western literature and who was also into acting, pitched in with them. He, too, was a wealthy man, and later he himself went on to establish a theatre. Kaliprasanna Sinha, another landholder interested in drama, also joined this group. Contact with so many educated and wealthy drama enthusiasts turned around the fortunes of Michael and Bengali drama.

Sharmistha was enacted on the same stage as *Ratnabali* had been. Those who acted in it were all amateurs in the true sense of the word. Keshab Ganguly, whom Michael called the Garrick of his time, was also among them. But the actors who would 15 years later make it to the professional stage had not yet emerged. After the successful run of *Sharmistha*, Michael wrote three other plays one after another and two satirical skits. All of them were dramatised, though it took them a few years to go on stage because of social reasons. Michael's true contribution was to set an ideal for stage-worthy drama. Later plays by other dramatists that were put up on stage had to reach a certain standard.

So far we have noted that plays were staged under the patronage of one rich man or another. They did of course derive enjoyment from staging dramatic performances, but through such exercise they also attempted to gain social recognition and respect as cultured and patrons of culture. One by one, therefore, the Tagores of Pathuriaghata and Jorasanko and the influential 'royals' of Shobhabazar came forward to join the initiatives around dramatics and stagecraft. After the Paikpara theatre folded up, Jatindramohan Tagore established the Pathuriaghata Natyalaya (Pathuriaghata House of Drama) in 1865. His brother Sourindramohan Tagore was with him in this. This theatre began its journey with Jatindramohan Tagore's play *Vidya-Sundar* and his skit *Jemon Karma Temon Phal* ('As You Sow, So You Shall Reap'). These were staged some seven or eight times over a couple of months beginning in December 1865. Plays and skits were staged quite a few times, though irregularly, in this theatre until 1871. But this theatre, dependent as it was on the whims of rich men, did not last very long.

The Shobhabazar Private Theatrical Society started functioning in 1865. Their first performance was the skit *Ekei ki Bole Sabhyata?* ('Is This Called

Civilisation?'). The skit ran on July 27 and 29. That apart, *Krishnakumari* was staged in 1867 at the initiative of this group. Despite staging several plays, however, the group was not able to play any very significant role in the history of Bengali dramatics. The theatre initiatives by the Jorasanko Tagores were not able to play such a role, either. The Jorasanko group did stage a couple of performances, but it was not able to take Bengali dramatics forward through regular stage performances.

The dramatic performances that were organised at the initiative of wealthy families had another limitation. Only guests invited for the shows were able to watch them. Yet there was a growing interest in dramatics among the general educated classes. In this context some significant changes came about in dramatics in the late 1860s. The biggest change was that middle-class people got together at this time to set up amateur theatre groups. Two such theatre groups were the Bowbazar Banganatyalaya and Bagbazar Amateur Theatre. The Bowbazar Banganatyalaya was established in 1868 by two gentlemen, Baladeb and Chunilal Dhar. The first play that they staged was Manomohan Basu's *Ramabhishek* (Ram's Coronation). Organising stage performance was extremely expensive, and it was not easy for this group to keep on at it without the patronage of the wealthy.

The Bagbazar Amateur Theatre in comparison played a far more significant role in taking Bengali dramatics forward. This group started functioning in 1867 and it staged seven plays in all. Staging so many plays was by no means an easy thing to do in those days. But there were some factors that made this group successful. Well known actors such as Girish Ghosh and Ardhendushekhar Mustafi worked with this group. It is not enough to say that these men loved acting. Theatre was what breathed life in them. Notwithstanding all the obstacles that came their way, they continued to act until the end of their lives and immensely enriched Bengali dramatics as they pursued their calling. They also displayed discernment in their choice of plays. The plays that they staged dealt not only with social issues, but also with nationalist, Puranic themes and aspects of folk culture. The presence of these two different aspects attracted viewers. Thus this group showed the way for future dramatics in Bengal.

The Bagbazar Amateur Theatre staged two plays by Dinabandhu Mitra with great success. It staged *Sadhabar Ekadashi* for the first time in 1868 during Durga Puja, and then again at the time of the Lakshmi Puja that is held a week later in Bengal. In 1870 the play was staged for the fourth time. The playwright Dinabandhu Mitra himself was among the audience. Delighted with Girish Ghosh's performance as Nimchand and Ardhendushekhar Mustafi's performance as Jibonchandra, he commented that their rendering was an improvement of the original. The group staged *Sadhabar Ekadashi* for the seventh time during Durga Puja in 1872. A skit by the same playwright, *Biye Pagla Burho*, was also staged alongside.

Notwithstanding the successful staging of *Sadhabar Ekadashi*, this group was unable to meet the demand for regular dramatic performances. In the absence of a regular stage and enough resources, they could not hold as many shows as they might have wanted to. But the successful performance of Dinabandhu Mitra's *Leelavati* in Chinsura earned them enthusiastic applause from viewers and also impressed upon them the fact that regular shows might attract viewers. Armed with this new realisation, they put on *Leelavati* under the open sky on the grounds of Rajendra Pal's house in Calcutta, for the first time on May 11, 1872. They repeated the performance with great success on the two following Saturdays.

Leelavati was a love story. There was a noticeable interest in the play among general viewers. Nevertheless, it was not possible for the group to put up regular shows because it did not have a stage of its own, nor enough money. The group, therefore, planned to fund shows through the sale of tickets, making use of the interest in theatre that *Leelavati* had generated. It was decided that this theatre group would henceforth be known as National Theatre. A sense of nationhood had emerged around the Hindu Mela initiatives a few years before, and the word 'national' was at this time added to all kinds of efforts beginning with Nabagopal Mitra's *National Paper*. The name chosen for the theatre also reflected this general tendency. The greatest actor associated with this theatre, Girish Ghosh, was not in favour of funding shows through the sale of tickets. He therefore parted ways with the group after it was decided that National Theatre would be set up on a commercial basis. He realised soon enough, however, that there was no alternative to running a theatre group on funds generated by the sale of tickets. Besides, theatre and drama were the air that he breathed in, they filled his mind and heart. He was not able to stay away from the theatre group for very long.

In the absence of a dedicated stage, the group had put up a stage at Madhusudan Sanyal's house on Chitpur Road and this was where they put up shows. The group started functioning on December 7, 1872. For their first show they had chosen Dinabandhu Mitra's *Neeldarpan.* Although Madhusudan Dutt was the greatest playwright of the time, Dinabandhu was the most popular. Ordinary theatre-goers could identify with the situations in his plays and his themes appealed to general educated Bengalis. The high art of Madhusudan's Puranic and historical drama did not quite have the same appeal for a general viewership. Until February 1 the following year, it was the plays of Dinabandhu that got staged, one after another, one show every week with only two exceptions. These plays were *Jamai Barik, Sadhabar Ekadashi, Nabin Tapaswini, Leelavati* and *Biye Pagla Burho.* Apart from Dinabandhu's plays, however, this group also put up Madhusudan Dutt's *Krishnakumari, Burho Shaliker Gharhe Ron* and *Ekei ki Bole Sabhyata?* Ramnarayan Tarkaratna's plays also contained the kind of contemporary realities and clowning that made them suitable for the consumption of ordinary viewers. This was why the group also chose some of his skits for their shows. The plays of Sisir Kumar Ghosh, Kiran Chandra Bandyopadhyay, Jyotirindranath Tagore and other contemporary dramatists were also staged at the initiative of this group.

The shows ran fairly regularly until May 1873. There were even some weeks when two shows were put up. Yet, National Theatre did not survive for very long owing to the absence of a permanent stage and factiousness among actors. The group split into two—National Theatre kept running under Girish Ghosh's leadership, while the dissenting group led by Ardhendushekhar Mustafi was called the Hindu National Theatre. Towards the end of 1873, however, some actors of the Hindu National Theatre came back to National Theatre, which was then rechristened Great National Theatre. Henceforth the group held on to its existence under various names. It did indeed play a true pioneering role in Bengali dramatics.

Bhubanmohan Niyogi had helped with funds when the Great National Theatre was established, while Dharmadas Sur accepted its managerial responsibilities. They constructed a stage for this theatre on Beadon Street in Calcutta. Apart from plays such as *Neeldarpan, Bidhoba-Bibaha, Krishnakumari, Sadhabar Ekadashi,* a few plays based on Bankimchandra's stories were also performed on this stage. Plays by Lakshminarayan Chakraborty, Manomohan Basu, Nagendranath Bandyopadhyay, Kiran Chandra Bandyopadhyay and Haralal Roy were also staged.

The Expansion of Theatre

Once the ideal of staging plays on a commercial basis was established, it did not take long for National Theatre to acquire rivals. Groups such as Oriental Theatre, Bengal Theatre and Indian National Theatre came up one after another within a couple of years. The Hindu National Theatre under Ardhendushekhar's leadership had started out with Madhusudan's *Sharmistha.* They also staged the most popular play of the time, *Neeldarpan.* They even put up *Mohanter Ei Kee Kaj,* a play based on a scandal surrounding a temple priest and thus totally contemporaneous. Yet the theatre still ran in fits and starts until it closed down permanently by September 1873. As we have already mentioned, Ardhendushekhar and some other actors then returned to National Theatre and founded the Great National Theatre.

Compared with the first three professional theatres, Bengal Theatre emerged as far more successful and truly long-lasting. Sharat Chandra Ghosh, a grandson of one of the richest men of Calcutta, Ashutosh Deb, established this theatre in Beadon Street. He was both wealthy and interested in drama, and hence this initiative. His personal enthusiasm and sacrifices were what helped his theatre to stay afloat for so long. Instead of using a makeshift stage as National Theatre did, Bengal Theatre erected a permanent one. The later theatre groups realised that a theatre needed a permanent stage to keep running. They all therefore followed the example of Bengal Theatre in constructing permanent stages.

Like Hindu National Theatre, Bengal Theatre also started out with Michael's *Sharmistha,* on August 16, 1873. The poet himself was unable to watch the performance—he had died on June 29. Apart from *Sharmistha,* the group also staged his *Krishnakumari, Mayakanan* and *Padmavati.* Indeed, it was at the request of Bengal Theatre that Michael wrote *Mayakanan* despite his failing health. The group even got plays written on the basis of *Meghnadvadh Kavya* and *Tilottama Sambhav Kavya* and staged them. With minor changes in its management, the group lasted until 1901 and staged over a hundred plays in this period. Among the dramatists whose work they staged were Dinabandhu Mitra, Ramnarayan Tarkaratna, Jyotirindranath Tagore, Upendranath Das, Manomohan Basu, Sisir Kumar Ghosh, Rajkrishna Ray, Girish Chandra Ghosh, Amritalal Basu and Kshirodprasad Vidyavinod. Tagore's plays were also performed by Bengal Theatre.

The two main obstacles that dramatics in Bengal faced were the lack of good plays and the absence of stages. The efforts of Michael and Dinabandhu to some extent addressed the first problem. The second was also partially addressed when Bengal Theatre erected a permanent stage. Another major obstacle, however, still remained—the want of actresses. Indeed, female roles presented one of the main problems for show organisers in those days. We know from Michael's letters that right at the stage of writing his plays he worried about how many female roles he could afford in his play and which contemporary male actors would be able to play them. Bengal Theatre got around the problem by getting women to act on the professional stage. Acting was in those days not a little problematic for women. For one, it was rare to find a woman who was able to act. For another, viewers were not used to seeing women on stage, and many did not even wish to see them. Ishwarchandra Vidyasagar and Shibnath Shastri were not only social reformers, they genuinely wanted a better life for women. Both of them also loved to watch plays. Yet after Bengal Theatre introduced women's acting on the professional stage, neither of them ever went to watch a show again. It is possible that there were others like them among drama audiences.

Despite this resistance and hostility to women's acting in a section of society, Bengal Theatre's initiative in having female roles played by women opened up new horizons in dramatics. Apparently when the group requested Michael to write *Mayakanan*, the poet himself supposedly advised the organisers to get women to play women's roles. It is not impossible that it was partly his advice that enthused Bengal Theatre to appoint, right at the beginning of its journey, four women, called Jagattarini, Golapsundari, Elokeshi and Shyama, to act in female roles. Though they might not have had any training in acting, all four of them could sing and dance. They were all, however, prostitutes by profession. Bengal Theatre had not only introduced women on stage, these were also women who sold their bodies for a living—these two things led many newspapers and magazines to vehemently criticise the group. But Bengal Theatre, notwithstanding all the criticism, was able to last relatively long probably because of, among other things, its use of women actors.

It must be mentioned here that women had been participating in the rural theatrics of *jatragan* from much earlier. That is why, when women came on the theatrical stage, the *Hindu Patriot* said in its criticism that by bringing women into theatre the organisers were pushing theatre down to the level of the *jatra*. A measure of how bold and how significant Saratchandra Ghosh's move to appoint women actors in his theatre was can be glimpsed from something that happened another 40 years later. When Dadasaheb Phalke made his first movie in 1913, he had to use a male restaurant chef in the heroine's role. In 1958, the government of East Bengal allowed the performance of the play *Beder Meye* on the condition that no women would act in it. In this context, Saratchandra Ghosh's role was bold and historic.

It is no use denying that women acting in female roles had become inevitable after the establishment of the professional stage. And once Saratchandra had stared down society's bloodshot gaze to introduce women on his stage, all theatre groups were forced to follow his example. When in the 1880s, Tagore's family organised performances of plays including *Balmikipratibha, Kalmrigaya* and *Raja-o-Rani* for their private stage, the Tagore women participated in them. It would take several decades, however, for women of 'decent' families to act on the professional stage.

Women in those days had no scope to receive any training in acting, but that many of them were born with natural acting talents was established soon enough. Golapsundari had joined Bengal Theatre's second show, on August 23, 1873. She was an accomplished singer, especially of kirtan. Within a short time, she displayed her expertise in acting, playing many different kinds of roles with aplomb. Ardhendushekhar Mustafi was with Bengal Theatre at that time, and he trained her up very well.

Among the plays in which Golapsundari acted was Upendra Nath Das's *Sarat-Sarojini* staged by the Great National Theatre. In January 1875 she acted in the role of a female character called Sukumari in this play. Her rendering of the role was so perfect that viewers started calling her Sukumari, and it was by this name that she became fairly well known. Upendra Nath Das was at that time the manager of this theatre. One of his actors was a young man called Gosthobehari Datta. He was romantically involved with Golapsundari and, at Upendra Nath's initiative, married her. After that Golapsundari became known as Sukumari Datta. That the son of a bhadralok family had married a former sex worker generated such heated criticism in society that Gosthobehari abandoned Sukumari and fled, not only from Calcutta but from the country. He sailed to England as a sailor (*khalasi*) on a ship. Sukumari, on the other hand, not only stayed on with the theatre group, she continued to act. Indeed, financial constraints compelled her to go on performing for a long time. It was not long before she herself came up with an autobiographical play called *Apurba Sati*. It is sometimes said that Upendra Nath Das wrote the play under her name. It ran successfully on March 23, 1877, at this theatre. In 1883 she set up an all-women theatre group called the Hindu Female Theatre and got it to stage a play called *Shumbha Samhar* ('The Killing of Shumbha').

Even in 1898, Sukumari acted in several plays in Bengal and Minerva Theatres. Her performance in roles such as Bimala in *Durgeshnandini*, Rani Oilobala in *Purubikram*, Sarojini in *Sarojini*, Birajmohini in *Surendra-Binodini*, Girijaya in *Mrinalini*, Malina in *Asrumati* and Surjamukhi in *Bishbriksha* earned praise from theatre critics.

Though Golapsundari acquired considerable fame, the most well known actress in the first phase of the Bengali professional stage was Binodini. She worked for a while with Sukumari in the Great National Theatre. Apart from her acting skills, she could also sing very well. She had, moreover, a fair degree of literary talent. Among the autobiographies written by women, her *Amar Katha* ('My Story') is especially remarkable for its candidness and simplicity of language. Apart from the autobiography, she also published some poems. She made her stage debut in December 1874 in the role of a friend of Draupadi. She was then only 13 or 14 years old. Her salary was Rs10 a month. Nothing is reliably known of her family, and she has repeatedly referred to herself as a *barnari* or as *barangana*, meaning prostitute.

Within a short time she started touring north India extensively with the Great National Theatre. After two years she joined Bengal Theatre and stayed with it for nine months. At Girish Ghosh's behest, however, she quit Bengal Theatre in 1877 and returned to National Theatre. Her contact with Girish Ghosh proved immensely enriching for her, for it was under his tutelage that her acting skills were polished and refined. Ardhendushekhar was the other iconic actor of the time, and Binodini learnt from him, too.

Binodini Dasi

A few years later, in early 1883, Binodini established Star Theatre with Girish Ghosh. A Marwari trader, Gurmukh Ray, provided the funds. His real objective was Binodini, rather than theatre. Though she was what was called a 'loose' woman, it was not easy for Binodini to give herself up to Gurmukh Roy. For, she was already 'kept' by a wealthy landowner, and she loved him. This landowner, too, regarded Binodini as a lover. He had no objection to her acting in theatre. The problem lay elsewhere. A non-Bengali businessman called Pratap Chand Jahuri was the proprietor of National Theatre, for which Girish Ghosh and Binodini worked. Theatre was not for him a passion but simply a business enterprise. It was not easy for actors to work independently under him. Girish Ghosh, therefore, set about trying to establish a new theatre.

He could not however put together the money required for a new theatre. In this situation the young Gurmukh Ray in his early twenties came forward to help. As we have already said, he had more interest in Binodini than in theatre. He made over 50,000 rupees in cash to Binodini and asked her to forget about setting up a new theatre. But theatre was the centre of Binodini's life. It was only on condition that she would be able to build up a new theatre that she agreed to leave her lover for Gurmukh Ray. Indeed, the personal sacrifice that Binodini made for the sake of theatre was quite extraordinary. Yet, in an irony of fate, in spite of her huge sacrifice, opposition from some of her colleagues drove her away from Star Theatre in less than three and a half years. Gurmukh Ray was not around to support her, for he had died a year after Star started running. The unkindest cut of all was that Girish Ghosh was among those who worked for her removal. Binodini had reached the peak of her fame while working for Star Theatre. Her name lives on over a hundred years later, although she was forced to retire when she was just 24 or 25. It is doubtful that her potential had been fully realised by the time she stopped working.

Girish Ghosh

The Star Theatre years were when Girish Ghosh started writing plays prolifically. He wrote many different kinds of plays including Puranic and religious ones. He had even started a translation of Shakespeare. In the initial days of this theatre, Binodini played the title role of his play *Chaitanyaleela.* In 1885 Ramkrishna Paramhansa came to watch the performance of this play. Moved by Binodini's extraordinary and deeply emotional acting, he blessed her before he left. In an age when Vidyasagar stopped watching plays altogether after the arrival of women actors on stage, the presence of a religious leader like Ramkrishna among the audience watching Binodini's performance and his blessing the actor earned in Hindu society a sort of legitimacy for women acting on the professional stage. Vivekananda, too, used to watch dramatic performances. Binodini had acted in over 50 plays. Her roles in religious and Puranic plays were particularly memorable. Conservative Hindus did not just watch her performances, they relished the experience. Binodini thus played a historic role in making women's acing acceptable to Bengali society.

Some other well known women actors of the time may be mentioned in this context. Kiranbala was some five years younger than Binodini. She too was born to a sex worker in Calcutta's prostitute quarters. When in 1887 Binodini was forced to quit acting and permanently take up the life of a 'mistress' to rich men, Kiranbala started playing the roles that had once been hers. Kiranbala was able to live up to the ideal that Binodini had set in her rendering of those roles. But the most famous actress after Binodini in those days was Tinkori Dasi. Her mother, too, was a prostitute. She, too, had taken to acting, driven by financial want. She was coached in acting by Girish Ghosh. In 1893 she earned praise from drama critics for her role as Lady Macbeth in his play *Macbeth.* Kusumkumari (1876? – 1948) was a few years younger than Tinkori. She performed creditably in many theatres including Grand, Classic, Kohinoor and Star. She was the first actress to coach others in dance as well as acting. She was also a good singer. Norisundari was roughly the same age as Kusumkumari. Like the women actors who came before her, she, too, was a prostitute's daughter. In 1884 she joined Star Theatre with Binodini's help, at the age of seven. She later displayed such skill in acting that at one phase she was known universally as the empress of theatre.

Nobody could even imagine in those days that women of decent families could act on stage. Yet the Tagores of Jorasanko defied this rigid social convention to encourage their wives and daughters to take part in their private dramatic performances. There were a number of reasons that made it possible for this family to take such an extraordinarily bold step. Their position in society made it possible for them to ignore social disapproval. In religious faith, too, they were somewhat removed from mainstream Hindu beliefs. Above all else, the stage that the Tagore women performed on was the family's private stage. It was not open to the general public. By getting their women to act on stage, the Tagores were able to make two important points. First, this served as an example for subsequent generations. A quarter century later, this was the example that women of respectable families followed to perform on stage, this was what gave them the heart to do so. Second, the Tagore women eschewed the exaggerated histrionics of the *jatra* form and instead brought an everyday naturalness to the rendering of their dramatic roles. This, too, turned into an example to be imitated by later generations.

Dramatic performances on the Tagores' private family stage started with *Balmikipratibha* in February 1881. Tagore himself played Balmiki, while his niece Pratibha played Saraswati. Tagore's sister Saratkumari Devi's daughter Susheela acted in Lakshmi's role. Several performances of *Balmikipratibha* were subsequently staged, spread across the entire 1880s. Women of the Tagore household and the larger extended family participated in each of these performances. Some other girls including Indira Devi took part in the performance of *Kalmrigaya* in 1882. *Mayar Khela* was enacted at Bethune College in 1888 at the initiative of the Tagore women. Only women acted in it, and a couple of them were unrelated to the Tagores. When *Raja-o-Rani* was put up in October 1890, not only young girls but also Jnanadanandini Devi and Tagore's wife Mrinalini Devi acted in it. In sum, the Tagores played a pioneering role in the matter of respectable women taking part in dramatic performances, as they had done in so many other areas.

Though Star Theatre played the longest-running role in the history of the professional stage, it was not able to function for very long in the house where it was first established. In 1887 Gopal Shil bought the house, and in October that year he got together the old National Theatre actors and set up a new group called Emerald Theatre. Ardhendushekhar Mustafi was also among them. Within a short while Gopal Shil persuaded Girish Ghosh to join this theatre, too. Relations between Ardhendushekhar and Girish Ghosh were marred by personal envy. Ardhendushekhar, therefore, left the group after Girish Ghosh joined it. Girish Ghosh was not able to stay with this group for very long, either. He, therefore, went back to Star. Gopal Shil had been the first to light up his theatre electrically by installing a dynamo. Notwithstanding this novelty, Emerald Theatre cannot be said to have contributed a great deal to Bengali professional theatre. In April 1897 it closed down.

After Emerald Theatre shut shop, Amarendra Nath Datta set up a new theatre in Gopal Shil's house. He belonged to an aristocratic family and was well educated. He was also a good actor, and this was what led him to take up the management of a theatre. He launched his Classic Theatre with a play by Girish Ghosh. After that he put up Hariraj based on *Hamlet.* He also staged Tagore's *Raja-o-Rani.* He was more interested in good theatre than in commercial success. He did not however have a strong business instinct. Notwithstanding sufficient support from viewers, therefore, it was largely because of his thriftlessness that Classic Theatre had to close down in

1906. Now another theatre called Kohinoor was established in the house by a zamindar. This theatre started running in 1907, and actors such as Girish Ghosh and Ardhendushekhar Mustafi and actresses such as Tinkori Dasi and Tarasundari were among those who worked with it at different times. Yet it did not last for more than five odd years.

Star, on the other hand, survived its eviction from its original stage in 1887. It started afresh the very next year in a house on Cornwallis Street. Girish Ghosh returned to Star at this time and worked with it for 10 continuous years. During this phase of his theatrical career, Girish Ghosh maintained a very high standard of acting and also wrote a number of new plays. Indeed, his efforts established Star on a strong foundation.

Bengal Theatre's contribution in the history of the Bengali professional stage is by no means paler than that of Star. Overall, this theatre raised acting and theatre production to a certain level of expertise and professionalism. It made such a good reputation for itself within a few years that not only did it count Indian princes and nobles among its patrons, but even a Viceroy – Lord Lytton – went to watch one of its shows with his wife and friends. Queen Victoria's husband, Albert, also watched a Bengal Theatre performance during his Calcutta visit in 1890. After this rare honour, Bengal Theatre modified its name to Royal Bengal Theatre. Bengal Theatre was Bengal's first truly commercial theatre. Though it did sometimes display a certain loyalty to the country, it did not stage any play that might offend the government. It thus significantly differed from the kind of dramatics practised by National and Great National Theatre.

Another commercial theatre, known as Minerva Theatre, was established during the lifetime of Star. After National Theatre closed down in 1883, Bhubanmohan Niyogi took charge of the theatre and staged a few plays. Yet his efforts to revive the theatre could not continue for very long. After it was auctioned off, Star Theatre was born in its place. But as we have already noted, Star did not run from this property for very long. In 1893, Minerva Theatre was set up there with considerable fanfare, on the strength of Bhubanmohan Niyogi's efforts and funds provided by a grandson of Prasanna Kumar Tagore. Girish Ghosh was unattached at that time. He joined Minerva on Bhubanmohan Niyogi's request, and it was with his translation of *Macbeth* that Minerva was rolled out on January 28 that year. Ardhendushekhar Mustafi, too, joined Minerva at this time and played four different roles in the same production of *Macbeth.*

New Dramatists and Dramatic Themes

Once the professional stage started functioning, the playwrights whose work got the most frequent dramatic representation were Ramnarayan Tarkaratna, Michael Madhusudan Dutt and Dinabandhu Mitra. But once the supply dried up from these dramatists, there appeared a severe dearth of new plays. The men who moved in to fill the vacuum were Manomohan Basu, Jyotirindranath Tagore, Upendra Nath Das, etc. Not all plays, however, were equally stage-worthy or appealing to viewers. The search for gripping narratives led to the dramatisation of Bankimchandra's novels and of the narrative poems by Michael, Hemchandra and Nabin Sen. This spring, too, was bound to dry up sometime, and the absence of new plays was keenly felt when it finally did. In this environment, the actors themselves took up the pen. The most famous of these actor-playwrights was Girish Ghosh. But the first to show the way had been Kiran Chandra Bandyopadhyay. Another remarkable actor-playwright was Amritalal Basu.

A change also crept into the dramatic themes at this time. The chief reason was contemporary social and political thinking. We noted in the chapter 'Bengali Culture under Western Impact' that after Nabagopal Mitra inaugurated the Hindu Mela in 1865, a patriotic consciousness grew into a powerful tide in the 1870s. This newly awakened patriotism strongly influenced contemporary drama and theatre. This was the environment in which the first professional stage was christened National Theatre. The group was not just 'national' in name, quite a few of the plays it staged were inspired by nationalist thinking.

And it was not just National Theatre. Indeed, in keeping with changing social awareness, other theatres also staged, beginning in 1878, a number of patriotic and nationalist plays. The plays of Dinabandhu or Michael were no longer considered sufficient for the expression of this nascent patriotism. New playwrights now came forward to write drama informed with the nationalist consciousness. Particularly remarkable among this crop of plays were Kiran Chandra Bandyopadhyay's *Bharatmata*, Jyotirindranath's *Purubikram*, Haralal Ray's *Banger Sukhabasan*, Nagendranath Bandyopadhyay's *Gaekwad*, Upendra Nath Das's *Surendra-Binodini* and *Sarat-Sarojini*, Ramesh Chandra Datta's *Bangabijeta* and Amritalal Basu's *Heerakchurna*. Of these, Upendra Nath Das's *Sarat-Sarojini* and *Surendra-Binodini* created quite a storm. In sum, the repeated and frequent performance of patriotic plays produced a close link between theatre and nationalism. This connection in turn made the theatre popular with the general viewer.

Notwithstanding the nationalist plays that were being written, making a direct display of opposition to colonial rule was not quite so easy. Just a decade earlier, a court case had been lodged over the publication of *Neeldarpan* in English and Rev. James Long had been punished and fined. The memory of this episode was still fresh in people's minds. Dramatists also probably remembered the rioting by the English in Allahabad in response to the staging of *Neeldarpan*. Despite this phobia of the British, however, dramatists such as Upendra Nath Das introduced English characters in their plays. The British did not take too kindly to the performance of these plays. Jyotirindranath Tagore, therefore, chose a different route for expressing patriotic feelings. For instance, he based his *Purubikram* on Jean Racine's play *Alexander the Great*. He could not make bold to depict the English in the role of the aggressor, so he glorified a native monarch's standing up to a foreign invader in this play. It should be noted that the name of the original makes evident exactly where the dramatic stress lies—it is Alexander's greatness that is sought to be emphasised. Jyotirindranath, on the other hand, seeks to impute greatness to the dignified courage of the defeated Puru, or Porus. Jyotirindranath changes tack in his *Sarojini*, which too is a free translation of a play by Jean Racine. In this play the invading outsider is the Muslim sultan Alauddin Khilji.

When the Prince of Wales, Britain's crown prince, visited Calcutta in early 1876, the distinguished High Court advocate Jagadananda Mukhopadhyay held a reception for him at his home, which was attended by the women of his family. Many of his fellow Indians found this to be an anti-patriotic act. Jagadananda, therefore, found himself the target of a satirical attack in the play *Gajadananda O Jubaraj* (Gajadananda and the Crown Prince) staged by the Great National Theatre. It was in response to this play and some other developments that followed that the colonial government in 1876 passed the Dramatic Performances Act, which gave the government the 'power to prohibit certain dramatic performances'. Even after the adoption of this piece of legislation, however, patriotic plays continued to be performed, either by defying the law or by taking advantage of loopholes in it. Seen in this perspective, history was created in Bengali dramatics in less than two decades beginning with 1857, and the dramatic performances held during this phase stoked the newly awakening patriotism among Bengalis.

Other dramatists were inspired by the way Jyotirindranath fired up the spirit of patriotism through his depiction of a Muslim sultan as the invading outsider. It was indeed easier to express love for the motherland through criticism of Muslim rule than through opposition to the British. Hence the unabashed Muslim bashing in many plays written at this time. Another way of stoking a sense of nationhood was to glorify Hinduism through Puranic narratives. Starting from the 1870s, innumerable such plays were written, and the ones that were actually put on stage became quite popular.

It must be said here that though many plays got written at this time, most of them were not stageable. Actors like Girish Ghosh, Amritalal Basu and Kiran Bandyopadhyay had direct experience of the stageability of plays, that is, how fit they were to be put on stage. Girish Chandra was the most skilled and popular actor of his time. He knew what the viewers were looking for. Besides, just as he had mastered the art of acting in *jatra*, he had also mastered, and with greater expertise, the art of acting in plays. He was also equally familiar with both English and Bengali dramatic literature. He had not read Lebedoff's comment on the Bengali character made some 70 years earlier, yet, he, too, had reached the same conclusion. He knew that the easy way to win the hearts of Bengali viewers was through songs and clowning. He had both in his own plays. He was also himself an accomplished singer. We have noted in the previous chapter that he wrote some 1,300 plays. And the character of the fool or the zester is present in his tragedies. He also imported the spirit of folk theatre, or *jatra*, in his plays. Above all, he could always tell which way the wind was blowing.

It was because of his direct experience with the stage and dramatics and his unfailing understanding of what the audience wanted that Girish

Ghosh repeatedly went back to Puranic narratives. He often used material from the *Ramayana* and the *Mahabharata*. The playwright also wrote quite a few plays on religious themes. Being a Vaishnava devotee, he wrote a few plays on Chaitanyadev and on Vaishnava religious themes. He was influenced by the assertion of Hindu religious identity that started in the 1870s and himself contributed not a little to it. Then again when it was patriotism that caught the prevailing wind at the turn of the century, he was able to make a contribution to that trend, too. Indeed, measured by the yardstick of popular appeal, no one else in those days wrote plays that were quite as successful as his were. Social, Puranic, historical, and patriotic—he wrote all kinds of plays with remarkable success. Amritalal Basu was also associated with theatre and wrote stageable plays to meet the demands of professional theatre. So did Amritlal Mitra and Kshirodprasad Vidyavinod.

Ramkrishna Paramhansa brought new life into the Hindu religious movement. No one else after Chaitanyadev had perhaps been able to produce such a tidal wave of enthusiasm in Hinduism. A nationalist political environment was also created alongside in the last 25 years of the 19th century. Moreover, the orthodox Hindu revivalist movement started in the 1880s. This cultural environment encouraged the writing of Puranic and nationalist historical plays. The political movement that started building up at the dawn of the 20th century, particularly around the 1905 partition of Bengal, also greatly influenced dramatic literature. And it can be said that just as, on the one hand, the social and political environment provided a fillip to dramatic literature and theatre, on the other, drama and theatre also inspired educated sections with a new political awareness.

The example of the movement around the partition of Bengal is particularly significant in this context. It turned the attention of educated society to Hindu-Muslim relations. The indifference and distaste that playwrights once harboured towards Muslims vanished almost overnight in this background. Plays were now written even about characters such as Siraj-ud-Daulah, Mir Qasim or even Aurangzeb, to whom Hindus had previously been severely opposed. In the 1860s, Michael Madhusudan Dutt had tried more than once to write a play about Razia Sultana, but his friends advised him against it. At the end of the century, however, Razia did finally become the subject of a play. A dramatist of the calibre of Dwijendralal Ray wrote two great plays on Shah Jahan and Noor Jahan. More importantly, these plays ran successfully on stage and attracted audiences.

Twentieth Century Theatre

The first Bengali play was published in 1852, and, leaving Lebedoff aside, the first dramatic performance was held in 1857. Within half a century, Bengali drama and dramatics recorded remarkable progress, much of its success owing to the arrival of the professional theatre. The trend continued unbroken in the 20th century. Notwithstanding occasional dry spells, drama and theatre had by that time acquired enough momentum of their own and so did not have to depend on individual sponsors. The anti-partition movement had come as a tidal wave and shaken up Bengali drama and theatre. Yet, a sort of low tide seemed to set in as early as the second decade of the century. There were several reasons for this. Girish Ghosh did his last show in 1911 and died a few days after it. Dwijendralal died in 1912. After that, Bengal was left with no truly great dramatist apart from Tagore. Tagore's plays, despite their literary excellence, were not staged too often in professional theatre, for they did not have much appeal for ordinary viewers. This was also the time of the arrival of cinema. Dadasaheb Phalke's *Raja Harishchandra* was released in 1913.

In the absence of powerful playwrights, talented actors and resourceful managers, plays of the old type and the old-style acting were not able to retain their viewership. In this decade, therefore, films started being shown alongside stage shows of plays. This decade can be said to mark the worst time ever for Bengali theatre. The person who redeemed Bengali theatre from the doldrums was Sisir Kumar Bhaduri. Not only did he come from an educated background and was a professor of English, he was also a great actor and director. His acting talents were first revealed during his student days. But it was in 1911 that he charmed audiences with his rendering of the role of Chanakya in Dwijendralal Ray's *Chandragupta*. It was from the next decade that he started making his truly unique contribution to theatre.

Star, Minerva and Manomohan Theatre somehow managed to run through the 1910s, but all these three old theatres folded up early in the next decade and later resurfaced in a changed form or with a changed name. Minerva burnt down in 1922. It started running again after a couple of years and even got a fresh shot of life after Ahindra Choudhury joined it. The control of Star Theatre, on the other hand, passed into the hands of Art Theatre, and Manomohan Theatre made way for Natyamandir. Star was totally remodelled by the producer who set up a completely new kind of theatre under the name of Art Theatre. This group staged *Karnarjun* in 1923 with extraordinary success. The play ran for 250 continuous nights, something that was unimaginable until then.

So three old theatres passed into the hands of new managements and thus acquired a new look, Madan, a producer and distributor of films, lent support to theatre, which had been pushed into a corner by cinema. He probably hoped that combining the drama form based on dialogue with cinema in single shows would help his silent films to succeed better. In 1921 he established the Cornwallis Theatre and invited Sisir Bhaduri to join it. In the 1920s, then, Bengali theatre can be said to have turned a corner again.

Cornwallis Theatre started out with Kshirodprasad Vidyavinod's play *Alamgir*. Sisir Kumar played the title role and his acting won the viewers' hearts. There was a quality in his acting that attracted both ordinary and discerning viewers. He in fact introduced a new and unique style in Bengali dramatics. So high indeed was the standard of his acting that Dwijendralal's son Dilip Kumar Ray wrote in a critical piece that it was better than even the kind of acting he had seen Europe. Sukumar Sen has said that Sisir Bhaduri had before him a high ideal of acting and direction in Tagore's production of *Phalguni*.

Sisir Bhaduri, however, did not have a completely free hand in Madan's Cornwallis Theatre. Yet he had his own strong views on theatre and acting. Disillusioned, he left it the very next year, in 1922. When two years later he took up the management of Manomohan Theatre, he rechristened it as Natyamandir. In August 1924 he rolled out his new theatre with the play *Sita*. One of his distinctive traits was that he always showed good taste in the plays that he chose for production. Apart from plays by popular dramatists such as Dinabandhu Mitra, Girish Ghosh, Dwijendralal Ray and Kshirodprasad Vidyavinod, he also staged several of Tagore's plays. He got actors of the calibre of Ahindra Choudhury, Durgadas Bandyopadhyay, Naresh Mitra, Susheelasundari and Krishnabhamini to act for him. He also played a role in persuading young women of decent families to join theatre. Among the women whom he thus persuaded to take up acting, two sisters – Kankabati and Chandravati – became very well known. They were daughters of a Brahmo zamindar and honorary magistrate and had been born in Muzaffarpur. Kankabati had graduated from Bethune College.

Natyamandir folded up at the end of the decade, having run out of lease. Sisir Bhaduri then joined Art Theatre. It was with the Art Theatre group that he travelled to the United States to hold shows. His *Sita* got reviews in New York in 1931.

Two new theatres started running in 1931. One of these was Rangmahal, and Sisir Kumar joined it after he returned from America. Less than two years later, however, he acquired a lease for Star Theatre and in early 1934 he got it running again as Naba Natyamandir. But he could run it for only about three years. He had relatively far greater success in early 1941 when he started directing the theatre group called Srirangam and kept it running for 15 years.

Tagore was one of the greatest dramatists in Bengali literature. He also had a keen interest in the production of plays and was himself a good actor. He staged his own plays with remarkable success. Yet his contribution to professional Bengali theatre was not much to speak of. In theme and mood, his plays were way beyond the comprehension of ordinary viewers. The kind of environment in which his plays might have got lively representations was also not available in his lifetime. The play that got staged several times in Bengali theatre during his time was *Raja-o-Rani*. However immature, excessively emotional and overdramatic the play may appear in a literary assessment, it was this play among all of Tagore's plays that drew Bengali theatre-goers most. Bengali theatre was not yet quite ready for the far superior *Bisarjan, Achalayatan, Raktakarabi, Raja, Dakghar* and *Muktadhara*. Theatre producers might even have felt that some of these plays would hurt the religious sentiments of Hindu audiences. Sisir Kumar Bhaduri did stage *Bisarjan* after 1925, but it did not attract viewers. Yet this play was successfully staged in the 1960s. By that time, not only had theatre and dramatics recorded sufficient progress, the theatre audience had also become far more discerning and sophisticated. Religious sensibilities in particular were no longer quite so vulnerable, nor were tastes so old-fashioned. The Bahuroopi group staged with roaring success not only *Bisarjan* but also such allegorical plays as *Raktakarabi* and *Raja.*

Sisir Bhaduri

Indeed, many of Tagore's plays got staged in the 1960s and 1970s. Seen in this context, Tagore must be acknowledged to have been far too advanced for his time. One reason for professional theatre's new interest in him was the birth anniversary celebrations in 1961. Many of his plays including *Dakghar, Achalayatan, Tapati, Muktadhara* and *Kaler Jatra* were now successfully staged. It must also be remembered, however, that the bulk of the theatrical performances of Tagore's plays were done by amateur rather than professional theatre groups.

Professional theatre in the late 1930s faced a crisis of good plays. There were no truly great playwrights at this time, nor theatre directors of the stature of Sisir Bhaduri. Nor did any famous actor appear in Bengali theatre in this decade. Yet this was a time of keen political consciousness, with the freedom movement gaining momentum on the one hand and interest in Marxism growing among young people on the other. At this moment of crisis, the Indian People's Theatre Association, or IPTA, an organisation of Marxist writers, journalists and artists, came forward to give expression to the new political consciousness. These progressive votaries of culture expressed empathy for the lower rungs of society. Nor was their empathy simply humanistic; ideologically it belonged to the leftist end of the political spectrum.

In this environment, the play *Nabanna* ('New Harvest') brought about a revolution in Bengali drama. The play was written by Bijon Bhattacharjya.

In the year after the great famine during the Second World War, that is, in 1944, he had written a one-act play called *Jabanbandi* ('Statement') and it was staged in Star Theatre. It told the piteous story of how a poor peasant family found itself pushed into even greater poverty. Memories of the recent famine were still perhaps fresh in people's minds, and the one-act play created quite a stir. Encouraged by this success, he now wrote a full-length play on the same theme – *Nabanna*, which produced a new movement in Bengali theatre.

Nabanna was enacted in 1944, at the initiative of the IPTA artists, who believed in revolutionary thinking. The playwright himself along with Shambhu Mitra directed the play. The play was received with far greater enthusiasm than they had expected. The play ran to packed audiences at Srirangam Theatre. Though the stage was ordinary, the stagecraft was novel. There was none of the old-style sets, wings, drop scenes and all the various stage props and artificial devices used in theatrical productions. The simple and unaffected acting and stage set-up were appreciated by viewers. Despite the packed hall, however, the play did not run beyond seven nights at Srirangam Theatre. For, envious and orthodox managers of professional theatre feared that it would force them to change their style of staging plays. Nor were they keen to see an amateur theatre group take over the space occupied by professional theatre. So *Nabanna* had to stop running at Srirangam. In the absence of a dedicated theatrical stage, the directors of the play now started putting it up in various halls and in spite of this limitation met with remarkable success. About 7,000 people are claimed to have watched an open theatre performance of the play in 1945. Around 1950, the IPTA staged over a hundred plays and made drama an immensely popular form.

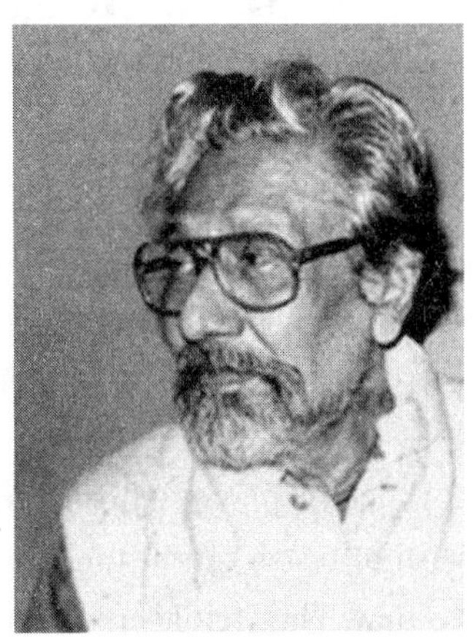
Shambhu Mitra

Notwithstanding his empathy for the common man, Shambhu Mitra was unable to remain restricted by the IPTA's leftist ideology for very long. He, therefore, slowly removed himself from this organisation. But the success that he had tasted while staging *Nabanna* encouraged him to form a new theatre group. With a group of young men and women interested in drama, he set up a new group called Bahuroopi in 1948. The group debuted with Tulsi Lahiri's play *Chenrha Tar* ('The Snapped Chord'). The play had thematic similarities with *Nabanna.* After this, however, Shambhu Mitra lost faith in drama dominated by the message of class struggle. He now turned his attention to drama for its own sake, motivated by his faith in the ideals of humanism, truth and beauty. This started with his adaptation of Tagore's *Char Adhyay* (Four chapters) in dramatic form in 1951. The spectacular success of this play made Bahuroopi famous as an amateur theatre group and gave it a permanent place in the history of Bengali theatre. The group eventually enacted quite a few of Tagore's plays with great success, including such symbolic plays as *Raktakarabi* (1954) and *Raja* (1964).

Whatever the progress of Bengali theatre and dramatics, the dearth of competent playwrights was never removed. The Bahuroopi group did not wish to restrict itself to Tagore's plays, and nor is it possible for any group to do that. They felt keenly the need for new plays. Yet, this need could not have been fulfilled with home-grown plays. Shambhu Mitra, therefore, looked to the West, turning his gaze to even classical Greek drama. Astonishingly, his group staged a play like *Oedipus* with extraordinary success. Among foreign plays, this group also enacted, with great expertise, *Putul Khela* adapted from Ibsen's *A Doll's House* and *Dashachakra* adapted from *The People's Enemy.* The Bahuroopi group brought about an epochal change in Bengali dramatics by snatching drama from professional theatre and handing it to amateur theatre. Indeed, it was Bahuroopi's success that established the idea of 'group theatre' on a strong foundation in Bengal. Thereafter, group theatre began to show the way in Bengali dramatics, whereas professional theatre got left behind.

Shambhu Mitra was perhaps the greatest actor in 20th century Bengali theatre. He had started his acting career in professional theatre, though he later virtually brought about the end of professional theatre. He, indeed, founded a whole new tradition in Bengali dramatics. Of course, he had a pool of inspired actors including Tripti Mitra. He also had excellent technical support in his stage designer Khaled Choudhury and lighting expert Tapas Sen.

Utpal Dutt

Another major theatrical talent emerged in Bengal in Shambhu Mitra's time, though occupying a position at the other end of the dramatic spectrum. He was Utpal Dutt. He started off with Shakespeare but did not stay restricted to Shakespeare. In 1947 he built up his own theatre group—The Little Theatre group. A few years later he came into the possession of Minerva Theatre. Consequently, he never again had to worry about a stage for his shows.

Utpal Dutt was influenced by leftist politics. He did not find plays to uphold the leftist political ideal in the existing literature, so he ended up writing a number of plays himself. Not all his plays can be said to have attained a high literary standard. But then, that was not his aim anyway. His objective was to reach out to the masses through these plays. He even wrote plays in the *jatra* mould, believing, perhaps not unreasonably, that *jatra* was the easiest and the surest way of appealing to ordinary viewers.

Utpal Dutt culled his themes from Indian and international situations in order to convey to the people the political ideal he believed in. The discrimination against blacks in the United States; the war of liberation in Vietnam; the revolution in Russia; the situation in Germany just before Hitler's rise to power; the naval mutiny in India—these were among the varied subjects that he chose for his plays, sometimes with immense success. He also showed the way for the plays and *jatras* that were written to help the leftist movement that in the 1960s progressively gained strength in West Bengal.

Quite a few other group theatres that were sympathetic to the leftist cause, though not rigidly leftist but rather, committed to the ideals of truth and beauty, came up in the 1960s. Among these, Nandikar deserves special mention. It was established right at the beginning of the decade. Led by Ajitesh Bandyopadhyay, this theatre group was not able to make commercial gains but it raised the standard of Bengali dramatics. Like Shambhu Mitra,

Ajitesh, too, keenly felt the dearth of good plays. He adapted Brecht's *Three Penny Opera* into *Tin Paysar Pala* (1970) with remarkable success. Another of his achievements was the adaptation of a short story (Cherry Orchard) by Chekhov as the play *Manjari Amer Manjari.* Bengali theatre in the early 1970s was immensely enriched by performances such as Utpal Dutt's *Tiner Talowar,* Ajitesh's *Bhalo Manush* and Badal Sircar's *Shatabdi.* Badal Sircar's *Ebong Indrajit* also created a stir. Another playwright and director as successful as Badal Sircar was Manoj Mitra.

It was group theatre, then, that led Bengali dramatics and took it forward in the second half of the 20th century. But professionally run commercial theatre continued to exist. Rang Mahal and Srirangam kept on running alongside the old Star Theatre. Such theatres tried to keep afloat by getting cine actors to perform for them and staging plays such as *Bar-Badhu,* which were sexually titillating.

Theatre outside Calcutta

Though Bengali dramatics started in the capital Calcutta in the 1850s, within a single decade the mofussil was also touched by the new wind. It was not just that the amateur groups of Calcutta started to take their shows to the districts, plays were also staged at local initiatives. For instance, we know that in 1863, Durgaprasad Kar's *Swarnasrinkhal* was enacted in Barisal. And in Dhaka a theatre called Purbabanga Rangabhoomi was established in 1865. Dramatic performances must have been held in Dhaka even before this, otherwise a theatre would not suddenly have emerged from nowhere. By 1900, in fact, a good number of theatres had been established not only in Dhaka but all the big cities of the province. More importantly, even when a permanent stage was not available, dramatic performances were held at venues ranging from schoolrooms to Durga Puja mandaps by the amateur theatre groups. Whereas drama had once been unfamiliar and practically unknown in Bengal, scores of plays began to be written in the province no later than the second half of the 19th century and a keen interest in dramatic performances was created among educated people.

When Hindus, who were the mainstay of dramatic performances, migrated from East Bengal on a mass scale after the Partition of 1947, dramatics practically came to an end in Dhaka, even though the city now became the provincial capital. That a strong theatrical tradition had not developed in Dhaka was probably because of religious orthodoxy. It should be mentioned in this context that Muslim writers rarely wrote plays. Mir Mosharraf Hussein did write *Zamidardarpan* in the 1870s, when memories of *Neeldarpan* were still fresh, but this was a rare exception in the 19th century.

But though dramatics in Dhaka temporarily came to an end after Partition, the writing of plays and dramatic performances did not stop for ever. When Bengalis began to cherish their language and literature, and indeed Bengali culture as a whole, with renewed affection in the wake of the language movement, the pursuit of theatre started afresh. Munir Chaudhury was arrested during the language movement. He had a keen interest in dramatic literature and also loved acting. During his time in jail he wrote his famous short play *Kabar* ('Grave') and arranged to have it staged at Dhaka Central Jail on February 21, 1953. *Kabar* had flashes of brilliance, but it was not too rich in literary merit. It is beyond doubt, however, that Munir Chaudhury played a historic role in writing and enacting this play. Later, quite a few of Tagore's plays were staged in Dhaka in 1961 as part of the birth centenary celebrations. In 1962-63, Munir Chowdhury took the initiative of staging Michael's *Krishnakumari* and his own *Raktakto Prantar* ('Bloody Fields'). Nurul Momen was also particularly enthusiastic about writing plays, and he did write quite a few. Plays were also written to meet the needs of Dhaka Radio and, after 1964, television, and those plays were enacted, too. Notwithstanding such fragmented and discrete efforts, no permanent theatre was established in Dhaka, and nor was there any theatre group.

Dhaka got its professional theatre in 1972, after the war of liberation. Two things made this happen. First, theatre enthusiasts hoped that the pursuit of Bengali culture would be possible with renewed fervour in liberated Bangladesh and they expected official patronage. That apart, their exposure to the theatre of Calcutta as refugees in that city just a year earlier had immensely enthused them to organise dramatic performances. They lacked a stage, but this they made good by using the stage of a women's association. A theatre movement now developed in Dhaka very fast and plays began to be successfully staged. Dhaka never really had any dearth of talent.

It did not take very long for the theatre of Dhaka to almost catch up with that of Calcutta in terms of standard. One cannot help but wonder at the way people like Ghulam Mustafa, Ramendu Majumdar, Firdausi Majumdar, Ali Zakir, Abul Hayat, Abdullah Al Mamun and Mamunur Rashid started producing plays with remarkable success in spite of the limitations within which they functioned. Equally amazing were the people who, like Syed Shamsul Haq, started writing plays. Plays such as *Payer Awaj Pawa Jae* ('Footsteps') and *Nur Al Diner Sarajibon* ('The Whole Life of Nur Al Din') are remarkable in Bengali literature as a whole.

Bioscope in Bengal

The city was not just the capital of India; Calcutta was the largest city in the entire British empire. For this reason, the ripples emitted by all technological innovations lapped against its shores first. The first film was screened in France, in 1896. Within a few months it was screened in Calcutta. Many people at that time referred to cinema as 'bioscope', and it was in fact this word that had greater currency in Bengal in the initial years.

The companies that held bioscope shows were initially all foreign. Very soon – in 1898 – a Bengali gentleman set up a bioscope company. He was Hiralal Sen. He did not just hold shows for bioscopes made by others, he started making his own films from 1901. To do this he filmed scenes from the plays that ran in the theatres of Calcutta—for instance, *Alibaba, Sarala, Sitaram* and *Buddha*. In 1901 itself these fragmentary images were screened in Classic Theatre. But there was something more important that he did: in those early years of moving images, he made documentary films using snippets that he had made by filming events of the anti-Partition and Swadeshi movements, the coronation ceremony for George V in Delhi, and people bathing at the pond in his village. He was from Dhaka, and so, though he had set up his company in Calcutta, it was in various locations in East Bengal that he started screening bioscopes from 1911. He even took initiatives to screen bioscopes beyond Bengal, in Assam and Bihar.

Films in those days were silent. It was not easy to either tell a story or to depict characters through them. Yet even these silent films generated a lot of popular interest. In response to this demand, several movie halls were built in Calcutta. Companies were also formed to distribute these films. In 1902 a Parsi gentleman called Jamshedji Fremji set up such a company, called Madan Theatre. He started out by screening bioscopes in tents at various places in Calcutta. Needless to say, he screened English movies. But after Dadasaheb Phalke made *Raja Harishchandra* in 1913, he started showing Hindi films as well. This company also played a historic role in making Bengali films. The first Bengali feature film, *Bilwamangal*, was made at its initiative in 1919. After that it made movies such as *Nal-Damayanti, Mahabharat, Dhrubacharitra, Paper Porinam* ('Consequence of Sin') and *Matrisneha* ('Mother's Love'). The two Bengalis who translated the plan of making the first Bengali feature film, *Bilwamangal*, into reality were Priyanath Ganguly and Jyotish Bandyopadhyay. Priyanath Ganguly went on to direct a few other movies. Dhirendranath Ganguly also directed a number of films in the age of silent cinema.

The first Bengali talkie, *Jamai Shasthi*, was also made by Madan. The film earned immediate success after its release on April 12, 1931. Encouraged, Madan made five other films within a short time, including one in Hindi. After that, however, the company folded up for some unknown reason.

An engineer who had completed his studies in England came forward to fill the vacuum left by Madan—he was Birendra Nath Sarkar. Whatever his original profession or skills might have been, he became addicted to cinema while in England. That is why he set up a company called International Film Crafts immediately after returning from England in 1930 and made two silent films. The following year, he built up a company called New Theatres in order to make talkies.

Birendra Nath Sarkar attempted to use in his organisation the technological innovations that he had come across in England and the cinematic progress that he had witnessed there. He also fortunately found quite a few brilliant individuals to help him. All of them together took forward the nascent art of cinema in Bengali, some through their mastery of technology, and others through their music, acting or directorial abilities. Birendra Nath had Debaki Basu as his director, and later Pramathesh Barua. As for technology, cameraman Nitin Basu and sound engineer Mukul Basu deserve first mention. In music there were people like Raichand Boral, Krishna Chandra Dey, Pankaj Mullick, Kundan Lal Saigal and Kanan Devi.

Nazrul Islam, Sachin Dev Burman, Kamal Dasgupta, Himanshu Dutta, Ajoy Bhattacharya, Shailen Roy and Anupam Ghatak also later worked for films. Pramathesh Barua, Pahari Sanyal, Chhobi Biswas, Saigal and Kanan Devi acted in New Theatres films. New Theatres, in fact, left a contribution in the history of Bengali cinema that was far more significant than the role played by Madan, and it did so with the help of these talented individuals.

Kanan Devi

Within a year of the establishment of New Theatres, five films were made on behalf of this organisation, one after another. The first of the five was based on Saratchandra's *Dena Paona.* It was directed by Premankur Atorthi. The film was released in 1931. The following year, New Theatres made *Pallisamaj,* also based on a novel by Saratchandra. The organisation's first successful film, however, was *Chandidas* (1931-32). That apart, in 1932, *Natir Puja* enacted by the students of Santiniketan and directed by Tagore himself was filmed. Just as in the case of Bengali theatre it had been the plays by famous dramatists that made an impact, in Bengali cinema, too, a link with the famous names of Bengali literature was formed in the early years.

Indeed, Tagore and Saratchandra between them provided much material to Bengali cinema in its first phase. The sentimental narratives of the films adapted from Saratchandra's novels strongly drew Bengali movie-goers of the time. It is difficult to say how much of Tagore's greatness is left in his stories once they are stripped of his magical language. Nevertheless, even in the era of silent films a movie was made on the basis of one of his stories, at the initiative of Dhirendra Nath Ganguly. This film, made in 1921, was called *Manbhanjan.* Quite a few of Saratchandra's stories were also turned into films in the silent era. These were *Andhare Alo, Debdas* (1929), *Chandranath, Srikanta* and *Swami.* That apart, in 1931, Saratchandra had his *Charitraheen* made into a film under his own supervision and directed by Dhirendra Nath Ganguly. But this movie sans dialogue did not turn out to be particularly popular.

Saratchandra Chattopadhyay

Until 1947, a good number of films were adapted from stories by Saratchandra and Tagore, at the initiative of New Theatres. Other producers also came forward to make films based on the works of these two writers. Among the Saratchandra stories that were made into films were *Pallisamaj, Debdas, Grihadaha, Datta, Pandit Mashai, Barodidi, Parineeta, Kashinath, Ramer Sumati, Birajbou* and *Pather Dabi.* In the same period films were also made based on Tagore's *Chirokumar Sabha, Chokher Bali, Gora, Shodhbodh, Sheshrakkha* and *Noukadubi*, though not many among ordinary viewers could really get the hang of his narratives.

Though early Bengali cinema kept going back to these two towering personalities of Bengai literature for its stories, the film *Chandidas* turned out to be far more popular than the films adapted from the books. Its director was Debaki Basu. The film was lovingly done, the director himself being influenced by the Vaishnava philosophy. Dominated by its songs, the movie earned immense popularity. The kirtans sung by Krishna Chandra Dey in this film have not lost their appeal even after 80 years. The film's music director was Raichand Boral. In 1937 Debaki Basu made *Bidyapati*, in the mould of *Chandidas.* This film, too, was dominated by songs and was very popular. Debaki Basu continued to make many other successful movies for another quarter century.

Made three years after *Chandidas*, in 1935, *Debdas* far outstripped the former in popularity. The most successful actor of the time, Pramathesh Barua, was able to make full use of the sentimental and tragic story of love in this Saratchandra novel. Afterwards, too, films of this title and based on the same story were made in Bengali and Hindi at least five times. Even a Tamil version was made in 1936. There were also two Telugu versions in four decades. According to many critics, however, the 1935 *Debdas* was the best. Barua had borrowed only the outlines of Saratchandra's plot. The story he told, however, was largely his own interpretation. Indeed, he was able to turn this early sentimental and tragic story of Saratchandra into a veritable personal tragedy of the main characters, Debdas and Parbati. Barua was also able to establish a new benchmark in acting. He rejected the old affectedness and overly dramatic acting and introduced a more realistic style. Through this film he established himself as an actor and a director and at the same time gained recognition for New Theatres as one of the major studios of India.

Pramathesh Barua's next most well known Bengali film was *Mukti*, which was screened in 1937. In this film, too, he played the hero's role. Kanan Devi acted in the heroine's role. Like *Debdas*, this film, too, had a tragic ending. The success of *Debdas* had made Barua aware of Bengali viewers' taste for tearful sentimentality. In *Mukti*, too, he used this sentimentality. The hero – a young artist – sets his wife free by feigning suicide. His wife subsequently gets married to another man. Eventually he does actually die while trying to rescue her from a gang of kidnappers. In this film he also used the other Bengali weakness—for songs. The film had quite a few good songs, including some Tagore songs. Kanan Devi was then very young—a teenager just stepping into womanhood. Even when so young, however, she excelled in both acting and singing. The songs she sang in this film were very well received in their time. She had learnt a wide variety of songs from people like Bhishmadev Chattopadhyay, Raichand Boral, Nazrul Islam, Anadi Dastidar and Pankaj Mullick. Not just modern Bengali songs, she was also instrumental in making many Tagore songs popular. For instance, she plucked the song '*Aji sabar range range meshate hobe*' from the bhadralok drawing room and took it to every Bengali home across the social classes. Among the most popular songs of the time were '*Akashe helan diye paharh ghumae oi*', '*Jodi bhalo na lage to diyo na mon*', '*Ami banaphul go*' and '*Anadi kaler strote bhasa*'.

In this context, Kanan Devi's contribution to Bengali cinema must be mentioned. Her father died when she was nine or 10 years old. Her mother, widowed with two daughters, found herself thrown into extreme poverty. She herself has said that the family could not afford two square meals a day. But Kananbala's wealth was her extraordinary beauty. It was this that she banked on when one day she turned up at Madan Studio, having got a kindly gentleman to take her there. The feature film with which she secured her position in the world of cinema was the 1935 movie *Manmoyee Girls School.* By that time she was a mature young woman. Film historian Rabi Basu has written that many young and not-so-young men found their hearts beating faster at her sight. There was a time when her photographs, laid out on jute sheets, were sold on the pavements of Calcutta. In beauty and in fashion, she set the trends for her time. Women copied the kind of saris and blouses that she wore and imitated the design of her earrings. Not only did cinema make her popular, she in turn vastly increased the appeal of Bengali cinema with her beauty, her acting and her singing.

It was *Mukti* (1937) that fetched her the greatest fame in the first phase of her life. *Bidyapati* and *Sathi* in the following year were also popular. In the early 1940s she got the award for Best Actress twice in a row for *Parichay* and *Shesh Uttor.* Her glorious years as a heroine were between 1937 and 1944, and this was the time when she turned from Kananbala to the redoubtable Kanan Devi.

Thereafter, Kanan Devi in her thirties seemed better suited to play the wife and mother, rather than the heroine. She set an extraordinary ideal of motherhood with her quiet, dignified beauty. Viewers seemed to see in her the image of Saratchandra's heroines that they carried in their minds. Kanan Devi herself was aware of this. That is why she herself set up a film company called Srimati Pictures in 1948. Most of the movies she made were adapted from Saratchandra's stories.

Among the films for which Pramathesh Barua acquired fame in the 1930s, apart from *Debdas* and *Mukti,* were *Manjil, Adhikar, Rajat Jayanti, Zindagi* and *Shesh Uttor.* Barua was perhaps the most famous name in the first phase of the history of Bengali cinema. He was a popular romantic hero and at the same time a successful film director. His keen interest in the medium had brought him to the world of cinema. No matter whose story it was that he chose for his movies, he always wrote the script himself, thus reinterpreting the original narrative. He also gave a free hand to his actors.

The story of his own life can indeed be made into a film. He began life as a handsome prince, the son and heir of a family owning a large landed estate in Assam's Gauripur. After passing out of Presidency College in Calcutta in

1924, he proceeded to England for higher studies. But cinema, more than books, attracted him in the West. In London and Paris he was exposed to the work of well known film-makers. Once back in the country, he entered the film industry in Calcutta. After an initial phase of struggle, he joined New Theatres as an actor. It was during his association with New Theatres that he made his famous film *Debdas.* The film *Debdas* had a Bengali and a Hindi version. Barua himself played the hero in the Bengali film, while Saigal played the role in the Hindi movie. The Hindi version was released in the same year, that is, in 1935. Pramathesh Barua did not live long. He died at just 48 in 1951.

New Theatres was able to get hold of another film-maker: Nitin Basu. As an youngster Basu had been able, with his father's encouragement, to acquire a movie camera. He started directing films in the 1930s. He quickly learned the skill and in the following decade came up with some reasonably good films such as *Parichay, Lagan, Noukadubi* and *Milon.* He went on making movies into the 1970s, though he was never really able to strike out on a different or distinctive path.

The age of New Theatres was over at the start of the 1940s. The other smallish film companies that were around continued to make feature films, but they made only run-of-the-mill commercial films. These films had a concoction of religious, Puranic and musical elements, along with an eminent absence of realism. IPTA, the organisation of progressive writers and artists, now came forward to play a meaningful role. The idea was to retrieve cinema from the stranglehold of Puranic narratives and utopia and locate it in everyday reality and contemporary society. Among those who contributed to this effort in the early phase, Khwaja Ahmed Abbas, Bimal Roy, Nimai Ghosh and Ritwik Ghatak deserve particular mention. Khwaja Abbas's *Dharti ki Lal* was an extremely praiseworthy film. Made in 1946, the theme of this film was the famine that had taken place three years earlier. Khwaja shows with great expertise the way in which the famine shattered the way of life in villages. Balraj Sahni, Ravi Shankar, Shambhu Mitra and Krishan Chander were all associated with this film. The movie anticipates Satyajit Ray's *Ashani Sanket.*

Bimal Roy's *Udayer Pathe* was made in 1944, and two years later it won an award at the Cannes Film Festival. Nimai Ghosh made his *Chinnamool*

(1950) on the heart-rending story of the homeless people who migrated from East Bengal after Partition and sought refuge in West Bengal. Ghosh was assisted by Ritwik Ghatak in making this film. Two years later Ritwik on his own made the film *Nagarik*, on the same theme. Bimal Roy made *Do Bigha Zamin* in 1953. These films were thematically different from the commercial films of the time and pointed to a new direction in film-making.

It was Satyajit Ray who led the way in making films that were even more radically different, followed soon after by Ritwik Ghatak and later by Mrinal Sen and Aparna Sen. Ray's family background had helped in the development of his genius. His grandfather Upendrakishore Raychaudhury was a well known writer and a musician. He was also the first Bengali to travel to England in 1899 to study photography. His son, Sukumar Ray, occupies a distinctive and unique position in Bengali literature. He, too, studied photography in England. His son was Satyajit. Like his father and grandfather, Satyajit was also a writer and was well-versed in music. Like them again, he travelled to England to study, though not photography but the art of film-making. He had also studied art at Santiniketan. All this added up to the process that eventually made him a world-renowned film director. He regularly watched movies and also read up voraciously on cinema. He met the French film-maker Jean Renoir when the latter arrived in Bengal in 1948-49 to make his film *The River*. He chose Satyajit as his assistant director. Satyajit acquired first-hand experience of the practical aspects of film-making while working on this movie.

Satyajit Ray

Soon after this he went to England, only for a few months. But he managed to take in some film or the other almost every day during that time. He is said to have watched 99 films in four and a half months. He watched with close attention the movies made by the greatest contemporary European and American directors. One film in particular fascinated Ray—the Italian movie

Bicycle Thieves. The influence of this film can be detected in his very first movie, *Pather Panchali.* But Ray was also influenced by the realism of films that had been made in the 1940s and in the early 1950s. Some critics have claimed that even the play *Nabanna* had made an impression on him. *Pather Panchali* does not have any song sequence, something so dear to Bengali viewers. There is no sentimental love story in it, nor the glitter or wealth of cities. What it has is the prosaic story of a rural family grappling with extreme poverty, described by critics as neorealist representation. The film, therefore, got no recognition from viewers at home before it won awards abroad. The film that Ray had in mind was apparently so unappealing that he was not able to find a producer for it and had to struggle to find the money to make it. It is doubtful whether he would be able to complete the film had he not eventually received a favour from the Chief Minister, who had been a friend of his father's. *Pather Panchali* is a major milestone not just in Bengali cinema but in Indian cinema as a whole.

After the success of his first film, Ray continued to make one remarkable film after another and placed Bengali, indeed Indian, cinema on the global map. He made *Aparajito* ('The Unconquered') the year after *Pather Panchali* was released in 1955. The following year came *Parash Pathar* ('Philosopher's Stone') and *Jalsaghar* in the year after that. In 1559 he completed the Apu Trilogy with *Apur Sangsar* ('Apu's World'). *Mahanagar* was one of his notable films. In this film he beautifully represented the urban middle-class family's struggle for survival in a big city. Immediately after it he made *Charulata.* The Apu Trilogy still occupies a special place in the history of world cinema, as does this 1965 film, *Charulata.* Working on it some 10 years after the release of his first film, Ray surpassed himself in this film—such was the mastery that he showed in the script, scene sequencing, use of camera, editing and music. Ray himself has also claimed that *Charulata* is his best film. *Charulata* differs from the original story, *Nastaneerh,* in the focus that Ray chose for it. In *Nastaneerh,* Tagore drew a brilliant and detailed picture of how the home of Charulata and Bhupati was destroyed with a nuanced psychological analysis. In *Charulata,* however, it is not Bhupati but the lonely, childless Charu, deprived of her husband's company and with nothing to keep her occupied, whose personal tragedy is depicted.

Ray continued with his experimenting after *Charulata* and came up with ever new films. Particularly remarkable among these are *Ashani Sanket, Jana Aranya, Shatranj ke Khilari, Shakha Prashakha* and *Agantuk. Ganashatru* based on Ibsen's *Enemy of the People* is also a notable name in Bengali cinema. Ray founded yet another new tradition by making a few movies for young viewers. The first, and perhaps the best, of these was *Gupi Gain Bagha Bain* (1968). Among the others, *Sonar Kella, Jai Baba Phelunath* and the *Gupi Gain* sequel *Heerak Rajar Deshe* are also noteworthy. He also made movies based on Tagore's stories, including *Tin Kanya. Charulata* of course was the greatest of these.

A contemporary of Ray who was also richly talented was Ritwik Ghatak. As we have already mentioned, he was associated with the making of *Chinnamool* in 1950. He then made a film of his own in 1952. Ray and Ghatak really held completely different points of view. The family and educational backgrounds of the two men were also quite different. Ray was a product and inheritor of the liberal tradition of the 19th century. His ideal was the humanism of Tagore, and his aim was the pursuit of art. It was art that he sought to create in his movies. His objective was not to preach any dogma or ideology. Ghatak, on the other hand, belonged to a lower-middle-class family, and leftist humanism was for him a more powerful impulse than liberal thinking. His work contains loving portrayals of the struggles in the lives of people at the bottom of society. He, too, sought to create art through cinema, but expressing empathy for the down and out and upholding leftist ideals were to him not any less important than art.

Partition and the human tragedies that appeared in its aftermath come back repeatedly in his creations. Both Ray and Ghatak were originally from East Bengal, but the two could not have been more different in temperament. Ray's is the ultimate expression of the cultural excellence that had Calcutta at its centre. Whereas Ghatak seems to carry the scent of the soil. Working people, their struggles for survival and even the regional dialects in which they talk come alive in Ghatak's films. Yet he was not as great a craftsman as he was an artist. Though there are flashes of brilliance in his films – in dialogue, script, editing and in acting – there are also flaws in sequencing, presentation and editing. In allowing himself to be carried away by feeling, he has sometimes compromised the restraint that art demands and broken the rules of craftsmanship. His genius thus seems to recall that of Nazrul Islam. *Ajantrik, Titas Ekti Nadir Nam, Meghe Dhaka Tara, Komal Gandhar, Subarnarekha, Jukti Takko Gappo*—an observation that they all bear out, to a greater or a lesser extent.

Though not quite as original a genius as either Ray or Ghatak, Mrinal Sen also made movies that were works of art rather than commercial films. Like Ghatak, he, too, showed an interest in making movies on ordinary people. His *Akaler Sandhane, Kharij, Ekdin Pratidin,* etc., may well command noteworthy positions in Bengali cinema. Aparna Sen has also been making art films since the late 20th century.

Bengali cinema, however, would not have survived as an industry if art films in the mould of Ray, Ghatak, Mrinal Sen and Aparna Sen were the only kind of movies produced, as they catered to a clutch of select viewers. Very few viewers actually watched Ray's films. Most directors and producers came forward to make the kind of films that drew the crowds. Among the directors who made the best and the most appealing films using popular gimmicks such as sentimental narratives, clowning, song-and-dance sequences, sexual titillation and violence were Pramathesh Barua and Debaki Basu in the first phase of Bengali talkies. But after Bengali cinema came into its own in the 1950s, it was Ajay Kar, Asit Sen and Tapan Sinha who gained recognition as the most successful directors. Although Ajay Kar did make the commonplace *Barhdidi* and *Atal Jaler Ahbhan* early in his career, he later directed such extremely popular movies as *Harano Sur, Saptapadi* and *Sat Pake Bandha.* The most notable films of Asit Sen were *Swaralipi, Uttor Phalguni, Deep Jwele Jai* and *Jibontrishna.* The best known films of Tapan Sinha are *Kabuliwala, Atithi, Hasulibanker Upakatha, Jatugriha, Galpo Holeo Sotyi, Ekhoni,* etc. The Agradoot group and Sudhir Mukherjee also made a good number of successful commercial films. The mention of just one film made by each of them should suffice in the context: *Agni Pariksha* by Agradoot and *Shapmochan* by Sudhir Mukerjee.

Directors and producers have played a historic role in cinema history by making films. Many actors, likewise, have also played a historic role. Not only have they taken Bengali cinema forward, they have wielded significant influence in the everyday lives, clothes and deportment of Bengalis. The first generation of actors who made this kind of impact included Pramathesh Barua, Chhobi Biswas, Pahari Sanyal and Kanan Devi. From the 1950s, however, we got such extraordinary heroes and heroines as Suchitra Sen and Uttam Kumar. Just as the Kanan-Pramathesh partnership had left a powerful impact on the minds of cinema-goers in the first phase of Bengali films, the Suchitra-Uttam partnership left a similar, or maybe we should say much greater, impact.

Between 1953 and 1975, Suchitra Sen and Uttam Kumar partnered as co-stars in a total of 30 movies. But it was the first four or five movies that established them as the most popular screen couple in the over 80 years of Bengali cinema. The Suchitra-Uttam films seemed to shower a veritable feast of dreams that had remained unfulfilled in Bengali middle-class and lower-middle-class lives. Ordinary viewers thronged the movie halls to taste those dreams. Their first film together was *Sare Chuattor* (1953). But they became popular through their second film in the following year, *Agni Pariksha*. There may be a difference of opinion on Suchitra Sen's acting abilities, but both she and Uttam Kumar were so good-looking, their romantic roles felt so natural and unaffected, and their partnership was apparently so perfect, that audiences accepted them far more as a screen couple than separately, as individual actors. Suchitra Sen set a new ideal in the representation of the heroine's role. Her extraordinary beauty, style of talking, smart clothes, the loving gaze that she turned on the hero and her unabashed intimacy with him set an ideal of the courting couple in the minds of young people. In the roles enacted by the Suchitra-Uttam partnership, they observed a reflection of something that was absent in their own middle class families but which they deeply desired and tried to imagine. Suchitra Sen's popularity did not just enhance her own stature, it also immensely helped Bengali cinema. In particular, the 30 films that she did with Uttam Kumar drew audiences away from Hindi movies to Bengali films.

Uttam Kumar was a good-looking and competent actor. No one in Bengali cinema has in fact surpassed him in fame and popularity as a hero. He did 27 movies with Sabitri Chattopadhyay, too, but these movies did not acquire sufficient popularity. Likewise, the films that Suchitra Sen acted in with Ashok Kumar, Basanta Choudhury, etc., had only limited success. I have already said this earlier in the chapter 'Traditions of Music in Bengal', but it bears mention again in this context that in most Suchitra-Uttam movies the playback singers for the couple were Hemanta and Sandhya Mukhopadhyay. The appeal of their singing seemed to vastly increase through the way in which Uttam Kumar presented Hemanta Mukhopadhyay's songs and Suchitra presented Sandhya Mukhopadhyay's. The mention of just a couple of instances, those of *Agni Pariksha* and *Shapmochan*, should be enough in the context.

Cinema of Dhaka

All major ventures in the colonial era were centred in the capital. The film industry, too, developed in Calcutta. But the hinterland for the businesses and industrial activities of the capital comprised vast areas dotted with villages, small cities, towns and market towns. The majority of the cinema audiences lived in the mofussil. It did not therefore take long for movie halls to come up in the district headquarters, away from Calcutta.

The first movie hall outside Calcutta was perhaps set up in Dhaka. In 1913-14 a movie hall by the name of Picture House started functioning there. Regular shows were not held yet. What was screened when there was a show cannot really be described as cinema. After the formation of Pakistan, this hall became known as Shabistan. The second hall that Dhaka got was called Picture Palace, which was later renamed as Roopmahal. This hall started functioning in 1924. In the district towns of East Bengal away from Dhaka, nearly 80 halls were established even before Partition.

Not just movie halls, efforts to make films also started in Dhaka in the age of silent cinema itself. Curiously enough, it was a conservative Muslim family that in 1928-29 took the initiative—the family of the Dhaka nawabs. The silent film that got made then was titled *Sukumari*. An employee of Jagannath Collage, Ambuj Gupta, directed the film. The role of the hero was played by a son of the nawab family, Khwaja Nasrullah. But the Muslim society of the time was so hostile to anything to do with acting that no woman could be found to play the heroine's role. The heroine's role was, therefore, played by a young man called Syed Abdus Sobhan. This short film was not screened for the public. But what the private screening of the movie within the nawab's family circles proved was that it was possible to make movies in Dhaka. It should be mentioned in this context that hostility to acting was so intense in Muslim society that the few Muslims who were associated with cinema in Calcutta suppressed their real names. For instance, Ata-ur-Rahman became Pinaki Roy, Obawedul Haq became Himadri Choudhury, Fateh Lohani became Kiran Kumar and Anwara Begum became Banani Choudhury.

Whatever that may be, Ambuj Gupta and the Nawab's family, enthused by their success in making a film, now decided to make a full-length feature film. Work on the film started in 1929. Titled *The Last Kiss*, this film, too, had young people from the Nawab's family, including Nasrullah, acting in it. The producers realised that for cinema to be successful, women's roles would have to be played by women. The female cast for the movie, therefore, was chosen from among prostitutes. A woman called Lalita played the heroine. It took the film two years to be released after it was made. In 1931 it was screened in what was then called Mukul cinema. It was a silent film, and apart from Bengali, it was subtitled in English and Urdu as well.

But the age of silent films was over. In the same year, the first Bengali talkie was released in Calcutta. No other film, therefore, was made in Dhaka. Even when after Partition Dhaka became the capital of East Bengal, conditions favourable for a film industry to develop did not immediately emerge. In the first place, the kind of skill needed for the making of films was not readily available in Dhaka. There were no directors, actors, photographers or technicians, and nor were there laboratories or other technological infrastructure to make movies. On top of everything else, Islamic attitudes to dramatics were hostile. This, too, perhaps held back the growth of cinema in East Pakistan.

The first feature film that got made in East Pakistan was titled *Mukh o Mukhosh* (1956; The Face and the Facade). To make this film, however, technicians had to be brought in from outside. There was still no studio in Dhaka, and no laboratory, either. Dhaka got its first film laboratory in 1958. So much of the work on the film had to be done in Karachi.

In the Pakistani regime, quite a few films were made during the 1960s. Though some of these dealt with contemporary urban realities, the themes were chiefly drawn from folk narratives and from life in the countryside and often had scant connection with realism. *Mukh o Mukhosh* was made in East Pakistan at a time when in West Bengal Satyajit Ray was established as an internationally acclaimed director. As in literature, music and drama, so in cinema, too, East Bengal was behind West Bengal by half a century or even longer. These films gave joy because ordinary people were able to identify with them, just as they could identify with folk music. Yet the excellence that had developed in folk music was absent in the cinema of East Bengal.

❋❋❋

ARCHITECTURE, ART AND CRAFT

As in the Bengali language, literature and music, thc last 1,000 years saw a flowering of architecture, art and craft. What should, however, be kept in mind at the outset is that because of the adverse climatic conditions in this part of the world, a consistent and continuous tradition of architecture could not grow in Bengal. Moreover, from the time of the Pala regime in the 8th century, architecture in Bengal was repeatedly exposed to external influences and, consequently, often changed character. However, a certain unity of design is manifest through the ages in the thatched mud huts of the Bengal countryside. The differences consist in the building materials—people have built mud houses in northern Bengal and in the Rarh plains of the west, which are areas of scanty rainfall; but in the heavy-rainfall areas of eastern and southern Bengal, bamboo and straw have been used to build homes. The extreme simplicity of the design and building technique of these dwellings drew the attention of people in other parts of India. For instance, the mud-and-straw homes of Bengal crept into the Gujrati language in the form of 'bungalows'. The mud-and-straw huts of Bengal still do not show any noticeable changes in design and layout. With the arrival of tin in recent times, the homes of relatively well-off families in the countryside show a shift in the building materials but not any changes in style.

In urban Bengal, on the other hand, external influences have been pervasive in the homes built by and under the regimes of the sultans and the rajas. In century after century, therefore, new traditions in architecture have constantly been created. A close look at the architecture shows that the soft clayey soil, heavy rainfall and a topography criss-crossed with rivers and canals not unexpectedly left a defining mark on Bengal's building styles. For instance, a deep foundation and extremely thick walls had to be built for any permanent construction. The walls of many medieval mosques have been found to be 6 to 8 feet thick. The materials used determined the building methods. Stones were not as easily available in Bengal as they were in northern India. Bricks were therefore used instead of stones. Edifices made of bricks must necessarily be different from those built with stones. More importantly, the impermanence of older instances of architecture that might have served as models left the architecture of Bengal with no paradigms that could be followed. Architectural styles consequently kept on changing with changing times. To explain with a counterexample, a certain continuity can be seen in the architecture that evolved over the centuries in Persia, Egypt, Greece and Rome. The columns that were built in Greece and Rome centuries before the time of Christ have not disappeared after the passage of more than 2,000 years. Not so in Bengal. The climate of Bengal and the materials used in building combined to ensure that ancient architecture did not survive very long.

Moreover, regimes kept changing in Bengal throughout history. The rulers often came from outside Bengal—some came from southern India, some from the Middle East and Central Asia, and some from distant Europe. The constructions that they undertook and patronised as the ruling class initially bore the stamp of the lands that they came from. But the intensity of the influence was bound to wear off in this frontier province and eventually yield to regional characteristics peculiar to Bengal. Under the sultans, for instance, Bengal's rulers for good measure largely rejected the architectural styles of Delhi in their efforts to repudiate the authority of their nominal overlords in Delhi. The defiance of Delhi's political authority more or less meant an acceptance of local as well as West and Central Asian influences. Besides, the ruling classes of foreign origin had to depend on local craftsmen for all their constructions. Above all, Bengal's culture of assimilation left a deep imprint on the region's architecture.

Since most early samples of Bengal's ancient architecture and art are lost because of climatic conditions and the nature of the building materials, the pattern of evolution in architecture and art cannot be clearly pointed out. It is not even known how far back into antiquity the history of Bengal's architecture stretches, or how wide the geographical area over which it was spread. But at least two remarkable specimens that have survived bear evidence that noteworthy constructions were getting built in Bengal from ancient times. One of these is Chandraketugarh, or Chandraketu Fort, while the other is Mahasthangarh. Both date back to the pre-Christian era. Word about Chandraketugarh travelled to Europe in its own day. European scholars have referred to Chandraketugarh in their writings in the first two centuries after Christ.

Architecture of Ancient Bengal

Chandraketugarh is situated some 25 kilometres from Calcutta, in 24 Parganas of West Bengal. The area also goes by the name of Berhachanpa. It is not known how the place came to be called Chandraketugarh. The formidable size of the site suggests that it was a capital city, and there is evidence indicating that it survived as such for several centuries. The site is almost two miles long. The ruins suggest that it was a city of many mansions and was ringed by a boundary wall on all sides. Ancient coins, figurines, utensils, ivory ornaments and various other things have been found here. Sculptures in the Graeco-Roman style, specimens of the Brahmi script of Mauryan times and a range of seals have been found too. The ancient coins that have been found at the site were all cast in moulds. Figurines of the snake deity (Naga devi) and of the Yaksha have been found, but none of the Buddha. That makes it appear that the place had Hindu kings. Any Mauryan influence would have been of an indirect nature. The place served as a capital for these kings during the age of the Guptas, too. The remains of a large temple of the Gupta age have survived in Chandraketugarh, and some scholars believe that these are the oldest of all the temple ruins that have been found in Bengal.

The city had a system of drainage, which decisively proves that the town planners had access to developed technology and belonged to a society that had made significant civilisational advances. Excavations have unearthed terracotta pipes of diameters of 5 and 8 inches quite deep below the surface.

The other ancient archaeological site in Bengal is Mahasthangarh, situated eight miles from Bogra town in the district of that name in Bangladesh. Stretching over nearly one square mile on the bank of the Karotoya river, the ancient ruins of Mahasthan were discovered during British rule. This fort, too, must have been the capital of a kingdom. In 1879, Alexander

Cunningham identified it as Pundranagara or the capital of Pundravardhana. Archaeologists had earlier assumed that the fort was built sometime around the time of the birth of Christ. But a stone inscription in the Brahmi script, dating back to the 4th century BC and carrying a mention of Pundranagara, has been found at Mahasthan. This shows that the town was at that time under Mauryan rule, which means it was founded in an even earlier age. The technology of carbon-dating has since been used to tell the age of this archeological site with greater accuracy. The oldest finds of the site have been found to be dating back to 400 years before the birth of Christ, that is, pre-dating Mauryan rule. However, the city was built not in one particular historical period but gradually over many centuries. The various parts of the city were built in the Mauryan, Sunga, Kusana, Gupta and Pala ages, and parts of it were even built in the Indo-Muslim age. Most of the archaeological finds of the site belong to the Pala age.

There are not many finds that pre-date the Mauryan age, however. The little that has been found of earlier times is mostly an assortment of utensils including coloured pottery. On the other hand, finds of the Mauryan and Kusana periods include, apart from pottery, bronze mirrors, lamps, clay artefacts and statuettes, silver coins, ornaments and jewels. That apart, brick houses have been found. It was at this time, that is, during the time of the Mauryans and the Kusanas after them, that *surkhi*, or lime mortar (crushed bricks with lime), was used for the first time as an important building material in masonry. Among the finds of the Gupta age are stone vessels, brick houses, terracotta artefacts and figurines and glass ornaments. Most of the houses found at Mahasthan belong, however, to the time of the Pala kings. Three gateways to the fort belonging to the Pala period have been discovered, and each of these had quarters for guards on its inner side. Nothing has been found that can be said to be indisputably belonging to the Sena era. But there is evidence to show that constructions were undertaken here in Indo-Muslim times. Mosques discovered at the site are among the noteworthy finds.

Excavation at Mahasthan started in 1928-29, and it was around this time that most of the archaeological discoveries were made here. The next notable phase of exploration at the site was in the 1990s, with French collaboration. Yet much remains to be unearthed at Mahasthangarh—in particular, the mysteries of the many mounds near and around the site remain unresolved.

Excavation work recently carried out in the larger Dhaka district uncovered an ancient city in the Wari-Bateshwar area which was built during the rule of the Mauryan dynasty. These 2,500-year-old ruins near the old course of the river Brahmaputra are a significant archaeological discovery. Among the artefacts found here were silver punch-marked coins, different types of earthen pots, roulette ware, knobbed ware, northern black polished ware, black-slipped ware, common ceramics, semiprecious stone beads. Iron articles included brooms, hand-axes, spearheads, knives, nails and slugs, melted pieces of iron. A 180-metre long, 6-metre wide road with 21–35 cm surface thickness indicates that urbanisation in East Bengal started much earlier than it was generally believed. Moreover, recent excavation in the old Bikrampur area has brought to light another site with the ruins of a Buddhist vihara believed to have been the birthplace of the great Buddhist teacher and philosopher Atish Deepankar. Excavation work has also been done in West Bengal at various places, including Ballal Dhipi, Dihar, Mangolkot and Rajbari.

The discoveries at Chandraketugarh and Mahasthangarh are useful mainly to determine the time when brick-and-stone constructions started in Bengal. But these give no reliable indicators of how developed architecture was in ancient and medieval Bengal, or how well the architecture at these sites fared in comparison with that of other regions. Such indicators are available to a certain extent in the Buddhist viharas found at Paharpur and in the Mainamati and Lalmai hills of Comilla in Bangladesh. The Somapura Mahavihara was built at Paharpur in the 8th century at the time of Dharmapala. The vihara was novel in its design and huge in its dimensions. A contemporary Sanskrit sloka describes it as the only thing worth seeing in the world. It is the biggest of the innumerable Buddhist viharas that have been discovered in the Indian subcontinent.

The Somapura Mahavihara was built in the shape of a square—about 300 square yards in area. It was ringed by a high wall, and hugging the wall on its inner side were 177 rooms which served as the living quarters of the Buddhist *bhikshus* (mendicants). Further in, there were the monastery kitchen, dining rooms and many other smallish rooms. There were big wells and also a system of drainage. But what made this vihara truly extraordinary was the 69 feet tall temple that stood at its centre. The temple layout resembles the Christian cross. There are also similarities with the ground layout of many European cathedrals. There is no evidence of any earlier construction using this novel design anywhere else in India. However, an earlier temple, called Vasu-Vihara, which Hiuen Tsang saw in the 7th century, was shaped somewhat like a cross and was not very far from Mahasthan. This earlier temple may have served as a model for the temple at Somapura, which was shaped entirely like a cross. The existing height of the temple is about 23 yards, the height of a six- or seven-storey building in our time.

It is not just the size of the Somapura Vihara that marks it out as special. The ornamentation of the edifice was also quite novel. The brick walls of the vihara were decorated with terracotta tiles. Some 3,000 tiles have been found, both plastered to the walls and loose. Most of the tiles measure a little under one square foot. The distinctiveness of these tiles consists in the figurines carved on them. Some of these tiles are exquisite examples of artistry. However, most tiles are not very beautiful, and some historians believe that they might have been produced by ordinary craftsmen. But what makes these tiles invaluable in reconstructing the cultural history of Bengal is that they provide a glimpse into contemporary ways of life. They also provide an idea of contemporary religious beliefs and of religious syncretism.

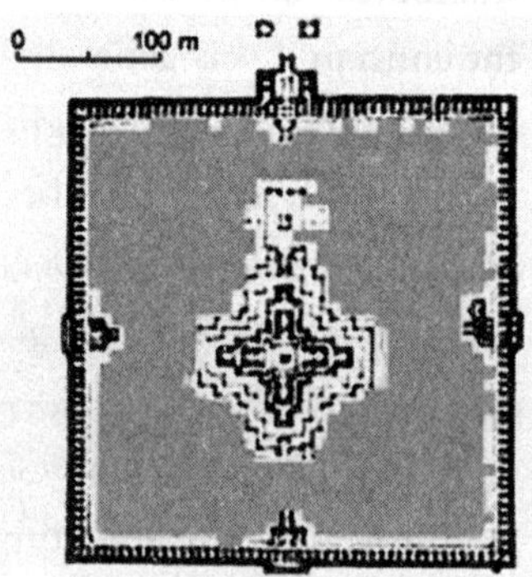

Paharpur Vihara Plan

The figures carved on these tiles are of men and women going about their work routines. The farmer with his plough slung over his shoulder; the hunter carrying his arrow; the huntress with the carcass of her prey; the magician performing his tricks; male musicians with their instruments and female instrumentalists; dancing women; stick-wielding sentinels; the Brahmin officiating at the ritual of worship; the warrior riding his chariot; men and women carrying weapons; old man slouching under the weight of utensils on his shoulder; woman drawing water from a well while carrying a child; woman returning home with a pot of water; etc. There are also many images of courting young couples, including leaf-clad couples of the Shabara tribe. However, nothing like the couples locked in sexual union that are depicted on the walls of Hindu temples of later centuries have been found in Paharpur. There are images of animals and also mythical creatures carved on the tiles. The animals include tigers, lions, deer, elephants, monkeys, foxes, fish, ducks and rabbits. Among the mythical creatures are *gandharva*s, *kinnara*s and *daitya*s and *danava*s.

Yet another group of tiles carries images of deities, mostly Hindu gods and goddesses. Among the Hindu deities depicted on the tiles are Brahma, Vishnu, Shiva, Ganesha and the Sun. Gautam Buddha himself had repudiated the concept of a Creator, let alone gods and goddesses. His followers, however, turned him into a deity and gradually opened their imagination to other gods and goddesses. Thus the Paharpur tiles carry images of deities such as Hevajra and Tara apart from Bodhisattva and Manjusri.

A section of the tiles depicts Puranic narratives such as the *Ramayana* and the Jataka tales. It is not known whether the tradition started in Paharpur. But it was widely followed in Hindu temples over the following 1,000 years. The use of Hindu deities and mythology in a Buddhist vihara is certainly significant. It indicates not only the coexistence of the two communities but also the extent of religious assimilation between them. The Hindu acceptance of the Buddha as the ninth avatara also points to a syncretistic culture.

Sixty-three stone sculptures have been found on the walls of the foundation of the vihara at Paharpur. When these sculptures were made has not yet been ascertained through carbon-dating. But historians believe these to be belonging to an earlier age. Most of them were probably of the Gupta age. Unlike most of the terracotta tiles, these sculptures are rich in beauty and refinement. Significantly enough, almost all the sculptures, attached though they are to the foundation of a Buddhist temple, are of Hindu gods and goddesses. Prominent among them is Krishna. One Buddhist sculpture of particular interest is of Hevajra embracing Shakti.

There is no explanation of why sculptures of Hindu deities belonging to an earlier period were attached to a Buddhist temple. It is not known whether there had been a pre-existing Hindu temple at the site or whether the Buddhist temple was built with stones culled from a Hindu temple.

But these possibilities cannot be entirely dismissed. A comparison with the Salban Vihara of Mainamati particularly reinforces these possibilities. Although many statuettes have been found at the Salban Vihara, none has been found of any Hindu deity. This is so even though terracotta tiles at this vihara depict images of Hara-Gauri, Vishnu, Radha-Krishna, Surya, Ganesha and Jagaddhatri, all Hindu deities. Though it cannot be indisputably inferred that the Somapura Vihara was built at the site of a pre-existing Hindu temple, a bronze inscription found at Paharpur have led historians to surmise that a Jain temple might have existed at the site at some point.

The vihara at Paharpur testifies to the excellence of architecture in pre-medieval Bengal. The layout, size and ornamentation of the vihara earned praise at home and abroad in its own time. The Salban Vihara was modelled on the Somapura Vihara and was built soon after it. Even some Hindu temples borrowed the Somapura design. The remains of one such temple have been found at Birat in Rangpur district of northern Bangladesh, though this temple did not have a cross-shaped structure at its centre. But terracotta tiles were used here, too. The temple measured 195 feet in length and 150 feet in breadth. Close imitations of the Paharpur architecture, including of the cross-shaped temple, can be observed in South East Asia—particularly in Cambodia and Indonesia.

The history of how and when the Buddhist vihara and educational centre at Paharpur closed down and were reduced to ruins is not known. However, it has been surmised that their decline started under the Hindu rulers of the Sena dynasty owing to the absence of patronage or hostility towards Buddhists. That was also the time when Buddhism in Bengal faced a general decline. Subsequently, the religion was virtually wiped off in the Indo-Muslim period. We have noted before that when Bakhtiyar Khilji attacked Adandapuri, the capital of Gobindapala, he ransacked the Buddhist vihara there and massacred the Buddhist *bhikshus*. It is not known whether any Muslim ruler mounted a similar attack on Paharpur. But there is indirect proof that the monastery survived for several centuries after the establishment of Muslim rule in Bengal. Some 16th century coins of the Bengal sultanate have been found at the vihara. Talking of coins, it should be mentioned here that a gold coin struck in AD 788 and belonging

Mainamati Vihara, aerial view

to the regime of the Abbasid Caliph Harun-ur-Rashid of Baghdad has been found at the vihara. But it has not been determined whether the coin arrived at the vihara around that time or later. The possibility that it might have reached the vihara at a later date cannot be ruled out.

It is clear from the blueprint, technology and raw materials that were used in the construction of the vihara that architecture was quite well developed in Bengal in the 8th century. Over a thousand years after it was built, the brick structure has not caved in. It is not known for certain what the architects and masons of Paharpur used to bind the bricks, but the temple still stands some 70 feet tall—testimony to an extraordinary feat of building technology.

The same can be said of the Salban Vihara of Mainamati. The Salban Vihara and some other viharas of varying size in the Lalmai hills have been discovered close to Comilla town. The biggest and the most remarkable is the Salban Vihara, which was modelled on the vihara at Paharpur. In size it is slightly over half of the Paharpur Vihara. In shape, however, it is a square, like the Paharpur Vihara, about 550 feet in both length and breadth. In this vihara, too, there is a row of rooms running along the inner side of the boundary walls. There are 115 rooms in all. At the centre of this vihara, too, there is a temple shaped like a cross. But the temple has collapsed, so it could not be determined how tall it was.

In a comparison between the vihara at Paharpur and those at Mainamati and Lalmai, a few differences stand out. The first thing to note is that whereas

Paharpur had a single large monastery, there were quite a few viharas, big and small, at Mainamati. These were not all built in the same period. It is believed that they were built over a period of 400 years, between the 8th and the 12th centuries. From the location of these viharas, it would not perhaps be far-fetched to infer that Buddhism in Bengal was gradually retreating to the south-east in the face of the might of first the Vedic religion and then of Islam.

But the viharas in and around Mainamati bear a more important indication. Whereas the Paharpur ruins record a forceful presence of Hindu gods and goddesses and point to religious syncretism, no such thing is evident in Mainamati. Some 150 small bronze figurines have been found at Mainamati, but they are all images of the Buddha and of other Buddhist deities. A number of stone figurines have also been found. Two large statues of the Buddha surrounded by followers have been unearthed. But no representations of Hindu deities have been found here. It may well appear from this that although assimilation between the Hindu and Buddhist faiths had taken place in northern Bengal to a certain extent, such syncretism did not reach the more remote stretches of south-eastern Bengal in pre-medieval times, at least not to a significant extent. The figurines and statues of Mainamati are also different in their raw material. Figurines and statues that have been found in other parts of Bengal are made of black stone from the Rajmahal hills of Jharkhand. The Mainamati statuettes, however, are made of hardened clay from the Comilla-Chittagong area.

As in the other Buddhist viharas, hundreds of terracotta tiles have been found at Mainamati. Though smaller in number than the Paharpur tiles, these are not lacking in variety and can be seen as exquisite examples of folk art. Among the images carved on these tiles are men and women in different postures, birds and animals, mythical creatures, gods and goddesses and the mythological *kinnaras*. But the pictorial representation of the *Ramayana* and Jataka tales that have been found in Paharpur are absent in Mainamati. Though there are Hindu gods and goddesses depicted on terracotta tiles in Mainamati, there are not too many of these. Among the Hindu deities depicted are Hara and Gauri, Vishnu, Radha and Krishna, Surya, Ganesha and Jagaddhatri.

In comparison with Paharpur, excavations at Mainamati and Lalmai have produced a richer harvest of archaeological finds. Among these are 12 copper plates with inscriptions, 227 gold coins, 224 silver coins, bronze statuettes and bells. There are also stupas made of bronze. Two of the gold coins are of the Gupta age, one belonging to Samudragupta's reign and the other to Chandragupta's. That is, both are of the 4th century. It has been claimed that a coin belonging to King Sashanka's time, that is, the 7th century, has been found in these ruins. But if there is room for some doubt about this coin, there is no doubt about the coins belonging to the kings of the Pattikera area. Two gold coins belonging to the Abbasid caliphs of Baghdad have been found. These finds point to how long this vihara survived. But what the Mainamati ruins tell us, more than anything else, is that a rich tradition of architecture existed in ancient and early medieval Bengal.

Buddhist viharas are believed to have been built not just in Paharpur and Mainamati but also in other places of Bengal. In the 7th century the Chinese traveller Hiuen Tsang saw a stupa built by the Emperor Asoka in Pundravardhana in what is now Bogra district of Bangladesh. The oldest stupa in Bengal, made of metal, has been found at Ashrafpur in Dhaka district. The stupa is made of mixed metals along with the copper plates of King Devakharaga.

The rich possibilities for architecture in Bengal that were evident in Paharpur and Mainamati were thwarted after the end of the Buddhist era because of the lack of favourable conditions. There is, however, no reason to believe that constructions stopped totally during the Sena regime. The skills in building and ornamentation that architects and builders would have inherited and passed on from generation to generation also surely did not vanish overnight. The remains of at least one major construction have survived between Gaur and Pandua, about two miles to the west of the Malda railway station. According to Alexander Cunningham, these are said to be the ruins of Ballal Sena's palace. Signs have survived of the many temples that were built during Sena times. These temples differed from Buddhist viharas in their structure and building plans. The ruins of one such temple have been found in Deopara, not far from Rajshahi town. Known as the Pardyumneswara temple, it is mentioned in the Deopara *prasasti*, a eulogy to the Sena ruler Vijaya Sena (reign: AD 1095-AD 1158).

The Sena dynasty ruled – mainly in the western part of Bengal – for less than two centuries. They built some temples, but they were unable to establish any permanent style of architecture. There were mainly two kinds of temples that were built during Sena rule. One was what was known as *bhadra deul* or *peerha deul*, *deul* meaning temple. The other kind was known as the shikhar (meaning tower or spire) mandir (temple), or the *rekha* mandir. These two kinds of temples differed mainly in the shape and structure of their roofs. In the *bhadra deul*, the roof tapered off in steps, progressively narrower as it went up. The ruins of a temple of this kind have been found in Bankura. In the shikhar temple, on the other hand, four slanting sides from the four walls taper upwards until they merge together, forming a tower. These towers carried much ornamentation, which also served to form several categories of the shikhar temples on the basis of the kind of ornamentation used. A marvellous sample, built perhaps centuries after the fall of the Sena dynasty, has survived at Barakar in Burdwan district. The extraordinary beauty of the stone tower of this temple reminds one of the Parashuram temple in Bhuvaneswar. There are remains of two other similar temples at Dehar in Bankura. In sum, a new architectural style of temple-building had begun to develop in Bengal during the Sena regime in post-Buddhist times. And like the Sena kings themselves, this new architectural style came from outside Bengal.

We noted at the outset that the architectural styles of Bengal kept changing with the changing regimes. The Buddhist architectural styles of the Pala regime, for instance, did not find continuity under Sena rule. The shikhar temples, introducing a style imported from Odisha and northern India, were instead the new vogue. Building skills and technologies also seem to have gradually advanced to keep pace with changing traditions. At least the ornamentation of the towers of the shikhar mandirs bear testimony to great advances in construction technology. Architects and builders did not find themselves out of work when there was a pause in temple-building in the Indo-Muslim age. Men with a reserve of inherited building skills came forward to build mosques in the new age. In consequence, a certain degree of continuity in building technology can be noted in the mosques, though Bengal's architects were also bringing about a new tradition of architecture according to the directions of their Turkish overlords.

Architecture of Indo-Muslim Rule

In the 1st century of Muslim rule after the fall of Gaur to Turkish forces, 25 sultans seized power one after another. In the initial years these sultans were obliged to prove their authority to their overlords in Delhi and to the local 'rajas' and other influential people. Neither of these was easy. But since Bengal was a frontier province, the expression of their loyalty to Delhi often required little beyond the payment of revenue. To establish their authority with the local elite, who spoke a different language and practised a different religion, however, was not so simple. The sultans adopted a range of initiatives to this end, apart from the display of force. The introduction of coins and the construction of mosques and mazars were among these strategies. The destruction and/or desecration of places of worship belonging to the vanquished population were powerful symbolic actions to assert authority and prove the might of the conquerors. After the fall of Constantinople in 1453, the Turks built four turrets or minars at the four corners of the Hagia Sophia Church (Aya Sophia in Turkish) and converted it into a mosque. In Bengal, too, Muslim rulers not only razed many temples but also turned a number of them into mosques.

In the second chapter we noted that Bakhtiyar Khilji was in power for only two years after taking Gaur. In that short time he struck his own gold coins to prove his authority. He also built several mosques, mausoleums and *khanqahs* (Sufi retreats). It is doubtful whether this scale of construction was required to meet the needs of the handful of Muslims in the province at that time. But Bakhtiyar Khilji needed to build these spaces of Muslim religious practice in order to make his presence felt and to enforce his authority. Like him, the 24 sultans who sat on the throne of Bengal after him in that century also built mosques, mausoleums, dargahs and *khanqahs*. Yet samples of architecture commissioned by these sultans did not survive for very long. Hence, there is now no way of telling where they were built, and what is more important, what style of architecture they followed.

The oldest extant Indo-Muslim edifices that survived for over 700 years were Zafar Khan's mosque at Tribeni in Hooghly district of West Bengal and a minar at Chhoto Pandua. The mosque was built in 1298. In the chapter 'Cultural Transformation in the Indo-Muslim Era' we noted that there was nothing really novel about the architecture of this mosque. It was modelled on the mosques that were built in Delhi at that time, combining the styles of the Middle East and the Indian subcontinent. Yet it was novel in the context of Bengal—it introduced in the province a hitherto unknown style of building with domes and arches.

The mosque measured almost 77 feet X 34.5 feet in length and breadth. The five east-facing doorways of this mosque are matched by five mihrabs on the western wall—niches shaped like doorways that indicate the qiblah, the direction that Muslims must face while praying. As we will see later, this tradition of putting in mihrabs on the western walls of mosques, their number matching the number of doorways in the eastern wall, was followed everywhere in Bengal with a few exceptions until the arrival of the Mughal era. There are 10 low domes on the roof of the mosque, matching the five doorways in front and two each on its northern and southern sides. This practice of the number of doorways determining the number of domes in a mosque was also followed extensively until the start of the Mughal age. Even the low domes shaped like half-spheres used in this mosque became a defining characteristic of Bengal's Muslim architecture for the next 200 years and more

But it cannot be said of the domes that they reflected any remarkable architectural excellence. Magnificent domes had been built many centuries earlier in Turkey and Persia. The technology and knowledge that was used in building them had not travelled to Bengal. It also appears unlikely that there were skilled masons available to give shape to an architect's blueprint. What is more likely is that construction workers with inherited knowledge of building technology and skills passed on through generations built the mosque with directions from a Muslim architect. It is this perhaps that explains the considerable local influence in the ornamentation used in the mosque.

Apart from the mihrab and the dome, the other new element that the mosque introduced in Bengal's architecture was the *khilan* or arch. The expertise of building proper arches had been absent in the region's building tradition before this. Muslims, on the other hand, were familiar with the ancient architecture of Greece, Rome, Byzantium, Assyria and Persia. Along with the dome and the arch, they also introduced minarets and vaults in Bengal. These building styles did not thereafter remain confined to mosques and influenced local constructions, too. But Zafar Khan's mosque, though it introduced new elements in Bengal's architecture, did not reflect any distinctively local trait in its construction. Nor, for that matter, did his mausoleum, which was located not very far from the mosque.

The two other samples of 13th century Muslim architecture that have survived are the Minar of Chhoto Pandua and the Barhi Masjid near it. In terms of its design, the tower was not unique at all. Such towers had been built in Afghanistan and in Delhi much earlier. In terms of size, it comes nowhere close to the Qutb Minar of Delhi. But in the Bengal of those times, there was no other construction that was quite so high or so striking. It was close to 125 feet in height, tapering upwards in five steps, each narrower than the one below. The base tower measures 60 feet in diameter, while the topmost one is 12 feet in diameter. An internal stairway goes all the way up to the top.

Chhoto Pandua Minar

There is no definite information about exactly when the tower was built. But many historians believe that it was built either in the second half of the 13th century or at the beginning of the 14th, as an icon signifying a sultan's victory. The location of the huge (231 feet x 42 feet) mosque 175 feet from the tower has also led to the inference that the tower was used for delivering the azan, the Muslim call to prayer. So it may have also served a religious objective. But most historians agree that a triumphant sultan attempted to broadcast his prowess and greatness among the local population through the tall and imposing tower.

It should be noted in this context that over 200 years after this tower was built, another tower or minar known as the Firoze Minar was built in Gaur. It measured 84 feet in height. This, too, was built in five steps. In ornamentation, however, this later minar was far superior to the older one.

In terms of size, the largest house of worship in Bengal's architectural tradition after the Buddhist viharas is the mosque of Adina. Iliyas Shah's son Sikandar Shah built this huge mosque in 1375 in his capital Adina in what is now Malda district of West Bengal. Measuring 565 feet in length and 317 feet in breadth, this was India's biggest mosque in history. The size of the Muslim population in Adina at that time did not justify the construction of such a huge mosque. It is obvious that Sikandar undertook a construction on this scale to impress the greatness of his own power and fame on the people of Bengal, as well as on his nominal overlords in Delhi. The mosques that were built in Bengal in later years were all less than 100 feet in length. By that time, presumably, the sultans of Bengal no longer found it necessary to prove their own superiority in competition with Delhi. In these later mosques, therefore, the need for imposing doorways and multiple domes in addition to the main prayer hall was not felt.

The distinctive architectural style of the mosque at Adina was new in its time in Bengal. Sikandar did not import this style from Delhi. He imported it from Persia, the seat of the greatest flowering of medieval Muslim art and culture. But the style that he imported from Persia was not a contemporary one. It belonged, instead, to pre-Islamic Persia—somewhat on the lines of the Taq-i-Kisra Palace. Some historians have noted similarities that the mosque apparently shares with the Al-Walid mosque of Damascus. There was nothing in India until then comparable to the huge barrel vault at the heart of Adina Masjid. The mosque also boasted a giant arch and 390 low domes, only six of which survive today. The main wing of the mosque was built of stone and bricks, some of which were from abandoned or broken Hindu temples. In its walls there still exist carved images of Hindu deities.

But size is not the only remarkable thing about Adina Masjid. In this mosque Sikandar Shah brought about a significant synthesis of Central Asian and local styles. The niches set in its walls and its terracotta ornamentation reflect Pala era traditions. As seen in the photograph, the decorations

Adina Mosque façade. *Photo courtesy: Ajit Kumar Majhi (commons.wikimedia.org)*

included hanging lamps, hanging lotus petals as well as the lotus flower—all exquisitely carved on stone. Calligraphic writings of verses from the Quran are also beautifully carved on stone and put on the doorways and mihrabs. The motif of bells and chains, had, however, started appearing from the time of Zafar Khan's mosque. Adina Masjid gives us a fair idea of the time when assimilation between Islamic and local cultures began taking place and also of the kind of assimilation that happened.

The mingling of traditions became more pronounced some decades later, at the start of the 15th century, when the Iliyas Shahi dynasty was in decline. It was a time of major political upheavals. We noted in the second chapter that a Hindu king was in power at this time—Raja Ganesh. Though he himself remained a devoted Hindu, his son Jalal-ud-din was not a Muslim only in name. He appears to have shaped up as a devout Muslim and attempted to obtain legitimacy for his reign from Muslims at home and abroad. As a person of local origin, however, he had an opportunity to forge an extraordinary synthesis of the local culture with the Islamic culture that had come from distant shores—it was an advantage that the earlier sultans did not have. Earlier sultans would have looked to the regimes in Delhi and in the Middle East for acknowledgement of the legitimacy of their rule. Jalal-uddin, too, was not free of this compulsion. Still, he was the first to turn his gaze away from the Middle East and back to the land of his birth in many matters of culture. For instance, he started actively promoting the local language and culture. But he left the greatest imprint of his efforts towards cultural syncretism in mosques that he built and particularly in his own mausoleum.

Although these mosques have not survived, his mausoleum, known as Eklakhi, still stands, bearing testimony to an unprecedented synthesis of the architectural traditions of Bengal and of the Middle East. It exerted such abiding influence on the Hindus and Muslims of the land and on Muslim immigrants who came from distant lands that many mosques and temples of later years were modelled on this mazar. Historians believe that Jalal-ud-din got his mazar built during his lifetime, in 1432.

A single giant dome sits on this brick-built mazar, not multiple domes as on the mosques built in earlier centuries. The dome instantly stands out as a specimen of Muslim architecture. Yet its true uniqueness lies elsewhere. It emulates the design of the thatched-roof huts of the Bengal countryside. This imitation is evident in the curved cornices. There are four octagonal towers at the four corners of the tomb, much like the four poles of a hut, though this is not exactly typical of Bengal constructions. The outer wall of the mazar was decorated with window-shaped blind niches (*kulungi*) and terracotta and painted tiles. The structure was a square, like the old Buddhist viharas. The

Eklakhi Tomb, a trendsetter. *Photo courtesy: Ajit Kumar Majhi (commons.wikimedia.org)*

giant dome rested on the strength of walls of extraordinary thickness on the northern and southern sides and corners that curved inside, masonry filling up the hollows of the curve. Consequently, though the mazar looked like a square from outside, the inner chamber was octagonal.

The use of curved cornices in this mausoleum, resembling the thatched roofs of the Bengal countryside, appears completely novel. No earlier specimen of this particular style of architecture has been found. Still, some historians surmise that the style may have existed earlier. According to David McCutchion, imitating thatched mud homes in stone and brick was an ancient tradition. The claim may be correct. While Eklakhi imitated just the curved cornice, temples built hereafter adopted not only the bent cornice but the entire design of thatched mud homes, instead of using domes. It may well appear from this that this style of building was not new.

Notwithstanding such surmises by historians, in the absence of specimens proving them, with Jalal-ud-din must rest the credit for copying the thatched mud-hut design in architecture. Besides, whether or not the idea originated with him, once the style was used in his mausoleum, it became the standardised Bengal style of building. It did not remain confined to the construction of mosques but was also followed extensively in temples. What is more, after a certain time, it was followed more in temples than in mosques. Though Jalal-ud-din's use of the dome did not find popularity in the construction of temples, the arches, vaults and curved cornices of his edifices were widely accepted and copied. Jalal-ud-din extensively used terracotta tiles. He also put three statues of the Hindu god Ganesha (also his father's name), now defaced, on the front doorway. Eklakhi mausoleum, then, can be considered an extraordinary milestone in Bengal's architectural tradition. Subsequently, a few temples in the Bengal style were built elsewhere in India.

Among the mosques and mazars of varying sizes that came to be built on the lines of Eklakhi was Khan Jahan Ali's mausoleum. It is not known exactly when it was built. But Khan Jahan Ali died in 1459. So it must have been built soon after that date. Like Eklakhi, this mazar is also a square and has a large dome, four turrets in its four corners and even a bow-like cornice. Among the mosques that show an unmistakable resemblance with Eklakhi are the Shah Safiullah Masjid (1477); the Chika Masjid of Gaur, West

Bengal; the Bahram Sakkar Masjid of Burdwan, West Bengal (1562); the Singra Masjid, Bibi Begani Masjid, Ranbijoypur Masjid and Zindapir Masjid, Chunkholar Masjid, all five in Bagerhat, Bangladesh; the Goaldi Masjid in Sonargaon, Bangladesh; Sadi Masjid in Egarosindur, Bangladesh; the Gorai and Tenga Masjids in Jessore, Bangladesh; and the Dara Masjid of Dhaka. All these mosques are either squares or almost squares. They all have four turrets hugging the four corners, a large domed roof and a curved cornice. The four turrets at the corners and a large dome in the middle later provided the model for the *pancharatna* temple at Bishnupur in Purulia, West Bengal.

Some other mosques were built on almost the same lines, their structures squarish, but with a verandah branching off from the eastern side that has three small domes on its roof. In all other ways these mosques differ little from the Eklakhi style. The first such mosque was the Chamkati Masjid in Gaur built in 1475. This mosque is square in shape, with a carpet area of nearly 24 sq feet, but with a 10-feet wide verandah attached to it. A rare distinction that marks this mosque is that though the eastern side has three doorways, there is just one mihrab on the western wall instead of three. The Masjidbari mosque (1465) is likewise square in shape, with an attached verandah and a large dome on the roof.

Lattan Masjid

To this category of mosques also belongs the Lattan Masjid, situated a mile away from the palace premises of Gaur. This mosque is also quite remarkable for other reasons. According to Cunningham, 1475 was the year of its construction, though most historians believe it was built during the time of Hossein Shah, that is, between 1493 and 1519. The mosque has nothing to boast of in terms of its size. But like the Chamkati mosque located a short distance to its north, this mosque has a verandah attached to it. The main mosque carries, like Eklakhi, a large dome on its roof, but there are three other domes above the verandah. Of these three domes, the middle one is shaped like the four-sided domes of Shat Gombuz Masjid (literally, 60-dome mosque). Lattan Masjid stands out as a shining example of the inter-mingling of traditions in architecture. Four

Shat Gombuz Masjid. *Photo courtesy: Rajesh Mondal (commons.wikimedia.org)*

turrets stand at the four corners of this mosque, too, but these turrets are circular and not octagonal. The mosque is not quite a square when measured externally, but the inside is a square. Alexander Cunnigham, who saw the mosque in the latter half of the 19th century, was profuse in his praise of its ornamentation.

Subsequently, mosques modelled on Chamkati Masjid and Lattan Masjid were built in different parts of Bengal. These mosques were all square in shape, but they all had a verandah branching out from one of the sides. The main mosque carries a large dome, while the verandah carries three smaller ones. These mosques also have a turret in each of the four corners, circular in some mosques and octagonal in others. The mosques are varied in their ornamentation, but their main structures show an unmistakable resemblance. The Gunamanta and Khaniadeeghi mosques of Gaur, the Sura Masjid of Dinajpur and Atiah Masjid of Tangail are all built in this style. The last one, Atiah Masjid, constructed in 1609, has a pronounced bow-like cornice and is decorated with elaborate terracotta tiles bearing Bengali motifs and geometric patterns. No other mosque built during Muslim rule in Bengal was quite as influenced by Bengali architectural style as this one was.

The Shat Gombuz or Sixty Dome mosque of Bagerhat was built some 20 to 25 years after Eklakhi. The mosque shows resemblances with Adina Masjid, mosques built in the Tughlaqi style in Delhi, and with local architectural traditions. But this synthesis between imported and local traditions is not manifest in the mosque's ornamentation, for it is practically bare of decorations. But the mosque is unique in its array of domes. Although called Shat Gombuz, there are actually a total of 77 domes in 11 rows, seven in each row, on its roof. The seven domes in the middle row, running over the stretch from the doorway in front to the mihrab facing it, are four-sided Bengali hut-like domes similar to the ones of Chhoto Sona Masjid and Lattan Masjid. But this mosque was built 20 to 40 years earlier than the other two. It is with this mosque, then, that the credit for the innovation of the four-sided dome must rest. The mosque also stands out in its size. Although smaller than Adina Masjid, it is the biggest mosque in eastern Bengal.

Khan Jahan Ali was an extremely influential warrior-saint and ruler of southern Bengal. The influence of his Sixty Dome mosque is quite evident in many of the mosques built during his time and also in the decades following his death (1459) in Jessore, Khulna, Bagerhat and Barishal. Notable examples of mosques showing this influence are the Nine Dome and Ten Dome mosques of Bagerhat, the mosque at Masjidkurh in Khulna, the mosque at Shailakupa, the Masjidbarhi mosque and the Hammad Masjid.

The Darasbari Masjid of Gaur, though not as distinctive in style as Eklakhi or the Sixty Dome mosque, is accorded particular importance by historians because of its grandeur and the wealth of its embellishments. Not only were its mihrabs intricately decorated, the entire mosque was adorned with terracotta tiles. The mosque was built during the reign of Yusuf Shah, in 1479. There were nine domes on the main structure, which was more than 100 feet in length, and seven on its 10.5-feet-wide verandah. The construction plan was more or less modelled on Adina Masjid, but some historians have said that there are resemblances with Zafar Khan's mosque. In the mosques built around this time, the number of mihrabs on the western wall usually corresponded with the number of doorways on the eastern side. In this mosque, however, there are seven doorways in the eastern wall but nine mihrabs in the western wall.

The Tantipara Masjid, which has ten domes, is slightly smaller than the Darasbari mosque. Closely following in the tradition of elaborate ornamentation that marked the Darasbari Masjid, this one was built a year later. But although similar in embellishments, the two mosques were not similar in design and structure. There was no verandah in the Tantipara mosque; its cornices were curved, in the style of Eklakhi; and the number of mihrabs matched the number of doorways. Cunningham found this mosque to be above all others in Bengal in the excellence of its ornamentation.

Mosques built in the time of Hossein Shah are noticeably and significantly different in style. Among the first mosques built at this time was Chhoto Sona Masjid. Located at the far south of Gaur (13 miles from the railway station at modern Malda if one draws a straight line south of it), this mosque may be considered as an extremely remarkable specimen of architecture during the time of Hossein Shah, showing a striking assimilation of local and Muslims styles. But the style is quite different from that of Eklakhi. This mosque is not square in shape, its length being significantly greater than its breadth (82 feet x 52 feet). Nor is it built entirely of brick. Its brick walls are covered with stone both on the inner and outer sides. In an important variation from Eklakhi, the roof carries not a single large dome but several small domes in keeping with the number of the doorways, as in Adina Masjid and Sixty Dome mosque.

In size, the Chhoto Sona Masjid is a little bigger than Lattan Masjid. There are octagonal turrets standing like posts in the four corners, and the cornice is curved. It is the domes and the embellishments of this mosque that most noticeably reflect a mingling of local and Middle Eastern traditions. In symmetry with its five doorways in front and three on each side, there are 15 domes on the roof, three in each of five rows. The domes in the middle row are four-sided hut-like domes and not half-spheres like the rest. As we have already noted, this innovation of design was first seen in Khan Jahan Ali's Shat Gombuz Masjid in Bagerhat. The Lattan Masjid also had a four-sided dome.

The ornamentation in Chhoto Sona Masjid also unmistakably reflects a mingling of local and imported cultures. The stone plastering on the external walls of the mosque carries not just geometrical designs in the Islamic tradition but also floral motifs, suspended chains and bells, hanging rose petals, lamps and so on. The rose is considered iconic of Islamic culture in India. But in the embellishments of the mosques of the Indo-Muslim age, the lotus shares space with the rose. It was with Adina Masjid that the use of the lotus motif started. In Chhoto Sona Masjid, the word 'Allah' is carved on the lotus motif.

Chhoto Sona Masjid, an example of synthesis between Bengali and Islamic architectural styles

Though the mosque was built at the time of Hossein Shah, the exact date of its construction is not known. But in 1500 the Baro Goaldi Masjid at Daudkandi was built in near total imitation of this mosque. Chhoto Sona Masjid, therefore, must have been built a few years earlier. In Sylhet, too, a mosque was built in its image. Later, the Hetamabad Masjid in Dinajpur was also modelled on it. These examples bear testimony that Chhoto Sona Masjid drew attention to itself in its own time as an architectural ideal to be followed. The domes of Chhoto Sona Masjid are said to have been gilded once, which is how it got its name. However, in 1526, Hossein Shah's son Nusrat Shah built, almost five miles to the north, on the western side of the palace complex, another golden-hued temple that was double the size (168 feet x 76 feet) of the older one. That mosque consequently became known as Boro Sona Masjid (Big Golden mosque), while this one became popular as Chhoto Sona Masjid. Boro Sona Masjid boasted many more domes than Chhoto Sona Masjid did—it had 33 domes on the main structure and another 11 on its verandah. The multiple domes and the sheer length of the mosque may perhaps evoke memories of the Adina Masjid. Apart from the characteristic four turrets at the four corners, the mosque had two extra turrets, one on either side of the front courtyard. The 19th century architectural historian James Fergusson praised Boro Sona Masjid as the most beautiful mosque of Gaur.

Speaking of ornamentation, it can be said that with time Bengal's local styles and traditions of embellishment progressively influenced Muslim architecture. The Bagha Masjid and Kusumba Masjid of Rajshahi were built shortly after Chhoto Sona Masjid. The geometric designs and floral motifs of these mosques have a distinct character. Islam forbids artistic representations of living beings. Upon a close look at the floral motif ornamentation of Bagha mosque, however, the eye seems to detect bird-like creatures among the flowers and leaves. What is more, a hint of the peacock and peahen can be noted in the ornamentation above the mihrabs. The decorative designs of Kusumba mosque even depict a familiar fish species—the *makor*.

In 1532, Nusrat built, just outside the palace complex on the southern side, not a mosque but a tomb known as Qadam Rasul. It is claimed that a black stone preserved at the tomb carries the imprint of the Prophet's foot. The tomb subsequently wielded wide influence on the region's architecture, particularly on account of the terracotta work on its façade and its domes. The dome standing in the middle of its roof is not like the low half-sphere of Adina Masjid, nor is it like the high and huge half-sphere of Eklakhi. The top of the dome tapers up into a narrow, pointed tip, somewhat like an onion. This subsequently became the most widely followed ideal in the design of domes. According to David McCutchion, the narrow spires on top of the turrets standing at the four corners of Qadam Rasul are the precursors of the *ratna* or 'pinnacle' of Hindu temples in later years.

The mosques of the Hossein Shahi regime that are important architectural landmarks include Rajshahi's Bagha 1523) and Kusumba (1535) mosques; Pabna's Nabagram Masjid (1526); Jhanjhania Masjid (1535); the 10-dome Patrail Masjid of Faridpur and the Sura Masjid of Dinajpur. We have already mentioned the distinctiveness of the ornamentation of Bagha Masjid. Many historians have noted similarities that the Sura Masjid and the 15-dome Nabagram Masjid share with Lattan Masjid, especially in ornamentation. In structure the Sura Masjid resembles Eklakhi, though this mosque has a verandah. Jhanjhania Masjid deserves a special mention because its dome is shaped like that of Qadam Rasul, that is, like an onion. The other remarkable thing about this dome is that it looks like a lotus kept face down. In subsequent years, similar pinnacles were used in many temples.

After the time of the Hossein Shahi dynasty and the Afghans, the Mughals arrived in Bengal, and they brought new styles of architecture. But it took 30 years for the Mughals to consolidate their reign, and even longer to put down roots in the land. Though the Mughal style was evident even in the initial years in a few mosques built with the direct patronage of the new ruling class, elsewhere the Sultani style of building mosques continued to be followed. For instance, the Qutub Shahi tomb of Gaur (1582), the Gorai Masjid of Mymensingh and the Atiah Masjid of Tangail (1609) were built after the start of Mughal rule, but their structures and their ornamentation imitate the traditions followed under the sultans. But once mosques and other edifices began to be built in the new architectural style under the Mughal rulers, the old ideal of building was gradually phased out.

Before we move on to a discussion of the Mughal era mosques, a few remarks about some other kinds of architecture in the Sultani age are in order. It was not as if only mosques were built under the sultans. But the sultans, or perhaps their officials, eager to secure their position in the afterlife, do not seem to have taken while building their own palaces the kind of care that they took in building mosques and mazars. Though remains of their palaces have been found, they have not been found in a condition that would allow us to comment on the architecture. But there is no doubt that many palaces and mansions of varying sizes were built in that age. In Gaur, the sultans also built quite a few giant doorways, the size of which continue to inspire awe. The 275 feet long and 27 feet wide bridge that they built in Gaur reflects the excellent standards of construction achieved by them. Ruins of Sultan era forts have also been found in different places.

Mughal Era Architecture

The first mosque constructed by the Mughal administration in the province was Jama Masjid in Rajmahal (now in the Indian state of Jharkhand), built in 1592 on Man Singh's orders. A glance at the mosque, which was modelled on the imperial constructions at Fatehpur Sikri, is enough to tell how different it is from the mosques built in the preceding four centuries. The Mughal style is also quite unmistakably evident in the Jama Masjid that was built four years later at Old Malda. The structures of these two mosques bear no resemblance with Adina Masjid, Eklakhi, Shat Gombuz Masjid, or the Hossein Shahi Masjid. Man Singh introduced in Bengal the style of building that had developed in Delhi over several centuries, particularly in the Mughal era. This new style can be noted in the edifices that were hereafter built under Mughal patronage in difference places, especially in the province capital. But the construction carried out without the subedar's or governor's direct patronage continued to reflect the old styles. The differences between the old style and the new Mughal style were quite apparent. The curved cornice, which was a style that had developed over a couple of centuries, was rejected by the Mughals. The Mughals also rejected the old Bengali tradition, almost a thousand years old at this time, of using terracotta tiles for ornamentation in architecture. Instead, they used plaster for ornamentation, with carved motifs. The tradition of using domes shaped like half-spheres that started with Zafar Khan's mosque also underwent a change. Although Mughal domes do bear some resemblance to the onion-like dome of the Qadam Rasul, they are higher and the tips are more tapering and pointed. Admittedly, the Mughal domes were more imposing.

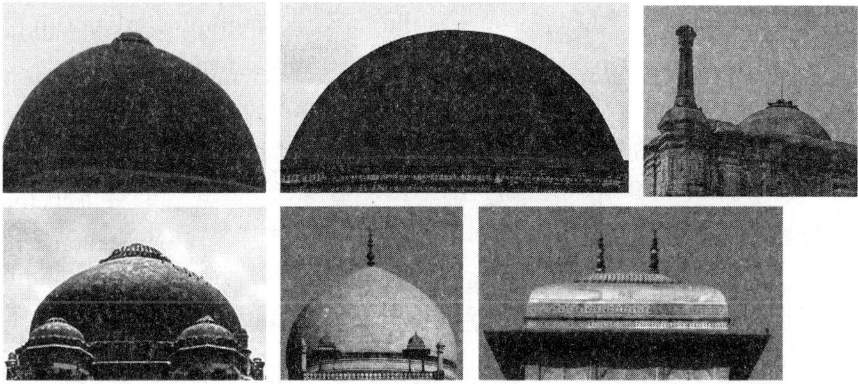

Differences between the old style (top line) and the new Mughal style (bottom line) architecture

The Mughals shifted the province capital from Gaur-Pandua in Malda to Dhaka. Consequently, the flowering of Mughal architecture in Bengal was centred around Dhaka, whereas architecture in the Sultani era had developed around Gaur-Pandua. But it was not as if the Mughals did not build anywhere else, especially in the initial years of their reign. Shahzada Shuja, for instance,

Shah Niyamatullah Mosque, an example of Mughal architecture in Bengal

got quite a remarkable palace built in Rajmahal, replete with the diwan-e-aam (hall for public audience), diwan-e-khas (hall for private/elite audience), Macchi Bhavan and haveli (private residential quarters). He even put in a lake close to the palace for private use. In Gaur, too, he undertook several constructions. The most notable of these was the Shah Niyamat Ullah Masjid, which was quite distinctively Mughal in its style. The same style is manifest in Lalbag's Bibi Pari Masjid and Narayanganj's Bibi Miriam Masjid, which came later. The geographical mapping of architecture changed with the new regime. Mosques and mazars in the Sultani era were built mainly in Gaur-Pandua, Rajshahi, Pabna, Dinajpur, Jessore-Khulna and Barishal. Under the Mughals, however, mosques and mazars were built in far greater numbers in eastern Bengal. One reason for this was that the Mughals established their capital in eastern Bengal. The other reason was the rapid demographic expansion of Muslims in eastern Bengal from the end of the 15th century.

Many of the mansions, forts, mosques, mausoleums and other edifices that were built in Dhaka during the Mughal era still stand even after 400 years. Though Boro Katra was used as a private residence, its appearance suggests that it was perhaps initially meant to serve as Shahzada Shuja's palace. The structure included two huge doorways. The edifice was built in the 1640s. It was called Boro (Big) Katra because another *katra* was later built some 200 yards away. This became known as Chhoto Katra and was built by Shayasta Khan in 1664. Shahzada Muhammad Azam got the fort in Lalbag built in 1678-79 during his time as the subedar. But the construction was interrupted when he left the province and was never completed. Of the several doorways of this fort, the elevated entrance on the south-western side is a truly remarkable specimen of Mughal architecture.

Quite a few religious constructions were undertaken in the time of Shayasta Khan. He himself had a mausoleum built for his deceased daughter,

Pari Bibi, and also a mosque in her name. It was during his governorship that Haji Shahbaz Khan built, in 1679, a beautiful mosque behind what is now the High Court of Dhaka. Four turrets stand at its four corners, and three large domes crown the roof. In this mosque, as in the Shah Niyamat Ullah Masjid and Lalbag Masjid, the central dome is bigger than the two on both sides. Indeed, this feature turned into a widely followed style and in later years was used in many mosques. Apart from the turrets at the four corners, the courtyard of Shahbaz Khan's mosque has two relatively narrower turrets flanking it. One look at the mosque is enough to tell that it was not built during the time of the sultans. The domes, the cornices, the ornamentation—all the details are different. Dhaka's famous Sat Gombuz (Seven Dome) Masjid was also built during Shayasta Khan's time. Although it is named Sat Gombuz, it would be more correct to call it Teen Gombuz because the main structure carries three domes on its roof. But the design of this mosque stands out in the way in which each of the four turrets carries a large dome, almost competing in size with those on the main mosque. All the domes are beautifully embellished. Small, ornamental blind niches are set in the walls near the entrance. Lotus-petal ornamentation hugs the base of the domes as well as the top of the front wall. The mosque does not show any local influence except to an extent in its ornamentation.

Kartalab Khan's mosque in Dhaka's Begum Bazar area was built several decades after Shayasta Khan's time, during the regime of Murshid Quli Khan. The mosque shows certain similarities with Haji Shahbaz's mosque. There are five domes on its roof, in symmetry with the five doorways in its eastern wall, and there are four turrets in the four corners. That apart, there are two smaller turrets flanking each of the doorways. The mosque was one of its kind in at least two ways. It was built above a cluster of rooms. Attached to the mosque on its northern side is a cottage with a two-sided roof like a *dochala* hut typical of Bengal. Some historians have inferred that the imam of the mosque resided in this cottage. A previous instance of a home with a double-sided roof on the northern side of a mosque already existed in the Shah Mohammad Masjid of Egarosindur, and it looked pretty much like a *dochala* temple. Though built at the end of the 17th century, the huge dome

Kartalab Khan's mosque in Dhaka's Begum Bazar

that caps the Shah Mohammad Masjid evokes memories of the Eklakhi mausoleum. The mosques of Khan Muhammad Mirdha and Bibi Miriam were built shortly afterwards, both quite remarkable in terms of beauty and distinctive architectural style.

Apart from mosques and mansions, a number of forts got built in Bengal during the Mughal era. The Mughals had wrested the province from the Bara Bhuinyas, a group of 12 powerful chieftains who ruled like kings over their territories. But though the sway of the Bara Bhuinyas faded during the time of Islam Khan, new security challenges arose in the form of Portuguese and Arakan pirates. The Hajiganj fort near Narayanganj was built to meet these new threats, most probably on the orders of Islam Khan. The fort is located at the confluence of the Burhiganga and Sheetalakhya rivers. The Sonakanda fort was built on the other side of the Sheetalakhya. The Munshiganj fort was built at a later time. The Mughals also built a few bridges in and around Dhaka. On the whole, however, the progress and expansion of architecture that took place under the Bengal sultans did not continue unimpeded in the Mughal age. The Mughal rulers did not assume any very remarkable initiative to create architectural edifices. They could not help undertaking a certain amount of construction in Bengal, but nothing was built quite on the scale of the forts at Agra, Lahore and Delhi or the Jama Masjid.

In comparison with the age of the sultans, fewer religious edifices were built at the administration's initiative during the Mughal era. More remarkably, the native influences that had made themselves felt in the religious architecture under the Bengal sultans disappeared under the Mughals. Curiously, though the mosques lost the native touch, the curved cornice and some other native styles began to be used more than ever before in the construction of mazars. The temples built in the Mughal era also powerfully reflect native styles and influences.

Temple Architecture

Although Bakhtiyar Khilji captured power by overthrowing the Hindu king Lakshman Sena, he and other Muslim rulers had to depend on the Hindu elite and Hindu officials for governing the native population who spoke languages unknown to the invaders and followed religions other than Islam. Nonetheless, Muslim monarchs apparently continued destroying Hindu temples and Buddhist viharas, even though the number of such instances was small. In their iconoclastic zeal, the sultans might have also banned the construction of new temples and viharas in the areas under their control. Outside these areas, however, new temples and viharas continued to be built. For example, the Malla kings of Bishnupur built a temple at Dehar in the early 14th century. They also built another temple in Thakurpara in the early 15th century. Later in that century, the Malla kings constructed two other temples – Gopal and Ekeshwar temples – at Banki. The independent kings of Dinajpur, too, are known to have constructed temples during this time. Located far from the Muslim capital of Gaur, the Buddhists must have built new viharas in south-eastern Bengal.

As mentioned earlier, the cooperation and understanding between the sultans and the local 'kings', that is, big landlords, deepened during the 2nd century of the Muslim rule. The clout of the Hindu elite peaked in the early 15th century when Ganesh, a Hindu minister of a weak sultan, briefly became the king after removing his master. In order to consolidate his grip on power, he converted his adolescent son, Jadu, to Islam and named him Jalaluddin Mohammad. New temples started being built during the rule of Ganesh and his son. The king himself is said to have built a number of temples and even broken at least one mosque. A century later, there came another wave of temple construction after Chaitanyadev brought about a tide of Hindu regeneration in general and of Vaishnavism in particular. With the advent of Mughal rule in Bengal in the late16th century, there was a spurt in the number of new temples because the new dispensation pursued the principle of not interfering in the religious matters of the local people.

It is important to note that the temples constructed in the 15th century and later were, from the point of view of architecture, of a new type, as architectural styles had significantly changed during the previous two centuries. The old style curvilinear *rekha deul* temples as well as pyramidal *bhadra* or *pirha deul* temples continued to be built, but architects started experimenting with both the structure and the external as well as internal decoration of these temples. Apart from these experimentations with shapes and styles, these temples used new materials and building techniques brought

Top: Zafar Khan Masjid
Left: Shah Niyamat Ullah Masjid

by the Muslims. For example, the model of the curved cornice was almost universally imitated by temple architects. In the early years of Muslim rule, the dome, a symbol of Muslim architecture, was left out.

Unlike the flat roofs of mosques, temples had curved and gabled roofs and looked like rural huts with thatched roofs or *chala*. These temples, therefore, were called *chala* mandirs. Once *dochala* mandirs with two sloping faces of roof, joined together by a gable, were constructed, architects increasingly looked for variations. They thus built *chauchala*s with four faces of roof, and then *aatchala* with one smaller *chauchala* on the top of a large one. These *chala*-mandirs were later classified according to the number of faces of the roof. Thus a *dochala* mandir has a roof with two faces, *chauchala* has four and *aatchala* has eight. They can also have 12, 16 and even 20 *chala*s, giving them a pyramidal look.

Dochala temple

A *dochala* temple is the easiest to build. Hence the first chala mandirs were all *dochala*s. However, the oldest *dochala* temples did not survive. Among the oldest surviving ones are the Gopalbari temple (1644) in Jessore, Bardhankutir temple in Rangpur and two other temples at Madhabpasha in Barisal. These were all built in the 17th century. The earliest extant *chauchala* temple, the Singhabahini temple in Ghatal (Medinipur), however, dates back to 1490. The Henry Martin Pagoda in Serampore, which was initially an *aatchala* temple, was built in the 16th century. This suggests that the simpler *dochala* temples were built significantly earlier than 1490.

Among *chala* mandirs, Jor-Bangla temples are an important type. Jor-Bangla temples are so called because they are units of two *dochala*s joined together side by side. The earliest extant Jor-Bangla temples were all constructed in the 17th century. Among them were a temple in Chandrakona, Medinipur, the Radha-Krishna temple in Beernagar (Nadia) and the Gopinath temple at Kalachandpur (Pabna). The Kestaray temple in Bishnupur, built in 1655, is also a Jor-Bangla type temple, but it has a *chauchala* on its top. It is the oldest extant temple of its kind. It is also remarkable for its elaborate terracotta decorations. This suggests that Jor-Bangla temples started to be constructed much earlier than 1655. There is another Durga temple at Bali in

Chauchala temple

Hooghly which is unique for its innovative planning. It is basically a Jor-Bangla temple with an *aatchala* and nine *ratna*s (narrow domes) on its top. However, this temple was built in fairly recent times—in the 19th century.

A good number of *chala* temples have survived, but none of them was built earlier than the 17th century, except one—the Singhabahini temple at Ghatal. The Basudev temple at Basudevpur (Bankura) was built in 1626, the Shiv temple at Ghurisa (Birbhum) in 1633, the Kapileshwar temple at Tarash (Pabna) in 1635 and the Khatial Shiv temple in Howrah are the oldest surviving temples of this type. The Raja Ram temple at Khalia (Faridpur), built in the 18th century, is notable for its innovative planning. It has three parts—a *dochala* in the middle and two *chauchala*s on two sides. This *dochala* has three entrances and the two *chauchala*s have one entrance each. A temple at Puthia (Rajshahi) also has such a combination of *dochala* and *chauchala* structures.

The earliest *chala*-mandirs must have been the *dochala*s or temples with double-faced roofs, but then architects sought to introduce variations to the design. They did so by joining two *dochala*s (Jor-Bangla), adding two extra faces to the roof (*chauchala*), putting a smaller *chauchala* on the top of a larger *chauchala* (*aatchala*), and then experimenting with different combinations of *chala* mandirs. When they exhausted all their options by varying the number of *chala*s, they turned to narrow domes, called *ratna*. An early example of architecture using such narrow domes was the 16th century tomb called Qadam Rasul. Their use in an Islamic structure was quite unique. Temple architects, however, widely followed the example of these narrow domes.

The oldest surviving *aatchala* is the Henry Martin Pagoda, which was built in the 16th century. None of the other extant *aatchala* temples was built earlier than the 17th century. Notable examples of such temples are the Madan Mohan temple at Mellok (Howrah) built in 1651, the Lakshmi-Narayan temple at Balsi (Bankura), 1652, the Dogachiya Gopinath temple in Burdwan (1654), the Bishnupur Radhabinod temple (1659) and the Balaram temple in Bankura (1662). Among this type of *aatchala* temples, the Shyamchand temple in Shantipur is noteworthy for its size. Built in 1726, it has five front entrances. It is elaborately decorated on the two sides and the front. The Damodar temple at Jhikira in Howrah is, perhaps, the most beautifully decorated temple of this type. The terracotta plaques in this temple are exquisite. The Kantaji temple in Dinajpur and the Basudev temple in Puthia are also distinguished for their beautiful terracotta decoration.

Ratna Mandirs

Initially, mandir architects deliberately avoided domes to give temples a different look from that of mosques. However, they could not avoid the dome altogether for very long. A domed roof looks far better than a flat one. Architects could, however, make the temple dome look different by building it narrow and tall or giving it an angular or pyramidal shape, or even the shape of a four-sided tower. There were also temples with mosque-type domes, such as the Bhairavi temple at Bindol (Dinajpur), the Adinath and Keeriteshwari temples in Murshidabad and the Harihar temple at Gangabas (Nadia). Some temples in Coochbehar, too, had domes that looked very similar to mosque domes, although they were called *ratna* instead of *gombuz* (dome).

Temples with *ratna*s on the roof were called *ratna* mandirs. They were further classified by the number of *ratna*s they had, such as, *ekratna* (single-domed), *pancharatna* (five-domed), or *navaratna* (nine-domed). The *ratna*s on *ekratna* temples are, indeed, variations of the mosque-dome, such as the *ratna* of the Kalanjay Shiv Mandir in Bankura. The Shyamsundar temple at Memanpur and the Burha Shiv Madnir at Shingi (Burdwan) are not *ekratna* but *pancharatna* temples. All five *ratna*s of these two temples, nevertheless, look very much like the mosque-type domes. The same comment can be made about the *ratna*s of the Damodar temple in Dhanbad. The central *ratna* of the Parbatinath temple at Chandrakona in Medinipur, too, is similar. It can, thus, be said that even though the temple architects did not directly or widely imitate the Islamic dome, they were, nevertheless, influenced by its beauty.

Ekratna Mandir

A number of domes looking like inverted lotuses were built on mosques during the time of the sultans. Similar domes were later built on some Hindu temples, for example, on the Jora Mandir at Lalbagh, the Bhavanishwar

Mandir at Baranagar, the Shiv Mandir in Kashimbazar, the Shiv Mandir at Baliar in Rajshahi and on the Ras-Mancha in Puthia (Rajshahi). The *chala* mandir called Jora Shiv Mandir at Dohazari in Khulna was built in such a way that a small *chauchala* on its top looked like a dome. Generally speaking, however, architects and founders of temples were reluctant to use the Islamic dome.

The number of *ratna*s in temples corresponds to the number of *chala*s. A *chauchal*a mandir would have a large *ratna* or dome in the centre of the roof and four smaller ones in the four corners. A *navaratna* temple would have four *ratna*s in the four corners of the lower tier of the temple, and four in the upper tier and a large *ratna* in the centre of the top roof. *Navaratna* i.e. nine-domed temples proved to be the most popular.

Among the single-domed temples, the Jadavray temple at Jadavnagar (Bankura), built in 1650, was identified to be the oldest. However, two five-domed or *pancharatna* temples have been identified to have been built respectively in 1639 and 1643. The first one is the Gokulchand Mandir located at Gokulnagar, and the other one is the Shayamray Mandir on

Pancharatna temple

Bishnupur. If *pancharatna* or five-domed temples were built in 1639, single-domed on *ekratna* temples must have been built significantly earlier. Among the surviving *ekratna* temples, the Kalachand Mandir in Bishnupur, buit in 1656, seems to be the oldest, followed by Lalji Mandir (1658), Muralimohan Mandir (1665), Basudev Mandir at Bansberia (1679), Madanmohan Mandir (1694) and the Shyamaray Mandir at Daspur, Medinipur (1699). Among these *ekratna* temples, Jadavray Mandir at Jadavnagar is worth mentioning for its *ratna* or dome. Its dome is very large, like the one of the Eklakhi Mazar, and occupies almost the whole of the temple. The *ratna* or dome of the Jagannath Mandir at Mohanpur (Medinipur) is noteworthy for its beauty. Its dome is high and has horizontal ridges. The dome of the Kalanjay Shiv Mandir in Bankura has, on the contrary, perpendicular ribs.

Among the two most notable 17th century *pancharatna* or five-domed temples which have survived the onslaught of time are the temples located in Gokulnagar and Bishnupur (Shyamray). Apart from these two, the Shyamchand temple at Baital in Bankura (1660), Madangopal temple in Bishnupur (1665), Singhabahini temple at Sangkar in Burdwan (1662), Radhagobinda temple at Chechua-Gobindanagar in Medinipur (1682) and Shyamsusndar temple at Memanpur in Hooghly are also noteworthy. The *ratna*s of the temple at Memanpur are beautifully shaped, even though a bit too tall. The *ratna*s of the Govinda temple at Puthia are worth mentioning because unlike mosque-type domes, they are small *chauchala*s. This temple was built in the 18th century.

Puthia temple complex

A temple in Calcutta, built in the early 18th century, was perhaps the largest and tallest temple of that time. It was built by Govindaram Mitra, popularly known among the English as the 'Black Zemindar'. The temple later came to be known as the Black Pagoda. From the painting of Thomas Daniel (1792) it can be seen that the Black Pagoda was, indeed, a temple complex consisting of two *dochalas*, a flat-roof temple, an *aatchala* and a *navaratna* temple. The tallest *ratna* of this temple was even taller than the 165-ft-tall Ochterlony Monument built by the English a few years before the Black Pagoda. Its arches and round *ratnas* were very similar to those of mosques.

Black Pagoda

In their quest for innovation, temple architects even constructed twin *pancharatna* temples joined together, like Jor-Bangla temples. Several such twin *pancharatna* temples were built in and around Calcutta in the 18th and 19th centuries. *Jora navaratna* – pairs of nine-domed temples – were also built later. The famous temple scholar David J. McCutchion was unable to find any *navaratna* temple built earlier than 1700. The *navaratna* temple at Potajia (Pabna), he reckoned, was built in 1700. The Kantajiu temple in Dinajpur and the temple at Hatikumrul in Pabna, both *navaratna*, were, in his opinion, built in the early 18th century. The *navaratna* temple at Bardhankutir (Rangpur) was also built in the 18th century. It is surprising that even though western Bengal led in temple-building, *navaratna* temples were built first in the East Bengal districts. Among the *navaratna* temples in western Bengal, only the temple at Raghunathbari (Medinipur) was built in the 18th century. The Radhabinod temple at Kenduli is also relatively old among the *navaratna* temples of West Bengal.

The Kantajiu temple is thought to have been the most beautiful of all the *navaratna* temples. It lost its towers as well as some of its beauty because of an earthquake. But a picture of the temple as it was before the earthquake suggests that it was quite exquisite. The Shyamsundar temple at Sonabaria (Khulna) was built in 1767 and can thus be considered quite old. Other *navaratna* temples notable for their beauty were built in the 19th century. Among them are three temples of Medinipur: the Radhagobinda temple at Dheola, Shiva temple at Chandrakona and Brindabanchandra temple at Ghatal, and Bura Shiva temple at Singi (Burdwan). The last one was built in the 1790s. An excellent example of the *navaratna* temple is the Bhabatarini Kalimandir at Dakshineswar (near Kolkata). It was built fairly recently—in the second half of the 19th century.

Navaratna temple

Once *navaratna* temples became popular, temple architects endeavoured to introduce innovations by planning *trayodashratna* or 13-tower temples. They did not stop there and went on to build 17-tower, then 21-tower and even 25-tower temples. The increasing number of towers did not, however, add to the beauty of these temples. On the contrary, too many towers made them look messy; they lacked the simple beauty of the *pancharatna* or *navaratna* temples.

The pre-Muslim *deul* type temples, *rekha* and *pirha deuls* continued to be built, though in fewer numbers. However, with the knowhow that the Muslims had brought in, these temples excelled both in shape and ornamentation. The architects experimented with the shikhar, i.e. the tower, and made it more beautiful than it was before. Various designs were engraved on it, including patterns of curves cut around the shikhar both horizontally and perpendicularly. The oldest extinct shikhar temple dates back to 1461. This Shiva temple is located in Barakar (Burdwan). Although built so long ago, it was beautifully decorated. *Rekha deuls* came into fashion after the 16th century. Moreover, a few *pirha deuls* were also built during this time. As the scope of ornamenting a *pirha deul* was restricted (compared with the shikhar *deul*), only a small number of temples of the latter type were built. There were instances of shikhar and *pirha deuls* built close to each other.

Mosques tend to be large in size in order to accommodate congregations praying on their premises. Temples, on the other hand, can afford to be smaller in size because only the Brahmin priest performs the rituals before the deity, while the lay worshippers can pray outside. The size of temples, however, gradually became relatively large, perhaps as a result of the influence of mosques. Temple architecture also underwent other significant changes

A terracotta tile on the wall of Kantajiu Mandir

during colonial rule and accommodated European styles. But for centuries, temple architecture relied heavily on terracotta for ornamentation. How extensively terracotta was used and how beautiful and sophisticated it became can be seen from the Bahabpur Shyamsundar temple, Damodar temple at Bahirgarh, Krishnamandir at Baidyapur, Shivmandir ar Raypara, Basudev temple at Banshberia, Ratneshwar temple at Bhattamati, Keshtaray, Shyamaray and Madan Mohan temples in Bishnupur, Ramchandra temple at Guptipara, Radhaballabh temple in Krishnanagar, Gobindamandir in Puthiya, Gopinath temple at Radhakantapur, Sridhar temple at Sonamukhi, Sitala temple at Suratput and other such temples. However, the terracotta work at the Kantajiu temple in Dinajpur is almost without any comparison. The temple itself was constructed as a *navaratna* or a nine-domed structure in the middle of the 18th century. However, its towers were removed after being severely damaged in an earthquake towards the end of the century. It survives as an *aatchala* temple. Even though it is bereft of the beauty of its nine towers, it is still renowned for the beauty of its terracotta work.

Significant stylistic differences began to appear between temple and mosque architecture during Mughal rule. Nevertheless, it will be wrong to say that the temples built during this time were not influenced by Mughal architecture at all. Indeed, apart from the use of construction material and technology, structural influences can also the noticed. For example, there are undeniable similarities between Mughal mosques and five-domed temples.

David McCutchion called the Taj Mahal a *pancharatna* or five-domed temple. Mughal traits are noticeably clear in the multi-domed *rasamancha* built in the 19th century at Gopalpur in the district of Medinipur.

In particular, flat-roofed temples known as *dalan*-temples came to be built during the Mughal period. They had not existed before. The oldest extant example is the Govinda Mandir at Gazipur in Howrah, built in 1714. It had a slightly higher and smaller flat roof over its broader flat roof. This suggests that flat-roofed temples started to be built much earlier, though the older temples did not survive. The Gazipur temple had three entrances and the terracotta ornamentation above and by the sides of these entrances was similar to that of the earlier temples.

Once flat-roofed *dalan* temples became fashionable, many such temples were built. The Radhagobinda temple at Bamanpara in Burdwan (1745), the Rupeshwar temple at Kalna (1765), the Damodar temple at Kotalpur in Bankura (1769), the Radhagobinda temple at Chandakona in Medinipur (1781), the Shyamsundar temple at Paikbheri and Radhabinod temple at Perua in Birbhum were all constructed in the 18th century. *Ratna*s or towers on the flat roof, a variety of entrances, and curved cornices below the flat roofs were some of the innovations introduced by the architects of these temples.

After the establishment of British rule, Western influence on temple architecture became apparent, particularly in the 19th century. For example, the Bhutnath Shivmandir at Laoda in Medinipur had not only a flat roof but also European columns. It is not known exactly when this temple was built, but most probably in the second half of the 19th century. Some temples also had European spear towers along with *ratna*s. We will later notice that such European influences on temples were mostly seen in 19th century temples in Calcutta.

Architecture in Colonial Times

The nawabs moved their capital from Dhaka to Murshidabad in 1704. A period of semi-independent rule by the nawabs started in 1716 during the time of Murshid Quli Khan. But the British seized power from the Bengal nawabs before a distinct tradition of architecture could be established in Murshidabad. By 1773, Calcutta was the seat of power.

Job Charnock founded the city of Calcutta in 1690. Kolkata, Govindapur and Sutanuti were just villages at that time. There was no accommodation available when Charnock arrived in Sutanuti on August 24, so he lodged in a boat with his companions. Four days later, East India Company officials decided to build a few absolutely essential houses. Clearly, though Calcutta was formally founded in 1690, there was no architecture of any kind there at that time, let alone Western-style architecture. Nor had the East India Company traders brought any architects with them. After Job Charnock's death on January 10, 1693, therefore, his son-in-law Charles Eyre was not able to build a European-style tomb for him. The tomb that was built over his grave in 1695 was a double-domed, eight-cornered structure reminiscent of the Muslim architecture of past centuries.

Apart from Charnock's tomb, the notable constructions undertaken by the East India Company were all essential buildings such as a fort to secure personal safety, a factory to carry out trade, a church to cater to the religious needs of Company officials and a hospital for medical treatment. The construction of Fort William was completed in 1712. This 700-ft-long fort was not a remarkable feat of architecture. Its walls were 40 feet thick and 18 feet high. The Company also built homes for its civilian employees. There was not yet a Governor in Calcutta, but quite a grand mansion was built for the Company's chief official in the city. The Company's directors in London actually sent a warning against the prodigal extravagance of Company officials in Calcutta.

No matter how ordinary the fort was in terms of architecture, the first church of the British in Calcutta, built around the same time as the fort, can be considered quite a remarkable specimen of architectural excellence. The church was dedicated to Saint Anne in 1709, but work on its exceedingly high spire was finished only in 1716. It was a square tower surmounted by a tapering steeple. A lightning strike in 1724 left the tower damaged. Then in 1737 the tower collapsed in a tornado. It was never properly repaired. Eventually, new constructions came up in 1777 on the site where the church once stood.

Going by the 1730 drawing made by George Lambert, the church appears to have been a beautiful edifice. Although by this time churches in the shape of the Christian cross had become popular, this church was

St Paul's Cathedral (1847), Kolkata. *Photo courtesy: Ankitesh Jha (commons.wikimedia.org)*

a basilica, an oblong building of the kind used in ancient Rome for law courts and public assemblies. The sides of the roof were curved like bows. Along each of the two long sides of the church were five tall, arched windows, and each window was capped by a small round window above. The central part or nave of this basilica was 20 feet wide and 80 feet long. There were aisles on the two sides of the nave, divided into five sections. The rear wall was rounded, with five full-length windows, but the drawing does not show the façade. What can be guessed from the drawing is that there was an open verandah in front supported by a colonnade, that is, a row of evenly spaced columns.

Around the time when the church was built, a factory was built within the fort premises. A hospital was built, too. In Lambert's drawing, we catch a glimpse of the first floor of the factory. The first floor had an open verandah with 16 classical columns (most probably Ionic pillars). The two wings of this house had tall Palladian windows. There are two other houses on the right of this building in the picture, both with tall windows reaching up close to the ceiling. The stamp of an able architect is clear in the image of the three buildings.

A few Armenians and Portuguese, most probably traders, had started living in Calcutta even before the English had properly set up a colony in the place. They too built a couple of churches. Two sketches made in 1747 give us an idea of what they looked like. The spire of the Armenians' Church of Saint Nazarath was rounded, tapering off into a pointed steeple. The Church of Virgin Mary of the Portuguese had a square tower with a pointed steeple. Apart from the spire, it is hard to say to what extent the edifice reflected European styles of architecture.

As its trade gradually expanded, the East India Company was becoming involved with many kinds of work. In 1727 the Company set up a court called the Mayor's Court. The Company in fact had to build many buildings for similar administrative purposes in the first half of the 18th century. The Englishmen who arrived in Calcutta to make their fortunes overnight also started building homes here. These houses were all built around the 'park' area near the fort. We know from a report of 1707 that there were in the village of Kolkata alone residences built over an area of 400 bighas (bigha is a unit of measurement in eastern India including Bengal; it roughly equals one third of an acre) and that the Company regularly received taxes on these properties. Sutanuti and Govindapur were not yet quite as built up then; only 5 per cent of the area in both villages had homes built on them. In just 5 years, however, the population of the city of Calcutta quadrupled, and the number of homes increased accordingly. In short, the city was expanding fast.

The house occupied by Lord Clive some 40 years later was built by the East India Company. Characteristics of European architecture are evident in the ruins of this house. There were twin Doric pillars and a triangular pediment over an open verandah supported by pillars. The house also had Venetian windows. These features were absent in Muslim and Hindu architecture. John Clavering's home was built in the middle of the century. An open verandah resting on pillars was part of its front façade, too. The mansion known as Hasting's House was built around 1770. Its high, open verandah rested on Tuscan pillars. Ionic pillars were also used in this house. The house was divided into bays. Reza Khan's house built in 1775 also had 12 Tuscan pillars.

Hasting's House

European Influence in the Constructions of the Bengali Elite

The new building styles of the Europeans naturally drew the attention of native residents. Some wealthy traders and landlords began to imitate these styles. The family of Sabarna Choudhury and Nabakrishna Deb of Shovabazar were among the first to build homes showing European architectural influence. The platform for worship (puja mandap) attached to Sabarna Choudhury's house at Barisha in Calcutta had Ionic pillars. Nabakrishna Deb's home was even more remarkable in terms of architecture. Remarkable, because of the way in which it shows the gradual expansion of European influence among the indigenous population. Indian, Islamic and European styles were assimilated in this house. It had a *navaratna* temple and also a Durga mandap, that is, a roofed platform for the worship of the goddess Durga. There was also a *naatmandap*, a roofed space for dance and dramatic performances of religious content, which had Islamic gateways (toran). There was an open verandah on twin Ionic pillars and a sculpture of a lion on it. The windows on the ground floor were all arched.

Home of Nabakrishna Deb at Shovabazar

The Sinha family house built in 1760 had a similar assimilative style. The puja mandap had Islamic arches and Ionic pillars. The Tagores of Jorasanko and the rajas of Bhukailash were among the families who built European-style homes. The Bhukailash family home had a verandah on high pillars and a massive gateway. It also had a *chauchala* temple. Ionic pillars were used in the house that Ram Mohan Roy built, probably in 1800. Rani Rasmani's house was built in 1803. What was new for native homeowners in this house was that it had a triangular pediment surmounting Ionic pillars in its façade.

A Firm Trend

Thus, well before the 18th century was over, European architecture flourished in Calcutta in the constructions by both Europeans and Indians.

The Belvedere Palace at Alipore was built probably by Mir Zafar in the 1760s in the Italian Renaissance style and reflects how firmly European-style architecture had taken root in Calcutta by that time. The new trend became firmly established through the building of the new Fort William (1778), Writers Building (1780), the New Court House (1787), St. Thomas's School (1787), St. John's Church (1788), Council House (1788), the Sadar Dewani Adalat (1790), the Portuguese Church (1799), etc. The Chowringhee area can be clearly recognised as a European neighbourhood from the picture of it drawn by Thomas Daniel in 1787. The New Court House and St. John's Church were two of the noteworthy architectural specimens of this time. The open first-floor verandah of the New Court House instantly attracts attention. Twenty-two high Ionic pillars supported it. Divided into three sections, the verandah had its central section slightly jutting out. The doors were Georgian. The architecture of St. John's Church was simpler. But its high open verandah resting on eight Tuscan towers, its full-length windows and its imposing spire deserve mention.

The Government House built in 1802-1803, a civilian construction, can be considered a major architectural feat of colonial Calcutta. This huge mansion with 137 rooms was modelled on the English country house Kedleston Hall of Derbyshire. The three-storey house is built approximately in the shape of the English 'E'. A massive stairway leads up from the entrance to the first floor, where six huge Ionic pillars support an open verandah surmounted by a pediment. The windows are Georgian. A large, low dome sits atop the semi-circular verandah to the south-east of the edifice. An impressive gateway with two pairs of Tuscan pillars is part of the façade and is surmounted by an ornamental entablature with a sculpture of a lion. On each side of this gateway is a smaller entrance built in a similar design. The Governor General's Barrackpore House, built in 1808, had an open verandah surmounted by a triangular pediment and supported by Corinthian pillars.

Government House

Hundreds of European-style buildings built at government initiative followed the construction of the Government House. Quite a few of them were remarkable for their architectural excellence. For instance, Bank of Bengal (1806), Asiatic Society (1808), Town Hall (1813), St. Andrew's Church (1818), the Kolkata Madrasa (1820), the Baptist Chapel (1823), Old Mint (1828), Sanskrit College (1826), Ochterlony Monument (1828), Metcalf Hall (1844), St. Paul's Cathedral (1847), Medical College (1852), General Post Office (1868), the Calcutta Port Trust headquarters (1871), High Court (1872) and Collectorate (1890). The Babu Ghat (1838), Princep Ghat (1840), Bengal Club (1845), Chartered Bank (1857), Cossipore Club, etc. were also well known architectural landmarks.

Town Hall, St. Paul's Cathedral, Medical College and the High Court building deserve special mention. The open verandah at the centre of Town Hall was modelled on the temple of Minerva at Athens. Medical College has an open verandah in front supported by eight Corinthian pillars and surmounted by an entablature and pediment. The similarity of design with the Old Mint House and Cossipore Club is quite unmistakable. All three were

High Court building and Medical College

in fact modelled on the Parthenon. Like the Parthenon, Old Mint House was built with Doric pillars. It has open verandahs resting on pillars on all four sides. The edifice may well be seen as the first instance in Calcutta of the Greek Revival in architecture that swept Europe in the 18th and 19th centuries.

St. Paul's Cathedral was easily the most beautiful church built by the English in Calcutta. It was designed by William Forbes, the architect who created Old Mint House. This was Calcutta's first Gothic-style edifice. It had a square tower surmounted by a high steeple with four smaller steeples surrounding it. The tower collapsed in 1938 and was never rebuilt. There are 38 narrow towers around the church, 16 on each side and three each on two ends. There are also 15 full-length windows on each side. The church is embellished with beautiful ornamentation and the windows are paned with painted stained glass. The top ends of the windows are narrow, and ornamentations stretch all the way up to the ceiling from the narrow ends of the windows.

The High Court was built in the Gothic Revival style in 1872. It was built in the image of Stadthaus at Ypres in Belgium. It has a tower resembling the old tower of St. Paul's Cathedral. Many narrow towers ring the edifice on all four sides. The windows taper off at the top.

The Victoria Memorial is the greatest architectural feat of the British in Calcutta in the 20th century. It is remarkable for its undoubted

Victoria Memorial

beauty, but more so because of the assimilation of different architectural styles in its construction. There is a popular view that this memorial was built in imitation of the Taj Mahal. Beautiful as this white marble edifice certainly is, there cannot be any reasonable comparison to the Taj Mahal. However, its dome and its many small and big turrets may well bring the Taj Mahal to the mind. Built in the European Renaissance style, the memorial also clearly reflects traits of Islamic architecture.

Nineteenth Century and Thereafter

Over the 18th and 19th centuries, the British introduced and fostered a totally new style of architecture in and around Calcutta, pushing away older styles of building. It would not have been possible to recreate such a minuscule 'Blighty' had they chosen as their capital either Dhaka or Murshidabad, which were already built-up. But they built Calcutta from scratch. The natives who made the city their home were not able to ignore the new architectural style. On the contrary, the well-off among them more or less imitated the colonial styles while building their own homes. We have already mentioned how people like Sabarna Choudhury, Nabakrishna Deb and the Tagores followed the new style in the construction of their homes in the 18th century. As the Western influence grew in the 19th century and the number of wealthy local residents swelled in Calcutta, the native residents of the city started taking to the new styles more than ever before. The classical European pillars became so popular among them that a Bengali name was coined for them. *Hutom Pyanchar Naksha* calls it the *kolagechhe thaam* (the pillar that resembles a banana tree). Apart from the pillar, the European influence can be seen in the doors, the windows, the open verandahs, the high stairways leading up to the upper floor from the entrances and in the ornamentation of the native homes of colonial Calcutta.

Among the rich native residents who built homes influenced by Western architecture around the middle of the 19th century, the most notable were Rajendralal Mullick of Chorbagan, Khelat Ghosh, the Mullicks of Jorasanko, Sukhomoy Roy, Jadunath Mullick, the Tagores of Jorasanko, Prasanna Kumar Thakur, the Mitra family in Shyambazar, Bhabanicharan Laha, Digambar Mitra and the Roys of Jorasanko. Marble Palace, the mansion built by Rajendralal Mullick, really does look like it has been imported from Europe. Built in the classical European style in 1835, it was modelled on London's Burlington House. Both storeys of the house are fronted by long end-to-end verandahs, each supported by 14 Tuscan pillars. A low, triangular pediment sits like a crown at the centre of an ornamental entablature. There are sculptures scattered around the front garden.

The European influence was not exactly uniform in the homes built by native residents, but this section collectively changed the cityscape of Calcutta.

Marble Palace

The trend defined the kind of doors, windows and ornamentation that were used in the city's homes. Open verandahs and Venetian windows became the norm. The Calcutta of the late 19th and early 20th century was indeed a very Western-looking city.

European Influence on Religious Buildings

People are usually more conservative about religious matters, including, perhaps, religious architecture. Though the techniques of Islamic architecture were widely used in temples, there was scant use of the features that were exposed to the public gaze, such as domes and turrets (minar) at the four corners seen in Muslim edifices. Likewise, notwithstanding the use of Western architectural trends in homes, these were long eschewed in the construction of temples and mosques. Indeed, until Calcutta came to be known as the capital city in the second half of the 18th century and British colonial power was irrefutably established, Bengalis did not start imitating the colonial style of architecture. Mosques, temples and homes continued to follow the older styles for some decades.

Hence the famous temples that were built in Calcutta in the early years of the city were all constructed in the traditional Bengal style. The Kali temple at Kalighat, for instance. From a drawing by Thomas Daniel, dated (approximately) 1792, the temple can be identified as an *aatchala* temple with a *chauchala* entrance. But the temple that was built anew in the early 19th century (1809) was an ordinary *aatchala* structure. It was the kind of temple that was built in Bengal for the preceding two centuries—their architects had perfected the art of building it. The Kalighat temple is a flawless specimen of the *aatchala* temple. But the structure built as an extension to the temple shows European influence in its pillars, arches and cornices.

The Kali temple at Kalighat

Towards the end of the 18th century and the beginning of the 19th, many among the native residents of Calcutta came to possess a great deal of wealth. This section built temples in the pursuit of virtue and renown, so there was a veritable surge in temple-building in Calcutta at this time. Some among these rich men, not happy with building just one temple, built clusters of temples. The Black Pagoda built by Gobindoram Mitra, for instance is one such. Quite a few twin *aatchala* temples were built in Calcutta. A family of Ghoses built a cluster of four *aatchala* temples at Tollygunge in the late 18th century. The family of Sabarna Raychaudhury built a cluster of as many as six *aatchala* temples on the banks of the Adi (Old) Ganga. On the other side of the river stands an extraordinary complex of 12 temples. On Tollygunge Road, too, there is a cluster of 10 *aatchala* and two *pancharatna* temples. Rani Rasmoni and Joy Mitra had also constructed a cluster of 12 temples. Twin *pancharatna* and twin *navaratna* temples were also built in this pursuit of novelty in temple-building. Stranger still was the Gopaljiu temple at Tollygunge, which had a *navaratna* temple between two *pancharatna* ones.Likewise, the layout of a temple cluster in the north of Calcutta has a *navaratna* temple at the centre of six *chauchala* temples. The *navaratna* temple has 12 Corinthian pillars surmounted by a pediment in the foreground. Pilasters, rectangular columns projecting from walls, have been used near the entrances to the temples.

The construction of a *navaratna* temple was a more complicated affair than building a *pancharatna* one, but a high level of expertise was achieved in the 19th century in the building of these temples. The *navaratna* temples built in Calcutta during this time were remarkable in every way—in size, in ornamentation, in the sense of proportion displayed in the relative sizes of the lower and upper *chauchalas*. Talking of ornamentation, an easily discernible pattern is the steady decline in the use of terracotta tiles and plaques in temples from the 18th century. The Mughals had put a stop to the use of terracotta ornamentation in Muslim architecture, but the new practice did not immediately affect Hindu temples. Terracotta plaques continued to be widely used in temples for another 200 years after the consolidation of Mughal rule in Bengal in the early 17th century. But their use started dwindling from the latter half of the 18th century and ceased completely in the 19th. A notable instance of the new trend was the Kali temple at Dakshineshwar. Rani Rasmoni got this delightful *navaratna* temple built in the late 19th century at a cost of six lakh rupees. Though this temple has square recesses in its walls suitable for terracotta decoration, there are no terracotta plaques or tiles filling them up. Burnt-earth decorations having fallen out of vogue, artisans skilled in the production of terracotta tiles might well have been unavailable by that time.

From the middle of the 19th century, however, the Western influence started to make itself felt in Calcutta's temples and mosques. For instance, a number of Tuscan pillars and pilasters were used in the Gopal Jiu temple built in Tollygunge by the Mondal family in mid 19th century. Another example is the Bhabatarini Kali temple of the late 19th century in Shyambazar. One cannot but notice the European influence in the pillars flanking the three entrances of the temple. The Annapurna temple of Barrackpore-Talpukur also has clusters of pillars flanking the entrance. The worship area (*thakur dalan*) of the Bosu-Mullicks of Patoldanga has pillars and pilasters on both sides of the entrance. Tuscan pillars and pilasters have been used in the Radhakanta temple in Gopikrishna Pal Lane.

Nakhoda Masjid

Pillars and pilasters have been used, too, in the Bhabatarini Kali temple of Dakshineshwar. The European influence can also be spotted in the ornamentations used in some temples, such as in the nude sculptures in the entrance of Gokul Mitra's temple.

The European influence was also evident in mosques, but at a later date. It can be seen in the arched windows, turrets and pillars of Ghulam Mohammad's mosque in Dharmatolla Street. It is even more pronounced in the Ghulam Mohammad mosque at Tollygunge. The European influence is also clear in the open verandah, arches, windows, turrets and domes of Nakhoda Masjid. The stamp of a completely non-native architecture is also quite evident in the Pareshnath temple of the Jains built in 1867. Islamic and European architectural styles have been assimilated in the construction of this temple.

Outside Calcutta, the European influence was most evident in areas close to the city, in Hooghly, Barrackpore, Chinsura and Chandannagore. The European-style homes and offices at Chinsura and Chandannagore were built at French and Dutch colonial initiative. In the district headquarters of western Bengal, the British administration followed Western styles as much as possible in the construction of offices and courts. After Calcutta, however, it was in Dhaka where the British undertook constructions on a large scale. One reason was that Dhaka became the capital of the province comprising East Bengal and Assam at the beginning of the 20th century. But Dhaka already had a rich architectural tradition when it became a provincial capital under British colonial rule. Hence, European architecture did not flourish here as it had in Calcutta. Moreover, it did not remain the provincial capital for very long. Consequently, the boom in construction ebbed before Western architecture got a chance to get firmly rooted in the city. Nonetheless, the offices and homes built there at colonial initiative more or less reflected European influence. It was of course far less pronounced than in Calcutta. There were, instead, many instances of an assimilative style combining Mughal and European traditions. Unlike in Calcutta, for example, classical pillars, pediments and entablatures can be hardly seen in Dhaka. The European influence is seen instead in domes, doors and windows, open verandahs, staircases, bays jutting out from the main structure and square towers. But though it grew slowly, European architectural influence did leave its mark on Dhaka.

Two examples of the gradual expansion of European influence in Dhaka are Husseini Dalan and Ahsan Manzil. The old Hussaini Dalan was a Mughal edifice. But there is little of Mughal architecture in the new Husseini Dalan that was built after the old one collapsed in the earthquake of 1917. Instead of Mughal features we see pillared verandahs, bay windows and square towers. Ahsan Manzil was built in 1872 as the seat of the Dhaka Nawab family. The stairs in front leading straight up to the upper floor, the two bays with low square towers jutting out at the two ends of the palace, and the large dome in the centre unmistakably point to European influence. This became more pronounced when the palace was rebuilt after the damage inflicted by the tornado of 1888. Northbrook Hall, built at the same time as Ahsan Manzil, also shows an assimilation of Mughal and European styles.

Like the nawabs of Dhaka, many landowning families (zamindars) in western and eastern Bengal built European-style homes in the 19th and 20th centuries—the *rajbari*s (royal houses belonging to large zamindars) of Mymensingh, Jaydevpur, Dinajpur and Muktagachha, the Murhapara rajbari of Narayanganj, the Baliati rajbari of Manikganj, etc. The seat of the Natore zamindars at Deehgapatia can be clearly recognised as a colonial edifice. The dome at the rear of the building shows resemblances with the dome of Calcutta's Government House. The arches and the doors and windows of the mansion also follow European traditions. But the mansion is essentially a motley of various European styles.

Some constructions show a veritable blending of European with local and Islamic styles. It happened particularly in the government buildings constructed in Dhaka after the partition of Bengal in 1905. The most notable of these was Curzon Hall. If the Victoria Memorial was the greatest feat of British colonial architecture in Calcutta, Curzon Hall can perhaps claim that status in Dhaka. A seamless blending of European and Mughal traditions can also be seen in Fazlul Haq Hall, Dhaka Hall, Salimullah Muslim Hall, Carmichael College in Rangpur, etc. The European influence was more pronounced in the High Court building of Dhaka, built at an earlier phase. It is something of an exception in Dhaka in the use of classical pillars. The dome surmounting the

Curzon Hall

pillars is also European, and not Islamic. The European influence was quite emphatic in Burdwan House and other buildings that were constructed in what is now known as the Dhaka University area after the 1905 partition of Bengal. Still, the cityscape of Dhaka never quite acquired the Western looks of Calcutta. Some European-style buildings, forming exceptions rather than the norm, also came up in the district headquarters of eastern and western Bengal and in other places. The Anglican Church at South Point in Darjeeling, for instance, is a simple but beautiful specimen of Gothic architecture.

Over half a century has elapsed since the Partition of 1947, but no distinctive tradition of architecture has developed either in West Bengal or in Bangladesh in these decades. The influence of modern Western style of construction is progressively growing. The rapid increase of population and the tremendous pressure on the cities have ensured that the efficient use of space rather than beauty is the most important consideration in new constructions, as the tall apartment buildings of Dhaka and Calcutta bear testimony. Most of the apartment buildings and other private homes do not bear the mark of any attempt at ornamentation. However, government buildings constructed over large areas at considerable expense are usually planned by able architects and show some attempt at ornamentation.

Baitul Moqarram Mosque

In the modern edifices built in Dhaka and Calcutta in recent decades, shapes such as those used in modern Western architecture are predominant—spheres, cylinders, cubes, circles, triangles, etc. The most noteworthy example of modern architecture in Dhaka is the Jatiyo Sangsad Bhaban, or the National Parliament House, designed by the renowned architect Louis Kahn. He started working on it in the early 1960s, well before Bangladesh became a free country. He spent many years in Bangladesh to complete the project. The building was completed in the late 1970s, several years after his death. No comparable construction of this scale has taken place in Calcutta in recent years. Some religious structures, including the Baitul Moqarram mosque, are also worth mentioning. Among secular structures, the Shahid Minar and the Jatiya Smriti Soudha (National Memorial Monument) are beautiful and innovative.

The Italian Renaissance of the 14th and 15th centuries found one of its chief expressions in architecture and art. Just as there was a revival in the study of ancient texts that were given a new, humanist interpretation, there was also a revival of ancient Greek and Roman architecture, which formed the foundation of a new tradition. Many historians have not been willing to accept the Bengal Renaissance as a renaissance at all because the architecture of colonial Bengal, centred in Calcutta, was not a revival or reinterpretation of past traditions. There is no denying, however, that colonial rule brought about a construction boom in Calcutta and introduced European styles of building. Not so in art. Historically, Bengalis lagged behind in art.

Art

Not much is known about art in ancient and medieval Bengal. The main reason is the climate. The drawings and paintings by ancient and medieval artists have not survived. Besides, the ingredients used by them were not of the kind to last for very long. The oldest extant drawings are ornamentation in old texts and wooden covers for texts. These wooden frames had drawings on the outside as well as inside. The manuscripts were also decorated with pictures. But these were written on palm leaves, and there was only so much that could be drawn in such limited space. Still, any account of the art of ancient and medieval Bengal cannot but rely on the pictures found in manuscripts.

Some palm-leaf manuscripts by Buddhist scholars have been preserved in the British Museum. These were written during the Pala era or just after. These contain drawings of the Buddha in many poses and in many of his names—such as Amitabha, Bodhisatva Shakyamuni, Bodhisatva Padmapani, Bodhisatva Maitreyi, etc. There are also drawings of goddesses. The chief goddess is Tara—in many names and forms, such as Shyamtara, Bajratara, Sit-tara, etc. There are drawings of some minor gods and goddesses of the Vajrayana Buddhist sect. These pictures were believed to possess the power to protect both the manuscripts and their owners from harm. One such text was the *Astasahasrika Pragyaparomita*, with versions written at various times. Several copies of the text have been found. In one of these, thought to be written around 1220, there is a drawing of Bodhisatva Samantabhadra, with Tara and Bajrapani. The style of the drawing shows unmistakable similarities with the cave drawings of Ajanta. In another version of *Astasahasrika Pragyaparomita*, preserved in the British Museum and written in the second half of the 10th century, there is a drawing of Mahasree Tara. In keeping with the custom of the times, the representation of the Buddha and other male figures in these drawings is remarkably feminine in physical attributes, posture, clothes and ornaments.

Manuscripts were inserted inside wooden covers to protect them from wear and tear. The drawings on these covers were called *patachitra*. The oldest extant *patachitra*, preserved in the British Museum, is with a manuscript of *Vishnupuran*, written approximately in 1499. It was found in the district of Bankura. Another *patachitra* found in Bankura and dating back to 1647 is also preserved in the British Museum. The first of these contains a drawing of the 10 avataras (incarnations of the divine), while the second contains a drawing of Vaishnavas singing devotional songs (kirtan). In the first *patachitra*, the Buddha is shown as the ninth of the 10 avataras. That means that the idea of assimilating Buddhists within the Hindu fold was firmly established by that time. Though only a handful of the oldest *patachitra*s have been found, many dating from the late 17th century onwards have survived. Though rich in their pictorial content, they are quite small in size and therefore restricted in their scope for drawings.

That Bengal was ruled by Muslims at the time when Bengali culture is believed to have come into its own did not help the cause of art. Just as music was thought to be against the scriptures by the Muslims, the pictorial representation of the created world was thought to be anti-religion. They did not, consequently, patronise art. The local tradition of art might have been discouraged in the face of opposition from the rulers. But not all Sultans were equally iconoclastic or opposed to art. A shining exception was, for instance, Hossein Shah's son Naseeruddin Nusrat Shah (1519-32). He patronised art as well as literature. A copy of the Persian poet Nizami's *Iskandarnama* (1531; 'Book of Alexander') was prepared for him. Preserved in the British Museum, it contains pictures in the Persian style. The extraordinary thing about it is that the people, animals and plants represented in these pictures reflect local characteristics. This suggests an assimilation of local art with imported traditions. Nusrat Shah's example, however, was an exception.

It is not as if Bengal had no folk tradition of art outside the sphere of royal or religious patronage. The folk tradition flourished among the *patua*s of Bengal, a community of artisans who drew their hearts out in a variety of mediums. From time to time they set out with their paintings on scrolls, made of rolled-up coarse cloth, and travelled from village to village showing their art to zamindars and rajas, that is, the big landholders. Their livelihood consisted in their art and its itinerant display to wealthy clients. It was mostly religious narratives that they depicted in their art. Not just stories from the *Ramayana* and the *Mahabharata*, they also drew popular local folk deities such as Manasa and Chandi. No pictures by medieval *patua*s depicting secular themes have been found.

In a previous chapter we have noted how Chaitanyadev infused the Hindu faith with new life with his Vaishnava preaching during the time of Hossein Shah. In those heady days of devotional emotion, many pictures of Chaitanyadev and his chief followers were produced. Many drawings were made, too, of sessions of devotional music or kirtan. Some of those pictures have survived. Several such pictures have been reproduced in the book *Arts of*

Bengal (edited by R. Skelton and Mark Francis) and also Dinesh Chandra Sen's *Brihat Banga.* A picture depicting Chaitanyadev in the Ajanta style has been found (see chapter 'Society and Religion of Bengal'). This Vaishnava tradition of art does not seem to have gained wide currency in society. Nor did it leave any lasting artistic heritage. But once the Vaishnava faith became popular, *patuas* started depicting the story of Radha and Krishna in their drawing. Their pictures, however, were far removed from the pictorial depictions of Chaitanyadev produced by the Vaishnavas.

The Mughals started ruling in Delhi a few decades after the time of Hossein Shah. In comparison with other contemporary Muslim rulers of their stature, the Mughals were in fact quite exceptional in their patronage of art, particularly Akbar and Jahangir. The tradition of miniature painting flourished under Mughal patronage. Historians believe this tradition to have combined Indian, Persian and even European trends. The Mughal rulers commissioned paintings of historical incidents, their courts and other worldly matters and their own portraits (*tasveer*). These pictures differed in their secular content from the local tradition of drawings on religious themes.

The Mughals conquered Bengal towards the end of the 16th century. But this did not immediately or even long afterwards cause the Mughal tradition of painting to have any impact in Bengal. From the end of the 17th century, however, some portraits were produced of the Mughal rulers of Bengal and later of the independent nawabs—Shaista Khan, Meer Zumla, Murshid Quli Khan, Alivardi Khan, Siraj-ud-Daulah, and so on. Alivardi Khan, in particular, is known to have encouraged the art of painting. But the art produced in Bengal under the nawabs did not strictly follow the Mughal tradition of miniature painting; instead, the creators of these paintings struck out on their own to produce a local style. 'Madhumadhavi Rangini', 'Alivardi Khan and his two companions' and 'Alivardi Khan in a hunt' are three beautiful examples of this style reproduced in *Arts of Bengal.* All 3 quite noticeably differ from the Mughal style. Who painted them is, however, not known.

A Scottish doctor called William Fullerton worked in Patna from 1744 to 1766. He got an artist from Murshidabad called Deep Chand to paint a number of portraits of his family. These pictures are reminiscent of the Mughal style influenced by local techniques. But since Deep Chand was commissioned by

Fullerton to produce these portraits, some European elements have found their way into them. Deep Chand's is one of the very few names that have come down to us among the painters of his time. The name suggests, however, that he was not a Bengali. Other officials of the East India Company, and not just Fullerton, engaged local artists to get their own portraits painted and to paint scenes from nature and local lifestyles. The artists of Murshidabad moved somewhat away from their own distinctive styles in order to produce paintings to suit the tastes of their foreign paymasters. A certain local style influenced by European trends grew among them from the end of the 18th century. The only other contemporary painter we know of was Bhabani Das. He was from Patna but worked in Calcutta towards the end of the 18th century. Another contemporary painter who worked in Calcutta was Sheikh Zai-nal-deen. His 1780 painting of Lady Impey (see chapter 'Attire', on sartorial history) has survived. The work bears testimony to his able craftsmanship.

As the capital and a rising city, Calcutta far outstripped Murshidabad in status and significance towards the end of the 18th century. Many artists now made their way to Calcutta in search of work. Able artists like Hicki and Daniel had started arriving in Calcutta by this time. These foreign artists drew likenesses of influential local individuals such as Ram Mohan Roy and Dwarkanath Tagore. Native artists must have seen their work and can be reasonably surmised to have been influenced to an extent by their technique and style. Sheikh Mohammad Ameer from the Kareya area of Calcutta, who became quite well known in the second half of the 19th century, is said to have mastered new styles and techniques through his association with European artists. His 'Two Dogs' reproduced in *Arts of Bengal* and picture of Government House reproduced in Jeremiah P. Losty's *Calcutta, City of Palaces* point to European styles.

The folk tradition of the *patua*s also seems to have grown in strength in the 18th century. The art found its most notable expression in the *pat*s of Kalighat. It is not just that many of these pictures were undoubtedly beautiful; their artists also developed a distinctive style that was later adopted by Jamini Roy (1887-1972). The earliest Kalighat *pat*s engaged exclusively with religious themes but the tradition did not eventually limit itself to religion. Social realities, aspects of everyday life and even the animal world started making their way into the art of the *patuas* in the 19th century. The sensational 1873 case of the rape/seduction of a young Bengali housewife called Elokeshi by a *mahant* (priest) of the Shiv temple in Tarakeshwar, a pilgrimage town near Calcutta, and her subsequent decapitation by her husband became the theme of innumerable *pats*. The craft gradually lost out in competition with the printing press in the second half of the 19th century and was virtually erased in the 20th.

Although not quite able to make the mark that the Kalighat *pats* did, a similar art known as the *ghazir pat* (pictures of the ghazis) gained currency among Muslims. These represented religious personalities such as ghazis, pirs and the folk deity Dakshin Ray. The animal world, too, intruded into these pictures. The *jadu pats* of the Santhals were a similar medium of local art. The advent of modern lifestyles slowly eased out the different traditions of *pat* art in Bengal. The printing press was one of the reasons for their disappearance.

The printing press, however, also stoked the tradition of pictorial art in Bengal in many ways. Illustrations for books and book covers began to appear in the 19th century. Limitations of printing technology placed certain restrictions on such illustrations in the initial years, and there was also no scope for printing colour pictures. But the arrival of lithograph printing in the late 19th century in Calcutta pushed down the cost of printing pictures, even coloured illustrations. Many beautiful illustrations for books and book covers were produced in Bengal in the 19th and 20th centuries. The likes of Abanindranath Tagore, Jamini Roy, Satyajit Ray and Quamrul Hassan left testimony to their formidable artistic abilities in the book covers that they designed.

However, the flowering in the language and literature of Bengal that followed the colonial encounter did not have a comparable counterpart in art. This is intriguing, especially when we look at artists such as Ravi Varma who used European techniques to produce reasonably good art. Bengali artists, too, could not indefinitely keep the European influence at bay. This influence started telling on their work at the end of the 19th century and the dawn of the 20th.

The artist who in one powerful wrench pushed the art of Bengal to a different plane altogether was Abanindranath Tagore (1871-1951). He learnt his craft from two European artists, an Italian and an Englishman. They taught him how to use water colours, oil paints and pastels. But though they taught him techniques and the use of different raw materials, he was more attracted to Indian styles of art. He was influenced by the folk and miniature styles of Ajanta, Rajput, Persian, Mughal and tribal hill art. He even learnt Japanese techniques from a Japanese artist. The combination of such myriad influences gave variety to his work but also at times acted as a weakness. The presence of so many styles at once meant critics of no one school found his work completely satisfying. Also, he was able to produce few works that can be recognised unmistakably as bearing his own stamp.

'Ganesh Janani' by Abanindranath Tagore

Attracted by Abanindranath's extraordinary genius, E.B. Havell, the Principal of the Calcutta Art College, persuaded him to accept the post of Vice Principal there. The post earned him quite a following. Together, the artists who gathered around him stoked interest and enthusiasm in art and also created a new school that can be termed the Bengali school of art. The most famous of his followers were Nandalal Bose, Asit Haldar (1890-1964), Abdur Rahman Chughtai and Mukul Dey. Hemendranath Majumdar was a contemporary of Asit Haldar. He displayed a special skill in paintings of women.

Gaganendranath Tagore (1867-1938) was the elder brother of Abanindranath. He took drawing lessons from a Bengali and a Japanese artist. He was also tutored in the European technique of using water colours. Unlike Abanindranath, he did not follow the old Indian styles. He was influenced by French styles. His pictures also bear the imprint of the contemporary Cubist movement. Gaganendranath also showed a flair for the modern art of cartoons.

Sunayani Devi, a younger sibling of Gaganendranath and Abanindranath, made a name for herself through her pictures in traditional Indian styles. At least one famous artist later started out by imitating her style—Jamini Roy.

Rabindranath Tagore threw all rules to the wind to produce drawings and paintings of a completely different kind. He came to the medium late, at the age of 67, but his work is deeply individualistic and bears the stamp of his genius. He had no formal training in the craft, which was at once a strength and a weakness. His figures, of humans as well as of birds and animals, often display a flawed sense of proportion and therefore appear distorted. His work was displayed at quite a few exhibitions in the West. The critics who saw them either enthusiastically praised his distortions of proportion or dismissed his art as worthless.

Jamini Roy and Zainul Abedin (1917-76) took forward the Bengal school of art. Jamini Roy was born in Bishnupur, a place with traditions of sculpture, architecture, art and craft going back many centuries in history. These formed Jamini Roy's artistic heritage. Still, the work of his early phase shows European influences because he was taught by a European artist at Calcutta Art College. Later, he based his art in the tradition of the Kalighat *patua*s and developed a style that makes his work instantly recognisable as belonging to him. He drew his subjects from the lives of Santhals and folk traditions, everyday realities and religious narratives. Even his paintings of Jesus are done in the style based on the craft of the *patua*s that he had made his own. His renderings of Krishna, Yashoda, Santhals—all bear his unmistakable style.

The first artist of renown among Bengali Muslims was Zainul Abedin. It was not easy for Muslims to practise art. Zainul Abedin, who was a student of Calcutta Art College, had to overcome much opposition in order to stick to his chosen path. After graduating from Art College, he started teaching there. He played a leading role in the establishment of an art college in Dhaka after the 1947 Partition. Indeed, he made the pursuit of art acceptable among Bengali Muslims by his own example and by helping to start an art college. He chose his subjects from the everyday lives of the ordinary people of Bengal, and his work reflects his social awareness. His pictures of the 1943 famine brought him instant fame. He was deeply moved by the destruction caused by the tidal waves of 1972 and produced a series of pictures and scroll paintings on it.

Quamrul Hassan also drew upon the folk traditions of Bengal in his art. His pictures of Bengali women are individualistic and show a simple beauty. Another noteworthy artist of post-Partition eastern Bengal was Safiuddin.

After 1947, artists from both Bengals have not infrequently travelled to the West to learn their craft. This has exposed them to the use of different media and raw materials. Many of their pictures reflect modern as well as folk traditions. Yet, none of them has been acclaimed by critics as an artist of international stature. Bengalis, indeed, have not been able to make in art the kind of contribution that they have made in literature and music.

Folk Art and Crafts

A rich and valuable tradition of folk art and craft has developed over generations everywhere in Bengal. Driven chiefly by necessity, such art makes use of easily available and inexpensive raw materials. Pots and pans and other utensils, for instance, have always been in demand for cooking and storing food. In ancient and even in more recent times, such needs were met by producing earthenware. The continued practice of the craft over generations created a skilled community of potters. There also developed a tradition of painted earthenware. Producing earthen vessels thus turned into a cottage industry, churning out not only vessels but painted pots and dishes, and also dolls. Women were often closely associated with the craft.

The different traditions of craft that developed in the villages of Bengal often retained distinctive local characteristics in their raw materials and technique, unlike urban artisan traditions that were more cosmopolitan in the influences they imbibed. The demand for crafts in modern times and the arrival of modern methods of production that make them more easily available have, to an extent, converted these crafts into mass-produced commodities. Nonetheless, they still retain some of their traditional properties, if not all.

The intricately worked *kantha*, for example. The *kantha* was initially the handiwork of women in Bengal's villages who poured their creativity and their dreams into criss-crossing handmade quilts with colourful running stitches, sometimes in simple patterns, sometimes working the stitches into elaborate motifs, transforming an article of everyday use into a thing of beauty. As, for instance, we see in Jasim Uddin's narratives. Now, *kantha* hangings grace the drawing rooms of the urban elite and *kantha* saris make an industry worth crores. The *kantha*, thus, has become a commercial commodity and it is doubtful whether it can be called folk art anymore. Both the raw materials and the threads used have changed; *kantha* artisans now experiment with fabric and design to cater to a niche client base that can afford their products. The designs are still beautiful, often boldly innovative, but they have lost the simple spontaneity of motifs created by women who once poured their creative energies into the art in gaps squeezed out of overworked domesticity.

Nakshi kantha

Though the *nakshi* (literally, designed) *kantha* was made in both eastern and western Bengal, the districts of Jessore, Faridpur and Rajshahi in East Bengal were most famous for their *kantha*s. In Bangladesh, the Nawabganj area of Rajshahi is now a major centre for the production of *kantha.* In West Bengal, *kantha* products, both saris and quilts, are produced in villages around Santiniketan in Birbhum district. It is a tradition that started in the 1940s with Tagore's daughter-in-law Pratima Devi's rural reconstruction programme centred in Kala Bhavan of Santiniketan.

Alpona, the art of covering floors and walls with floral and geometric designs with a solution of rice flour, has evolved in its own way. (The *kollam* is the South Indian cousin of the Bengali *alpona*, kept much more alive in urban life in South India than in Bengal and still gracing the space outside the front door of almost every Hindu home.) In Bengal, *alpona* was traditionally used by Hindu women for *vrata*s, an exclusively female domain of worship using ritual and narrative recitals. Sometimes, the *alpona* depicted the deities being appeased through the ritual and narrative details relating to the story around it. It was for long almost completely a craft practised and innovated by women. Apart from adding a touch of beauty to the *vrata*s, the *alpona* also graced spaces used for the worship of mainstream Hindu deities and was on display during weddings, the 'turmeric ceremony' preceding marriages, and the rice-eating and naming ceremonies held for infants. With time, the craft has lost much of its religious associations and is now widely used by Bengali Muslims in Bangladesh during weddings and pre-wedding rituals such as the turmeric ceremony. The streets of Dhaka and the area around the Shahid Minar sport elaborate *alpona* every year on February 21, the anniversary of the martyrdom of language activists in 1952 and on the occasion of the Bengali New Year. Particularly, the mile-long *alpona* on the road (a recent practice) in front of Jatiyo Sangsad Bhaban (parliament house) is a wonder. Bengalis never saw anything quite like it. Recently, however, the *alpona* on the road started being painted.

All this has produced a need for '*alpona* artists', inevitably eroding the exclusively female nature of the activity. Talking of the *alpona*, it would be unfair not to include a word about the little boys and girls in West Bengal's government schools who pour their hearts out in drawing elaborate floral *alpona*s every year on Vasant Panchami (the fifth day in the bright fortnight of the month of Magh, sometime in late January/early February) when Bengali Hindus celebrate Saraswati Puja. The entry of the *alpona* in secular spaces has changed it in many ways, even in the raw material used for it. Rice flour is increasingly jettisoned in favour of coloured powders of various kinds. In its changed and colourful form, however, the *alpona* continues to be firmly linked to 'Bengaliness' in the minds of most Bengalis and therefore finds its way into many modern festivities, religious and secular. Inevitably, it is a part of the Panchise Baishakh (the birth anniversary of Tagore, on the 25th of the month of Baishakh) celebrations in both Bengals.

Somewhat like the *alpona*, but on a smaller scale, is the art of painting earthenware with colourful designs and pictures of deities. Curved earthen dishes (*soraa*) with their convex sides painted with pictures of gods and goddesses were once widely used (and continue to be used in many parts of Bengal) for the annual worship of the goddess Lakshmi seven days after Vijaya Dasami. At the end of the rituals, the plate was hung up on the wall in the belief that it placed the household under the benign watchfulness of the goddess of prosperity and good fortune. And there it stayed until it was displaced by a new one next year. Now non-Hindu Bengalis also decorate their homes with such plates, painted with secular motifs. Like the *alpona*, the *soraa* has lost its old rural associations. Though the *soraa* used for the worship of Lakshmi was produced by craftsmen all over Bengal, the area around Dhaka was particularly known for it. Manasa the snake goddess being popular in western Bengal, such earthen dishes depicting Manasa used to be produced in the Rarh area.

The use of the *mangal ghot* or *mangal kalsi* in auspicious occasions such as marriages was prevalent in Bengal from ancient times. A rimmed, narrow-necked wide-bottomed pot, whether of metal or earthen, decorated with mango leaves and a green coconut and marked with vermilion was believed to bring good luck and prosperity. The belief was also quite entrenched among Bengali Muslims. That is why in many Muslim families pots were kept filled up, with water or milk, when a new bride was welcomed into the household. Though the practice initially had Hindu religious associations, those associations have now largely given way to a general trend of using painted pots to decorate homes. Painted pots are hence produced in large numbers, especially in Bangladesh.

Though plastic dolls are now all the rage, earthen dolls were produced all over Bengal until a few decades ago. The earthen dolls, likenesses of both humans and birds and animals, show a remarkable continuity of design with the dolls produced in ancient times. Extremely simple in structure, outline and ornamentation, some of these dolls are just barely recognisable as what they are supposed to represent. But then there were also dolls such as those made in Krishnanagar, which were quite lifelike imitations of their originals, ranging from birds and animals to insects and bugs. The tradition has not entirely faded out. William Hunter, writing in the early 1870s, said that earthen dolls from Nadia were displayed at exhibitions in London and Paris and even won prizes. Rasasundari Devi has written in her autobiography that she once made a snake that got people alarmed until one of them made bold to hit it with a stick. Only when the snake was smashed did people realise that it was a fake. Rasasundari had not of course received any training in doll-making. What she had was an aptitude for crafting likenesses with clay. It was this natural flair for the craft that made women in Bengal's villages fashion dolls out of clay.

Bengal indeed had a tradition of clay artefacts right from ancient times. The innumerable terracotta plaques and tiles found in the viharas of Paharpur and Mainamati bear testimony to the excellence and range that this tradition had achieved. Many earthen objects have also been found at

Chandraketugarh, Mahasthan and Vasuvihara. Objects of daily use such as pots and pans have also been churned out by generations of artisans. In their shapes and in techniques of production, these objects stand out from similar articles made in other parts of India. Bankura and Nadia districts were most well known for clay objects and artefacts in the 19th century. The craft was well developed also in Barishal, Mymensingh, Rajshahi and Rangpur.

Terracotta sculptures and images of deities made for worship are the most remarkable of earthen objects produced in Bengal. In particular, the skill and the aesthetics that go into the making of images of the goddess Durga are undoubtedly extraordinary. It is a skill that artisans have acquired through

Goddess Durga with her four children

generations of image-making, over many centuries. Images of the goddess Lakshmi are made in far greater number than the Durga images, Lakshmi being worshipped in almost every home. Images of Kali and Saraswati are also produced in relatively smaller numbers. In innovation and beauty, the Durga images far outstrip the others. The way in which the goddess is imagined in the popular consciousness, as a daughter visiting her parental home with her four children on their different mounts, and the mother goddess herself mounted on a lion and slaying the buffalo demon, allows ample scope for artisans to give free rein to their creativity. Apart from these mainstream deities, there are other deities that are worshipped by specific communities or in particular locations. Images of these deities are also produced. Those who work with tools, for instance, worship Vishwakarma. Vastu Puja was once a big affair in Barishal, and the paraphernalia included life-size clay likenesses of tigers, lions and crocodiles.

The kind of ornamentation used in clay images differed from region to region. Just as the clay images of Bengal show resemblances with ancient sculptures, they also show similarities with paintings. There are similarities, too, with ideas of beauty expressed in Sanskrit *alankara shastra*, that is, the theory of rhetoric in Sanskrit. Such images also inevitably reflect the styles of their own time. In recent times, for instance, some images show remarkable similarities with popular heroines. The changes that have taken place in the clothes and jewellery of Bengali women in the last 200 years have influenced the way clay images are conceived. The images of gods and other kinds of sculpture produced in Katoa and Bishnupur are particularly noteworthy.

Apart from clay, other easily available materials such as wood, cane and bamboo have been used for centuries in Bengal's villages to produce innumerable kinds of artefacts. Each of these raw materials has produced its own particular tradition of art objects. Wood endures better than cane and bamboo and is also easy to carve. From ancient times therefore people in Bengal have worked with timber to make pillars, doors, windows, thresholds in doorways, shutters, beaded wooden curtains, fences, containers, large vessels to hold rice/paddy, ornate chests, palanquins, or covered litters carried by men, and so on. Wood was also used to make local stringed musical instruments, hookahs to smoke tobacco and moulds for making steamed sweets and milk sweets. Many different kinds of wood were used to make furniture, especially those that were both durable and easy to saw and carve. Timber has been imported, too. The chairs, tables, sofa sets and beds made in modern times show efforts to create beauty through intricate designs. Just as the architecture and terracotta plaques of Bengal began to reflect Western influences from the 18th century, Western motifs and designs began to appear in woodwork. Zeenat Mahrukh Bano's book *Bangladesher Darushilpo* (Wood Art of Bangladesh) has excellent pictures and designs of objects made of wood. Such objects are not just functional, they also reflect attempts to create beauty.

Wooden dolls have also been made in Bengal from ancient times. They are of two kinds: toys or playthings of children are the first kind, whereas the second are almost like sculptures in wood and are usually images of gods and goddesses. Until about just 50 years ago, children used dolls chiefly of clay and wood. In particular, wooden horses and clays animals of various kinds were much loved by children. Artisans worked on these throughout the year in order to sell them at fairs.

A pair of *topor* worn by Hindu grooms and brides

Talking of dolls, mention must be made of dolls made of *shola*, or the soft, white pith of Indian cork. Until about half a century ago, many kinds of dolls and toys made of shola were available in village fairs. *Shola*, however, is chiefly used for making wedding headgears for Hindu grooms and brides in Bengal. The conical *shola* hat (*topor*) worn by Hindu grooms is a very old tradition. Dhaka was a well known centre for *shola* objects and artefacts. The 1872 Census revealed that there were many *shola* artisans residing in Dhaka. Barishal and Faridpur also had a fair sprinkling of *shola* artisans.

People in Bengal have from ancient times made use of bamboo to make not only different kinds of flutes but also many articles of everyday domestic use. The poles that were used to support huts, fences and doors were made of bamboo. Bamboo was used even to make vessels and furniture, and paint was sometimes used to make these more attractive. Another widely used object was the basket made of interwoven strips of cane or bamboo. William Hunter mentioned Nadia, Jessore, Rangpur and Rajshahi as places where artisans excelled in making these baskets. The use of bamboo in making furniture seems to have increased in modern times, especially in Bangladesh. One reason could be that bamboo is more affordable than wood.

Eastern Bengal has a tradition of cane craftsmanship, and especially Sylhet is quite unparalleled in the field. Among the places mentioned by William Hunter as centres for cane craftsmanship were Dhaka, Rangpur and

Nadia. Cane is now being used to make low seats, chairs, tables, sofa sets and other kinds of furniture. It is easy to make furniture from cane because cane can be curved easily. It is also cheaper than wood. Both these factors make it a popular material for making furniture.

Grass mats (*madur*) were widely used in Bengal for people to sit and sleep on. The mat has not totally faded out in villages. Different kinds of grass were used to make these mats, and the most well known centre for mat-making was Medinipur. Mats were also made in Nadia, Rangpur, Dhaka, Noakhali and Faridpur.

A far richer cousin of the grass mat was the *sitalpati* (literally, cool mat), made of green cane. It was much more expensive and it was almost a luxury to own one. Barishal, Comilla, Noakhali, Mymensingh and Sylhet were well known for their green-cane mats. But Hunter wrote that those of Faridpur were the best. The mats woven by the women of Faridpur were so highly prized that girls who had mastered the skill were sought after in marriage alliances. Mats woven out of *hogla* leaves are also produced in large numbers, especially in southern Bengal, and decorated with a variety of patterns. These mats, however, do not quite match up to the other two kinds of mats made in Bengal.

Jute has been grown in Bengal since ancient times. Apart from ropes and gunnysacks, jute was used for making fabric. Bengal was also well known for a fabric made out of jute and cotton fibres. Jute was used, too, to make ropes to hang up food and other objects at home. It was women who usually made these, creating things of beauty out of these simple everyday articles. Hanging ropes made of jute were particularly popular in eastern Bengal.

Bengal's cloth industry was famous right from medieval times. In quality and fineness, the muslins and mulmuls of Dhaka were well known. Legend has it that the Mughal emperor Aurangzeb once chided his daughter Zeb-un-nissa that the dress she had on did not quite cover her modesty. She retorted that she was wrapped in seven folds of muslin. The veracity of the story cannot be ascertained. However, muslin from Dhaka was sent to the Great Exhibition of the Works of Industry of All Nations, or the Great Exhibition, that was held in London in October 1851. On October 24th, the *Morning Chronicle* wrote that a 10-yard piece of muslin woven by one Habibullah weighed just over 3 ounces and that it could pass through a wedding ring. After the establishment of British rule, the cloth-making tradition of Bengal led to the establishment of a factory for making cloth in Dhaka. It was from Dhaka that muslin was supplied for the families of the courtiers in Mughal Delhi and in Murshidabad. Muslin was also produced in Mymensingh and Nadia. The best muslins were *shabnam* and *ab-rawan*. More valuable than even muslin was chikan, muslin worked with white thread. The Muslim women of Dhaka were skilled in the craft. They also embroidered on muga and *tussar* fabrics. The *kasida* muslin woven by them used to be exported to the Middle East. The fabric was used for turbans. Silk fabrics worked with cotton and zari threads were also produced in Malda. It was muslin that was most in demand in West Asia and Europe, and it was also incredibly expensive. The Mughal general Mirza Nathan wrote in his Farsi chronicle *Baharistan-i-Ghaibi* that he bought a muslin apparel for 10,000 rupees in the early 17th century. After the start of the industrial revolution in late 18th century, the import of muslin was from time to time banned in England. The import duty on muslin was also very high. Consequently, the demand for it slowly fell. The population of Dhaka, which was around 2,00,000 at the start of the 19th century, fell to 68,000 within just 50 years. Many weavers migrated to Calcutta in search of work; several of them started producing embroidered handkerchiefs and other such things that found a market among the English sahibs and their memsahibs in the capital.

The silk industry of Bengal was also quite developed. Silks of Bengal had a large market abroad. Murshidabad and Malda were in particular known for their silks. In these two districts the East India Company established factories to produce silk, even before it came to seize political power. The Baluchari saris of Murshidabad were extremely reputed and sold at very high prices. But the tradition slowly faded out. Weavers in Murshidabad started mixing cotton threads with silk to produce fabric that was more affordable. Yet, the silk-making tradition of Murshidabad never totally died out and to this day various kinds of silks are produced in Murshidabad, Malda and Rajshahi. The *garad* and *tussar* fabrics of Murshidabad and the *matka* fabric of Rajshahi are quite distinctive. The silk industry is also still alive in Bankura and Bishnupur.

The *jamdani* sari constitutes another famous industry of Dhaka and has a tradition stretching far back into history. But these saris are now produced on a large scale and therefore have inevitably lost the care and creativity that the weavers of old used to bestow on these saris. However, the modern *jamdani*s are rich in their designs and the quality of the raw materials used. The census report of 1872 said that over 5,000 women were engaged in weaving saris in Dhaka. The saris and dhotis of Tangail, Mainamati, Chandrakona and Pharashdanga also had a long and rich tradition. The saris of Shantipur and the intricately worked ones of Bishnupur also retain their old reputation.

Cloth was used in Bengal not just for making clothes but also many other articles of daily use. It was women who produced these, and though these objects did of course have their use in various household needs they also provided an outlet for women to release their creative energies into. The *nakshi kantha*, for instance, or the cloth dolls. Women also made pillow covers, handkerchiefs, fans, curtains, all kinds of embroidered covers, and large cloth napkins to serve food on (*dastarkhwan*). They used many-coloured threads to beautify these articles; in particular, they used threads culled from the borders of saris. These threads were worked into various motifs that gave expression to untold thoughts, and love sometimes found its way into threaded messages such as *Mone rekho* (remember) and *Bhulo na* (do not forget) on handkerchiefs. Cloth hangings with moral platitudes such as *Samsar sukher hoy ramonir gune* (a woman's virtue makes for a happy home) embroidered on them were hung up on walls. *Dastarkhwan*s were made exclusively by Muslim women. Muslim women also made prayer mats, or *zainamaz*, for offering namaz. Saris were often intricately embroidered, and they still are.

Ivory objects were also made in Bengal. There is a view that ivory objects started getting made only in the 18th century. But there were elephants in Bengal even in ancient times, and it is unlikely that ivory was not harvested and turned into artefacts. Ivory ornaments have in fact been unearthed at Chandraketugarh. Ivory furniture made for East India Company officials in the second half of the 18th century have been found. The high degree of excellence and intricacy of design that these objects show would suggest a skill born of the practised craftsmanship of generations of artisans.

Murshidabad was particularly known for its ivory workmanship. The nawabs and their staff based in the capital must have patronised the craft. But ivory was not easily available. Consequently, small objects such as containers and combs were produced in an abundance that was not possible in the case of furniture.

Conch bangles

Much more widespread than the art of working on ivory was the craft of using conch shells to produce various objects. The Oxford dictionary describes conch as a tropical marine mollusc with a robust spiral shell which may bear long projections and have a flared tip. Conch shells worth about 5,000 pounds were imported almost every year during the decade of the 1870s from the Maldives, Ceylon and also Madras because these were not so widely available in Bengal. But they were widely used. Married Hindu women, in particular, wore conch bangles which served to signify their married status. One of the factors that helped the conch shell industry to flourish was that it did not require much infrastructure. Apart from bangles, containers and decorative pieces for household use were made from conch shells. These often had intricate patterns carved on their surfaces. Dhaka and Bishnupur were most well known for the craft. Pabna, too, is said to have had many artisans who worked with conch shells.

The comb is a household article that is put to use every day. Wood and buffalo horns were used to make combs. Once the art of straightening and cutting horns was mastered, it was not difficult to fashion combs out of them and to cover them with ornate details. The people of some regions, however, turned out to be particularly skilled in the art. Jessore was well known for its combs, particularly its ivory combs.

Bengal also had a tradition of producing metal objects. Murshidabad was known for its utensils made of bell metal (called *kansa* in Bengal; an alloy of copper and tin, but with a higher concentration of tin than bronze, which is also an alloy of copper and tin); Bishnupur was known for its copper and brass utensils; Burdwan and Dhaka were known for utensils of copper; and Calcutta was known for its copper utensils and statuettes. The welding of statues at Nabadwip was well known. William Hunter has mentioned Jessore and Rangpur as places where good-quality copper objects were produced. Nadia, Rajshahi, Rangpur, Dhaka and Mymensingh were famous for their bell metal goods. The gold and silver filigree work of Dhaka and the golden and enamelled jewellery of Calcutta had earned a good reputation. Those who could not afford gold used silver jewellery, which was usually chunkier and heavier that gold jewellery.

Criss-crossed as it is with rivers and canals, Bengal always had a tradition of boat-building, which became a skilled activity in parts of southern Bengal including Dhaka. Ships were also built in these areas. The stems and bows of these vessels were beautifully painted or carved. The tradition is dying out fast, but racing boats and small rafts still sport ornate decorations.

In sum, the tradition of folk art and craft that existed in Bengal from ancient times was rich and wide in scope and distinctive in its regional characteristics. The industrialisation that has taken place in the last 100 years has no doubt thwarted this tradition. Yet, the old rural handicrafts and the old designs continue to be imitated in modern workshops, and much of what was once exclusively handcrafted is now produced on a mass scale using modern means. In a way these mass-produced products are fake, they lack the earthiness of the originals they imitate. Still, visually they remain largely true to the traditions that they try to recreate. And that, perhaps, is the way in which the ancient craft traditions will stay alive in the future.

ATTIRE

The kind of clothes that people wear depends chiefly on climate and culture. It is also linked to economic conditions. Contact with other cultures brings about changes in attire. Above all, attire is related to the development of technology and of systems of production. The kind of clothes worn by the people of Bengal has changed considerably in the past 2,000 years, notwithstanding the more or less unchanged climate during this period. The arrival of people belonging to a number of ethnic groups in the land, each with its own distinctive culture, is responsible for this. Systems of communication and improvements in technology have also over the ages left their mark on clothes. But though we know how attire evolved in the recent centuries, we do not have quite as clear an impression of the kind of clothes that people wore in Bengal in the centuries preceding them.

It is not possible to infer from the oldest extant samples of Bengali literature, the *Charyapada* poems, how men and women of the time dressed. We do, however, get some idea of the clothes worn by the people of Bengal from the sculpture of ancient and medieval times, the terracotta slabs of Paharpur and Mainamati, and pictures in manuscripts. In most cases these clothes were quite minimal, constituting the least that people must have needed to cover their shame and protect themselves from the weather. The clothes worn by men and women in those early times were, therefore, quite similar.

Nihar Ranjan Ray and Ramesh Chandra Majumdar have described this attire thus: both women and men wore a single piece of clothing, a sari or a dhoti. The difference between a sari and a dhoti was that the sari was longer and broader. Men higher up the social order wore dhotis that fell a little below their knees. But ordinary people wore extremely short dhotis which generally stayed well above the knees. One end of the dhoti was drawn between the legs and tucked behind at the waist. Terracotta slabs at Paharpur bear evidence

Terracotta slabs of Paharpur. *Photo courtesy: kazi Rashed Abdallah (ommons.wikimedia.org)*

of this kind of minimalist clothing. But since rich men wore their dhoti somewhat longer, they pleated a part of it in front. Women, on the other hand, wore their saris extending almost up to their ankles.

Both women and men left the upper parts of their bodies uncovered, though women of the upper classes occasionally used a thin shawl during festivals or other social gatherings. They also sometimes wore a kind of short shirt covering their breasts and upper arms. It may be inferred that in the winter men and women covered themselves with a piece of cloth that was something like a shawl. But ancient sculpture bears no testimony to such wrappers. Men and women depicted in these sculptures are always bare-bodied from waist up. In sculptures and in terracotta slabs, the only covering for women's breasts consists of an assortment of jewellery.

In the picture of the terracotta slabs found in Paharpur, note the short dhoti length and the array of ornaments worn on the upper part of the body. The sculpture has no breasts, otherwise there is little to distinguish it from the female form. It may be compared with the sculpture of Purneshwari, a mother goddess.

Both women and men wore ornaments around their necks and on their ears. They often wore multiple necklaces and chains. Neither men nor women covered their heads in ancient Bengal. Gods and courtiers wear crowns in sculptures, but not hats, turbans or any other kind of cloth headwear.

Citing slokas from the works of poets of the Sena era, Sukumar Sen has described the attire of rich women of the time. Dhoyi, for instance, has written that women wore thin mulmuls. According to a sloka by Sarbananda, some upper class women even wore underwear. Lokkhidhar has said in a sloka that women covered their heads with one end of their saris (*ghomta*), their faces and eyes always lowered and bashful, their gait slow and their sparse words softly and sweetly spoken. Yet the sculptures and the images found in contemporary manuscripts yield no evidence of women veiling their heads with their sari ends. Poets have said that women wore earrings made out of tender banana leaves and gold chains round their waists. They greased their hair with scented oils, wore it coiled into pointed buns and wrapped strings of flowers around them. They blackened their eyes with kohl and reddened their lips with *alta*, a red vegetable dye squeezed out of betel leaves. Drops of sandalwood paste decorated their foreheads. Going by the description of the poet Govardhan, even in ancient Bengal married women smeared their parting with vermilion. In the poet Chandrachandra's account we see women of well-to-do families in villages wore kohl bindis, bangles made of lotus stems and earrings made of tender *ritha* (soap nut) flowers. They decorated their plaits with sesame leaves. Yet such clothes and ornaments do not seem to have been generally prevalent beyond elite social circles. Rather, we learn from poets' descriptions of poor women that they covered their lean bodies with torn, ragged pieces of cloth, which they mended with needles that had to be borrowed from neighbours.

Significant changes in attire can be seen in the Indo-Muslim age, presumably owing to Muslim influence. Muslims had come from lands of extreme climatic conditions. Also, the kind of clothes they wore was linked to religious regulations. They therefore continued to wear those clothes even after they arrived in Bengal. There is usually a conservative reaction against accepting new styles of attire, so clothes in Bengal did not change immediately after the advent of the differently-clothed Muslim rulers. Over time, however, people in Bengal starting wearing the new kind of clothes introduced by Muslims—just as, in the 19th century, Western clothes became fashionable as people imitated the English in their attire. Muslim attire in the Middle Ages were initially fashionable in the courts of the *badshahs* and in cities. Over a few centuries, however, it was slowly adopted in villages, too, especially among the rich.

It cannot however be said with any certainty exactly when this sartorial change took place. We hear of Muslim-influenced people such as Jagai and Madhai, who lived at a relatively later time—early 16th century. Sanatan Goswami was at that time the chief minister in Hossein Shah's court and his brother Roop Goswami was *dabir-e-khas,* or chief secretary. The brothers later repented their contact with *javans* (Muslims) and their service under them, but I have not anywhere seen any mention of what they wore to court while in the sultan's employment. It was presumably during the 14th and 15th centuries that Muslim clothes slowly started making their way into people's lives. These subsequently became widely accepted among the elite sections, and for the next 500 to 600 years it was the court apparel of the Muslim rulers that was recognised as being the attire of the aristocracy. Notwithstanding some Sufi influence on the Vaishnava faith, Vaishnavas and Muslims did not generally have much love lost between them. Nevertheless, it is Mughal clothes that women seem to wear in the pictures of Radha-Krishna and of the *gopis* (milkmaids) in late 16th-century manuscripts. Even Krishna's crown looks much like the Mughal turban. That apart, the turbans and *taj* (Muslim cap) seen in *patachitras* (illustrated wood jackets for medieval manuscripts) that I mentioned before suggest the widespread use of Muslim clothes. In the second half of the 16th century, Jayananda Das in his *Chaitanyamangal* hints at the increasing popularity of Muslim attire. It is evident from what he says that by that time many people had started wearing even socks as they had seen Muslims do.

There is evidence of people in ancient Bengal wearing a single article of clothing, but in medieval literature as many as three articles of clothing are mentioned—one to cover the upper part of the body, one for the lower part and something to cover the head. Mukundaram clearly writes about the turban in his *Kabikankan Chandi.* Foreign travellers who passed through the land have also written about three articles of clothing. Foreign travellers came in contact with wealthy city dwellers, the majority of whom were Muslims of foreign origin. All this seems to suggest that though

A manuscript jacket (*patachitra)* found in Bankura district

headwear was unnecessary in view of the climatic conditions of Bengal, people in cities used it in imitation of the court customs of the time. In the manuscript illustrations in *Iskandarnama*, which was written down in the 16th century, and in the 17th century *Shahnama*, all heads without exception are covered. But the subjects of these illustrations are not native, and so they cannot be used as historical evidence. On a manuscript jacket (*patachitra*) found in Bankura district and thought to date back to 1647, one of the four men depicted as singing and dancing is turbaned and two wear the *taj*. Two women have their hair piled high, and the raised buns are covered with a small piece of cloth. From the percussion instruments (*khol* and *kartal*) depicted in it, the picture appears to be a Vaishnava one. This shows that Muslim attire in those days was not limited to courtiers but had spread out among ordinary people. Even people of other religions wore Muslim clothes at quasi-religious functions.

Eighteenth-century pictures that have been found also provide evidence of heads being almost universally covered. In George Lambart's painting of what was then Calcutta's only church, done around 1730, all natives are either turbaned or have their heads covered with a piece of cloth. A picture of Alivardi Khan and his friends, done around 1750, also has everyone wearing a Mughal turban. The back of this turban was shaped like a bun and was slightly suspended. One end of the turban was tilted backwards, like a feather. It might appear from the picture that all heads are turbaned because it depicts a court scene. That is however not right. A more important picture is Sheikh Zainuddin's painting of Lady Impey surrounded by servants, belonging to roughly 1780. In this picture, too, all heads are turbaned. Even

Sheikh Zainuddin's painting of Lady Impey surrounded by servants, belonging to roughly 1780

the boy standing bare-bodied from waist up wears a turban. The universal use of turbans can also be noted in the late 18th century paintings of Thomas Daniell and Fracois Solvyns. We will later see that despite its diminishing use the turban continued to be worn by the elite in Bengal right up to the end of the 19th century.

Despite the widespread use of the turban, it can be safely inferred that those who did not have money to spend on turbans or cloth to cover their heads made do with two articles of clothing. Among the poor in the countryside, the custom was to wear just a single article of clothing, not even two. People wore either a dhoti or a sari. Those who could not afford a full-length dhoti wore very short ones, or even thin, checked towels (*gamchha* or *gamochha*, literally, a piece of cloth used to wipe the body) around their waists. The practice continued well into the 20th century for the major part of society. There is a 1795 Francois Solvyns painting of a Calcutta *patua*, who can be reasonably supposed to have been more solvent than the rural poor. Yet, we see him wearing just a dhoti, and that too going down only to his knees.

In the painting of a Muharram procession in Dhaka (dated approximately 1820), which is preserved at the Dhaka Museum, we see all the palanquin-bearers, otherwise turned out in turbans, girdles, cummerbunds and long overcoats, wearing their dhotis short with one end drawn between the legs and tucked behind. In almost all the paintings by Thomas Daniell, Francois Solvyns, James Frazer, James Moffat, Thomas and William Princep, Sheikh Zainuddin and Sheikh Mohammad Amir, dating from 1786-87 right up to the 1840s, we see ordinary people wearing such short dhotis, their heads covered with a piece of cloth. Most of those without turbans are Oriyas, and Brahmins. The women in these pictures wear either just a sari or a sari/long, pleated skirt (ghagra) and a shawl covering their chests, their heads usually veiled slightly.

From Mukundaram's works we learn that during his time, that is, in the late 16th century, well-to-do Muslims wore pyjamas. *Shunyopuran* gives a humorous description of Hindu sages adopting the pyjama and overnight becoming Muslims. There is of course exaggeration in this account, but it indicates that Hindus too had started wearing pyjamas under Muslim influence. Even Lausen in *Dharmamangal* is seen to be wearing a pyjama. That apart, there is mention in *Dharmamangal* of Muslims wearing long dresses and turbans. But this was not what converted Muslims in the countryside wore. Those people do not seem to have dressed very differently from the Hindus. Many Muslims wore what is now called a lungi, a piece of cloth that was shorter than the dhoti. Though the word lungi is of Burmese origin, the concept of the Muslim *tahband* is not much different from that of the lungi. Lungi is mentioned even in Mukundaram. We meet a village mullah in Bijoygupta's *Manasamangal.* That he wore dhotis is evident from the description of how he loosened this garment when he sat down to slaughter chickens. Nowhere do we find any mention of Hindu and Muslim women in villages dressing differently.

Before the Indo-Muslim era, Bengali society was not familiar with stitched clothes. It was Muslims who introduced them. We know from medieval literature that this was also the time when a certain kind of skilled workers – tailors – emerged. But the resistance to innovations among the religiously inclined kept alive the custom of wearing unstitched clothes among

A Muharram procession in Dhaka (dated approximately 1820)

Hindus of the time, and also to an extent in more recent times. Particularly in religious ceremonies and in semi-religious ones such as weddings, stitched clothes are forbidden. Even now priests are clothed only in a dhoti while they officiate at religious rituals and functions, the upper parts of their bodies being left bare. Syed Mujtaba Ali has written in one of his stories that the pandit in his school did not even wear an undershirt (called *gunjee* in Bengali) in the second decade of the 20th century, let alone a shirt. For, the *gunjee* is also a stitched garment. That apart, both the undershirt and the word *gunjee* were imports from Europe and thus carried associations with *javan*s and *mlechchha*s.

Shoes do not appear to have been much used in ancient Bengali society. Though *panai* and *paduka* (basic wooden sandals) are mentioned, medieval literature does not have any evidence of Bengalis wearing leather shoes. In the illustration of a battle scene in *Iskandarnama*, written in 1531, mounted cavalry are seen to be barefoot. But soldiers have their feet in shoes in the manuscript drawing in *Shahnama* (preserved in the Dhaka Museum), which was committed to writing in 1677. This shows how the practice of wearing shoes slowly became popular in the Indo-Muslim age. Nevertheless, ordinary people had not yet taken to wearing shoes on a mass scale. Only a couple of men wear shoes in the 1820 painting of the Dhaka Muharram procession, the rest are all barefoot. An Eid painting belonging to the same time also depicts barefoot people, though they are dressed in turbans, long overcoats and cummerbunds. This shows that they are not poor, yet their feet are bare. It appears from what *Hutom Pyanchar Naksha* describes that even in the middle of the 19th century those who wore shoes to visit community pujas had to hire them; they did not possess shoes of their own. People in villages do not seem to have taken to shoes even then. It was probably only in the 20th century that shoes became common in the countryside.

Just as the sartorial influence of the new ruling class began to make itself felt ever so gradually after the start of the Indo-Muslim age, in the same way European sartorial styles began to make an impact some 70-80 years after the start of British colonial rule. Even before that, however, some articles of European clothing had begun to make their way into Bengal. Woollens, for instance. Woollen clothes were among the commodities imported by the European traders who started doing business in the subcontinent at the time of the Mughals. It may appear from this that very few people in the land in those days used woollen clothes.

Photograph of some Hindu leaders, 1846

The first few decades of the 19th century hardly saw any change in what people wore, though the English had by then consolidated their presence. Even in 1835 The *Samachar Darpan* claimed: 'Babus and zamindars, *serestadars* and vakils and other such personages with due esteem use *jama, nima, kaba, korta,* that is, Hindustani apparel.' The expression 'Hindustani apparel' is actually used here to mean Muslim or Mughal attire. In the oil paintings of Ram Mohan Roy and Dwarakanath Tagore, this is what they are seen to wear. In an 1846 painting by W. Taylor, this is also what is seen to be worn by the leading and most aristocratic men of contemporary Calcutta, including Radhakanta Deb, Prasanna Kumar Tagore, Ashutosh Deb, Kalikrishna Tagore and Pratap Chandra Sinha. They all wore long kurtas/*chapkans*/*jubbas*, and on their heads they wore turbans or caps. In the description of Pyalanath Babu in *Hutom Pyanchar Naksha* (1862-64), he, too, is always seen wearing a cap. Some men wore caps worked with zari, which was called a *taj.*

Indeed, this was the formal attire of the elite in those days. Debendranath Tagore (died 1905) continued to wear such clothes until the end of his life. Bankimchandra is not known to have been too kindly disposed towards Muslims. Nevertheless, a likeness of his done in 1882 shows him wearing the old Muslim-era clothes—a turban covering his head and a long, buttoned up high-necked *chapkan* covering his body. This was what he wore as long as he lived. It was also what Tagore wore, though with some modifications. In an 1896 photograph of Pradyot Kumar Tagore, he is dressed in a turban, a *chapkan* and a *jubba,* cummerbund, churidar pyjamas and pointed *nagrai* shoes. This attire can be called the standardised outfit of an age that was on its way out, and it left its mark even on Vivekananda's clothes. Indeed, this was what the bhadralok in those days was expected to wear.

Pradyot Kumar Tagore

This was perhaps why Bankimchandra while describing his heroes wrote about their chained watches and rings but did not describe their clothes. Tagore, too, in his early novels and stories wrote of watch chains, rings, other ornaments and spectacles, but not so much of his characters' clothes. These writers took it for granted that their readers would know exactly what their characters would wear. It was rather other articles of personal use that they commented on to show how unaffected or how self-indulgent their characters were.

Needless to say, the clothes of the age of the nawabs slowly lost their appeal in the colonial era. *Hutom* says that most of those who still wore turbans were clerks. According to this book, once they retired, turbans would no longer adorn the heads of babus. It was indeed at this time that clothes in Bengal began to look different. There is a hint of this in *Hutom*'s description of people going out to attend community pujas. The clothes that *Hutom* describes as being worn by these people comprise pleated dhoti, clean, uncrumpled kameez, a short crepe shawl thrown over the shoulder and a net shawl. What was called a kameez was probably the same as what was meant by *ramjama*—a long shirt. This was what perhaps evolved into the punjabi, which does not appear to have any connection with Punjab and is actually known there as 'Bengali kurta'.

Social attitudes to clothes are usually conservative, so those who try out something different are often exposed to ridicule. Many people in the colonial era saw the British as saviours for having replaced Muslim rule by a new system of governance. Yet social conservatism about clothes made sure that Western clothes did not have an easy entry in Bengali society. This sartorial orthodoxy was of course even more pronounced and rigid in the case of women. The formal attire of urban and wealthy men had noticeably changed in the five and a half centuries of Indo-Muslim rule. But society at large did not accept corresponding changes in the clothes worn by women. We see a similar attitude at work during the colonial period. Within 150 years of British rule, many men turned sahibs in their clothes, but the women were not able to imitate the memsahibs. In the following discussion we will see that women's clothes were scant, and in some cases even indecent. Nevertheless, Western influences could not easily make a mark on women's clothes. Even at the end of the 20th century, women's clothes would appear more conservative when compared with the clothes of men.

Like modern thought, it was through the Hindu College route that Western attire gained acceptance among men. A *Sambad Prabhakar* report said in July 1831 that the students of this college dressed like *firangis*. The magazine also said that these youngsters were giving up wearing their dhoti and crepe shawl in the traditional way. It appears from this magazine report that young men of the time were actually adopting Western apparel. Yet there is no evidence of this. What the writer of the *Prabhakar* report said while describing the sartorial trends among youngsters was really less about clothes and more about conduct. It can be seen from the magazine account that the only thing about Western attire that the youngsters had adopted was *firangi* footwear. A new style of wearing the dhoti or discarding the crepe shawl cannot be construed as adopting Western clothes. What the magazine perhaps meant to convey was that youngsters were displaying irreverence to traditional customs through the way they dressed.

The author of the *Prabhakar* report further said that young men left their heads bare, did not wear garlands, and also that they urinated standing. He also described what according to him constituted the ideal attire for men. In his opinion, young men should not wear *firangi* shoes; they should wear their dhoti and chador, hang garlands round their necks and have sandalwood smeared on their foreheads. From another report published in the *Samachar Chandrika*, we find that some young men had started wearing socks. That leaving one's head bare was a weighty issue is also evident from a write-up in the Young Bengal magazine the *Enquirer*.

Michael Madhusudan Dutt was probably the first among Hindu College students to wear Western clothes. His friends have written that one day in early 1843 he startled everyone at college by turning up in *firangi* apparel. In that phase of his life, however, he must have worn such clothes only once in a while. For, it is quite clear from the way he wrote to his friend Gourdas Basak from Madras in 1849 about dressing like a *firangi* in Western clothes that he had not earlier been in the habit of wearing these on a regular basis. Western clothes were indeed still quite exceptional. That it was so is also the impression that one gets from the 1849 edition of *Sambad Bhaskar*. One of its reports says that the attire of English-educated youngsters consisted of shoes, *izar* (loose trousers), *chapkan*, turban, chain and watch. That is to say that it was not yet Western apparel that young men wore, but clothes belonging to an earlier time and described by many as 'Hindustani attire'. The only new additions were the chain and the watch. In 1885, Tagore called it Muslim, rather than Hindustani, attire.

Given the vast improvements in the communication system during the colonial era, Western clothes spread relatively quickly among people who came to Calcutta to study or to trade. The prevalence of Western attire began to rise in the second half of the 19th century. In particular, those who went to England to study often continued to wear Western clothes even after they returned. This was more or less true of men such as Surja Goodiv Chakraborty, Satyendranath Tagore, Manomohan Ghosh, Jnanandramohan Tagore, Gobindachandra Datta, Umesh Chandra Banerjee, Shashipada Bandyopadhyay, Ramesh Chandra Datta and Debendra Nath Das. At the dawn of the 20th century, Tagore's description of a drunken Blighty-returned young man in the story *Mastermoshai* (Teacher) has him wearing a hat and coat. Trousers are not mentioned. It would not be unreasonable to assume that relatives of such England-returned people, and others inspired by the example they set, had also started adopting Western attire. With sewing machines becoming fairly common, it also became quite easy to get such clothes stitched. And so it was that Western clothes made their way deep into society.

The practice of wearing woollens during winter also rapidly caught on during this time. That this was so is evident from reports of women's knitting, though it is not really known exactly what they knitted. Tagore mentions *galabandho* (literally, a wrap for the neck) in *Nashtaneer*, which is surely the same as what is now called a muffler (pronounced 'maflar' in Bengali). That apart, women also knitted woollen slippers to be worn at home. In this context it may be mentioned that woollen clothes first began to be used in the Mughal era, probably as a result of Western influence. But the use of woollens was limited then, and mainly restricted to the wealthy.

Notwithstanding the growing popularity of Western clothes during the age under discussion, *Tatwabodhini Patrika* in 1876 expressed this opinion on what constituted ideal attire: dhotis should be worn at home, but *chapkan* and turban were more suitable for formal dressing. It appears from this comment that clothing of the age of the nawabs, or at least some articles of it, continued to be in use for another few decades in society at large.

In Tagore's description of the young Apurba in the 1893 story *Samapti* (The End), we see that though he wears a dhoti and thin shawl at home; for the formal occasion of meeting a prospective bride he is dressed in turban, *chapkan*, *jubba* and polished shoes. There is no mention of what covered his lower body; it would probably be pyjamas. But wearing *chapkan*s or even coats over dhotis slowly became popular. There was indeed little that was quite 'Bengali' in the sartorial hotchpotch that prevailed in the late 19th century, a confused mixing of the native dhoti-chador with the Muslim *izer-chapkan* and Western coat and trousers. *Somprakash Patrika*, therefore, commented in 1881 that one could tell other nations by their clothes, but not Bengalis.

It appears from a passage in a Tagore novel that early in the 20th century the dhoti and chador had gained considerable acceptance as formal attire and Western clothes had started being used as a mark of extravagance and as a means of showing off to others.

> There was something a bit novel in the way he had dressed today. Instead of the festive dhoti and chador, he had a Parsi coat and pantaloons on his plump frame and a cap on his head. Pearls and precious stones glittered on his fingers. His watch, suspended by a thick gold chain worn around the neck, was inserted in his chest pocket. Beneath his coat sleeves, a diamond button on his shirt sleeve was visible.

In a story written soon after this one, Tagore describes another young man who wears no shoes but has a turban and a shirt on. He describes him as belonging to a respectable family, pointing to the turban on his head.

The collared shirt is now much used among Bengalis. Yet it does not appear to have become fashionable before the 20th century. No male character in late 19th century stories and novels is seen to be wearing it. But in a 1905 photograph of a public meeting held in protest against the partition of Bengal, some men can be seen wearing collared shirts (the photograph is reproduced in Siddhartha Ghosh's book *Chhobi Tola*, or Taking Pictures).

I have also looked closely at a photograph of the huge funeral procession that followed Tagore's hearse in 1941. The proportion of shirt-wearing men is far higher than in the 1905 photograph. There are even men who paired dhotis with their shirts. Some of the shirts are half-sleeved. In most of the photographs of the child Ray dated before 1930 and printed in his childhood memoirs, he is dressed in the loose collar-less kurta that Bengalis call 'punjabi'. But in a 1934 photograph with other boys, everyone has a shirt on. This gives us an idea of when and how fast, or how slowly, Western clothes made their way into Bengali society. Thus the shirt replaced the *nima*, *phatua* (a short, collar-less, loose and informal upper garment with buttons in front but not all the way down, usually made of cotton) and the kurta, while the coat replaced the *chapkan*. There is mention of the buttoned-up coat in a Tagore story written in the second decade of the 20th century. However, a quarter century before this story was written, Tagore himself is seen to be wearing such a coat in several photographs clicked in the 1880s and 1890s. The buttoned-up coat is also seen in photographs, taken around the same time, of Neelmadhav Dey and of the royal family of Tripura. The widespread use of trousers without coats did not probably begin before the 1930s.

Even before the 19th century was over, Western attire, or at least some articles of it, had infiltrated English-educated circles. In society at large, however, traditional clothes still prevailed. Mainly dhoti, punjabi and chador. This continued to be the bhadralok attire in the first half of the 20th century, and it was worn both at home and outside. Educated Muslims also wore dhotis. Muslim-run newspapers and magazines criticised the practice in the early years of the 20th century. The language used in such criticism seems to suggest that most Muslims, particularly those in villages, wore lungis instead of dhotis. Educated Muslims were exhorted to wear pyjamas instead of dhotis. For a very short time after Partition, the dhoti disappeared in East Bengal, even among Hindus. Lungis replaced dhotis, perhaps because, among other things, it is easier to wear. The curious thing is that in the second half of the 20th century, lungis have largely replaced dhotis even among Hindus in the villages of West Bengal. The dhoti lost its usefulness in the fast-paced life of the new age. Many people have in fact forgotten the art of draping the dhoti stylishly. The dhoti in West Bengal, too, has therefore been touched by the winds of change. You now get dhotis with ready-made pleats and fitted with a belt, all designed to make the dhoti easier to wear. Young men wear such dhotis at semi-religious functions.

Even in this age of changing values, a certain loyalty to tradition seems to linger in women's clothing. Previous centuries, too, had shown a similar conservatism. For instance, men now wear clothes that are not Bengali in origin, but women continue to dress traditionally in saris. Men, too, expect to see their women in saris, and in most cases women comply. Even in the age of the nawabs or in the early years of colonial rule, no Bengali woman was ever seen to wear anything other than a sari. The women clad in north Indian clothes that artists in Calcutta had painted in the late 18th and early 19th centuries were all either courtesans or non-Bengali. They are seen to be wearing a long, flared skirt (ghagra) paired with a short blouse, with their heads veiled with a dupatta.

The description and illustration of the woman of wealth in Fanny Parkes's book *Wanderings of a Pilgrim in Search of the Picturesque* (1851) shows that such women, though rich, covered themselves with only a sari. In the cold months they had the additional protection of a shawl. The practice of wearing an in-skirt or petticoat underneath the sari had not yet started, though it had been a couple of centuries that the *saya* had arrived in Bengal with the Portuguese. The word, too, is of Portuguese origin. Blouses, too, were not worn for much of the 19th century, not even by aristocratic women. The sari, especially the fine saris worn by rich women, therefore hid little, and this was criticised by Fanny Parkes. But it was not only in the 18th century that women wore transparent saris. In the Middle Ages, too, Bengali weavers created fine fabrics such as muslin, which enhanced the beauty and sensual appeal of wealthy women.

No matter how beauty-enhancing fine fabrics might have been, they were not quite able to ensure decency. In the 1863-64 book *Dekhe-shune Akkel Gurhum* ('Enough to Put One Off'), Rajkumar Chandra wrote that the clothes that women wore were best not called clothes. According to him, women remained all but naked in the 10-yard saris that they used. Satyendranath Tagore, too, wrote in 1864 that 'the kind of clothes that our women wear, they might as well not take the trouble of wearing them at all'. This attire might not have seemed all that inadequate as long as women did not venture out of the domestic space. But it was no longer considered enough once women started acquiring an education and felt the need to go out. Satyendranath Tagore, for instance, was in 1863 extremely keen to have his wife, Jnanadanandini Devi, join him in England. He wrote to her saying that she would require an overhaul of her wardrobe if she was to travel to England. The trip did not materialise, so Jnanada Devi did not have to don shoes and socks or any new type of clothes just yet.

After returning to the country, Satyendranath wanted to take her to Ahmedabad, where he was posted. He had to get decent clothes made for her, because just a sari worn without a blouse or an in-skirt was not suitable for a woman to appear in company. He got a dress stitched by a French tailor, who came up with an innovation that combined oriental and occidental styles. Somewhat like a gown, so complicated was this dress that Jnanadanandini was not able to put it on by herself. She had to take Satyendranath's help every time she wore it.

Jnanada Devi stopped for a few months at the home of a Parsee gentleman called Maneckjee Cardosjee in Bombay before going on to Ahmedabad. It was a Western-influenced family. Enthusiastic about women's education, Cordosjee had even established a school for girls. Satyendranath requested the two finely educated daughters of this family to coach his wife in the manners and etiquette required to move in refined social circles, especially among the English. It was in the company of these ladies that Jnanada Devi first came across petticoats and full-sleeved blouses as articles of women's clothing. Their blouses followed European styles, and they tied the sari in the west Indian way—with one end of it folded and draped over the right shoulder. These were the two things that Jnanada changed when she devised a new way of tying the sari, but it was the women of this family from whom she borrowed her ideal of feminine attire.

In 1867, it was her own modification of this attire that she wore to the Governor-General's party, which she attended on her own, without her husband. Two years later she wrote in *Bamabodhini Patrika* that if any woman was interested in the dress that she had devised, she would send her an

Jnanada Devi

illustration and even a sample if she asked for one. Satyendranath's friend Manomohan Ghosh got his wife, Swarnalata, an unlettered girl, to wear a gown like the memsahibs after he came back from England. Another member of the Brahmo Samaj, Shashipada Bandyopadhyay, took his wife, Rajkumari, to Europe in 1868 in order to introduce her to modernism. He, too, needed to get his wife a new wardrobe, but it is not known exactly what clothes she travelled in.

Notwithstanding the rigid orthodoxy regarding women's clothes in contemporary society, the feminine dress supported by blouse and petticoat that Jnanada Devi devised was so superior to the sari that was draped around women's bodies without any supporting garments that other Tagore women also adopted it before long. Many Brahmo women not belonging to this family also adopted it. *Bamabodhini Patrika* mentioned how in 1865 the 13-year-old Rajalaskhmi Maitreya attended a school prize distribution ceremony in this reformed attire. Socially progressive leaders such as Keshab Sen, Shibnath Shastri, Rakhaldas Roy of Barishal, Durgamohan Das—they all had to introduce this new reformed feminine attire in their families. A photograph of Annette Akroyd, with the students of the school that she opened in Calcutta for the 'higher education' of girls in 1874, was published in her famous son Lord Beveridge's book *India Called Them.* The photograph shows that the girls of this school had also started wearing this dress. Nor did the trend stop with them. Within a few years, women of some elite, educated Hindu families of Calcutta adopted this way of dressing. Indeed, it did not take too long for the awareness to take hold that women would not be able to go out in decent company without considerable reform in the scant clothing that they had traditionally worn.

Indira Devi and Rabindranath Tagore

Jnanada Devi did not wear her sari pleated in front in the way women started doing in the 20th century. In her photograph with Kadambari Devi (Jyotirindranath's wife) taken in the early 1880s, or in the 1910 photograph of Tagore with his son, daughter-in-law and two daughters, the sari does not appear pleated in front but folded twice. In more than one photograph of the actress Binodini taken in the 1880s, the sari is folded and not pleated in front. But she wore a long-sleeved blouse with her sari. A white petticoat can be noticed underneath her sari. I have not been able to ascertain exactly when women started pleating their saris. One of Keshab Sen's daughters also came up with a distinctive way of tying the sari, but it did not become as popular as the style introduced by Jnanada Devi.

Jnanada Devi, Satyendranath, Jyotirindranath (seated) and Kadambari Devi, 1882

Notwithstanding the adoption of a reformed way of wearing the sari, shoes and socks took much longer to be accepted. Society does not appear to have easily accepted the idea of women wearing shoes and socks. In the poem that Ishwar Gupta wrote ridiculing women's progress on the occasion of the establishment of Bethune School, among the undesirable changes that education would supposedly bring about was that girls would now take to shoes! The idea of women wearing shoes was so extraordinary that when Satyendranath proposed to have his wife join him in England, he warned her right at the beginning that she would be required to wear shoes and socks. Those who started wearing shoes in those early days were indeed exceptional. It appears from a 1903 piece in *Bamabodhini Patrika* that even then it was particularly Brahmo women and prostitutes who wore shoes. This social attitude continued to be in place for some more time. Nirad C. Chaudhuri, describing the situation in the early 20th century, wrote that when his mother went out in shoes, she often had to explain to curious onlookers that she was

Meera Devi, Rathindranath, Rabindranath, Pratima Devi and Bela, 1910

Brahmo. In the photograph above, though Tagore and his son Rathindranath are in shoes, the women – Bela, Meera Devi and Pratima Devi – are barefoot.

Since Jnanada Devi introduced the blouse to be worn with the sari, in the mid 1860s, fashions in this garment repeatedly changed. Initially she wore full-sleeved blouses. The blouses that we see her and Kadambari Devi wearing in the 1882 photograph on the previous page are not only long-sleeved but also have pronounced collars. In the photograph that has survived of the actress Binodini Dasi, also belonging to this time, she, too, is seen wearing a long-sleeved blouse. Sleeve-ends soon climbed up to the elbow, subsequently giving way to sleeves that came down to just above the elbow. Even after that blouse sleeves continued to get shorter and shorter until sleeveless blouses made their appearance. Different fashions were also tried out with blouse sleeves. The puffed sleeve, for instance, or the entire sleeve arranged in overlapping layers.

Other innovations in blouse designs included different necklines and experimenting with how much of the back and neck could be left exposed. There was also much experimenting with the length of the blouse. What once extended to below the waist sometimes climbed up to a length that just about covered the breasts. In-skirts also show evidence of continuous changes as new fashions are tried out. Even the length of the sari *anchol*, the pleated end that is drawn over the left shoulder and allowed to hang, keeps changing, sometimes hanging below the knees and sometimes worn much shorter.

Family restrictions on Hindu women were not a little rigid in the early 20th century, let alone in the 19th century. But purdah among Muslims was relatively far more stern. For, purdah is prescribed in Islam. It is probably for this reason that though we have some pictures and descriptions of clothes worn by Hindu women at that time, no corresponding pictures or descriptions of aristocratic Muslim women are available. Notwithstanding Rokeya Sakhawat Hossein's humorous accounts of Muslim women wearing the burkha and ornaments, she has not given any detailed analysis of their clothes. A 1920 photograph of her survives. It shows her wearing a pleated sari with her blouse sleeves extending to her elbows, and with shoes on her feet. There is a photograph of Faziltunnesa clicked more or less around the same time, in which she is seen in a V-necked blouse and wearing earrings and a pendant on a chain, one end of her sari drawn lightly over the head.

On the whole it can be said that despite the religious divide, Hindu and Muslim women in Bengal did not differ much in the clothes they wore. The little difference that did exist was in the case of elite and urban women. For instance, though Urdu-speaking, aristocratic Muslim women even then wore salwar-kameezes, all Bengali-speaking Muslim women in villages, whether rich or poor, wore saris.

One other thing must be borne in mind in the context of the practice of wearing saris. The women who first started wearing the reformed version of the sari were all, Hindu or Muslim, either wealthy or educated or lived in cities. They formed a tiny proportion of the total population of women. Ordinary, poor and rural Hindu and Muslim women mostly draped just a sari around their bodies. Even now, many women in Bengal's villages wear nothing but a sari. They do not wear their sari pleated in front, but folded twice over. This is true of both Hindu and Muslim women. The religious divide introduces changes in men's clothes, but not in women's.

A certain contradiction always existed in the attitudes to clothes. This ensured that Bengali men adopted Muslim attire in the Muslim era and Western clothes during colonial rule, but women all along wore saris. This thousand-year-old practice, however, has been breaking down in recent times. It is difficult to say exactly why. Globalisation, improvements in the communication system and the wide reach of cinema and television could be among the factors that have made this possible. Indeed, nowhere in the world are local cultures able to retain their distinctiveness anymore. That apart, women in recent times have in increasing number been forced to venture out of home, and to do this they use various kinds of transport, particularly public transport. Women, thus, are negotiating spaces for which the sari is not really a suitable garment. More than anything else, many women now occupy senior positions in offices and courts and play leading roles in their working lives. Consequently, their positions in both family and society are now much improved than before. With the greater personal autonomy and influence that this has brought for women, they are now no longer constrained to accept diktats from their husbands or in-laws regarding what they will wear. They choose their own clothes according to their taste and convenience. Women's clothes, therefore, are looking more and more non-traditional. The salwar kameez is the garment through which women have in the major part broken with tradition. Yet, here, too, a certain conservatism is at play. Women may have stopped wearing only saris, but most have not adopted Western clothes in the way their husbands have done. They have largely limited themselves to clothes belonging to the Indian subcontinent.

Some people imagine a close connection between Bollywood movies and the increasing popularity of the salwar kameez. This is however not true. Bollywood movies have long featured the salwar-kameez-clad woman, but it is only recently that Bengali women have taken to this garment. Admittedly, when Bengali women finally did start wearing salwar-kameezes, they accepted Bollywood styles. But the source of the motivation to embrace this new way of dressing clearly lay elsewhere. In this context it should also be remembered that young girls, especially school and college students, had even earlier worn salwar-kameezes, though it was usually Muslim girls who did so. Hindu girls generally wore frocks. Hindu girls in their early teens wore frilly frocks that ensured that their breasts were not sharply outlined. Muslim girls used dupattas over their kameezes. It was perhaps in the 1960s that this religious divide over the salwar-kameez started getting blurred. At present girls of all communities wear the salwar-kameez, and there is nothing to distinguish between the two Bengals in this respect. What was new at the end of the 20th century was that married women, and also women in their late middle age, started being seen in salwar kameezes. Elderly women, however, tend to wear saris at home even if they are in a salwar-kameez at their workplace or when out on errands. For women above a certain age, it is still customary to wear a sari when visiting people. In recent times, young girls in Dhaka and Calcutta are sometimes seen in trousers and T-shirts. Initially limited to families that had spent some years abroad, the practice is now slowly spreading further in society. But it is still not a very common sight in mofussil towns.

Urban and educated Bengali women may have started breaking with tradition in their clothes, but keeping breasts and legs safely out of sight is still an entrenched sartorial habit. Wearing a dupatta with the salwar-kameez is therefore still almost mandatory, whether or not it serves to conceal feminine curves. Girls in trousers and tops have of course done away with the dupatta, though some do use stylish stoles even with Western clothes. Though school students can be seen in skirts, adult women generally don't because their legs would show. Society does not any more object to non-traditional outfits that keep breasts and legs well concealed.

Women's hairstyles, like their clothes, have considerably changed. There was a time when much of the beauty of Bengali women consisted in their long black tresses. A woman's beauty was often measured in direct proportion to the length, thickness and blackness of her hair. Now, however, wearing one's hair short and having it cut in various styles is in fashion. It is hard to put an exact date on when this trend first started. In the 1940s, actors such as Kanan Devi did not wear their hair short. In the 1950s, however, some actors – Suchitra Sen, for instance – introduced the style of wearing a few locks cut short and loosely framing the face, though this marked an exception at that time and not

Suchitra Sen

the general trend. Many urban women now wear their hair cut to shoulder length. The ideal of what is beautiful in hairstyles has indeed changed so much that women now dye their black hair in various colours.

The Bengali woman's bun, the coiled heap at the back of her head and called a *khonpa* in Bengali, has undergone many changes in fashion. I do not know when the custom of doing up women's hair in different kinds of buns started. But women in the 19th century tried out various kinds of buns. From *Hutom*'s description it appears that something called a *firangi khonpa* imitating Western women's hairstyle was then quite popular among elite women. Such was the appeal of this particular bun that even Durga idols were seen sporting it.

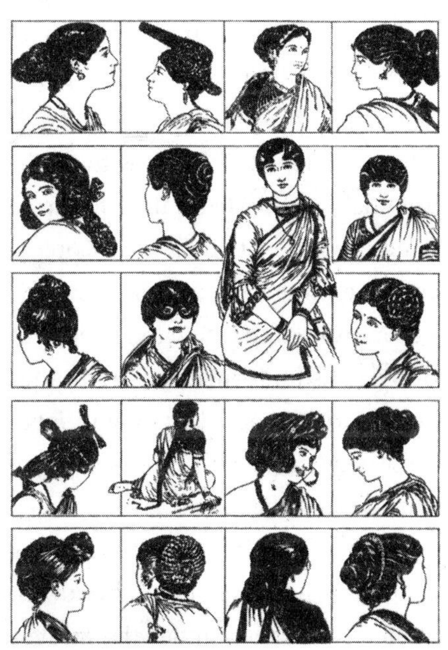

Different kinds of bun

The 'Albert' fashion was the 'in thing' in men's hairstyles at this time. Many also dyed their hair and moustaches. But the dye that was used, called *kalap*, had not come with the English. It had come during Mulim rule. The origin of *kalap* was the Arabic *kalaf.* The beard is not seen in ancient sculptures of Bengal. But bearded men are seen in some medieval manuscript illustrations. This seems to indicate Muslim influence. In the early 19th century, distinguished Hindus such as Ram Mohan Roy, Dwarakanath Tagore and Radhakanta Deb did not wear beards. In the painting of the Dhaka Muharram procession that I mentioned before, only two of the 63 men in it sport beards. All of them, on the other hand, are moustached. In the mid 19th century, however, growing beards became fashionable. Michael Madhusudan Dutt, Debendranath Tagore, Rajnarayan Basu, Bhudeb Mukhopadhyay, Dwijendranath Tagore, Umesh Chandra Banerjee, Upendrakishore Raychaudhuri, etc. grew beards or sideburns, probably under British influence. It is hard to say whether it was family tradition that Tagore followed when he grew a beard or if he did so under British influence.

Spectacles are not seen in paintings belonging to the age of the nawabs, but they can be seen in 19th century paintings. Many people at that time had started getting spectacles made, in imitation of the English, even if there was nothing wrong with their vision. Spectacles seem to have grown an association in people's minds with education and intellect.

Religion has a link with the symbolism of clothes, which is why people who make a living through religion as well as those who abide by religious proscriptions still wear particular kinds of clothes. There are Vaishnavas who even now use shawls with the names of Krishna printed on them, sport a sandalwood paste on their foreheads and wear garlands round their necks. Among Buddhists there are people who use unstitched saffron clothes, but they are only a handful in number. A large section of Muslims wear long kurtas extending below the knee with a lungi to go with it, replaced by a pair of pyjamas on formal occasions. Many Muslims also always wear a cap. The fascination for beards, caps and *jubba*s seems to be on the rise now. Some of these peddlers of faith even use turbans, while some wear achkans or sherwanis. Turbans and sherwanis have become fashionable in weddings among wealthy, urban Muslims. In the context of Muslim clothes, it may be mentioned that in a society where the purdah broke down in the mid 20th century, the burkha made a comeback under the influence of the fundamentalist movement at the end of the century.

The clothes of men and women in cities may no longer have anything distinctively Bengali about them anymore, but such distinctiveness still exists in the extended Bengal countryside, though even there the rich and the poor do not dress alike. Hindus and Muslims do not exactly dress alike, and neither do clothes in the West and East Bengal look completely identical. Many of men in Bengali villages still wear just a dhoti or a lungi in the summer, and a vest with it. For formal dressing they use a punjabi, *phatua*, or a shirt. A shawl in the winter is the only additional protection against the cold. The minimal dressing among men, thus, does not significantly differ from that of the past. For rural women, however, there has been a change—they try to wear an in-skirt and a blouse with their saris. As for the clothes of the rich, though there may be differences in refinement and sophistication between urban and rural areas, there is not much difference in the kind of clothes worn. In sum, Bengali clothes have evolved through the ages, with communities casting influences on each other's clothes and different regions also effecting a give-and-take between them. In the age of globalisation, sartorial fashions are turning to the wider world outside. And yet, a Bengali can still perhaps be told from the way he or she looks and dresses.

BENGALI FOOD

The 19th century poet Ishwar Gupta commented on the Bengali love for the fish-and-rice meal in one of his poems. Paddy cultivation arrived in Bengal from South East Asia some 5,000 years ago. Paddy was grown in dry land in China and in many places in South Asia. It was perhaps in India that paddy was for the first time grown in land immersed in water. This kind of rainfed lowland cultivation of paddy was peculiarly suited to Bengal's climatic and geographical condition. It is no wonder therefore that over time rice became the staple food of Bengalis. The *Charyapada* poems mention rice and no other grain, though by that time wheat had started growing in eastern India. So cherished and central is rice in the Bengali diet that Bengalis acquire the major part of their daily calorie intake from rice. This is all the more true of the poor. A 1940 government estimate showed that the poor got over 3,500 of the 3,600 calories that they needed every day from rice. The report also said that many people in the province ate half a seer of rice (one seer = 0.933 kilogram) every day. Eating large quantities of rice is also fairly common among the wealthy. Most Bengalis still prefer rice to rotis, the unleavened wheat breads that are the staple in northern India.

There is no specific information on when the people of Bengal started eating fish, but fish was probably eaten all along in this land criss-crossed by rivers, canals and lakes. Rice and fish are therefore inseparable from Bengali lives. A slab with the image of a fish on it has been found at Chandraketugarh. In Nihar Ranjan Ray's opinion, this slab dates back to the 4th century. Fish images also appear in many of the terracotta slabs that got made at Paharpur and Mainamati from the 8th century. There are even images of fish being cut for cooking and getting transported in wicker baskets. Such finds reflect the love that the people of this land have for fish. People of many other provinces of India, however, do not view this fish-eating habit of Bengalis too kindly. Many people in the subcontinent still do not eat fish.

Back in the days when the terracotta slabs were being made at Paharpur, Bengal's god-fearing Brahmins perhaps refrained from eating fish. According to Sukumar Sen, fish and meat in ancient Bengal were popular not among Brahmins but among the other castes. Fish was, besides, always taboo for orthodox Buddhists. It was not however easy to forever resist, in the name of religion, the delicious yield of river fish, or even a widely accepted food culture. In the 10th or 11th century, therefore, a Bengali scriptural scholar, Bhabadeb Bhatta, tried to establish the benefits of eating fish and marshalled many arguments in its favour. Fish has also been praised in the *Brihadhdharmapuran.* This text said that Brahmins could eat the rohu (*rui* in Bengali), the swamp barb (*punti*), the snakehead murrel (*shoul*), and other white and scaly fish. Jeemutbahan was also not against eating fish and he praised the hilsa (*ilish*, as Bengalis call it) and its oil. Sarbananda, too, did not forget the hilsa when he slammed fish-eating in his *Teekasarbasya* in the 12th century. The Udbhat Slokas are said to have been written in the 12th century or a little later. These describe the joys of eating fish. Fish-eating is richly advocated in *Prakritpaingal.* One of its poems says: 'Fortunate is the man whose wife serves freshly cooked rice, clarified butter from cow's milk, leaves and a gravy of sardines every day on plantain leaves'.

Rohu, swamp barb, snakehead murrel and hilsa

The Bengali love for fish led Bengali homemakers to experiment with many different ways of cooking fish. The oldest cookbook in Bengali, *Pak Rajeshwar*, was published in the 19th century. The next was Bipradas Mukhopadhyay's *Pak-Pranali* ('How to Cook'), published in 1923. Both these books describe various ways of cooking fish. Later, Prajnasundari Devi of the Jorasanko Tagore family offered 58 fish recipes in her cookbook. This gives an idea of the strength of the Bengali attraction for fish.

This love of fish has from ancient times earned Bengalis much contempt as fish-eaters. Sarbananda was among those who criticised Bengalis for their fish-eating ways. He wrote in *Teekasarbasya* that dried fish was a favourite food of the people of lower Bengal, a habit which provoked abuse from him. In the chapter 'Cultural Transformation in the Indo-Muslim Era' we discussed that Mughal officials who lived in Bengal were also contemptuous of the fish and rice that Bengalis ate. Isa Khan and his son Musa Khan were disdainfully described by them as fisherfolk (*jele*). Mughal officials were not able to discard this scornful attitude even after the start of colonial rule, as Ghulam Hossein Selim betrayed in his *Riyaz-us-Salatin* in the 1780s. He wrote: 'The people of this land, both high and low, all love to eat fish, rice, mustard oil, curds, fruits and sweets. They like huge quantities of red chillies and salt in their food. They do not at all eat wheat or barley rotis. Nor can they digest goat meat or fowl cooked in ghee.'

Dals, or lentils, now compete with fish in the Bengali diet. The *Charyapada* poems do not mention dals, nor does any other source of the time. This led Nihar Ranjan Ray to conclude that lentils were then not grown in this part of the world. Lentils used to be imported from northern India. Yet the popularity of dals can be noted in Mukundaram's *Chandimangal*, written a few hundred years after the *Charyapada* poems. Surely this popularity could not have developed in a couple of years. Nor is it reasonable to suppose that ordinary village folk could easily afford lentils that had travelled across a large stretch of India to reach local markets. Kalketu, the hero of *Chandimangal*, belongs to the lower orders of society. That he lives on husks and lentils suggests that lentils formed one of the chief foods of the poor. Apart from *Chandimangal*, several kinds of dals are mentioned in other medieval literary texts—particularly black gram, dehusked white lentils, and red and yellow lentils. The split Bengal gram is also mentioned.

Bengalis in ancient times do not appear to have been too enthusiastic meat-eaters. Among the bottom half, however, squids, crabs, cocks, ducks, pigs and many kinds of birds are known to have been popular sources of meat. Those higher up the social order ate the meat of deer, goats, lambs and turtles. According to Bhabadeb, even the flesh of hedgehogs and rabbits was not taboo. Images of deer hunts can be seen in the Paharpur slabs. It was the job of Shabars to hunt down various animals. Muslims ate meat foreign travellers passing through the land have left testimony. The meat eating habits of Muslims are also hinted at in Mukundaram's *Chandimangal* and Narayan Deb's *Padmapuran.* There is evidence in Mukundaram and in Bijoy Gupta's *Manasamangal* that Muslims ate the flesh of cocks and that mullahs got money for slaughtering them. We also hear of Muslims eating beef. Mukundaram says butchers who sell the flesh of cows would not be welcome even in hell.

A fairly clear picture of what Bengalis ate before the colonial era emerges from *Chaitanyacharitamrita*, Mukundaram's *Chandimangal*, Narayan Deb's *Padmapuran*, Bijoy Gupta's *Manasamangal* and Bharatchandra's *Annadamangal. Chaitanyacharitamrita* tells us that 10 different kinds of leaves were cooked at Sarbabhouma's kitchen for Chaitanyadev. But Chaitanyadev's mother cooked 20 different kinds of greens for him. It is unlikely that even today there are more than 20 varieties of greens! In this text and in other medieval poems, the greens that we hear of inlclude water spinach (*kolmi*), green amarnath (*notey*), margosa (*neem*), leaves of pointed gourd (*potol*), jute leaves (*paat shaak*), spinach (*paalong/paalak*), basella leaves or the creeping climbing spinach (*puin*), the tender stem and leaves of bottle gourd (*lau daga*) and water cress or marsh herb (*helencha*).

The descriptions of fish available in medieval literature are extensive. Bharatchandra's list, in particular, is quite lengthy. Leaving aside some varieties of fish that have been imported in recent times, most of the other fish that Bengalis are familiar with are mentioned in medieval literature.

It is not just the names of a widely varied range of fresh water fish that we learn from medieval literature, but also the many different ways in which fish was cooked to pamper taste buds. In *Chandimangal*, for instance, Mukundaram lists the different fish dishes that were prepared after Khullana was brought back home:

> Fatty pieces of *chitol* (clown knifefish) fried in mustard oil; a gravy of *rui* (rohu) cooked with red pumpkin, potatoes and dried lentil balls; *koi* (climbing perch) marinated in juice of ginger and fried in mustard oil; *katla* (catla) in a gravy; *khorsula* (corsula), fried; *shoul* (snakehead murrel), deboned and cooked with green mangoes.

Among the vegetables mentioned in medieval sources were *ole* (elephant yam), *kochu* (taro/arum root), *kala* (banana), *kankrole* (tease gourd), *kanchkala* (green plantain), *kanthal bichi* (jackfruit seeds), *kumro* (red pumpkin), *neem* (margosa), *potol* (pointed gourd), *barbati* (string beans), *begun* (aubergine), *mula* (horse radish), *lau* (bottle gourd) and *sheem* (Indian flat beans). In ancient times, and for much of the Middle Ages, people in this part of the world were not familiar with potatoes. The potato arrived in Bengal only in the mid 17th century, with Portuguese traders. The medium of cooking in medieval times was not just mustard oil; sesame seed oil was also used.

Since widows and some other sections in society did not eat non-vegetarian food, women introduced greater variety and innovation in vegetarian cooking and in making sweets than in the cooking of fish. Among vegetarian dishes mentioned in medieval literature were *labra* and *chachchori* (both dishes of mixed vegetables, without gravy), pepper gravy; *mochar ghonto* (cooked banana blossom, a moist dish but without gravy); *mocha bhaja*, or fried banana blossom; red pumpkin balls; and *bharta*, dishes made from boiled and mashed vegetables. An example from Mukundaram's *Chandimangal* will give an idea of the astounding variety in medieval Bengali vegetarian cooking. It is women who usually decide the daily fare in Bengali households, and have probably always done so. But one day Shiva asks Ganesh's mother to prepare a feast for him. The dishes he asks for cannot fail to arouse interest. The list is also an indicator of what constituted a lavish spread in those days. This was what Shiva ordered:

A bitter gravy with margosa, Indian flat beans and aubergine; red pumpkin and aubergine, cooked in large quantities; green amaranth (*notey shaak*) and jackfruit seeds cooked with juice of ginger and flower-shaped dried lentil cakes (*phoolbori*); mustard leaves and allgood/goosefoot leaves cooked in mustard oil; cooked red lentils with a squeeze of lime; mixed vegetables with fried balls of the leaves of ash gourd; giant taro cooked with pumpkin balls and powdered seeds of jackfruit; spinach cooked with clarified butter and cumin seeds. Shiva's dessert menu included sweetened *karamcha*, a kind of local cherry; flower-shaped dried lentil cakes fried in ghee and

cooked in milk; sweetened split Bengal gram soup cooked over a slow fire and kheer (thickened and sweetened milk).

A few vegetarian dishes may be mentioned from among the spread that Kalketu's mother asked for at the feast celebrating her pregnancy and the imminent birth of her son (*sadhbhakshan*, roughly the equivalent of a baby shower): ripe elephant apples (*chalta*) cooked in a gravy; water cress (*helencha*), water spinach (*kolmi*), kangkong (*gima*), all greens of different kinds; tender stem of creeping/climbing spinach (*puin daga*), taro (*mukhi kochu*) and flower-shaped cakes of dried lentils (*phoolbori*) in a pepper gravy; radishes cooked with aubergines and flat beans. Apart from vegetable dishes, medieval Bengalis also excelled in sour gravies, called *ambal*, literally meaning sour, and eaten at the end of a meal. Example: a sour gravy of ripe banana.

Bengalis have always been fond of sweets. Desserts such as the *payesh* (rice pudding) and *pithe* (sweets with a coconut filling wrapped in varied batters of rice, lentils or semolina and even refined flour—either steamed or fried) have been widely eaten from ancient times. Extensive information on a wide range of sweets and sweetened dishes is available in medieval literature. Certain kinds of vegetarian cooking and some particular sweets have in fact become inseparable parts of Bengali culture. Let us name a few of these—signature Bengali preparations such as *shukto* (a gravy of vegetables with one bitter ingredient, such as bitter gourd or margosa) and *kasundi*, the Bengali mustard sauce, on the one hand, and sweets such as the *rasogolla* and sandesh on the other. Medieval literature tells us about many different kinds of kasundi, flavoured variously with green mangoes, ginger or pepper. Bengali wives also made a wide variety of pickles. It is hard to say for how long the savouries and snacks that are now popular with Bengalis have been around—puris (deep fried wheat flat breads); *kachuri* (stuffed puris); *luchi* (deep fried flat breads made of maida); *nimki* (fried wheat/maida savouries); *parota* (roasted wheat/maida flat breads); *ruti* (roti in Hindi, unleavened wheat breads); *papad*s

Indian flat beans

Elephant yam

Green plantain

Red pumpkin

Aubergine

(flat lentil discs that are fried or roasted); *piyanji* (onion dipped in chick pea batter and fried); *beguni* (thinly sliced aubergines dipped in chick pea batter and fried); *singara* (a cousin of the north Indian samosa, spicy potato filling in a maida wrapping, shaped somewhat like a pyramid and deep fried). Some of these appear to have come from northern India during Muslim rule. Some may even have come during colonial times. Though *ruti* finds mention in medieval Bengali literature, the other items on the list do not.

Medieval literature mentions various kinds of *narus*, the Bengali equivalent of laddus, spherical sweets made of varied ingredients such as rice flour, coconut, puffed rice. Camphor was widely used to flavour these sweets. In the Middle Ages, as now, Bengalis indulged themselves with sweet *pithes*. Many of the sweets and sweetened foods that were popular in the Middle Ages were mentioned in *Chaitanyacharitamrita*. Among these were dried mango, sweets made of thickened milk, a sweet and sour drink of whipped and diluted curd called *ghol*, milk-and-coconut sweets, fried balls of cottage cheese, cottage cheese, curd, flattened rice with milk, *payesh* or rice pudding, sweets of thickened milk, fried balls of sweetened, soaked and ground black lentils, and *pithe*. Bengalis have for centuries relished the juice of dates, collected in mud pots tied to date palms and left overnight. Date palm jaggery is made out of this juice, the different varieties marking the various stages of extraction. There has also always been a tradition of making sweet *pithe* by mixing grated coconut and other ingredients with rice flour.

Gopal Haldar once joked that Bengali culture was a culture of the *rasogolla* and sandesh. A joke it may be, but these two sweets do rank very high in the food preferences of Bengalis, and people of other regions in the subcontinent identify these as Bengali sweets. Curiously enough, however, there is no mention of either of these in the literature written a few hundred years ago. The *rasogolla* was not even mentioned, and even if sandesh was, the word did not then mean what it does now. Fried wheat sweets dipped in sugar syrups and sent by relatives were known as sandesh.

It is not known exactly when the *rasogolla* came into being. But it seems to have made its appearance before the start of the colonial era. It was in the 19th century that the *rasogolla*'s inseparable link with Bengal was established. It must have taken a few centuries for the *rasogolla* to gain recognition as a peculiarly Bengali sweet. Bengali confectioners have created many other sweets that are variations of the *rasogolla*– for instance, *rajbhog* (a giant-sized *rasogolla*), the *swarajbhog* of Kanthi, the *rasogolla* chutney, *kamalabhog* (rasogolla with orange food colour), *rasomalai* (mini rasogollas in a base of sweetened milk). Among the dry versions of the *rasogolla* are *danadar, kheermohan, chamcham* and *chhanabarha* (fried pieces of cottage cheese). The *chhanabarha* (*chhenabarha*) is mentioned in medieval literature, particularly in *Chaitanyacharitamrita*, which has led Bijonbehari Bhattacharjya to infer that it was this *chhanabarha* that was the ancestor of the *rasogolla.*

Patishapta, a type of *pithe*

Rasogolla

Like the *rasogolla*, the sandesh is also a trademark Bengali sweet. Bijonbehari Bhattacharjya thinks that the *manohara* mentioned in *Chaitanyacharitamrita* is an early version of the sandesh as we know it. Both *chhana*, or cottage cheese (obtained by curdling the milk and separating the cheese from the whey) and kheer (milk boiled until it thickens into a sweet semi-solid state) are used to make sandesh. With several centuries of sandesh-making behind them, Bengali confectioners have not only perfected the art but have also introduced considerable variety in it. With small variations here and there, the same sandesh is sometimes known by different names in different parts of Bengal, and some places have become known for their speciality in making some versions of the sandesh. For instance, though the *kanchagolla* (uncooked sandesh, that is, the cottage cheese is not stirred over a flame) is made everywhere, Natore confectioners specialise in making it. The *manda*, too, is made in various locations in Bengal, and each place usually makes it in a different way. But Muktagachha in Mymensingh has a particular reputation for its *manda*, a milk sweet made of cottage cheese and thickened milk. The liquid date palm jaggery (*nalen gurh*, literally, new jaggery) collected at the beginning of the season in winter is used to make *manda* in some places of West Bengal. The sandesh in its different versions is variously known as *kalakand, karha pak* (sandesh that has been 'cooked' to yield a less soft sweet), *dim* (shaped like an egg or dim), *barfi* (diamond-shaped) and so on. The *pyanra*, a flat sandesh made of kheer, is chiefly a West Bengal sweet. But there are now versions of the *pyanra* that are made of *chhana*.

The *pantua*, which is basically a fried *rasogolla*, was surely conceptualised as a variation of the latter. It is mentioned in Jati Ramananda's *Chandimangal* written in the 18th century and in Jainarayan Ghosal's *Karunanidhanbilas* completed in 1813. That would mean that the *rasogolla* goes further back into the past. Once the *pantua* lost its novelty, newer variations were not long in making their appearance. One of these was the *ledikeni* or Lady Keny (Lady Canning). The name suggests that this sweet was first made sometime in the mid 19th century. The *golapjam* and the *kalojam* are also variations of the *pantua*. The *jilipi*, a cousin of the north Indian *jalebi*, is another favourite and fairly cheap Bengali sweet, versions of which are eaten all over the subcontinent. It is not known when Bengalis started eating *jilipi*, but perhaps towards the end of Muslim rule. The *jilipi* is mentioned in Jainarayan's book.

It must be mentioned here, before we quit the discussion on sweets, that though it is not known exactly when Bengali confectioners started curdling their milk to make sweets such as *rasogolla* and *chhana* sandesh, it must have marked some breaking of taboo and certainly a departure from custom because splitting of milk was once ritually forbidden, and continues to be so for many Hindus in India. Apart from the *chhanaporha* (*chhenaporh*) of Odisha, the Bengali *rasoglla* and sandesh and their variations are probably the only milk sweets that are made by splitting milk, at least by Hindus. We know from Jyotirmoyee Devi's autobiographical books that even in her youth, that is, in the early 20th century, *chhana* sweets were not offered to the gods. It may appear from this that such sweets are of relatively recent origin, and therefore, perhaps, the ritual resistance to its use in worship. It must also be borne in mind that kheer sweets have longer life and may have been the automatic choice in pre-refrigeration days, especially in the summer. But then, that *chhana* sweets started being made well before refrigeration is a possibility too, and maybe even before ice started being imported. Was it contact with the Europeans who came with their cheeses that encouraged Bengali confectioners to experiment with cottage cheese? That is an interesting idea, but there is no historical evidence to support it. Besides, people seem to have been familiar with the *pantua* at least as early as the time of *Chaitanyacharitamrita.*

Medieval poets mentioned many fruits in their works, though there is no reason to assume that all of these fruits grew in Bengal. Grapes, for instance, were not locally grown. There were not too many oranges growing in Bengal either. But mangoes, gooseberries, bananas, jujubes, kesur tubers, dates, figs, quinces, coconuts, almonds, plums such as the *jam* or *jamrul*, sugar palm fruits, citrons, pomegranates appear to have grown abundantly. The mango is mentioned even in ancient literature. Medieval poets have left particular mention of the variety called *chanpa* banana.

Bengali society of the medieval period was not familiar with the wide range of spices that we are now used to. But poets have mentioned the spices that were ordinarily used. Ginger, cardamom, camphor, kababchini, cumin, coriander, pepper, fennel and clove. Green mangoes, dried mango powder, jujubes and june plums or hog plums were used to cook *ambal*s, the sour gravies eaten at the end of meals. Other sour fruits were gooseberries, local cherries, limes, tamarind and shaddocks (*jamir*). Bengali cooking is usually hot, but chilli peppers were not available in Bengal, or in the whole of India for that matter, before the 17th century. Chillies, like potatoes, were introduced by Portuguese traders.

There do not seem to have been too many differences between Hindus and local Muslims in the matter of everyday food like fish and rice and most other kinds of daily fare. That cannot however be said about meat-eating. Many Muslims, especially the city dwellers among them, not only ate meat but they also ate beef. We have already noted how the mullah received money for slaughtering poultry and goats. Some differences in the dietary habits of Hindus and Muslims can be inferred from this. But Shakta Hindus, that is, worshippers of the mother goddess, ate the flesh of a wide range of animals including goats, deer and turtles. Low-caste Hindus seem to have been in the habit of eating the flesh of hedgehogs, pigs and a kind of giant lizard (*godhika*). In Mukundaram's *Chandimangal*, Kalketu's mother asks him to eat roasted hedgehog meat and *godhika.*

This varied range of food listed above was, needless to say, chiefly the preserve of well-to-do families. In society at large, the staple even in medieval times was rice that had been soaked and allowed to ferment a little. The historian and Portuguese friar Sebastian Manrique passed through Bengal in the 16th century. He wrote that the poor of the land ate their rice with salt and greens and could only occasionally afford gravies. Mukundaram's description of the diet of the impecunious hunter Kalketu around the same time as Manrique's visit also gives an idea of how the poor ate. Kalketu ate a viscous soup boiled from broken rice (*khuder jau*). The accompaniments were red lentils cooked with bottle gourd, elephant yam (*ole*), taro (*kochu*) and june plums (commonly called ambarella or *aamra* in Bengali). Once in a while there was even curd. It is evident from the way it is written of that curd was a favourite of both the rich and the poor. Just as Kalketu is pleased to have curd on his plate, quite a few scriptural scholars have praised a meal of steaming rice, greens and curd. But the poor did not always have access to curd. *Ghol*, or sweetened buttermilk, was also popular, though maybe not as coveted as curd.

People at the bottom of society for ever battled with want. As a *Charyapada* poem said, there was never any rice in the pot, and fasting was a daily affair. Several poets including Mukundaram have written of people eating *khuder jau* or broken bits of rice that got damaged at the time of husking. Towards the close of the Middle Ages, too, Bharatchandra's writing hints at the poverty of the masses. He describes Annada, the goddess of plenty, in her 'poor' avatar as being 'skin and bones, in the absence of food'. There was no dearth of people who went hungry in Bharatchandra's time though rice sold for one maund (1 maund = 37 kg, roughly) a rupee. Many workers of the time got less than a rupee a month as wages. Bharatchandra has also described the food of the wealthy. A comparison of the foods that he lists with that of *Chaitanyacharitamrita*, written some 150 years earlier, shows only minor differences.

Paan, bits of areca nuts and other sweet spices in a wrapping of betel leaf, and fennel seeds were eaten after meals as mouth fresheners. The *Charyapada* poems mention paan (betel leaf) and camphor. In Mukundaram we hear of areca nuts (*gua*). Consumption of alcohol is mentioned in a wide range of texts beginning from the *Charyapada* to works of medieval Muslim poets. The Vaishnava Padavalis mention women's drinking, too. Yet drinking does not seem to have been very open or prevalent in all sections in the Middle Ages. There was enough tippling among the wealthy. The juice of date and toddy palms and also rice were fermented into alcoholic drinks. Mahua flowers also yielded fine alcoholic drinks. Even the rice soaked in water that was the staple of the poor provided a certain alcoholic high. Drinking among the rich continued unabated during Indo-Muslim rule. The post of '*khaas sharaabdar*', or official-in-charge of the royal cellar, existed during the Hossein Shahi period. That would suggest that not only was drinking an accepted custom among the sultans it was a regular affair. According to Mamtazur Rahman Tarafdar, the *badshah*s of Delhi and the sultans of Bengal maintained a tradition of employing staff to serve drinks. Many Muslims, however, did not drink because of religious reasons. They even went so far as to try to prevent others from drinking. Notwithstanding religious prohibition, however, drinking and other kinds of addiction were practised. For instance, housewives often soaked a handful of rice in a pot, which was allowed to ferment and then cooked and eaten. This, needless to say, was but a variation of alcohol consumption.

Even though religious regulation did not encourage drinking, rich Muslims and the urban elite among them were quite liberal in this respect. Drinking is known to have been common among the officials and courtiers (amirs and omrahs) of Islam Khan, the subahdar or governor of Bengal in the early 17th century. But since Islam Khan himself was against drinking, his courtiers knocked off their drinks well before he joined the gatherings and tried to hide the smell with attar. It should be mentioned in the context that Islam Khan's childhood friend and master, the Emperor Jahangir, drank copiously. Images inscribed on his coins show the emperor carrying a drink in his hand. There are images, too, of Nur Jahan carrying a drink. Apart from alcohol, Jahangir regularly used opium.

Many Bengali Hindus openly got high on bhang (intoxicating drink made from the cannabis plant) during religious festivals such as Durga Puja. The custom is not totally discarded even now. Ganja or marijuana (the dried and crushed seeds, flowers and stems from the same plant) was also widely used in smoking. We learn from William Hunter's book that marijuana was cultivated on a large scale in the Nawgaon area of Rajshahi district. Many people consumed opium. We encounter opium addicts in *Hutom Pyanchar Naksha* and in Bankimchandra's works. I have come across many advertisements for opium and the auctioning of opium in late 18th century newspapers. Much of the opium produced was exported. It was not as if opium was not used in Bengal at all, but Bengal or the rest of India never took to opium in the way that the British succeeded in making it popular in China. The curious range of addictions in 19th century Calcutta is discussed with humour in Arun Nag's book *Chitrito Padme.*

Muslim Influence on Bengali Food Habits

The arrival of Muslims in Bengal introduced a novel dietary tradition in a section of society. New kinds of food ingredients were also imported as a result of Muslim conquest. The seeds of a slow change in food habits were thus sown. Yet in a society where even sniffing and inhaling the aroma of food was considered as partaking of food, in however limited a way, and could lead to people losing caste, orthodox Hindus were not easily influenced by Muslim food.

The *badshahs*, nawabs and the amirs and omrahs who came into Bengal brought with them culinary traditions from northern India and even perhaps from Persia and Central and West Asia. Some of their food seems to have trickled out first to the native, lowborn and poor Muslims. The wealthy Hindus who converted to Islam or who, holding positions in the new administration, came in close contact with Muslim rulers also gradually accepted Muslim food. But the process, it is reasonable to suppose, must have taken a few hundred years. There is no clear evidence of exactly when Muslim food penetrated the larger Bengali society, irrespective of the religious identities of its people. But Mughlai food is not mentioned in the works of non-Muslim poets up to Bharatchandra. We may infer from this that until the time of Bharatchandra, Muslim food was not eaten in Hindu households. In the mid 19th century, however, the poet Ishwar Gupta mentioned *polao* and *kalia* (a rich gravy, usually of fish or meat). The *palanna* that he mentioned was, I suppose, a local version of the pulao and biryani.

The *ghee-bhat* served on formal occasions was nothing but a local version of the pulao. Apart from the evidence in Ishwar Gupta's work, we will see in the following discussion that the pulao became a much-loved food in many Hindu households.

Muslims introduced fruits such as the watermelon. It cannot be said with certainty whether onions and garlic were grown in Bengal before the Muslims came or if these were new crops brought in by the new rulers. There is no doubt, however, that it was the Muslims who introduced the custom of using onions and garlic in food. Bengali Hindu society did not just have a stiff resistance to eating onions and garlic, this resistance lasted for a very long time and in fact well into the 20th century. There are still dishes in which Hindus do not use onions and garlic though Muslims do. Hindu widows, for instance, did not traditionally eat onions and garlic. Onions and garlic are still never used in food that is offered to gods or is served at functions associated with religious ceremonies. The foods listed as *naibedyo* or 'offering' at the Puri temple do not include onion. The onion, on the other hand, is among the foods mentioned in the *Ain-i-Akbari*. The strong hostility to garlic ensured that the use of this herb remained unfamiliar to much of society for a long time. *Rasun*, the Bengali word for garlic, was so little used that Haricharan Bandyopadhyay's dictionary published in the fourth decade of the 20th century entered the word as *loshun*, which is closer to the Hindi *lehsun*.

Portuguese and British Influences

New kinds of food also came in with the Portuguese. They brought to the land many European and South American fruits and vegetables and also some European foods that were not easily perishable. The most notable vegetable import was the round potato. Though there are at present some 150 kinds of potatoes in the world and though the potato is now the staple in many countries, there were no potatoes in India before the 17th century. The Spanish had brought the potato to Europe from the Bolivia-Peru region in the second half of the 16th century. The Portuguese brought it to India from Europe. Tagore has written of trying to grow potatoes on farmland owned by the Tagore family estate in what is now the Kushtia district in Bangladesh, headquartered in Shilaidaha village, sometime in the late 1890s. The tone of his writing suggests that it was a new thing that he was experimenting with, implying that the potato was not yet a widely grown crop. The poet ended up sinking a small fortune in trying to grow it, unsuccessfully, despite using all the fertilisers prescribed in the agricultural department. A peasant in his zamindari, however, managed to produce a bumper crop on a much smaller farm plot than the one in which Tagore was trying out his experiment and without paying attention to expert advice. Tagore's son Rathindranath has also written of growing potatoes, this time with more success, in Shilaidaha. He, too, writes in a way that suggests that this was a new thing being tried out. The peasants, he says in his book *Pitrismriti* (Memories of My Father), were 'taught' to grow the potato and they soon mastered the crop and grew it with success. This second experiment with potatoes by the Tagores must have taken place after 1910, which was the year Rathindranath settled down in Shilaidaha with his new wife and took over the management of the landed estate in Kushtia.

Potatoes

The most important fruit brought by the Portuguese was the pineapple or *ananas*, which became *anaras* in Bengali, probably because of the rich juiciness of the fruit. *Ras* in Bengali is 'juice'. The sugar apple, custard apple and cashew also came with the Portuguese. They also probably gave us the *chiku.*

Two other very important farm products that came in with the Portuguese were chilli peppers and tobacco. These farm products did not inspire the kind of intense and long-standing hostility that onion and garlic had attracted. On the contrary, Indians enthusiastically seized chilli peppers and tobacco and made them part of their everyday lives. So well liked, indeed, were these two imports that they spread all over the subcontinent within some 50 years of their arrival.

Bread, called *paunruti* in Bengali, also seems to have been brought by the Portuguese because *paun* is Portuguese, not English. Biscuits are also thought to have first come with the Portuguese. As we will see later, native hostility to these two bakery products turned out to be intense and long-standing.

Vegetables of what is called the mustard family – *kopi* in Bengali – became quite popular with Bengalis in the 20th century, if not in the 19th. The cauliflower, cabbage and turnip—none of these came out of South America; these were crops grown in different parts of Europe. They might well have been introduced by the British, but that Bengalis chose to call the cabbage *bandha kopi* and the cauliflower *phul kopi* suggests that these too were brought by the Portuguese. For, in the Portuguese language these are called *kobi.*

The British, too, brought in many new foods. Bread and biscuits apart, the chop, cutlet and the patty were among the foods that penetrated circles of English-educated young Bengali men. Beef-eating is usually associated with Muslims. It was during British colonial rule that beef seems to have become popular among Hindu youngsters, and not earlier. This was because Muslim rule had not introduced the kind of liberalism or education leading to the disowning of institutional religion that students of the Hindu College were exposed to in the 19th century. The word 'mutton', too, found its way into Bengali literature in the mid 19th century.

Though the Portuguese brought their own wines and alcoholic drinks, the habit of drinking is also closely associated with British rule. For, it was during colonial rule that the educated middle class took to drinking. Ram Mohan Ray started drinking right at the beginning of the 19th century. It is hard to say how much of it was done in imitation of the prevailing fashion, and how much from an actual addiction to alcohol. Drinking quickly became popular with the first generation of English-educated young men in the 19th century. Like Ram Mohan, Dwarakanath also drank—far more heavily, in all probability. So harmless, in fact, was drinking regarded to be by this first generation of English-educated young men that Rajnarayan Basu's father used to ask his son to drink with him. The father had hoped that the licence to drink at home would prevent the son from imitating his bibulous friends and drinking excessively. Rajnarayan Basu, however, drank with his father at home and also outside, without his father's knowledge. Excessive drinking broke his health in 1846 while he was still in college.

Some scholars have claimed that Rajnarayan's classmate Michael Madhusudan Dutt got into the habit of taking one drink every night while still a student, early in the 1840s. Some have said that he did so with his father's permission. But one of Michael's letters seems to deflate this claim. Debendranath Tagore, notwithstanding the saintly image reflected in his 'maharshi' title, also drank. There were indeed few teetotallers among those who had been students of the Hindu College in the 1830s and 1840s. Many well known individuals of the time, including Harish Chandra Mukhopadhyay, Kaliprasanna Sinha, Pratap Chandra Sinha, Dinabandhu Mitra and Michael Madhusudan Dutt died early mainly because of unrestrained drinking. Bankimchandra, too, was not averse to alcohol. He, too, did not live very long, though he did not spare the bibulousness of English-educated sections of his ridicule. Notwithstanding his own weakness for alcohol, Madhusudan Dutt subjected the drinking habits of the youth to biting sarcasm in his skit *Ekei ki Bole Sabhyata?*.

There is evidence in contemporary newspapers and journals that apart from the educated classes who sought to imitate an European way of life, drinking also became a widely accepted custom among little-educated wealthy sections. Indeed, it appears from what was written in various papers and magazines and from dramatic literature such as *Ekei ki Bole Sabhyata?* and *Sadhabar Ekadashi* that Bengalis were not social drinkers but that they drank because they were addicted to alcohol. It was not wine that they drank, but hard alcoholic drinks. The Portuguese had brought madeira. The British introduced brandy, whisky, sherry and champagne. Whisky however was not at all popular with Bengalis in the initial years. It was in the late 19th century that it became a well-loved drink.

Drinking remained fashionable and an aspect of modernism among educated youngsters right up to the end of the 19th century. From the 1850s, however, people started becoming aware of the harmful effects of drinking. Rajnarayan Basu, once an excessive drinker who disowned Hinduism through a symbolic act of drinking at the time of his conversion to the Brahmo faith, later gave up alcohol. Debendranath Tagore, too, gave up drinking in the 1850s under the influence of Akshay Kumar Datta. Like Rajnarayan Basu, his classmate Pyaricharan Sarkar became drawn to the agenda of social reform.

The way in which these men, not satisfied with just giving up their own drinking, started an anti-alcohol campaign in the 1860s also provides indirect evidence of how widespread the practice of drinking was in contemporary Bengali society.

Though they introduced some non-perishable foods, the British did not bring with them new fruits and vegetables in the way the Portuguese had done. The only notable exception was the tomato, now extremely popular with Bengalis and much used. Like the potato, the tomato, too, had its original home in South America. It probably arrived in Europe from Mexico in the first half of the 16th century. But it was not the Portuguese who brought this fruit to India. It arrived with the British, and that too quite late. The word 'tomato' is not there in Subal Mitra's dictionary published in 1906 or in Haricharan Bandyopadhyay's dictionary published in 1933. But Radhaprasad has mentioned the tomato among the foods that were according to him consumed in Calcutta in the early 20th century. Rathindranath, too, grew tomatoes at Shilaidaha in the second decade of the 20th century and successfully taught peasants to grow the crops. The seeds, he has written in *Pitrismriti*, were imported from the United States. I remember eating tomatoes as a young boy back in my village home in East Bengal, sometime around 1948, as far as I can recall. It was however known as 'sour aubergine' (*tauk begun*) among people in the countryside.

Restaurant Culture

One of the things that made forbidden foods and food not eaten in Bengali households so popular among youngsters during British colonial rule was that restaurants started making their appearance in Bengal, as early as the 18th century, in order to cater to English customers. English-educated young men began frequenting these places in the 1830s, and thus started what can be called a 'restaurant culture' in Bengali society. Young men patronised restaurants to eat what they could not get at home. Rajnarayan Basu wrote of eating beef kebabs in the 1840s and Madhusudan Dutt of buying meat dishes, patty and biscuits, also in the 1840s. They also named shops that sold cooked food.

It will not be unreasonable to assume that the first cooks and chefs at the Calcutta restaurants were English. Later, however, Muslim *bawarchi*s became available to do the cooking at restaurants. It had been *bawarchi*s, and not women, who in the Indo-Muslim age cooked unfamiliar north Indian dishes. And from that time there had come up among Muslims a professional class of *bawarchi*s. Chops and cutlets, poultry and mutton, they cooked everything without any cultural inhibitions holding them back. It was they, again, who baked bread and turned out biscuits. One of the things that long made Hindus see bread and biscuits as ritually forbidden was that these were made by Muslim *bawarchi*s.

Nor were these *bawarchi*s satisfied with cooking just English dishes. Especially when they opened their own restaurants in the mould of the English ones, it was Mughlai food and not Continental dishes that they served there. And so it came about that Bengali society in the 19th century started becoming familiar with kebabs, kormas, pulaos, biryani and other kinds of Muslim food. So tasty in fact were these kebabs made of beef that Rajnarayan Basu and his friends, in their impatience to savour these delicacies, jumped over the college walls to get to the shop that sold them. Rajnarayan Basu's *Atmacharit* ('My Story') gives an indication of how popular Mughlai food had become among Bengali Hindus. He mentions in this book that in the 1850s, when he lived in Medinipur, one of his neighbours was Brajendranarayan Deb, the grandson of the orthodox Hindu leader of an earlier generation, Radhakanta Deb. This man's hard-drinking friends regularly met at his house, and pulao was served at these gatherings. It would not be unreasonable to infer that the cooking was done by Muslim *bawarchi*s.

Until the 18th and also a part of the 19th century, the consumption of Muslim food was confined initially to subedars, nawabs, amirs and omrahs, and later among elite non-Bengali Muslims. Once Mughlai food started becoming available at restaurants in Calcutta, there took place a limited expansion of its reach in the city. Indeed, the extent to which Mughlai and Continental food found acceptance in Calcutta through the city's restaurants is indicated in the description of a feast that was held at the residence of the Chorbagan Mitras. There were 117 dishes on the list of foods that Debashish Bandyopadhyay has mentioned in his book *Banedi Kolkatar Ghar Barhi* as the fare that was served at this feast in April 1917. Among these were Mughlai foods such as kebabs, kofta, *kalia*, but also traditional Bengali vegetarian dishes. Fries, grilled foods, chops, cutlets, croquettes and lemonades were not left out either.

Mughlai food started gaining wide acceptance among the Muslim middle classes in the 20th century. The emergence of Pakistan as a separate nation also encouraged Mughal cuisine in East Pakistan because a close link was at that time established with West Pakistan. English culinary traditions, on the other hand, do not seem to have ever gained much currency in Bengal. The foods that Western contact made popular were in the nature of snacks—bread, chops, cutlets, cake, biscuits, patties and such like. Apart from a few restaurants in Calcutta, restaurants elsewhere that served English food folded up almost as soon as the British departed. We know from Tapan Raychaudhuri's writing that in his father's family a Muslim *bawarchi* prepared Mughal and European dishes in the early 20th century.

Changes in Food Habits in the Twentieth Century

The discovery of life-saving drugs, antibiotics and vaccines in the 20th century led to a rapid increase in population and also in poverty levels. Cropping patterns changed, too. This had an impact on food habits, particularly those of the poor. Many Bengalis in the second half of the century gave up rice, the staple of over a thousand years, for wheat. There was a story in a medieval poem of how a cruel Muslim feudal lord made Hindus lose caste by forcing them to eat rotis! There is no mention in medieval literature of natives of the land willingly eating rotis.

Restaurants serving Chinese food came up in Calcutta even before Partition. In other parts of Bengal, however, restaurants selling Chinese and other foreign cuisine appeared after Partition, slowly introducing greater variety in the food that people ate. South Indian and Punjabi food is available in Calcutta, and, in this age of hotch-potch, one even gets traditional Bengali food in restaurants like Aheli. Dhaka, too, now has restaurants offering traditional Bengali food. Whether or not the food in Chinese restaurants has anything very 'Chinese' about it, these are now favourite places to celebrate birthdays and anniversaries in, and also to take out girlfriends for meals. And that is not where the changing food fashions stopped, either. The latest is to eat Western fast foods such as hamburgers, spaghetti or hot dogs in cities like Dhaka and Calcutta. The children of those who went abroad on scholarship to pursue higher studies in the 1970s or 1980s continued to seek the food flavours they had grown familiar with in the West even after coming back home. This was the demand that spurred the growth of low-quality restaurants serving foreign foods in Dhaka and Calcutta. Notwithstanding the poor quality of the food served in these joints, the young Bengali global citizens patronise them and buy hamburgers and hotdogs under the sheer spell cast by the magic in these names. It is not only fashionable to eat these foods, but flattering to one's self-image and vanity. With spectacular progresses in the media of communication, the world is now fast shrinking. It is therefore not surprising that food cultures of different countries should impact each other.

But it must be said that though Bengali food has been amenable to various influences at different times, Bengalis continue to hold on to certain traditional foods that have become part of the Bengali cultural identity. Bengalis of all communities and all regions continue to be as attached as ever to their fish and rice and their lentil soups and their varied vegetarian cuisine. But of course differences continue to exist between Bengali Hindu food and Bengali Muslim food. Differences between the food cultures of East Bengal and West Bengal are not negligible, either.

Beverages

There is no detailed historical information of beverages used in early Bengali society. Did they drink milk then, or was milk mixed with rice and eaten as a meal? It is hard to say. Medieval literature mentions '*paana*', which was something like a sherbet. Sherbets had come with the Muslims. Sherbets, especially lime sherbets, are still widely used as part of Muslim hospitality.

Paan-supari, tea and tobacco are some of the things other than food that are offered to guests. As we have mentioned before, paan, or betel leaf, was mentioned in the *Charyapada* poems and even in earlier texts. Areca nut, too, is mentioned in the earliest Bengali literary texts. It is evident, then, that the paan-supari mouth freshner has been part of Bengali culture for the past thousand or more years. Medieval literature also has instances of fennel seeds being offered to guests after a meal. Tea, however, was a much later addition to the Bengali food culture. The British introduced tea, though it was neighbouring China that tea came from.

Bengal's links with China go back many centuries. Chinese travellers and state envoys from China have since ancient times repeatedly visited Bengal, for religious reasons. But there is no evidence to suggest that tea arrived in Bengal in ancient or medieval times. Tea eventually arrived through a circuitous route.

The first tea shop was set up in London in 1657, though it did not immediately become popular. Coffee was then the preferred beverage of the English people. In other European countries, however, tea was already quite popular. There was therefore a high demand for tea as a commodity of import. It was to pay for this expensive import that the East India Company introduced opium in China. It became a standard practice to export opium in order to import tea. But it is not known whether supplies of tea arrived for Englishmen living in Calcutta as soon as the city was founded. That tea started arriving in Calcutta by the middle of the 18th century is, however, beyond doubt. There is unmistakable evidence in Upjohn's English-Bengali dictionary published in 1793 that the word 'cha' entered the Bengali vocabulary at the end of this century. Not only was the word 'cha' entered in this dictionary, it also had the compound expression 'cha-pani'. That English officials of the time drank tea is clear from John Miller's book *Shikhyaguru* published in 1797. The sahib in this book asks his dewan, through his servant, to wait until he finishes his tea and is free to see him.

But though the sahibs drank their tea, before 1823 they were not aware of the fact that tea could grow on Indian soil. Tea shrubs were discovered in Assam in that year, growing wild, like weeds. Eleven years later, Lord Bentinck permitted trade in tea in India. Gradually, tea cultivation started in the newly established tea gardens. There was a movement in the late 1850s against the exploitation of peasants by indigo planters. Tea garden workers did not get organised into any such movement. The chief reason was that it was not possible to grow tea on ordinary farmland by getting peasant owners into a contract. But tea garden workers were also an exploited lot. Their plight was written about in newspapers and journals in the late 1860s. At least one short

Bengali play on how tea garden owners exploited workers was published, indicating that the tea gardens were growing in size and number and making their presence felt.

There is no clear evidence of exactly when Bengalis started drinking tea. But that it must have been in the second half of the 19th century is incontrovertible. It was the urban, English-educated section that first took to drinking tea. Prabhat Kumar Mukhopadhyay wrote a short story called *Nishiddho Phal* ('Forbidden Fruit') at the start of the 20th century. The story, however, was set in Bankimchandra's time, that is, three decades before it was written. A fictitious friend of Bankimchandra called Ray Bahadur exhorts him to write not on love but some other issues. This, according to the friend, would be more edifying for society. One of the themes he suggests is the inadvisable habit of drinking tea that educated Bengalis have cultivated. The suggestion shows that by Bankimchandra's time, tea-drinking was more or less a regular practice among urban, educated people. Ordinary people, too, would have heard of the beverage. Otherwise, Tagore would not have mentioned it in his novels *Chokher Bali* ('Grain of Sand') and *Noukadubi* ('Boat Capsize'). In *Chokher Bali* he has Mahendra and his friend Behari drinking tea at a picnic. The novel was written around 1902. In *Noukadubi* written two years later, the subject of tea appears on the first page and then makes repeated appearances.

It is almost certain that tea-drinking rapidly became an accepted practice among educated sections in the cities. Some cultural resistance against a product of foreign origin was perhaps possible, and most probably such resistance did exist. But it did not prevent people from taking to tea. Whether for cultural inhibitions or for other reasons, many people expressed fears that tea was harmful for health. In the third decade of the 20th century, the patriotic scientist Prafulla Chandra Ray published a book titled *Cha Paan, Na Bish Paan?* ('Tea, or Poison?'). Notwithstanding his worries, however, tea became more and more popular. Tagore sang its praises in a famous song in 1924. The scholar, the scientist, the poet, the

Tea garden in Assam

geographer, the singer, the painter, the legislator, the public official—the poet invites all to taste the pleasures of the tea boiling in the kettle. Sometime later Nazrul Islam, too, wrote a song about tea.

The companies that sold and distributed tea played an active role in making tea popular. These companies spread the word about the many beneficial effects of tea through advertisements in newspapers and magazines. That apart, for a long time they carried out a campaign of distributing cups of tea absolutely free in villages and market towns and weekly markets in the mofussil, and then handing out free packets of tea. As a young boy, I, too, witnessed such a campaign in a market in Barisal in 1951. Coffee preceded tea in Bengal, though not among ordinary people. Historians have mentioned that Alivardi Khan drank coffee.

Christopher Columbus had his first brush with tobacco soon after setting foot in South America. It was not long before he got into the habit of smoking it. It was he who introduced tobacco in Europe. It is however not known whether tobacco cultivation started in his time. The man whose name is most closely linked with the large-scale use of tobacco in Europe was Jean Nicot, the French ambassador in America. It was after him that the addictive stimulant in tobacco was later named nicotine. Tobacco was introduced in Spain, Portugal, France and England in the sixth decade of the 16th century. Not long afterwards, the Portuguese brought tobacco to India. Within 50 years, it had spread all over India. Even Emperor Akbar started smoking tobacco. Though his son Jahangir did not like tobacco, Shah Jahan did. Some of the Nawab-era paintings that have survived in Bengal depict people puffing at the hookah. Alivardi Khan, in particular, was fond of tobacco. In this context it must be said that the mention of Muslims using the hookah in Bipradas's *Manasamangal* cannot but be a later interpolation. It was not only the rich who savoured this new addiction; it also became popular among ordinary people.

Tobacco was initially called *tamaku* by Bengalis. Then in the 19th century, which was the age of the Sankritisation of the Bengali language, *tamaku* gave rise to the pseudo-Sanskrit word *tamrakut*. This gives an indication of the kind of acceptance that tobacco had gained in society. This is also reflected in literature. The hookah and tobacco are mentioned in Bipradas's *Manasamangal*, but it is unlikely that tobacco had arrived in Bengal when this text was composed. The relevant passage looks like an interpolation. On the other hand, the description of 'fourteen hundred dervishes walking with *albola*s in their hands' by Dwija Shahsthibar in the 18th century gives an idea of the popularity of tobacco among Muslim religious personalities. Dwija Ramananda also sang of the glories of marijuana and tobacco in his songs. But the poets Sheikh Sadi and Afzal Ali criticised tobacco. Ramprasad, Shantidas and Sito Karmakar in their verse narratives *Tamaku Mahatmya*, *Tamakupuran* and *Hookahpuran* described various beneficial and ill effects of tobacco. Apart from the promise of cure for various diseases, the beneficial effects of tobacco that were listed in these poems included a guarantee against death from unnatural causes.

Such were the glories of tobacco. Yet the idea that smoking it in the presence of elders was disrespectful to them took hold in the first half of the 19th century. Madhusudan Dutt's friends were taken aback to see him smoking in his father's company in the early 1840s. By the end of the century, not smoking tobacco began to be regarded by some as a sign of a sound character. One of Tagore's stories describes the hero as being of such salutary moral character that he does not even indulge in an addiction to tobacco. Presumably, since it was initially the nawabs and their amirs and omrahs who smoked tobacco, smoking by their subordinates or other people in the presence of these royals and their high-ranking officials was considered as a violation of etiquette.

Though tobacco was brought by the Portuguese, the hookah was introduced by Muslim rulers. With time, the hookah came to be widely used by elderly people irrespective of whether they were Hindus and Muslims. Social excommunication of families that transgressed rules of ritual purity was signified by a phrase that meant, in a literal sense, that the family would lose access to rural service-providers such as the barber and also the right to enjoy the hookah in the company of others of the community. And this phrase is by no means of recent origin. Cigarettes came much later, around the middle of the 19th century. And this time it was not older people but the young who showed the way in making the cigarette their own. One of the early users of cigarettes was Michael Madhusudan Dutt.

Bengali food has so far retained its own distinctiveness despite the many changes in food, drinks and modes of hospitality over the past 1,000 years. But the way in which science and the campaign for high-yielding strands are changing food crops in both Bengals, and what with all kinds of synthetic drinks invading the market and the world growing smaller with immense leaps in technology, it is hard to say how much longer traditional Bengali foods and drinks will be around. Particularly among the upper and middles classes in the city. The easing of the once rigid caste structure and the greater mobility of families in choosing where to live and work also reduces the local and communal distinctiveness of food. Still, it looks unlikely that rice is going to lose its place as the chief staple.

Unchanging, too, is the Bengali delight in food and the association of food with hospitality. There is no end to celebrations in Bengali social life, and all occasions are associated with food. Various kinds of foods are prepared and eaten during all the different pujas and the Muslim festivities including Eid. Festivities celebrating harvests, weddings and births are all linked with various kinds of food. Hindus, especially Hindu women, have many fasts that follow the movement of the stars, and the breaking of these fasts are again linked to particular kinds of food. Muslims, too, have similar customs. There are specific foods that are expected at the time of breaking the Ramzan fast. Eid comes with its own food expectations. Delicacies such as vermicelli puddings are served on Eid. The two Eids have different foods associated with them. In sum, religious and quasi-religious ceremonies come with a wide array of food arrangements without which the festivities fall flat.

THE DISTINCTIVENESS OF BENGALI CULTURE

In the long discussion on Bengali culture, we have noted that notwithstanding similarities with other cultures in the Indian subcontinent, it has distinctive qualities of its own. The subcontinent is marked by assimilation and cultural exchange among various ethnic and anthropological groups and language groups. This has resulted in a confusing variety of physical features in the Indian people, and also in a bewildering multiplicity of languages. The subcontinent is claimed to have some 800 spoken languages. These languages have had many points of exchange among themselves, and so many of them strongly resemble each other. It is above all the quality of assimilation and syncretism that most strongly marks the cultures that the intermingling of people of different anthropological and linguistic groups has given rise to.

This is also a quality that is eminently manifest in Bengali culture. In the discussion on religion we noted how all religions that came to Bengal from other regions took on a particular character. The Hinduism of Bengal is a Bengali Hindu faith. Vaishnavism of Bengal has its own characteristics and hence is called Goudiya Vaishnavism, meaning a Vaishnava religious movement centred in Gaur. The rituals and customs that mark the Hindu faith in Bengal are quite noticeably different from those prevailing elsewhere in India. Even the gods and goddesses worshipped are sometimes different. The autumnal worship of Durga is for Hindu Bengalis the biggest religious festival, but it is not so elsewhere in India. Buddhism in Bengal is also quite distinct. Between the 7th and the 11th century, philosophers from the region largely changed the character of Buddhism.

It was not easy to either reform or distort a young and written faith like Islam. Yet even Islam took on a Bengali form in Bengal. It was Sufi Islam rather than the Sunni persuasion that was more popular in Bengal in the first few centuries after the arrival of Muslims. Moreover, there even took place a process of assimilation between the Sufi faith and the local non-dualism (*advaita vedanta*). There was, so to speak, no hard-line or purist zeal in this version of Islam, as is evident in the writings of many people including Syed Sultan. The devotional content of this faith outweighed the stress on correct observance of rituals. It was perhaps Bengal's situation as a frontier province that made it possible for its Muslims to be recognised as such even though they more or less ignored the Islamic regulations of the Arab world. Indeed, followers of the kind of Islam that prevailed in village after village in Bengal even at the dawn of the 20th century are best described as having been Muslims only in name. Thus, for instance, though music, particularly instrumental music, is forbidden in Islam, Bengali Muslims in the countryside lovingly nurtured their folk musical traditions.

The emergence of various cult communities that we observe in Bengal – Sahajiya, Nathyogi, Baul, Kartabhaja, Sahebdhani, Murshidi, Maijbhandari, etc. – must also be attributed to this quality of assimilation in Bengal's religious life. Satya Pir alias Satyanarayan; Banadurga alias Banabibi; Dakshin Ray a.k.a. Gazi Pir—all these divinities with blurred communal identities emerged from the soft soil of Bengal's syncretism. An 18th-century poet produced by this soil was thus able to think of a divinity that was half Krishna and half Muhammad. The Bengali folk poet had noticed that milk was always white, so what if there were cows of different colours.

Bengal's geographical situation, sufficiently removed from northern and central India, has also given a certain distinctiveness to its culture. Bengal was more than a thousand miles away from the areas in which the first Aryans made their settlements. Bengal's many rivers and dense forests also made it inaccessible and remote. So the Brahmanical, Buddhist and Jain faiths had to traverse a considerable distance in order to reach Bengal. And for the Muslims who came from Central Asia, Bengal, when compared with north and central India, was located right at the outer edge. That was the reason for their late arrival in Bengal. That was also why they did not look further east.

Bengal was far removed from the centre of political power in India, Delhi. This was why the rulers of Bengal were able to repeatedly defy the authority of Delhi. This distance from the centre was partly responsible for the frontier quality of the culture that developed in Bengal, distinct from the culture of the mainland. It is a more flexible culture, bound by fewer rigidities. It was not only religion, therefore, but also architecture, art and music that could not retain the purity of the forms that existed in mainland India. We noted in the chapter 'Architecture, Art and Craft' how the architecture of Bengal differed from that of Delhi. Local, non-Aryan cultures have impacted it.

Bengal is a land of rivers, lakes and canals. In consequence, communication between the various areas of Bengal was never quite easy from ancient times. The various regions of Rarh, Gaur, North Bengal, South Bengal, East Bengal, South-East Bengal, North-East Bengal were each like a country on its own, the language of each region quite distinct from the languages spoken in the others. Other differences developed in various areas of everyday life, including food and cuisine. Regional particularities can also be noticed in religious matters. For instance, Vaishnavism and Brahmanism did not prosper in East Bengal as much as they did in Rarh, Gaur and Barendra regions. The Baul faith flourished in middle Bengal. It was in Gaur that the Muslims began their rule, but it was East Bengal that eventually developed as a Muslim-majority area. Dharma Thakur is a Rarh divinity, and not of East or North Bengal. Badar Pir belongs to East Bengal. The culture of river-washed East Bengal is again somewhat different from the culture of the dry terrain of Rarh.

Notwithstanding all the regional differences, what has come to be recognised as Bengali culture is defined by language. What binds Bengalis together despite all the fragmentations is their language. Take away this linguistic identity, and you take away the defining characteristic of this culture.

Another notable feature of Bengali culture is that it is rooted in agriculture and in the countryside. Now, in the early 21st century, about 30 per cent of the population in the two Bengals lives in cities. Still, the roots of this ethno-linguistic group are rural, as Bengali literature and music clearly reflect. This is true of even modern literature, especially in drama. The city-dwelling novelist and playwright keep turning their gaze back at the village. More stories and plays have been written in recent times about life in villages than about life in the city. The same may be said about poetry. Folk music continues to be more popular than urban music, and city-dwelling poets keep looking to rural landscapes for inspiration.

Despite the many similarities that Bengalis share with the people living in other regions of India, there are some popular notions about the Bengali character and behaviour. Bengalis are generally thought to be weak, polite and soft-natured. The oldest written comments on Bengalis can be found in the works of Vatsayan, the Chinese traveller Hiuen Tsang and Kalidasa. Bengalis had of course not yet made their appearance as a distinct ethno-linguistic group when these writers wrote their comments. It was the people living in what we now call Bengal that they commented on. It is not clear whether they were commenting on the Aryans who came to Bengal from the north and west or on the indigenous inhabitants of the land. Their comments are in part prompted by experience, and in part by legend. Such generalised comments about an entire people do not really mean much. Over the last 1,500 years, many Indian and foreign writers have in various ways evaluated the Bengali character and the defining Bengali qualities—some of these are partly true, some are exaggerated. May be we can look at some of the negative comments to begin with.

The well known 19th century English official and writer Thomas Babington Macaulay remarked that Bengalis were lazy and baulked at the prospect of physical labour. Among Indian writers, Bankimchandra Chattopadhyay criticised what he saw as a reluctance to work and empty talk. Tagore, too, was not sparing in his ridicule of these qualities. His image of the tame, timid, well-mannered, idle Bengali attached to the comforts of home in the poem *Duranto Asha* written in the late 1880s was echoed by Swami Vivekananda some 12 years later. According to the Swami, Bengalis were work-shy, lacked enterprise, and were intolerant of their successful countrymen. All they wanted to do was to somehow keep body and soul together and live for the moment. This may appear somewhat rude, yet many Bengalis do display an extraordinary willingness to accept the circumstances of their lives. Bengalis, said Vivekananda, were shiftless and resembled the proverbial frog in the well. The comment is presumably not meant for the peasants and labourers who work their backs off for two square meals a day. But it does largely apply to a vast section of the lower middle classes. The Bengali distaste for hard work and enterprise also drew comments in *Somprakash Patrika* in 1885: 'Bengalis will starve to death at home and yet refuse to go out and look for food.'

Until recently, in fact, Bengalis had little interest in venturing out to seek their fortune in strange new lands. They had little interest, too, in trade or industry, though there were some notable exceptions in the early 19th century. Men like Ramdulal Dey and Motilal Sheel chose to build up their own businesses instead of seeking employment with the East India Company. Dwarakanath Tagore trod on the completely unfamiliar terrain of industrial entrepreneurship. He also tried his hand at banking, though with only limited success.

But these instances of Bengali enterprise were so exceptional that towards the fag end of the 19th century Tagore appealed to 'Banga Mata' (Mother Bengal) to push her sons out of their homes. The scientist Prafulla Chandra Ray in his autobiography written in the early 20th century sharply criticised the lack of enterprise among Bengalis. He wrote that people coming in from other regions to Bengal made their fortunes by engaging in business but Bengalis were happy to be exploited by these fortune-seekers. He established the Bengal Chemicals company to provide a hands-on example of business enterprise.

Prafulla Chandra Ray

The Bengalis of East Bengal also silently bore with the exploitation of Bihari businessmen in the years after Partition. But the Bengalis of independent Bangladesh seem to be changing. Many of them have become traders and industrialists. With little or no leeway for foreign traders or industrialists in a sovereign state, the Bengalis of Bangladesh had no option but to meet the demands of trade and industry with their own limited experience and insufficient capital.

Despite making headway in trade and industry, however, Bengalis continue to be keen on buying land if they come into money. Prafulla Chandra Ray had noticed this habit a century ago and condemned it in strong language. It was probably the Permanent Settlement that gave rise to this mindset. In any case, land is still considered by most people, rich and poor, to be the safest and most valuable investment. The increasing landlessness and soaring real estate prices have made people more attached to land.

In the Middle Ages Bengalis engaged in foreign trade and were skilled in building ships, even though it is not known what proportion of the Bengali population was engaged in foreign trade. But this tradition of travelling overseas came to an end before the start of colonial rule. Beginning in the 16th-17th centuries, first the Portuguese and then the British, French and Danish companies seized control of foreign trade and edged Bengalis out. Portuguese pirates also emerged as a major obstacle in the way of trade by sea routes. In this environment, prejudices against crossing the dark waters became entrenched in society. Transgressions of the taboo invited social ostracism right until the end of the 19th century. A write-up in *Somprakash Patrika* in 1881 regretfully observed that people who had travelled to Europe held their own society in contempt while society, in turn, did not accept them back until they performed expiatory rites of ritual purification.

Now, in the early 21st century, the old attitudes to foreign travel have been turned on their head. Whereas earlier exile was equated with death, now not only are Bengalis ready to try their luck abroad, but doing so has turned into a major object of aspiration. This is partly fuelled by population pressures, unemployment and increasing levels of poverty. Bengalis now have no qualms about engaging in menial jobs in foreign lands in order to earn money and are actually willing to adopt every means, honest or otherwise, to be able to do so. Far from facing social ostracism, people who have travelled abroad are now admired and envied. Grooms settled abroad are highly sought after, showing the extent to which social attitudes have changed. At present about 10 million Bangladeshis live and work abroad; and the Bengali diaspora is ever expanding.

The work-shy nature of Bengalis is in keeping with their easy-going lifestyles. Many centuries ago Ibn Batuta had compared Bengal to a granary. It was perhaps the abundance of produce that kept Bengalis from developing into a hard-working people. They do not generally make any extra effort if they are able to go on leading the life that they are used to. We noted how Tagore ridiculed the habit in a poem. Fifteen years earlier, an article in *Somprakash Patrika* had said much the same thing: 'Bengalis are not inclined to engage in trade, there is no momentum in their life struggle, they have no stomach for anything that requires hard work, they like their soft beds and their sleep-inducing food, and so it is self-indulgence that they are in love with.'

To give an example, the post-lunch nap complements this indolence and work-shyness. The afternoon siesta is a daily affair for Bengalis who do not need to work in the afternoons for a living. The warm climate of Bengal and the heavy midday meal of rice are perhaps responsible for this habit. However, this habit is now quickly changing as both men and women have to work for a living. It is only those who do not have to go out to work who can afford the luxury of the afternoon siesta.

There is much debate over the etymological meaning of the Bengali word 'adda'. It means a lively conversation between friends. Whatever may be the source of the word, adda is now one of the chief ways in which modern Bengalis spend their leisure and largely defines the Bengali character. In the mid 19th century *Alaler Gharer Dulal* (1854-58), the word adda signified a place of residence. The meaning of the word is slightly different in *Hutom Pyanchar Naksha* (1861-63). A babu is said to spend his nights at his own home but has his adda at the Sens'; that is, he spends time with friends at the Sens'. So adda no longer means place of residence, it means friendly conversation between like-minded people. In 1888, Tagore seemed to criticise this Bengali habit of engaging in unending discussions on everything under the sun. Half a century later, Buddhadeb Basu was not able to take such a high moral ground on adda. On the contrary, he himself was part of long sessions of adda and spoke highly of them.

Adda was indeed one of the principal platforms for the educated, urban middle class that emerged in the mid 19th century to air its views and fill its hours of leisure. For the first three decades of this century, one's inner circle consisted of relatives and family. From the middle of the century, however, we can see many notable examples of relationships forming on the basis of friendship. A friend was one with whom joys and sorrows could be shared, and friendship a meeting of minds. Adda was where friends could meet and exchange ideas. Everything could be discussed in the adda, from spiritualism to the deliverance of the nation and even what one's neighbours were up to. In praising adda, Buddhadeb Basu said that it thrived in Bengal and not so much elsewhere in India because of Bengal's mild climate and easy-going lifestyle.

There was a link between adda and the emergence of the urban educated middle class. Members of this class often lived away from their families, wherever their jobs took them. In the absence of family, it was colleagues and neighbours with whom they began to form close relationships. The men usually did not do housework, which was done by women and also in part by domestic servants. Moreover, the women were not educated and so unsuitable for refined conversation. In this situation it became customary for the men to meet up with friends in the evening in search of stimulating conversation, and it is this that in time became known as 'adda'. However, in spite of its popularity, adda, too, is becoming a luxury these days when everybody is busy earning money, whether through honest means or otherwise.

The adda, however, sometimes had a negative connotation. *Hutom Pyanchar Naksha* talks about an adda of opium addicts. The 1930-published *Bangiyo Shabdokosh* ('Bengali dictionary') gives one of the meanings of the word as a meeting of scoundrels. The more recently published *Samsad Bangala Abhidhan* said the use of the word adda was negative. No matter how enjoyable an adda might be, it was, according to the compilers of the dictionary, a waste of time.

The other traits for which Tagore reproved Bengalis were sycophancy and empty arrogance and boastfulness. Bengalis, the poet said, might proudly recall their valiant Aryan ancestry in the comfort of their own homes, but they were fawning and servile in all negotiations with their superiors and happy to collect the crumbs and morsels contemptuously thrown to them. The comment may be exaggerated, but not entirely untrue. Vivekananda made much the same point when he described Bengalis as licking the feet of the powerful and acting like the personification of death itself for the weak. But what was it that produced this mentality of abject subservience in Bengalis?

Even before the time that we have claimed as truly marking the beginning of the history of the Bengali people, Bengalis, that is, people living in what we know as Bengal, were under the Sena rulers who had come from the Deccan. These rulers were zealous Hindus, but most of their subjects were Budhhists. In this situation, those who worked for the royal administration had no option but to make adjustments and compromise in order to make their way in life. Next came the Muslim rulers. They were very different from the locals not only in their religion but also in their language. The divide, indeed, was deep in customs and rituals, food, clothes and many other things that separated two distinct ways of life. Yet, thousands of local people had to learn the language used by the new rulers and accept jobs under them. The zamindars and their managers in the villages were reduced versions of the sultans and the kings, and they used brute force to assert their authority over their tenants. 'Human rights' was an unknown concept.

Muslim rule was replaced by British colonial rule, which lasted for some 200 years. The British colonialists brought European ways of thought. The ideals of rationalism and liberalism had taken root in Europe before the British arrived in India. The American War of Independence and the French Revolution took place within three decades of the establishment of East India Company's rule in Bengal. Lord Cornwallis, who was a general serving England during the American War of Independence, came to India as Governor General. He did not just carry his administrative experience to his new posting, he brought ideas that were perhaps far more liberal than those of Lord Clive or Hastings. That apart, the colonial administration established courts and introduced secular legislation. The rule of law was gradually established during the colonial era. It was in this environment of respect for law that an indigent man like James Hicky had the stomach to criticise the Governor General and the Chief Justice in his capacity as the proprietor of a newspaper. It was not even as if his criticisms were always just or decent. Yet he got away with just a prison term. Any opposition to the previous Mughal rulers or the sultans before them would have cost him his head.

The Mughal ideal of equating the ruler of Delhi with the Almighty crumbled under British colonial rule, and with it also crumbled the ideal of might as right. This environment might have weakened the master-servant relationship between the British and Bengalis. But the colonial mindset of the British came in the way. Nor did the Bengalis' long history of subservience and compromise help to bring about any change in this relationship. Though a liberal ideal started taking hold among educated Bengalis after the institutionalisation of education in the 19th century, we have seen how those who came in contact with the sahibs expressed deference and loyalty by claiming the sahibs were like parents to them, and also how they compromised on their own religious customs in order to work in offices run by the British. There were few as upright as Ram Mohan Roy, Dakshinaranjan Mukhopadhyay, Debendranath Tagore, Ishwarchandra Vidyasagar or Harish Chandra Mukhopadhyay. There emerged a certain class of government employees who obsequiously wrung their hands before their English masters and behaved like tyrants with their own weaker compatriots. Thus the tradition of fawning subservience thrived in this new era, too, and became widespread among the salaried sections. The rest of society more or less followed suit.

The tradition did not spare Bengal's villages, though there it travelled by a different route. The lords and masters of the countryside were the large and petty landlords and their managers. Under the Permanent Settlement, they turned into centres of power that controlled the destinies of the rural population. The newspapers and magazines of the 19th century carried detailed reports on how these people exploited their tenants. The story can also be gathered from contemporary plays and skits. Though a landlord himself, Tagore drew a fine sketch of the zamindar's relationship with destitute peasants in the poem *Dui Bigha Jomi* ('Half Acre of Land' in William Radice's translation). This indeed was the pattern of power relationships everywhere in society. The way in which people behaved with domestic servants was also described vividly by Tagore in another poem, *Puratan Bhritya* ('The Old Servant'). The denial of human dignity to subordinates and the poor is indeed a centuries-old tradition in Bengali society. This was more or less also how the upper castes treated people lower down in the caste hierarchy.

The bottom heap was therefore forced to adopt an attitude of subservience in order to survive.

But the self-abasing and cringing behaviour of subordinates in the presence of their social or workplace superiors by no means reflected any real deference or regard. The keen awareness of working for someone else fostered a culture of bitter complaining behind the backs of people in power.

Years of working under foreigners may well breed a certain kind of work-shyness, a tendency of getting away without putting in one's best efforts into the task at hand. However, the growth of socialism and the role of trade unions in the 20th century strengthened this mindset. Trade unions became particularly powerful in West Bengal after the Left Front came to power there and in Bangladesh after the country won its independence through a war. The efforts of these trade unions have certainly led to better working conditions and improved rights for workers. Trade unions have also played positive and significant roles in movements for higher wages. Yet trade union activities have had an indirect effect on people working in petty and menial jobs. The positive side of this effect is that such people are now more aware of their rights and have greater confidence in themselves. The negative side is negligence in work and disrespect for one's superiors.

Bengalis display a certain suicidal rage directed at public property instead of protectiveness. There is a saying *sarkari mal, dariya me dal*, meaning 'if it's government property toss it into the sea'. This is the mindset that is at play when people make knife incisions into the foam on train seats. The perpetrator gains nothing from this kind of vandalism, but harm is done to public property. It is hard to say how this mindset emerged. But the anti-partition movement in the first decade of the 20th century may have something to do with it. The movement against colonial rule over the next few decades would have strengthened these attitudes. The violent movement against Pakistan in East Bengal, which culminated in the struggle for independence, entrenched attitudes of hostility to government property in Bangladesh. The Naxalite movement in West Bengal might have played a similar role. Not just public property, many Bengalis also nurture envious feelings about the possessions of others and would not shy away from inflicting harm on the possessions of people whom they have nothing against or even completely unknown people.

Another habit of the mind has been increasingly evident among Bengalis from the second half of the 20th century—disregard for the law. The factors that produced hostility and contempt for public property are also perhaps responsible for this disdain for law. There are also those who are not just indifferent to the law but actually take the law into their own hands.

Enviousness of the good fortune of others is quite pronounced among Bengalis. A culture of competitiveness has also taken shape in recent times. Unlike in the first half of the 20th century, Bengali society is now marked by intensely materialistic preoccupations with who earns how much, who keeps a fashionable home, who owns a car and how expensive it is and who has relatives living abroad. Honesty, scholarship, literary or musical talents are not quite as important. Money and degree are now more important than acquiring knowledge, and it does not matter if the money has been obtained through dishonest means.

In general we can say that though there has been noticeable material progress in Bengali society, a decline in values can be unmistakably observed in recent times. There was a time when educated and deserving individuals became university vice chancellors. Now the post goes to people best able to play politics. There was a time when teachers and professors were widely respected, and they, too, were inspired by ideals of service to society. The Ramtanu Lahiris, the Vidyasagars and the Shibnath Shastris were of course always rare. Yet innumerable idealistic individuals embraced the profession of teaching in the 19th century and the first few decades of the 20th century. Notwithstanding the greater development of talents at present, it is hard to come by teachers for whom teaching is a calling.

Even half a century ago, the best of students who took up teaching did not do so entirely for the sake of money. Now the most successful students try to land jobs abroad or seek administrative positions. Teaching frequently becomes the last resort of people who are not able to find any other job. Very few choose teaching for its own sake. The literary critic and theologian

Shashi Bhushan Dasgupta spent his vacations at his family home in Barisal. There he worked with villagers to repair roads and bridges and clean out ponds. He also taught every day at the village school. This ideal of social service is now very rare. Those who are engaged in social service get their work funded by government or other agencies. Politician ambitions also fuel social work for some.

Politicians also once served society. Now political activities are driven by ambitions of becoming ministers or legislators or of using political power for material gains. Some leftist politicians however still display commitment to serving society. Yet the ideal of serving the poor and the destitute is not typically a leftist attitude but a humanistic and liberal one. It first manifested itself among educated middle class individuals in the mid 19th century. It is this liberal philosophy of empathy for the poor that inspired Dinabandhu Mitra's *Neeldarpan* and Harish Chandra Mukherjee's writing in favour of the struggle of the peasants resisting the exploitation by indigo planters. The plight of common people, the struggles of tea garden workers and even of sex workers were all written about in those days. Shibnath Shastri and his friends brought out a journal called *Sramajeebi* ('Living on Labour') in the 1870s.

The empathy that Tagore showed for ordinary people in his short stories and poems in the late 19th century was also an expression of this attitude. On the other hand, the increased awareness about the conditions of the working people and greater concern for them after the Bolshevik Revolution early in the 20th century came not from this liberal humanistic world view but from leftist ideology. A comparison of Tagore's *Dui Bugha Jomi* with Nazrul Islam's poem *Kuli-Mazur* makes evident this change in attitude. Tagore's poem expressed sympathy for a destitute man, but his sympathy was not informed by an egalitarian ideal. Nazrul's poem carries traces of that ideal. It is hard to say whether he was initiated into Marxism, or how much. But many young men in the 1920s and 1930s extensively read Marxist literature and turned into committed Marxists. Many of these young men also joined the Communist Party. There were also those who brought their communist leanings to bear on the movement for freedom from colonial rule.

It became quite fashionable in fact to be associated with leftism in the 1930s and the 1940s. To be recognised as 'progressive' in educated circles one must now more or less repose faith in leftist ideology. Even if one has not read the works of Marx, one must know the fundamental principles of Marxist philosophy and thus occupy a left-of-centre political position. This ideological position can be widely observed among writers, professors and journalists, that is, people who are known as intellectuals. Such people are to a large extent armchair leftists. They take leftist positions in their writings, while talking at various meetings and forums, and in drawing room conversations, but not so much in inheriting, acquiring or enjoying the fruits of private property. In their beliefs and in their personal lives, they are not truly leftist. This is why leftist leaders sometimes worship at temples before joining a movement or in Bangladesh socialist leaders come up with slogans such as 'dharma, karma, *samajtantra*' (religion, work, socialism).

The long Bengali tradition of emotional dependence on religious beliefs, and the stress on devotion (bhakti) rather than knowledge in religious life, may be responsible for this effort to find a meeting ground between Marxism and religion. Belief in supernatural powers and in all kinds of superstitions have struck deep root over many centuries. The uncertainty of life in ancient and medieval times also entrenched these beliefs. The depth and intensity of these beliefs can be gauged from the sheer range of gods and goddesses that were traditionally worshipped in Bengal—there were divinities associated with snakes, crocodiles, tigers, rivers and also poxes and other diseases. Among Muslims, too, there was no dearth of ritualistic cleansing of spirits or of worship of pirs and *nabi*s. Nevertheless, it is hard to say how loyal ordinary village people were to institutional religion or how well-versed they were in its precepts. The Sahajiya, Nath Jogi, Baul and Kartabhaja sects did not worship any gods or goddesses. There was deep devotion and loyalty in the way the Shaktas related to their gurus, Vaishnavas to their *gonsai*s and Muslims to their pirs. Many people were prepared to give up or do anything to please these religious leaders. *Hutom Pyanchar Naksha* mentions how women were offered to *gonsai*s as gestures of loyalty. This account is probably exaggerated. But there is no doubt that ordinary Hindus looked up to Brahmin priests and Muslims to pirs.

In the 19th century, loyalty to institutional religion deepened among many people, both Hindus and Muslims. This interest in formal religion further intensified in the 20th century under the influence of nationalism. It must be said, however, that the increased enthusiasm about institutional religion is not matched by any such interest in humanism. Bengalis have in fact lost interest in the kind of humanism that believes in the universal in human experience and is therefore an assimilative and unifying force.

The section of society that in early 19th century Calcutta grew rich through trade showed a tendency to show off their wealth through lavish celebrations of religious festivals. Rich households sometimes offered hundreds of beasts in ritual sacrifice. Such extravagance was motivated more by a desire to impress fellow humans than to placate the goddess. It is hard to now even imagine the kind of money that rich men at that time spent on pujas and funeral ceremonies. Some 150 years down the line, many rich people still engage in similarly lavish religious observances to display their wealth. Though they are keen to seek publicity by making donations in the name of religion, they are not quite as enthusiastic about helping the cause of public service. There is no dearth of people who earn in billions in Bangladesh following its emergence as a free nation. Some of these people have built mosques and set up madrasas, but none of them thought of establishing a hospital. Unlike the zamindars of old, no one even thought of laying a road or constructing a bridge. Prasanna Kumar Tagore and hundreds of others had donated lakhs of rupees to Calcutta University. No one comes forward anymore to donate money for education.

Bengalis in recent times do not seem to have registered much progress in their moral lives. The ideals of honesty, truthfulness and public service that many individuals were able to set in the 19th century are now practically absent. It will be difficult now to find someone who, like Debendranath Tagore, would be willing to accept a late father's financial liabilities without any written proof of debts. On the contrary, there are enough instances everywhere of people making money through dishonest means. Bribes and supplementary incomes were common enough in the 19th century, but the scale of these things is now much higher.

Whatever might have been the origin of caste divisions, these are closely associated with religion and rules of commensality, and also to hereditary occupations. Although not as rigid as in South India or in Bihar, caste divisions were from ancient times universally accepted in Bengali society. There are indications of this even in the *Charyapada* poems, which were written about a thousand years ago. Brahmins were at the top of the caste hierarchy, irrespective of social position or financial situation. In this caste-divided society, questions such as whom one could share a meal with, whom one could marry or even so much as touch were all questions that were determined at the moment of birth. But in the 19th century, caste divisions began to weaken. The old rigidities of commensality and social mingling have now slackened at all levels. The gap, in fact, has narrowed even between Hindus and Muslims. In marriages, however, Hindus still largely abide by caste rules. Family elders are not yet able to happily accept matrimonial alliances with families lower down the caste order.

Hindus and Muslims in Bengal have been living side by side for hundreds of years. But society still does not look kindly upon marriages between Hindus and Muslims. Though both communities speak in Bengali, not all words are used by everyone. *Jal* and *pani* are both words of Sanskrit origin. And yet Muslims use only *pani* and never *jal*, and Hindus use only *jal* and never *pani*. This kind of distinction does not exist in northern India, but in Bengal it lives on, or it might have been created in modern times. The words signifying family relationships are also different for the two communities. Though many Muslims now choose so-called 'Hindu' names for their offspring, Bengali Hindus never opt for Arabic or Farsi names, no matter how beautiful they may be in meaning and sound. Clearly, though caste divisions may have eroded, communal identities are still intact.

In the 1830s Thomas Babington Macaulay denounced Bengalis as being 'feeble' and 'effeminate'. His observation reflects his own colonial prejudices more than anything else. Otherwise, he might have thought of the Sanyasi movement and the Chuar revolt and also of the revolt by Santhals before making such a comment. It is hard to detect realism in Titu Mir's strategy, but his plan of taking on the colonial forces from a bamboo fortress did show his nerve and daring. And this uprising took place when Macaulay was in Calcutta. Seven decades after Macaulay wrote his remarks on 'sedentary' and 'languid' Bengalis, scores of Bengalis who joined the terrorist movement for freedom and the communists proved themselves capable of dauntlessness and extreme self-sacrifice. There may certainly be controversy over the way chosen by Subhas Chandra Bose, but not over his patriotism, courage and heroism. The ideal of heroism, fortitude and self-sacrifice that thousands of liberation soldiers set during Bangladesh's war for freedom in 1971 is extraordinary by any yardstick. Hundreds of thousands of people died during the war. Few nations in the world have earned freedom at such cost.

It is sometimes claimed that during British colonial rule, and later under Pakistani colonial rule in East Bengal, Bengalis were too faint-hearted to join the armed forces. That this was baseless has been amply proved in the past half century by Bengalis of both West Bengal and Bangladesh. The Indian Army had enough recruits from West Bengal after the 1947 Partition, and at least one of them became the army chief. Across the border, not many people from East Pakistan, it is true, joined the Pakistan Army, but those who did proved their credentials despite the discrimination that they faced. The situation changed further after Bangladesh became a free nation. Hundreds of thousands have joined the army. Nor have women fallen behind.

Bengalis are also said to be a sentimental people. Many commentators ranging from Macaulay to the linguist Suniti Kumar Chattopadhyay, and more recently Nirad C. Chaudhuri, have said Bengalis are given to excessive emotions. Some of them saw this as a blameworthy trait, some meant it as a compliment. In favour of this view, it is pointed out that there are many poets among Bengalis, both successful and those not-so-successful, but not enough scientists. Nevertheless, in intellectual achievements in general, Bengalis have not lagged behind others in the subcontinent. Many well known philosophers were born in ancient Bengal. Particularly in the development of Buddhist philosophy, many of them played leading roles. During his visit to Bengal in the 7th century, Hiuen Tsang was much impressed by the scholarship of Shilabhadra and became his disciple. This scholar born in East Bengal headed the greatest institution of learning in ancient India, Nalanda. Another scholar from Bengal obtained the headship of Nalanda in the early 8th century. He was Shanta Rakshit and was born in Dhaka. He wrote several valuable books of philosophy and Mahayana Buddhism. The ruler of Tibet founded a monastery named after him in the capital Lhasa.

The famous scholar Atish Dipankar of the 10th-11th centuries is considered as one of the chief exponents of Buddhism. Born in Bikrampur of Dhaka district, he wrote a number of books on Buddhist philosophy in several languages including Sanskrit. He travelled to Tibet and even to China to preach the Buddhist faith. In Tibet he was seen as an incarnation of the Buddha. In the 11th century Jnanashrimitra wrote quite a few books on Buddhist law. Many leading gurus of Mahayana Buddhism were residents of Bengal. This was perhaps why there were many more Buddhist viharas in ancient Bengal than in other regions of India.

Buddha

Many Hindu scriptural scholars and philosophers were also born in ancient Bengal. Scholars such as Bhabadev Bhatta, Jeemutvahan, Aniruddha, Ballalsen and Halayudh produced many important religious texts and gave interpretations in different branches of Hindu philosophy. During the time of the Sena rulers, Bengalis also made extraordinary contributions to Sanskrit literature. Poets such as Sriharsha, Sharan, Dhoyi, Umapati Dhar and Acharya Gobardhan produced many well known works. Jaydev's *Gita Govinda*, in particular, won hearts all over India.

A few centuries later, Chaitanyadev added a fresh chapter to the history of Hinduism. The faith he preached was in large measure his own interpretation of what the Vaishnava faith had been before. His philosophy was novel, and finely nuanced. This religious philosophy made its mark over a large area in the subcontinent. Chaitanyadev himself did not live long. After his death his *goswamis* gave even more subtle interpretations of his teachings. In a different branch of Hinduism, another Bengali, Krishnananda Agambagish, gave a new interpretation of the Shakta faith. The philosophies of both the Mahayana branch of Buddhism and Hinduism were in fact immensely enriched by contributions by Bengali scholars. The poet Krittibas turned Ram and other mythological characters into Bengalis in his version of the *Ramayana* story. Sahajiya cults such as that of the Bauls are exclusively Bengali.

Bengalis have displayed their intellectual edge in modern times, too. For the past two centuries therefore the rest of the subcontinent has looked upon the educational advances of Bengalis with respect and admiration. This is an image that developed in the 19th century when Bengal was taking rapid strides in Western education. The rest of the subcontinent has made immense progress in education, science and technology. Yet Bengalis are still associated with intellectual pursuits.

Not much is known about the contribution of Bengalis to music in medieval times. But they did create at least one unique school of music—the tradition of kirtan, devotional songs sung by Goudiya Vaishnavas. In the modern age, Bengalis were the first to create a new kind of music influenced by Western vocal and instrumental traditions. In theatre and drama, too, Bengalis have often played leading roles. In the world of thoughts and ideas, Bengalis have made their greatest contribution through literature. We have discussed earlier how innumerable Bengali poets enriched Bengali literature in the Middle Ages. The literary tradition saw an unprecedented flowering in the colonial era and Bengali writers were the first in the subcontinent to create a modern literary prose tradition. Tagore put Bengali firmly in the international literary map, and the Nobel prize in 1913 (no other Indian writer received it in the over 100 years that have elapsed since) served to create an international awareness of the literature produced by the Bengali-speaking people. In this age of communal disharmony and heightened cultural and religious rigidities, we will also do well to remember how Tagore's work inspired several generations of Hindu and Muslim Bengalis to draw closer on the basis of their shared linguistic identity. The ideal of a liberal, secular and humanist universalism that formed the underpinning of Tagore's work and his world view continues to inspire progressive Bengalis today.

Karnaphuli river in full expanse; Chittagong district, Bangladesh
Photo courtesy: Faisal Akram (commoms.wikimedia.org)

AFTERWORD AND ACKNOWLEDGEMENTS

A few years ago, I produced a serialised programme on Bengali culture for the Bengali Service of BBC Radio. While working on the project, I realised that there was no reliable, informative book on the various aspects of Bengali culture. I felt that such a book was needed. While reading up on the history of Bengal, I also noticed that most historians had written a partisan as well as partial history of Bengal. Bengali society is endlessly divided, the two major stakeholders being Hindus and Muslims. Historians have written either histories of Bengali Hindus or histories of Bengali Muslims, not comprehensive works covering the shared destiny of the entire Bengali-speaking people. Religious identities are often too forceful for it to be possible to write objective accounts. Even the handful of writers who are markedly above communal allegiances have ended up writing rather biased histories of the Bengali-speaking people as they do not know enough of the 'other' community. Consequently, the vision continues to remain fragmented in works of history.

I do not identify myself with any particular race, caste, community or country. I like to think of myself as a human being—an international person. In this book I have tried to write a history of Bengalis from a perspective beyond all boundaries and barriers. Not a political history but a cultural one. In writing about the varied and various aspects of the culture of the Bengali-speaking people, I have sought out the assimilative and syncretic aspects of that culture and those special characteristics that mark out the people of the Bengali-speaking world as Bengalis. How successful I have been in this endeavour—that is for my readers to judge.

My greatest debt of gratitude in writing this book is to Professor Tapan Raychaudhuri. Although he generously supplied me with information for the book, I could not always use it in a way that he would like. The interpretation of the information he shared with me is my own. I have profited, too, from my discussions with Professors Shibnarayan Ray, Rabindra Kumar Dasgupta, Amlan Datta, Asim Roy and Anisuzzaman. Hassan Azizul Haque, Sudipta Kabiraj, Anis Ahmed, Amalendu Biswas, Saifuddin Chowdhury and M.A. Aziz have helped me with valuable comments after reading, or listening to, excerpts from the book. Purabi

Bose, Shafi Ahmed and Swarochish Sarkar, however, read the entire book with great patience and made some extremely insightful observations. No expression of thankfulness would suffice to clear my debt of gratitude to them.

I have attended seminars in Dhaka, Kolkata, Rajshahi and Jahangirnagar with discussions on some themes in the book. The discussions at these seminars have given greater clarity to my thoughts.

The first five chapters of this book were serialised in the newspaper *Prothom Alo* by Sajjad Sharif. Sharif published three other chapters in an Eid issue of *Prothom Alo*. My heartfelt thanks to him. I am grateful, too, to Zafar Ahmed. Publication in a newspaper opened up my book to a wide readership and many people were able to read it. Many of them commented on the book in emails sent to me. Of the few hundred emails that I received, the three that moved me most were much the same in what they said – their senders do not much enjoy reading history but they enjoyed reading my book. Many readers sent their comments to *Prothom Alo*. I am grateful to all of them.

It was Dr Syed Mahmud Ali of the Bengali Section of BBC World Service who first suggested writing such a book. Alamgir Rahman published the book with great interest and enthusiasm. My heartfelt thanks to both of them.

It would be unfair not to include my wife, Eliza, in this note of thanks. Without her tireless nursing and care during my long illness, this book would not progress beyond the stage of planning.

Ghulam Murshid
London, December 2005

Acknowledgement for the English Edition

This book was very well received in both Bengals by critics and readers alike, and has been reprinted many times. However, it has been limited to the Bengali readership only. It was not even accessible to the large communities of expatriate Bengalis, not to speak of non-Bengali readers. I am sincerely grateful to Sarbari Sinha of *Frontline* magazine for, first, offering to translate and, then, translating this not too short book into English. I am also grateful to Niyogi Books for bringing out the English edition.

Ghulam Murshid
London, January 2017

SELECTED BIBLIOGRAPHY

(The list of books below is for readers who wish to dig deeper into Bengali cultural history. It is only a selected list. Many of the books I have used are not on this list. In particular, I have not included biographies and autobiographies in the list, though I have referred to them multiple times in the book. I have made brief comments on some of the books in the list, in the hope that this will help readers to choose the books they want to read. Some of the books are so well known that I felt it would be redundant to provide publishing details for them.)

A

A. Chakrabarty, *Muslim Identity and Community Consciousness.* Calcutta: Minerva Associates, 1993.

A. Karim. *Social History of the Muslims of Bengal.* Dhaka: Asiatic Society, 1959.

A. Roy. *The Islamic Syncretistic Tradition in Bengal.* Princeton: Princeton University Press, 1983 (a very important book).

A.F.S. Ahmed. *Social Change and Social Ideas in Bengal.* Leiden: E.J. Brill, 1965 (a valuable book).

A.F.S. Ahmed and B.M. Chowdhury ed. *Bangladesh National Culture and Heritage.* Dhaka: Independent University, 2004.

A.H. Dani. *Muslim Architecture in Bengal.* Dhaka: Asiatic Society, 1961 (a very important book).

A.K. Mukhopadhyay. *Uday Shankar: Twentieth Century's Nataraja.* New Delhi: Rupa & Co., 2004.

A.K.M. Zakaria. *Bangladesher Pracheen Keerti* [Ancient Feats of Bangladesh]. Volumes 1-2. Dhaka: Bangladesh Shishu Academy, 1987.

A.R. Mallik. *British Policy and the Muslims in Bengal.* Dhaka: Bangla Academy, 1977.

Abanindranath Tagore. *Banglar Broto* [Rituals in Bengal]. Kolkata: Visva Bharati Gronthalaya, 1960.

Abul Momen. *Bangla O Bangalir Katha* [The Story of Bengal and Bengalis]. Third reprint. Dhaka: Sahityaprokash, 2000. (A book written from a secular point of view, very useful for general readers.)

Ahmed Sharif. *Banglabhasha-Samskar Andolan* [The Bengali Language Reform Movement]. Dhaka: Bangladesh Bhasha Samiti, 1986.

___, *Modhyojuger Sahitye Samaj O Sanskritir Roop* [The Contours of Society and Culture in the Middle Ages]. Dhaka: Somoy Prokashon, 2000. (The writer has not ascertained the facts in many cases.)

___, *Sahitya O Sanskriti Chinta* [Literature and Cultural Thinking]. Dhaka: Agami Prokashoni, 2001.

Akhileshwar Bhattacharjee. *Moder Garob Moder Asha* [Our Pride, Our Hope]. Kolkata: Ananda Publishers, 1995. (An easy-to-read and racy discussion on the Bengali language.)

Amalesh Tripathy. *Italir Renaissance, Banglar Samskriti* [The Italian Renaissance & The Culture of Bengal]. 2nd ed. Kolkata: Ananda Publishers, 1996.

Anil Tapadar. *Kolkatar Chhoto Lucknow.* Kolkata: Subarnarekha, 2002.

Aniruddha Roy and Ratnabali Chattopadhyay ed. *Modhyojuge Banglar Samaj O Sanskriti* [Society and Culture of the Medieval Bengal]. Kolkata: K.P. Bagchi, 1992. (A valuable collection of essays.)

Anisuzzaman. *Atharo Shatoker Bangla Godyo* [Bengali Prose in the Eighteenth Century]. Dhaka: Chittagong Vishvavidyalaya Bangla Samiti, 1982.
___ed. *Muslim Banglar Samayik Patra* [Periodicals of Muslim Bengal]. Dhaka: Bangla Academy, 1969. (A selection from Muslim-run magazines.)
___*Muslim Manas O Bangla Sahitya* [The Muslim Mind and Bengali Literature]. Dhaka: Lekhak Sangha, 1964.
___*Swarooper Sandhane* [In Search of Identity]. Dhaka: Jatiyo Sahitya Prokashoni, 1976. (A slim but invaluable book.)

Annadashankar Roy. *Rabindranath, Pramatha Choudhary O Sabujpatra* [Tagore, Pramatha Chaudhary and Sabujpatra]. Kolkata: Paschimbanga Bangla Akademi, 1999.

Annadashankar Roy. *Samskritir Biborton.* 2nd ed. [The Evolution of Culture]. Kolkata: Banishilpa, 1989.

Apareshchandra Mukhopadhyay. *Rangalaye Trish Batsar* [Thirty Years in Theatre]. First published in 1933. Kolkata: Papyrus, 1991.

Arun Nag. *Chitrito Padme.* Kolkata: Subarnarekha, 1999.
___ed. *Sateek Hutom Pyanchar Naksha* [Sketches by Hutom the Owl, Annotated]. 2nd ed. Kolkata: Subarnarekha, 1997. (An extraordinary representation of 19th-century Bengali society, enriched by Arun Nag's annotations.)

Ashok Bhattacharjee. *Banglar Chitrakala* [Art in Bengal]. Reprint. Kolkata: Paschimbanga Bangla Akademi, 2002.
___ed. *Paschimbanger Patachitra* [Scroll painting in West Bengal]. Kolkata: Loksamskriti O Adisamskriti Kendra, 2001.

B

Badruddin Umar. *Bangla Bhasha Andolan O Tatkaleen Rajneeti* [The Bengali Language Movement and Contemporary Politics]. Vols. 1-3. (The best book on the language movement.)

Bankimchandra Chattopadhyay, *Rachonaboli* [Collected Works of Bankimchandra Chatterjee] Vols 1-2. Kolkata: Sahitya Samsad.

Bhabani Prasad Chattopadhyay. *Deshbibhag: Paschat O Nepathyo Kahini* [Partition: The Backstage Story]. Kolkata: Ananda Publishers, 1993.

Bhabatosh Datta. *Bangalir Manob Dharma* [The Humanity of Bengalis]. Kolkata: Mitra & Ghosh, 1999. (The writer uses 'Bangali' to mean only Bengali Hindus.)
___ed. *Ishwarchandra Gupto Rochito Kobijeeboni* [The Poet's Life Authored by Ishwarchandra Gupta]. Kolkata: Paschimbanga Bangla Akademi, 1998.

Binoy Ghosh. *Banglar Samajik Itihaser Dhara* [The Social History of Bengal]. Kolkata: Pathabhavan, 1968.
___*Paschim Banger Sanskriti* [The Culture of West Bengal]. Vols. 1-4. Kolkata: Prakash Bhavan. (A district-wise survey of the culture of West Bengal.)
___*Samoyikpatre Banglar Samajchitra* [Bengali Society as Portrayed in Periodicals] Vols. 1-6. Kolkata: published by various publishers, 1962-64. (A collection of several important Bengali journals including *Sambad Prabhakar, Tatwabodhini Patrika* and *Somprakash.*)

___*Vidyasagar O Bangali Samaj* [Vidyasagar and Bengali Society]. Kolkata: Orient Longman, 1993. (A valuable book on Vidyasagar and 19th century society and the Bengal Renaissance.)

Bireshwar Bandyopadhyay. *Paschimbanger Loukik Deb-Debi O Lokbiswas* [Folk Deities and Folk Worship in West Bengal]. Kolkata: Loksanskriti O Adibasi Sanskriti Kendra, 2001.

Brajendranath Bandyopadhyay. *Bongiyo Natyoshalar Itihas* [History of the Bengali Theatre]. 7th ed. Kolkata: Bangiyo Sahitya Parishad, 1998.
___*Sambadpatre Sekaler Katha* [The Yesteryear as Seen in Newspapers]. Vols. 1-2. Kolkata: Bangiya Sahitya Parishad. (Collected from the newspapers of the first half of the 19th century. Extremely valuable in the reconstruction of Bengal's history.)

Brindavandas Goswami. *Sri Sri Chaitanyabhagabat* [Biography of Sri Chaitanya]. Ed. by Mahendranath Gupta. Kolkata: Rajendra Library, date not given.

C

Chintaharon Chakraborty. *Banglar Palaparbon* [Rituals of Bengal]. Kolkata: Visva Bharati Granthalaya, 1952. (The writer uses the word 'Bangali' to mean Bengali Hindu.)

Chittaranjan Bandopadhyay ed. *Dui Shatoker Bangla Mudron O Prokashon* [Printing and Publishing of Bengal Over Two Centuries]. Kolkata: Ananda Publishers, 1981. (A valuable collection, recommended in particular for those who wish to read about the development of Bengali printing.)

D

D. Zbavitel. *Bengali Literature.* Wiesbaden: Otto Harrassowitz, 1976. (A short but important book.)

Darshan Choudhury. *Gananatyo Andolan* [People's Theatre Movement]. 2nd ed. Kolkata: Anustup Prakashani, 1994.

David McCutchion. *Late Medieval Temples of Bengal.* Calcutta, 1972. (There is no more informative book than this one on the temples of Bengal. The writer has categorised each and every temple. The book also has many rare pictures. Among the writer's works, the one most enriched by pictures is *Brick Temples of Bengal,* 1983, edited by George Mitchell.)

David Kopf. *British Orientalism and the Bengal Renaissance.* Berkeley: University of California Press, 1968. (A very important book.)
___ *The Shaping of the Modern Indian Mind: History of the Brahmo Samaj.* Princeton: Princeton University Press, 1981. (A valuable book.)

Deb Kumar Bose ed. *Shatobarsher Aloke Sisirkumar* [Sisirkumar in the Perspective of Hundred Years]. Kolkata: Deb Kumar Bose, 1991.

Debajit Bandopadhyay. *Banglar Manchageeti* [Stage Lyrics of Bengal]. Kolkata: Subarnarekha, 1999. (Informative and valuable.)

Debashish Bandopadhyay. *Banedi Kolkatar Ghar-Barhi* [Homes of the Kolkata Elite]. 2nd reprint. Kolkata: Ananda Publishers, 2002. (A valuable book with many pictures.)

Debnarayan Gupta. *Banglar Nat-Nati* [Dancers of Bengal]. Vol. 1. Kolkata: Sahityalok, 1985.

Dhrubajyoti Banerji. *European Calcutta: Images and Recollections of a Bygone Era.* New Delhi: UBS Publishers, 2005.

Dinesh Chandra Sen. *Brihat Banga* [Greater Bengal]. Vols. 1-2. Kolkata: University of Calcutta, 1934. Reprinted by Dey's Publishing, Kolkata. (An extremely valuable book, but some of the scholarship is now outdated.)

E

E.D. Potts. *Baptist Missionaries in Bengal.* (An important book for information on the missionaries of Serampore.)

Enamul Haque. *Islamic Art Heritage in Bangladesh.* Dhaka: Bangladesh National Museum, 1983. (An important book with many rare pictures.)

G

Gautam Bhadra and Partha Chattopadhyay ed. *Nimnabarger Itihas* [Subaltern History]. 2nd ed. Kolkata: Ananda Publishers, 1999.

Ghulam Murshid. *Kalantare Bangla Godyo: Ouponibeshik Amole Bangla Godyer Roopantar* [The Transformation of Bengali Prose in Colonial Times]. Kolkata: Ananda Publishers, 1992. (A recently revised edition of this book, renamed as *Ouponibeshik Amoler Bangla Godyo: Unmesh O Bikash*, published by ABOSAR, Dhaka, is available.)
___. *Rabindrabiswe Purbabanga: Purbabange Rabindranath* [East Bengal in Tagore's World, Tagore in East Bengal]. 2nd ed. Dhaka: Bangla Academy, 1993. (The first part of the book is about Tagore, but the second part deals with the social history of Bengali Muslims. A revised edition, recently published by ABOSAR, Dhaka, is available.)
___. *Rassundari Theke Rokeya: Nari Progotir Eksho Bachhor* [From Rassundari to Rokeya: Hundred Years of Women's Liberation]. 2nd ed. Dhaka: Bangla Academy, 1999.
___, *Samaj Samskar Andolan O Bangla Natok* [The Social Reform Movement and Bengali Theatre]. Dhaka: Bangla Academy, 1984.
___. *Sankocher Bihobholota: Adhunikotar Obhighate Bangaramonir Protikriya.* 2nd ed. Kolkata: Naya Udyog, 2001. (The book was originally written in English with the title *Reluctant Debutante: Response of Bengali Women to Modernization*, Rajshahi: Sahitya Samsad, Rajshahi University, 1983.)

Gopal Haldar. *Gopal Haldarer Shrestha Prabhandha* [The Best Essays of Gopal Haldar]. Kolkata: Nabark, 1985. (Contains quite a few valuable essays on culture. In particular, the essays 'Banglar Culture' [Culture of Bengal] and 'Musalman Bangalir Culture' [Culture of Muslim Bengalis] are extremely valuable. The writer does not adopt an ultra-Marxist or communal stance.)

Gourangaprasad Ghosh. *Sonar Dag* [Stain of Gold]. Kolkata: Jogomaya Prokashoni, 1982. (An informative book about cinema, theatre and actors and contains many good pictures.)

H

Hahib Rahman, ed. *Muslim Sahitya Samajer Barshik Adhibeshan: Sabhapatider Bhashon* [Presidential Addresses of Muslim Literary Society Annual Conferences]. Dhaka: Bangla Academy, 2002. (A useful book to read on what educated, progressive Muslim young men were thinking in the 1920s.)

Harisadhan Mukhopadhyay. *Kalikata Sekaler O Ekaler* [Kolkata, Old and New]. Kolkata: P.M. Bagchi, 1991 [1995].

J

J. Sarkar. *The History of Bengal.* Vol 2. 2nd ed. Dhaka: Dhaka University, 1972.

J.H. Broomfield. *Elite Conflict in a Plural Society: Twentieth-Century Bengal.* Berkeley: University of California Press, 1968. (An extraordinary book on the Hindu-Muslim conflict in 20th century Bengal.)

J.P. Losty. *Calcutta: City of Palaces.* London: British Museum Library, 1990.

(An informative book with many valuable pictures.)

Jogesh Chandra Bagal. *Jatiyo Andolane Bango Nari* [Bengali Women in the National Movement]. Kolkata: Visva Bharati Granthalaya, 1954.

K

K. Raha. *Bengali Theatre.* Kolkata: NBT, 1997. (A brief but fine discussion.)

Karunamoy Goswami. *Sangeetkosh* [Music Encycopaedia]. Bangla Academy, 1985. (Rich in facts.)

Krishnadas Kabiraj Goswami. *Sri Sri Chaitanyacharitamrita* [The Life of Sri Chaitanya]. 6th reprint. Sukumar Sen and Tarapada Mukhopadhyay ed. Kolkata: Ananda Publishers, 1995.

Kshitimohan Sen. *Banglar Sadhona* [Tradition of Worship in Bengal]. Reprint. Kolkata: Visva Bharati Granthalaya, 1954. (An extremely valuable booklet.)
___. *Bharate Hindu-Musalman Jukto Sadhona* [The Linked Tradition of Worship of Hindus and Muslims in India]. Kolkata: Visva Bharati Granthalaya, 1950. (A slim but valuable book.)

L

Lokeshwar Basu. *Amader Padobeer Itihas* [The History of Our Surnames]. 4th reprint. Kolkata: Ananda Publishers, 1986.

M

M. Ali. *History of the Muslims of Bengal.* 3 vols. Riyadh: Imam Muhammad Ibn Saud Islamic University, 1985. (An informative book, but written from an Islamist point of view. Attempts to glorify Muslims and show Hindus in a poor light.)

M. Borthwick. *The Changing Role of Bengali Women.* Princeton: Princeton University Press, 1984. (An important book.)

M.G. Kabir. *Changing Face of Nationalism: The Case of Bangladesh.* Delhi: South Asia Books, 1996. (An important book on the question of identity of Bengali Muslims. Should be read particularly for the history of how the nationalistic thinking of Bengali Muslims evolved in the years between 1940 and 1990.)

Mamtazur Rahman Tarafdar. *Hosseinshahi Bangla* [Bengal Under Hossein Shah]. Dhaka: Bangla Academy, 2001.

Mohammad Abdul Jalil. *Modhyojuger Bangla Sahitye Bangla O Bangali Samaj* [Bengali Language and Bengali Society in the Bengali Literature of the Middle Ages]. 1st reprint (1996). Dhaka: Bangla Academy. (An informative and valuable book.)

Mohammad Mokammel Hossein Bhuinya. *Pracheen Banglar Porhamatir Shilpa* [Terracotta Art in Ancient Bengal]. Dhaka: Dibya Prakash, 2003.

Moinuddin Khaled. *Bangladesher Chitrashilpa* [Art in Bangladesh]. Dhaka: Dibya Prakash, 2000.

Muhammad Abdul Hai. Anwar Pasha, ed. *Ishwar Gupter Kobita Songroho* [Collected Poems of Ishwar Gupta]. 3rd reprint. Dhaka: Mowla Brothers, 1998.

Muhammad Enamul Haque. *Islamic Art Heritage in Bangladesh.* Dhaka: Bangladesh National Museum, 1983. (An important book with many rare pictures.)
___. *Muslim Bangla Sahitya* [The Literature of Muslim Bengal]. 2nd reprint. Dhaka: Pakistan Publications, 1965. (A valuable and pioneering work on the Muslim contribution in Bengali literature. Not very analytical, and in quite a few instances the writer has not ascertained his facts.)
___. *Bange Sufi Probhab* [The Sufi Influence in Bengal]. Kolkata: Mohsin & Co., 1935. (A scholarly work.)

Muhammad Shahidullah. 'Bangla Bhashar Itibritto' (History of the Bengali Language). *Sahitya Patrika*, 4th issue.
—. *Hazar Bachchor Purano Bangalae Siddha Kanupar Geet O Doha* [Thousand-

Years-Old Songs and Couplets of Siddha Kanupa]. Dhaka: 1925.

Muntassir Mamoon, ed. *Unish Shatoke Bangladesher Sambad Samayikpatra* [Newspapers and Periodicals in Nineteenth- Century Bengal]. Vols. 1-5. Dhaka: Bangla Academy, 1984-93. Binoy Ghosh had collected magazines that were published in Kolkata. Muntassir Mamoon collected magazines that were published in Dhaka and elsewhere in East Bengal, including *Grambarta Prakashika* and *Dhaka Prakash*. These magazines have now made it easier to reconstruct the social history of 19th century Bengal.)

Mustafa Nurul Islam. *Abohoman Bangla* [Bengali Down the Ages]. Dhaka: Anyaprokash, 1999. (A collection of essays by different writers.)
___. *Samayikpatre Jeebon O Janamot* [Life and Opinion as Seen in Periodicals]. Dhaka: Bangla Academi, 1976. (A seminal work.)

N

Narayan Choudhury. *Bangla Gaaner Jagat* [World of Music in Bengal]. Kolkata: Firma KLM, 1961.
___. *Sangeet Parikrama* [Music Round-up]. Kolkata: Indian Associate Publishing, 1953.

Nihar Ranjan Ray. *Bangalir Itihas* [History of Bengalis]. 3rd ed. Kolkata: Dey's Publishing, 2001. (Best available history of ancient Bengal. Unfortunately, the author did not go on to write a book on medieval history.)

Nirad C. Chaudhuri. *Atmaghati Bangali* [The Suicidal Bengal]. Vol 1. 2nd reprint. Kolkata: Mitra & Gosh, 1989.
___*Bangali Jeebone Ramonee* [Women in Bengali Life]. Kolkata: Mitra & Ghosh, 1968. (A valuable book on a subject no one had previously written on.)

Nirmalendu Mukhopadhyay. *Bharatchandrer Annadamangal* [Bharatchandra Ray's *Annadamangal*]. 5th ed. Kolkata: Modern Book, 2002-03.

Nirmalya Acharya and Dibyendu Palit ed. *Shatobarshe Chalochitro* [Hundred Years of Cinema]. Kolkata: Ananda Publishers, 1996.

Nishith Kumar Mukhopadhyay. *Bangla Sahitya O Bangla Chalochitro* [Bengali Literature and Bengali Cinema]. Kolkata: Anandadhara, 1986.

Nizamuddin Ahmed. *Buildings of the British Raj*. Dhaka: Dhaka University Press Ltd., 1986. (A very valuable book.)
___. *Discover the Monuments of Bangladesh*. Dhaka: Dhaka University Press Ltd., 1984. (An informative book.)

P

P. Sinha. *Nineteenth Century Bengal: Aspects of Social History*. Calcutta: Bookland, 1965.

Pabitra Sarkar ed. *Bangadarpan*. Vols. 1-2. Kolkata: Samaj Roopantar Sandhani, 2001-03. (Includes quite a few insightful essays.)
___. *Bhasha Desh Kal* [Language, Land, Time]. Kolkata: Mitra & Ghosh, 1999.

Parthapratim Bandopadhyay. *Bharatiyo Chalochitrer Rooprekha* [The Outline of Indian Cinema]. Kolkata: Banishilpa, 1997.

Prabhat Chandra Gangopadhyay. *Banglar Nari Jagoron* [Women's Awakening in Bengal]. Kolkata: Sadharon Brahma Samaj, 1946.
___. *Rabindrajeeboni* [Life of Tagore]. Vols 1-4. Kolkata: Visva Bharati Granthalaya. (The book provides insightful discussions on not just Tagore but also on contemporary society, culture and literature.)

Purabi Bose and Haroon Habib. *Bangali* (collection of essays). Dhaka: Bengal Foundation, 1992.

Pearychand Mitra. *Alaler Ghare Dulal* [The Spoilt Brat]. First published in 1858. (A valuable book on 19th century society and family life.)

R

R. Ahmed. *The Bengal Muslims: A Quest for Identity*. Delhi: Oxford University Press, 1996. (A very important book.)

R. Eaton. *The Rise of Islam and the Bengal Frontier*. Berkeley: University of California Press, 1996. (A scholarly work, written from an objective and non-partisan point of view. One of the most important books on Bengali Muslims in the medieval era.)

R. Skelton and M. Francis. *Arts of Bengal: The Heritage of Bangladesh and Eastern India*. London: Whitechapel Art Gallery, 1979. (A slim but very important book.)

R.V. Baumer, ed. *Aspects of Bengali History and Society*. Hawaii: University Press of Hawaii, 1974. (Contributions include important essays by Tapan Raychaudhuri, David Kopf, Blair King and John Broomfield.)

Rabi Basu. *Smritir Saronite Bangla Chalochitrer Ardho-Shatabdi Satrango* [Bengali Cinema, A Half-Century of Memories]. Vol. 2. Kolkata: Dey's Publishing, 1998.

Rabindra Kumar Dasgupta. *Bangali Ki Atmoghati O Anyanyo Rachona* ['Are Bengalis Suicidal' and Other Essays]. Kolkata: Paschimbanga Bangla Akademi, 2000.

Rabindranath Tagore: Poems, songs, short stories, novels, plays and essays.

Radha Prasad Gupta. *Machh Aar Bangali* [The Bengali and His Fish]. Kolkata: Ananda Publishers, 1989. (An informative and humorous discussion on not just fish in the Bengali diet but also of other foods and beverages and even clothes.)

Radharaman Mitra. *Kalikata Darpan* [A Mirror to Kolkata]. Vol. 1. 3rd edition. Kolkata: Subarnarekha, 1988.

____. Vol. 2. Kolkata: Subarnarekha, 2004.

Rajat Kanti Ray. *Palashir Sharhajantro O Sekaler Samaj* [The Conspiracy at Plassey and Contemporary Society]. 2nd ed. Kolkata: Ananda Publishers, 1998.

Rakhaldas Bandyopadhyay. *Bangalar Itihas* [History of Bengal]. Vols. 1-2. 3rd reprint. Kolkata: Dey's Publishing, 1998 [1917].

Ramakanta Chakraborty. *Bangalir Dharma Samaj O Sanskriti* [The Religion, Society and Culture of Bengalis]. Kolkata: Subarnarekha, 2002. (By 'Bengali' the author means Bengali Hindu. Also neglected is the fact that Hindu Bengali culture has imbibed Muslim influence.)

Ramesh Chandra Majumdar. *Bangla Desher Itihas* [The History of Bengal]. Vol. 1. 9th ed. Kolkata: General Printers & Publishers, 1998.

____. Vol. 2. 5th ed. Kolkata: General Printers & Publishers, 1998.

____. Vol. 3. 4th ed. Kolkata: General Printers & Publishers, 1996. (Ramesh Chandra. Majumdar was a great historian. This book, in three parts, is rich in facts and analysis. In the second part, however, the writer's aversion to Muslims leads him to make comments not borne out by facts. The sentiment is naturally absent in the first volume, which deals with a period preceding the arrival of Muslims in Bengal.)

Ramkumar Mukhopadhyay. *Bangali Sanskritir Ayoton* [The Range of Bengali Culture]. Kolkata: Pratibhas, 2003.

S

S. Sarkar. *On the Bengal Renaissance*. Reprint. Calcutta: Papyrus, 1985.

____. *The Swadeshi Movement in Bengal*. Delhi: People's Publishing, 1973. (An informative book on the Swadeshi movement during the first partition of Bengal.)

S. Sinha. *The Quest for Modernity and the Bengali Muslims.* Calcutta: Minerva Associates, 1995.

S.C. Mukherji. *The Changing Face of Calcutta: An Architectural Approach.* Calcutta: Government of West Bengal, 1991.

S.N. Amin. *The World of Muslim Women in Colonial Bengal.* Leiden: E.J. Brill, 1996. (The first important book on Bengali Muslim women.)

S. N. Ray. *Bengal Renaissance: The First Phase.* Calcutta: Minerva Associates, 2000.

Saifuddin Chowdhury. *Early Terracotta Figurines of Bangladesh.* Dhaka: Bangla Academy, 2000.

Shailesh Kumar Bandopadhyay. *Dangar Itihas* [A History of Riots]. Kolkata: Mitra & Ghosh, 1993.
___. *Jinnah/Pakistan: Notun Bhabna* [Jinnah/Pakistan: New Thoughts]. 4th ed. Kolkata: Mitra & Ghosh, 1994.

Shankar Sengupta. *Bangali Jeebone Bibaho* [Marriage in Bengali Life]. 2nd ed. Kolkata: Indian Publishing, 1991.

Sheila Basak. *Banglar Nakshi Kantha* [The Patterned Quilts of Bengal]. Kolkata: Ananda Publishers, 2002.

Shibnarayan Ray. *Bangalitwer Khonje O Onyano Alochona* [In Search of Bengaliness and Other Discussions]. Kolkata: Dey's Publishing, 2004.
___. ed. *Jignyasa*, collected vol. Kolkata: Papyrus, 1992. (Several notable essays on Bengali culture are included in the volume.)

Shibnath Shastri. *Ramtanu Lahiri O Tatkaleen Bangosamaj* [Ramtanu Lahiri and Bengali Society of His Time]. (Different publishers have at various times published this book.)

Siddhartha Ghosh. *Chhobi Tola* [Clicking Photographs]. Kolkata: Ananda Publishers, 1988. (Valuable information and pictures.)

Somnath Nandy. *Bulbul Larhaier Sekal Ekal* [Bird Fights, Then and Now]. Kolkata: Ananda Publishers, 1994.

Sripantha. *Keyabat Meye* [What A Girl!] Kolkata: Ananda Publishers, 1988. (The writing is not very cohesive but the book gives valuable information and contains good pictures.)
___. *Oitihasik Onaitihasik* [The Historical and the Non-historical]. Kolkata: Ananda Publishers, 2002. (Contains valuable information and pictures.)

Sudhir Chakraborty. *Bangla Filmer Gaan O Satyajit Ray* [Bengali Film Music and Satyajit Ray]. Kolkata: Pratikshan Publications, 1994.
___. *Bangla Gaaner Char Diganta* [The Horizons of Bengali Songs]. (Kolkata: Anustup, 1992.
___. *Bangla Gaaner Sandhane* [In Search of Bengali Songs]. Kolkata: Aruna Prakashani, 1990.)

Sukumar Bandopadhyay and Bishwapati Choudhury, ed. *Bharatchandrer Annadamangal* [Bharatchandra Ray's Annadamangal]. Reprint. Kolkata: University of Calcutta, 1996.

Sukumar Sen and Subhadra Sen. *Bangalir Bhasha* [The Language of Bengalis]. 2nd ed. Kolkata: Paschimbanga Bangla Akademi, 1994. (A brief and easy-to-read discussion.)

Sukumar Sen. *Bangla Sahityer Itihas* [History of Bengali Literature]. Vols. 1-5. Kolkata: Ananda Publishers, 1991-99. (The most valuable book on the history of Bengali literature, in terms of both information and analysis. However, the writer ignores completely the massive contribution of Bengali Muslims in Bengali literature. A separate book on the subject, *Islami Bangla Sahitya*, has not been able to redeem this narrowness of approach.)
___. *Charjageeti Padabali* [The Charja Songs]. Reprint. Kolkata: Ananda Publishers, 2002 [1956].

___. *Islami Bangla Sahitya* [Bengali Muslim Literature]. First pub. 1951. Kolkata: Ananda Publishers,1994.
___, *Pracheen Bangla O Bangali* [Bengal and Bengalis in Ancient Times] (Kolkata: Visva Bharati Granthalaya, 1962.)

Sunil Kanti Dey, ed. *Muslim Samajchitra: Samyabadi Samayikpatre* [Muslim Society: Through Communist Periodicals]. Dhaka: Bangla Academy, 1994

Suniti Kumar Chattopadhyay. *Bangalir Sanskriti* [The Culture of Bengalis]. 4th reprint. Kolkata, Paschimbanga Bangla Akademi, 1998. (A collection of valuable articles.)
___ *Sanskriti* [Culture]. Vols. 1-4. (A very informative piece of writing. The last two parts are published by Ananda Publishers.)
___. *The Origin and Development of the Bengali Language.* Vols. 1-3. Calcutta :Rupa, 1975.

Surama Ghatak. *Ritwik.* Kolkata: Anustup, 1996.

T

Tapan Raychaudhuri. *Bengal under Akbar and Jahangir: An Introductory Study in Social History.* Reprint. New Delhi: Munshiram Manoharlal, 1969.
___. *Europe Reconsidered: Perceptions of the West in the Nineteenth Century.* 2nd impression. Delhi: Oxford University Press, 1989.

Tarapada Santra. *Kolkatar Mandir-Masjid: Sthapotyo-Olonkoron-Roopantor* [Temples and Mosques of Kolkata: Architecture-Ornamentation-Transformation]. Kolkata: Ananda Publishers, 2001. (An informative discussion.)
___. *Paschimbanglar Dhormiyo Sthapotyo: Mandir O Masjid* [Religious Architecture of West Bengal: Temples and Mosques]. Kolkata: Paschimbanga Bangla Akademi, 1998. (A valuable book.)

U

U. Banerjee. *Bengali Theatre – 200 Years.* Publications Division, Ministry of Information and Broadcasting, Govt. of West Bengal, 1999. (Informative essays written by various contributors.)

Utpala Goswami. *Kolkatae Sangeetcharcha* [The Cultivation of Music]. 2nd edition. Kolkata: Paschimbanga Rajyo Sangeet Academi.; (A short but informative discussion.)

W

W. Hunter. *A Statistical Account of Bengal.* Vols. 1-10. London: Trubner and Co., 1870. (An extraordinary and informative book covering myriad aspects of Bengal in the early 1870s, ranging from the population and geographical parameters of the different districts to industry and trade.)

Z

Zinat Mahrukh Banu. *Bangladeshe Darushilpa* [Wood Carvings of Bangladesh]. Dhaka: Bangladesh Jatiya Jadughar, 2003. (An informative book with good pictures.)

INDEX

A

C

D

E

F

G

K

L

M

N

O

P

Q

R

S

T